Lecture Notes in Computer Science 2495
Edited by G. Goos, J. Hartmanis, and J. van Leeuwen

Springer
Berlin
Heidelberg
New York
Barcelona
Hong Kong
London
Milan
Paris
Tokyo

Chris George Huaikou Miao (Eds.)

Formal Methods and Software Engineering

4th International Conference
on Formal Engineering Methods, ICFEM 2002
Shanghai, China, October 21-25, 2002
Proceedings

Springer

Series Editors

Gerhard Goos, Karlsruhe University, Germany
Juris Hartmanis, Cornell University, NY, USA
Jan van Leeuwen, Utrecht University, The Netherlands

Volume Editors

Chris George
United Nations University
International Institute for Software Technology
Casa Silva Mendes, Est. do Engenheiro Trigo No. 4
P.O. Box 3058, Macao
E-mail: cwg@iist.unu.edu

Huaikou Miao
Shanghai University
School of Computer Engineering and Science
149 Yanchang Road, Shanghai 200072, P.R. China
E-mail: hkmiao@yc.shu.edu.cn

Cataloging-in-Publication Data applied for

Bibliograhpic information published by Die Deutsche Bibliothek
Die Deutsche Bibliothek lists this publication in the Deutsche Nationalbibliografie;
detailed bibliographic data is available in the Internet at http://dnb.ddb.de

CR Subject Classification (1998): D.2.4, D.2, F.3, D.3

ISSN 0302-9743
ISBN 3-540-00029-1 Springer-Verlag Berlin Heidelberg New York

This work is subject to copyright. All rights are reserved, whether the whole or part of the material is
concerned, specifically the rights of translation, reprinting, re-use of illustrations, recitation, broadcasting,
reproduction on microfilms or in any other way, and storage in data banks. Duplication of this publication
or parts thereof is permitted only under the provisions of the German Copyright Law of September 9, 1965,
in its current version, and permission for use must always be obtained from Springer-Verlag. Violations are
liable for prosecution under the German Copyright Law.

Springer-Verlag Berlin Heidelberg New York
a member of BertelsmannSpringer Science+Business Media GmbH

http://www.springer.de

© Springer-Verlag Berlin Heidelberg 2002
Printed in Germany

Typesetting: Camera-ready by author, data conversion by Steingräber Satztechnik GmbH, Heidelberg
Printed on acid-free paper   SPIN: 10870708   06/3142   5 4 3 2 1 0

Preface

This volume contains the proceedings of the Fourth International Conference on Formal Engineering Methods: ICFEM 2002. The conference was held in Shanghai, China, from 21 to 25 October 2002.

Formal methods for software development have been extensively researched and their use in industry is increasing. Recent applications to the development of safety-critical, security-critical, and mission-critical systems have significantly increased trustworthiness, without increasing overall development costs. ICFEM encourages the exchange of ideas on recent advances in formal methods and software engineering.

The conference received 108 papers submitted from 24 different countries and regions. A total of 43 regular and 16 short papers were accepted. All papers were reviewed by three or four members of the program committee or other reviewers. The conference would not have been possible without their voluntary and dedicated work.

The conference had a number of excellent keynote speakers: Prof. Ralph-Johan Back of Abo Akademi University, Finland, Dr. Mark A. Hale of Interwoven Inc., USA, Dr. Richard Jüllig of CommerceNet Consortium, USA, Prof. Shaoying Liu of Hosei University, Japan, and Prof. Jim Woodcock of the University of Kent, UK. They provided a balanced view of advanced formal methods and software engineering from their research programs and experience.

We are pleased to have successfully organized this conference. However, it could not have been successful without the hard work and efforts of the members of our program committee and organizing committee, reviewers, authors, and support from different countries and regions. We would particularly like to thank Xiang Jugu for handling the finances, Qing Wei for handling local arrangements, Liu Jing for handling paper reviews, Chen Yihai for taking care of our publicity, and Sandy Lee for her help in preparing these proceedings. Finally, our thanks to Springer-Verlag for their help with the publication.

ICFEM 2002 was sponsored by Shanghai University, the United Nations University International Institute for Software Technology (UNU/IIST), and the National Natural Science Foundation of China, in cooperation with the China Computer Federation, China Software Industry Association, Shanghai Computer Association, and East China Normal University, and was organized by Shanghai University.

ICFEM 2002 coincided with the 10th Anniversary of UNU/IIST, which has been promoting formal engineering methods since 1992. We wish it every success in the future.

October 2002

Chris George
Miao Huaikou

Program Committee

Paul Ammann
Sten F. Andler
Keijiro Araki
Richard Banach
Jonathan Bowen
Barrett R. Bryant
Michael Butler
Dan Craigen
Jim Davies
Dong Jin Song
Feng Yuling
John Fitzgerald
Marc Frappier
Andy Galloway
Chris George
Henri Habrias

Ian Hayes
Huang Guoxing
Peter Lindsay
Liu Junbo
Wayne Luk
Míchéal Mac an
  Airchinnigh
Mei Hong
Dominique Mery
Miao Huaikou
A. Jeff Offutt
Yakup Paker
Qian Leqiu
Augusto Sampaio
Jeff Sanders
Thomas Santen

Klaus-Dieter Schewe
Song Guoxin
Sun Yongqiang
Paul Swatman
T.H. Tse
Sam Valentine
Wang Farn
Wang Yingxu
Wu Gengfeng
Wu Jie
Xu Baowen
Xue Jinyun
Yu Namsrai
Sijing Zhang
Zheng Guoliang
Zhu Hong

Other Reviewers

Bernhard K. Aichernig
Marc Aiguier
Pascal André
Cao Fei
Christian Attiogbé
Mikhail Auguston
Zeki Bayram
Juan Bicarregui
Marcus Brohede
Phil Brooke
Peter Burton
David Carrington
Sergio Cavalcante
Alessandra Cavarra
Antonio Cerone
Chen Yihai
Charles Crichton
Dang Van Hung
Sebastien Faucou
Colin Fidge

Gao Xiaolei
Mats Grindal
Lindsay Groves
Stefan Gruner
Sanny Gustavsson
Dan Hazel
Maritta Heisel
Steffen Helke
Tomasz Janowski
Roland Kaschek
Marie Christine Lafaye
Birgitta Lindström
Sebastian Link
Liu Chuchang
Liu Shaoying
G. Louis
Alexandre Mota
Muan Yong Ng
Robert Nilsson
Richard Paige

Sibylle Peuker
Brian Ritchie
Neil Robinson
Peter Robinson
Gwen Salaün
Graeme Smith
Soon Keong Kim
Andrew Simpson
Sun Jing
Sun Meng
Paul Strooper
Kenji Taguchi
Alexei Tretiakov
Mark Utting
Wang Hai
Luke Wildman
Xie Liang
Zhao Wei

Table of Contents

Invited Talks

SFI: A Refinement Based Layered Software Architecture 1
    Ralph-Johan Back

Developing Quality Software Systems
Using the SOFL Formal Engineering Method 3
    Shaoying Liu

Maintaining Referential Integrity on the Web 20
    Mark A. Hale

Formal Methods in Enterprise Computing 22
    Richard Jüllig

Unifying Theories of Parallel Programming 24
    Jim Woodcock, Arthur Hughes

Component Engineering and Software Architecture

ABC/ADL: An ADL Supporting Component Composition 38
    Hong Mei, Feng Chen, Qianxiang Wang, Yaodong Feng

The Description of CORBA Objects Based on Petri Nets 48
    Hong Zheng, Shi-xian Li

Toward a Formal Model of Software Components 57
    Maritta Heisel, Thomas Santen, Jeanine Souquières

A Specification-Based Software Construction Framework for Reuse 69
    Jing Liu, Huaikou Miao, Xiaolei Gao

Specifying a Component Model
for Building Dynamically Reconfigurable Distributed Systems 80
    Xuejun Chen

Three-Tiered Specification of Micro-architectures 92
    Vasu Alagar, Ralf Lämmel

Modeling the Architecture for Component-Based E-commerce System 98
    Jiayue Chang, Huadong Ma

Component Specification and Wrapper/Glue Code Generation
with Two-Level Grammar Using Domain Specific Knowledge 103
  *Fei Cao, Barrett R. Bryant, Rajeev R. Raje, Mikhail Auguston,
  Andrew M. Olson, Carol C. Burt*

Method Integration

Abstract Specification in Object-Z and CSP 108
  Graeme Smith, John Derrick

Mechanization of an Integrated Approach:
Shallow Embedding into SAL/PVS 120
  J. Christian Attiogbé

Specification Techniques and Languages

Concept Use or Concept Refinement:
An Important Distinction in Building Generic Specifications 132
  David R. Musser, Zhiqing Shao

An Overview of Mobile Object-Z 144
  Kenji Taguchi, Jin Song Dong

Z Approach to Semantic Web 156
  Jin Song Dong, Jing Sun, Hai Wang

Hardware/Software Partitioning in Verilog 168
  Shengchao Qin, Jifeng He, Zongyan Qiu, Naixiao Zhang

A Formal Methodology to Specify E-commerce Systems 180
  *Adriano Pereira, Mark Song, Gustavo Gorgulho,
  Wagner Meira Jr., Sérgio Campos*

Model-Based Specification Animation Using Testgraphs 192
  Tim Miller, Paul Strooper

An Abstract Model for Scheduling Real-Time Programs 204
  Alvaro E. Arenas

A Specification and Validation Technique
Based on STATEMATE and FNLOG 216
  Olfa Mosbahi, Leila Jemni, Samir Ben Ahmed, Jacques Jaray

Formal Representation and Analysis of Batch Stock Trading Systems
by Logical Petri Net Workflows 221
  Yuyue Du, Changjun Jiang

A Calculus for Mobile Network Systems 226
  Jinfeng Huang, Ad Verschueren, Henri Aalderink, Johan Lukkien

Modelling Real-Time Systems with Continuous-Time Temporal Logic 231
  Guangyuan Li, Zhisong Tang

On Concept-Based Definition of Domain-Specific Languages 237
  Ying Liu, Naixiao Zhang

Formal Specification of Evolutionary Software Agents................... 249
  Hong Zhu

Detecting Deadlock in Ada Rendezvous Flow Structure
Based on Process Algebra... 262
  Yuan Liu, Baowen Xu, Zhenqiang Chen

Formal Analysis of Real-Time Systems with SAM 275
  Huiqun Yu, Xudong He, Yi Deng, Lian Mo

Tools and Environments

Tool Support for Visualizing CSP in UML 287
  Muan Yong Ng, Michael Butler

Theorem Prover Support for Precondition and Correctness Calculation ... 299
  Orieta Celiku, Joakim von Wright

XML-Based Static Type Checking and Dynamic Visualization for TCOZ.. 311
  Jin Song Dong, Yuan Fang Li, Jing Sun, Jun Sun, Hai Wang

Refinement

μ-Chart-Based Specification and Refinement........................... 323
  Doug Goldson, Greg Reeve, Steve Reeves

Towards a Refinement Calculus for Concurrent Real-Time Programs 335
  Sibylle Peuker, Ian Hayes

Refinement Algebra for Formal Bytecode Generation 347
  Adolfo Duran, Ana Cavalcanti, Augusto Sampaio

Applications

Formal Modelling of Java GUI Event Handling 359
  Jessica Chen

A New Algorithm for Service Interaction Detection.................... 371
  Ana Cavalli, Stéphane Maag

Specification of an Asynchronous On-chip Bus 383
  Juha Plosila, Tiberiu Seceleanu

Analysis of a Security Protocol in μCRL 396
  Jun Pang

Developing a Spell-Checker for Tajik Using RAISE 401
  Gafurov Davrondjon, Tomasz Janowski

M2Z: A Tool for Translating a Natural Language Software Specification
into Z 406
  Zarina Shukur, Abdullah Md. Zin, Ainita Ban

Validation and Verification

Abstract Interpretation with a Theorem Prover 411
  Hugh Anderson

Formal Reasoning about Hardware and Software Memory Models 423
  Abhik Roychoudhury

Slicing Hierarchical Automata for Model Checking UML Statecharts 435
  Ji Wang, Wei Dong, Zhi-Chang Qi

Formal Verification of a SONET Telecom System Block 447
  M. Hasan Zobair, Sofiène Tahar

Enabling Hardware Verification through Design Changes 459
  Amr T. Abdel-Hamid, Sofiène Tahar, John Harrison

Specification-Based Test Generation for Security-Critical Systems
Using Mutations 471
  Guido Wimmel, Jan Jürjens

A Formal Definition of Function Points
for Automated Measurement of B Specifications 483
  Hassan Diab, Marc Frappier, Richard St-Denis

Machine Code Type Safety 495
  Fan Guo, YiYun Chen, RongGui Hu

UML

On the Formalized Semantics of Static Modeling Elements in UML 500
  Yan-Bing Jiang, Wei-Zhong Shao, Zhi-Yi Ma, Yao-Dong Feng

From a B Specification to UML StateChart Diagrams 511
  *Ahmed Hammad, Bruno Tatibouët,
  Jean-Christophe Voisinet, Wu Weiping*

Formalizing UML Models with Object-Z 523
  Huaikou Miao, Ling Liu, Li Li

Using Transition Systems to Unify UML Models 535
  Zhiming Liu, Xiaoshan Li, Jifeng He

A Formal Metamodeling Approach to a Transformation
between the UML State Machine and Object-Z 548
   Soon-Kyeong Kim, David Carrington

A UML Approach to the Design of Open Distributed Systems 561
   Behzad Bordbar, John Derrick, Gill Waters

A Semantic Model of Real-Time UML 573
   Subash Shankar

Research on Ontology-Oriented Domain Analysis on MIS 578
   Zhong Ming, Shi-xian Li, Xiu-rong Fang

A Requirements Description Model Based on Conditional Directed Graphs 583
   Zaobin Gan, Chuanbo Chen, Xiandeng Pei

Semantics

Introducing Reference Semantics via Refinement 588
   Graeme Smith

Soundness, Completeness and Non-redundancy of Operational Semantics
for Verilog Based on Denotational Semantics 600
   Huibiao Zhu, Jonathan P. Bowen, Jifeng He

Towards a Time Model for *Circus* 613
   Adnan Sherif, Jifeng He

Author Index **625**

SFI: A Refinement Based Layered Software Architecture

Ralph-Johan Back

Åbo Akademi and Turku Centre for Computer Science
Lemminkainenk 14, 20520 Turku, Finland
backrj@abo.fi

Abstract. *Refinement calculus* [1,5] is a formal framework for reasoning about program correctness and correctness preserving program refinements. It serves as the foundation for an object-oriented software architecture and construction method that we refer to as *stepwise feature introduction (SFI)* [3]. Characteristic for this approach is that each software module is described in terms of thin layers. Each layer extends the software with some new feature, in a way that preserves the features that have been introduced by earlier layers. This amounts to requiring that the new layer is a *superposition refinement* [4] of the layers below. The modules are interconnected using interface specifications, usually providing a more abstract view of the module state than what will actually be implemented. The implementation is required to be a *data refinement* [9,6] of the interface specification. SFI is based on structuring software with these two basic mechanisms, *modularization* and *extension*, while the refinement calculus provides the formal framework for reasoning about the correctness of software constructed in this way.

We use *UML* [8] to describe the software architecture, with refinement calculus providing a rigorous mathematical semantics for the UML constructs employed. This will also give us a formal framework for reasoning about UML class diagrams, in essence using these as proof schemes when arguing about software properties.

SFI goes well in hand with an *extreme programming (XP)* [7] approach to constructing software, with feature introductions corresponding to the iteration cycles in XP. We can look at SFI as providing a general software architecture for XP, and we can look at XP as providing a software process for SFI. We will report on some experiments where these two approaches have been combined [2]. We will also discuss in more detail how the notions of *unit tests* in XP can be generalized to requirement specifications in SFI.

References

1. R.J. Back. *Correctness Preserving Program Refinements: Proof Theory and Applications*, volume 131 of *Mathematical Centre Tracts*. Mathematical Centre, Amsterdam, 1980.
2. R.J. Back, L. Milovanov, I. Porres-Paltor and V. Preoteasa. A Experiment on Extreme Programming and Stepwise Feature Introduction. TUCS Technical Report no 451 (http://www.tucs.fi/Research/Series/techreports/), 2002.

3. R.J. Back. Software Construction by Stepwise Feature Introduction. In *ZB 2002: Formal Specification and Development in Z and B*, Eds. D. Bert, J. Bowen, M. Henson and K. Robinson, Springer LNCS 2272, 2002.
4. R.J. Back and K. Sere. Superposition Refinement of Reactive Systems. *Formal Aspects of Computing*, 8(3):324–346, 1996.
5. R.J. Back and J. von Wright. *Refinement Calculus: A Systematic Introduction*. Springer-Verlag, 1998.
6. R. J. Back and J. von Wright. Encoding, decoding, and data refinement. *Formal Aspects of Computing*, 2000.
7. K. Beck. *Extreme Programming Explained* Addison-Wesley, the XP Series, 1999.
8. G. Booch, J. Rumbaugh and I. Jacobson. *The Unified Modeling Language User Guide*. Addison-Wesley, 1998.
9. W.P. de Roever and K. Engelhardt. *Data Refinement: Model-Oriented Proof Methods and their Comparison*. Cambridge Tracts in Theoretical Computer Science 47, 1998.

Developing Quality Software Systems Using the SOFL Formal Engineering Method*

Shaoying Liu

Department of Computer Science
Faculty of Computer and Information Sciences
Hosei University, Tokyo, Japan
sliu@k.hosei.ac.jp
http://www.k.hosei.ac.jp/~sliu/

Abstract. *Formal Engineering Methods* are a bridge from Formal Methods to industrial applications. In this paper I describe the relation between formal engineering methods and formal methods, and present a specific formal engineering method SOFL (*S*tructured *O*bject-Oriented *F*ormal *L*anguage) for developing quality software systems. I explain how SOFL can be applied in practice through examples.

1 Introduction

Formal methods have made significant contributions to the establishment of the theoretical foundation for software development over the last thirty years by emphasizing the use of mathematical notation in writing system specifications and the employment of formal proof based on logical calculus for verifying designs and programs [1-6]. However, we should also clearly recognize the reality that formal methods are facing strong challenges to their acceptance by industrial users, although a few exceptions have been reported [7]. According to my observations, students who have studied formal methods at university hardly ever apply them in practice when they start to work in industry; some try initially, but most eventually give up.

There may be various reasons for this unfortunate situation, but the fact itself indicates that education in formal methods alone is insufficient to solve the problem. I believe that formal methods need to be developed further to address many important engineering issues so that they can be applied to development of real systems in industrial environments. For example, how can formal specifications, especially for large-scale and complex systems, be written so that they can be easily read, understood, modified, verified, validated, and transformed into designs and programs? How can the use of formal, semi-formal, and informal methods be balanced in a coherent manner to achieve the best quality assurance under practical scheduling and cost constraints? How can

---

* This work is supported in part by the Ministry of Education, Culture, Sports, Science and Technology of Japan under Grant-in-Aid for Scientific Research (B) (No. 11694173) and (C) (No. 11680368).

formal proof and testing, static analysis, or prototyping techniques be combined to achieve rigorous and effective approaches to the verification and validation of formal specifications, designs, and programs? How can the refinement from unexecutable specifications into executable programs be effectively supported? How can software development projects using formal methods be managed so that they can be well predicated before they are carried out, and well controlled during their implementations? And how can effective software tools supporting the use of formal methods be built so that the usability of formal methods can be improved and the productivity and reliability of systems can be enhanced?

To attack these problems, we may need to compromise some of the original principles of formal methods. If we treat formal methods as an effective "medicine" for curing the "disease" of software crisis, but one which is too bitter for most people to swallow at the moment, then a compromise solution is to provide a "sugar coating". Although this may reduce the effectiveness of the "medicine", it allows most people to be able to take it and therefore to gain a trade-off between its effectiveness and accessibility.

Since research to provide possible solutions to these questions addresses different aspects of the problem, I call this area *Formal Engineering Methods* (FEM). In other words, formal methods focus on the power of mathematical notation and calculus to increase the rigor of software development, without paying much attention to human factors (e.g., capability, skills, and education background) and other practical constraints (e.g., accuracy and completeness of requirements, changes in both specifications and programs, and the scale and complexity of systems), whereas formal engineering methods advocate the incorporation of mathematical notation into the software engineering process to substantially improve the comprehensibility and effectiveness of commonly used methods for development of real systems in the industrial setting. In this sense, formal engineering methods are a further development of formal methods, not towards achievement of more expressive power, but towards improvement of their usability for industrial applications. They should support the integration of compatible informal/semi-formal and formal methods for the construction of formal specifications in a user-friendly manner, and rigorous but practical verification of software systems.

Over the last ten years, I have been working on a specific formal engineering method known as *SOFL*. SOFL stands for *S*tructured *O*bject-Oriented *F*ormal *L*anguage; it achieves practicality of formal methods while preserving their rigorous features by integrating conventional Data Flow Diagrams [8], Petri Nets [9], VDM-SL [10], as well as Object-Oriented approach [11] in a coherent manner for specification constructions, and by integrating formal proof with static analysis and testing in order to review and test specifications. It also supports the use of *refinement* and *evolution* as the underlying principle for developing formal design specifications from informal and then semi-formal user requirements specifications. By refinement I mean the technique for resolving nondeterminism in the specification, while by evolution I mean a technique for either extending or modifying the specification.

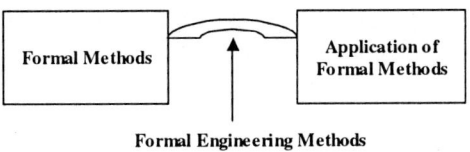

Fig. 1. An illustration of formal engineering methods

The remainder of the paper is organized as follows. Section 2 gives a detailed description of formal engineering methods. Section 3 introduces the SOFL specification language, while section 4 focuses on the discussion of the SOFL method. Section 5 and 6 describes, respectively, two verification and validation techniques: rigorous review and specification testing. Finally, in section 7, I offer some concluding remarks and outline the future research.

2 Formal Engineering Methods

Formal Engineering Methods aim to support application of formal methods to the development of large-scale and complex computer systems; they are neither equivalent to applications of formal methods, nor equivalent to formal methods themselves. Rather, they are a *bridge* between formal methods and their application, as illustrated in Figure 1. How to build the bridge therefore becomes the primary task of formal engineering methods.

As mentioned in the introduction, integrations of formal notation with commonly used graphical notations and formal proof with commonly used verification and validation techniques may provide a solution to this problem. Attempts at integrations should be made to achieve accessibility or usability of formal methods. For this reason, the use of formalism should be limited to the level at which they help to increase clarification of ambiguity, and should be kept as simple as necessary. In principle, formal engineering methods should have some or all of the following features:

- Adopting specification languages that integrate properly graphical notation, formal notation, and natural language. Graphical notation is suitable for describing the overall structure of a specification comprehensibly, while formal notation can be used to provide precise abstract definition of the components involved in the graphical representation. Interpretation of the formal definitions in a natural language facilitates understanding of them.
- Employing rigorous but practical techniques for verifying and validating specifications and programs. Such techniques are usually achieved by integrating formal proof and commonly used verification techniques, such as testing [12], reviews [13], inspection [14], and model checking [15].
- Advocating the combination of prototyping and formal methods. A computer system has both dynamic and static features. The dynamic features, including the usability of a GUI and system performance, are apparent only

during the system operation. Prototyping can be effective in capturing the user requirements for some of the dynamic features in the early phases of system development and provide a basis for developing an entire system using formal methods.
- Supporting both refinement and evolution rather than only strict refinement in developing specifications and programs. Evolution of a specification, at any level, means change, and such change does not necessarily satisfy strict refinement rules (of course, it sometimes does). The interesting point is how to control, support, and verify changes of specification during software development in a practical manner.
- Deploying techniques for constructing, understanding, and modifying specifications. For example, effective techniques for specification construction can be achieved by integrating existing requirements engineering techniques with formal specification techniques, and techniques in simulation and computer vision can be combined to create visual simulation technique to help specification understanding and explore the potential behavior of the ultimate system.
- Adopting intelligent software tools to support formal specification and rigorous verification in such a way that the process of either building a specification or conducting a verification is guided by the tools, so that the developer is under the "control" of the tools and may not necessarily need to directly manipulate formal notations as well. Thus, the efficiency, productivity, and correctness of software development can be substantially enhanced.

In summary, formal engineering methods embrace integrated specification, integrated verification, and all the supporting techniques, with the purpose of providing user-friendly formal notations and methods for automation of specification construction, transformation, and system verification and validation. To put it simply,

FEM = Integrated specification +
Integrated verification +
Supporting techniques

Effective formal engineering methods would have to be realized by means of software supporting tools. Fortunately, the precise syntax and semantics of formal specification languages provide great advantages over traditional informal or semi-formal languages, allowing the construction of powerful tools that support software development in depth and systematically. I believe that the quality of software tools is the key to success in making formal specification and rigorous verification techniques more accessible to industry at large.

3 The SOFL Specification Language

The SOFL specification language was designed by integrating Data Flow Diagrams (DFDs), Petri Nets, the formal specification language VDM-SL (Vienna

Development Method - Specification Language), and the features of object-oriented programming languages [16, 17]. A DFD is intended to describe the architecture of a specification (e.g., system requirements specification and design specification), while a Petri Net is used to provide an operational semantics for the DFD. Such a formalized DFD is called a CDFD (condition data flow diagram) in SOFL. To provide precise definitions for the components of the CDFD, such as processes, data flows, and stores, VDM-SL is adopted, with necessary extensions or modifications. To support data abstraction and object-oriented features, such as encapsulation, information hiding, reusability, and polymorphism, classes are allowed to be defined and their objects are allowed to be used as either data flows or stores in CDFDs.

A specification in SOFL is a hierarchy of condition data flow diagrams (CDFDs), resulting from decomposition of the processes involved. A CDFD at each level is associated with a module for formal definitions of the components of the CDFD, as shown in Figure 2. In fact, a module can be perceived as a self-contained structure with a certain behavior (or functionality) that is represented by the associated CDFD.

A process models a transformation from its input to its output; a data flow indicates a data item moving from one process to another; and a store represents a data depository (such as a file or database). A module plays the same role as both data dictionary and process specification in conventional data flow diagrams [8], but the difference is that all the definitions are given in a formal textual notation to achieve preciseness and conciseness: all the data flows and stores are defined with types and invariants, and processes are defined using either a pair of pre and postconditions or explicit specifications. The general structure of a process specification is as follows:

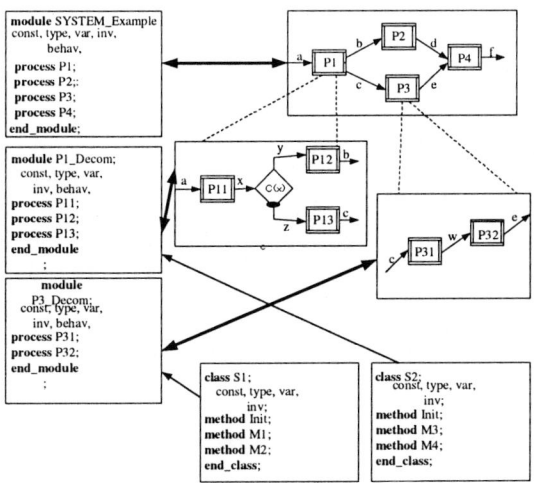

Fig. 2. The outline of a SOFL specification

```
process ProcessName(input) output
ext ExternalVariable
pre PreCondition
post PostCondition
decom LowerLevelModuleName
explicit ExplicitSpecification
comment
end_process
```

A process specification starts with a process name *ProcessName*, its input data flows *input*, and output data flows *output*. If the process deals with external variables (state variables defined in the **var** section of the module), they need to be listed after the keyword **ext**. The functionality of the process can be defined by either a pair of pre and postconditions, usually known as *implicit specification*, or an explicit specification *ExplicitSpecification*, which is formed by using the predicate logic together with the sequential, conditional, and iteration constructs available in most programming languages. A complex process may be decomposed into the next lower level CDFD whose associated module must be written after the keyword **decom** for good traceability in the documentation. To facilitate understanding of the formal specification of the process, informal comments may be written to provide a proper explanation. It is worth noting that all the parts of a process specification, except its signature (i.e., process name, input and output data flows), are optional.

A class in a specification is treated as a user-defined type from which objects can be instantiated for being used as data flows and/or stores in CDFDs. A class shares the similar structure with a module, but differs from the module in several ways. First, objects can be derived from a class but cannot be derived from a module. Second, a method in a class can have only one output, whereas a process may have many. Finally, a class has no associated CDFD, but a module is associated with a CDFD.

4 The SOFL Method

The SOFL method is composed of a *software process model* and *techniques for specification* and *verification*. The former provides an overall control of software development process, while the latter provides specific techniques to support activities involved in the development process.

4.1 The Process Model

Development of software systems using SOFL combines the approaches of the waterfall model [18] and the transformation model [19], as shown in Figure 3. The process is similar to the waterfall model in emphasizing the necessity of requirements analysis, design, and coding, but differs from the conventional transformation model in the way that transformations from high-level specifications

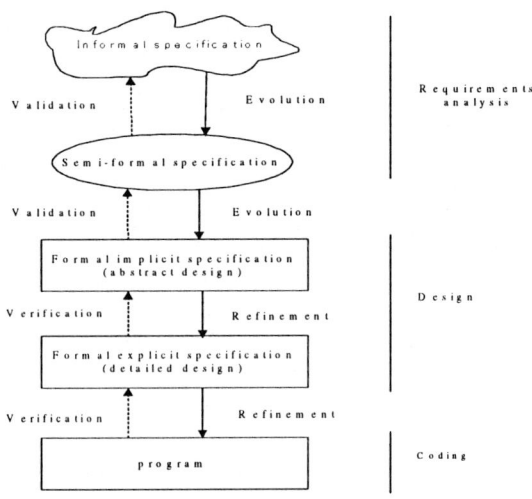

Fig. 3. The software development process using SOFL

to low-level ones may not necessarily be strict refinements: they can be either *evolutions* or refinements, depending on the phase of the development.

One of the important features of the process model is the use of a *three-step approach* for building formal specifications: *informal, semi-formal,* and *formal specification.* Developing an informal specification helps the analyst (the person who carries out requirements analysis) study the domain knowledge and identify what data items and operations are necessary for the system to be built. Transforming an informal specification into a semi-formal one helps the analyst clarify ambiguities in the concepts involved, understand the required operations in more detail, and set up a well-organized and comprehensible specification.

Since informal and semi-formal specifications are suitable for use in communications between the user and the developer, they are normally used for documenting requirements. On the other hand, a complete formalization of the semi-formal specification allows the designer to understand the user requirements and clarify ambiguities in the semi-formal specifications, and it will also help to build a firm foundation for implementation. Therefore, a formal specification should be achieved to represent design, including both abstract design and detailed design. The abstract design focuses on the architecture of the system and the functionality of related operations, which are suitable for being defined with pre and postconditions, whereas the detailed design is intended to provide algorithms and data structures to facilitate implementation using a specific programming language (e.g., Java).

In fact, it is a common phenomenon nowadays that companies conducting requirements analysis and writing requirements specifications are different from the companies designing and implementing the systems, for economic reasons (e.g., the cost of design and implementation by another company is much lower).

Therefore, there is a strong need for the companies conducting design and implementation to study the requirements thoroughly and clarify potential ambiguities. The three-step approach of the SOFL method can help enhance the quality of the communications, understanding, and the documentations in such a process.

The SOFL process model also emphasizes that transformations from informal specification to semi-formal specification and then to formal specification can be achieved by evolution, which means any of three activities: refinement, extension, and modification. It also requires that transformations from the abstract design to the detailed design and then to the final program be a strict refinement process. Thus, it can be ensured that the final program meets the design specification and, hopefully, the requirements specification as well.

To ensure the quality of evolution and refinement, rigorous but practical techniques are advocated to support validation and verification of specifications produced in various phases. Validation aims to make sure that the written specification does reflect accurately the user's conception of requirements while verification ensures the consistency within a specification or between different specifications.

4.2 Example

I take a simplified ATM (Automated Teller Machine) as an example to illustrate how a system can be formalized by taking the three-steps introduced above. First, an informal specification that contains all the desired functions is written as follows:

(1) Select the service of *displaying* the balance of an account or *withdraw* from the account.
(2) Insert a cashcard and supply a password.
(3) If *displaying* the balance is selected, the current balance is displayed.
(4) If *withdraw* is selected, the amount of the money to withdraw is properly provided.

To gain a thorough understanding and clarify the potential ambiguities in the specification, we develop it into a semi-formal specification. Since the scale of the problem is rather small, I use a single module to model the system in which the functional specification of the desired processes, data types, and communication between processes are described. The functional specification is given in the form of pre and postconditions, but in the manner that both pre and postconditions are basically defined informally. Data types are defined using SOFL built-in data types or the user-defined classes, but *given types* are allowed. The communication between processes is modeled using a CDFD, as shown in Figure 4. The outline of the semi-formal specification of the system is given as follows:

    module SYSTEM_ATM;
    type
    Account = **composed of**

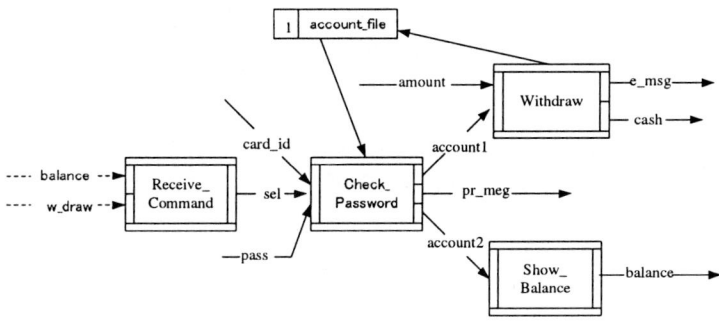

Fig. 4. The CDFD modeling an ATM

        account_no: **nat0**
        password: PassWord
        balance: **real**
      end
PassWord = **given**; /*The type PassWord will be finalized in the formal
            specification. */

var
ext #account_file: **set of** Account; /*this variable contains data in a file. */
behav CDFD_1; /* Assuming the CDFD of the ATM is numbered 1. */

process Init()
end_process; /* The initialization process has no specific function because
        there is no local store in the CDFD to initialize. */

process Receive_Command(balance: **sign** | w_draw: **sign**) sel: **bool**
...
end_process;

process Check_Password(card_id: **nat0**, sel: **bool**, psas: PassWord)
              account1: Account | pr_meg: **string** |
              account2: Account
...
end_process;

process Withdraw(amount: **real**, account1: Account)
            e_msg: **string** | cash: **real**
ext wr account_file
pre "account1" exists in "account_file".
post if the balance of "account1" is greater than or equal to "amount", then
    assign "amount" to cash and reduce "amount" from the balance of
    "account1"; otherwise, if "amount" is greater than the balance of

"account1", then issue an message to indicate the lack of sufficient
money to withdraw from "account1".
end_process;

process Show_Balance(account2: Account)
                    balance: real
...
end_process;
end_module;

The next step is to design the system based on the semi-formal requirements specification. The focus of this step is on the architecture of the system and the formalization of its every component. For this reason, the structure of the module, including its associated CDFD, processes, and data variables in the semi-formal specification may need to be evolved to suit the design purposes (e.g., to achieve high efficiency and good usability of the system). Following this line we derive the following formal design specification, with necessary omission for the sake of space:

module SYSTEM_ATM;
type
...
PassWord = nat0; /* the precise definition of PassWord is finalized. */
...

inv
forall[x: Account] | 1000 <= x.password <= 9999;
 /* The password of every account must be a natural number with four
    digits in the range between 1000 and 9999. */
...
process Withdraw(amount: real, account1: Account)
                e_msg: string | cash: real
ext wr account_file
pre account1 inset account_file
post (exists[x: account_file] | x = account1 and
                                x.balance >= amount and
                                cash = amount)
    and
    account_file = union(diff(~account_file, {account1}),
        {modify(account1, balance -> account1.balance - amount)})
    or
    not exists[x: account_file] | x = account1 and
                                  x.balance >= amount and
                                  e_meg = "The amount is too big")
comment
If the balance of "account1" is greater than or equal to "amount", then assign

"amount" to cash and reduce "amount" from the balance of "account1"; otherwise, if the "amount" is greater than the balance of "account1", then issue an message to indicate the lack of sufficient money to withdraw from "account1".
end_process;
...

end_process;
end_module;

In this formal design specification we adopt the semi-formal specification in comments of processes to help explain the meaning of the formal specification for future maintenance or system evolution. Also, we decide to define the given type PassWord in the semi-formal specification as **nat0** for passwords are required to be a natural number with four digits. In this particular case, we do not need to evolve any process or the entire CDFD, but this does not mean there is no need to do so in general.

Note that several operators defined on set types and composite types are used, such as **union**(), **diff**(), **modify**(), etc. Briefly speaking, the operation **union**(x, y) is the union of two sets x and y; **diff**(x, y) yields the set whose elements belong to x but not y; and **modify**(x, f -> v1) yields a new composite object from the given composite object x by replacing the value of its field f with v1. The detailed discussion of these operators can be found in [16].

5 Rigorous Review

Review is a traditional technique for static analysis of software to detect faults that undermine its reliability. Basically, software review means to *check through* software in an appropriate manner, either by a team or an individual. Since software means both program and its related documentations, such as specification and design, a review can be conducted for all level documentations. Various review methods have been proposed and/or applied in practice with different names, such as *active design reviews* [13] and *inspection* [14], and more importantly, many studies have shown that detecting faults in specifications helps to substantially reduce the cost and risk of software projects [20]. When dealing with specifications with no formal semantics, the review techniques have to be applied intellectually based on reviewers' experience, and may not be supported systematically in depth. However, for formal specifications more rigorous review techniques can be developed and applied. To make reviews effective and efficient, especially for large-scale and complex systems, it is important to use a systematic method that allows the reviewer to focus on a manageable component at a time and provides an automatic analysis based on the review results of all the related components. In this section I describe a specific technique for rigorous reviews of SOFL specifications with those features.

5.1 Steps for Rigorous Reviews

A review of a specification takes four steps:

1. derive all the necessary properties to be reviewed from the specification, and to express them as predicate expressions.
2. build a *Review Task Tree* (RTT) to present all the review tasks graphically and logically.
3. perform reviews for all necessary tasks in the tree.
4. evaluate the review results to determine whether any fault is detected or not.

Review is intended not only to verify the consistency of the specification, but more importantly to validate the specification. For this reason, a review task tree must show a clear logical relation between the top task and other review tasks. The evaluation of review results of all the individual tasks will be properly used to determine whether the property under review is correct.

There might be many kinds of properties for a specification, but the most important ones include

- *internal consistency,*
- *satisfiability,*
- *validity.*

Definition 1. *A specification is said to be internally consistent if and only if there is no contradiction with the syntax and semantics of SOFL language in the specification.*

Definition 2. *A specification is satisfiable if and only if there exists an output satisfying the postcondition for a given input satisfying the precondition.*

Such a specification ensures the existence of a program that implements it.

Definition 3. *A specification is valid if and only if it satisfies the user's conception of requirements.*

Since the conception of requirements is not a formal concept, the formalization of the "validity" concept is almost impossible. This nature presents a challenge to reviews of specifications for their validation, and there seems no radical solution yet to this problem.

5.2 Properties of Specifications

To conduct rigorous reviews of the properties described above, we first need to express them as predicate expressions. For the sake of space, I focus on the consistency between a process and the related invariant as an example to explain the procedure of a rigorous review.

Let $P(x; y; s) : [pre\_P, post\_P]$ denote a process and $I = \forall_{x \in X} \cdot Q(x)$ a related invariant defined in module M. Then the consisteny between P and I is defined as follows:

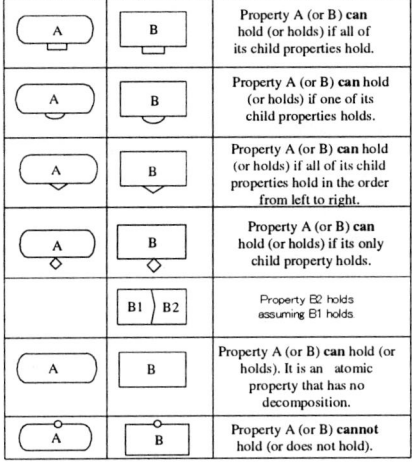

Fig. 5. The main components of RTT

Definition 4. *A process P and invariant I are consistent if and only if the following conditions hold:*

(1) $\neg(pre\_P \wedge I \Leftrightarrow false)$
(2) $\neg(pre\_P \wedge post\_P \wedge I \Leftrightarrow false)$

In other words, invariant I must not be violated before and after the execution of process P, according to its pre and postconditions, for the invariant is required to be sustained throughout the module and the related parts in the entire specification.

To review these predicate expressions, we build a *review task tree* (RTT) drived from the expressions. Figure 5 shows all the most important nodes of the review task tree notation. Each node represents a *review task*, defining what to do with a property, and it may be connected to "child nodes" in different ways, depending on the type of the node. There are two kinds of review tasks: one is "the property involved **holds**" and another is "the property involved **can hold**".

The result of reviewing a task has three possibilities: *positive, uncertain*, and *negative*. A positive result means that no fault in the property involved is detected; an uncertain result provides no evidence to either support or deny the property; and a negative result indicates that the property contains faults.

Let us take the process **Withdraw** and the only invariant, known as I, for type **Account** in the ATM system as an example to illustrate how a RTT can be built to support a review of their consistency. Figure 6 shows a RTT built based on the formal expression of the consistency:

    1000 <= account1.password <= 9999 **and**
    forall[x: account_file] | 1000 <= x.password <= 9999

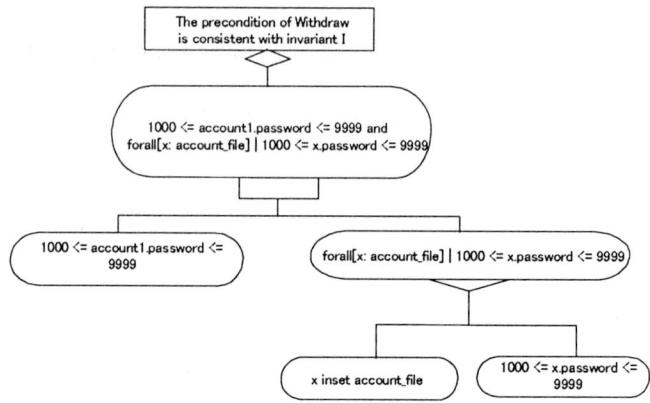

Fig. 6. A RTT for the consistency between the process Withdraw and invariant I

Reviews and Evaluation of a RTT. In principle review of a RTT is done by human reviewer, possibly with support of software tools. The question is how to help the human reviewer to perform reviews effectively and comprehensively. In SOFL we adopt the technique called *walk through with sample data*. By this technique we first produce some sample data, similar to test cases for program testing, for the variables involved in the predicate expressions under reviewing and then let human reviewer check whether the evaluation of the expressions are satisfactory or not. The key point of this technique is the generation of the sample data that could provide the most effective aid to the reviewer for examining every aspect of the expressions.

For example, to review the expression 1000 <= account1.password <= 9999, given in Figure 6 as an atomic task, to decide whether it can hold, we need to check whether it is possible to have such an account1 meeting the condition. For this purpose, we examine the types of account1 and its field password to see whether we can find a value for password that is greater than or equal to 1000 and less than or equal to 9999. This is easy to be proved because, at least, we can find the following value for account1:

account1 = mk_Account(20021425, 1010, 100.50)

where mk_Account is a *make function* that yields a value account1 of type Account such that account1.account_no = 20021425, account1.password = 1010, and account1.balance = 100.50.

To determine whether the top task of the RTT in Figure 6 is performed successfully (i.e., the top property holds), we only need to know whether all the atomic tasks are performed successfully, because the truth of their properties (or expressions) determines the truth of the top property according to the RTT logic. The atomic tasks are represented by the three nodes, respectively, in Figure 6 that contains the following expressions:

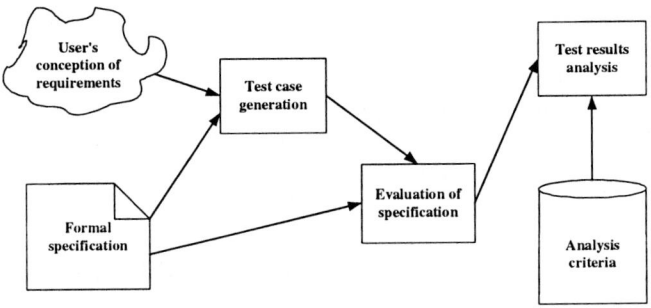

Fig. 7. The process of specification testing

- 1000 <= account1.password <= 9999
- x inset account_file
- 1000 <= x.password <= 9999

This decision process can be automatically supported by a software tool because it is entirely syntactical.

6 Specification Testing

By specification testing I mean an activity of detecting faults in specifications with *test cases*. Testing is complementary to the rigorous review technique in the sense that the former focuses on the examination of input and output relations of processes while the latter emphasizes the importance of examining the structure of process specifications. Also, rigorous reviews are usually done *statically* (i.e., without the need to "execute" specifications) whereas testing are usually performed dynamically (i.e., with the need to "execute" specifications).

Specification testing usually takes three steps: *generating test cases, evaluating the specification or necessary logical expressions with the test cases*, and *analyzing test results*. In fact, the idea of specification testing is similar to that of program testing; the only difference is that in the former there is no need to run any program, but in latter execution of program is necessary.

Figure 7 shows a process of specification testing. The most important task of testing is to generate test cases that will help to effectively uncover faults in the specification. Two methods for test case generation can be used. One is to generate test cases based on the specification itself. This shares the principle of the *white-box* testing of programs. Such test cases are usually expected to detect faults leading to the violation of consistency properties of the specification. For example, satisfiability of a process and the consistency between process specifications and invariants in a module. Several criteria are given in our previous publication [21] for generating test cases based on specifications. Another way is to generate test cases based on the user's conception of requirements. This method is similar to the *black-box* testing of programs, aiming to validate the specification.

Testing of an entire specification can be conducted on two levels: *unit testing* and *integration testing*. Unit testing aims to detect faults in components, which can be invariants and/or processes, and to ensure their reliability. The reliability of components must be ensured before they are used in the testing of the entire specification, because the reliability of the specification depends on that of its components. Integration testing tries to uncover faults in the interfaces between components. The targets of integration testing are CDFDs. For the sake of space, I cannot discuss the details of the specification testing technique. Readers who are interested in testing *unexecutable* specifications can refer to my previous publication [21].

7 Conclusions

While emphasizing the importance of improving the accessibility of existing formal methods to practitioners in general, I have introduced a specific formal engineering method known as SOFL that includes a specification language and a method for constructing and verifying specifications. The specification language is intended to strike a good balance between suitable and compatible graphical notations (e.g., DFDs) and formal notations (e.g., Petri Nets and VDM-SL), and to utilize the advantages of both the structured and object-oriented methods. The method is intended to provide a framework for incorporating formal methods into the software development process. Specifically, for constructing specifications the method adopts a combination of refinement and evolution in achieving accurate and complete functional specifications, and follows a three-step approach to achieving formal specifications of systems. For verification and validation, the method includes two techniques: rigorous review and testing. Both techniques aim to be practical, but rigorous, for detecting potential faults in the specification and validating the defined functionality of the system. I believe that theoretical achievements in formal methods are important, but formal engineering methods could be an effective means to realize the ideal of formal methods in practice.

The focus of our future research will be on the further development of techniques and supporting tools for requirements engineering with SOFL, rigorous review, testing, and transformation of SOFL specifications, and for verification and validation of Java programs based on SOFL specifications.

References

1. C.A.R. Hoare and N. Wirth. An Axiomatic Definition of the Programming Language PASCAL. Acta Informatica, (2):335–355, 1973.
2. Cli. B. Jones. Systematic Software Development Using VDM. Prentice-Hall International(UK) Ltd., 1990.
3. Jim Woodcock and Jim Davies. Using Z: Specification, Refinement, and Proof. Prentice-Hall Europe, 1996.

4. Ralph-Johan Back and Joakim von Wright. Refinement Calculus - A Systematic Introduction. Springer-Verlag, 1998.
5. Steve Schneider. B-Method. Palgrave, 2001.
6. Mike Gordon and Andrew Pitts. The HOL Logic and System. In J. Bowen, editor, Towards Verified Systems, volume 2 of Real-Time Safety Critical Systems series. Elsevier, 1994.
7. Dan Craigen, Susan Gerhart, and Ted Ralston. An International Survey of Industrial Applications of Formal Methods. Technical Report NISTGCR 93/626, U.S. Department of Commerce, Technology Administration, National Institute of Standards and Technology Computer Systems Laboratory, Gaithersburg, MD 20899, 1993.
8. Edward Yourdon. Modern Structured Analysis. Prentice Hall International, Inc., 1989.
9. Wilfried Brauer, Grzegorz Rozenberg, and Arto Salomaa. Petri Nets - An Introduction. Springer-Verlag, Berlin Heidelberg, 1985.
10. John Dawes. The VDM-SL Reference Guide. Pitman, 1991.
11. Meilir Page-Jones. Fundamentals of Object-Oriented Design in UML. Dorset House Publishing, 2000.
12. G. Bernot, M. C. Gaudel, and B. Marre. Software Testing based on Formal Specifications: A Theory and a Tool. Software Engineering Journal, 6(6):387–405, 1991.
13. Dave L. Parnas and David M.Weiss. Active Design Reviews: Principles and Practices. In Proceedings of the 8th International Conference on Software Engineering, pages 215–222, Aug. 1985.
14. E. A. Meyers and J. C. Knight. An Improved Inspection Technique. Communications of the ACM, 36(11):50–61, Nov. 1993.
15. Edmund M. Clarke, Orna Grumber, and Doron Peled. Model Checking. MIT Press, 2000.
16. Shaoying Liu, A. Je. Offutt, Chris Ho-Stuart, Yong Sun, and Mitsuru Ohba. SOFL: A Formal Engineering Methodology for Industrial Applications. IEEE Transactions on Software Engineering, 24(1):337–344, January 1998. Special Issue on Formal Methods.
17. Shaoying Liu, Masashi Asuka, Kiyotoshi Komaya, and Yasuaki Nakamura. An Approach to Specifying and Verifying Safety-Critical Systems with Practical Formal Method SOFL. In Proceedings of Fourth IEEE International Conference on Engineering of Complex Computer Systems (ICECCS'98), pages 100–114, Monterey, California, USA, August 10-14 1998. IEEE Computer Society Press.
18. Douglas Bell. Software Engineering. Third Edition, Person Education Limited, 2000.
19. Carroll Morgan. Programming from Specifications. Prentice-Hall International(UK) Ltd., 1990.
20. B.W. Boehm. Software Engineering Economics. Prentice-Hall, 1981.
21. Shaoying Liu. Verifying Consistency and Validity of Formal Specifications by Testing. In Jeannette M.Wing, Jim Woodcock, and Jim Davies, editors, Proceedings of World Congress on Formal Methods in the Development of Computing Systems, Lecture Notes in Computer Science, pages 896–914, Toulouse, France, September 1999. Springer-Verlag.

Maintaining Referential Integrity on the Web

Mark A. Hale

Interwoven, Inc
803 11th Avenue, Sunnyvale, CA 94089
mark.hale@interwoven.com

Abstract. The Web has proven itself as a capable tool for establishing business practices around information exchange and application access. There is an underlying shift in web application technology that must be addressed to insure systems integrity for businesses. Web services allow us to consider the development of independent task-driven applications that mix both code and content. For example, modern Portal servers use portlets to embody presentation, personalization, logic, and security as code. These portlets also connect to a content source such as a news feed, file system, or directory server. Both the code and content source must be integrated and functioning at all times to deliver the expected user experience.

High Value Applications

Further compounding the business challenges, these web applications have not been given the due diligence afforded to installed applications. Installed applications are programmed by dedicated teams over a course of months or years with rigid program reviews and checkpoints. Web applications are built by disconnected users over several days or weeks. These applications are often unmanaged. This is an unfortunate consequence because these short development and rapid turnaround projects often have significant business impact. The average portlet is used enterprise-wide and businesses cannot afford to have it fail. They are developed at a marginal cost but have considerable value in the enterprise.

Web Application Management

Key to maintaining system reliability is to integrate development, test, and deployment of both code and content. This is called *Web Application Management* (WAM). The code is tested within a staging server that executes the code and provides access to content sources such as databases, file systems, and channels. After testing, both the code and the content are pushed to production simultaneously. Content must be fully synchronized with the application code during deployment to insure that the application code continues to work with the current schemas. A surprising number of portlets fail in production because database schemas are changed without notice to application developers. Simultaneous deployment will alleviate stoppages and Web Application Management includes the notion of controlled release schedules for both code and content.

Referential Integrity

Virtualization is an essential technology for testing within the staging environment. Ideally, uses would like to use production links in all of their applications rather than temporary links for staging that are mapped to their final form at deployment. A proxy server acts as an intermediary in staging to map production links back to the staging server. Therefore, both code and content developers alike are working as though they are in production. Virtualization maximizes reliability of deployed applications.

Next Step: Web Services

Web services are the model to build these applications in the future. It is implicitly assumed that these services are easily transferred from one organization to the next, through either redirection or moving the actual code. This model is very difficult to realize in practice because the content driving the applications are neglected and it ignores the accepted practice of testing for system reliability in mission critical applications. Rarely do databases and file systems exist in the same server configuration from one organization to the next. Web applications, including new Web service applications, must be transferred into a staging environment for integrating testing and deployment.

Failure to accommodate the referential integrity in back-end schemas is a well-understood challenge in business-to-business environments and leads to considerable expenses in services and support. Its challenges should not be underestimated as applications are proliferated across the Web with web services. Web application management and virtualization will insure the integrity of the integrated application code and sources of content for better business environments.

Formal Methods in Enterprise Computing

Richard Jüllig

169 University Avenue
Palo Alto, CA 94301, USA
Richard@commerce.net

Extended Abstract

The impact of formal methods on enterprise computing historically has been fairly small. This may be about to change. Current business and information technology trends present both opportunities and challenges for the application of formal methods in enterprise computing.

Although the end to the first wave of e-business and e-commerce shattered many naïve dreams, the major impact of networked computing technologies, including the Internet and the World Wide Web, on businesses is yet to come. The business community now realizes that networked computing technologies can form an *enterprise nervous system* that in turn enables the *real-time, adaptive enterprise*. The real-time, adaptive enterprise has up-to-the-date or even up-to-the-minute visibility into its own state. It is able to respond efficiently to changes in its business environments, be it changes in product demand or breakdowns in production or distribution infrastructure, by adjusting its supply, production, and distribution channels appropriately to optimize chosen business objectives, e.g. customer satisfaction, market share, or profit.

Computing networks as a high-capability, low-cost computing, information, and communication infrastructure change the nature of businesses and business relationships in several ways. They precipitate the transformation of tightly integrated enterprises into loose federations of highly focused enterprises, and with it the mutually reinforcing trends of business process automation, dynamic business partner relationships, and increasing intelligence in the enterprise computing network.

The promise of the potential economic benefits currently fuels a dizzying array of activities toward a new generation of distributed enterprise computing technologies. The work on Web Services and related technologies is very much driven by practical interests and objectives; nevertheless, it could benefit substantially from the concepts and tools developed by the formal methods community.

Salient issues include information interoperability, business process specification, and business process execution. Information interoperability addresses the problem of relating semantically equivalent but syntactically different descriptions of business objects and services. This issue is at the heart of the integration problem of product catalogs and business service directories, the search over such catalogs and directories, and the dynamic composition of Web Services. Automated yet flexible complex business processes call for structuring techniques supporting both global and local views, e.g. process phases and role-specific views, and for the specification of invariants, constraints, and objectives. These invariants, constraints and objectives can serve to statically establish desired properties, or to dynamically bind to specific services and resources, or to monitor the health and soundness of the ever-changing enterprise system.

The talk will go into some detail on the application of specification structuring and mapping concepts realized in the Specware™ system to information interoperability and search. By viewing an XML schema as a specification, and an XML document as a model of such a specification, the notions of specification morphisms and interpretations carry over straightforwardly. Many of the information mapping and search problems then amount to finding or constructing a suitable interpretation.

The talk will conclude with a discussion of some of the factors that may inhibit or create special challenges for the use of formal in enterprise computing.

Unifying Theories of Parallel Programming

Jim Woodcock and Arthur Hughes[*]

University of Kent at Canterbury, UK
{J.C.P.Woodcock,A.P.Hughes}@ukc.ac.uk

Abstract. We are developing a shared-variable refinement calculus in the style of the sequential calculi of Back, Morgan, and Morris. As part of this work, we're studying different theories of shared-variable programming. Using the concepts and notations of Hoare & He's unifying theories of programming (UTP), we give a formal semantics to a programming language that contains sequential composition, conditional statements, while loops, nested parallel composition, and shared variables. We first give a UTP semantics to labelled action systems, and then use this to give the semantics of our programs. Labelled action systems have a unique normal form that allows a simple formalisation and validation of different logics for reasoning about shared-variable programs. In this paper, we demonstrate how this is done for Lamport's Concurrent Hoare Logic.

1 Introduction

Concurrent programming is hard and shared-variable programming is very hard. In the sequential world, the refinement calculi of Back [2], Morgan [10], and Morris [11] have been very influential in helping to understand the development of programs from their specifications. We want to extend this successful calculational style to the development of shared-variable programs. In order to build on previous research, we are formalising a number of logics for reasoning about shared-variable programs. The objective is to contrast and compare the different approaches, combining the best ideas into our proposed calculus.

We give a formal semantics to a shared-variable programming language by translation into labelled action systems. The semantics of labelled action systems is expressed using the alphabetised relational calculus from Hoare and He's unifying theories of programming (UTP) [5].

Programs in our language have a unique normal form as a labelled action system. This normal form allows a simple formalisation of several logics. In this paper we consider Lamport's Concurrent Hoare Logic, giving as an example of its application, an invariance proof of a mutual exclusion algorithm. We use our model to validate all the rules of the logic; this validation demonstrates the calculational power of the alphabetised relational calculus. A technical report contains a full account of this work with all its proofs [13].

---

[*] This work has been supported by the QinetiQ grant CU009–019346 on "Advances in formal modelling and concurrency as represented by the *Circus* language."

2 Unifying Theories of Programming

The semantic domain for unifying theories is an alphabetised form of Tarski's relational calculus. Here, sequential composition is relational composition; the conditional is a Boolean connective; nondeterminism is disjunction; and parallelism is a restricted conjunction. The miracle of the refinement calculus is the empty relation; abortion is the universal relation; and an assertion is a conditional abort. Refinement is simply implication, and all the laws of the relational calculus are valid for reasoning about correctness.

The auxiliary variables describe observations shared with the real world. For example: *clock* denotes the current time; l denotes the value of the program counter; *okay* denotes whether the program has terminated in a stable state; *ref* denotes the actions that cannot happen next; *resource* denotes the number of resources currently in use; *tr* denotes the trace of events that have happened so far; and *wait* denotes whether a process is awaiting interaction with its environment.

Alphabetised relations are similar to Z's schemas, but are somewhat simpler, as their variables are untyped. The alphabetised relational calculus is based on Tarski's calculus, with significance attached to the choice of free variables mentioned in the specification of each relation. A relation $P, Q, \ldots,$ **true** is a pair $(\alpha P, P)$, where every free variable of P must be found in its alphabet. In the manner or Z, variables may be decorated to distinguish their initial and final values: $\alpha P = in\alpha P \cup out\alpha P$. A condition $b, c, d, \ldots,$ **true** has an empty $out\alpha$. The calculus has a number of primitive notions, such as **true**, negation, disjunction, and existential quantification; operators such as composition are defined in terms of these primitive concepts. Relations are used to model programs, with refinement as relational inclusion.

The conditional relation is described using a distfix notation. For relations P and Q and condition b, instead of writing "**if** b **then** P **else** Q **fi**" we write "$P \triangleleft b \triangleright Q$". The conditional has a simple definition: if $\alpha b \subseteq \alpha P = \alpha Q$, then

$$P \triangleleft b \triangleright Q \ \widehat{=}\ (b \wedge P) \vee (\neg b \wedge Q) \quad \text{and} \quad \alpha(P \triangleleft b \triangleright Q) \ \widehat{=}\ \alpha P$$

Many useful properties are expressed nicely using the distfix notation.

Relational composition is defined in the usual way: there must exist an intermediate state that is produced by the first relation and consumed by the second. If the output alphabet of P is v' and the input alphabet of Q is v, then we have

$$P(v')\ ;\ Q(v) \ \widehat{=}\ \exists v_0 \bullet P(v_0) \wedge Q(v_0) \quad \text{if} \quad out\alpha P = in\alpha P' = \{v'\}$$

$$in\alpha(P(v')\ ;\ Q(v)) \ \widehat{=}\ in\alpha P \quad \text{and} \quad out\alpha(P(v')\ ;\ Q(v)) \ \widehat{=}\ out\alpha Q$$

Composition satisfies two important laws: it's associative and it distributes leftwards through the conditional.

The assignment $x := e$ has a simple semantics: it equates the final value of x with e; no other variable in the alphabet is changed by this assignment. For alphabet $A = \{x, y, \ldots, z, x', y', \ldots, z'\}$ and $\alpha e \subseteq A$, we have

$$x :=_A e \ \widehat{=}\ (x' = e \wedge y' = y \wedge \cdots \wedge z' = z) \quad \text{and} \quad \alpha(x :=_A e) \ \widehat{=}\ A$$

A special case of assignment leaves all variables in the alphabet unchanged; it's called "skip": if $A = \{v, v'\}$, then

$$\mathit{I\!I}_A \ \widehat{=}\ (v' = v) \quad \text{and} \quad \alpha \mathit{I\!I}_A \ \widehat{=}\ A$$

Skip (with the right alphabet) is a left and right unit for composition.

In the alphabetised relational calculus, nondeterminism is simply disjunction.

$$P \sqcap Q \ \widehat{=}\ P \vee Q \quad \text{and} \quad \alpha(P \sqcap Q) \ \widehat{=}\ \alpha P$$

The bottom element in the lattice is the full relation **true**, and the top is the empty relation **false**.

$$\bot_A \ \widehat{=}\ \mathbf{true} \qquad \alpha \bot_A \ \widehat{=}\ A \quad \text{and} \quad \top_A \ \widehat{=}\ \mathbf{false} \qquad \alpha \top_A \ \widehat{=}\ A$$

The relation $\bot$ is called "abort": it can do absolutely anything. The relation $\top$ is called "miracle": it can achieve the impossible.

Iteration of a relation is defined in terms of recursion, conditional, and skip.

$$b * P \ \widehat{=}\ \mu X \bullet ((P \mathbin{;} X) \triangleleft b \triangleright \mathit{I\!I})$$

A comprehensive set of laws for all these operators is contained in [5].

An assumption is something that makes a condition true: the assumption c behaves like skip if c is true, and like a miracle otherwise. An assertion behaves like skip if c is true, and like abort otherwise.

$$c^\top \ \widehat{=}\ \mathit{I\!I} \triangleleft c \triangleright \top \quad \text{[assumption]} \quad \text{and} \quad c_\bot \ \widehat{=}\ \mathit{I\!I} \triangleleft c \triangleright \bot \quad \text{[assertion]}$$

In [10], these are called coercions and assumptions, respectively.

The Hoare triple $p\,\{Q\}\,r$ describes the specification that a program Q is required to satisfy: given precondition p, it must establish postcondition r.

$$p\,\{Q\}\,r \ \widehat{=}\ [\,Q \Rightarrow (p \Rightarrow r')\,]$$

An important subtheory of relations allows the separation of preconditions from postconditions, in the manner of B, VDM, and the refinement calculus. It allows us to model the total correctness of programming constructs using relations.

We introduce two distinguished variables into the alphabet of relations: $okay$ records the observation that a program has started; $okay'$ records the observation that the program has terminated. A design is a pair of predicates $P \vdash Q$, where neither predicate mentions $okay$ or $okay'$. It has the following meaning:

$$(P \vdash Q) \ \widehat{=}\ (okay \wedge P \Rightarrow okay' \wedge Q)$$

where P is the precondition and Q is the postcondition. The separation of precondition from postcondition allows us to write a specification that has a more generous precondition than simply the domain of the relation used as a specification. Specifically, we can describe the miracle: **true** $\vdash$ **false**, which is always guaranteed to terminate, and achieves the impossible when it does.

The theory of designs forms a complete lattice, with miracle $\top_D$ as the top element, and abort $\bot_D$ as the bottom element.

$$\top_D \,\widehat{=}\, (\,\textbf{true} \vdash \textbf{false}\,) \qquad \bot_D \,\widehat{=}\, (\,\textbf{false} \vdash \textbf{true}\,)$$

$\top_D = \neg\, okay$ and $\bot_D = \textbf{true}$, and abort is a left zero for sequential composition. If one design refines another, then we have the familiar proof obligations.

$$[\,(P_2 \vdash Q_2) \Rightarrow (P_1 \vdash Q_1)\,] \quad \text{iff} \quad [\,P_1 \Rightarrow P_2\,] \text{ and } [\,P_1 \wedge Q_2 \Rightarrow Q_1\,]$$

The definition of assignment must be reinterpreted in the theory of designs.

$$(x := e) \,\widehat{=}\, (\,\textbf{true} \vdash x' = e \wedge y' = y \wedge \cdots \wedge z' = z\,)$$
$$\mathit{II} \,\widehat{=}\, (\,\textbf{true} \vdash x' = x \wedge y' = y \wedge \cdots \wedge z' = z\,)$$

If the expression contains the application of partial functions, then the precondition may contain suitable definedness conditions instead of simply being **true**. There are four healthiness conditions associated with designs.

H1 $R = (okay \Rightarrow R)$
H2 $[\,R[false/okay'] \Rightarrow R[true/okay']\,]$
H3 $R = R\,;\,\mathit{II}$
H4 $R\,;\,\textbf{true} = \textbf{true}$

This conditions are motivated and explained in [5].

3 Action Systems

A guarded command [4] is a condition-design pair gP. If g is true, then the guarded command behaves like P; if g is false, then P is not started.

Definition 1 (Guarded command). *For condition g and design P,*

$$gP \,\widehat{=}\, g^\top;\,P$$

An action is just a guarded command.

An action system [1] consists of a state, an initialisation, and a number of actions. First the initialisation is performed; then, repeatedly, a command whose guard is true is selected and executed. If several guards are true, then one of them is selected and its corresponding command is executed.

Definition 2 (Action system). *If v is a vector of state variables and e is a vector of their initialisations, and $g_1\,C_1, \ldots, g_n\,C_n$ is a collection of actions, then the following is an action system.*

$$\textbf{var }\, v := e;\; (true) * (\,(g_1\,C_1) \vee \cdots \vee (g_n\,C_n)\,)$$

See [1] for further information on action systems.

4 Labelled Action Systems

We use a restricted form of action system to describe the behaviour of programs in our shared-variable language; these action systems are similar to labelled transition systems. The basic actions that we use are triples ($l : P \mid n$), consisting of a program label l, a design P, and a continuation label n.

Program statements are translated into these actions, and the program counters are simulated, keeping track of the execution state. To do this, we introduce a new observational variable ls, called the label set, which contains the labels of program statements which may be executed next, one for each of the currently executing threads in the program.

A program action ($l : P \mid n$) is a guarded command, where the guard ensures that the label set ls contains the label l. The correct sequencing of commands requires us to do some housekeeping to update the label set. We use the notation $ls \oslash (l, n)$ to denote the update $(ls \setminus \{l\}) \cup \{n\}$, and where it is clear that we're using sets, $ls \oslash (L, N)$ to denote the update $(ls \setminus L) \cup N$.

Definition 3 (Program action). *If P is a design and l and n are labels, then a program action is defined by*

$$(l : P \mid n) \;\widehat{=}\; l \in ls \, P;\; ls := ls \oslash (l, n)$$

A conditional continuation is a quadruple ($l :\mid m \triangleleft b \triangleright n$) consisting of a statement label l and a conditional continuation: control passes to m if b is true, otherwise it passes to n. Labelled atomic conditions within a program are given a semantics using labelled condition actions.

Definition 4 (Conditional continuation). *For labels l, m, and n and condition b, the conditional continuation is defined by*

$$(l :\mid m \triangleleft b \triangleright n) \;\widehat{=}\; l \in ls \, ls := ls \oslash (l, (m \triangleleft b \triangleright n))$$

The observational variable ls contains a set of program labels in order to model concurrency: each label in ls represents an active thread of control. Multi-program actions allow us to fork and join this control flow in an appropriate way: a multiple continuation provides the fork; a multiple label provides the join.

We use a program action system to compute the operational semantics of our concurrent programs. A program action system is defined in a similar manner to an action system. It starts with the declaration of the state variables and the observational variable ls. This is followed by an assignment that initialises ls with the initial labels of the action system. This is followed by a while loop whose body contains the disjunction of the program actions, and repeats as along as the observational variable ls does not contain the final labels of the program.

Definition 5 (Program action system). *If v is a vector of state variables, P is a disjunction of program actions, I is a set of initial labels, and F is a set of final labels, then a program action system is defined by*

$$\textbf{var } v, ls := I;\; (F \not\subseteq ls) * P$$

Program action systems are the basis of our semantics for shared-variables

5 Syntax and Semantics

A labelled program is a finite, nonempty list of symbols whose syntax is characterised by the following BNF-notation.

program	::=	statement : label
statement	::=	assignment | wait | sequence | conditional | iteration | parallel
assignment	::=	label : varlist := exprlist
wait	::=	label : **wait** predicate
sequence	::=	statement ; statement
conditional	::=	label : **if** predicate **then** statement **else** statement **fi**
iteration	::=	label : **while** predicate **do** statement **od**
parallel	::=	(statement || statement)
block	::=	label : [statement]

A labelled program is given a semantics as a program action system. We first give the atomic operations of assignment and conditional evaluations a semantics using program actions and conditional continuations. Then each of the program constructors is given a semantics in terms of its components, using conditional continuations and disjunction. The control flow of the nested statements is not lost, but is modelled by the labels and continuations of the actions and the execution of the enclosing loop of the action system. For example, actions with multiple continuation labels are used to initiate each thread of a parallel composition, whilst actions with multiple labels are used to terminate them.

The function αlab yields the statement labels for a program; since there may be multiple labels, the function returns sets of labels. A necessary healthiness condition for a program P is that these sets are pairwise disjoint.

The assignment statement is one of the two atomic operations in our programming language. An atomic multiple assignment is allowed.

Definition 6 (Assignment). *If x is a vector of variables and e is a vector of expressions, and L_1 and L_2 are sets of labels, then an assignment is defined by*

$$L_1 : x := e; \; L_2 : \; \widehat{=} \; (\, L_1 : x := e \mid L_2 \,)$$

and the label functions are defined over an assignment by

$$\alpha init(\, L_1 : x := e; \; L_2 : \,) \; \widehat{=} \; L_1 \quad \text{and} \quad \alpha fin(\, L_1 : x := e; \; L_2 : \,) \; \widehat{=} \; L_2$$
$$\alpha lab(\, L_1 : x := e; \; L_2 : \,) \; \widehat{=} \; \{L_1\} \quad \text{and} \quad \alpha loc(\, L_1 : x := e; \; L_2 : \,) \; \widehat{=} \; L_1 \cup L_2$$

The wait statement is also atomic. The statement **wait** b cannot proceed unless the condition b is true; in other words, it's a guard.

Definition 7 (Wait). *If b is a condition, and L_1 and L_2 are labels, then*

$$L_1 : \textbf{wait} \; b; \; L_2 : \; \widehat{=} \; (\, L_1 : b \mathit{II} \mid L_2 \,)$$

and the label functions are defined over a wait by

$$\alpha init(\, L_1 : \textbf{wait} \; b; \; L_2 : \,) \; \widehat{=} \; L_1 \quad \text{and} \quad \alpha fin(\, L_1 : \textbf{wait} \; b; \; L_2 : \,) \; \widehat{=} \; L_2$$
$$\alpha lab(\, L_1 : \textbf{wait} \; b; \; L_2 : \,) \; \widehat{=} \; \{L_1\} \quad \text{and} \quad \alpha loc(\, L_1 : \textbf{wait} \; b; \; L_2 : \,) \; \widehat{=} \; L_1 \cup L_2$$

The first program combinator to consider is sequential composition. In $P \; ; \; Q$, P's final labels must be Q's initial ones and their label sets must be disjoint. In this way, when P terminates, control will be passed to Q.

Definition 8 (Sequential composition). *If P and Q are programs with*

$$\alpha\mathit{fin}(P) = \alpha\mathit{init}(Q) \quad \text{and} \quad (\bigcup \alpha\mathit{lab}(P)) \cap (\bigcup \alpha\mathit{lab}(Q)) = \emptyset$$

then their sequential composition is defined by $P \; ; \; Q \;\hat{=}\; P \vee Q$ and the label functions are defined over a sequential composition by

$$\alpha\mathit{init}(P \; ; \; Q) \;\hat{=}\; \alpha\mathit{init}(P) \qquad \text{and} \quad \alpha\mathit{fin}(P \; ; \; Q) \;\hat{=}\; \alpha\mathit{fin}(Q)$$
$$\alpha\mathit{lab}(P \; ; \; Q) \;\hat{=}\; \alpha\mathit{lab}(P) \cup \alpha\mathit{lab}(Q) \quad \text{and} \quad \alpha\mathit{loc}(P \; ; \; Q) \;\hat{=}\; \alpha\mathit{loc}(P) \cup \alpha\mathit{loc}(Q)$$

In the conditional statement l : **if** b **then** P **else** Q **fi**, the condition is evaluated at a control point at the beginning of the statement. In the semantics, l labels a conditional action that chooses a continuation between the initial labels of P and the initial labels of Q. So, the control flow splits after the evaluation of b; it is brought back together by P and Q having the same final labels.

The definition of iteration is similar to that of the conditional, except that the conditional action chooses between a continuation to the start of the body and one to the statement following the iteration.

Definition 9 (Iteration). *If b is a condition, L, M and N are sets of labels, and P is a program, such that*

$$\alpha\mathit{init}(P) = M \quad \text{and} \quad \alpha\mathit{fin}(P) = L$$
$$L \notin \alpha\mathit{lab}(P) \quad \text{and} \quad N \notin \alpha\mathit{lab}(P)$$

then an iteration is defined by

$$L : \textbf{while } b \textbf{ do } P \textbf{ od} \;\hat{=}\; (\, L :|\; M \triangleleft b \triangleright N \,) \vee P$$

and the label functions are defined over an iteration by

$$\begin{aligned}
\alpha\mathit{init}(\, L : \textbf{while } b \textbf{ do } P \textbf{ od} \,) &\;\hat{=}\; L \\
\alpha\mathit{fin}(\, L : \textbf{while } b \textbf{ do } P \textbf{ od} \,) &\;\hat{=}\; N \\
\alpha\mathit{lab}(\, L : \textbf{while } b \textbf{ do } P \textbf{ od} \,) &\;\hat{=}\; \{L\} \cup \alpha\mathit{lab}(P) \\
\alpha\mathit{loc}(\, L : \textbf{while } b \textbf{ do } P \textbf{ od} \,) &\;\hat{=}\; L \cup \alpha\mathit{loc}(P) \cup N
\end{aligned}$$

If two programs P and Q have disjoint locations, then their parallel composition is simply the interleaving of their atomic actions. In the parallel composition, the programs are started simultaneously and the termination of the composition requires both programs to terminate. We get this semantics by insisting that all the component programs' initial labels are present before their parallel composition can start, and that all their final labels are present before the composition can terminate. With these requirements, the parallel operator has a remarkably simple semantics: just disjunction.

Definition 10 (Parallel composition). *If P and Q are programs such that*

$$\alpha locs(P) \cap \alpha locs(Q) = \emptyset$$

then the parallel composition is defined by $P \parallel Q \mathrel{\widehat{=}} P \vee Q$, and the label functions are defined over a parallel composition by

$$\begin{aligned}
\alpha init(P \parallel Q) &\mathrel{\widehat{=}} \alpha init(P) \cup \alpha init(Q) \\
\alpha fin(P \parallel Q) &\mathrel{\widehat{=}} \alpha fin(P) \cup \alpha fin(Q) \\
\alpha lab(P \parallel Q) &\mathrel{\widehat{=}} \alpha lab(P) \cup \alpha lab(Q) \\
\alpha loc(P \parallel Q) &\mathrel{\widehat{=}} \alpha loc(P) \cup \alpha loc(Q)
\end{aligned}$$

The atomic components of a program are assignments and wait statements, which are both translated into program actions. The program combinators are all restricted forms of disjunction. If we apply the semantic definitions often enough, we can reduce a program to an action system consisting of a disjunction of atomic labelled actions. There is an atomic operation for each label set in $\alpha lab(P)$. This reduction is unique up to commutativity of disjunction.

Theorem 1 (Normal form). *If P is a program, then it can be expressed as a disjunction of program actions, one for each atomic operation in the program:*

$$P = \bigvee \{\, i : \alpha lab(P) \bullet P_i \,\}$$

where each P_i is of the form: ($L : gx := e \mid M \triangleleft b \triangleright N$).

The labelled, guarded assignment with conditional continuation is the general form of a labelled assignment, a labelled wait, or a conditional continuation.

6 Concurrent Hoare Logic

In reasoning about about concurrent programs, Lamport [9] introduces three location predicates: $at(P)$ means that program control resides immediately before the first statement in the program P; $in(P)$ means that program control resides either immediately before the first statement in P, or somewhere within P; $after(P)$ means that control resides immediately after P's last statement.

Lamport and Schneider [8] claim that either location predicates or auxiliary variables in the style of Owicki and Gries [12] are need to verify concurrent programs in the assertional style. We give a formal definition of location predicates using the functions and the observational variable ls.

Definition 11 (Location predicates). *If P is a program, then location predicates are defined by*

$$\begin{aligned}
at(P) &\mathrel{\widehat{=}} \alpha init(P) \subseteq ls \\
in(P) &\mathrel{\widehat{=}} (\bigcup \alpha lab(P)) \cap ls \neq \emptyset \\
after(P) &\mathrel{\widehat{=}} \alpha fin(P) \subseteq ls
\end{aligned}$$

Hoare [6] described a logical system for proving the partial correctness properties of sequential programs. Hoare's logical system is based on a three-place predicate called a Hoare triple denoted by $a \{ P \} b$ where a is the precondition, P is a sequential program, and b is the postcondition. A valid Hoare triple states that: if the precondition a is satisfied when the program P is begun, then the postcondition b will be satisfied if and when the program P terminates.

Hoare presented a collection of rules for deriving valid Hoare triples for arbitrary sequential programs P. These rules may be divided into two classes: general rules applicable to all programs; and rules that define the partial correctness semantics of the programming language constructs.

Lamport [9] extended Hoare's method to proving partial correctness properties of concurrent programs. He did this by introducing a three-place predicate called a concurrent Hoare triple denoted by $\{ a \} P \{ b \}$ where a is the invariant, P is a concurrent program, and b is the postcondition. A valid concurrent Hoare triple states that: if execution is begun anywhere within P with a true, then executing P will leave a true while control is inside P, and will make b true if and when P terminates.

In a similar way to Hoare's logical system Lamport presents a collection of rules for deriving valid concurrent Hoare triples for arbitrary concurrent programs. These rules may also be divided into two classes:

1. General rules applicable to all programs:
    (a) rules to relate a Hoare triple $a \{ P \} b$ with a concurrent Hoare triple $\{ a \} P \{ b \}$ when P is an atomic statement;
    (b) rules that generalise the rules of consequence for concurrency; and
    (c) rules to reason about program-location predicates.

2. Rules that define the partial correctness semantics of the concurrent programming language constructs; each construct has two classes of rules:
    (a) a rule to introduce a concurrent Hoare triple containing the program construct that requires the validity of concurrent Hoare triples containing the components of the program construct, and
    (b) rules to reason about location predicates and the program construct.

We formally define a concurrent Hoare triple $\{ a \} P \{ b \}$ over our normal form as a conjunction of Hoare triples involving each atomic action.

Definition 12 (Concurrent Hoare triple). *If a and b are conditions, and P is a program, then the concurrent Hoare triple is defined by*

$$\{ a \} P \{ b \} \triangleq \bigwedge \{ i : \alpha lab(P) \bullet a \{ P_i \} (a \triangleleft in(P) \triangleright b) \}$$

where $P = \bigvee \{ i : \alpha lab(P) \bullet P_i \}$.

Rule 1 bridges the gap between Concurrent and Sequential Hoare Logic. It states that the partial correctness semantics of an atomic statement is simply the semantics in a sequential program: there can be no interference.

Rule 1 (Atomic statement) *If a and b don't depend on location predicates, and P is an atomic operation, then*

(a) $\dfrac{a\,\{\,P\,\}\,b}{\{\,a\,\}\,\langle P \rangle\,\{\,b\,\}}$.   (b) $\vdash in(\langle P \rangle) = at(\langle P \rangle)$

We can use rule 1 to prove the correctness of an atomic assignment statement, or even the correctness of a compound statement that is required to be atomic.

In Sequential Hoare Logic, the rules of consequence allow us to prove facts about programs by changing their specifications. For example, if we want to show that $a\,\{\,S\,\}\,c$ is valid, then it's permissible to weaken the precondition. So, if $b\,\{\,S\,\}\,c$ is valid, and if $a \Rightarrow b$, then the original triple is also valid. There are similar rules of consequence for Concurrent Hoare Logic.

Rule 2 (Consequence) *There are four rules of consequence.*

(a) $\dfrac{\{\,a\,\}\,P\,\{\,b\,\} \quad b \Rightarrow c}{\{\,a\,\}\,P\,\{\,c\,\}}$ (b) $\vdash \{\,false\,\}\,P\,\{\,false\,\}$

(c) $\dfrac{\{\,a\,\}\,P\,\{\,b\,\} \quad \{\,c\,\}\,P\,\{\,d\,\}}{\{\,a \wedge c\,\}\,P\,\{\,b \wedge d\,\} \quad \{\,a \vee c\,\}\,P\,\{\,b \vee d\,\}}$ (d) $\dfrac{\{\,a\,\}\,P\,\{\,b\,\} \quad a \Leftrightarrow c}{\{\,c\,\}\,P\,\{\,b\,\}}$

Note that the first predicate in a concurrent Hoare triple is an invariant, so the rule of consequence requires that it is replaced by an equivalent predicate.

A feature of Concurrent Hoare Logic is the technique for reasoning about program locations.

Rule 3 (Location) *There are four rules for reasoning about program locations.*

(a) $\vdash \{\,true\,\}\,P\,\{\,after(P)\,\}$ (b) $\vdash \{\,in(P)\,\}\,P\,\{\,true\,\}$

(c) $\dfrac{\{\,in(P) \wedge a\,\}\,P\,\{\,b\,\}}{\{\,a\,\}\,P\,\{\,b\,\}}$ (d) $\vdash \{\,ls \setminus \alpha locs(P) = X\,\}\,P$
$\{\,ls \setminus \alpha locs(P) = X\,\}$

Rule 3(d) requires that P cannot enable or disable any program statement other than those within its own body. It is stated using a logical constant.

Rule 4 (Wait) *We have added the wait-statement to the language. It has the property that it preserves any invariant (it doesn't actually do anything), and if it terminates, then the awaited condition must be true.*

(a) $\vdash \{\,a\,\}\,\mathbf{wait}\,b\,\{\,a \wedge b\,\}$ (b) $\vdash in(\mathbf{wait}\,b) = at(\mathbf{wait}\,b)$

If we wish to prove the correctness of $P\,;\,Q$, we do so in the context of an invariant a for P and an invariant c for Q.

Rule 5 (Sequential Composition)

(a) $$\frac{\{a\}P\{b\} \quad \{c\}Q\{e\} \quad b \wedge at(Q) \Rightarrow c}{\{a \triangleleft in(P) \triangleright c\}(P \,;\, Q)\{e\}}$$

(b) (i) $\vdash in(P \,;\, Q) = in(P) \oplus in(Q)$ (ii) $\vdash at(P \,;\, Q) = at(P)$

(iii) $\vdash after(P \,;\, Q) = after(Q)$ (iv) $\vdash after(P) = at(Q)$

When P terminates, it must establish a condition b, which, with the information that the control is now at Q, establishes c. When Q terminates, the overall postcondition must be satisfied.

Rule 6 (While statement)

(a) $$\frac{\{a\}b\{c\} \quad \{d\}P\{a\} \quad c \wedge at(P) \wedge b \Rightarrow d}{\{a \triangleleft in(b) \triangleright d\}(\textbf{while } b \textbf{ do } P \textbf{ od})\{c \wedge \neg b\}}$$

(b) (i) $\vdash in(\textbf{while } b \textbf{ do } P \textbf{ od}) = in(b) \oplus in(P)$

(ii) $\vdash at(\textbf{while } b \textbf{ do } P \textbf{ od}) = at(b)$

(iii) $\vdash after(b) = at(P) \oplus after(\textbf{while } b \textbf{ do } P \textbf{ od})$

(iv) $\vdash after(P) = at(b)$

The inference rule for parallel combination is very simple. To prove that a parallel combination respects an invariant, including on termination, each component must do the same.

Rule 7 (Parallel composition)

(a) $$\frac{\{a\}P\{a\} \quad \{a\}Q\{a\}}{\{a\}([P \parallel Q])\{a\}}$$

(b) (i) $\vdash in([P \parallel Q]) = (in(P) \vee after(P)) \wedge (in(Q) \vee after(Q)) \wedge \neg(after(P) \wedge after(Q))$

(ii) $\vdash at([P \parallel Q]) = at(P) \wedge at(Q)$

(iii) $\vdash after([P \parallel Q]) = after(P) \wedge after(Q)$

We have elided most of the proofs of validity, but we give this one for parallelism.

Theorem 2 (Validity of rule 7). *The proof of correctness of this rule follows.*

$\{a\}(P \vee Q)\{a\}$
$= \{a\} \bigvee\{i : \alpha lab(P \vee Q) \bullet (P \vee Q)_i\}\{a\}$ [normal form]

$$
\begin{aligned}
&= \bigwedge \{\, i : \alpha lab(P \vee Q) \bullet a\,\{\,(P \vee Q)_i\,\}\,(\,a \triangleleft in(P \vee Q) \triangleright a\,)\,\} && \textit{[CH triple]} \\
&= \bigwedge \{\, i : \alpha lab(P \vee Q) \bullet a\,\{\,(P \vee Q)_i\,\}\,a\,\} && \textit{[idemp of conditional]} \\
&= \bigwedge \{\, i : \alpha lab(P) \bullet a\,\{\,P_i\,\}\,a\,\} \wedge \bigwedge \{\, i : \alpha lab(Q) \bullet a\,\{\,Q_i\,\}\,a\,\} && \textit{[conjunction]} \\
&= \bigwedge \{\, i : \alpha lab(P) \bullet a\,\{\,P_i\,\}\,(\,a \triangleleft in(P) \triangleright a\,)\,\} \wedge && \textit{[idemp of conditional]} \\
&\quad \bigwedge \{\, i : \alpha lab(Q) \bullet a\,\{\,Q_i\,\}\,(\,a \triangleleft in(Q) \triangleright a\,)\,\} \\
&= \{\,a\,\} \bigvee \{\, i : \alpha lab(P) \bullet (P)_i\,\}\,\{\,a\,\} \wedge && \textit{[CH triple]} \\
&\quad \{\,a\,\} \bigvee \{\, i : \alpha lab(Q) \bullet (Q)_i\,\}\,\{\,a\,\} \\
&= \{\,a\,\}\,P\,\{\,a\,\} \wedge \{\,a\,\}\,Q\,\{\,a\,\} && \textit{[normal form]}
\end{aligned}
$$

The proof of correctness is remarkably simple, due to the simplicity of the rule and the operational semantics of the construct.

7 Example

Consider the following gross simplification of the mutual exclusion problem, taken from Lamport [9]. Suppose that we have two processes labelled 0 and 1, each with the following code (for $i = 1, 2$).

α_i: $x_i := \textit{true}$;
β_i: **wait** $\neg\, x_{i \oplus 1}$;
cs_i: $\langle$critical section$\rangle$;
δ_i: $x_i := \textit{false}$

Clearly, it's not possible for both processes to be in their critical section at the same time. It's also clear that if the x_i's start off *false*, then both processes could advance as far as their wait-statement; the parallel combination would then deadlock. In the logic that we're considering, however, we may reason only about safety properties, so our proof of correctness is only partial. We now consider proving the safety-correctness of this little algorithm.

In any assertional method, proof of correctness of an assertion P proceeds by finding a global invariant I such that: I is true of the initial state; I implies P; I is invariant over any program step. In our example, the assertion is that it is not possible for both processes to be at their critical sections at the same time; that is, $\neg\,(at(cs_0) \wedge at(cs_1))$. This assertion may be strengthened to find a suitable invariant. The additional information that is needed to prove correctness concerns the values of the x_i variables: if process i is at either β_i or cs_i, then its x_i is *true*. So our proposed invariant is:

$$ I \,\widehat{=}\, \neg\,(at(cs_0) \wedge at(cs_1)) \wedge \bigwedge \{\, i : \{0, 1\} \bullet at(\beta_i) \vee at(cs_i) \Rightarrow x_i\,\} $$

We prove a stronger invariant assertion, justified by consequence and location.

$$ \{\, I \wedge at(\beta_i)\,\}\, \beta_i : \textbf{wait}\, \neg\, x_{i \oplus 1}\, \{\, I \wedge at(cs_i)\,\} \qquad\qquad (*) $$

Consider

$$ I \wedge at(\beta_i) $$

$$= \neg\,(at(cs_0) \wedge at(cs_1)) \wedge \bigwedge \{\, i : \{0,1\} \bullet at(\beta_i) \vee at(cs_i) \Rightarrow x_i \,\} \wedge at(\beta_i)$$
$$= at(\beta_i) \wedge x_i \wedge (at(\beta_{i\oplus1}) \vee at(cs_{i\oplus1}) \Rightarrow x_{i\oplus1})$$

$I \wedge at(cs_i)$
$$= \neg\,(at(cs_0) \wedge at(cs_1)) \wedge \bigwedge \{\, i : \{0,1\} \bullet at(\beta_i) \vee at(cs_i) \Rightarrow x_i \,\} \wedge at(cs_i)$$
$$= at(cs_i) \wedge x_i \wedge \neg\, at(cs_{i\oplus1}) \wedge (at(\beta_{i\oplus1}) \Rightarrow x_{i\oplus1})$$

So, $(*)$ is equivalent to

$$\left\{ \begin{array}{c} at(\beta_i) \wedge x_i \\ at(\beta_{i\oplus1}) \vee at(cs_{i\oplus1}) \Rightarrow x_{i\oplus1} \end{array} \right\} \beta_i : \mathbf{wait}\ \neg\, x_{i\oplus1} \left\{ \begin{array}{c} at(cs_i) \wedge x_i \\ \neg\, at(cs_{i\oplus1}) \\ at(\beta_{i\oplus1}) \Rightarrow x_{i\oplus1} \end{array} \right\}$$

which follows from rule 4.

8 Conclusion

This paper contains an operational semantics in the style of Hoare and He's unifying theories of programming [5], and we used it to formalise Lamport's Concurrent Hoare Logic. Lamport published the logic as the axiomatic semantics for his parallel language; here we have been able to validate this axiomatic semantics by finding a suitable model. Elsewhere, we have carried out the same process for Jones's logic of rely and guarantee conditions [7]. A comprehensive survey of for shared-variable verification techniques may be found in [3].

References

1. R-J. R. Back and R. Kurki-Suonio. Decentralization of process nets with centralized control. In *Proc 2nd Annual Symposium on Principles of Distributed Computing*, Montreal, 1983.
2. R. J. R. Back and J. Wright. *Refinement Calculus: A Systematic Introduction.* Graduate Texts in Computer Science. Springer-Verlag, 1998.
3. Willem-Paul de Roever, Frank S. de Boer, Ulrich Hannemann, Jozef Hooman, Yassine Lakhnech, Mannes Poel, and Job Zwiers. *Concurrency Verification : Introduction to Compositional and Noncompositional Methods.* Number 54 in Cambridge Tracts in Theoretical Computer Science. Cambridge University Press, 2001.
4. E. W. Dijkstra. *A Discipline of Programming.* Prentice-Hall International, 1976.
5. C. A. R. Hoare and He Jifeng. *Unifying Theories of Programming.* Series in Computer Science. Prentice Hall, 1998.
6. C. A. R. Hoare. An axiomatic basis for computer programming. *Communications of the ACM*, 12(10):576–583, October 1969.
7. C. B. Jones. *Development methods for computer programs including a notion of interference.* PhD thesis, University of Oxford, 1981.
8. Leslie Lamport and Fred B. Schneider. The 'Hoare Logic' of CSP, and All That. *ACM Transactions on Programming Languages and Systems*, 6(2):281–296, April 1984.

9. Leslie Lamport. The 'Hoare Logic' of Concurrent Programs. *Acta Informatica*, 14:21–37, 1980.
10. C. C. Morgan. *Programming from Specifications*. Prentice-Hall, 1990.
11. J. M. Morris. A Theoretical Basis for Stepwise Refinement and the Programming Calculus. *Science of Computer Programming*, 9(3):287–306, 1987.
12. Susan Owicki and David Gries. An axiomatic proof technique for parallel programs I. *Acta Informatica*, 6:319–340, 1976.
13. Jim Woodcock and Arthur Hughes. Validation of Lamport's Concurrent Hoare Logic. Technical report, Computing Laboratory, University of Kent, Canterbury, UK, 2002.

ABC/ADL:
An ADL Supporting Component Composition

Hong Mei, Feng Chen, Qianxiang Wang, and Yaodong Feng

Department of Computer Science and Technology, Peking University, Beijing 100871, P.R.China
{meih, chenfeng, wangqx, fengyd}@cs.pku.edu.cn

Abstract. Architecture Description Language (ADL) is one of the keys to software architecture research, but most attention was paid to the description of software structure and high-level analysis of some system properties, while the ability to support refinement and implementation of Software Architecture (SA) models was ignored. In this paper, we present the ABC/ADL, an ADL supporting component composition. Besides the capability of architecting software systems, it provides support to the automated application generation based on SA model via mapping rules and customizable connectors.

1 Introduction

As an effective and practical way to solve the software development crisis, component-based software reuse is an important research area in current software engineering. A systematic and integrated approach to guide the process is desired but still under research.

In nature, software architecture provides a top-down mechanism for component-based software reuse. But current SA research pays most attention on how to effectively describe system structure and reason the behaviours of software, ignoring how to guide the development of applications. Therefore, as the basis of software architecture research, most ADLs lack the ability to help refinement and implementation of the high-level design model.

In [1], we propose the architecture-based component composition (ABC) approach that employs SA descriptions as frameworks to develop components as well as blueprints for constructing systems, while using middleware as the runtime scaffold for component composition. An ADL, called ABC/ADL, is also defined to support component composition.

The rest of this paper is organized as follows: section 2 introduces the primary features of ABC/ADL, section 3 describes the constructs of ABC/ADL, section 4 illustrates the supporting toolkit, section 5 discusses some relate work, and the last section concludes this paper.

2 Features of ABC/ADL

An example of a distributed scheduling system, shown in Figure 1, is used in the rest of this paper.

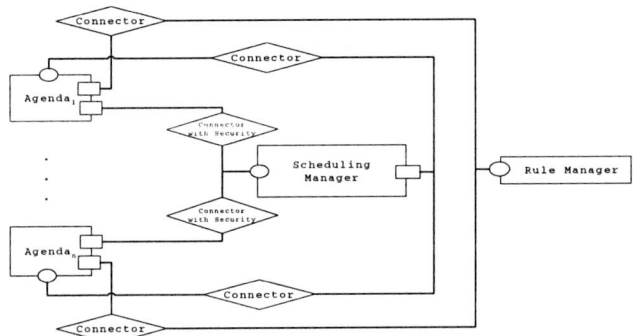

Fig. 1: Architecture of distributed scheduling system

In this system, each agenda is on behalf of a client. The scheduling manager carries out a negotiation among invitees via their agendas. Before the client requests services of the scheduling manager, he should be authenticated and authorized.

2.1 Component Model

A component model is the kernel in software component technology. Different models should be provided to meet different needs. [2] proposed classification of current component models according to their usage: model for component description/classification; model for component specification/composition; model for component implementation. In ABC, the component model is defined in Figure 2 to meet the requirements of composition.

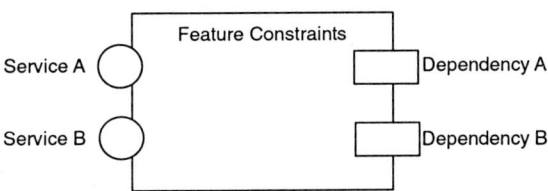

Fig. 2: Component Model in ABC

This component model is divided into two parts: external interfaces and feature constraints. External Interfaces describe services that a component provides to other components and dependencies that are requested by the component itself, while feature constraints specify constraints on component's interior structure, semantic model of the component and some nonfunctional features, e.g., security, throughput limitation.

2.2 Design Principles

ABC/ADL follows some sound design principles: balance between simplicity and understandability; concision – no more constructs that do not serve for the component composition exist in order to keep the language simple; open framework for extension.

ABC/ADL uses a three-layer structure to support the extensible framework. The meta-language layer provides abstract constructs to define templates and architectural styles. The definition layer provides concrete language constructs to define components, connectors, and generic architectures. The instance layer provides abstractions to define the interconnection of component and connector instances.

2.3 Type and Instance

ABC/ADL distinguishes component definitions and instances clearly. This separation enables us to handle architectural issues both at the definition level e.g. connection constraints, and at instance level e.g. multiplicity and dynamic.

Besides, the methods in the component's interfaces are divided into two groups: type related methods and instance related methods. Because some methods are bound to the component type such as creation and finding, while others should be executed by instances. This classification depicts the component more accurately, and helps in understanding and developing applications. It also facilitates transforming ADL description into Enterprise Java Bean (EJB) and CORBA Component Model (CCM) models.

2.4 Architecture, Composite Component and Component Evolution

In ABC, architecture is a group of interconnected component and connector instances that comply with the constraints of architectural styles. It models the application's overall structure and is the blueprint for composing components. A component can have its own interior architecture. Such components are called composite components. With this concept, we can refine the architecture gradually and make the design process more controllable. Moreover, composite component can be reused and composed as well.

In order to enhance the capability of system refinement and evolution, there are two kinds of component type relationships in ABC/ADL. The first is subtyping (a new component inherits and extends the old one's interfaces) and the second is refinement (the new component and the old one are identical in interfaces while different in interior architecture).

2.5 Pluggable Style

Style is another important concept brought by SA. [3] A number of engineering benefits can be obtained by introducing style [4]. In addition, the study of architectural styles can guide developers to choose proper architecture in practice since different styles possess different features. Some efforts towards the style handbook have been made, e.g. [3]. In some other efforts, the styles in use are limited to simplify system reasoning and facilitate code generation, e.g., Unicon [5] and C2 style [6]. As a more general solution, ABC/ADL allows users to define their own styles according to their experiences and specific requirements.

2.6 Complex Connector

Although the connectors are viewed as the first-class entities in SA, they are simple and have no interior structure in most SA study. However, in practice, communication between components may be quite complex, e.g., FTP protocol between server and client. To model such interactions, ABC/ADL introduces complex connectors, which are the connectors that provide some functionality and have interior architectures. The complex connector appears similar to the composite component, but it describes communication instead of functions.

2.7 Aspect

Recently, research on aspect has become an attractive topic. Aspect is a way to encapsulate and modularize crosscutting concerns that used to be scattered over the whole system [7]. Implementations can be more modular, easier to understand and better aligned with requirements with the application of aspect. Application servers such as J2EE have implemented some common crosscutting features as system services, including transaction, security, logging, and so on. In substance, such services can be best expressed as aspects. We introduce aspect into ABC/ADL, and a special kind of composition, named weaving, is also defined. For the scheduling system, the connector between agenda and scheduling manager is the connector with a security aspect.

3 Constructs in ABC/ADL

3.1 Component and Connector

In ABC/ADL, a component or connector must be based on a type of architecture style template. Architecture style casts addition constraints on components and connectors. To accommodate different requirements, a component can integrate several styles.

Interface specification is composed of players that incorporate head declaration and several method specifications. Head declaration defines the type of the player (provide or request) and the template style (definition of style refers to 3.3) on which the player must be based. Each player consists of two kinds of methods: type-method and instance-method, as discussed in section 2.3.

On the definition of method, we refer to the definition of CORBA/IDL for the purpose of compatibility and facilitating the generation of glue code to construct and deploy the system based on COTS middleware.

Table 1: Part of the description of scheduling manager

```
Component SchedulingManager is BLACKBOARD.BlackBoard {
Interfaces {
provide player SchedulingManager is BlackBoard.Entry {
  type-method{
  SchedulingManage findByPrimaryKey(Object id);}
  instance-method{…}
}
request player Agenda is BlackBoard.Notification {
…}}
Attributes {…}
Properties {…}
Dependencies {…}
SemanticDescription{…}
```

Attribute section designates the attributes the component will use in the interaction with others. Property section describes additional information of the component, e.g. security, version. Dependency section describes the relationship between the provide players and in the request players. And semantics description section describes the semantics information of the component. (Refer to section 3.4 for details.)

The specification of connectors has a similar structure with components. (Table 2)

Table 2: Description of a connector of scheduling system

```
Connector J2EEConnector is DEFAULT.Connector{
Interfaces {
  provide player Callee is Connector.Callee{*}
  request player Caller is Connector.Caller{*}
}
Properties{Platform = J2EE;}
Dependencies{Callee depends on Caller;}
SemanticDescription {Caller includes Callee;}}
```

In this specification, the use of "*" in the player definitions denotes that the player's methods are the same as the component player that connects to it.

Besides, users can define the aspect and attach them to components or connectors:

Table 3: Description of connector with secured aspect

```
Aspect SecuredAspect {
Interfaces {
  provide player PreInvocation{
    instance-method {BOOL authorize()}
}}}
Connector SecuredConnector is DEFAULT.Connector {
Interfaces {
  provide player Callee is Connector.Callee{*}
  request player Caller is Connector.Caller {*}
}
Weaving {SecuredAspect.authorize weaves Callee.*;}}
```

Table 4: Description of Scheduling System

```
Architecture DS_Architecture{
uses{
Component agendas : Agenda[];
Component schedulingManager : SchedulingManager;
Connector agendaToSchedulingManager :
SecuredConnector[];
Connector schedulingManagerToAgenda :
DefaultConnector[];
Variable i : int;
...}
Config main{
agendas[i]. SchedulingManager connects
agendaToSchedulingManager[i].Callee;
agendaToSchedulingManager[i].Caller connects
schedulingManager. SchedulingManager;
schedulingManager.Agenda connects
schedulingManagerToAgenda[i].Callee;
schedulingManagerToAgenda[i].Caller connects
agendas[i].Agenda;
...}
SemanticDescription{ }
}
```

```
Component Scheduling_System is System{
Structure {architecture DS_Architecture}
mapping {self.makeMeeting to
schedulingManager.makeMeeting}
}
```

3.2 Architecture

Architecture specification comprises two sections. In *uses* section, all instances of components and connectors used in the system are declared from the defined types. *Config* section depicts the topologic layout of instances in the system, which must conform to the style constraint. Moreover, to improve flexibility and adaptability, ABC/ADL allows a system has multiple configurations, so multiple *config* sections can exist. Users designate a configuration at the late phases of the composition process according to requirement.

In a complete system description, an architecture description will not be stand-alone, but should be attached to some composite components using the *structure* section in component specification. Besides, the interface of the composite component is determined by its interior components. The *mapping* section specifies how to connect the interface of the composite component with its internal components.

Table5: Definition of Blackboard Style

```
Style BLACKBOARD_STYLE{
COMPONENT_TEMPLATE Blackboard {
PROVIDE_PLAYER_TEMPLATE Entry {multicity=n};
REQUEST_PLAYER_TEMPLATE Notification {multicity=n};}
COMPONENT_TEMPLATE Client {
PROVIDE_PLAYER_TEMPLATE Notification {multicity=n};
REQUEST_PLAYER_TEMPLATE Entry {multicity=1};}
CONNECTION_SPEC {
Client.Entry :: DEFAULT.Connector.Callee
DEFAULT.Connector.Caller :: Blackboard.Entry }
CONNECTION_SPEC {
Blackboard.Notification :: DEFAULT.Connector.Callee
DEFAULT.Connector.Caller :: Client.Notification}}
```

3.3 Style

Every definition of style includes component templates, connector templates and connection specifications. Component and connector templates describe the basic frameworks of the components and connectors, including players and some properties. And connection specifications restrict the relationship between components and connectors.

3.4 Semantic Description

The semantic description is not a standalone element in ABC/ADL, but scattered over every specification of elements, using *SemanticDescription* key word to mark. Some automated system verification and validation can be achieved based on formal methods.

Every semantic description section contains multiple segments, each of which uses a kind of formal language or natural language. Before the semantic segment, the name of used language must be designated, according to which the analysis tool will pass the content of that segment to corresponding module.

Table 6: Semantics Description of Scheduling Manager, using UML-OCL

```
Component Agenda is BLACKBOARD.Client {...........
SemanticsDescription{...
OCL{
Self.timetable is Sequence of TimeSlice
Invariants {
Self.timetable->ForAll(t1,t2|t1<>t2 implies
t1.starttime>=t2.endtime or t2.starttime>=t1.endtime
)}... ...
```

4 Tool Support

A prototype of ABC tool has been implemented to support the ABC/ADL. ABC tool allows users to design applications in a visualized way (Figure 3). It also accomplishes some transformation of ABC/ADL, e.g. generating IDL and Java code from ADL description. In addition, it can automatically construct applications from existing components based on some COTS middleware specifications, including CORBA and J2EE.

Before generating applications, the system model will be validated. in three layers: syntax layer, implementation layer (e.g compatibility with the specified platform and type-matching check between component invocation), and semantic layer (e.g. style constraints and some behaviour reasoning based on some formal methods)

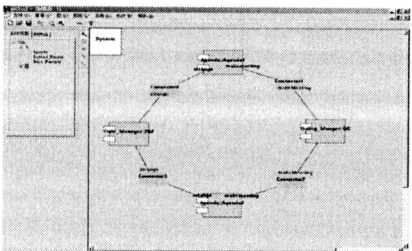

Fig. 3: Graphic Modeling

5 Related Work

5.1 Other ADLs

There exist many kinds of ADLs for different objectives, e.g., Wright [8], Unicon [5] and ACME [9].

Wright is regarded as one of the most representative ADL. It adopts CSP to describe behaviours so as to formally verify some aspects of the architecture description. But, Wright is only a language for specification and don't support system development.

UniCon is a step toward the system realization, because it realizes a set of predefined connectors so that makes it possible to generate system from architecture. But it is limited for only the predefined connectors can be utilized.

ACME is an architecture description interchange language. It provides a structural framework for characterizing architectures, together with annotation facilities for additional ADL-specific information [9]. On the basis of ACME, different ADLs can share a set of kernel capabilities and set up their own capability via the open framework. But ACME is not a practical ADL to model application. ABC/ADL benefits from the structure of ACME.

5.2 Component Based Software Development (CBSD)

Based on the middleware and specification of runtime component, CBSD provides a practical bottom-up approach to construct systems from existing components. There have emerged some widely accepted runtime component models, e.g., EJB, CCM, Microsoft's distributed component object model (DCOM) and the newly web service model. These models provide the foundation for component development and composition. ABC/ADL adopts some features of them to enhance the ability of description and narrow the gap to implementation. But CBSD primarily puts emphasis on the interoperability of components in implementation layer, and lacks a systematic methodology to guide the developing process. As a result, it's unable to help the component composition at the higher level of abstraction, which is just an advantage of ABC/ADL.

6   Conclusion

This paper presents an architecture description language supporting component composition. By separating run-time and design-time configurations, supporting composite components and complex connectors, introducing aspects, it effectively support the ABC approach. Besides, it provides an open framework to allow user extend the language. A supporting tool, ABC Tool, has been implemented.

One of the future works is to setup an XML-based framework for ABC/ADL. XML provides a standard way to define the ADL, facilitating understanding and transforming ADL. Another significant work is to transforming ABC/ADL into UML. As a high-level abstraction of applications, SA does not describe how to implements its components and connectors. A good mapping between ABC/ADL and UML can greatly benefit the development process of ABC approach.

Acknowledgements

This effort is sponsored by the State 863 High-Tech Program, and Natural Science Foundation of China.

References

1. Feng Chen, Qianxiang Wang, Hong Mei, Fuqing Yang, "An Architecture-Based Approach for Component-Oriented Development", in *Proceedings of CompSAC 2002*.
2. Mei, H. "A Component Model for Perspective Management of Enterprise Software Reuse", Annals of Software Engineering 11,219-236, 2001.
3. Bass L., Clements P. and Kazman R., "Software Architecture in Practice", Published by Addison-Wesley in the SEI Series, 1998.
4. Abowd G., Allen R. and Garlan D., "Using Style to Understand Descriptions of Software Architecture", in *Proceedings of SIGSOFT'93: Foundations of Software Engineering, Software Engineering Notes* 18(5), 1993.
5. Shaw M., Deline R., Klein D.V., Ross T.L., Young D.M. and Zelesnik G., "Abstractions for Software Architecture and Tools to Support Them", in *IEEE Transactions on Software Engineering*, April 1995.
6. Taylor R., Medvidovic N., and Anderson K., "Component- and message-based architectural style for GUI software", in *IEEE Transactions on Software Engineering*, June 1996.
7. Kiczales, G., et al., "Aspect-Oriented Programming", In *Proceedings of the European Conference on Object-Oriented Programming (ECOOP)*. Springer-Verlag, Finland, 1997.
8. Allen R. And Garlan D., "A formal Basis for Architectural Connection", in *ACM Transactions on Software Engineering and Methodology*, July, 1997.
9. Garlan D., Monroe R. and Wile D., "ACME: An Architecture Description Interchange Language", In *Proceedings of CASCON'97*, November 1997.

The Description of CORBA Objects Based on Petri Nets

Hong Zheng and Shi-xian Li

Department of Computer Science, Zhongshan University ,Guangzhou 510275, P.R. China
zhjenny@21cn.com, lnslsx@zsu.edu.cn
Institute of Software, Chinese Academy of Sciences, Beijing 100080, P.R. China

Abstract. OMG has provided a set of Common Object Services (COS), which help users to build large-scale distributed CORBA applications, but Common Object Services Specifications (COSS) don't contain integrated formal descriptions. Petri-nets are a powerful instrument for modeling, analyzing, and simulating dynamic systems with concurrent and non-deterministic behavior. This paper introduces a high-level Object-oriented extended Petri nets to express the behaviors of individual objects as well as the concurrency between different objects and concurrency internal to an object in the context of CORBA, and gives an example for formal description of CORBA Objects.

1 Introduction

The Object Management Group (OMG) [6] is the world's largest software consortium with a membership of over 800 vendors, developers, and end users. Established in 1989, its mission is to promote the theory and practice of Object Technology (OT) for the development of distributed computing systems. A key goal of OMG is to create a standardized object-oriented architectural framework for distributed applications based on specifications that enable and support distributed objects. Objectives include the reusability, portability, and interoperability of object-oriented software components in heterogeneous environments. CORBA(Common Object Request Broker Architecture) is a set of open standards proposed by the OMG in order to promote interoperability between distributed object systems[1].

CORBA reaches several operational goals: language and platform independent through the use of a common Interface Definition Language (IDL), promote cross-platform, cross-language interoperability between heterogeneous application systems, and provide a seamless integration with popular object-oriented and non-object-oriented programming languages such a C, C++, or Java.

The paper is organized as follows: In section 2, we first briefly review CORBA Objects and Services. We then present the importance of CORBA Objects formalism. In section 3, after reviewing Petri nets basics, we introduce a high-level Petri nets with object-oriented concepts to specify objects suited to CORBA. Then we illustrate a formal CORBA objects. Section 4 concludes our paper and suggests further issues.

2 CORBA

CORBA[1,6] defines the programming interfaces to the OMA ORB component. An ORB is the basic mechanism by which objects transparently make requests to and receive responses from each other on the same machine or across a network. A client need not be aware of the mechanism used to communicate with or activate an object, how the object is implemented, nor where the object is located. The ORB thus forms the foundation for building large scale applications from distributed objects and for interoperability between applications in both homogeneous and heterogeneous environments.

And the OMG Interface Definition Language (IDL) provides a standardized way to define the interfaces to CORBA objects The IDL definition is the contract between the implementers of an object and the client. The IDL is a strongly typed declarative language that is programming language-independent. Language mappings enable objects to be implemented and sent requests in the developer's programming language of choice in a style that is natural to that language.

2.1 The CORBA Object Model

CORBA provides a layer of abstraction between low level complexity of network environments, and the construction and delivery of object services, through the provision of an object model which describes the interfaces and interactions available to services within a distributed heterogeneous environment.

CORBA object interfaces is described by the IDL, while the object services used by clients and the servers provided by systems are defined on the IDL. The OMG provides language mappings to generate language specific interfaces for most common programming languages and platforms.

The provision of a common data representation for CORBA types, and a comment InterORB communication protocol allows CORBA to interoperate over a wide variety of distributed applications, from large mainframes running COBOL, to desktop machines running Java Virtual Machines.

2.2 CORBA Object Services

Object Services are general purpose services that are either fundamental for developing useful CORBA-based applications composed of distributed objects, or that provide a universal-application domain-independent basis for application interoperability.

Object Services are the basic building blocks for distributed object applications. Compliant objects can be combined in many different ways and put to many different uses in applications. They can be used to construct higher level facilities and object frameworks that can interoperate across multiple platform environments.

Adopted OMG Object Services are collectively called CORBA services, CORBA services are a standardization of the various basic services that any large-scale distributed application is expected to require, and CORBA services include Naming, Events, LifeCycle, Persistent Object, Relationships, Externalization, Transactions, Concurrency Control, Licensing, Query, Properties, Security, Time, Collections, and Trading Services. The Object Request Broker, is the core of the CORBA. It provides the basic mechanism for making and receiving calls. Combined with the Object Services, it ensures meaningful communication between CORBA compliant applications.

2.3 CORBA Specification

In order to facilitate the modeling and development distributed systems in CORBA, the specification of the CORBA services (COSS) is provided by the OMG in the form of a mixture of IDL (for the definition of the interfaces) and English text (for the specification of the behavior). The specification can be considered as a "semi-formal" specification [8]. CORBA IDL covers only the syntactic aspects of the possible use of a remote object. The interface details the services supported and their signature: a list of parameters with their IDL type and parameter-passing mode, the IDL type of the return value, the exceptions that may possibly be raised during the processing of the service. Therefore, rigorous specifications of CORBA objects are required to understand clearly the intention of users and providers in a precise and abstract manner.

However, CORBA IDL does not cover any semantic or behavioral description of the remote object (by English text), while this information is very important for the clients. For example, two concurrent services are not always concurrent in practice, but implementers can not get enough information to decide the order of two services execution, and the conditions under which an exception might be raised when a service is provided. These show CORBA has not specified the semantics of an IDL interface without constraining its implementation by formal methods. Although this limitation can be viable in the domain of concurrent systems, in our opinion, it presents a serious drawback in the field of distributed heterogeneous systems such as CORBA.

interface Account {
exception insufficientbalance;
void deposit(in float amount);
void withdraw(in float amount);
float getBalance(inout float amount);
raises (insufficientbalance) ;
};

Fig. 1. An IDL interface

Fig.1 first defines a simple account object interface expressed in CORBA IDL. The interface (Account) includes three services: deposit, withdraw and getbalance. In addition, The figure illustrates the syntax for the two kinds parameter-passing modes (in, or inout) and of the exceptions. The keyword exception defines an exception type (insufficientbalance) that might be thrown during processing, while the keyword raises specifies what types of exceptions may be raised by a service.

The main goal of our efforts is to provide a suitable and operational means for behavioral aspect specifications of distributed objects, in the context of CORBA.

3 CORBA Objects Formalism

Distributed systems are the most challenging and the most complex systems that are practically developed. Such kinds of systems need well adapted and easy to use formal models. And the importance of providing behavioral specifications suited to the OMG object model as been recognized by several researchers. Sankar [9] argued that the introduction of formal methods could help maintaining the current level of software quality while the complexity of software increases due to the presence of distributed objects. He also noted that formal methods are more likely to be accepted in the field of distributed object systems.

Petri nets are widely used in various application domains because of its simplicity and flexibility in depicting dynamic system behaviors, and its strong expressive and analytic power of system behaviors[2,3]. In this paper, we use mainly a high-level Object-oriented extended Petri net (HOOEP) that supports object-oriented concepts to model CORBA objects.

3.1 Petri Nets Basics

Petri nets were introduced by C.A. Petri in 1962 [7]. Petri nets have been studied for a long time as a mathematical formalism for the modeling of concurrent systems [4]. The classical Petri nets are a directed bipartite graph with two node types called *places* and *transactions*. The nodes are connected via directed *arcs*. Connections between two nodes of the same type are not allowed. Places are represented graphically by circles and transactions by rectangles or bars. Places many contain zero or many *tokens*, drawn as black dots. The number of tokens may change during the execution. A place p is called an input place of a transaction t if there exists a directed arc from p to t; p is called output place of t if there exists a directed arc from t to p. A transaction is called *enabled* if each of its input places contains 'enough' tokens. An enabled transaction can *fire*. Firing a transaction refers to consuming tokens from the input places and producing tokens for the output places.

Fig.2 shows a classical Petri nets. The classical Petri net has many limitations in modeling complex systems, as it tends to be complex and extremely large in describing real systems. To solve these problems, many extensions have been made to enhance the modeling capacity of Petri nets[5,10].

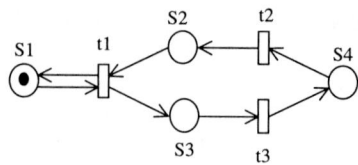

Fig. 2. A classical Petri net representation.

In the paper, a High level Object-oriented extended Petri Net(HOOEP) is introduced to describe the behavioral specification for CORBA system. The HOOEPs are expressed by extending Object-oriented Petri nets. Our approach has been inspired from two ideas. The first is practicability of Object-Oriented Petri nets(such as CPN) and successful use in many different application areas[3,10]. And Object-Oriented Petri nets support the representation of objects structure, information hiding through optimized interfaces and abstract places, inheritance through properties shared among classes, polymorphism through dynamic binding of abstract tokens, and communication between objects. The second is the description style of CORBA IDL. In fact, an IDL provides an executing frame of object models.

3.2 CORBA Object Description Based Petri Nets Rules

In this sub-section, a high-level object-oriented extended Petri net is defined to model and analyze the behaviors of CORBA system.

Definition 1. A High-level Object-Orented extended Petri net (HOOEP) is a 2-tuple HOOEP=(SD,CPN), where

(1) SD is the specification description of a modeled system.
(2) CPN=(Σ, P, T_1, T_2, A, N, C, G, E, I) is the coloured Petri net satisfying the requirements below:
   Σ is a finite set of non-empty types, called colour set.
   P is a finite set of places.
   T_1 is a finite set of guard transitions.
   T_2 is a finite set of action transitions, and $T_1 \cap T_2 = \phi$.
   A is a finite set of arcs.
   N is a node function. It is defined from A into P×($T_1 \cup T_2$) $\cup$ ($T_1 \cup T_2$) ×P.
   C is a colour function. It is defined from P into Σ.
   G is a guard function. It is defined from T_1 into logical expressions.
   E is an arc expression function. It is defined from A into expressions.
   I is an initialization function. It is defined from P into closed expressions such that
   $$\forall p \in P: Type(I(p))=C(p)_{ms}$$
where $C(p)_{ms}$ represents the multi-set of C(p).

In fact, HOOEP is divided into two parts. One of parts is a specification description. The other part is a kind of Object-oriented Petri nets, which is consisted of places, transitions, typed token and arcs. In the CORBA system, places are derived from a defined IDL interface, and the Exception places introduced are only used if the service is defined to raise an exception. The Token-type sets of the places will be described in terms of CORBA IDL, and the expressions on the arcs will be an IDL-defined type. The Token types of the input places are all of the IDL types of all in and inout parameters of the service; The Token-type of the output places are all the IDL type of the result returned by the service (if any), the list of the IDL types of all out and inout parameters of the service. The Token-type of the Exception is <Exception>, where Exception is the super-type of all IDL exception types. Two kinds of transitions are guard transitions (represented by rectangle with two lines) and action transitions (represented by rectangle). Guard expressions are evaluated during transition firability testing. Exception transitions are also action transitions (represented by black rectangle). There must be no side effect. It only allows atomic decision if the transition can or cannot be executed. CORBA objects interact with one another by invoking services defined by the IDL interfaces they support.

On the other hand, action transitions are also evaluated during transition execution (such as the call of a service). With respect to the HOOEP, the flow of one token from input place will eventually result later on in exactly one token being deposited either in the output place or in the exception place. Each arc is inscribed by a tuple of variables, with a given multiplicity as multiplicity*<v1,...vn> in terms of a defined IDL.

Definition 2. Firing rules of the transitions in HOOEPs.

$\forall t \in T1$, t is said to be enabled if $\forall p \in \bullet t$, $Type(E((p,t))) \subseteq C(p)ms$, where $\bullet t$ represents a set of all input places of t.

$\forall t \in T2$, t is said to be enabled if $G(t)$ is evaluated to be true, after all variables in $G(t)$ are substituted by the bindings in $\bullet t$.

From the definition above, a transition is firable if it satisfies the following requirements:

A substitution of its input variables to values stored in the tokens of its input places can be found,

The multiplicity of each substituted token in the input places is superior or equal to the multiplicity of the input arc,

The precondition of the transition evaluates to true for the substitution.

The firing of a transition will execute the transition's action, remove tokens from input places, compute new tokens and store them in the output places of the transition. We now gives the behavior specification of an IDL in Fig.1 based on the HOOEP.

Fig.3 describes a sensible behavior for the account interface. The close place is added as a start place. The start place can be provided with an initial marking which is an account. From the initial marking described in Fig. 3, Td transition is always viable for a deposit service. On the other hand, if the withdraw amount is less than the balance in this amount, Tw transition is enable, or else the Exception is raised. That is, the Account HOOEP specifies conditions under which exception might be raised. This invocation to the account object is ended normally by close place or an exception occurrence. We can also find some concurrency and synchronization constrains. For instance, when an account is opened, Transition Tc and Transition Tb are unable simultaneously. Transition Tc is enable only when the deposit operation has been performed.

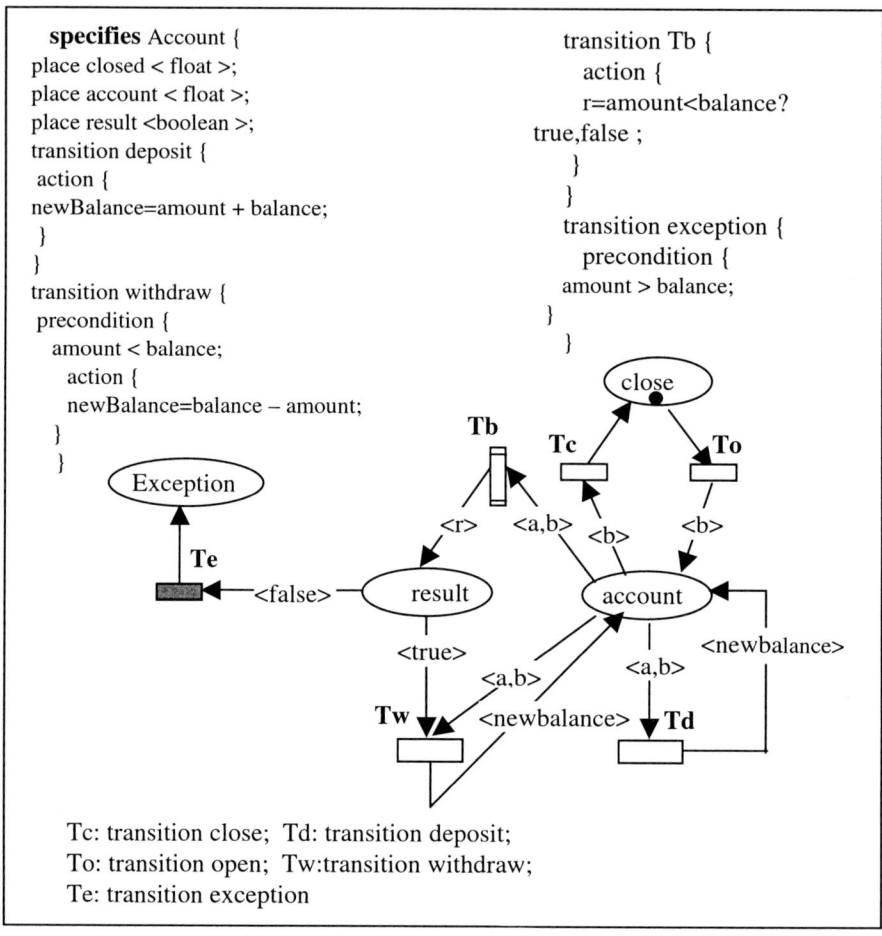

Fig. 3. HOOEP model of the behavior specification of the Account interface

From Fig.3, we can conclude the results in terms of its reachable graph as follows:

Proposition 1. If a user want to withdraw from his account, and the withdraw amount is no more than the balance of the account, then he can eventually execute the operation.

Proof: By Fig.3 and its reachable graph, transition Tw is enabled after transition Tb fires, based on the suppositions of the proposition. Therefore, there exists a firing transition sequence: To→Tb→Tw from the initial marking. Firing Tw accomplishes the operation of the withdraw from the account.

The following propositions can be proved similarly.

Proposition 2. There is no limitation to a user's execution of his deposit.

Proposition 3. If a user wants to withdraw amount more than the balance, this can't take place.

As a result, we can conclude under any circumstance that the dynamic behavior of the HOOEP is in accordance with the specification of the Account interface.

4 Conclusions

The CORBA systems show complex concurrent and interactional behavior that frequently cannot be well understood, though CORBA has standardized features described by IDL. The graphic nature of Petri nets is an intuitive understanding. The HOOEP presented here is a high level object-oriented extended Petri nets which offers the following benefits:
- integration of object-oriented concepts into Petri-nets;
- formal behavioral specifications that support simulation and execution;
- the usefulness of Petri net analysis techniques.

Object behavioral specification helps the development of CORBA system. While our research offers a methods to analyze distributed objects, Future works will be carried out in the description of the semantics of HOOEP will be extended and improved, especially concerning the refinement aspects.

Acknowledgements

We are pleased to acknowledge the National Natural Science Foundation of China and Guangdong Education Department. This research is supported by the National Natural Science Foundation of P.R.China (No. 79910161989) and the Software Technology Key Laboratory Research Foundation of Guangdong Education Department. The authors are also grateful to the anonymous referees for their insightful and valuable comments and suggestions.

References

1. The Common Object Request Broker:Architecture and Specification, CORBA 2.4.2 (February 2001)
2. Hong, J.-E., Lee, N.H., Cha, S.D., Bae, D.H.: Towards reusable colored Petri nets. In: Proceedings of International Symposium on Software Engineering for Parallel and Distributed,Systems, Kyoto, Japan (April 1998) 223-229
3. Lakos, C.: The object orientation of object Petri nets. In: Proceeding of the International Workshop on Object-oriented and Models of Concurrency Turin, Italy (June 1995)
4. Lakos, C., Keen, C.D.: LOOPN++: a New Language for Object-Oriented Petri Nets. European Simulation Multiconference, Barcelona, Spain (June 1994)

5. Maier, C., Moldt, D.: Object Coloured Petri Nets - a Formal Technique for Object Ori-ented Modelling. In: Farwer, B.; Moldt, D.; Stehr, M.-O. (Eds.): Petri Nets in System Engineering, Modelling, Verification and Validation. University of Hamburg (1997) 11-19
6. Object Management Group: Deployment and Configuration of Component-based Distributed Applications, OMG Document: orbos/2002-01-19 (2002)
7. Petri, C.A.: Kommunikation Mit Automaten. PhD Thesis, Institut fur Instrumentelle Mathematik, Bonn (1962.)
8. Rémi, B., Philippe, P.: Modeling a Groupware Editing Tool With Cooperative Objects, Concurrent Object-Oriented Programming and Petri Nets. Gul A.Agha, and Fiorella De Cindio, editors. Wien: Springer-Verlag (1998)
9. Sriram, S.: Introducing Formal Methods to Software Engineers Through OMG's CORBA Environment and Interface Definition Language, Algebraic Methodology and Software Technology. In: 5th International Conference, AMAST '96, Munich, Germany, July 1-5, 1996. Martin Wirsing, and Maurice Nivat, Editors. ed. Lecture Notes In Computer Science, no. 1101. Springer (1996) 52-61
10. Verkoulen, P.A.C.: Integrated Information Systems Design: An Approach Based on Object-Oriented Concepts and Petri Nets. PhD Thesis, Technical University of Eindhoven, the Netherlands (1993)

Toward a Formal Model of Software Components

Maritta Heisel[1], Thomas Santen[2], and Jeanine Souquières[3]

[1] Technische Universität Ilmenau, Germany
maritta.heisel@tu-ilmenau.de
[2] Technische Universität Berlin, Germany
santen@acm.org
[3] LORIA–Université Nancy2, France
souquier@loria.fr

Abstract. We are interested in specifying component models in a way that allows us to analyze the interplay of components in general, and to concisely specify individual components. As a starting point for coming up with a technique of specifying component models, we consider JavaBeans. We capture the JavaBean component model using UML class diagrams, Object-Z, and life sequence charts.

1 Introduction

Component-based software engineering [20] is an emerging field of great interest in research and practice. Its goal is to develop software systems not from scratch but by assembling pre-fabricated parts, as is done in other engineering disciplines. These pre-fabricated parts are called components.

Components are independently deployable pieces of software. Several *component models*, such as *JavaBeans* [17], *Enterprise Java Beans* [18], *Microsoft COM* [12], and *CORBA* [13] have been proposed. A component model is designed to allow components to interoperate that are implemented according to the standards set by the model. Building a system from components means selecting components that adhere to a particular component model and composing them in a way that is suitable to achieve the desired system behavior.

To ensure the interoperability of components, a component model must address the following aspects: the *syntactic conventions* for building component interfaces (often called the "interface specification"); the *dynamic behavior* describing allowed and forbidden flows of events between connected components; and the *semantics* of operations of a component, e.g. registering a call-back procedure with a component has an effect on the state of the component, although that may not be immediately visible.

An analysis of a component model must demonstrate that the interplay of components fulfills the expectations described in the component model in any case, i.e. that the component model is consistent (components can interoperate), and that it is complete (all possible behaviors are covered).

For an individual component, a concise way of instantiating the component model (saying that it *is* a component) is needed. Additionally, a specification describing the specifics of the individual component is necessary to analyze whether a specific way of composing individual components actually achieves a desired system behavior.

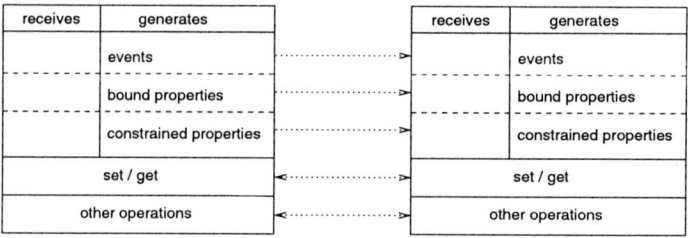

Fig. 1. The JavaBean Interface

The general aim of our research is to come up with a technique of specifying the different *semantic* aspects of a component model, capturing the dynamic behavior and the effects of operations in sufficient detail for analyzing consistency and completeness of the model. A component model specification should be easily instantiable to yield a concise, easily extensible specification of concrete components. We use a combination of UML class diagrams [14], an extension of sequence diagrams called life sequence charts (LSC) [6], and the formal specification language Object-Z [15] to capture the different aspects of a component model. In the present work, we focus on the JavaBean component model [17]. JavaBeans are a well-established technology. The JavaBean component model is reasonably simple to allow us to illustrate our general approach to specifying component models without obscuring the presentation with the technical detail of a more elaborate component model.

2 Introduction to JavaBeans

JavaBeans is a component model originally introduced by Sun in 1996. It has an event-based communication model between components, which are called *Beans*: a Bean notifies registered listener Beans about the events that it generates, and it registers with other Beans to be notified about their events. As we will see in Section 3, cooperating Beans thus realize three variants of the *observer* design pattern [8].

More specifically, the main aspects of the Bean model include [20]:

- A Bean can generate and receive arbitrary *events*.
- A Bean has a number of *properties*, which are manipulated with specific setter and getter operations.
- Changing a property may generate an event. For a *bound property*, a Bean generates a change event whenever the value of that property changes. For a *constrained property*, the Bean generates a change event like for a bound property. Additionally, the listeners to that event may *veto* the change, causing the Bean to revert the value of that property to the one before the change.
- In addition to the operations implementing the event-based communication between Beans, a Bean may provide an arbitrary number of ordinary operations in its interface.

Figure 1 illustrates the interfaces of two Beans and their connections. For the events, an interface is divided into two parts: one to receive events, and one to generate them.

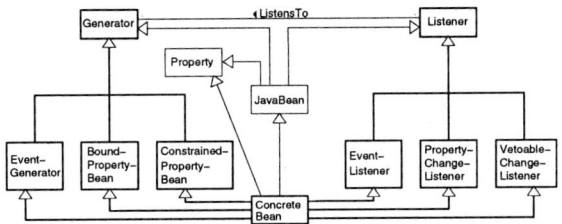

Fig. 2. Overview of the JavaBean component model

When connecting Beans, the generating side of an interface can be connected to several receiving sides of other Beans that will be notified of events. The set and get operations, and other operations provided by a Bean can be called by other Beans in an arbitrary fashion.

3 The JavaBean Component Model

In order to adequately specify all relevant aspects of the JavaBean component model, we use several complementary formalisms: UML class diagrams [14] describe the static structure of the component model. Because of their graphical nature, class diagrams provide a readily accessible overview of the component model. Object-Z [15] serves to specify the detailed semantics of the classes contained in the class diagram and their features. In particular, it states properties such as class invariants, and it specifies the effect of operations. As the information shown in the class diagrams is also contained in the Object-Z specification, the class diagrams are not strictly necessary. However, they are useful to provide an overview of the component model. Life sequence charts (LSCs) [6] specify the behavioral aspects of the component model. Such aspects cannot be expressed in languages like Object-Z in a satisfactory way. We use LSCs instead of message sequence charts [10] or UML sequence diagrams, because, first, they have a formal semantics [11], and second, they are more expressive than message sequence charts or UML sequence diagrams. In particular, we need to distinguish between optional and mandatory behavior, and we need to use activation conditions and forbidden messages.

3.1 Top-Level Model

We now present a formal specification of the JavaBean component model. Figure 2 shows the top-level class diagram of the component model. In general, a JavaBean comprises the functionalities of generators, listeners and properties (c.f. Figure 1). The class *JavaBean* in the center of Figure 2 illustrates this fact. It specializes the three abstract classes *Generator*, *Listener*, and *Property*, and thus serves as a focus relating those three classes.

Corresponding to the three variants of events (simple events, change events for bound properties, and for constrained properties), there are three specializations on the generator and on the listener sides of the class diagram. A concrete component *ConcreteBean* will specialize those classes rather than the abstract classes *Generator* and *Listener*. Therefore the class *JavaBean* and its associated generalization / specialization- relations are not strictly necessary in the component model.

A Bean can take the role of a generator and of a listener at the same time. This results in multiple inheritance in two ways: first, a concrete Bean can inherit from the descendants of the class *Generator* as well as from the descendants of the class *Listener*. Second, it may have several bound properties or listen to several events, for example. Hence, multiple inheritance – with a suitable renaming – from the same class will occur.

For the specification of the component model, we are not interested in the question whether the programming language in which the components are implemented (in our case Java) supports multiple inheritance. We rather aim at clearly describing the essentials of the component model.

3.2 Constrained Properties

In the following, we present the part of the component model describing constrained properties in more detail. The specification of events, simple properties, and bound properties can be found in [9].

Class Diagram. Figure 3 shows the class diagram for JavaBeans with constrained properties. Each Bean having constrained properties incorporates an object *vcs* of class *VetoableChangeSupport*. That object is responsible for registering and de-registering listeners, and for notifying the listeners of an intended change of a constrained property. A *ConstrainedPropertyBean* also incorporates a number of objects of class *ConstrainedProperty*. Each *ConstrainedProperty* has a name, a value, and getter and setter methods to query and change that value. The object *vcs* is responsible for notifying registered listeners of an intended change of a constrained property. For that purpose, the object *vcs* maintains references to the registered listeners, which are objects of class *VetoableChangeListener*. Each *VetoableChangeListener* incorporates objects of the class *ObservedProperty*. This class provides an operation *VetoableChange* to process change events. Processing a change event may amount to vetoing the proposed change.

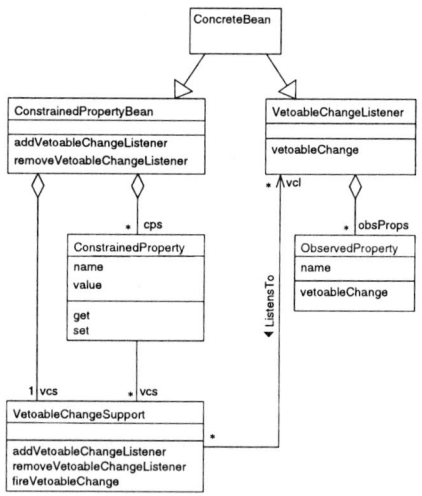

Fig. 3. Constrained properties

As in Figure 2, we indicate in Figure 3 that a concrete Bean can multiply inherit from both classes *ConstrainedPropertyBean* and *VetoableChangeListener*.

Property Specification. The following Object-Z specification gives a precise meaning to all classes, attributes, and methods mentioned before.

In Object-Z, each class is defined using a "box" that shows the class name at its top, e.g., *ConstrainedPropertyBean*. The symbol "↾" is used to specify which attributes and operations of a class are publicly visible. Following the export list, the constant attributes of a class are specified (for example, *name* and *vcs* in the class *ConstrainedProperty* below). The unnamed box inside a class box contains the specification of the mutable attributes of the class. These are declared above a horizontal line. Below that horizontal line, the *class invariant* is given. It states integrity constraints that each object of the class must satisfy. The state box of a class definition is followed by the definition of the class operations.

The class *ConstrainedPropertyBean* offers the operations *addVetoableChangeListener* and *removeVetoableChangeListener* to its environment. It contains two private attributes, namely an object *vcs* of class *VetoableChangeSupport* and a set (expressed by the powerset operator $\mathbb{P}$) of objects of the class *ConstrainedProperty*. The class invariant stipulates that the same *vcs* object be used by all objects belonging to the set *cps*. The operations of the class *ConstrainedPropertyBean* are defined to be the promotion of the operations provided by the *vcs* object.

A *ConstrainedProperty* has two constant attributes: the *name* of the property, and a reference *vcs* to the *VetoableChangeSupport* that handles its change messages. The *value* of the property is its mutable private attribute. The operation *get* copies the *value* to its output *v!*. In Object-Z, there is a convention to decorate output variables with an exclamation mark, and input variables with a question mark.

―― *ConstrainedPropertyBean* ――――――――――――――――――――――――
↾ (*addVetoableChangeListener*, *removeVetoableChangeListener*)

vcs : *VetoableChangeSupport*	*addVetoableChangeListener* $\widehat{=}$
cps : $\mathbb{P}$*ConstrainedProperty*	*vcs.addVetoableChangeListener*
∀ *cp* : *cps* • *cp.vcs* = *vcs*	*removeVetoableChangeListener* $\widehat{=}$
	vcs.removeVetoableChangeListener

The operation *set* is defined as a combination of several auxiliary operations. First, *get* is invoked to provide the current *value* as an input to *vcs.fireVetoableChange*, which also takes the name of the property as an input. The sequential composition operator ⨾ pipes outputs of its first argument to inputs of its second argument that have the same base name.

A boolean value *veto!* is the output of the operation *vcs.fireVetoableChange*. It indicates whether the change of the property has been vetoed by one of the listeners. Depending on the value of *veto!*, one of the operations *setSuccess* and *setVetoed* is invoked. The operation *setSuccess* has a precondition ¬ *veto?*, whereas *setVetoed* has a precondition *veto?*. Therefore, the choice operator *setSuccess* [] *setVetoed* invokes *setVetoed* in case of a vetoed change, and *setSuccess* otherwise. The operation *setVetoed* has no effect: it does not mention a Δ-list, and therefore it cannot change the state of the bean. The operation *setSuccess* changes *value* as indicated by Δ(*value*). The new *value'* is determined by the input parameter *v?*.

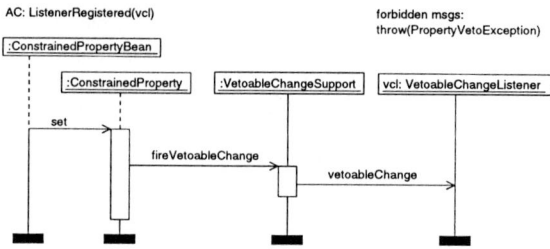

Fig. 4. A Non-Vetoed Property Change

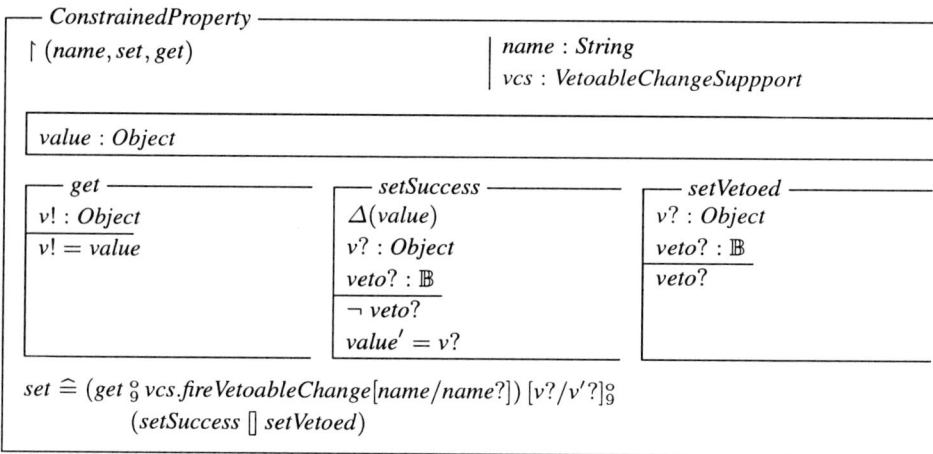

Component Collaboration. To specify how intended changes of a constrained property are processed, we need life sequence charts that show which objects send which messages in which order. Figure 4 shows how a property change is handled when no veto occurs. The expression "forbidden msgs: throw(PropertyVetoException)" states that no veto may occur in the sequence of messages in Figure 4. The possibility to state such negative conditions is a means of expression not available in message sequence charts.

Moreover, the chart has an *activation condition*, which means that it is only invoked if the corresponding condition holds. In this case, we must require that the object *vcl* of class *VetoableChangeListener* be registered for the *ConstrainedPropertyBean* whose constrained property is to be changed.

Once a listener *vcl* has been registered, it will receive appropriate property change events whenever the operation *set* for a constrained property is invoked. The object *vcl* prototypically stands for all registered listeners. Here, we see that the Object-Z and the LSC specifications are complementary. In the LSC, it cannot be expressed that the *vetoableChange* message must be sent to *all* registered listeners. This fact is stated in the Object-Z specification of the class *VetoableChangesupport*, however.

Figure 5 shows the more complex behavior in the case that one of the listeners vetoes the change of a constrained property. In that situation, we need to consider two proto-

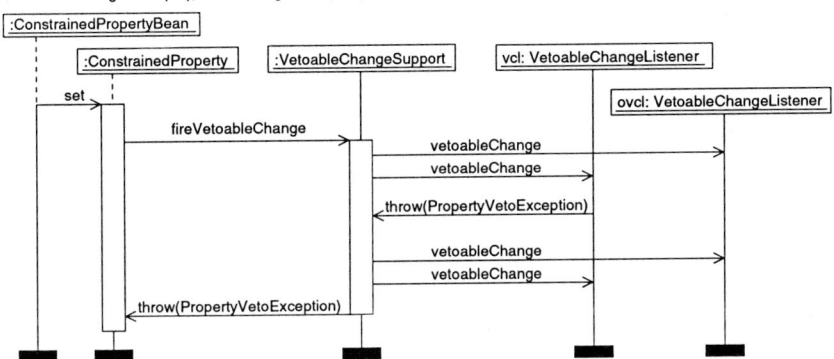

Fig. 5. A Vetoed Property Change

typical listeners, *vcl* and *ovcl*. An invocation of *set* causes a call to *fireVetoableChange*. All listeners, i.e. *vcl* and *ovcl* are notified of the proposed change. Vetoing the change, *vcl* throws a *PropertyVetoException*. As a consequence, all listeners must be notified of the veto. A way to do so [7] is to notify all listeners of a change of the property's value *back* from the new value to the previous one. This may indeed be the only way to notify listeners of a veto, because the JavaBean component model does not enforce explicit confirmations of (vetoable) changes. Therefore, a listener must assume that a change is not vetoed unless it receives a *vetoableChange* message reverting the value of a property back to its previous one.

The class *VetoableChangeSupport* defines the general infrastructure for the generator side of vetoable changes. The class definition expresses crucial information about processing vetoable changes that cannot be expressed in LCSs or are not expressed in the LSC specification for reasons of conciseness and readability. For example, the parameters of all operations are not given in the LSCs, but only in the Object-Z specification.

In addition to the set of listeners *vcl*, the boolean state variable *veto* holds the status of veto for an execution of *fireVetoableChange*. Several private operations manipulate *veto*.

The operations *addVetoableChangeListener* and *removeVetoableChangeListener* just add or remove a new listener to or from the set *vcl*.

The definition of *fireVetoableChange* reflects the complexity of catching a veto and possibly notifying all listeners of a change back to the old value of a property. The operation *mkVCE* [1] constructs a vetoable change event *evt!*, which is input to the first invocation of *vetoableChange* on all members of *vcl*. It also returns *evtRev!*, a change event reverting the value of the property back to its previous value. The invocation of *vote* in parallel with each *vetoableChange* serves to accumulate possible vetoes: if one call to *vetoableChange* returns *veto!* = *true*, then the attribute *veto* becomes (and remains) true.

---

[1] The definition of *mkVCE* can be found in [9].

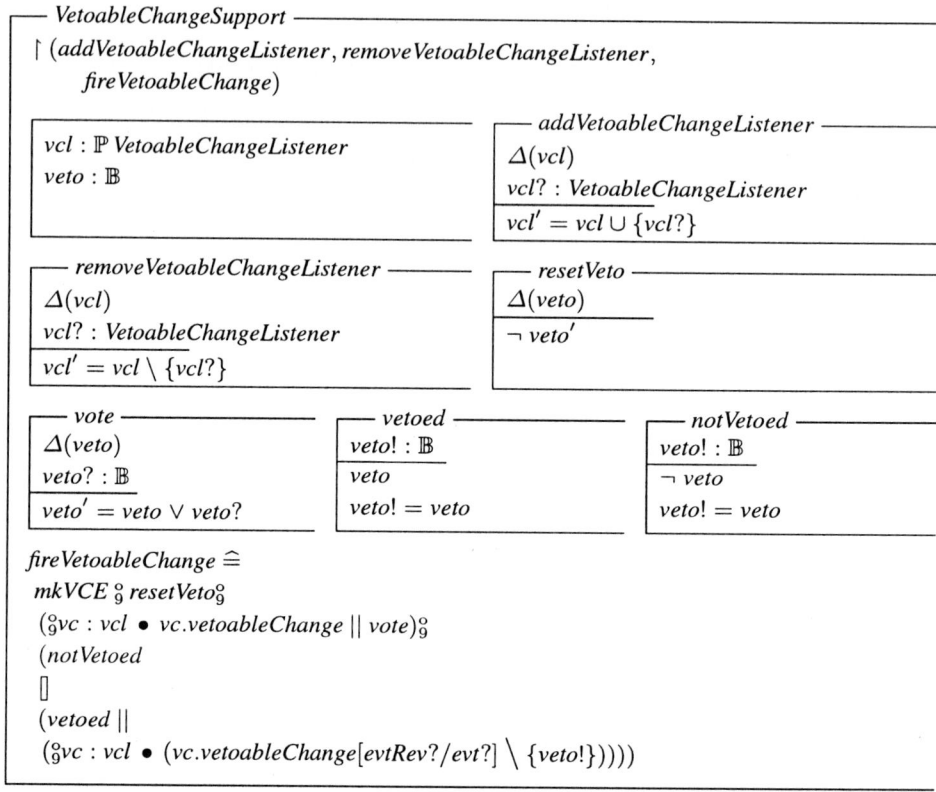

The choice *notVetoed* [] (*vetoed* ...) processes a possible veto. If *veto* is false, the left branch is taken and the property change succeeds, because *notVetoed* is a no-op with precondition ¬ *veto*. If *veto* is true, then all listeners are notified of the reverse change event *evtRev*!. In this case, hiding the output *veto*! of *vetoableChange* prevents a veto to the reverse change from succeeding.

Here, an unresolved issue of the JavaBean component model has become obvious: what happens if one of the listeners vetoes the second *vetoableChange* that reverts the first vetoed change? In our Object-Z specification, we have decided to forbid that kind of behavior.

The specifications presented in this section give the reader an impression of how the formal specification of component models might look. The specifications of the other classes shown in Figure 3 can be found in [9].

4 Specification of a Bean

This section illustrates by way of an example how our JavaBean component model can be instantiated to specify individual Beans very concisely, without repeating all the details already stated in the component model specification.

The simple Bean *MyButton* implements a text button for a graphical user interface [19]. The button has a text field of a certain size which displays the *label* of the button.

```
┌─ MyButton ─────────────────────────┐      ┌─ MyButton ──────────────────────┐
│ ↾ (paint, fireAction,              │      │ ConstrainedPropertyBean         │
│     isLargeFont, getPreferredSize) │      │ ...                             │
│ generates event action of ActionEvent │   ├─────────────────────────────────┤
│ receives event pressed, clicked,   │      │ label : String                  │
│     released, ... of MouseEvent    │      │ ∃ cp : cps | cp.name = "label"  │
│ text_xpad, text_ypad : ℕ           │      │     ∧ cp.value = label          │
├────────────────────────────────────┤      ├─────────────────────────────────┤
│ text_xpad = 12                     │      │ getLabel ≙                      │
│ text_ypad = 8                      │      │     [cp : cps | cp.name = "label"] • get │
├────────────────────────────────────┤      │ setLabel ≙                      │
│ sized, down : 𝔹                    │      │     [cp : cps | cp.name = "label"] • set │
│ bound properties                   │      └─────────────────────────────────┘
│ debug : 𝔹                          │
│ font : Font                        │
│ fontSize : ℕ                       │
│ foreground, background : Color     │
│ constrained properties             │
│ label : String                     │
└────────────────────────────────────┘
```

Fig. 6. A component specification and its expansion

Using the mouse pointer, which is implemented as another Bean, the button can receive a number of events signaling the status of the mouse pointer and the mouse button. An instance of *MyButton* generates an event called *action* if the mouse button is pressed while the mouse pointer is on the button.

We specify an individual Bean such as *MyButton* in Object-Z augmented by some keywords, as the left-hand side of Fig. 6 shows. Replacement rules define the meaning of those keywords. There is no need to give additional class diagrams or repeat any of the LSCs of the component model. Specializing operations inherited from the component model describes their effect particular to the individual Bean.

The specification of *MyButton* declares the generated and received events *action*, *pressed*, *clicked*, etc. The phrases declaring those events mention the classes *ActionEvent* and *MouseEvent*. These classes – which we do not show here – implement the type of information those events carry: an *ActionEvent* identifies the source of the event, which is an instance of *MyButton*; a *MouseEvent* carries the coordinates of the mouse pointer.

The state box declares the mutable attributes of *MyButton*: *sized* and *down* are private boolean flags; *debug*, the font and color information (*font*, *fontSize*, *foreground*, *background*) are bound properties, and the text *label* displayed by the button is a constrained property.

We exemplify the keyword translation process by considering the expansion of the declaration of *label*, which the right-hand side of Fig. 6 shows, leaving out the parts concerning the other attributes of the Bean.

The value of each property is stored in a mutable attribute. Therefore, the declaration of *label* remains part of the state box. Because *label* is a constrained property, *MyButton* inherits from *ConstrainedPropertyBean*. This provides all the infrastructure discussed in Section 3.2. In particular, *MyButton* has attributes *vcs* and *cps*. An invariant relates the attribute *label* to a member of *cps*, namely one with the name "label". It also relates the *value* of that *ConstrainedProperty* to *label*. Finally, to conform to the naming conventions for JavaBeans, the operations *getLabel* and *setLabel* are defined to be promotions of the *get* and *set* operations of that object.

This example shows how the keywords related to JavaBeans hide formal noise in the Object-Z specification of a Bean. It also shows that we are actually working at the specification level: how an implementation ensures that *label* is realized as a constrained property is of no interest at this level of abstraction; it suffices to *require* that the attribute *label* be related to a constrained property including all the necessary operations.

5 Related Work

Although much has been published about component-based software engineering, the formal specification of components in general and JavaBeans in particular has not yet been undertaken by many researchers.

Cimato [4, 5] proposes an algebraic specification technique for Java objects and components, where the term "component" does not denote an independently deployable piece of software – as in the context of component-based software engineering – but an entity of computation that is connected to other components in a software architecture Consequently, Cimato focuses on architectural issues in his specification of JavaBeans. A Bean architecture consists of Beans as components and adapters as connectors. A configuration specifies how these are connected. These architectural descriptions do not describe the interaction of Beans as we have done in Section 3 using life sequence charts. Properties, bound properties, and constrained properties are not dealt with.

Brucker and Wolff [2] use UML class diagrams annotated with OCL formulas to support the run-time checking of constraints on Enterprise Java Beans. They do not attempt to specify the component model of Enterprise Java Beans as such, but they exploit the structure of interfaces that the component model imposes on Beans to generate specific run-time checks of Java code from OCL constraints that annotate the various parts of the class diagram for a Bean. They observe that the constraints on the implementation of an abstract enterprise bean interface should be a data refinement of the constraints on the interface, and they exploit that observation when checking constraints at run-time.

Beugnard [1] and Cariou [3] use UML to describe communication components called mediums. A medium is a means to define communication services needed in distributed applications, offering a specific interface, transportation services and specific services (shared memory, configuration, quality of service). They specify components by collaboration diagrams, OCL for class invariants and service specifications, and state diagrams for temporal and synchronization constraints. In contrast to our work, Beugnard and Cariou do not aim at specifying component models in general, but propose a specific component model.

6 Conclusions

A component model is the basis for many applications. Therefore, it deserves a thorough analysis based on a precise description of its semantics. Our approach of specifying component models provides such a precise description. As we have seen for the example of the JavaBean component model, just specifying a component model can make contradictions and omissions in the informal description explicit: the literature [7, 17, 19] does not resolve the problem of "vetoed vetoes". We are probably not the first to detect that problem, but setting up a specification systematically leads one to ask the questions that make problems as this one obvious.

We specify components independently of a target programming language. In the JavaBeans case, for example, we do not restrict inheritance in specifications, even if it is restricted in Java. Component specifications should provide all necessary information concerning the component that is needed either to incorporate the component in a system or to implement the component.

Not referring to specific features of a programming language, specifications of component models support the comparison of different component models – a research that may lead to improved interoperability between different component models.

There inevitably is some "formal noise" in a formal specification. We believe this is acceptable for a component model, because the goal of interoperable components requires a consistent and complete description of the infrastructure that they can build on.

For an individual component, however, the specification highlights the specific services, abstracting from details of the component model by means of specific key-phrases. Specifications of individual components – and the underlying component model – can be the basis for advanced assembly tools that analyze components not only on the level of interface syntax but also on the level the semantics of the services that components provide, and their interaction in a specific system. Such an analysis cannot be provided based on the code alone.

Future Work. We have presented a way of formally describing component models with the motivation of analyzing those models for consistency and completeness. The question how such an analysis is best conducted and what appropriate tool-support for analyzing component model specifications is must still be addressed. An embedding of Object-Z in the logic of a theorem prover [16] can be a starting point to come up with mechanized support for component models analysis.

A long term goal of this research is to find a general understanding of what the characteristics of components are by way of specifying and comparing different component frameworks. This understanding could serve as a basis for unifying component frameworks and allowing components of different frameworks to interoperate.

To reach this goal, it is necessary to investigate other, more complex component models such as EJB and CORBA. It will also be necessary to take the process of composing systems from components into account.

References

1. A. Beugnard. Communication Services as Components for Telecommunication Applications. In *Proc. 14th European Conference on Object-Oriented Programming, ECOOP'2000*. Sophia Antipolis et Cannes (F), 2000. http://www-info.enst-bretagne.fr/medium.
2. A. Brucker and B. Wolff. Testing distributed component based systems using UML/OCL. In M. Wirsing, editor, *Workshop on Integrating Diagrammatic and Formal Specification Techniques*, pages 17–23. LMU München, 2001. http://www.pst.informatik.uni-muenchen.de/GI2001/gi-band.pdf.
3. E. Cariou. Spécification de composants de Communication en UML. In *Proc. Objets, Composants, Modèles (OCM'2000)*, 2000. http://www-info.enst-bretagne.fr/medium.
4. S. Cimato. *A Methodology for the Specification of Java Components and Architectures*. PhD thesis, University of Bologna, 1999. http://www.cs.unibo.it/~cimato/www/papers/sty.ps.gz.
5. S. Cimato. Specifying component-based Java applications. In P. Ciancarini, A. Fantechi, and R. Gorrieri, editors, *Proc. 3rd Conf. on Formal Methods for Open Object-Based Distributed Systems (FMOODS)*, pages 105–112, 1999.
6. W. Damm and D. Harel. LSCs: Breathing life into message sequence charts. In *Proc. 3rd Conf. on Formal Methods for Open Object-Based Distributed Systems (FMOODS)*, 1999.
7. D. Flanagan. *Java in a Nutshell*. O'Reilly, 1999.
8. E. Gamma, R. Helm, R. Johnson, and J. Vlissides. *Design patterns: Elements of reusable object-oriented software*. Addison-Wesley, 1995.
9. M. Heisel, T. Santen, and J. Souquières. On the specification of components – the JavaBeans example. Technical Report A02-R-025, LORIA, Nancy, France, 2002.
10. ITU-TS, Geneva. *ITU-TS Recommendations Z.120: Message Sequence Chart (MSC)*, 1996.
11. J. Klose and H. Wittke. An automata based interpretation of live sequence charts. In T. Margaria and Wang Yi, editors, *Proc. TACAS'2001*, LNCS 2031, 2001.
12. Microsoft Corporation. *The Component Object Model Specification, Version 0.9*, 1995. http://www.microsoft.com/com/resources/comdocs.asp.
13. The Object Mangagement Group (OMG). *The Common Object Request Broker: Architecture and Specification, Revision 2.2*, February 1998. http://cgi.omg.org/library/corbaiiop.html.
14. J. Rumbaugh, I. Jacobsen, and G. Booch. *Unified Modeling Language Reference Manual*. Addison-Wesley, 1997.
15. G. Smith. *The Object-Z Specification Language*. Kluwer Academic Publishers, 1999.
16. G. Smith, F. Kammüller, and T. Santen. Encoding Object-Z in Isabelle/HOL. In D. Bert, J. P. Bowen, M. C. Henson, and K. Robinson, editors, *ZB2002: Formal Specification and Development in Z and B*, LNCS 2272, pages 82–99. Springer-Verlag, 2002.
17. Sun Microsystems. *JavaBeans Specification, Version 1.01*, 1997. http://java.sun.com/products/javabeans/docs/spec.html.
18. Sun Microsystems. *Enterprise JavaBeans Specification, Version 2.0*, 2001. http://java.sun.com/products/ejb/docs.html.
19. Sun Microsystems. *JavaBeans Tutorial*, 2001. http://developer.java.sun.com/developer/onlineTraining/Beans/beans02.
20. C. Szyperski. *Component Software*. ACM Press, Addison-Wesley, 1999.

A Specification-Based Software Construction Framework for Reuse*

Jing Liu, Huaikou Miao, and Xiaolei Gao

The School of Computer Engineering and Science, Shanghai University
Shanghai, 200072, P. R. China
liujingh@hotmail.com, hkmiao@online.sh.cn

Abstract. Software reuse includes low-level components reuse, high-level components reuse and system architecture reuse. High-level components reuse and software architecture reuse are still limited to some domain specific models, while low-level components reuse is constrained by machine's retrieve ability. This paper proposes a mechanism that builds software in three levels, namely software system, high-level components and low-level components. Each level has a unique structure and organization manner. The focus of the paper is on the construction of high-level components and their matching and composition approaches. Design pattern is proposed for building generic high-level components with large number of alternatives. Once a pattern model of high-level component is constructed, it can be directly used or generalized. Design space incorporated with formal specification technology is introduced to not only precisely describe the relationship between high-level components but also easily analyze components matching and composing. The method is illustrated with a debugger example.

1 Introduction

The concept of reuse is fundamental to all engineering disciplines. Components provide levels of software abstraction used to effectively construct increasingly complex systems. Large enterprises have thousands of large-scale, complex, packaged and custom applications. Interoperation between these applications is essential for the flexibility and evolution needed by enterprises to build new software, compose software, offer new services, meet regulatory requirements, reduce time to market, reduce costs, and execute business mergers. In fact, software reuse was described by Mili et al. as the "only realistic approach" to meet the needs of the software industry [1].

The potential of software reuse is not limited to source code, algorithms, or object classes. It also includes high-level components, software architectures, and program transformation [2]. The benefits of software reuse have extended beyond the design phase to the analysis and maintenance phase of development. However, the potential benefits of software reuse are far from reaching, in practice software reuse has not flourished. One major technical barrier is lack of approaches to provide software construction framework with which reuse process is easy to practice. To produce software by reuse, we need reuse-oriented software framework, specific design ap-

---

* This work is supported by National Natural Science Foundation of China (No. 60173030)

proach, components matching, retrieving and composing rules. Formalization of component gives component users a good understanding, and ensures its rigor [14]. As a specification based construction framework is formal, it will be unambiguous and can be analyzed to ensure its internal consistence. We may start with analyzing the process in which software system is constructed by reuse.

Software developers usually divide software development process into four steps. First, they design or reuse system architecture, second divide the system into several interconnected modules or high-level components, third design or retrieve and match (or develop) every module respectively, fourth compose the modules, finally a system is constructed. These activities are interdependent. Ideally, most components and system architecture can be automated retrieving, matching, adapting and composing. However, automation is difficult because reuse now is still limited to low-level components, while the number of low-level components is enormous and will cause retrieve problem. Integrating low-level components into high-level components will not only greatly reduce the number of components in order to release the retrieve difficult, but also partly reuse design. Whereas a reusable high-level component will have a lot of parameters and it lacks of a mechanism to manage.

This paper proposes a mechanism that builds software in three levels, namely software system, high-level components and low-level components. Each level has a unique structure and organization manner. The main focus of this paper is on the construction of high-level components and their matching and composition approaches. Design pattern is proposed and used as a template for building generic high-level components with large number of alternatives. Once a pattern model of high-level component is constructed, it can be directly used or generalized. Design space incorporated with formal specification technology is introduced to not only precisely describe the relation between high-level components but also easily analyze components matching and composing. The method is illustrated with a debugger example.

2 Construction Framework

It is generally agreed that formal models and techniques for formal analysis are cornerstones of a mature engineering discipline, but engineering disciplines use them in many different ways [3]. Formalisms can be used to provide precise, abstract models and to provide analytical techniques based on these models. Specification matching [4, 5, 6] applies formal prove to evaluate relationships between specifications. Given a formal definition of reusability, specification matching can be used to evaluate the reusability of a component with respect to a requirement specification. In addition, automated reasoning can be used to determine what changes are necessary to reuse a component and guide component adaptation. [7]

2.1 Reuse Oriented Framework

In recent years, the rate of component reuse in a software system has apparently increased, but it is still limited to specific domain. If we want to expand reuse beyond specific domain, a component framework with strong adaptive ability to various environments is essential.

Another problem for components' reuse is retrieving in enormous components. If large numbers of low-level components are integrated into high-level components, not only the retrieve problem can be solved but also the reuse granularity can be increased. Therefore, we provide a three-level model, as shown in Fig. 1, to represent a software construction framework.

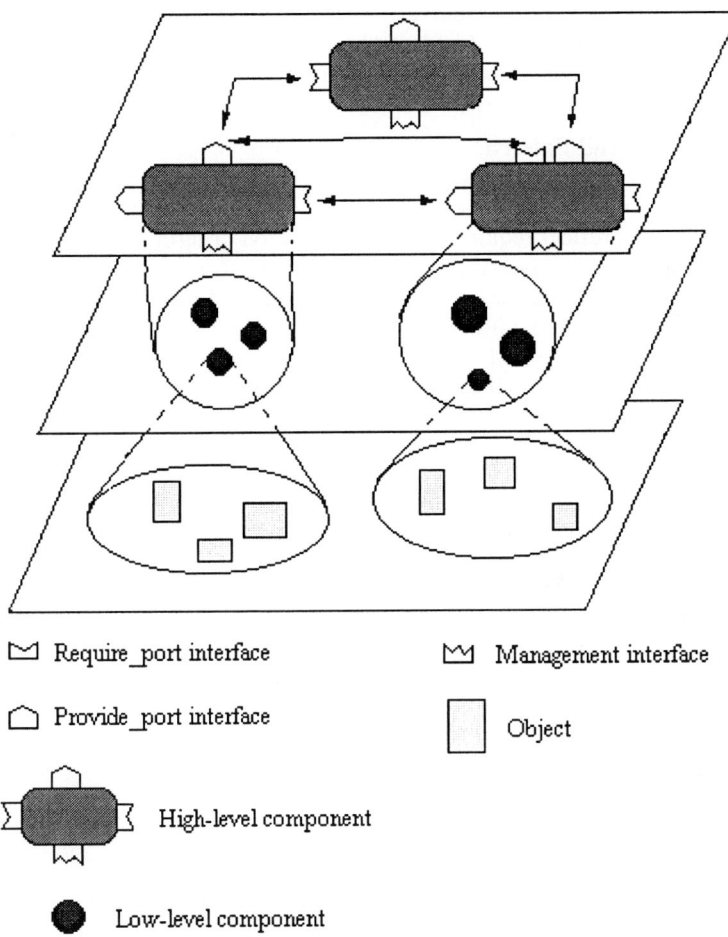

Fig. 1. An instance of software constructing framework

The top level allows the specification of coordination between high-level components. Components connected with arrows represent that the two components whose *Require* and *Provide* interface have been matched and bounded. The second, middle level shows the low-level components and their integration. The third, lowest level shows the low-level components are formed by integrating objects. The top level is the key level, in this level component body is very complex while the interface must provide a wide choice.

2.2 Design Space and High-Level Component Construction

As general purpose high-level components have many alternatives and much more complex than a low-level component, high-level components should have different framework from that of low-level components. High-level components must keep generic properties and high flexibility. By constructing a design space, we can describe and classify the architectural alternatives. Within a design space, we can formulate design rules that indicate good and bad combinations of choices, and use them to select an appropriate design based on functional requirements.

2.2.1 Design Space and Pattern

Multidimensional design space classifies all aspects of high-level component framework, with each dimension describes variation in one component aspect characteristic. Some dimensions reflect requirements or evaluation criteria (function and/or performance), while other dimensions reflect structure (or other available design choices). The dimensions that describe functional and performance choices make up the functional design space, while those that describe structural choices make up the structural design space. Different values along a dimension correspond to alternative requirements or design choices. It can be described in many ways.

One widely used formal specification language is Z. Z is a powerful analytical tool that facilitates system understanding through the development of a series of unambiguous, verifiable mathematical models [10, 13].

Design space is defined as a multidimensional space with functional dimensions and structural dimensions and large number of alternatives. A particular design space has its own name. The set of all valid functional dimensions DIMF can be defined as a given set DIMF, and the set of all valid structure dimensions DIMS defined as a given set DIMS. The set of all valid particular design space names defined as a given set NAME. Then, a design space can be modeled as a Z schema.

[DIMF, DIMS, NAME]

```
┌─ DesignSpace ─────────────────────┐
│ funcdim: ℙ DIMF                   │
│ strucdim: ℙ DIMS                  │
│ dr: NAME ↔ (ℙ DIMF × ℙ DIMF)      │
└───────────────────────────────────┘
```

The different dimensions are not necessarily independent. In fact, it is important to discover relationship between dimensions, in order to create design rules describing appropriate and inappropriate combinations of choices.

Pattern is used as a generic framework for a type of high-level components, such as *Debugger* or *User interface* component. A generic high-level component pattern has a large number of alternatives and can be instantiated to a real component in specific environment.

We define pattern as a particular design space that has a name and a number of functional dimensions and structural dimensions. The pattern is specified to a type of components. It can be modeled as:

```
┌─ DesignPattern ──────────────────────────┐
│  Designspace                             │
│  pattern_id: NAME                        │
│  fn, sn: ℕ                               │
├──────────────────────────────────────────┤
│  # funcdim = fn                          │
│  # strucdim = sn                         │
│  (funcdim, strucdim) ∈ dr (pattern_id)   │
└──────────────────────────────────────────┘
```

The same type of components usually has similar characteristics in structure and function. Father more, we can obtain a pattern by generalizing concrete components. The generic pattern is able to provide a number of alternatives for a component to select and it can also be easily instantiated to concrete components.

2.2.2 The Illustrative Example

Software system construction process can be divided into three steps. First, we construct a pattern of a high-level component in design space. Second, we instantiate the pattern to obtain concrete components. Third, we match and compose the high-level components to form a software system. To illustrate this we will consider the generic component pattern *DebuggerPattern*.

In *Debugger* pattern, the dimensions are divided into two groups: functional dimensions, structural dimensions. Functional dimensions represent the requirements for a debugger that greatly affects its functionality. We choose five functional dimensions, five structural dimensions.

Functional dimensions include: debugger adaptability across platforms dimension that expresses the range of platform support; system organization dimension that describes the surrounding computer system; external event handling dimension that reflects an application-imposed external requirement; user customizability dimension that reflects user-imposed external requirement and basic debugger class dimension that identifies the basic kinds of interaction supported by debugger system. There are several alternatives in every dimension. For example, in the dimension of debugger adaptability across platforms *adaptabilityacrossplatform*, we give three alternatives, including *none, loca_behavior_changes* and *globa_behavior_change*, to indicate the extent of change in debugger's behavior that may be required when changing to a different platform. We can use the similar method to choose alternatives for other dimensions as shown in Fig.2.

Debugger's five functional dimensions are named as ADAPT, SYSTM, EXTER, USERC and BASDE. The dimensions are described with schema: IfuncDim.

Structural dimensions include debugger definition notation dimension, control thread mechanism dimension, basis of communication dimension and platform interface abstraction level dimension. The dimensions are named as DEBDE, CONTR, BASIS, PLATE and MOTIT. Structure dimensions are described with schema named IStrucDim.

DIMENSIONS		VALUES						
Functional Dimensions	Adaptability across platforms	None	Local behavior change	Global behavior change				
	System organization	Uni-processing	Multiprocessing	Distributed processing				
	External event handling	No external events	Process events while waiting for input	External events preempt user commands				
	User customizability	High	Medium	Low				
	Basic debugger class	Breakpoints setting	Module property	Monitors expression	Debugger message			
Structural Dimensions	Debugger definition notation	Implicit in shared debugger code	Implicit in environment code	External declarative notation	External procedural notation	Internal declarative notation	Internal procedural notation	
	Control thread mechanism	None	Standard processes	Lightweight processes	Non-preemptive processes	Event handlers	Interrupt service routines	
	Basis of communication	Events	Pure state	State with hints	State plus events			
	Platform interface abstraction level	Interaction manager with fixed data types	Interaction manager with extensible data type	Extensible interaction manager	Abstract interface	Monolithic application program		
	Monitor representations	Natural language message	Form filling					

Fig. 2. An instance of design pattern

ADAPT, SYSTM, EXTER, USERC, BASDE: ℙ DIMF
ADAPT = { None, Local_behavior_change, Global_behavior_change }
SYSTM = { Uniprocessing, Multiprocessing, Distributed_processing }
EXTER = { No_external_events, Process_events_while_waiting_for_input,
          External_events_preempt_user_commands }
USERC = { High, Medium, Low }
BASDE = { Breakpoints_setting, Module_property, Monitors_expression,
          Debugger_message }

```
┌─ IFuncDim ──────────────────────────────────┐
│  adaptabilityacrossplatform: ADAPT          │
│  systemorganization: SYSTM                  │
│  externaleventhandling: EXTER               │
│  usercustomizability: USERC                 │
│  basicdebuggerclass: BASDE                  │
└─────────────────────────────────────────────┘
```

DEBDE, CONTR, BASIS, PLATF, MONIT: ℙ DIMS
DEBDE = {Implicit_in_shared_debugger_code, Implicit_in_environment_code,
         External_declarative_notation, External_procedural_notation,
         Internal_declarative_notation, Internal_procedural_notation}
CONTR = {None, Standard_processes, Lightweight_processes,
         Non-preemptive_processes, Event_handlers,
         Interrupt_service_routines}
BASIS = {Events, Pure_state, State_with_hints, State_plus_events}
PLATF = { Interaction_manager_with_fixed_data_types,
          Interaction_manager_with_extensible_data_type,
          Extensible_interaction_manager, Abstract_interface,
          Monolithic_application_program }
MONIT = {Natural_language_message, Form_filling }

```
┌─ IStrucDim ─────────────────────────────────┐
│  debuggerdefinitionnotation: DEBDE          │
│  controlthreadmechanism: CONTR              │
│  basisofcommunication: BASIS                │
│  platforminterfaceabstractionlevel: PLATF   │
│  monitorrepresentations: MONIT              │
└─────────────────────────────────────────────┘
```

The design pattern of debugger is modeled as a schema DebuggerPattern.

```
┌─ Debugger: NAME ─────────────────────────────────────────┐
│ ┌─ DebuggerPattern ──────────────────────────────────┐   │
│ │ DesignPattern                                       │   │
│ │ pf : IFuncDim                                       │   │
│ │ ps : IStrucDim                                      │   │
│ ├─────────────────────────────────────────────────────┤   │
│ │ pattern_id = Debugger                               │   │
│ │ funcdim = { pf.adaptabilityacrossplatform, pf.systemorganization, │
│ │ pf.externaleventhandling, pf.usercustomizability, pf.basicdebuggerclass } │
│ │ strucdim = { ps.debuggerdefinitionnotation, ps.controlthreadmechanism, │
│ │ ps.basisofcommunication, ps.platforminterfaceabstractionlevel, │
│ │ ps.monitorrepresentations }                         │   │
│ │ ( funcdim, strucdim ) ∈ dr (Debugger)               │   │
│ └─────────────────────────────────────────────────────┘   │
```

After a generic debugger pattern is constructed, we can easily obtain a concrete component of the type. We only need to select a set of alternatives of the generic pattern according to the requirements, then a type of concrete components is created.

3 Component Matching

In order to achieve correct interoperation among components by using composition and reusability, it is important to know how to match mutually useful components.

Specification matching is a process of determining if two software components can be integrated [15]. It is essential for component retrieve, substitution and integration.

3.1 Matching Function

The activity of components matching corresponds to that of interfaces matching. There are many ways to define component interface matching. In our paper, interface matching is based on the pre/post-conditions matching [15]. Match is determined by relationship R between the predicate pre/post-conditions of interface. Ideally, R is determined by user, but we also provide a default matching function $R = R_1 = R_2$.

We introduce a given type of interface represent a set of schemas:

[Interface].

I, J: Interface
R, R_1, R_2: (Interface × Interface) $\nrightarrow$ Boolean

$(R = R_1 \wedge R = R_2) \Rightarrow ((PreI \Rightarrow PreJ) \wedge (PostI \Rightarrow PostJ))$

R returns a boolean value that determines if each pre/post condition of a component specification implies each pre/post conditions of an existing component offers. PreI and PreJ represent the pre conditions of interface I and J respectively. PostI and PostJ represent the post conditions of interface I and J respectively.

3.2 Matching Definition

An interface I consists of the signature describing the statically-checkable type and the specification describing the behavior of the interface [12].
Given two interfaces I and J, we define a generic interface matching:

$$\text{Match}: (\text{Interface} \times \text{Interface}) \nrightarrow \text{Boolean}$$

$$\forall \text{I, J}: \text{Interface} \bullet R_1(\text{PreI}, \text{PreJ}) \wedge R_2(\text{PostI}, \text{PostJ}) \Leftrightarrow \text{Match}(\text{I, J})$$

Pre/post-condition matches relate to the pre/post-conditions of each interface. The relations R_1 and R_2 are restricted to either a binary relationship as equivalence ($\Leftrightarrow$), implication ($\Rightarrow$) or any functional or logical expression as seen in [9]. R_1 and R_2 are ideally provided by the user, but there is a default matching function as defined in section 3.1.

Given a component set and a specification matching predicate *Match*, the function *Retrieve* returns a boolean value which corresponds a set of components that each has an interface that match the given interface under the match predicate *Match*.

[Component]

$$\text{Search}: \text{Component} \rightarrow \mathbb{P}\ \text{Interface}$$
$$\text{Retrieve}: \text{Interface} \times \text{Component} \rightarrow \text{Boolean}$$

$\forall \text{component}: \text{Component}, \text{interface}: \text{Interface} \bullet$
Retrieve (interface, component) $\Rightarrow$
($\exists$ interfacex: Interface $\bullet$ interfacex $\in$ search (component) $\Leftrightarrow$
match (interfacex, interface))

In the above, *Search* is a function for searching all of the interfaces in a component. If we take all of the components that have any interface that matches the given interface as qualified component set, *Retrieve* is a function for searching qualified component set. The *Retrieve* is based on component matching.

4 Components Composition

Composition of components consists of specifying new components and reusing/building new components out of existing components. This implies that composition covers interoperability. Software composition is an integral part of interoperability.

Formalizing high-level components and their relationships can make the composition architecture precise. To formalize the high-level components' composition, we begin by selecting a basic component model with component name and component interface. The interface consists of require ports and provide ports. Given a set of component name, we use Z to describe the model.

[CNAME]

$$\begin{array}{|l} \text{Component} \\ \quad \text{name : CNAME} \\ \quad \text{require\_port, provide\_port : P Interface} \end{array}$$

An integrating system consists of a set of components and the relationship among them. Connection, *connect*, is a relation that associates one component to another.

$$\begin{array}{|l} \text{ComponentsComposition} \\ \quad \text{components : P Component} \\ \quad \text{connect : P Interface} \leftrightarrow \text{P Interface} \\ \hline \forall c_1, c_2 : \text{components} \cdot (c_1.\text{name} = c_2.\text{name}) \Leftrightarrow (c_1 = c_2) \\ \forall c_1, c_2 : \text{components} \cdot (c_1, c_2) \in \text{connect} \Rightarrow \\ \quad (\text{dom connect} \subseteq c_2.\text{require\_port} \land \text{ran connect} \subseteq c_1.\text{provide\_port}) \\ \forall \text{interfacex, interfacey} : \text{Interface} \cdot (\text{interfacex, interfacey}) \in \text{connect} \Leftrightarrow \\ \quad \text{match (interfacex, interfacey)} \end{array}$$

The invariant of *ComponentsComposition* asserts that the components in the system have unique names and *connect* relates *require* and *provide* ports that exist in the system. Only the components with matched interfaces can be connected together.

5 Conclusion

Specification-based method is one of the essential methodologies that can provide exact component integration to form a software system. Reuse, however, also requires that components be suitable for various environments and easy to move from one kind of environment to another. High-level component pattern can evade this bottleneck by giving a general framework. In the framework, all kinds of alternatives can be put into one design space.

In this paper, we propose a mechanism that builds software in three levels, namely software system, high-level components and low-level components level. We show that different frameworks must be applied to different levels of components and how the complex management of high-level components with large number of alternatives is practiced. The collection of necessary alternatives that influence the flexibility of a component is defined in design space. Design pattern is introduced as a template for building complex high-level components. Formal method used to precisely analyze and describe the relation between components. Once a pattern model is constructed, it can be directly used in or generalized to various environments, thus we can benefit from the high portability.

Specification matching brings the determination of inter-module connection beyond name matching . The formal notation for composition allows various levels of abstraction and ensures the preciseness and automation in producing software. Design space cooperated with formal specification can not only precisely describe the relation between high-level components but also easily analyze components matching and components composing.

Future work essentially concerns integrating fuzzy concepts into formal model forming, matching and composing. Fuzzy set theory is an established technique for representing uncertainty and imprecision and can be seen as a generalization of Boolean or crisp set theory [11, 16]. Given that Z is a set and logic based specification language then it should be possible to provide a notation that incorporates fuzzy set ideas within the language itself while at the same time retaining the precision of any Z model. A long-term goal is to develop support for automated component adaptation and integration.

References

[1]. Mili, H., Mili, F., and Mili, A. 1995. Reusing software: Issues and research directions. IEEE Transaction on Software Engineering, 21(6):528-562
[2]. Penix, J. And Alexander, P. 1999. Efficient Specification-Based Component Retrieval. Automated Software Engineering, 6, 139-170, Kluwer Academic Publishers
[3]. Shaw, M. And Garlan, D. 1996. Software architecture: perspectives on an emerging discipline. Prentice Hall.
[4]. Rollins, E.J. and Wing, J. 1991. Specifications as search keys for software libraries. In Proceedings of the Eight International Conference in Logic Programming.
[5]. Moormann Zaremski, A. And Wing, J.M. 1995. Signature matching, a tool for using software libraries. ACM Transactions on Software Engineering and Methodology (TOSEM).
[6]. Moormann Zaremski, A. And Wing, J.M. 1995. Specification matching of software components. In 3rd ACM SIGSOFT Symposium on the Foundations of Software Engineering.
[7]. Penix, J. and Alexander, P. 1997. Toward automated component adaptation. In Proceedings of the Ninth International Conference on Software Engineering and KE, page 535-542.
[8]. Rakotonirainy, A., Bond, A., Indulska, J. and Leonard, D., 2000, SCAF: A simple component architecture framework. IEEE 0-7695-0731-X/00
[9]. Zaremski, A.M., and Wing, J.M., 1995, Specification matching of software components. SIGSOFT'95 Pro of 3rd ACM SIGSOFT Symposium on the foundation of software Engineering – ACM Press
[10]. Jacky, J., 1997, The way of Z: Practical Programming with Formal Methods. Cambridge University Press
[11]. Matthews, C., and Swatman, P.A., 2000, Fuzzy Concept and Formal Methods: Some Illustrative Examples, IEEE 1530-1362/00
[12]. Zaremski, A.M. and Wing, J.M. 1993, Signature Matching: A key to Reuse, Proc. ACM SIGSOFT Symp. On the Foundations on Software Engineering
[13]. Miao, H., Li, G. and Zhu, G., 1999, Software Engineering Language — Z, (in Chinese), Shanghai Science and Technology Literature Press
[14]. Miao, H., Yu, C. and Li, L., 2000, A formalized abstract component object model — Z-COM$^+$, 36th International Conference in Technology of Object • Oriented Languages and Systems Tools- Asia, IEEE Computer Society Press
[15]. Zaremski, A.M. and Wing, J.M., 1997, Specification matching of software components, ACM Transactions on Software Engineering and Methodology (TOSEM), Vol. 6, No. 4, pages 333-369.
[16]. Matthews, C., and Swatman, P.A., 2000, Fuzzy concept and formal methods: a fuzzy logic toolkit for Z, in J.P. Bowen, S.E. Dunne, A. Springer-Verlag, Berlin, ISBN 3-540-67944-8, 491-510.

Specifying a Component Model for Building Dynamically Reconfigurable Distributed Systems[*]

Xuejun Chen [1,2]

[1] University of Stuttgart, Faculty of Computer Science, IPVS
Stuttgart, Germany
xuejun.chen@informatik.uni-stuttgart.de
[2] Nokia Networks, Research and Development,
Duesseldorf, Germany
xuejun.chen@nokia.com

Abstract. The growing popularity of wired and wireless Internet requires distributed systems to be more flexible, adaptive and easily extensible. Dynamic reconfiguration of distributed component-based systems is one possible solution to meet these demands. However, current component models do not offer adequate supports for dynamic reconfiguration of distributed systems. In this paper, we investigate the requirements of dynamic reconfiguration on component model. Based on that, we specify a component model that is more appropriate for dynamic reconfiguration of distributed systems. This component model specifies design rules and conventions that are imposed on component developers, in order to efficiently support dynamic reconfiguration of distributed systems.

1 Introduction

Today, not only conventional computers, but also many electronic appliances, such as PDAs, mobile phones, TV boxes, and telematics systems in vehicles are becoming "internet-enabled". The growing popularity of wired and wireless Internet requires that distributed application systems must be more flexible, adaptive, reliable, and easily extensible. Dynamic reconfiguration of distributed component-based systems is one possible solution to meet these demands, because the ability to dynamically reconfigure the applications enhances the flexibility, adaptability and extensibility of distributed systems. In addition, component-based software development is a promising way to increase reliability of systems and treat the increasing complexity of systems.

In long running distributed systems, for example, telecommunication systems and application servers for E-Business, it is difficult to decide which application components should be available throughout the whole lifecycle of the systems. It is also undesirable to fix the exact location of a component in such systems, since its operating conditions may change. In these cases, dynamic reconfiguration provides the necessary flexibility: a component can be dynamically loaded into the system, migrated from one location to another, and unloaded from the system at runtime. An

---
[*] This work was done while the author was at DaimlerChrysler Research.

additional advantage is that a component can be updated dynamically. Therefore, a dynamically reconfigurable component-based distributed system can quickly fulfill new requirements of customers and adapt to changing environmental conditions.

The current component models (e.g. CORBA Component Model [9], Enterprise JavaBeans [12], and Distributed Component Object Model (DCOM) [6]) or service frameworks such as OSGi [10] provide little support for dynamic reconfiguration of distributed systems. If a dynamically reconfigurable distributed system is built on these component models, the burden of carrying out a dynamic reconfiguration is completely placed on the component developer. However, the component developer should only concentrate on the application logic, not on dynamic reconfiguration of a component.

In this paper we describe a novel component model that specifies design rules and conventions that efficiently support dynamic reconfiguration. One of the most crucial problems of dynamic reconfiguration is: if a component is reconfigured, which other components are affected and how must the system treat this change? To answer this question we specify the static and dynamic dependencies among components in the component model and use a flexible communication mechanism for inter-component interaction.

The rest of the paper is organized as follows: Section 2 describes how a dynamic reconfiguration is carried out. Based on that, we determine the demands of dynamic reconfiguration on component model. Section 3 presents a novel component model that is more suitable for dynamically reconfigurable distributed systems. Section 4 surveys related work. The last section gives a summary of the main points and discusses issues for future work.

2 Dynamically Reconfigurable Component-Based Distributed Systems

In this section, we describe how a dynamic reconfiguration is carried out and discuss which demands must be met by a component model for supporting a dynamic reconfiguration.

In general, there are four forms of reconfiguration of distributed systems: addition of a component, removal of a component, replacement of a component, and migration of a component. Assume that we replace a component. The following example describes simply how a component is replaced. B is the target component, which will be replaced by a new version. B' is the new and compatible version of B. A is a client component of B. C is a server component of B. The replacement process is carried out as follows:

(1) install(B');
(2) treatLink(A, B);
(3) treatLink(B,C);
(4) transferState(B, B');
(5) link(A, B');
(6) link(B', C);
(7) remove(B);

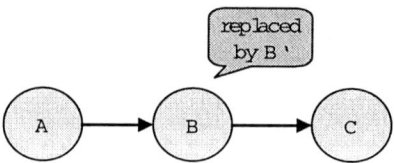

Fig. 1. Component replacement

This replacement process shows us the following points: (1) During dynamical update of a component, communication between the target component and other components must be treated (e.g. *treatLink()* and *link()*). (2) If the target component is stateful, the state of the old version of the target component must be transferred to its new version (i.e. *transferState()*).

The consistent state of a component has to be guaranteed during a dynamic reconfiguration of the component. How to treat interactions between the target component and other components during a reconfiguration can affect the consistency of the target components and other affected components. We define in this paper that a component is consistent, if the integrity of interactions between the component and other components is guaranteed. In other words, there are no pending interactions between the component and other components. Similar to the work [5], we define that a component can be consistently reconfigured, only when the following conditions are fulfilled:

- Its clients carry out no new invocation on it.
- The invocations of its clients on it have been completed.
- It carries out no new invocation on any other components.
- Its invocations on its server component have been completed.

When a component fulfills the above conditions, we say, the component reaches a reconfigurable state. However, how to recognize when the target component reaches a reconfigurable state is a challenge. To meet this challenge, the component model must use a certain communication mechanism that can treat the interactions among components during a dynamic reconfiguration. Before a dynamic reconfiguration is carried out, at first, we have to determine which interactions among components will be affected by the reconfiguration. Then, we must decide how we deal with these interactions, so that the target component reaches the reconfigurable state. Thus, we can carry out the reconfiguration safely. In addition, after a component was reconfigured, the references to the reconfigured component are not valid any longer. The component system should update such invalid references automatically.

If a consistent reconfiguration is guaranteed, there are still some optimization challenges in the reconfiguration process that we must take into account. First, we must try to minimize the interruption that accrues during the reconfiguration. Second, we must try to minimize the system overhead of the dynamic reconfiguration capability. Finally, the burden that component developers take for the dynamic reconfiguration must also be minimal, because the developers should only concentrate on the application logic.

In conclusion, a component model must meet the following demands to support a dynamic reconfiguration of component-based distributed systems:

(1) The component model must provide functions to load, control, and reconfigure components, for example, init(), start(), stop(), update(), extractState(), restoreState(), and destroy().

(2) The component model must clearly describe a component with respect to interface, type, and version of the component, in order to build a robust dynamically reconfigurable component system. In addition, the component model must specify the dependencies among components to support configuration check.

(3) For inter-component interaction the component model should use a flexible communication mechanism that can provide support for monitoring and treating interactions among components during a dynamic reconfiguration.

In the next section, we will describe how our component model meets the above-mentioned demands, in order to support dynamic reconfiguration of distributed systems efficiently.

3 Component Model for Dynamic Reconfiguration

A component model specifies design rules and conventions that are imposed on component developers. There is some terminological confusion in the literature concerning component models and frameworks. We follow the CMU/SEI terminology [1] which states that component-based systems rely upon well-defined standards and conventions (which is called a component model) and a support infrastructure (which is called a component framework). In this paper, we focus on a component model that supports dynamic reconfiguration of distributed systems.

3.1 Component Structure

A software component is a unit of composition with contractually specified interfaces [14]. In our component model, a component consists of the following elements (see Fig. 2):
- provided interfaces
- required interfaces
- service implementation
- management interfaces
- management implementation

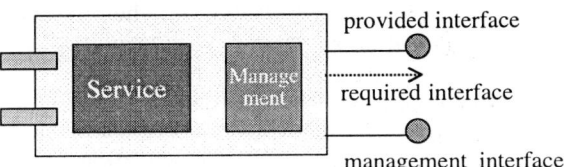

Fig. 2. Component structure

A component offers other components services through the service interfaces, so that the components can cooperate with each other. Conventional interface specification expresses functional properties that include services provided by a component and the signatures of these services - the types of arguments to the services and the manner in which results are returned from the services [1]. We call this kind of interface *service interface*. The *service interfaces* can be divided into *provided interface* and *required interface*. The *provided interface* is an interface that enables the component to provide the implemented functionality to other components. The *required interface* describes the functionality that must be provided by other components or by the system to the component.

The *type* of a component is specified by the set of its *provided interfaces* and the set of its *required interfaces*. When a client component looks up a server component by calling *lookup(component Type)*, the component framework uses a trading mechanism that returns a server component with the required type to the client component.

The *service implementation* ("*Service*") implements the services provided by a component. The *management implementation* ("*Management*") of a component allows the component framework to manage and reconfigure the components at runtime through the *management interface*, which defines the following methods: init(), start(), stop(), update(), extractState(), restoreState(), and destroy(). These methods must be implemented by the component developers, because the implementation of these functions needs component-special knowledge.

3.2 Static Dependencies Among Components

The current component models do not require explicit specification of dependencies among components and also do not manage the dependencies. However, if dependencies among components are not explicitly specified, it is difficult to build a robust component-based system, especially for a dynamically reconfigurable system. For example, without a dependence management, a new component probably cannot work after its installation, or the other components perhaps can not function after the installation of the component, because their requirements may not be fulfilled any more.

At design-time of a component, the component developer must determine on which components this component depends. Such dependency is defined as *static dependency*. The static dependencies of a component are specified by required interfaces of the component. The required interface of a client component and the provided interface of its server component conclude a contract between the client and the server. This contract states how the client uses the interface. It also states what the server has to implement to provide the services promised by the interface. We specify a contract between the client and the server by the use of pre- and post-conditions. Note that the use of pre-conditions and post-conditions is not the single way for the specification of a contract. Other techniques have also been used, for example, a set of rules that map sequences of input events to sequences of output events [1]. However, pre-conditions and post-conditions are the simplest way for the specification of a contract.

In our component model, static dependencies of a component are described in a separate XML-file. Figure 3 describes a component called *DC_Navigation* and its static dependency on the service *getLocation(Precision para)*, which gets location information from the component *LocationManager*.

```xml
<componentProperty>
    <componentName>DC_Navigation</componentName>
    <providedInterface>
        <method methodName="startNavigation">
            <pre-condition>True</pre-condition>
            <post-condition>returnValue=boolean</post-condition>
        </method>
        ....
    </providedInterface>
    ....
</componentProperty>
<dependency>
    <requiredComponent>
        <requiredInterface>
            <method methodName="getLocation">
                <pre-condition>para=precision</pre-condition>
                <post-condition>returnValue=location</post-condition>
            </method>
        </requiredInterface>
        ....
    </requiredComponent>
</dependency>
```

Fig. 3. The description of an example component *DC_Navigation*

The static dependencies among components construct a basis for building and checking a configuration. At compose-time of a component, for example, when loading a component into a system, the component framework has to fulfill the static dependencies of the component, in order to build a correct configuration. Similar to a program dependence graph, we can calculate the dependencies among components by the use of a component dependence graph. A component dependence graph is built by static dependence analysis.

3.3 Dynamic Dependencies among Components

At dynamic reconfiguration-time of a component, we must answer the following questions: when a component is reconfigured, which other components are actually affected? How must we deal with these components? The static dependencies of components can not offer sufficient answers to the above questions, because a component does not actually depend on the components described in its static dependencies at an arbitrary point of time. For example, component A needs a service offered by component B. Only when the component A calls a method of component B, A is in fact dependent on B. Before A calls a method of B or after the method call was terminated, component A does not really depend on component B. We define this kind of runtime dependency that happens in an invocation between two components as *dynamic dependency*.

The current component models do not distinguish between static and dynamic dependencies. Our component model specifies dynamic dependencies among components. By investigating the dynamic dependencies among components we can determine which components are actually affected by a reconfiguration. This is a necessary precondition to achieve such a dynamic reconfiguration that leads only to a minimal disruption of the system, because we only need to treat the interactions between the component to be reconfigured and the actually affected components. However, how to investigate dynamic dependencies among components is a challenge. The component model must use a special communication mechanism to meet the challenge. The following subsection describes the communication mechanism used in our component model.

3.4 Inter-component Interaction

Today's distributed component systems often use RPC or its object oriented variant RMI (Remote Method Invocation) as communication mechanism. However, the standard middleware, for example, Java RMI and CORBA, does not provide mechanisms to control and treat interactions among components for dynamic reconfiguration. Therefore, we suggest a novel approach in which a client component does not communicate with a normal stub of its server component, but with a *virtual stub* of the server component. A virtual stub is a local object that holds the real reference to the server component, and updates this reference immediately if the server component is reconfigured (see Figure 4).

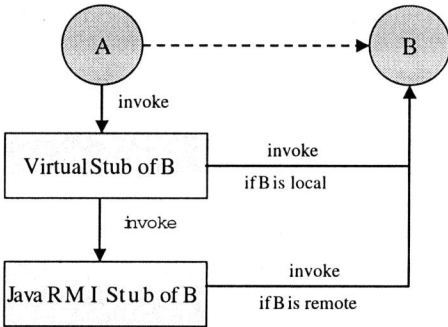

Fig. 4. Inter-component interaction

The advantages of a virtual stub are listed as follows: (1) A virtual stub can be manipulated by the component framework, for example, it can be dynamically loaded into the framework, and the real reference held in a virtual stub can be easily updated. (2) A virtual stub can automatically monitor and treat invocations between components, for example, registering the dynamic dependencies, blocking an interaction, and resuming it. (3) A virtual stub can be automatically generated by a compiler (similar to the Java RMIC) from the provided interface of a server component.

A programmer can use a virtual stub like a normal Java RMI stub. The example in Fig. 5 describes how a virtual stub *v_stub* is used in a program.

As mentioned in Section 2, a component can be consistently reconfigured only if it is in a reconfigurable state. Interactions among components must be monitored, so that we can determine when the target component reaches a reconfigurable state. Interactions that are affected by a reconfiguration are separated into two classes: newly initiated interactions and ongoing interactions. Before a dynamic reconfiguration, newly initiated invocations between the target component and other components are automatically blocked by the virtual stubs. After a dynamic reconfiguration, blocked invocations are rebuilt. On the other hand, ongoing interactions between the target component and other components must be completed. In order to monitor when these interactions are completed, we have designed two methods in the virtual stubs. They are *addDependency* and *removeDependency*:

- *addDependency()*: When a virtual stub invokes a method on the server component, the *dynamic dependency* between the client component and the server component is registered in a dependence list.
- *removeDependency()*: After a virtual stub has finished the method invocation on the server component, the registration of the *dynamic dependency* between the client and the server method is removed from the dependency list.

```
public void testCall(){
    String info;
    TestInterface v_Stub = (TestInterface)
            componentContext.lookup("TestServer");
    try {
        info = v_Stub.testMethod("a test call");
        System.out.println(info);
    } catch (Exception e) {
            e.printStackTrace();
    }
}
```

Fig. 5. An example for using a virtual stub

The following simple method illustrates how a virtual stub monitors dynamic dependencies.

```
public String testMethod(String info){
    ......
    TestInterface ref = (TestInterface)targetRef;
    addDependency();
    String str = (String)ref.testMethod(info);
    removeDependency();
    ......
}
```

Fig. 6. Monitoring dynamic dependencies in a method of a virtual stub

During a reconfiguration of a server component, the server component's virtual stubs check the dependency list periodically. If the dependency list is empty, that means that there is no ongoing interaction. Then the virtual stub informs the component system about it. Thus, the component system can know when the target component reaches its reconfigurable state.

Virtual stubs can not only update invalid reference and monitor interactions among components, but also distinguish between remote invocation and local invocation. When migrating a component, the relationships between the target component and other components are altered. In this case, the virtual stubs of the target component can automatically switch the invocations from local to remote and vice versa. Remote invocation is used only if two components are really in different locations. This approach improves the system performance significantly. For more details on the virtual stubs, see [3].

3.5 State Diagram of Components

As mentioned, in dynamically reconfigurable component-based distributed systems, a component can be loaded into the system, migrated from one location to another, and unloaded from the system at runtime. Moreover, a component can be replaced during its execution. In Figure 7, we describe a state diagram that specifies the states of a component through its lifecycle. Through the state diagram we show how a component can be transformed from one state to another.

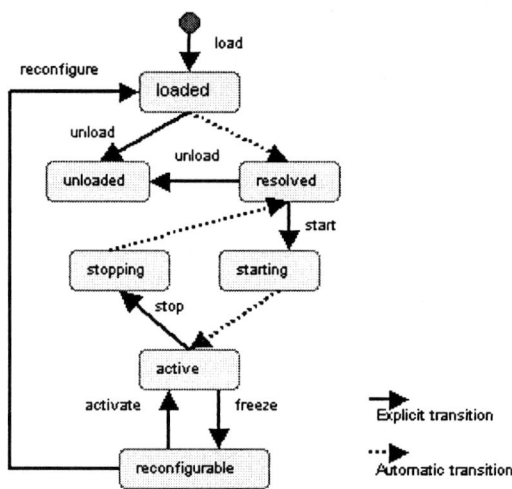

Fig. 7. State diagram of components

A component in a general component system is in one of the following states at any time: loaded, unloaded, resolved, starting, active, and stopping. The component framework is responsible for loading, starting, stopping, and unloading a component. When a component is loaded into a system, the framework has to fulfill the static dependencies of the component. After the static dependencies were resolved, the component is in the state *resolved*. Then the component framework calls the methods of the component *init()* and *start()*, in order to start the component. If the component is successfully started, it is automatically in the *active* state. When a component is stopped by calling its method *stop()*, the component is in the state *stopping*. If a component is not needed in the runtime environment any longer, the framework unloads it.

Besides the above states, we also specify a *reconfigurable* state of a component. A component can be safely reconfigured, only when the component is in a reconfigurable state. As mentioned in the last subsection, by treating interactions between a target component and other components, the target component can reach its reconfigurable state. We call this process as *freezing* a component.

In this section, we have described a component model that meets the three demands of dynamic reconfiguration listed in Section 2.

4 Related Work

In this section we describe related work in the areas of component models and dynamic reconfiguration of distributed systems.

4.1 Current Component Models

Currently, three major component models are well known in distributed systems: the Component Object Model (COM) [6], Enterprise JavaBeans (EJB), and the CORBA Component Model (CCM).

However, all of the above-mentioned component models do not support dynamic reconfiguration of components, because these component models only provide the infrastructure that forms the basic building blocks for component systems. The internal design of components, particularly the aspect related to component reconfiguration, is not addressed by the conventional component models.

Currently, a new component model called OSGi service platform is attracting the attention of industries. The Open Services Gateway Initiative (OSGi) created open specifications for the network delivery of managed services to local networks and devices [10]. OSGi service platform claims that it allows a component to be dynamically updated. However, this component model does not address the treatment of ongoing interactions between the target component and other components during a reconfiguration. Therefore, this component model can not consistently carry out a dynamic reconfiguration.

4.2 Dynamic Reconfiguration of Distributed Systems

Dynamic reconfiguration has been discussed in the research area of distributed systems. In work [5], Kramer and Magee defined that a node reaches a reconfigurable state, if this node is quiescent. However, in Conic, during the reconfiguration of a node, other nodes that require a service from the target node are completely blocked, where some activities are blocked unnecessarily. In work [5, 15], the co-operation among components is realized by atomic transaction that simplifies the treatment of interactions among components during a dynamic reconfiguration. However, communication based on transaction has restrictions: since not every system is transactional, a lot of applications need to take concurrency and partial failure into consideration [7].

Other research projects in this field, for example, work [2, 11] tried to minimize the system interruption during a reconfiguration of a component, where a configuration manager deals with the interactions among components. In such approaches, the centralized configuration manager is the bottleneck for communication among components. Work [4] introduced a *component configurator* that carried out a dynamic reconfiguration at the application level, consequence of which is that the programmers must implement a configurator of each component. In addition, configurators do not treat ongoing interactions between components.

5 Conclusions and Future Work

This paper has presented a component model that meets the demands of dynamic reconfiguration. The component model specifies both static dependencies and dynamic dependencies among components, and uses virtual stubs that not only realize location transparent invocations among components, but also dynamically monitor and manipulate interactions among components during a dynamic reconfiguration. By using this component model, not only a consistent reconfiguration is guaranteed, but also the disruption of the system is minimized, because only the actually affected interactions are treated.

We believe QoS is also an important aspect of system consistency. If an application demands QoS, it is possible that its QoS demands are not fulfilled during a reconfiguration. For example, an application has a demand on latency. During a dynamic reconfiguration, it can happen that this demand is not fulfilled because of system interruption. Certainly, there are also other demands on QoS that have to be fulfilled during a reconfiguration. In the next steps we will investigate how a component model specifies the QoS demands and what kind of support the component model can provide to guarantee the QoS of the component-based system during a dynamic reconfiguration.

Acknowledgments

The author thanks Martin Simons, Viktor Friesen, and Alexander Leonhardi for their helpful comments on earlier drafts of this paper.

References

1. Bachman, F. et al. Technical Concepts of Component-Based Software Engineering. Technical Report CMU/SEI-2000-TR-008, May 2000.
2. Bidan, Ch., Issarny, V., Saridakis, T., and Zarras, A. A Dynamic Reconfiguration Service for CORBA. In: Proceedings of the fourth International Conference on Configurable Distributed Systems, pages 35-42, Maryland, 1998.
3. Chen, X. Extending RMI to Support Dynamic Reconfiguration of Distributed Systems. In: Proceeding of the 22nd International Conference on Distributed Computing Systems (ICDCS 2002), pages 401-408, Vienna, Austria, 2002.
4. Kon, F. and Campbell, R. Dependence Management in Component-Based Distributed Systems. IEEE Concurrency, 8(1), pp. 26-36, January-March, 2000.
5. Kramer, J. and Magee, J. The Evolving Philosophers Problem: Dynamic Change Management. IEEE Transactions on Software Engineering, SE-16, 11, pages 1293-1306, 1990.
6. Microsoft, COM, http://www.microsoft.com/com.
7. Milojicic, D. Middleware's role, today and tomorrow. IEEE Concurrency, pages 70-80, April-June 1999.
8. OMG. CORBA, Object Management Group, http://www.omg.org, 1999.
9. OMG. CORBA Component Model, Object Management Group, http:// www.omg.org, 2000.
10. OSGi: Open Services Gateway Initiative. http://www.osgi.org, 2001.

11. Oueichek, I. and Rousset de P., S. Dynamic Configuration Management in the Guide Object-Oriented Distributed System. In: Proceedings of the third International Conference on Configurable Distributed Systems, pp. 28-35, Maryland, 1996.
12. Sun Microsystems. Enterprise JavaBeans, http://java.sun.com/products/ ejb/index.html, 1999.
13. Sun Microsystems. Remote Method Invocation, http://java.sun.com/products/ jdk/rmi/index.html, 2001.
14. Szyperski, C. Component Software - Beyond Object-Oriented Programming. Addison-Wesley / ACM Press, 1998.
15. Warren, I. and Sommerville, I. A Model for Dynamic Configuration which Preserves Application Integrity. In: Proceedings of the third International Conference on Configurable Distributed Systems, pages 28-35, Maryland, 1996.

Three-Tiered Specification of Micro-architectures
(Extended Abstract)[*]

Vasu Alagar[1,2] and Ralf Lämmel[3,4]

[1] Concordia University, Montreal, Canada
   alagar@cs.concordia.ca
[2] Santa Clara University, Santa Clara, CA, USA
   valagar@cse.scu.edu
[3] CWI, Amsterdam, The Netherlands
   ralf@cwi.nl
[4] Free University, Amsterdam, The Netherlands
   ralf@cs.vu.nl

Abstract. A three-tiered specification approach is developed to formally specify collections of collaborating objects, say micro-architectures. (i) The structural properties to be maintained in the collaboration are specified in the lowest tier. (ii) The behaviour of the object methods in the classes is specified in the middle tier. (iii) The interaction of the objects in the micro-architecture is specified in the third tier. The specification approach is based on Larch and accompanying notations and tools. The approach enables the unambiguous and complete specification of reusable collections of collaborating objects.

Keywords: object-oriented design, formal methods, micro-architectures, design patterns, frameworks, interaction, UML, reuse, evolution

1 Micro-architectures

An object-oriented system is a collection of encapsulated objects that collaborate among themselves to achieve specified tasks. The benefits of systems designed using OO principles include the potential for reuse, incremental extension and local modification. One can distinguish several levels of reuse and adaptation. At the lowest level, one reuses or adapts methods or *classes*. This level is often inadequate for reuse, and it does not appropriately scope adaptation activities since methods and classes are not "islands". They cannot be reused and adapted independently. At the highest level, one operates on entire application *frameworks*. This form does not account for application development with reuse of building blocks, neither does it restrict the scope of an adaptation. In fact, our target is the intermediate level of *micro-architectures*, that is, collections of collaborating objects. In Fig. 1, we sketch an example: the *WorldClock* micro-architecture. It deals with interacting *MasterClock* and *ZonalClock* objects such that the *MasterClock* object is responsible for maintaining the Greenwich Meridian Time, while the *ZonalClock* objects display the time in their respective zones.

---

[*] The full paper is available as *arXiv* Technical Report cs.SE/0205052 available from the authors' web pages or from http://arXiv.org/abs/cs.SE/0205052.

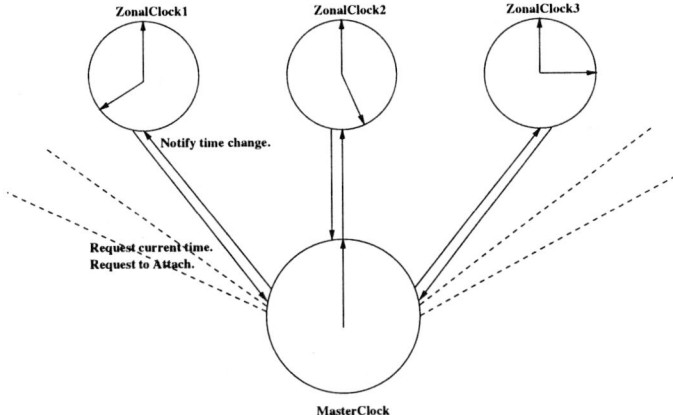

The *MasterClock* object can exist independently of the *ZonalClock* objects, but each *ZonalClock* object depends on the *MasterClock* object to maintain its zonal time. All the objects together maintain an invariant that any zonal clock displaying the time in its zone is consistent with the master clock's time. The *MasterClock* object notifies its associated *ZonalClock* objects whenever its time is updated. When a *ZonalClock* object is requested to update its zonal time, it queries the *MasterClock* object for the current time, and it updates itself if it observes a time change. Each *ZonalClock* object attaches itself to a *MasterClock* object upon its creation.

Fig. 1. The *WorldClock* micro-architecture

We consider micro-architectures to be the building blocks of object-oriented applications, especially of frameworks for domain-specific application development. We contend that micro-architectures provide the appropriate level for *reuse* and *adaptation* in object-oriented design and programming. Let us clarify our use of the term "micro-architecture" with regard to the related term "design pattern". A framework or an application contains several micro-architectures. In the actual code that embodies a framework, a certain class might contribute to more than one micro-architecture. By contrast, design patterns represent abstract, that is, application-independent designs. The operational meaning of design patterns is deliberately vague. We consider micro-architectures as concrete instances of design patterns within frameworks. To give an example, the *WorldClock* micro-architecture is a concrete instance of the *Observer* pattern. While the *WorldClock* micro-architecture deals with the notion of time, the more abstract *Observer* pattern only involves an abstract notion of state.

In need for a specification approach Informal explanations are *informative* for a developer who wants to reuse or to adapt a micro-architecture. However, in order to adequately deal with the complexity of design, improve productivity, and maintain acceptable levels of software quality the developer should also be provided with an *unambiguous* description of software components. The mainstream approach to specify designs is to use UML. One uses class diagrams to model the static structure of entities in the design, and one describes the collaborations using object collaboration diagrams. Specifications of object interfaces are given in pseudo-code. This semi-formal approach does not provide a clear description of object dependencies and inter-object behaviours.

2 Specification in Three Tiers

We contend that we need a *complete* and *formal* approach to the specification of collections of collaborating objects. We also want this approach to be *simple* and to allow for a *seamless integration with UML* visual modelling facilities. Because of space constraints, we only sketch the approach here while we refer to the full paper for details. In our approach, different aspects of micro-architectures are covered in three tiers:

(i) the *structural* properties to be maintained by the collaboration;
(ii) the *roles* of the collaborating objects in a black-box fashion;
(iii) the *interactive* behaviour in terms of the operation sequences and flow of control.

We use a designated notation for each tier.

2.1 Lowest Tier: Structure

The lowest tier specifies the structural aspects of the collaboration. Besides specifying the *data models* for the objects in the collaboration, it also specifies the *states of interest* of each object, and the *cardinality constraints* of the relationships among the collaborating objects. We use the Larch Shared Language LSL for the specification of this layer.

$WorldClock$: **trait**   **includes** $MutableObj(Time, MasterClock$ **for** $Obj[Time])$,
  $MutableObj(Zone, ZonalClock$ **for** $Obj[Zone]))$,
  $Set(ZonalClock, Set[ZonalClock])$
introduces
  $masterOf : ZonalClock \rightarrow MasterClock$
  $zonalClocksOf : MasterClock \rightarrow Set[ZonalClock]$
  $isConsistent : MasterClock, ZonalClock, State \rightarrow Bool$
asserts
  $\forall\, m : MasterClock, z : ZonalClock, st : State$
  $|zonalClocksOf(m)| \geq 0$
  $masterOf(z) = m == z \in zonalClocksOf(m)$
  $isConsistent(m, z, st) == (masterOf(z) = m) \wedge isUpToDate(m!st, z!st)$

Fig. 2. LSL specification of *WorldClock* trait

As for the *WorldClock* micro-architecture, we would need to define Larch traits for dealing with time data, zones, and with the mere collection of mutable clock objects. The latter trait is given in Fig. 2 as an illustration. We **include** other traits, we **introduce** several operators, and we **assert** properties of the operators. Here is a brief description of the operators declared in the *WorldClock* trait:

– *masterOf*: Given a *ZonalClock* object, returns the *MasterClock* object to which it is attached. The *ZonalClock* object depends on the *MasterClock* object for its current *zonalTime*. The totality of this function specifies the constraint that a *ZonalClock* object cannot exist independently of the *MasterClock*.

- *zonalClocksOf*: Given a *MasterClock* object, returns the possibly empty set of attached *ZonalClock* objects that depend on the *MasterClock*.
- *isConsistent*: Given a *MasterClock*, a *ZonalClock*, and a *State*, returns true if the two clocks are consistently related to each other in the state, and false otherwise.

2.2 Middle Tier: Roles

The middle tier in our three-tiered specification approach uses the data model defined in the lowest tier, and identifies the services required to specify the roles of the collaborating objects to specify their externally observable inter-object behaviour. All the operations of an object's role are specified using a behavioural interface specification language (BISL) — Larch/C++ in our case. While this concrete BISL interacts with C++, BISLs are also available for other programming languages, e.g., for Java.

We illustrate the notion of role specifications for the *ZonalClock* objects in our *WorldClock* example by the specification in Fig. 3 (the specification for *MasterClock* objects is omitted). There are the following services provided by a *ZonalClock* object. There is an interface for creation so that a new instance is attached to a *MasterClock* object, and it also provides an updating interface to keep its state, namely its zonal time, consistent with the *MasterClock*'s state via the methods *UpdateZonalClock* and *SetZonalTime*. The formal specification defines the **ensured** post-conditions for a service, and lists the **modified** or **constructed** objects. The formal specification directly implements our informal explanations. Note how the operations from the lowest tier are employed.

2.3 Highest Tier: Interaction

The highest tier employs the lower tiers to provide a specification of the interaction among the collaborating objects. The interaction between services provided in their roles must be specified in terms of operation sequences, and flow of control. These specify the state transformations of the object collaboration. In our formal specification approach, we use a simple designated action calculus for the interaction layer. There are action combinators for sequential collaboration ";", for independent collaboration "$\bigwedge$", guarded actions "**if** ...", and others.

The *WorldClock* example is continued in Fig. 4. We explain some elements of the specification in order to illustrate the action calculus and the overall purpose of the

---

ZonalClock : **role specification**

uses *WorldClock*

ZonalClock(*m*: *MasterClock*) { **contructs** *self*;
                                ensures $masterOf(self) = m$; }

UpdateZonalClock() { **modifies** *self*;
                           ensures $isConsistent(masterOf(self), self, post)$; }

SetZonalTime(*i*:*Int*) { **modifies** *self*;
                        ensures $self' = update(fromInt(i), self\hat{\,})$; }

Fig. 3. Role specification of *ZonalClock* objects using the *WorldClock* traits

third tier. In the specification of *SetZonalClocks*, the notation "$\bigwedge_{z \in zonalClocksOf(self)} \cdots$" is used for distributed independent collaboration to point out that the *UpdateZonalClock* methods can proceed for all the *ZonalClocks* independently of each other. In the specification of *SetChange*, sequential collaboration is used because it is essential that the *MasterClock* object invokes *SetSecond* and *SetZonalClocks* subsequently on itself. In the specification of the *UpdateZonalClock*, there is a guarded action to model that the role "*SetZonalTime(...)*" only needs to be invoked if an update is due. The guard relies on the operator *isConsistent* from the lowest tier. In order to retrieve the *MasterClock* object associated to *self*, we use another operator *masterOf* from the lowest tier.

3 Conclusion

Contribution. Our approach enables the reuser to understand the structural aspects (lowest tier), the behavioural aspects (middle tier) and the interactive aspects (highest tier) of collections of collaborating objects. The specification of behaviour in terms of roles depends on the specification of structural aspects. The specification of interaction between the collaborating objects in the highest tier invokes the roles of the objects specified in the middle tier, and operators from the lowest tier are used to query structural aspects. The three tiers achieve a separation of concerns. In each tier, a designated notation is favoured. Structural aspects are preferably specified in algebraic style as supported by LSL. Behavioural aspects are best described by contracts based on pre- and postconditions as supported by Larch/C++. Finally, the interaction of collaborating objects is best captured by an action calculus, say, a TLA-like logic. The approach adheres to a layered architecture principle (i.e., no up-calls). This design permits improved reuse of components, and it allows changes to components in one layer without affecting the components in lower layers. In previous studies, we have investigated the virtues of different variations on a three-tiered system architecture, and we have shown its expressiveness for the development of real-time reactive systems, E-Commerce systems, and evolving systems.

Perspective. Each tier in our specification approach gives rise to an implementation layer. Also, the presented specification approach allows for a seamless integration of the three tiers with UML visual modelling facilities, automated testing of Larch/C++ specifications, and verification of properties defined in terms of LSL traits. The components in

---

class *MasterClock* {
  method *SetZonalClocks*() { $\bigwedge_{z \in zonalClocksOf(self)}$ z.*UpdateZonalClock*() }
  method *SetChange*() { *SetSecond*(); *SetZonalClocks*() }

class *ZonalClock* {
  method *ZonalClock*(m : *MasterClock*) { m.*Attach*(*self*) }
  method *UpdateZonalClock*() { if $\neg$ *isConsistent*(*masterOf*(*self*), *self*, *pre*)
                                then let i : *Int* = *masterOf*(*self*).*GetTime*()
                                in *SetZonalTime*(i) }

Fig. 4. Interaction specification for *WorldClock* example

each layer can be individually analysed before composition, adaptation, or reuse. It turns out that one important notion is missing in our layered approach to the specification of micro-architectures: we lack a sufficiently expressive and automated model for reuse of class structures. That is, to actually deploy reusable micro-architectures or even design patterns in an actual application context, we need language constructs, tool support, and other means to adapt library structures, to replicate participants in a collaboration, to refine micro-architectures, and to compose behaviours of micro-architectures. In our on-going research, we attempt to reuse ideas from programming support for design patterns and corresponding ideas for tool support for OOA/OOD/OOP. In particular, we plan to base the syntactical notion of reuse on *superimposition of class structures* as defined in our previous work. This will eventually lead to a fully integrated software development method centred around the notion of micro-architectures.

Modeling the Architecture for Component-Based E-commerce System *

Jiayue Chang[1,2] and Huadong Ma[1,2]

[1] School of Computer Science & Technology,
Beijing University of Posts and Telecommunications, Beijing 100876, China
mhd@bupt.edu.cn
[2] Lab. for Computer Science,
Institute of Software, Chinese Academy of Science, Beijing 100080, China

Abstract. This paper introduces a reference architecture for component-based e-commerce system. Then, the authors propose a component dependency graph (CDG) for modeling the architecture of e-commerce system, which can be used to analyze the properties of an e-commerce application system in order to improve the design of e-commerce system. Finally, the paper discusses the future works.

1 Introduction

E-commerce becomes very popular as the number of Internet users grows explosively. To meet the complex requirements of e-commerce systems, the developers of e-commerce systems need a reference architecture to construct e-commerce applications, and available methods to analyze the properties of systems for improving the design of e-commerce systems. Component-based designing technique has been proved to be able to meet the need of today's software development. However, how to design and analyze a component-based e-commerce system is a key problem of the applications. The paper focuses on this problem.

2 The Reference Architecture of E-commerce System

2.1 Related Works

Researchers have done many works on e-commerce. EDI is the first standard to define formats in e-commerce frameworks. OBI [1] pays attention to the robustness of infrastructure so as to support users reliably and securely, and ensures interoperability and vendor neutrality. XPECT [2] is a simple framework for e-commerce. It specifies the application as a simple pay-per-view document server.

On the e-commerce architecture, S. Koushik and P. Toodi have made some endeavor on the design issues for e-commerce architecture [3]. F. Daoud described a general electronic commerce infrastructure [4]. Yu Li et al proposed

---

* The work reported in this paper is partly supported by the NNSF of China, EYTP of MOE and Lab for Computer Science, Institute of Software, CAS.

another infrastructure similar to F. Daoud's work. Meanwhile, people pay more attention to component technique. S. Pieere and N. Novisser [5] gave a methodology for reusing software components. Ye Wu et al have proposed a way for testing component-based software [6].

2.2 Classification of Component

An e-commerce application can be viewed as an integration of some components, which can be classfied into system component and business component. *System component* provides basic system services in both e-commerce and other distributed systems. This kind of component includes meta-component and adapter component. Meta-component fulfills a specific function such as storing data and communication; Adapter components are viewed as a bridge between meta-components for the connection of meta-components. *Business component* is responsible for providing all necessary services in business transactions. The functions vary with different types of business. The business components are common or specific components. Common components provide general services for e-business for a class of applications. A specific component is only for a given e-commerce application.

2.3 Reference Architecture of E-commerce System

In the light of ISO 7-layer networking model, we map the business logic into different layers to build the 7-layer reference architecture as follows:

User interface layer. It includes interface component and interface adapter. Interface component displays the information obtained from the back-end applications, and get the user commands or data required by the back-end applications. Interface adapter encapsulates the details of the distributed communication and locates the service.

Application adapter layer. This layer only contains business adapter component. It removes device- and client- specific information from incoming data and replaces the information when data returns to the user interface layer.

Business application layer. There are some common components in this layer. There are also some specific components different for each e-commerce application. This layer provides the basic business services.

Application support layer. This layer mainly provides necessary services for the upper layer. The components include session management, system monitor, conflict intercessor, failure recovery, and scheduling component. These components belong to system components.

Security layer. This layer is responsible for the security of whole system, and it consists of authentication component and attack monitor component.

Communication layer. This layer supports to communicate with other systems. It includes network management and communication component.

Resource layer. This layer contains the data and information for providing the business functions of applications. Typical components are database and resource adapter component.

3 Modeling Component-Based E-commerce System

3.1 Component Dependency Graph

We define the component-based system as a directed graph, called component dependency graph (CDG), G={(C,W_C),(E,W_E)}, where C={$c_1, c_2, c_3,...$} is a finite set of components; E={e_{ij}| iff there is a directed edge from c_i to c_j} is a set of edges; W_E={we_{ij}| i,j =1,2,3,...} is a set of weights, and we_{ij}={$et_{ij}, ep_{ij}, es_{ij}$} is used to describe the relationship between component i and j, where et_{ij} is the operation type between component i and j, ep_{ij} is the interface type between component i and j, es_{ij} is the size of data exchanged between component i and j; $W_C = \{wc_1, wc_2, wc_3,...\}$, and wc_i=(ct_i, cp_i, cs_i) is the weight of node i, where ct_i is the set of operation types that component i provides; cp_i is a set of interfaces to access component i; cs_i is the size of data that component i has to process, wc_i is used to describe the characteristics of a single component.

3.2 Layering of a Component-Based System

A layered structure has excellent scalability, flexibility and understandability. As we know, CDG can be represented by an adjacent matrix $A_{|V|\times|V|}$, whose element a_{ij} is 1 if $e_{ij} \in E$ otherwise 0. $P_{|V|\times|V|}$ is a reachable matrix, p_{ij} is 1 if c_i is reachable from c_j. We provide three steps to evaluate the layering of a component-based system.

Step 1. Finding strongly connected component in CDG
In order to judge whether two nodes are strongly connected or not, we first find P*=P ⊙ P^t, where P^t is the reverse of P, and ⊙ is an operator, it means $P^*_{ij}=P_{ij} \times P_{ji}$. c_i and c_j are strongly connected if $P^*_{ij}=P^*_{ji}=1$. Then, we get the blocked matrix P' from P* by some primitive transformations. For instance, we find 3 strong connected component sets (c_1, c_5),(c_2, c_4, c_6),(c_3) for Example 1 (shown in Fig. 1).

Step 2. Changing strongly connected component into one node
The strongly connected components obtained from Step 1 can be merged into a new node. Every edge originally directed to any of merged components becomes

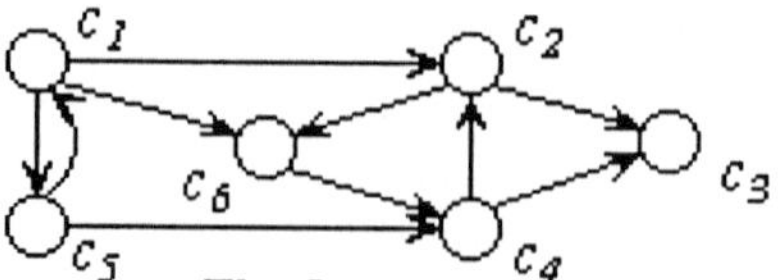

Fig. 1

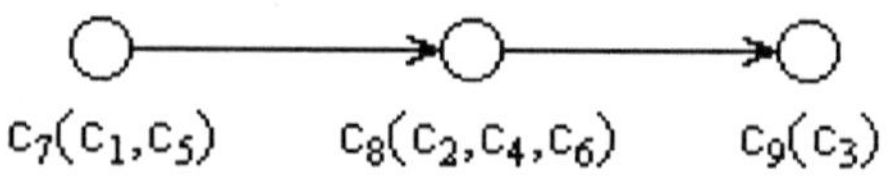

Fig. 2

$$P = \begin{vmatrix} 1 & 1 & 1 & 1 & 1 & 1 \\ 0 & 1 & 1 & 1 & 0 & 1 \\ 0 & 0 & 1 & 0 & 0 & 0 \\ 0 & 1 & 1 & 1 & 0 & 1 \\ 1 & 1 & 1 & 1 & 1 & 1 \\ 0 & 1 & 1 & 1 & 0 & 1 \end{vmatrix} \quad P^* = \begin{vmatrix} 1 & 0 & 0 & 0 & 1 & 0 \\ 0 & 1 & 0 & 1 & 0 & 1 \\ 0 & 0 & 0 & 0 & 0 & 0 \\ 0 & 1 & 1 & 0 & 0 & 0 \\ 1 & 0 & 0 & 1 & 0 & 0 \\ 0 & 0 & 0 & 1 & 0 & 0 \end{vmatrix} \quad P' = \begin{vmatrix} 1 & 1 & 0 & 0 & 0 & 0 \\ 1 & 1 & 0 & 0 & 0 & 0 \\ 0 & 0 & 1 & 1 & 1 & 0 \\ 0 & 0 & 1 & 1 & 1 & 0 \\ 0 & 0 & 1 & 1 & 1 & 0 \\ 0 & 0 & 0 & 0 & 0 & 1 \end{vmatrix}$$

an edge to this new node. Each edge whose source node is in any of the merged components should become an edge whose source node is this new node. The result for Example 1 is shown in Fig. 2.

Step 3. Evaluating system

From the viewpoint of layering, there is no dependency except two adjacent layers in a system. The below algorithm is to judge whether a system meets this requirement or not, where s_0, s_1, s_2 and s_3 are sets.

(3.1) Set s_0 and s_2 to null, and move the nodes whose in-degree are 0 to s_1, the other nodes are stored in s_3.

(3.2) Remove all elements adjacent to the nodes in s_1 from s_3, put them into s_2. Once there is a node adjacent to anyone in s_1 and it is not in s_3, then exit.

(3.3) Move the elements of s_1 to s_0, then set s_1 to s_2, and set s_2 to null. If s_3 is null then move s_1 to s_0 and exit, otherwise go to step 2.

If the algorithm ends in (3.2), the layering of system is not good. If the algorithm ends in (3.3), the system meets the requirement of layering.

The results of Example 1 processed by the above algorithm are as follows. It proved that the layering of this system is good.

(1) $s_0 = \phi$, $s_1 = \{c_7\}$, $s_2 = \phi$, $s_3 = \{c_8, c_9\}$; (2) $s_0 = \phi$, $s_1 = \{c_7\}$, $s_2 = \{c_8\}$; (3) $s_3 = \{c_9\}$, $s_0 = \{c_7\}$, $s_1 = \{c_8\}$, $s_2 = \phi$, $s_3 = \{c_9\}$; (4) $s_0 = \{c_7\}$, $s_1 = \{c_8\}$, $s_2 = \{c_9\}$, $s_3 = \phi$; (5) $s_0 = \{c_7, c_8\}$, $s_1 = \{c_9\}$, $s_2 = \phi$, $s_3 = \phi$; (6) $s_0 = \{c_7, c_8, c_9\}$, $s_1 = \phi$, $s_2 = \phi$, $s_3 = \phi$.

3.3 Finding Key Components

The key component refers to the component which has more functions or more data exchange than the others. We can find key components based on CDG. Let K be the importance degree of a component. $K = k_1T + k_2S + k_3D$, where T denotes the number of functions provided by the component, S denotes the total data processed by the component, and D denotes the number of components calling this component. k_1, k_2 and k_3 are three experience numbers, and they can be adjusted if necessary. Given CDG, finding the key component is as follows: (1) compute every node's indegree based on the adjacent matrix of CDG; (2) get every node's critical degree based on the weights of CDG and k_1, k_2 and k_3; (3) sort nodes by it's critical degree, the key component is the one with the maximum critical degree.

3.4 The Reuse of Component

Assume that there has been an e-commerce application called E-shop1, and it used the component Pay. If the developers want to develop other application E-shop2, can they reuse the component Pay?

CDG1 is a model of E-shop1, and the component c_i is Pay. Let $wc_i = (ct_i, cp_i, cs_i)$, then we can get two sets s_0 and s_1. $s_0 = \{et_{ij} | e_{ij} \in E\}$, $s_1 = \{ep_{ij} | e_{ij} \in E\}$, s_0 and s_1 are the functions and interfaces required by c_i. CDG2 is the model of E-shop 2. Assume that a virtual component c_v meet the requirements of E-shop2. Let $wc_v = (ct_v, cp_v, cs_v)$, if $ct_v \subseteq ct_i$ and $cp_v \subseteq cp_i$ then c_i

meets the requirement of E-shop2. Meanwhile, if all elements of s_0 and s_1 can be found in the W_C of CDG2, E-shop2 meets the requirement of c_i. If these two conditions are satisfied, c_i can be reused in E-shop2.

3.5 Connectivity of Component

All components in an e-commerce system should be reachable. In CDG, this connectivity can be judged based on the weakly connected graph. One method of judging this feature is described as follows.

First, change the directed graph into undirected graph called G. Let A be the adjacent matrix of G. We use $A^{(l)}$ to denote the matrix in which the element a_{ij} is 1 means there is a path with the length 1 between the nodes i and j otherwise a_{ij} is 0. Apparently, $A^{(1)}$=A, $A^{(2)}$=$A^{(1)} \cdot A^{(1)}$, $A^{(3)}$ and $A^{(4)}$ are found in the similar way. Note that "$\cdot$" and "+" used in the matrix computation are logic AND and OR, respectively. We can define the matrix
$$R^l = I + A^{(1)} + A^{(2)} + ... + A^{(l)} = (I+A)^l$$
For the number q ($q \leq |V|$), $R^q = R^q+1$, this matrix is called reachable matrix R. If all of the elements in R are 1, G is weakly connected.

See Example 1. We can find q=2 for it, and the matrix is weakly connected, so the system has good connectivity.

4 Conclusion and Future Works

We introduced a layered architecture for component-based e-commerce system, and proposed the component dependency graph for modeling e-commerce system. CDG can easily specify the features of e-commerce systems and can be used to analyze the problems in systems so as to improve the design of applications.

The future work includes three aspects: to use CDG model to describe dynamic features of e-commerce system; to find an available methodology to describe the communication scheme between two layers; to user formal method to validate layered architecture composed of components.

References

1. Open Buying on the Internet, OBI specification 1999. Http://www.openbuy.org
2. J. Andreoli, F. Pacull, R. Pareschi, XPECT: A framework for electronic commerce, IEEE Internet Computing, 1(4), July-Aug. 1997, pp. 40-48.
3. S. Koushik, Petelvodi, E-business architecture design issues, IT Professional,2(3), 2000, pp.38-43.
4. F. Daoud, Electronic commerce infrastructure, IEEE Potentials, Vol.19(1),Feb.-March 2000 , pp.30 -33
5. S. Pierre, N. Nouisser, A methodology for reusing software components in network design, IEEE Canadian Conf. on Electr. and Comp. Eng., Edmonton, May 1999.
6. Ye Wu, et al, Techniques for testing component-based software, 7th IEEE Int. Conf. on Engineering of Complex Computer Systems, 2001, pp.222 -232

Component Specification and Wrapper/Glue Code Generation with Two-Level Grammar Using Domain Specific Knowledge*

Fei Cao[1], Barrett R. Bryant[1], Rajeev R. Raje[2], Mikhail Auguston[3], Andrew M. Olson[2], and Carol C. Burt[1]

[1] Department of Computer and Information Sciences
University of Alabama at Birmingham, USA
{caof, bryant, cburt}@cis.uab.edu
[2] Department of Computer and Information Science
Indiana University Purdue University at Indianapolis, USA
{rraje, aolson}@cs.iupui.edu
[3] Computer Science Department
New Mexico State University, USA
mikau@cs.nmsu.edu

Abstract. UniFrame is a framework for seamlessly assembling heterogeneous distributed components. It's based on the Unified Meta-component Model (UMM) for describing components. Systems constructed by component composition should meet both functional and non-functional requirements such as the Quality of Service (QoS). We propose a Component Description Language (CDL) to specify the UMM components based on domain specific knowledge in the context of UniFrame using Two-Level Grammar (TLG). CDL is also used for wrapper/glue code generation. A simple case study is illustrated to show how CDL may be applied.

Keywords: Two-Level Grammar, Wrapper/Glue Code, Domain Specific Knowledge, Formal Specification

1 Introduction

Current software environments feature heterogeneous platforms, languages and applications over distributed systems. The trend of integrating software systems is already on the horizon. UniFrame [1] is a framework for seamless interoperation of heterogeneous distributed software components. It's based on the Unified Meta-component Model (UMM) [2] for describing components. Systems constructed by component composition should meet both functional and non-functional requirements such as the Quality of Service (QoS) [3]. A Generative

---
* This material is based upon work supported by, or in part by, the U. S. Office of Naval Research under the award number N00014-01-1-0746, and the U. S. Army Research Laboratory and the U. S. Army Research Office under the contract/grant number DAAD19-00-1-0350.

Domain Model (GDM) [4] is used to describe the properties of domain specific components and to elicit the rules for component assembly. In UMM, an infrastructure called "Headhunter" is proposed to actively detect the presence of new components in the search space, register their functionality and attempt matchmaking between client components (service requesters) and server components (service providers). As such, our specification should incorporate the mechanism of the Headhunter [5] to represent component information for retrieval and subsequent generative assembly. Here we adopt Gruber's view of ontology [6] to make the conceptualization of a domain explicit, and perform specification matching within a domain context using domain specific knowledge.

In this paper, we propose a Component Description Language (CDL) using Two-Level Grammar (TLG) [8] as the formalism not only to represent the UMM, QoS, and GDM, but also for wrapper/glue code generation in the component assembly process. We begin by briefly introducing the concept of TLG (section 2) and then apply the TLG into the context of component specification by describing our CDL over a simple banking example (section 3).

2 Specification with Two-Level Grammar

TLG was originally developed as a specification language for programming language syntax and semantics [7]. The name "two-level" of TLG comes from the fact that TLG contains two context-free grammars corresponding to the set of type domains and the set of function definitions operating on those domains. Though based on natural language, TLG is also a formal notation in the sense that it's strictly typed. Its semantics are embodied by rules in the function bodies. We will illustrate this in the CDL example below. For a detailed explanation of TLG, please see [8].

In this paper, we describe a CDL as a subset of TLG to describe both UMM components and generative rules for component composition with the output of wrapper/glue code. This includes two levels:

- User level
  Based on UMM, CDL specifies the following items, namely Computational Attributes, which include Functional Attributes such as Syntactic Contract and Implementation Technology; Cooperative Attributes; Auxiliary Attributes; and QoS. Examples of QoS metrics include Security, Availability, Throughput. Please refer to [3] for details. User-level specifications are provided by component developers.
- System level
  This level mainly specifies the rules of component composition. Specifications of this level are to be used by component assemblers. The above statements are illustrated in Figure 1.

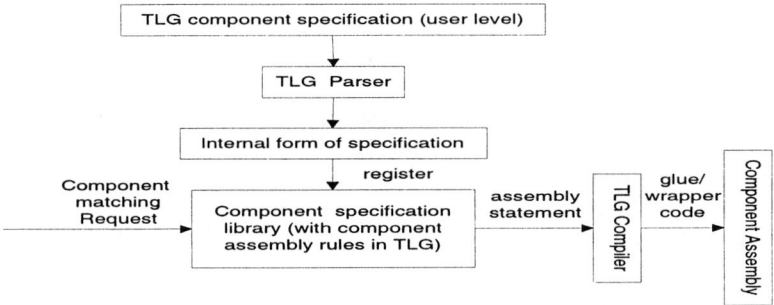

Fig. 1. Application of TLG for Component Assembly

3 An Example

Consider a CORBA component model for a simple banking system. The simple bank offers three services: withdrawing money, checking account balance and making deposits.

3.1 User Level Component Model Specification

For simplicity, assume this simple bank component uses string-form Interoperable Object Reference (IOR) for locating objects as an alternative to the Directory or Naming service [9]. Assume UMMComponent is the root specification of all components specified in the component repository.

```
component SimpleBank extends UMMComponent.
  Technology:: String.
  Domain:: String.
  IOR:: String .
  Amount :: Float.
  AccountNumber :: String.
  Pin :: String.
  Withdraw:: FunctionName.
  Balance:: FunctionName.
  Deposit:: FunctionName.
```

The specification above defines the type domain for the SimpleBank component. The domain variables all begin with an upper case letter, so do component names, function parameters and type identifiers. The following are the function definitions operating on those domains:

```
  init: Domain ::= ``Bank", Technology::="CORBA",
    IOR::="IOR:000000saji98898dss3322".
  export Withdraw with Amount AccountNumber Pin
    by classAccount returnType Boolean.
  export Balance with AccountNumber Pin by classAccount
    returnType Float.
```

```
    export Deposit with Amount AccountNumber Pin by classAccount
    returnType Boolean.
    /* Bank Domain Lexicon */
    lexicon of Withdraw: ''draw";"subtract".
    lexicon of Balance : ''check balance".
    lexicon of Deposit : ''credit";"save".
    /* static Quality of Service */
    qos availability: 90%. //the duration that a component is available
    qos delay: 10ms. /*the time between service invocation and completion */
  end component SimpleBank.
```
init is the initialization routine for the type domain. Note that the function body on the right side of ':' specifies the rules of the left hand side function signature, as you may see from the "ComponentRepository" specification in the next section. There may be no rules at all, like in the above example.

The *export* expressions indicate the syntactic contract specifications of components. They represent the services offered by components. Moreover, the precondition of service offering may be specified in the function body. Note "classAccount" represents a component (in the form of class) named "Account" that provides the above three services; "=" is a relational operator while "::=" is used to set values.

From the above example we can see that specification matching can be carried out by looking for such function signatures as directed by "export", "qos", "technology", etc. "Domain" is also a crucial tag that uniquely determines the context in which the domain knowledge may be applied against this component. By "lexicon of" we provide a thesaurus for a specific syntactic contract, so that "withdraw" is treated as equivalent service to "draw", while "balance" is treated as an equivalent service to "check balance", etc. During the process of component retrieval and assembly, if a component with expected service offerings doesn't satisfy the expected QoS, it is subject to be substituted for.

3.2 System Level Component Assembly Specification

In the following "ComponentRepository" specification, code generation rule is specified.
```
    UMM ComponentRepository
    ComponentN::UMMComponent.
    OperationName:: String.
    Package:: StringList. //the header files to be included/imported
    generate java wrapper code ComponentN
      OperationName using CORBA with Package :
      ComponentN get OperationName!= Empty,
      ComponentN init,
      ComponentN get Technology = ''CORBA'',
      ComponentN get IOR!= Empty,
      return CorbaClientCode.
    end UMM ComponentRepository
```

The above statement specifies wrapper code generation for a CORBA component to be used by a Java client. **return** *CorbaClientCode* directs the TLG compiler to generate the actual CORBA client code. Here the semantics for **generate java wrapper code** are based on CORBA's Dynamic Invocation Interface [9], which lets a client pick any target object at run time and dynamically invoke its method without requiring precompiled stubs. Because of the limited space, the code generation process and detailed generated code are not illustrated here - see [10] for more details.

4 Conclusion

In this paper we use Two-Level Grammar as a formalism to represent the Unified Meta-component Model of a simple banking domain example and to generate the wrapper/glue code based on the generative domain model. We illustrate some empirical techniques on building a Component Description Language using TLG and evaluate how TLG may be leveraged toward this goal.

References

1. R. R. Raje, B. R. Bryant, M. Auguston, A. M. Olson, C. C. Burt: A Unified Approach for the Integration of Distributed Heterogeneous Software Components. Proc. 2001 Monterey Workshop Engineering Automation for Software Intensive System Integration, 2001, pp. 109-119.
2. R. R. Raje: UMM: Unified Meta-object Model for Open Distributed Systems. Proc. ICA3PP 2000, 4th IEEE Int. Conf. Algorithms and Architecture for Parallel Processing, 2000.
3. G. J. Brahnmath, R. R. Raje, A. M. Olson, M. Auguston, B. R. Bryant, C. C. Burt: A Quality of Service Catalog for Software Components. Proc. (SE)^2 2002, the Southeastern Software Engineering Conf. (to appear), 2002.
4. K. Czarnecki, U. W. Eisenecker: Generative Programming, Methods, Tools, and Applications. Addison Wesley, 2000.
5. N. N. Siram, R. R. Raje, A. M. Olson, B. R. Bryant, C. C. Burt, M. Auguston: An Architecture for the UniFrame Resource Discovery Service. Proc. 3rd Int. Workshop Software Engineering Middleware (to appear), 2002.
6. T. R. Gruber: A translation approach to portable ontology specifications. Knowledge Acquisition, 5(2), 1993, pp. 199-220.
7. A. van Wijingaarden: Revised report on the algorithmic language ALGOL 68. Acta Informatica, 5, 1974, pp. 1-236.
8. B. R. Bryant, B.-S. Lee: Two-Level Grammar as an Object-Oriented Requirements Specification Language. Proc. 35th Hawaii Int. Conf. System Sciences, 2002, http://www.hicss.hawaii.edu/HICSS_35/HICSSpapers/PDFdocuments/STDSL01.pdf.
9. R. Orfali, D. Harkey: Client/Server Programming with Java and Corba. Wiley, 1998.
10. B. R. Bryant, M. Auguston, R. R. Raje, C. C. Burt, and A. M. Olson: Formal Specification of Generative Component Assembly Using Two-Level Grammar. Proc. SEKE 2002, 14th Int. Conf. Software Engineering and Knowledge Engineering, 2002, pp. 209-212.

Abstract Specification in Object-Z and CSP

Graeme Smith[1] and John Derrick[2]

[1] Software Verification Research Centre, University of Queensland 4072, Australia
smith@svrc.uq.edu.au
[2] Computing Laboratory, University of Kent, Canterbury, CT2 7NF, UK
J.Derrick@ukc.ac.uk

Abstract. A number of integrations of the state-based specification language Object-Z and the process algebra CSP have been proposed in recent years. In developing such integrations, a number of semantic decisions have to be made. In particular, what happens when an operation's precondition is not satisfied? Is the operation *blocked*, i.e., prevented from occurring, or can it occur with an undefined result? Also, are outputs from operations *angelic*, satisfying the environment's constraints on them, or are they *demonic* and not influenced by the environment at all? In this paper we discuss the differences between the models, and show that by adopting a blocking model of preconditions together with an angelic model of outputs one can specify systems at higher levels of abstraction.

1 Introduction

One strand of recent work on integrating formal methods has been the area concerned with combining state-based languages such as Object-Z [13,4] and Z [14] with process algebras such as CSP [6,9] and CCS [8]. A canonical example of this are the integrations of Object-Z with CSP. In such an integration, of which there have been a number of proposals [12,5,7,11], Object-Z is used to specify the components of a system, and CSP is used to describe how the components interact and communicate.

In developing such an integration, one is faced with a choice in terms of how *preconditions* and *outputs* are dealt with, and this choice effects the design approach one takes in the language.

The specific choice in terms of preconditions is whether to adopt a *blocking* or *non-blocking* model of an operation. That is, outside the stated or calculated precondition, is the operation unable to occur (blocking) or is it able to occur but its effect undefined (non-blocking)?

Z adopts the non-blocking approach and Object-Z the blocking approach (which is closer to an object-oriented and process algebraic interpretation). Different integrations of Object-Z and CSP have also taken differing interpretations. For example, [12,11] adopt a blocking model whereas [5,7] adopt a non-blocking model[1].

---

[1] Both non-blocking approaches [5,7] also extend the syntax of Object-Z to include *guards* so that operations can also be blocked.

The specific choice in terms of outputs is whether to adopt a *demonic* or *angelic* model of outputs. To understand this, consider a specification $A \| B$ where the components synchronise on an operation Op. In A, this operation has a non-deterministic output, matched by an input in the corresponding operation in B. The question is "Should B be able to control the output of A?".

In a demonic model of outputs the answer is "No". That is, the non-determinism of the value output by Op in A is entirely internal to A. So, if the chosen output is incompatible with the expected input in B, the composite operation's precondition is not satisfied (resulting in blocking or undefined behaviour). The contrasting angelic model of outputs, however, allows B to affect the non-determinism in A by choosing a value to synchronise on, if one can be found, thus allowing the operation to proceed normally if at all possible.

The majority of work on integrating Object-Z and CSP has used the demonic model of outputs. This work includes that of [5,7,11]. This is also the main approach appearing in other work on semantics of value-passing communication, e.g., Butler [1] places conditions on composed value-passing action systems which ensure that outputs are always accepted by the environment. The main reason for this bias is that since outputs can be controlled by the environment in the angelic model, they are effectively the same as inputs and hence cannot be strengthened during refinement. As a consequence, standard state-based refinement [2], which allows such strengthening, is not compositional.

In this paper, we show, however, that adopting an angelic model of outputs, together with a blocking model of operations, as is done in [12], allows us to specify at a higher level of abstraction. Consequently, specifications are simpler and therefore easier to understand and reason about. Furthermore, we show how the limitations of refinement for this interpretation of outputs can be overcome.

The structure of the paper is as follows. In Section 2, we illustrate the different interpretations of preconditions and outputs via a simple example. In Section 3 we show how, by adopting a blocking plus angelic model of operations, we are able to specify systems more abstractly. The consequences for refinement are dealt with in Section 4. Finally, we conclude in Section 5.

2 Illustrative Example

The differences between the approaches to the modelling of preconditions and outputs is best illustrated by considering a simple example. We assume the reader is familiar with both CSP and Object-Z, and the setting of our work is the Object-Z/CSP approach first proposed by Smith [12] and further developed by Smith and Derrick [11].

In this approach, which is similar in essence to other work in the area [5], Object-Z is used to describe the individual components which are combined with CSP operators by using, for example, parallel composition or interleaving.

Thus, in the following trivial example (more realistic examples are contained in [12,10,11,3]), two components A and B are given as Object-Z classes:

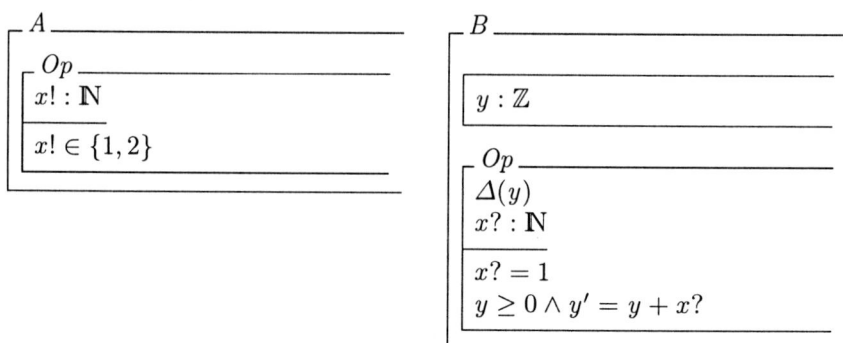

To illustrate the difference between the blocking and non-blocking model, let us first consider the component B on its own. The blocking model takes the view that outside its precondition ($y \geq 0 \wedge x? = 1$) the operation is not enabled and cannot occur. On the other hand, the non-blocking model views the operation to be enabled but the outcome is undefined, i.e., any after-state might result, including divergence or non-termination.

The complete Object-Z/CSP specification is given by the parallel composition of the two components:

$Spec = A \| B$

The effect of this specification is a system with one operation Op. Adopting the blocking model (as is done in Object-Z/CSP), how does it behave? The operations in A and B must synchronise, with agreement on the value communicated. Therefore, if this event does occur the value 1 will be communicated from A to B.

But does this event occur? Here, in addition to the issue of the precondition, we have a choice, which is the crux of the issue concerning outputs highlighted in the introduction. In particular, if A can non-deterministically output 2, then under these circumstances the precondition of Op will not hold. This interpretation is the one taken in [11] and [3] where the operation would be blocked. We shall call such an interpretation demonic.

The alternative is to view A and B as cooperating components, and allow the event to proceed *if it can*. That is, the non-determinism in A is restricted by what the environment is prepared to accept. This interpretation is less popular, but is the one taken in [12] and [10]. We shall call such an interpretation angelic.

3 Abstraction

The non-blocking interpretation of operations was developed (in Z, for example) predominantly for the specification of sequential systems. Such systems perform operations in a particular order. In concurrent systems where operations can occur at any time, specifiers using a non-blocking approach need to be more explicit about the exceptional behaviour that occurs when a precondition is not met. In many cases, this information is missing in a specification, leading to unintentional underspecification. For example, consider the following specification of a network node.

$[Message, Address]$

$\mid to, from : Message \to Address$

Node
$\mid address : Address$

$received : \text{seq } Message$

INIT
$received = \langle \rangle$

Receive
$\Delta(received)$
$msg? : Message$

$to(msg?) = address$
$received' = received \frown \langle msg? \rangle$

Send
$msg! : Message$

$from(msg!) = address$

The receive operation has a precondition that the incoming message is addressed to the node. In the case where the incoming message is not addressed to the node, the precondition is not met. Generally, we would not want our network to behave chaotically whenever a node detects a message which is not for it. A more suitable behaviour would be to ignore the message. Under a non-blocking interpretation, this would need to be specified explicitly as follows.

Receive
$\Delta(received)$
$msg? : Message$

$to(msg?) = address \Rightarrow received' = received \frown \langle msg? \rangle$
$to(msg?) \neq address \Rightarrow received' = received$

The blocking model, on the other hand, provides a way of specifying exceptional behaviour implicitly. This is only true when the exceptional behaviour is of the form that nothing happens. Other types of exceptional behaviour have to be specified explicitly as in the non-blocking model. As the node example illustrates, however, doing nothing is often what is required in concurrent systems.

This feature of the blocking model proves useful in the Object-Z and CSP context where it can be used to abstract away from implementation detail. For example, given a set of addresses $A : \mathbb{P}\,Address$, we can define a network as follows[2]. (The renaming of *Send* events ensures they communicate with *Receive* events with the same message.)

$$Network = \|_{a:A}\ Node_{\{address \mapsto a\}}[Receive/Send]$$

Adopting the blocking model for classes, the nodes only engage in events which concern them (i.e., where they are the sender or receiver). The specification abstractly models that such messages are not seen by other nodes (due to some routing mechanism in the network) or are simply ignored by them. The actual mechanism by which the network operates is not of interest at this level of abstraction.

It is not possible to similarly model at this level of abstraction with the non-blocking model since all events are in a given node process's alphabet regardless of the sender and recipient. Therefore, the network's operating mechanism needs to be explicitly specified as, for example, in the modified *Receive* schema above.

This ability to abstract from implementation details is further enhanced when we adopt the angelic model of outputs. This allows us to easily model cooperation between processes to produce an output. This allows us to abstract away from the actual cooperation mechanism which in general would require additional message passing. For example, a group of nodes can elect a "leader" by synchronising on an *ElectLeader* operation of the form

― *ElectLeader* ―――――――――――――――
| address! : Address
――――――――――――――――――――

which would be included in each *Node*. The leader is chosen by the identification of the *address!* outputs.

In the demonic model where outputs are chosen without reference to the environment, it cannot be guaranteed that all processes choose the same output. Hence, if the *ElectLeader* operation is required to occur, deadlock is possible. To avoid this, the actual protocol to elect the leader, which would typically comprise a series of communications, needs to be specified.

In general, the non-blocking interpretation of operations and demonic model of outputs reflect more closely the situation in an implementation: exceptional behaviour must be dealt with and outputs cannot be influenced by the environment. The penalty for this is that specifications tend to be less abstract, including additional details which may not be necessary to describe the essential functionality of the specified system. Introducing these details at an early

---

[2] $Node_{\{address \mapsto a\}}$ denotes the process corresponding to the class *Node* when its constant *address* is instantiated to a [12].

stage can complicate both the understandability and the ease of analysis of a specification.

4 Refinement

In this section, we examine the issue of refining specifications under the blocking plus angelic model of operations.

At first sight, this seems to provide a theory of refinement which is *not* compositional. Because Object-Z/CSP specifications are given a semantics identical to that of CSP specifications (i.e., a failures-divergences semantics) [12], we use the notion of refinement adopted for CSP (i.e., failures-divergences inclusion) [6]. Consider classes A and B from Section 2. Under the angelic model of output non-determinism the operation in $A\|B$ is always enabled since A and B cooperate on the choice of value communicated. Now consider refining A to the following class C:

$$
\begin{array}{l}
\rule{0pt}{0pt}\underline{C}\\
\quad \underline{Op}\\
\quad\quad x! : \mathbb{N}\\
\quad\quad\rule[0.5ex]{10em}{0.4pt}\\
\quad\quad x! = 2
\end{array}
$$

where, as in standard approaches to state-based refinement [2], we have reduced the non-determinism in the output.

Now, when we form the composition $C\|B$ we find the operation Op is blocked. We have thus introduced a *deadlock* into the specification, and therefore $C\|B$ is *not* a refinement of $A\|B$. We might conclude, therefore, that refinement is not compositional. However, closer inspection reveals a sleight of hand at play. The unstated assumption in this deduction was that the standard Object-Z downward simulation rule [2] (see Definition 1) is sound with respect to CSP refinement.

Definition 1 *Downward simulation in Object-Z*
An Object-Z class $C = (C.\text{STATE}, C.\text{INIT}, COp_i)_{i \in I}$ is a downward simulation of the class $A = (A.\text{STATE}, A.\text{INIT}, AOp_i)_{i \in I}$ if there is a retrieve relation R on $A.\text{STATE} \wedge C.\text{STATE}$ such that the following hold for all $i \in I$.

DS.1 $\forall\, C.\text{INIT} \bullet \exists\, A.\text{INIT} \bullet R$
DS.2 $\forall\, A.\text{STATE};\ C.\text{STATE} \bullet R \implies (\text{pre}\, AOp_i \iff \text{pre}\, COp_i)$
DS.3 $\forall\, A.\text{STATE};\ C.\text{STATE};\ C.\text{STATE}' \bullet$
$\quad R \wedge COp_i \implies (\exists\, A.\text{STATE}' \bullet R' \wedge AOp_i)$

However, this rule is sound with respect to the blocking plus *demonic* model, but it is not sound with respect to the blocking plus *angelic* model. Confirmation of this is found by noting that initially C cannot perform operation Op with

$x! = 1$ whereas A can. Refinement in CSP requires that the events which a process can refuse to perform at any stage of its evolution are a subset of those of any process it refines [6]. Thus, C is not, in fact, a valid refinement of A with respect to the angelic model of outputs.

The solution here is to adapt the simulation rules given above to produce rules which *are* sound with respect to the blocking plus angelic model. In fact, this adaption is easy. As detailed in [10], one has just to change the meaning of pre Op to include existential quantification of the after state only (and not the output), since we wish to exclude reduction of non-determinism of the output.

Thus, if we define Pre $\cong \exists \, State' \bullet Op$ for an operation Op defined over state space $State$, and use Pre in place of pre in the definition above, we produce a set of simulation rules sound with respect to the blocking plus angelic model. We call these rules (ba)-simulation rules for sake of easy reference.

Refinements in this model behave exactly as before, except non-determinism in outputs cannot be resolved. In fact, this is a by-product of how outputs are being used in this specification style. Specifically, the non-deterministic selection of outputs represents some sort of *required non-determinism* in the description (like external choice in CSP). Therefore, it would be an unacceptable refinement to reduce this non-determinism which was explicitly needed as part of the modelling paradigm.

We still do, however, achieve a compositional theory of refinement. That is, using the (ba)-simulation rules (where Pre has replaced pre), if C refines A then $C \| B$ refines $A \| B$.

4.1 Introducing an Explicit Communication Mechanism

Part of the motivation for using the blocking model with an angelic model of outputs was to model, at a suitable level of abstraction, cooperative communication between components. This it does successfully, allowing components to agree on values without having to describe explicitly how this agreement is achieved.

However, in an implementation the actual agreement mechanism used will need to be made explicit, and the natural question to ask, therefore, is whether the abstract description of the communicating components can be refined to an implementation-oriented view. In fact, we can perform this refinement, and we illustrate now how it can be achieved.

Consider a specification $Sys_1 = A_1 \| B_1$, where the cooperating communicating part of the components are as follows.

A_1
— Choose —
$x! : \mathbb{N}$
———
$x! \in \{1, 2\}$

B_1
— Choose —
$x! : \mathbb{N}$
———
$x! \in \{2, 3\}$

With the blocking model plus angelic model of outputs, the synchronisation of *Choose* in $A_1 \| B_1$ models agreement on a particular value for communication.

We wish to implement this design with an explicit mechanism which models finding the agreed value. In particular, we will refine Sys_1 to Sys_2, where

$$Sys_2 = (C \;_X\|_Y (A_2 \| B_2)) \setminus \{| \; Send \; |\}$$

where $X = \{| \; Send, Choose \; |\}$, $Y = \{| \; Send \; |\}$ and the components are given as:

─── A_2 ──────────────────────
  ─── $Send$ ────────────────
  │ $v! : \{1\}$
  │ $y! : \mathbb{P}\,\mathbb{N}$
  ────────────────────────
  │ $y! = \{1, 2\}$
  ────────────────────────

─── B_2 ──────────────────────
  ─── $Send$ ────────────────
  │ $v! : \{2\}$
  │ $y! : \mathbb{P}\,\mathbb{N}$
  ────────────────────────
  │ $y! = \{2, 3\}$
  ────────────────────────

─── C ──────────────────────────────────────
  │ $nodes : \mathbb{P}\{1, 2\}$
  │ $s : \mathbb{P}\,\mathbb{N}$

  ─── I_{NIT} ──────────────────────
  │ $nodes = \{1, 2\} \wedge s = \mathbb{N}$

  ─── $Send$ ──────────────────   ─── $Choose$ ─────────
  │ $\Delta(nodes, s)$ │ $x! : \mathbb{N}$
  │ $v? : \mathbb{N}$ ──────────────────
  │ $y? : \mathbb{P}\,\mathbb{N}$ │ $nodes = \emptyset$
  ──────────────────────────   │ $x! \in s$
  │ $v? \in nodes$
  │ $nodes' = nodes \setminus \{v?\}$
  │ $s' = s \cap y?$

In this description A and B now communicate with C via an operation $Send$, and C records, in the variable s, those values which are acceptable to both A and B. When both components have sent their preferences, C will communicate an acceptable chosen value via $Choose$. This operation can then be synchronised with a component taking in as input the values agreed by A and B.

Clearly, Sys_1 and Sys_2 have the same observable behaviour, and using *structural simulation rules* [3] which allow the structure of an integrated Object-Z and CSP specification to be altered in a refinement, we can show that Sys_1 is refined by Sys_2.

The structural simulation rules allow refinements to be verified even if the overall CSP structure of the integrated specification has been altered in a development step, and rules have been derived that allow components to be introduced and removed using each of the commonly used CSP operators. For example, there are simulation rules to refine a specification E into a specification $F \| G$ since, even though there is no correspondence between individual components, the simulation rules check whether the overall observable behaviour in $F \| G$ is consistent with that defined in E.

To verify the refinement above we proceed using four steps which, as we see in the following, introduce intermediate classes in order to verify the refinement ($\sqsubseteq$ denotes "is refined by"):

$$Sys_1 = A_1 \| B_1 \sqsubseteq D_1$$
$$\sqsubseteq D_2 \setminus \{| \ Send \ |\}$$
$$\sqsubseteq (C \ _X\|_Y \ D_3) \setminus \{| \ Send \ |\}$$
$$\sqsubseteq (C \ _X\|_Y \ (A_2 \|\| B_2)) \setminus \{| \ Send \ |\}$$

Full details of the form of structural simulation rules can be found in [3]. Here our purpose is to illustrate their use, and we do not give all the rules in full. First of all we note that the intermediate classes we need in the refinement are as follows.

─ D_1 ────────────────────────────
  ─ Choose ──────────────────────
  $x! : \mathbb{N}$
  ─────────────────────────────
  $x! \in \{1,2\} \cap \{2,3\}$
  ─────────────────────────────

─ D_3 ────────────────────────────
  ─ Send ────────────────────────
  $v! : \{1,2\}$
  $y! : \mathbb{P} \mathbb{N}$
  ─────────────────────────────
  $(v! = 1 \wedge y! = \{1,2\})$
  $\vee$
  $(v! = 2 \wedge y! = \{2,3\})$

─ D_2 ──

  $nodes : \mathbb{P}\{1,2\}$
  $s : \mathbb{P} \mathbb{N}$
  ───
  ─ INIT ─────────────────────
  $nodes = \{1,2\} \wedge s = \mathbb{N}$
  ───
  ─ Send ──────────────────────────   ─ Choose ──────────────
  $\Delta(nodes, s)$ $x! : \mathbb{N}$
  $v? : \mathbb{N}$ ──────────────────────
  $y? : \mathbb{P} \mathbb{N}$ $nodes = \varnothing$
  ───────────────────────────────── $x! \in s$
  $(1 \in nodes \wedge nodes' = nodes \setminus \{1\}$
  $\wedge s' = s \cap \{1,2\})$
  $\vee$
  $(2 \in nodes \wedge nodes' = nodes \setminus \{2\}$
  $\wedge s' = s \cap \{2,3\})$

Let us consider a few of the steps involved. To verify $D_2 \sqsubseteq (C_X \|_Y D_3)$, and hence the step $D_2 \setminus \{\!| \, Send \, |\!\} \sqsubseteq (C_X \|_Y D_3) \setminus \{\!| \, Send \, |\!\}$, we use the structural simulation rule shown in Definition 2 for introducing a parallel composition. This simplified form of the rule assumes that if an operation Op is shared between components F and G, then FOp has input $z?$ and GOp has corresponding output $z!$.

Definition 2 *Parallel downward simulation*
A CSP expression $F_A\|_B G$ is a downward simulation of the Object-Z class E if F and G satisfy the following for some retrieve relation R and each Op in both A and B.

PS.1 $\forall F.\text{INIT} \wedge G.\text{INIT} \bullet \exists E.\text{INIT} \bullet R$
PS.2 $\forall E.\text{STATE};\ F.\text{STATE};\ G.\text{STATE} \bullet$
$\quad R \implies (\text{Pre } EOp \iff \text{Pre } (FOp[z!/z?] \wedge GOp))$
PS.3 $\forall E.\text{STATE};\ F.\text{STATE};\ G.\text{STATE};\ F.\text{STATE}';\ G.\text{STATE}' \bullet$
$\quad R \wedge FOp[z!/z?] \wedge GOp \implies (\exists E.\text{STATE}' \bullet EOp \wedge R')$

(The derivation of a similar rule for demonic outputs can be found in [3]. Note however that by using the blocking plus angelic model, we do not place any restrictions on the outputs of the refinement as is done in [3].)

Application of this rule requires its verification for the initialisation and operations *Send* and *Choose*. To do so, we will use the identity retrieve relation. Since *Choose* does not appear in Y, the conditions with respect to that operation are easily discharged by the fact that *CChoose* is identical to D_2 *Choose* [3]. For *Send*, we are required to verify conditions such as **PS.2**:

$\text{Pre } D_2 Send \iff \text{Pre } (CSend[v!/v?, y!/y?] \wedge D_3 Send)$

The predicate of Pre $D_2 Send$ simplifies to $nodes \neq \varnothing$, as does the predicate of Pre $(CSend[v!/v?, y!/y?] \wedge D_3 Send)$. This condition is therefore easily discharged. Verification of correctness (**PS.3**) for *Send* is done in a similar fashion.

The structural rules allowing the introduction of an interleaving, as in $D_3 \sqsubseteq A_2 \| B_2$, are similar and we omit the verification here, as we similarly do for the step $A_1 \| B_1 \sqsubseteq D_1$.

The refinement step $D_1 \sqsubseteq D_2 \setminus \{\!| \, Send \, |\!\}$ which involves the introduction of a hidden operation, is slightly more involved. Here, under the assumption $D_2 \setminus \{\!| \, Send \, |\!\}$ contains no divergence, the relevant rule is (for our particular specifications):

Definition 3 *Weak downward simulation*
The CSP expression $D_2\setminus\{\!| \, Send \, |\!\}$ is a weak downward simulation of the Object-Z class D_1 if there is a retrieve relation R such that the following holds.

WS.1 $\forall D_2.\text{STATE} \bullet D_2.\text{INIT} \,\S\, Int_{Send} \implies (\exists D_1.\text{INIT} \wedge R)$
WS.2 $\forall D_1.\text{STATE};\ D_2.\text{STATE} \bullet R \implies$
$\quad (\text{Pre } D_1 Choose \iff \text{Pre } (Int_{Send} \,\S\, D_2 Choose))$
WS.3 $\forall D_1.\text{STATE};\ D_2.\text{STATE};\ D_2.\text{STATE}' \bullet$
$\quad R \wedge (Int_{Send} \,\S\, D_2 Choose \,\S\, Int_{Send}) \implies$
$\quad\quad (\exists D_1.\text{STATE}' \bullet R' \wedge D_1 Send)$

Here Int_{Send} represents the effect of the hidden event Send and is found by taking zero or more occurrences of Send, i.e., $Int_{Send} \cong \Xi D_2 State \lor Send \lor (Send \ \S\ Send) \lor \dots$. (This can, in fact, be written using the schema calculus, see [3, 2].)

The verification of this involves comparing the effect of Choose in D_1 with $Int_{Send}\ \S\ Choose\ \S\ Int_{Send}$ in D_2. In calculating $Int_{Send}\ \S\ Choose\ \S\ Int_{Send}$ in D_2 we note that Send can occur up to two times, then Choose will definitely be enabled. We then easily see that the effect of Choose in D_1 is the same as the effect of Choose in $D_2 \setminus \{|\ Send\ |\}$, and the conditions can be formally verified if necessary.

Putting the pieces together, we find that all the refinement steps in the sequence can be verified and, therefore, $A_1 \| B_1 \sqsubseteq (C\ _X\|_Y (A_2 \| B_2)) \setminus \{|\ Send\ |\}$.

In summary, what we have shown is that the blocking model with an angelic model of outputs has not constrained the design to necessarily adopt the abstract communication mechanism that motivated it. By using structural refinements, we can introduce explicit mechanisms to communicate and negotiate between the components. We can, therefore, move smoothly between an abstract view and a more implementation-oriented view of the same behaviour and, furthermore, this is achieved using the same angelic model of outputs throughout.

5 Conclusion

This paper has investigated a particular semantic interpretation of preconditions and outputs in the context of integrations of Object-Z and CSP. It has shown that by adopting a *blocking* model of operations, where operations cannot occur outside their preconditions, and an *angelic* model of outputs, where outputs may be influenced by their environment, we can specify concurrent systems at a higher level of abstraction. In particular, exceptional behaviours need not be specified in many cases and mechanisms for communication between processes can be largely ignored.

We have also shown that adopting an angelic model of outputs does not preclude compositional refinement, nor refinement to an implementation in which outputs are no longer influenced by the environment, i.e., are *demonic*. The latter is achieved by introducing an internal operation which "chooses" a value to output before the operation which outputs it. This approach can also be used when initially specifying systems providing the internal non-determinism associated with demonic outputs within the angelic interpretation.

Acknowledgements

This work was partially funded by a University of Queensland External Support Enabling Grant.

References

1. MJ. Butler. Refinement and decomposition of value-passing action systems. In E. Best, editor, *International Conference on Concurrency Theory (CONCUR'93)*, volume 715 of *Lecture Notes in Computer Science*, pages 217–232. Springer-Verlag, 1993.
2. J. Derrick and E. Boiten. *Refinement in Z and Object-Z, Foundations and Advanced Applications*. Springer-Verlag, 2001.
3. J. Derrick and G. Smith. Structural refinement in Object-Z/CSP. In W. Grieskamp, T. Santen, and B. Stoddart, editors, *2nd International Conference on Integrated Formal Methods (IFM'00)*, volume 1945 of *Lecture Notes in Computer Science*, pages 194–213. Springer-Verlag, 2000.
4. R. Duke and G. Rose. *Formal Object-Oriented Specification using Object-Z*. MacMillan, 2000.
5. C. Fischer. CSP-OZ - a combination of CSP and Object-Z. In H. Bowman and J. Derrick, editors, *Formal Methods for Open Object-Based Distributed Systems (FMOODS'97)*, pages 423–438. Chapman & Hall, 1997.
6. C.A.R. Hoare. *Communicating Sequential Processes*. Prentice Hall, 1985.
7. B.P. Mahony and J.S. Dong. Blending Object-Z and Timed CSP: An introduction to TCOZ. In *20th International Conference on Software Engineering (ICSE'98)*, pages 95–104. IEEE Computer Society Press, 1998.
8. R. Milner. *Communication and Concurrency*. Prentice Hall, 1989.
9. A.W. Roscoe. *The Theory and Practice of Concurrency*. Prentice Hall, 1998.
10. G. Smith and J. Derrick. Refinement and verification of concurrent systems specified in Object-Z and CSP. In M.G. Hinchey and Shaoying Lui, editors, *First International Conference on Formal Engineering Methods (ICFEM '97)*, pages 293–302. IEEE Computer Society Press, 1997.
11. G. Smith and J. Derrick. Specification, refinement and verification of concurrent systems – an integration of Object-Z and CSP. *Formal Methods in System Design*, 18(3):249–284, 2000.
12. G. Smith. A semantic integration of Object-Z and CSP for the specification of concurrent systems. In J. Fitzgerald, C.B. Jones, and P. Lucas, editors, *Formal Methods Europe (FME'97)*, volume 1313 of *Lecture Notes in Computer Science*, pages 62–81. Springer-Verlag, 1997.
13. G. Smith. *The Object-Z Specification Language*. Advances in Formal Methods. Kluwer Academic Publishers, 2000.
14. J.M. Spivey. *The Z Notation: A Reference Manual*. Prentice Hall, 2nd edition, 1992.

Mechanization of an Integrated Approach: Shallow Embedding into SAL/PVS

J. Christian Attiogbé

IRIN – Université de Nantes,
B.P.92208, F-44322 Nantes Cedex 3, France
Christian.Attiogbe@irin.univ-nantes.fr

Abstract. This paper describes a work on the systematic embedding into SAL of specifications written in the integrated approach of Configuration Machines. The final goal is to perform formal analysis. SAL is an intermediate language used as an input language of various formal reasoning tools and especially PVS. The Configuration Machine approach is a specification technique combining transition systems and state based data models. Our embedding technique, based on a systematic translation of the specifications into SAL, is presented, formalised and discussed.

1 Introduction

Real size systems often overwhelm the scope covered by mono-paradigm specification formalisms and techniques. The integration of methods to cover several paradigms appearing in systems requirements is a great deal to handle this shortcoming. Indeed, mono-paradigm formal specification approaches are now mature and current research efforts focus on the combination of these approaches and their specific tools in order to strengthen their impact on industrial systems treatment. Therefore, to make methods more practical and efficient in their use, their *mechanization* by providing powerful and operational development environments is an important challenge. This is the main motivation of our work. In this paper we focus on the mechanization of the Configuration Machine technique which is designed as an integrated specification approach combining transition systems and state based data models. We consider the embedding of the semantics of multi-paradigm specification within an appropriate logic as an effective mechanization approach which permits formal reasoning. We adopt this mechanization approach by embedding the specifications written in the Configuration Machine formalism into SAL [5] (Symbolic Analysis Laboratory). SAL is an intermediate language used as an input language of various formal reasoning tools like PVS [15], STeP [27], and Murϕ [10]. The motivation for using SAL is that it is close to Configuration Machine approach and is devoted to provide means for static analysis and for combining transition systems modules and tools for theorem proving and model checking. The technique for translating Configuration Machine specifications into SAL is a *shallow embedding*. Embedding techniques are introduced in [6] and are intensively used elsewhere [7, 1, 21]. The main contribution of our work is an effective method to mechanize integrated approaches by reusing mature proof systems such as PVS.

The paper is organized as follows. Section 2 presents the Configuration Machine approach. In Section 3, we give an overview of SAL. In Section 4, we formalize the general procedure for a systematic translation of Configuration Machine specifications into SAL. Section 5 reports on a complete experiment. Finally the Section 6 presents related works and concluding remarks.

2 An Overview of Configuration Machines

The *Configuration Machines* [2, 3] approach integrates, in a homogeneous framework supported by natural deduction, model based specifications of data and transition system models of behaviours. It is well-suited to the specification of multifaceted systems where the facets such as *data, transformation* (operations on data), *behaviour, interaction and reaction* are emphasized. The formalism combines basic concepts, simplicity, readability, and expressiveness. The current approach falls into a series of works [23, 29] combining model-oriented formalisms, especially *Z* with process algebras CCS or CSP. However, it avoids fixing the behaviour of components using process algebras; instead, the approach is comparable to *Actions Systems* [9] where the behaviour of components depends on guards. The specification unit of our formalism is a *machine type*, *machine* for short. It gathers both data and behaviour parts, and describes the type of components having the same data space (described by *configuration*) and the same behaviour. A configuration is the description of a global state including information about the environment of the system. The main methodological approach behind the Configuration Machine technique is the use of: *i)* *abstraction* to capture, as independent machines, the system parts which have a specific data model and a specific behaviour, *ii)* *composition* to reunite these different machines. The behaviour of a machine is expressed as a set of guarded transition rules (called *transactions*) relating the descriptions of an initial configuration (the guard) and a final configuration. A machine evolves repeatedly from one configuration to another one following enabled transactions. If several transactions are enabled, there is a nondeterministic choice. Larger machines (or systems) are built by extending or composing other machines. Composed machines communicate synchronously and interact via (parameterised) events exchange. Invariants are used to define global safety properties of systems. Some works related to Configuration Machines are Actions Systems [9], Event Calculus [25], μSZ [23], and CSP-OZ [12].

3 An Overview of SAL

SAL is a framework combining different tools for abstraction, program analysis, theorem proving, and model checking toward the calculation of properties of concurrent systems expressed as transition systems [5, 24]. SAL has been used recently for the Flight Guidance System case study [20], and for Java multi-threading programs analysis [22]. SAL is architectured around an intermediate language for specifying concurrent systems in a compositional way. This language serves as a common description for the interaction with different analysis tools. Apart from the intermediate language the main components of the SAL environment are the translators of the intermediate language to the input of the analysis tools. The outputs of the analysis tools are also translated into the intermediate language. The SAL language includes a *type* language, an *expression* language, a *module* language (a module is the basic construct of the intermediate language; it is a self-contained specification of a transition system), a *context* language and *properties* expressed in CTL (Computation Tree Logic).

SAL Modules. A module has a name and consists of a state type defined by four disjoint sets of input, output, local and global variables, an initialization condition on the state type, and a binary transition relation. The transitions of a module are specified by means of definitions (in the form *variable = expression*) or by guarded commands (in the form *boolean_expression → assignment_part*). Modules allow parameterisation. They can be composed synchronously with the operator || or asynchronously with the operator []. SAL modules composition supports a compositional analysis: modules properties are preserved through composition. Hiding and renaming operations can be applied to modules and their compositions. SAL includes constructs for stating module properties (safety and liveness) and abstractions between modules. CTL formulas are used for this purpose.

4 Systematic Translation of Specifications into SAL

We give in this section the guidelines of the procedure to translate Configuration Machines into SAL. This translation procedure and its semantics are based on the abstractions of configuration machines and SAL modules. We use a shallow embedding technique for the translation. With shallow embedding the constructs of one language are translated into semantically equivalent constructs in the target language. Nevertheless, the mapping from the language constructs to their semantic representations is part of the metalanguage (support of the source language). Shallow embedding can be contrasted with deep embedding in which both syntax and semantics of the embedded language are formalized inside the target language logic. That means, the mapping from language constructs to their semantic representations is part of the target language logic. Consequently, using shallow embedding, we do not need the syntactic constructs but rather the semantics to be translated into the target logic. The organization of the section reveals our method. First of all (sections 4.1 and 4.2), we give the abstractions corresponding to each formalism involved in the translation. This step underlines the constructs we have to translate. These abstractions make the expression of translation rules easier. Thereafter (section 4.3), we describe the semantic matching between the abstract constructs and we give the corresponding semantic rules to translate the constructs of one formalism to ones of the other. Finally in section 4.4, we focus on the translation of data into the SAL data language.

4.1 Abstraction of Configuration Machines

A Configuration Machine is made of

- a header part: the name of the machine and possibly some composition clauses;
- a data part: a Z schema which describes the state space;
- an initialization predicate;
- a behaviour part made of a set of action names and a transactions set;
- some communication constraints (defined as logical assertions). We do not consider these constraints here because they are not translated. However they are already in logical form and should be tractable.

Accordingly, an abstraction of a machine is a tuple of these components. In the following, we consider types as abstract sets. Let CM be the general type of machines and consider the types $NAME$, $Zdata$, $Expression$, $Transaction == Expression \times Expression$ as abstractions of each component. We have $CM \subseteq NAME \times Zdata \times Expression \times \mathcal{P}\, Transaction$. $Expression$ represents the set of all possible logic expressions according to the data part. Each component can be accessed via a function as described in the following table. All the functions have CM as their domain type.

Syntactic Component	Access Function	Type of the Component
name	m_name	$NAME$
datapart	$m\_datapart$	$Zdata$
initialization	$m\_initialization$	$Expression$
transaction	$m\_transaction$	$\mathcal{P}\,(Expression \times Expression)$

The constructs corresponding to these components will be translated. We detail now the abstractions represented by the types which are not basic ones.

The **data part** abstracted by $Zdata$ is essentially defined by a Z schema called *Config* which can use other Z data models. The Z schema semantics is a *set of bindings*. A binding is a tuple of variables with their values such that the predicate part of the schema is true. Therefore, each binding is supported by a characteristic tuple of variables with the associated types $\mathcal{P}\,(Var\_ID \times Var\_TYPE)$. Accordingly, $Zdata$ represents the abstraction of a signature (a set of couple s *(identifier, type)*) with a predicate. We use $signature(dp)$ and $predicate(dp)$ to refer to, respectively the signature and the predicate of a data part dp. The data part describes the configurations (states space) of a machine. Predicates are used to describe configurations. The abstraction of a configuration is a predicate as a conjunction of expressions.

The **transactions** abstracted by $\mathcal{P}\,(Expression \times Expression)$ express the behaviour of the machine via a transition relation between configuration descriptions. The initial configuration description is a guard.

The couple (*guard*, *new_configuration*) corresponds to the abstraction of a transaction. The *guard* member is a conjunction of expressions (equations describing the current state of variables). It is abstracted as a set of expressions linked with the logical conjunction: $l_1 = r_1 \wedge l_2 = r_2 \wedge l_3 = r_3 \wedge \cdots \wedge l_n = r_n$ (we note $\bigwedge_{i \in 1..n}(l_i = r_i)$ in the following wher i is a given natural). The *guard* may contain the expression `lr_event`$= evtname(\{prm\_name_j, prm\_type_j\}*)$ which deals with parameterised input events. The variable `lr_event` always holds the last event received by the machine. The *new_configuration* member is a conjunction of expressions (equations defining new values of state variables): $\bigwedge_{i \in 1..n}(l_i = r_i)$. It may contain the expression `ls_event`$= evtname(prm\_seq)$ which treats parameterised output events. We use $expr\_seq^1$ to denote a sequence of expressions. The variable `ls_event` always holds the last event sent by the machine. Parameters of output events are supplied with values from the machine environment such that each parameter *prm* of the sequence *prm_seq* can be given a type T from the scope of the current machine data part.

The **initialization** abstracted by *Expression* is a conjunction of expressions: $\bigwedge_{i \in 1..n}(l_i = r_i)$. Additionally, $alphabet(cm)$ denotes in the following the alphabet of a machine cm.

4.2 Abstraction of SAL Modules

A SAL module is made of eight components intuitively named *name*, *context*, *locvar*, *inputs*, *outputs*, *initialization*, *transitions*, *assertion*. In the following, we do not use the assertion component which is more related to properties checking. Let *SM* be the subset of the Cartesian product of the components types. Let us consider the basic types *NAME*, *Var_ID*, *Var_TYPE*, and *Expression* as the type of all possible logic expression. The following table describes the components, the access functions and their types.

Syntactic Component	Access Function	Type of the Component
name	s_name	NAME
context	s_context	Context
locvar	s_locvar	$\mathcal{P}(Var\_ID \times Var\_TYPE)$
inputs	s_inputs	$\mathcal{P}(Var\_ID \times Var\_TYPE)$
outputs	s_outputs	$\mathcal{P}(Var\_ID \times Var\_TYPE)$
initialization	s_initialization	$Expression \times Expression$
transitions	s_transitions	$\mathcal{P}(Expression \times Expression)$

Accordingly, if *sm* is a SAL module, $s\_inputs(sm)$ has the type $\mathcal{P}(Var\_ID \times Var\_TYPE)$ and denotes the set of couples *(identifier, type)* which constitute the inputs of *sm*. It works in the same way for the remainder of the module components. Now, we detail the abstractions represented by the types used for module components. The **context** of a module is a collection of PVS type and variable declarations. The **local** component, **input** component, and **output** component are collections of couples *(identifier, type)* which correspond to typed variable

---

[1] Formally $expr\_seq : Sequence[Expression]$.

declarations: $\mathcal{P}(\mathit{Var\_ID} \times \mathit{Var\_TYPE})$. The **initialization** component is a couple (*guard*, *new_expression*). It has the type *Expression* × *Expression*. The **transitions** abstracted by $\mathcal{P}(\mathit{Expression} \times \mathit{Expression})$ express the behaviour of the module via a transition relation between states. Each transition has a guard part and a statement part. The abstraction corresponding to a transition is then the couple (*guard*, *statement*), member of *Expression* × *Expression*. The guard part is either a simple expression or a conjunction of expressions: $\bigwedge_{i \in 1..n}(l_i = r_i)$. The statement part is a sequence of statements (equations defining new values of state variables). It is abstracted as an injective sequence[2] on a set of expressions: $iseq(\{i \in 1..n \mid l_i = r_i\})$; thus, it is an expression. Additionally, to preserve the events alphabet managed by the machines, we introduce into SAL modules an auxiliary component called *local_events* to hold the alphabet of events. This component is only used for the translation.

The abstractions of the source and target objects of our translation show some equivalent constructs: *Expression* in both abstractions, *Transition* and *Transaction*. Considering these abstractions, we give the semantics of the translation through the following rules.

4.3 Translation Rules

We have defined, based on the previous abstractions of machines and modules, the semantic rules that govern the systematic translation from machines to modules. The rules are expressed for each component involved. We cannot give here all these rules, but we focus on their main idea. Details can be found in [4].
Let *CM* be the type of any given configuration machine, *SM* the type of any SAL module resulting from a translation of a machine into SAL, and *Cm2Sm* the translation procedure defined over $CM \rightarrow SM$. In all the following rules, let *cm* be a machine (*cm* : *CM*) and *sm* be the SAL module (*sm* : *SM*) built from *cm* using *Cm2Sm*. Accordingly, we assume that $sm = Cm2Sm(cm)$.

Main Rules for Building Modules

We identify and formalize some general mechanisms for the embedding of machines into SAL, for example the way to build modules context knowing that some parts are shared. Every module translated from a machine contains a particular subtype Mod_EVENT of the type EVENT[3] in its context. We give here the rules for only three components.
Local Component. The data part of a machine is semantically equivalent to a module *s_locvar* component.

$$\frac{\begin{array}{c} sm = Cm2Sm(cm) \\ dp = m\_datapart(cm) \\ \texttt{T\_Config} = Z2PVS(dp) \end{array}}{(\texttt{config, T\_Config}) \in s\_locvar(sm)}$$

---
[2] Cannot contain duplicated elements.
[3] This font is used for types and variables.

Every module translated from a machine has a state variable corresponding to the configuration space of that machine. The idea of the function $Z2PVS$ consists in computing a PVS type from the signature and the predicate part of dp. The $Z2PVS$ function is more detailed in the section 4.4.

Input Component. The input parameters of the events received by a machine are input variables of the corresponding SAL module. A particular event c_event is needed to manage current event.

$$(\texttt{c\_event}, \texttt{Mod\_EVENT}) \in s\_inputs(sm)$$

Every module has c_event with the type Mod_EVENT in its input variables.

$$\frac{\begin{array}{c} sm = Cm2Sm(cm) \\ (guard, \bigwedge_{i \in 1..n}(l_i = r_i)) \in m\_transactions(cm) \\ \exists i \in 1..n \mid l_i = \texttt{lr\_event} \land r_i = evtname(typed\_prm\_seq) \\ j \in 1..\#typed\_prm\_seq \land (prm, type) = typed\_prm\_seq(j) \\ \alpha(prm, evtname, j) = newprm \end{array}}{(newprm, type) \in s\_inputs(sm)}$$

Each typed variable used as a parameter of a received event is part of the input component of the corresponding SAL module, after being renamed (by the function α) using its rank and the associated event name. This renaming enables us to treat the communication between modules. The idea is to relate input and output parameters that have the same names. The **Output** Component is treated in the same way.

Transition Component. Basically, transactions of machines are semantically equivalent to transitions of SAL modules. Configuration Machines and SAL modules have in common the use of transition systems model to specify behaviour. A transaction is a transition rule in the form of a couple of a guard and an expression. Then, the transactions form a transitions system equivalent to a SAL module, the components of which are described by the rules given above. The translation is then straightforward between their abstract forms. SAL uses the dash symbol (') to relate before and after state variable, for example in g --> sv' = sv + 1[4]. When translating a machine to a module, the right hand side of transactions are transformed by substituting sv' to each state variable sv appearing in left hand side of equalities. The function η_{left} is introduced for this purpose.

$$\frac{\begin{array}{c} sm = Cm2Sm(cm) \\ (guard, \bigwedge_{i \in 1..n}(l_i = r_i)) \in m\_transactions(cm) \end{array}}{(guard, iseq(\eta_{left}(\{i \in 1..n \mid l_i = r_i\}))) \in s\_transitions(sm)}$$

In the same way, and adding the guard TRUE to the predicate describing the initialization of a machine we obtain the equivalent construct of SAL module.

---

[4] An equivalent notation is next(sv) = sv + 1; this one is used in the generated code.

Now, we have the necessary rules for deriving the SAL module components from ones of machines. In the following, we give some details on the treatment of the data part.

4.4 Embedding of the Data Part into PVS: Z2PVS

The data language of SAL is mainly the PVS input formalism, then the translation of our data part into SAL results in a translation into PVS. This translation into PVS is not done from scratch. Indeed, a lot of works have been published on translating or embedding the Z language into PVS and HOL [1, 17, 7, 26]. Large parts of these works are profitably reused here. Note that by shallow embedding we have to translate constructs into equivalent constructs. *Schemas* are the basic structures of the Z language which is used by Configuration Machine formalism to describe data. The semantics of Z schema should be a *set of bindings*. However, schemas may be used in a more abstract way as predicates. Consequently, we use PVS types and theories as the equivalent constructs to describe data. Therefore, an important part of the translation process is the translation of Z schemas into PVS constructs.

Z Schema to PVS Type. A straightforward structural translation is as follows. A schema like

$$\begin{array}{|l}\hline \_SchName_____ \\ d1:\mathbb{Z};\ d2:\mathbb{Z} \\ \hline Predicate \\ \hline \end{array}$$

corresponds to the PVS type:
`DP_SchName: TYPE= [# d1: int, d2: int #]` followed by a subtyping

`SchName_T: NONEMPTY_TYPE= {e: DP_SchName | Predicate_on_e}`

Then, each declaration $var : SchName$ is translated by `var: SchName_T`.

Basic Types and Sets. Basic types (`integer`, `natural`, `real`, etc) are provided by PVS. Z given sets acting as types can be treated as basic types in PVS.

Expressions. Logical connectives, arithmetic operators and related basic expressions are rather the same in PVS and Z (up to a syntactic renaming).

Enumerated Types. Enumerated sets of Z are directly translated to PVS, up to a syntactic arrangement. The PVS type `T: TYPE= {E,F,G}` corresponds to the Z set $T ::= E \mid F \mid G$.

Finite Sets and Relations. PVS has a prelude (*i.e.* built-in theories) which provides finite sets, relations, functions, etc. As PVS uses a typed higher-order logic, sets are just predicates over a specific type rather than the richer notion used in set theory. A finite sets type is defined in the PVS `finite_sets` library as a subtype of the set type (predicate). Most operations on sets are already defined: set memberships, set union, set intersection, etc. The prelude also provides the `relations` theory useful for specifying binary relations.

Finite Sequences. A type of finite sequences is provided in the PVS library. We take care to sequences indexing which starts from zero in PVS and from one in Z.

Functions. PVS provides total functions; partial functions intensively used by Z are tractable via subtyping in PVS.

Axiomatic Definitions. Simple axiomatic definitions are treated with PVS subtyping. More general axiomatic definitions are treated via PVS theories.

4.5 Translation of Machines Composition

The synchronous parallel composition of SAL captures the semantics of machines parallel composition. The communication between machines which is handled by exchange of parameterized events is treated here by commonly named input variables (of one module) and output variables (of the other module). The events of both modules are related by renaming properly the variables.

5 An Experiment Report

A complete experiment is presented in [4]. It is a case study taken from [13] in which a ZCCS specification is given. It is about a two components system which samples the angle and radial position of an object, say a pen, from an instrument and outputs the corresponding Cartesian coordinates on a channel. First we write the complete specification using the Configuration Machine technique. Then, we do the complete embedding of the specification into SAL. We check the obtained SAL modules with the SAL experimental compiler[5] which generates PVS code from SAL. It results that this experimental SAL compiler cannot parse all the SAL modules generated by our translation procedure. This is because the data language treated by the compiler is a subset of the PVS language. Then, we have manually generated the PVS theory corresponding to our specification. The interpretation of the transition relation is done as a PVS relation over states. Therefore, we use successfully PVS to check directly the obtained modules. On this basis, liveness properties are stated and proved. This paper does not aim to cover directly verification aspects. We are preparing an accompanying paper on the verification possibilities offered by the translation into SAL/PVS.

6 Related Works and Concluding Remarks

We have mentionned numerous works on integrated approaches, for example ZCCS [13] and μSZ [23]. Most of them lack of effective tools support. It is this

---
[5] http://www.icase.edu/~munoz/SAL/sal.html

aspect we covered by our work and the choice of SAL as an intermediate language. Many other works use intermediate language for analysis purpose and to make tools communicate. There is a proposal [8] of a common intermediate language named IF for asynchronous systems. It can be viewed as a complementary concern since IF is particularly devoted to timed asynchronous systems. IF is an intermediate representation for SDL (System Description Language [28]) where a system is represented as a set of timed automata communicating asynchronously through a set of buffers or by rendez-vous through a set of synchronisation gates. IF uses mainly SDL as front-end formalism and has CADP/KRONOS [11] as formal analysis tool. Comparatively, SAL provides several back-end and front-end formalisms/tools. SAL also enables one to work with transition systems. In the other side IF provides support for timed asynchronous systems. The UniForM Workbench [18] supports the combination of formal methods and provides tools for development and analysis of hybrid, real-time or reactive systems. The UniForM Workbench enables one to integrate different formalisms or methods (Z, CSP, CSP-OZ, etc) in its environment and provides a new workbench for them. The input methods can have or not specific tools (for example FDR for CSP, Moby/OZ for CSP-OZ). We share some common idea with this project. The idea of a high level logic to handle the integration and support tools is the most important, but we can also underline the point on reusing existing mature proof systems to integrate methods and tools. However, in the UniForM project, HOL [14] is directly used as the intermediate language. That is a drawback. Indeed each time one have to integrate a system with transition systems for dynamic part, the translation of transition relation is done again. The advantage of choosing SAL is that it already provides transition relation for dynamic aspect.

We presented a general technique to translate Configuration Machines into SAL modules. PVS is used to typecheck the substantial part of the modules resulting from the translation. The encoding of Z into the PVS logic is not a simple concern. Some studies shown that coupling PVS and Z can leads to difficult proofs in PVS due to the difference between the specification styles they use [26, 19]. This would be a drawback of the translation into SAL if we had used a deep embedding. Using a shallow embedding, as we have done, helps to avoid these difficulties because the data are semantically translated and are no more tightly linked with the original Z. However, comparatively the deep embedding approaches enable reasoning on the whole formalism and not on specific properties as with shallow embedding. This work enables us to mechanize the Configuration Machine approach thanks to SAL/PVS and consequently to have at one's disposal a front-end to PVS. We cannot yet translate back from PVS. We gain by the facilities offered by SAL and PVS. Overall, we provide a cheap and reusable method for the mechanization of integrated approaches. More experiments are needed to improve the proposal through tools development, properties proving and user-friendly interfaces. Ongoing work focuses on these aspects.

References

1. A. W. Gravell and C. H. Pratten. Embedding a Formal Notation: Experiences of Automating the Embedding of Z in the Higher Order Logic of PVS and HOL. In *[16]*, pages 73–84, 1998.
2. C. Attiogbé. Configuration Machines: A Simple Formalism For Specifying Multi-faceted Systems. Technical Report 181, IRIN, University of Nantes, 1998.
3. C. Attiogbé. The Access Control System: Specification with Configuration Machines. In *Proc. of AFADL'2000*, pages 203–220, France, 2000.
4. C. Attiogbé. Mechanization of Configuration Machines: Shallow Embedding into SAL/PVS. Technical Report 01.8, IRIN, University of Nantes, 2001.
5. S. Bensalem, V. Ganesh, Y. Lakhnech, C. Muñoz, S. Owre, H. Rueß, J. Rushby, V. Rusu, H. Saïdi, N. Shankar, E. Singerman, and A. Tiwari. An Overview of SAL. In C. Michael Holloway, editor, *Proc. of the Fifth NASA Langley Formal Methods Workshop (LFM'2000)*, pages 187–196, Vancouver, 2000.
6. R. Boulton, A. Gorgon, M.J.C. Gordon, J. Hebert, and J. van Tassel. Experience with Embedding Hardware Description Language in HOL. In *Proc. of the International Conference on Theorem Provers in Circuit Design: Theory, Practice and Experience*, pages 129–156, North-Holland, 1992. IFIP TC10/WG 10.2.
7. J. P. Bowen and M. J. C. Gordon. A Shallow Embedding of Z in HOL. *Information and Software Technology*, 37(5-6):269–276, 1995.
8. M. Bozga, J. C. Ferandez, L.Ghirvu, S. Graph, J. P. Krimm, and L. Mounier. IF: An Intermediate Representation and Validation Environment for Timed Asynchronous Systems. In J. Wing and J. Woodcock and J. Davies, editor, *Proc. of the International Conference on Formal Methods (FM'99)*, volume 1708 of *Lecture Notes in Computer Science*, France, 1999. Springer-Verlag.
9. M. J. Butler and C. C. Morgan. Action Systems, Unbounded Nondeterminism, and Infinite Traces. *Formal Aspects of Computing*, 7:37–53, 1995.
10. D. L. Dill. The Murφ Verification System. In *Proc. of Computer-Aided Verification (CAV'96)*, volume 1102 of *Lecture Notes in Computer Science*, pages 390–393, New Jersey, USA, 1996. Springer-Verlag.
11. J-C. Fernandez, H. Garavel, A. Kerbrat, R. Mateescu, L. Mounier, and M. Sighireanu. CADP: A Protocol Validation and Verification Toolbox. In R. Alur and T. A. Henzinger, editors, *Proc. of the 8th Conference on Computer-Aided Verification (CAV'96)*, volume 1102 of *Lecture Notes in Computer Science*, pages 437–440. Springer-Verlag, 1996.
12. C. Fischer. CSP-OZ: A Combination of Object-Z and CSP. In H. Bowmann and J. Derick, editors, *Proc. of FMOODS'97*, volume 2, pages 423–438. Chapman and Hall, 1997.
13. A. Galloway. *Integrated Formal Methods with Richer Methodological Profiles for the Development of Multi-Perspectives Systems*. PhD thesis, University of Teesside - School of Computing and Mathematics, 1996.
14. M.J.C. Gordon. *Introduction to HOL: A Theorem Proving Environment*. Cambridge University Press, 1993.
15. J. Crow and S. Owre and J. Rushby and N. Shankar and M. Srivas. A Tutorial Introduction to PVS. In *Proc. of the Workshop on Industrial-Strength Formal Specification Techniques (WIFT'95)*. IEEE Press, 1995. Florida.
16. J. Grundy and M. Newey, editor. *Supplementary Proceedings of the 11th International Conference on Theorem Proving in Higher Order Logics: Emerging Trends, (TPHOL'98)*. Australian National University, 1998.

17. Kolyang, T Santen, and B. Wolff. A Structure Preserving Encoding of Z in Isabelle/HOL. In *Proc. of the International Conference on Theorem Proving in Higher Order Logic (TPHOL'96)*, volume 1125 of *Lecture Notes in Computer Science*, pages 283–298. Springer-Verlag, 1996.
18. B. Krieg-Brückner, J. Peleska, E. R. Olderog, and A. Baer. The UniForM Workbench, a Universal Development Environment for Formal Methods. In J. Wing and J. Woodcock and J. Davies, editor, *Proc. of the International Conference on Formal Methods (FM'99)*, volume 1708 of *Lecture Notes in Computer Science*, pages 1187–1205, France, 1999. Springer-Verlag.
19. A. Martin. Approaches to proof in Z. Technical report, University of Southampton, 1997.
20. C. Muñoz. Specification of the Flight Guidance System in (unofficial) SAL. Technical report, ICASE, http://www.icase.edu/~munoz/SAL/sal.html, 1999.
21. C. Muñoz and J. Rushby. Structural Embeddings: Mechanization with Method. In J. Wing and J. Woodcock, editor, *Proc. of the World Congress in Formal Methods (FM99)*, volume 1708 of *Lecture Notes in Computer Science*, pages 452–471, France, 1999. Springer-Verlag.
22. D. Park, U. Stern, J. U. Skakkebaek, and D. L. Dill. Java Model Checking. In *Proc. of the Fifteenth IEEE International Conference on Automated Software Engineering (ASE'2000)*, pages 253–256, 2000.
23. R. Büssow, R. Geisler, W. Grieskamp and M. Klar. The μSZ Notation, Version 1.0. Technical report, Teschnische Universität Berlin, Fachbereich Informatik, December 1997.
24. N. Shankar. Symbolic Analysis of Transition Systems. In Y. Gurevich, P. W. Kutter, M. Odersky, and L. Thiele, editors, *Proc. of the Workshop on Abstract State Machines: Theory and Applications (ASM'2000)*, volume 1912 of *Lecture Notes in Computer Science*, pages 287–302, Switzerland, 2000. Springer-Verlag.
25. W.J. Stoddart. An Introduction to the Event Calculus. In *Proc. ZUM'97*, volume 1212 of *Lecture Notes in Computer Science*, pages 10–34. Springer-Verlag, 1997.
26. D. W. J. Stringer-Calvert, S. Stepney, and I. Wand. Using PVS to Prove a Z Refinement: A Case Study. In J. Fitzgerald, C. B. Jones, and P. Lucas, editors, *Proc. of Formal Methods: Their Industrial Application and Strengthened Foundations (FME '97)*, volume 1313 of *Lecture Notes in Computer Science*, pages 573–588, Austria, 1997. Springer-Verlag.
27. Z. Manna and the STeP group. STeP: The Stanford Temporal Prover. In P. D. Mosses, M. Nielsen, and M. I. Schwartzbach, editors, *Proc. of Theory and Practice of Software Development*, volume 915 of *Lecture Notes in Computer Science*, pages 793–794. Springer-Verlag, 1995.
28. ITU Recommendation Z.100. Specification and Description Language SDL. Technical report, ITU, 1994.
29. C. FISCHER. How to combine Z with a Process Algebra. In J. P. BOWEN, A. FETT, et M. G. HINCHEY, éditeurs, *Proc. of The Z Users Meeting (ZUM'98)*, volume 1493 of *Lecture Notes in Computer Science*, pages 5–23. Springer-Verlag, 1998.

Concept Use or Concept Refinement: An Important Distinction in Building Generic Specifications

David R. Musser[1,*] and Zhiqing Shao[2,**]

[1] Computer Science Department,
Rensselaer Polytechnic Institute,
Troy, New York 12180
`musser@cs.rpi.edu`
[2] Department of Computer Science and Engineering,
East China University of Science and Technology,
Shanghai 200237, China `zshao@ecust.edu.cn`

Abstract. The Tecton concept description language provides constructs for building generic specifications incrementally, based mainly on the ability to *use* or *refine* concepts. This paper focuses on these constructs, the semantic distinctions between them, their role in determining the legality of concept instances, and their consequent role in motivating a certain style of specification. Differences in the legality conditions associated with instantiating a used or refined concept strongly motivate the specification writer toward a style in which concept use rather than refinement is favored.

Keywords: Specification techniques and languages, specification evolution and refinement, formal semantics.

1 Introduction

Tecton [8–10, 14] is a small language for describing and using abstract concepts in formal software development and hardware design. Special attention has been given in the design of Tecton toward supporting formal specification of generic software components such as those in the C++ Standard Template Library [12], the Matrix Template Library [17], and the Boost Graph Library [16]. Tecton omits many of the features of a comprehensive language like CASL (Common Algebraic Specification Language) [4], yet retains great expressive power, as has been demonstrated by concise Tecton specifications of many standard algebraic and relational concepts [13], software concepts such as generic sorting algorithms

---

* The first author's work is supported in part by the National Science Foundation (NSF) Next Generation Software Program, Grant 0131354.
** Most of the work of this paper was completed while the second author was visiting Rensselaer Polytechnic Institute and is supported in part by NSFC (Grant 69903004), CSC, EYTP, and China MOE Key Research Foundation.

and Standard Template Library containers and iterators [11], and a few hardware concepts such as generic adder circuits [8].

One of the main goals of Tecton and earlier formal specification languages like OBJ [6] and the Larch Shared Language [5, 7] is to reduce the need for proof. If one proof can be done at an abstract level, and the results can be used in a variety of instances without repeating the proof, there will be a substantial savings of effort. There is something to be proved when an instance is created, namely that the name or concept replacements made in the instance imply the assumptions made in the abstract-level proof, but generally these proofs will be simpler than if abstractions were not used and all proofs were done directly about concrete cases.

Reducing the proof burden is obviously also one of the goals of CASL. CASL is a synthesis of ideas from previous languages (including OBJ and Larch) and other research on algebraic specifications. It is a much larger language than Tecton; for example, CASL supplies several mechanisms for hiding part of a signature, while Tecton has none (except for marking some functions as private). Yet CASL, like most specification languages, does not directly address the question of conservative or nonconservative extension when combining or instantiating specifications (while users can use annotations to point out conservative extensions, these are optional).

Other specification languages that have made a strong distinction between conservative and nonconservative extension include Pluss [1] and GSBL [2, 3]. Tecton has much in common with these languages, including small size and similarities in abstract syntax (the concrete syntax is somewhat different), and, in the case of GSBL, provision for generic specifications without explicit parameters, where specific instances can be obtained by replacing some sub-specification by another one. Tecton differs from these languages mainly in the method of definition of its semantics. With GSBL, Pluss, CASL, and many other languages (if they have a formal semantics at all), the semantic definition is based on category-theoretic notions of which, to our knowledge, there is no available intuitively appealing description. Thorough understanding of the semantics of such languages seems likely to remain inaccessible to all but a few dedicated proponents of the category-theoretic approach. The semantics of Tecton concept descriptions, on the other hand, is defined in terms of a few set theoretic and algebraic notions. Furthermore, Tecton uses a nontraditional way of relating concept descriptions to concepts, which are sets of many-sorted algebras, resulting in a relatively simple way of defining the semantics of combinations of concept descriptions in terms of set intersections. I.e., many-sorted algebras are defined as usual in terms of a signature specified in the concept description, but instead of the conventional practice of saying that an algebra must have exactly the sorts and functions specified in the signature, we allow algebras in the concept to have additional sorts and functions.

Earlier definitions of Tecton [8, 10] introduced the basic ideas of this set-theoretic approach, but did not fully develop the details of the semantics relating to the legality of reusing existing concept descriptions. Further refinement and revision of these legality conditions, the main topic of the present paper, have led to even more flexible means of developing new concepts based on previously described concepts than in the previous versions of the language. The new legality conditions are designed to prevent certain ways of refining concepts that would otherwise be prone to later errors when combining specifications. In particular, two kinds of clauses, *uses* and *refines*, are provided for building new concept descriptions upon ones previously defined. Both have the same syntactic and type-checking role: the symbols that are available for use in a concept description are exactly those that are introduced directly in the description or indirectly from other descriptions via **uses** or **refines** clauses. Semantically, however, these clauses differ significantly. The difference is best explained in terms of two relations between concept descriptions, *preserves* and *modifies*.

In terms of the logical theory associated with a concept, "preserves" is a synonym for "conservatively extends" and "modifies" is non-conservative extension but is nonetheless conservative in some respects. These two relations, *preserves* and *modifies*, are important mainly because they determine the concepts that can be replaced in a concept instance and also influence the legality conditions that must be discharged when such a concept instance is created. A concept instance D in which a concept is replaced is written C [with B as A], where A, B, and C are names of concepts. The legality conditions for this concept instance are that

1. either C preserves A or C modifies A;
2. if C preserves A, then it is required that D preserves B;
3. if C modifies A, then it is required that D modifies B.

An immediate consequence of these conditions is that if C uses A, either directly or indirectly, then it would have been legal to have written B in place of A when originally writing C. Similarly if C refines A, either directly or indirectly, then it would been legal to have written B in place of A. Thus one can think of the replacement as being done by a simple textual substitution of B for A, since it causes no relabeling of the direct relations between concepts to be necessary.

While this correspondence is appealing to intuition, the legality conditions for guaranteeing the *preserves* and *modifies* relations are maintained as required would be very difficult to deal with in actual practice. Instead, we would like to be able to perform simpler, more localized checks when creating a concept instance, and a major part of the development of the semantics of concept instances in Section 5 is devoted to showing that this is possible.

2 Concepts and Concept Descriptions

Definition of concept. In Tecton a *concept* is a set of many-sorted algebras. Each algebra has a signature that consists of two disjoint sets of identifiers, called *sorts* and *function identifiers*. An *indexed family of sets* is a family of pairs (s, S), where s is a sort and S is a set. An *indexed family of functions* is a family $\mathcal{F}$ of pairs (σ, f), where f is a function and σ is a *function description*

consisting of a function identifier and an *arity*, which consists of two lists of sorts, called *domain sorts* and *range sorts*. Then a *(many-sorted) algebra* consists of
- an indexed family $\mathcal{S}$ of sets such that $\mathcal{S}$ is a mapping;
- an indexed family $\mathcal{F}$ of functions, such that $\mathcal{F}$ is a mapping and for each pair (σ, f) in $\mathcal{F}$, where σ has domain sorts $s_1, \ldots, s_n$ and range sorts $r_1, \ldots, r_m$, f is a function with domain $\mathcal{S}(s_1) \times \cdots \times \mathcal{S}(s_n)$ and range $\mathcal{S}(r_1) \times \cdots \times \mathcal{S}(r_m)$.

Overview of concept descriptions. Tecton permits statement of the requirements of a concept using a series of sentences called *concept descriptions*. These sentences take one of five forms:

```
Tecton sentence ::=  Tecton definition |  Tecton abbreviation
    |  Tecton lemma  |  Tecton extension  |  Tecton realization
```

Each of the sentence forms introduces or refers to a concept name, called the *subject* of the sentence. A definition, concept abbreviation, or realization defines its subject, an extension adds information about new identifiers to a concept while preserving the meaning it gives to other identifiers, while lemmas assert that certain properties follow from the definition of and extensions to the concept.

A concept description typically builds upon or modifies other concept descriptions, or both. It may name other concepts that it *refines* or *uses*, the distinction being based on whether it changes the meaning of identifiers in the other concepts, or merely uses the identifiers without any change in their meaning. Although identifier names are part of the semantics of concepts, new names can be substituted at any time. Such substitutions are introduced in *concept instances* of the form C [with y_1 as $x_1, \ldots, y_n$ as x_n], where C is a previously given name, $x_1, \ldots, x_n$ are identifiers, and each y_i is an identifier being substituted for x_i.

3 Tecton Definitions

A Tecton definition is a concept description of the form:

```
Tecton definition   ::=
    Definition:  concept-identifier  {   refines-clause } { ; }
        {   uses-clause } { ; } {   introduces-clause } { ; }
        {   generates-clause } { ; } {   requires-clause } .
```

An introduces clause declares sorts and functions. A requires or generates clause requires the sets and functions of an algebra to have certain properties. A uses or refines clause is often used to develop new concepts based on previous ones. The following is a simple example.

```
Definition: Segment
  uses Natural;
  introduces segments < naturals, max : -> naturals;
  requires (for n: naturals)
    n in segments = (n < max).
```

Syntactic and semantic concepts. We associate both a *syntactic concept* and a *semantic concept* with a definition with subject A and they are denoted by syn A and sem A respectively. When we use just the word "concept" we mean the semantic concept. The formal definitions of these sets of algebras will be given in several stages, first for the simplest cases of concept definitions and subsequently for more complex cases. In all cases, as one consequence of the definitions, we have sem $A \subseteq$ syn A. In the following we often write **A** for sem A.

Simple concept definitions. For the moment, we only consider *simple concept definitions*, which have no **refines** or **uses** clause. Given a simple concept definition D, an algebra $(\mathcal{S}, \mathcal{F})$ belongs to syn A if and only if the sorts introduced in D belong to dom $\mathcal{S}$, the subsort declarations are satisfied (i.e., $\mathcal{S}(s_1) \subseteq \mathcal{S}(s_2)$ when $s_1 < s_2$), and the function descriptions introduced in D belong to dom $\mathcal{F}$.

Note that there may be other sorts or function descriptions in $(\mathcal{S}, \mathcal{F})$ besides those introduced in D. This is a significant difference from the usual approach in which each algebra associated with a syntactic description, called a signature, has exactly the sets and functions named in the signature. By allowing additional symbols in the algebras we obtain a relatively simple way of defining the semantics of combinations of concept descriptions in terms of set intersections.

Semantics of simple concept definitions. Let C be a concept description and let $a = (\mathcal{S}, \mathcal{F}) \in$ syn C. We define an $\mathcal{S}$ *valuation* ν to be a mapping of declared variables to values, in which the value $\nu(v)$ is in $\mathcal{S}(s)$ if v is of sort s. The value $a^\nu(p)$ that ν assigns to p is defined as usual and a belongs to **C** if and only if:

1. it belongs to syn C;
2. for each p in the requires clause, $a^\nu(p) =$ **true** for any $\mathcal{S}$ valuation ν;
3. the **generates** clause, if any, is satisfied.

4 Inheritance from Previous Concept Descriptions

The **refines** and **uses** clauses allow reuse of previously described concepts.

```
refines-clause  ::= refines  ingredient -LIST
uses-clause     ::= uses     component  -LIST
```

Both ingredients and components are concept instances, which are described in full generality in the next section.

Semantics of concept description with ingredients or components. Given a concept definition C with **refines** or **uses** clauses, let $C_1, \ldots, C_n$ be all of the components and ingredients that appear in C. An algebra a is in **C** if and only if $a \in \mathbf{C}_1 \cap \mathbf{C}_2 \cap \ldots \cap \mathbf{C}_n$ and each property in the **requires** list of C is a true statement about the sets and functions of a.

Restriction requirements on ingredients and components. There are important semantic requirements on ingredients and components. To specify them, we first define *restriction*, *preserving*, and *modification*.

Definition of restriction. Let C and B be concept descriptions and $a \in \text{syn}\, C$. The *restriction* of a to B (notation: $a|_B$) is the subalgebra of a whose sorts and function descriptors are restricted to $\text{sig}\, B$ (the signature specified in B) and the restriction of $\mathbf{C}$ to B (notation: $\mathbf{C}|_B$) is defined to be $\{a|_B : a \in \mathbf{C}\}$.

Definition of preserving and modification. Let C and A be concept descriptions. We say that C *preserves* A if $\mathbf{C} \subset \mathbf{A}$ and $\mathbf{C}|_A = \mathbf{A}|_A$; and we say that C *modifies* A if $\mathbf{C}|_A \subset \mathbf{A}|_A$ and C preserves any concept description that A preserves.

Lemma 1. *Let B be a concept description and $a \in \text{syn}\, B$. Then*

$$a \in \mathbf{B} \quad \text{if and only if} \quad a|_B \in \mathbf{B}.$$

Lemma 2. *Let A, B, and C be concept descriptions. If $\mathbf{C} \subset \mathbf{B} \subset \mathbf{A}$, then*

$$(\mathbf{C}|_B)|_A = \mathbf{C}|_A.$$

Lemma 3. *(Transitivity) Let A, B, and C be concept descriptions.*

1. *If C modifies B and B modifies A, then C modifies A;*
2. *If C preserves B and B preserves A, then C preserves A.*

Lemma 4. *The* preserves *and* modifies *relations are strict partial orders.*

We now state the additional requirements on ingredients and components:

- If A is an ingredient of C, then it is required that C modifies A;
- If A is a component of C, then it is required that C preserves A.

In both cases, we have that C preserves any concept that A preserves. See Figure 1 for a graphical depiction of these requirements and relations.

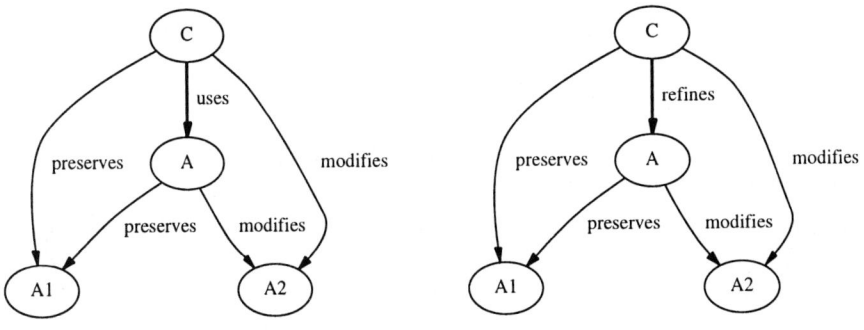

Fig. 1. Requirements on uses and refines clauses

In the following example

```
Definition: Binary-op
  uses Domain;
  introduces +(domain,domain) -> domain.
```

the semantic requirement on the Domain component is that

$$\text{Binary-op} \subset \text{Domain} \quad \text{and} \quad \text{Binary-op}|_{\text{Domain}} = \text{Domain}|_{\text{Domain}}$$

The proper subset relation between the concepts follows from the fact that there is one more function, +, in Binary-op than in Domain. Equality between the restrictions holds trivially because there is no requires clause in the description of Binary-op. However, in the following algebraic concept descriptions

```
Definition: Associative
  refines Binary-op;
  requires (for x, y, z: domain) x + (y + z) = (x + y) + z.

Definition: Commutative
  refines Binary-op;
  requires (for x, y: domain) x + y = y + x.

Definition: Identity
  refines Binary-op;
  introduces 0 -> domain;
  requires (for x: domain)
    x + 0 = x,
    0 + x = x.
```

Associative, Commutative, and Identity modify Binary-op with additional properties, thereby eliminating some algebras that were in Binary-op.

5 Concept Instances

Tecton definitions do not have explicit parameters; instead, one can treat many internal constituents of a definition as parameters subject to replacement. This gives the language user greater flexibility than if parameters had to be explicitly listed at the time of definition, for it is often difficult to anticipate which constituents it might be useful to substitute for in any subsequent use of the defined concept. At the same time, we want to prohibit replacements that could lead to syntactic or sort incorrectness, or to semantic inconsistency with the requirements imposed on ingredients and components. These considerations motivate the following definition of concept instance:

```
concept-instance ::= concept-name { [ with   replacement -LIST ] }
concept-name     ::= concept-identifier { by  concept-identifier }
replacement      ::= sort as sort
                   | function-descriptor as function-descriptor
                   | concept-name as concept-name
```

Below we address sort correctness and legality requirements on replacements.

5.1 The Simple Case

Syntactic and sort-correctness requirements. Let

$$C = B \; [\texttt{with} \; y_1 \; \texttt{as} \; x_1, \ldots, y_n \; \texttt{as} \; x_n],$$

where only sort and function replacements are applied. Since function descriptors are typed by sort lists, sort replacements must be processed in advance. First, we introduce the notion of *relabeling*: let c be a string or sequence of strings and $u_1, \ldots, u_n, v_1, \ldots, v_n$ be strings. Then by $c[v_1/u_1, \ldots, v_n/u_n]$, called a *relabeling* of c, we denote the result of simultaneous replacements of all occurrences (if any) of u_1 by v_1, ..., u_n by v_n in c.

Suppose now the replacement list is rewritten to

$$[\texttt{with} \; g_1 \; \texttt{as} \; f_1, \ldots, g_k \; \texttt{as} \; f_k, v_1 \; \texttt{as} \; u_1, \ldots, v_l \; \texttt{as} \; u_l],$$

where g_i and f_i are function descriptors ($i = 1, \ldots, k$), v_j and u_j are sorts ($j = 1, \ldots, l$). We require that if f_i is available with arity $(s_{i_1}, \ldots, s_{i_p}) \to (r_{j_1}, \ldots, r_{j_q})$, then g_i must be consistent with arity

$$((s_{i_1}, \ldots, s_{i_p}) \to (r_{j_1}, \ldots, r_{j_q}))[v_1/u_1, \ldots, v_l/u_l].$$

Semantics. We turn next to defining **C** from **B** and the replacement list. Let $a = (\mathcal{S}, \mathcal{F})$ be any algebra in **B**. Define $\mathcal{S}'$ and $\mathcal{F}'$ by

$$\mathcal{S}' = \{(s[y_1/x_1, \ldots, y_n/x_n], S) : (s, S) \in \mathcal{S}\}$$
$$\mathcal{F}' = \{(\sigma[y_1/x_1, \ldots, y_n/x_n], f) : (\sigma, f) \in \mathcal{F}\}$$

If $\mathcal{F}'$ is not a mapping, then we discard this algebra a. Otherwise, $a' = (\mathcal{S}', \mathcal{F}')$ is an algebra and we call a' *the relabeling of a using* $y_1/x_1, \ldots, y_n/x_n$. Now let a'' be any algebra $(\mathcal{S}'', \mathcal{F}'')$ such that $\mathcal{S}'' \supseteq \mathcal{S}'$ and $\mathcal{F}'' \supseteq \mathcal{F}'$. Then $a'' \in \mathbf{C}$, and the only algebras in **C** are those obtainable in this way, i.e.,

$$\mathbf{C} = \{a'' \mid a \in \mathbf{B}\}.$$

5.2 The General Case

More generally, let the concept instance C be

$$B \; [\texttt{with} \; B_1 \; \texttt{as} \; A_1, \ldots, B_m \; \texttt{as} \; A_m, y_1 \; \texttt{as} \; x_1, \ldots, y_n \; \texttt{as} \; x_n],$$

where $A_1, \ldots, A_m, B_1, \ldots, B_m$ are concept names and $x_1, \ldots, x_n, y_1, \ldots, y_n$ are sorts and function descriptors.

Syntactic and sort-correctness requirements. In addition to the requirements for the sort and function replacements [with y_1 as $x_1, \ldots, y_n$ as x_n], the following conditions must hold:

$$\text{sig } B_1 \cup \text{sig } B_2 \cup \cdots \cup \text{sig } B_m \supseteq \text{sig } A'_1 \cup \text{sig } A'_2 \cup \cdots \cup \text{sig } A'_m$$

where $A'_i = A_i$ [with y_1 as $x_1, \ldots, y_n$ as x_n] for $i = 1, \ldots, m$. With these assumptions, substituting B_i for A_i in B will not lead to lack of sorts or function identifiers which were originally used by B and will also be used in C.

Semantics. Let B^* be B [with y_1 as $x_1, \ldots, y_n$ as x_n]. Then we define **C** by

$$\mathbf{C} = \mathbf{B}^* \cap \mathbf{B}_1 \cap \cdots \cap \mathbf{B}_m.$$

5.3 Legality Requirements for Replacements

In the case of concept name replacements B_i as A_i, we have two further semantic requirements for **refines** and **uses** clauses respectively. The key point is to keep the semantic structure of B in C. Since A_i acts as a constituent of B, there must be some concept instance A'_i of A_i such that A'_i is preserved or modified in the concept development of B, i.e., $\mathbf{B} \subset \mathbf{A}'_i$. So, there is a (possibly empty) replacement list [with z_{i_1} as $w_{i_1}, \ldots, z_{i_k}$ as w_{i_k}] (which may also contain concept name replacements) such that

$$A'_i = A_i \text{ [with } z_{i_1} \text{ as } w_{i_1}, \ldots, z_{i_k} \text{ as } w_{i_k}], \quad \mathbf{B} \subset \mathbf{A}'_i. \tag{1}$$

Let $B'_i = B_i\,(([\text{with } z_{i_1} \text{ as } w_{i_1}, \ldots, z_{i_k} \text{ as } w_{i_k}])[y_1/x_1, \ldots, y_n/x_n])$. Recursively, we here assume the legality requirements for all A'_i and B'_i themselves have been satisfied already. Now, if

$$\mathbf{B}|_{A'_i} \subset \mathbf{A}'_i|_{A'_i}, \tag{2}$$

then A'_i acts as an ingredient of B and we require

$$\mathbf{C}|_{B'_i} \subset \mathbf{B}'_i|_{B'_i}. \tag{3}$$

and additionally C preserves any concept description that B'_i preserves.

This means that after replacement B'_i looks like an ingredient of C. Henceforth, B_i plays the same role in C as A_i does in B. But if

$$\mathbf{B}|_{A'_i} = \mathbf{A}'_i|_{A'_i}, \tag{4}$$

then A'_i acts as a component in B and we require

$$\mathbf{C} \subset \mathbf{B}'_i, \quad \mathbf{C}|_{B'_i} = \mathbf{B}'_i|_{B'_i}. \tag{5}$$

to guarantee that B'_i also acts as a component of C.

A sufficient condition for (1) to hold is that some concept instance A'_i of A_i be a component or ingredient in the concept description named by B. When B'_i and B have no common signature symbols other than sig A'_i, we may deliver simpler conditions for (3) and (5). If A'_i is an ingredient, then we require that either $\mathbf{B}'_i = \mathbf{A}'_i$ or B'_i refine some functions in A'_i in a different way from B, i.e.,

$$\mathbf{B}'_i \subseteq \mathbf{A}'_i, \quad \mathbf{B}'_i|_{A'_i} - \mathbf{B}|_{A'_i} \neq \emptyset,$$

which ensures condition (3). On the other hand, if A'_i is a component then the requirement (5) may reduce to

$$\mathbf{B}'_i \subseteq \mathbf{A}'_i.$$

In fact, we have the following lemmas which cover the most commonly occurring cases. The proofs can be found in [14].

Lemma 5. *Let A, B, and C be concept descriptions such that $\mathbf{C}|_A \subset \mathbf{A}|_A$, $\mathbf{B}|_A - \mathbf{C}|_A \neq \emptyset$, $\mathbf{B} \subseteq \mathbf{A}$, $\operatorname{sig} C \cap \operatorname{sig} B = \operatorname{sig} A$. If D is C [with B as A], then $\mathbf{D}|_B \subset \mathbf{B}|_B$.*

Lemma 6. *Let A, B, and C be concept descriptions such that C preserves A, $\mathbf{B} \subseteq \mathbf{A}$, $\operatorname{sig} C \cap \operatorname{sig} B = \operatorname{sig} A$. If D is C [with B as A], then D preserves B.*

In effect, the ingredients and components that appear in the process of developing a base concept description are formal parameters and can be replaced using other concept names as actual parameters. Even more generally, concepts not explicitly named in the base concept description, or even in the inheritance chain, can be treated as parameters so long as the legality conditions can be established for them. For example, in the following concept instance,

```
Exponentiation
   [with Natural as Mult-monoid,
        *(naturals, naturals)->naturals as *(domain, domain)->domain,
        1->naturals as 1->domain,
        naturals as domain],
```

it suffices for `Mult-monoid` to appear as a component in `Exponentiation`, the syntactic concept of `Natural` to be contained in that of `Mult-monoid` [with *(naturals, naturals)->naturals as *(domain, domain)->domain, 1-> naturals as 1->domain, naturals as domain], and all function identifiers in `Natural` to keep their meanings unchanged in `Exponentiation`.

5.4 Tecton Abbreviations

A concept abbreviation

```
Tecton abbreviation ::=
    Abbreviation: concept-name is concept-instance .
```

is just a way of naming a concept instance with a new name. For `Abbreviation: C is A`, we define $\operatorname{syn} C = \operatorname{syn} A$ and $\mathbf{C} = \mathbf{A}$. Below are a few examples:

```
Abbreviation: Semigroup is Associative.
Abbreviation: Monoid is Semigroup [with Identity as Binary-op].
Abbreviation: Commutative-monoid is Monoid
              [with Commutative as Binary-op].
```

In Tecton abbreviations are more than a convenience; when Tecton's strict legality conditions on **uses** and **refines** clauses prevent writing a specification one way, there is often an alternative in which one first writes an abbreviation. For example, suppose we are developing a `Sequence` concept where the sequence elements are required to have the properties of a `Monoid`:

```
Sequence uses Monoid ....
```

Now if we attempt to describe a concept X with

    Definition: X refines Sequence;
      requires (for some x, y: domain) not(x + y = y + x)

the legality conditions for the refines clause require that X preserves Monoid since Sequence preserves Monoid, but obviously X modifies Monoid. Thus this definition is illegal—which is good, because otherwise one could continue with

    Abbreviation: Y is X [with Commutative-monoid as Monoid]

with the result that Y is an empty (inconsistent) concept, because the requirements include both x + y = y + x and not(x + y = y + x).

Instead of defining X as above, we can write

    Definition: Noncommutative-monoid refines Monoid;
      requires (for some x, y: domain) not(x + y = y + x).
    Abbreviation: X is Sequence [with Noncommutative-monoid as Monoid].

This instance is legal because Sequence preserves Monoid and X preserves Noncommutative-monoid. In this specification style it is explicit that Monoid is being modified, and the resulting concept X cannot be instantiated with Commutative-monoid to produce an inconsistency. For example, if we try to define Y with

    Abbreviation: Y is
      X [with Commutative-monoid as Noncommutative-monoid]

this is illegal because X preserves Noncommutative-monoid, but Y modifies Commutative-monoid.

6 Concluding Remarks

The characterization of the semantic distinction between refines and uses constructs in terms of the *preserves* and *modifies* relations is part of a revision of the semantics of Tecton presented fully in [14]. These relations support an even more flexible way of developing new concepts based on previously described concepts than in previous versions of Tecton or in other languages such as CASL. The new legality conditions prevent certain ways of refining concepts that would otherwise be prone to later errors in combining specifications. Instead, an alternative style of specification is offered in terms of concept use, limited cases of concept refinement, and abbreviations, resulting in concepts that can be more safely combined and extended in later definitions. We are using this version of Tecton to rewrite concept libraries, mainly including algebraic systems, relations and orderings, and generic sorting algorithms, and find that many concepts may be described by abbreviations instead of refinements. One of the advantages of doing so is that one can translate such specifications more directly into C++ declarations using parametric polymorphism (expressed with templates) rather than subtype polymorphism (expressed with class inheritance), thus avoiding the inefficiencies of virtual functions. In fact, we have succeeded in writing C++ templates for most of the algebraic concepts in [15] that previously had been expressed in Tecton with refinement and correspondingly in C++ with inheritance.

References

1. M. Bidoit. The stratified loose approach, a generalization of initial and loose semantics. In sl Recent Trends in Data Type Specification, LNCS 332, 1–22, Springer-Verlag, 1988.
2. S. Clerici and F. Orejas. GSBL: an algebraic specification language based on inheritance. *Proc. 1988 European Conf. on Object Oriented Programming*, Oslo. LNCS 322, 78–92, Springer-Verlag, 1988.
3. S. Clerici and F. Orejas. The specification language GSBL. In Recent Trends in Data Type Specification, LNCS 534, 31–51, Springer-Verlag, April 1991.
4. CoFI Language Design Task Group. CASL—The CoFI Algebraic Specification Language—Summary, March 2001. http://www.brics.dk/Projects/CoFI/Documents/CASL/Summary/
5. S. J. Garland, J. V. Guttag, and J. J. Horning. Debugging Larch Shared Language Specifications. *IEEE Trans. Software Engineering*, 16(9):1990, 1044-1057.
6. J. A. Goguen, T. Winker, J. Meseguer, K. Futatsugi, and J.-P. Jouannaud. Introducing OBJ. In J. A. Goguen, D. Coleman, and R. Gallimore (eds). *Applications of Algebraic Specification using OBJ*, Cambridge University Press, 1992.
7. J. V. Guttag and J. J. Horning. Report on the Larch Shared Language. *Sci. Comput. Program.*, 6(2):103-134, 1986.
8. D. Kapur and D. R. Musser. *Tecton: a framework for specifying and verifying generic system components*. Technical Report TR-92-20, Computer Science Department, Rensselaer Polytechnic Institute, July 1992.
9. D. Kapur, D. R. Musser, and A. A. Stepanov. Tecton: a language for manipulating generic objects. In *Proc. of Program Specification Workshop*, University of Aarhus, Denmark, August 1981, LNCS 134, Springer-Verlag, 1982.
10. D. R. Musser, *The Tecton concept description language*, September 1998. http://www.cs.rpi.edu/~musser/gp/
11. D. R. Musser, *Tecton description of STL container and iterator concepts*, November 1998. http://www.cs.rpi.edu/~musser/gp/
12. D. R. Musser, G. J. Derge, and A. Saini. *STL Tutorial and Reference Guide: C++ Programming with the Standard Template Library, Second Edition*. Addison-Wesley, 2001.
13. D. R. Musser, S. Schupp, C. Schwarzweller, and R. Loos. *The Tecton Concept Library*. Technical Report WSI-99-02, Wilhelm-Schickard-Institute for Computer Science, Universität Tübingen, September 1999.
14. D. R. Musser and Z. Shao, *The Tecton concept description language (revised version)*, Technical Report TR-02-03, Computer Science Department, Rensselaer Polytechnic Institute, 2002.
15. S. Schupp, D. Gregor, and D. R. Musser. *Algebraic Concepts Represented in C++*. Technical Report TR-00-8, Computer Science Department, Rensselaer Polytechnic Institute, 2000.
16. J. G. Siek, L.-Q. Lee, and A. Lumsdaine. *The Boost Graph Library: User Guide and Reference Manual*. Addison-Wesley, 2002.
17. J. G. Siek and A. Lumsdaine. The Matrix Template Library: A generic programming approach to high performance numerical linear algebra. In *International Symposium on Computing in Object-Oriented Parallel Environments*, 1998.

An Overview of Mobile Object-Z

Kenji Taguchi[1] and Jin Song Dong[2]

[1] Department of Information Science, Uppsala University,
Kenji.Taguchi@dis.uu.se
[2] Computer Science Department, National University of Singapore,
dongjs@comp.nus.edu.sg

Abstract. Mobile Object-Z (MobiOZ) is an extended notation of Object-Z with mobile and communication primitives required for mobile agent applications. In this paper, we will give an overview of the MobiOZ language features and present its semantic foundation. We also demonstrate expressiveness of the notation through a number of examples.

1 Introduction

Recently, the notion of the *mobile agent* has been proposed in order to capture the new form of computation in communication networks. A mobile agent is a computing entity which can move around different hosts on the network, carrying its state and procedures. To support this new computation paradigm, many programming languages and systems have been developed, i.e., Telescript [16], Obliq [2] and Aglets [9]. However these languages and systems are not suitable to be applied at the specification and design level for mobile agents development because they are too involved with implementation details. Much higher level formalisms such as the π-calculus [11], Mobile Ambients [4] and, $D\pi$ [13] have been proposed. Although these formalisms are elegant and can capture the semantics of mobile agent behaviours, they generally cannot scale up for modelling complex mobile agent systems which often have complex data and state properties.

In this paper, we will give an overview of an extension of Object-Z [7, 14] for mobile agent applications (called MobiOZ), and present its semantic foundation based on labelled transition systems. MobiOZ includes mobile primitives inspired by Telescript [16], and communication primitives in process algebras. The design principle of the language has its source in the integrations of state-based and behavioural formalisms in Timed-CSP and Object-Z (TCOZ) [10], and CCS and Z [15].

The notion of locality is a key concept in mobile agent languages and systems. That is, agents can only directly communicate with each other at a common location. Our key idea in designing MobiOZ is to add a *locality* dimension to the Object-Z language with various mobile primitives (i.e. *go, send, here* etc) for capturing agent mobility. In an analogous fashion, many real-time modelling languages add a *time* dimension to the un-timed languages with explicit timing operators (i.e. *wait, timeout, deadline* etc) for capturing timing properties directly. With the support of the new MobiOZ primitives, many complex behaviours of mobile agents can be effectively modelled.

MobiOZ is based on the Agent-Place model advocated in Telescript, which has two essential entities, *agents* and *places*. The main difference in the roles of these entities is that agents can move around the network, while places cannot. Agents are to bring information and exchange it with other agents at places. An agent needs to move to some place to meet and interact with other agents. Places are stationary entities which host mobile agents and can be regarded as physical hosts or logical entities (domains in the communication network).

The agent-place model has an intuitive metaphor of distributed computation and simplifies the specification of mobile applications such as electronic commerce. The specification technique in MobiOZ is to specify a mobile agent as an Object-Z class together with its behaviour as process formulae, which include a special process for an entry point of execution. Process formulae are semantically interpreted at a place, which is a holder of processes with an explicit address.

This paper is organised as follows: the next section illustrates the basic syntax of MobiOZ and Section 3 presents its operational semantics. Some example specifications are given in Section 4. Section 5 discusses the language features of MobiOZ and finally section 6 compares related work and concludes this paper.

2 Syntax

In this section the syntax of MobiOZ is explained. We assume that the readers are familiar with Object-Z [7, 14].

A basic type *Address* is preserved, which designates the unique address in the network.

[*Address*]

The communication model adopted by MobiOZ is based on the following doctrine [3], which is slightly different from the one adopted in Telescript[1].

– Local communication is synchronous
– Remote communication is asynchronous

All communication is written in a manner similar to that found in process algebras, and polyadic communication in which a channel may have more than one parameter, is allowed. The most important difference between channels in process algebras and MobiOZ is that channels in process algebras are constants, whereas channels in MobiOZ are declared as state variables in a class which may be assigned concrete channel names later. Let com_1, com_2 be state variables declared as channels of the same type in different classes, then an input channel com_1 and an output channel $\overline{com_2}$ can communicate each other, provided they refer to the same channel name.

Remote communication is achieved by associating the destination address together with the channel name in the form of $addr :: \overline{com}$. Again address may be denoted by a state variable. Hence the channel name and the address used in the remote communication can be changed by a π-calculus [11] style of communication.

---
[1] In Telescript, only local communication was implemented. However the model [16] supports *connection* which is a remote communication between agents residing at different places.

The syntax of the channel is outlined below:

$x, x_1, \ldots$	variable name	e	$::= x \mid V \mid l$
$V, V_1, \ldots$	constant name	$expr$	$::= e \mid f(e, \ldots, e)$
f	function name	$input\_action$	$::= com(x, \ldots, x)$
com	input channel name	$output\_action$	$::= \overline{com}\langle expr, \ldots, expr\rangle \mid$
$\overline{com}$	output channel name		$l :: \overline{com}\langle expr, \ldots, expr\rangle$
$l, m, l_1, \ldots$	address name		

A channel is declared in the state schema of an agent with its types by using the keyword **chan**, which is the pre-defined type for channels. Both input and output channels are declared in the same manner, but when they are used in process formulae, output channels must have a line over the symbol. In order to support the polyadic channel, the notation is strengthened by the use of parameterised types. com : **chan**$[T]$ declares a channel com with type T.

A mobile agent in MobiOZ has the following primitives:

$go(l)$	moves to the address
$send(<l, \ldots, l>)$	sends multiple copies to the addresses
$here(x)$	obtains the current address
$kill()$	kills itself

The primitive $go(l)$ will move the subsequent process to the designated address and start its execution at that address. The primitive $send(\langle l_1, \ldots, l_n\rangle)$ takes a sequence of addresses and creates multiple instances with unique new identities. The subsequent processes will start to execute at those addresses. It has a different semantics from the one in Telescript and will be discussed later in section 5. The primitive $here(x)$ returns the current address of the place, i.e., the variable x is instantiated by the current address. Finally, The primitive $kill()$ simply kills itself, i.e., its state and execution thread.

These primitives may be used in process formulae, and their semantic interpretation will be given in section 3.

Process formulae are defined at two different levels (agent and place). We will only show the syntax for agent level in this section:

$Op(x_1, \ldots, x_n)$	Parametric operation schema name
;	sequential operator
□	choice operator
$P(x_1, \ldots, x_n)$	process constant
0	null process
G	state guard

$$Guard\_Expr ::= G \bullet Op(x_1, \ldots, x_n) \mid$$
$$G \bullet input\_action \rightarrow Op(x_1, \ldots, x_n) \mid$$
$$G \bullet output\_action \rightarrow Op(x_1, \ldots, x_n)$$

$$Mobile\_Op ::= go(l) \mid$$
$$send(\langle l, \ldots, l \rangle) \mid$$
$$kill() \mid$$
$$here(x)$$

$$Proc ::= 0 \mid$$
$$P(x_1, \ldots, x_n) \mid$$
$$Guard\_Expr \mid$$
$$Mobile\_Op \mid$$
$$Proc \ ; \ Proc \mid$$
$$Proc \ \Box \ Proc$$

The syntax of operation schema in Object-Z is modified to have substituent parameters, which excludes input/output annotation '?'/'!' of variables (as various forms of channels indicate the input and output). The semantics of operation schemas are remined as atomic actions.

The defining equation which associates a process constant $P(x_1, \ldots, x_n)$ with a process expression $Proc$ is denoted by $P(x_1, \ldots, x_n) \hat{=} Proc$.

As the syntax indicates, inter-class concurrency is avoided in MobiOZ.

An agent is a class which represents a computing entity that can move around the network. An agent is specified as an Object-Z class with process definitions. An agent class is given in the following form:

MozClassAgent
OZ_Definition
Process_Definition

where *OZ_Definition* is an Object-Z class definition which includes axiomatic definitions, state schema, initial schema, operation schemas, but excludes Object-Z operators: parallel composition, nondeterministic choice and sequential composition. Those operators are replaced by process formulae previously defined. *Process_Definition* is a set of defining equations.

We will not introduce a basic type for the unique identity of agents, since the reference semantics of Object-Z implicitly supports the unique identity of objects of a class which can also assure the unique identity of agents in MobiOZ.

Each agent with process definitions must have a particular process constant *Beh*, which designates an entry point of its execution.

3 Operational Semantics

In this section, we will present the operational semantics of MobiOZ based on labelled transition systems. In order to interpret mobile primitives in process formulae and subsequent state changes, we need to incorporate an explicit notion of locations and states with identity in the semantics.

Address denotes the set of all addresses, *State*, the set of all states, and *ID* the set of all implicit identities of Object-Z classes.

We will use the following symbols for this purpose:

$\sigma, \sigma', \ldots$ semantic function for state
$a, b, \ldots$ class identity

We first lift up the syntax of process formulae by assigning an address, a state and its identity.

$$[\![\cdot]\!] : Proc \longrightarrow Proc \times Address \times State \times ID$$

The state and location of each agent may be different from each other so that each semantic function which models the state of an agent is subscripted by its implicit identity and a process formula is associated with an address. We will use the notation $l[\![P]\!]_{\sigma_a}$ to denote the lifted process formula P with its state σ_a with an object identity a at an address l, where l is the address of a place where the process runs.

We will now define process formulae with explicit location and state with identity as below:

$$\mathcal{P}, \mathcal{Q}, \mathcal{P}', \ldots ::= 0 \mid l[\![P]\!]_{\sigma_a} \mid \mathcal{P} \parallel \mathcal{P}$$

where $\parallel$ is the parallel composition of explicitly located process formulae.

Mobile agents residing at the same address can be easily distinguished by this notation. For instance, $l[\![P]\!]_{\sigma_a} \parallel l[\![Q]\!]_{\sigma_b}$, where a and b stand for agent identifiers, σ_a and σ_b for their agent states and P and Q are process formulae owned by different agents. Each mobile agent class has its unique entry point of execution that is designated by the process constant *Beh* so that the execution of each mobile agent starts at some address $l[\![Beh]\!]_{\sigma_a}$.

The semantics of Object-Z classes is often given using a state transition model in which operations make an old (before) state evolve to a new (after) state. We use the convention for semantics functions in which σ stands for an old state and σ' for a new state, and the state evolution caused by an operation Op will be denoted by the following notation:

$$\sigma, \sigma' \models Op(V_1, \ldots, V_n)$$

which reads that an operation $Op(V_1, \ldots, V_n)$ is valid under σ, σ'. A guard expression G is evaluated under a single state so that

$$\sigma \models G$$

In case of parametric operation $Op(x_1, \ldots, x_n)$ which takes n arguments, we assume that all parameters $x_1, \ldots, x_n$ appear in Op, and the result of all values taken in $Op(V_1, \ldots, V_n)$ is the replacement of all variables by corresponding values.

We will only deal with monadic communication in the semantics for sake of brevity. Given the following actions:

$$\alpha, \beta ::= \tau \mid go(l) \mid send(\langle l_1, \ldots, l_n \rangle) \mid here(l) \mid kill() \mid com(V) \mid \overline{com}\langle V \rangle \mid l :: \overline{com}\langle V \rangle \mid Op(V_1, \ldots, V_n)$$

we can now define the labelled transition semantics $< \mathcal{P}, \{ \stackrel{\alpha}{\longrightarrow} \mid \alpha \in A \} >$, where A is the set of all actions defined above.

The operational semantics of MobiOZ is given by derivation rules and congruence relations.

Some primitives take their arguments from state variables defined in a class in the derivation rules. This makes the following derivation rules different from ones in process algebras in which only parameters are passed to process formulae.

We will introduce the following symbol for addresses in order to simplify rules for mobile primitives:

$addr, addr_1, \ldots ::= x \mid l$

[Go Primitive]

$$\frac{\sigma_a(addr) = m}{l[\![go(addr)\ ;\ P]\!]_{\sigma_a} \xrightarrow{go(m)} m[\![P]\!]_{\sigma_a}}$$

If $addr$ in $go(addr)$ is a state variable defined in that agent with the id a, then it enables the subsequent process to move to the address it denotes by the semantic function σ_a.

Note that $\sigma_a(addr) = addr$, if $addr$ is a constant.

[Send Primitive]

$$\frac{\sigma_a(addr_1) = k_1, \ldots, \sigma_a(addr_n) = k_n}{l[\![send(\langle addr_1, \ldots, addr_n \rangle)\ ;\ P]\!]_{\sigma_a} \xrightarrow{send(\langle k_1, \ldots, k_n \rangle)} k_1[\![P]\!]_{\sigma_{b_1}} \|\ \ldots\ \| k_n[\![P]\!]_{\sigma_{b_n}}}$$

If $addr_1, \ldots, addr_n$ in $send(\langle addr_1, \ldots, addr_n \rangle)$ are state variables defined in that agent with its identity a, the subsequent process will migrate to the addresses denoted by the semantic function σ_a. The subsequent processes are interpreted by the same semantic function with newly created identities $b_1, \ldots, b_n$.

[Here Primitive]

$$\frac{\sigma'_a = \sigma_a \oplus \{x \mapsto l\}}{l[\![here(x)\ ;\ P]\!]_{\sigma_a} \xrightarrow{here(l)} l[\![P]\!]_{\sigma'_a}}$$

The *here* primitive obtains the current address. If the x in $here(x)$ is a state variable defined in a class with an identity a, it causes a state change.

$\oplus$ is the function overriding symbol in Z. Hence $\sigma'_a = \sigma_a \oplus \{x \mapsto l\}$ means that σ'_a is the same as σ_a except an assignment of value l to a variable x.

[Kill Primitive]

$$\frac{}{l[\![kill()\ ;\ P]\!]_{\sigma_a} \xrightarrow{kill()} l[\![0]\!]_{\varnothing}}$$

The *kill* makes the agent's state empty and all subsequent processes are ignored.

We will denote substitution of variables $x_1, \ldots, x_n$ by $V_1, \ldots, V_n$ in a process P by $P\{x_1/V_1, \ldots, x_n/V_n\}$.

[Object-Z Operation]

$$\frac{\sigma_a \models G,\ \sigma_a, \sigma'_a \models Op(V_1, \ldots, V_n)}{l[\![G \bullet Op(x_1, \ldots, x_n)\ ;\ P]\!]_{\sigma_a} \xrightarrow{Op(V_1, \ldots, V_n)} l[\![P\{x_1/V_1, \ldots, x_n/V_n\}]\!]_{\sigma'_a}}$$

[Input Prefix]

$$\frac{\sigma'_a = \sigma_a \oplus \{x \mapsto V\},\ \sigma'_a \models G, \sigma'_a, \sigma''_a \models Op(V)}{l[\![G \bullet com(x) \to Op(x)\ ;\ P]\!]_{\sigma_a} \xrightarrow{com(V)} l[\![P\{x/V\}]\!]_{\sigma''_a}}$$

Input channel receives a value, which causes a state change as well as instantiating a value to the subsequent process.

[Output Prefix]

$$\frac{\sigma_a \models G, \sigma_a(expr) = V, \sigma_a, \sigma_a' \models Op}{l[\![G \bullet \overline{com}\langle expr \rangle \to Op \ ; \ P]\!]_{\sigma_a} \xrightarrow{\overline{com}\langle V \rangle} l[\![P]\!]_{\sigma_a'}}$$

Output channel may take some expression *expr* which will be evaluated under the semantic function σ_a.

[Asynchronous Output Prefix]

$$\frac{}{l[\![\overline{com}\langle V \rangle]\!]_\varnothing \xrightarrow{\overline{com}\langle V \rangle} l[\![0]\!]_\varnothing}$$

Asynchronous communication of MobiOZ is based on asynchronous π-calculus in which only a bare output channel without subsequent process is allowed. This bare output channel is only produced by the next rule which describes behaviour of asynchronous remote communication.

[Asynchronous Remote Communication Prefix]

$$\frac{\sigma_a \models G, \sigma_a(expr) = V, \sigma_a, \sigma_a' \models Op}{l[\![G \bullet k :: \overline{com}\langle expr \rangle \to Op \ ; \ P]\!]_{\sigma_a} \xrightarrow{k::\overline{com}\langle V \rangle} k[\![\overline{com}\langle V \rangle]\!]_\varnothing \ || \ l[\![P]\!]_{\sigma_a'}}$$

Once an agent sends a bare output channel to a designated address, the subsequent process remains at the same address. The bare output channel only carries a value without a state.

[Synchronisation]

$$\frac{l[\![P]\!]_{\sigma_a} \xrightarrow{com\langle V \rangle} l[\![P']\!]_{\sigma_a'} \ \ l[\![Q]\!]_{\sigma_b} \xrightarrow{\overline{com}\langle V \rangle} l[\![Q']\!]_{\sigma_b}}{l[\![P]\!]_{\sigma_a} \ || \ l[\![Q]\!]_{\sigma_b} \xrightarrow{\tau} l[\![P']\!]_{\sigma_a'} \ || \ l[\![Q']\!]_{\sigma_b}}$$

As the rule describes, two agents which communicate with each other must reside at the same place.

[Process Definition]

$$\frac{l[\![Proc\{x_1/V_1, \ldots, x_n/V_n\}]\!] \xrightarrow{\alpha} \mathcal{P}}{l[\![P(V_1, \ldots, V_n)]\!] \xrightarrow{\alpha} \mathcal{P}} \quad P(x_1, \ldots, x_n) \ \widehat{=} \ Proc$$

[Interleaving]

$$\frac{\mathcal{P}_1 \xrightarrow{\alpha} \mathcal{P}_1'}{\mathcal{P}_1 \ || \ \mathcal{P}_2 \xrightarrow{\alpha} \mathcal{P}_1' \ || \ \mathcal{P}_2}$$

[Congruence]

$$\frac{\mathcal{P} \equiv \mathcal{P}' \quad \mathcal{P} \xrightarrow{\alpha} \mathcal{Q} \quad \mathcal{Q} \equiv \mathcal{Q}'}{\mathcal{P}' \xrightarrow{\alpha} \mathcal{Q}'}$$

There are two kinds of congruence relations, one at the process level and another at the place level. For any $l \in Address$, any $\sigma \in States$ and any $a \in ID$,

$$l[\![0]\!]_\varnothing \equiv 0 \qquad\qquad \mathcal{P} \parallel 0 \equiv \mathcal{P}$$
$$l[\![P \Box Q]\!]_{\sigma_a} \equiv l[\![Q \Box P]\!]_{\sigma_a} \qquad\qquad \mathcal{P}_1 \parallel \mathcal{P}_2 \equiv \mathcal{P}_2 \parallel \mathcal{P}_1$$
$$l[\![(P \Box Q) \Box R]\!]_{\sigma_a} \equiv l[\![P \Box (Q \Box R)]\!]_{\sigma_a} \qquad (\mathcal{P}_1 \parallel \mathcal{P}_2) \parallel \mathcal{P}_3 \equiv \mathcal{P}_1 \parallel (\mathcal{P}_2 \parallel \mathcal{P}_3)$$
$$l[\![(0;\ P)]\!]_{\sigma_a} \equiv l[\![P]\!]_{\sigma_a}$$
$$l[\![(P;\ 0)]\!]_{\sigma_a} \equiv l[\![P]\!]_{\sigma_a}$$

It must be noted that $l[\![0]\!]_\varnothing$ and $l[\![0]\!]_{\sigma_a}$ have significantly different meanings, which will be discussed in the section 5.

4 Examples

In this section, we will show a number of examples of how mobile agent applications can be specified in MobiOZ. The given types for those examples include:

[*Data*, *Name*]

4.1 Forwarding

Travelling is the basic functionality of mobile agents. In this first example, we present a simple scheme which describes how travelling agents is informed the next destination from a stationary agent at a place. This scheme is called *forwarding*.

Firstly a basic agent consists of three attributes *dest* (next location), *home* (original location) and *com* (communication channel). A forward agent is defined by inheriting the *BasicAgent* and will move to the next destination, once it receives an address *next_dest* from a channel *com*.

─ *BasicAgent* ──────────────
| *dest* : *Address*
| *home* : *Address*
| *com* : **chan**[*Address*]
─────────────────────────

─ *FAgent* ──────────────
| *BasicAgent*
| ─ *SetDest*(*next_dest* : *Address*) ──
| $\Delta(dest)$
| $dest' = next\_dest$
| ─────────────────
| $Beh \;\widehat{=}\; go(dest)\ ;\ com(next\_dest) \rightarrow$
| $\qquad SetDest(next\_dest)\ ;\ Beh$
─────────────────────────

4.2 Tracking

In this example, we will specify a simple scheme called *Registration* in [9]. This scheme consists of two agents, *Finder* which plays a role as a searcher and *Traveller* as a travelling agent, and a stationary agent *DBAgent* playing a role as a database, which keeps track of travelling agents. The travelling agent will report the current address to the database whenever it travels to some other place and the searcher will make a query to the database to find out the current location of the traveller.

Itinerary. A simple itinerary may be used by a travelling agent.

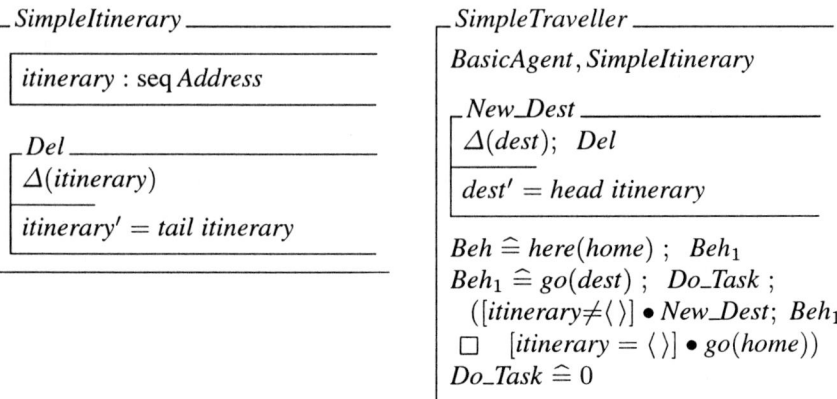

─ SimpleItinerary ─
itinerary : seq Address

─ Del ─
$\Delta(itinerary)$
$itinerary' = tail\ itinerary$

─ SimpleTraveller ─
BasicAgent, SimpleItinerary

─ New_Dest ─
$\Delta(dest);\ Del$
$dest' = head\ itinerary$

$Beh \mathrel{\hat{=}} here(home)\ ;\ Beh_1$
$Beh_1 \mathrel{\hat{=}} go(dest)\ ;\ Do\_Task\ ;$
$\quad ([itinerary \neq \langle\,\rangle] \bullet New\_Dest;\ Beh_1$
$\quad \Box\ [itinerary = \langle\,\rangle] \bullet go(home))$
$Do\_Task \mathrel{\hat{=}} 0$

In *SimpTraveller* class, an empty process definition *Do_Task* is introduced, which may be overridden by the specific subclasses of *SimpTraveller*.

─ Traveller ─
SimpleTraveller[**redef** Beh_1]

report : **chan**[Name, Address]
unreg : **chan**[Name]
db_addr : Address
name : Name

$Beh_1 \mathrel{\hat{=}}$
$\quad db\_addr :: \overline{report}\langle name, dest\rangle\ ;$
$\quad go(dest)\ ;\ Do\_Task\ ;$
$\quad ([itinerary \neq \langle\,\rangle] \bullet New\_Dest;\ Beh_1$
$\quad \Box$
$\quad [itinerary = \langle\,\rangle]\bullet$
$\quad db\_addr :: \overline{unreg}\langle name\rangle;\ go(home))$

─ Finder ─
BasicAgent

traveller_addr, db_addr : Address
traveller_name : Name
query : **chan**[Name, Address]
answer : **chan**[Address]

─ Get_Address(addr : Address) ─
$\Delta(traveller\_addr)$
$traveller\_addr' = addr$

$Beh \mathrel{\hat{=}}$
$db\_addr :: \overline{query}\langle traveller\_name, home\rangle;$
$answer(addr) \rightarrow Get\_Address(addr)$

The *Traveller* will be specified as a general subclass of the simple traveller. *Traveller* will use two remote communications to report the current address, and to notify that the traveller will no longer exist and the registry can be deleted. *db_addr* designates the address of the place where *DBAgent* will reside. *name* is the key of mobile agents on the database.

─ DBAgent ─
$db : Name \nrightarrow Address$
$report, query :$ **chan** $[Name, Address]$
$unreg :$ **chan** $[Name];\ answer :$ **chan** $[Address]$

$$
\begin{array}{|l}
\hline
\_Register(n : Name, current\_addr : Address)_____\\
\Delta(db)\\
\hline
db' = db \oplus \{n \mapsto current\_addr\}\\
\hline
\end{array}
$$

$Unregister(n : Name) \;\widehat{=}\; [\Delta(db) \mid db' = \{n\} \vartriangleleft db]$
$Beh \;\widehat{=}\; (report(n, current\_addr) \to Register(n, current\_addr)\square$
$\quad query(n, home) \to [n \in \text{dom}\, db] \bullet home :: \overline{answer}\langle db(n)\rangle\square$
$\quad unreg(n) \to Unregister(n))\; ;\; Beh$

Finder will use a channel *query* to make queries on the current address of the traveller, *answer* to receive the address.

Finally *DBAgent* will use a channel *query* to receive queries on the current address of the traveller, and *answer* to notify the address of the enquired mobile agent.

5 Language Features

MobiOZ can be best described as a *single-threaded* multi-agent with *strong mobility*. In this section, we discuss some of the language features of MobiOZ.

As was previously mentioned in the syntax section, MobiOZ does not allow interclass concurrency as agents are single-threaded. In this sense, MobiOZ is a formal specification language for single-threaded multi-agent systems. However, from a system point of view, it is multi-threaded.

The weak and strong mobility notions are used to describe the implementations of agent systems [5] and greatly affect the syntax of mobile agent languages [1]. Mobile agent systems and languages with weak mobility need to start execution at a remote host at the initial point of execution. Java based implementations of mobile agent systems such as Aglets [9] suffer this problem. Any statements followed by mobile primitives such as *go(addr)* will be ignored and re-start its execution at a specific entry point. In this sense, MobiOZ has a strong mobility.

MobiOZ supports asynchronous remote communication, but unlike the standard asynchronous communication which is characterised by unbounded FIFO queue of incoming messages, as our semantics shows that the asynchronous remote communication of MobiOZ behaves more non-deterministically.

It is easy to verify the following process formulae yields the same result by tracing transitions:

$here(x)\; ;\; go(m)\; ;\; \overline{com}\langle V\rangle\; ;\; go(x)\; ;\; P$
$m :: \overline{com}\langle V\rangle\; ;\; P$

A natural question arises why MobiOZ provides only one of them, if those two formulae will yield the same result. The main difference between the two comes into play at implementation level, not at the specification level. Mobile agent computation require very strict security and also consideration of the network load, which does not arise at the specification level. Remote communication is characterised as low security, but less network load. On the other hand messenger agents have high security and more network load.

Our aim was to design a wide spectrum formal specification language that can provide all necessary facilities for specifying of mobile agent applications. Hence we leave the choice to the specifiers which construct they would choose depending on their needs and requirements.

A mobile agent has its own thread of control and state so that the null process 0 which appears in a process formula does not necessarily mean that the agent's state is demolished (garbage collected) together with its process. In order to explicitly specify that its state as well as its process is abandoned, the *kill*() primitive is introduced in MobiOZ.

6 Related Work and Conclusion

There are a number of stateless basic formalisms such as mobile calculi which model several forms of mobility ranging from passing channel names in the π-calculus [11], to dynamic change of hierarchical structures in *Mobile Ambients* [4]. Indeed, our mobile and communication primitives, and their semantic interpretations are indebted to those works.

However we regard MobiOZ as a stateful high-level formal specification language in which mobile agents are stateful objects that carry their states and procedures while they are travelling around the network. Stateful mobile agents require more elaborate locking mechanisms for mobility than those stateless basic formalisms in order to avoid a circumstance in which some process migrates to other host while the rest of processes remain. This is why MobiOZ does not allow inter-object concurrency.

We have witnessed that the main trend of stateful high-level languages for mobile agents is based on Linda which includes LLinda [6] and LIME [12]. LLinda enhances the Linda model with distributed and multiple tuple spaces with access controls. LIME is equipped with reactive programming primitives, in addition to location sensitive access controls.

Another notable example is MobileUnity [8], which is an extension of Unity with mobile and reactive primitives, and their associated proof methods. Mobility is achieved by attaching a distinguished variable for location to each program and change of location is mimicked by assigning a new location to that variable.

Even they are powerful enough to simulate main mobile features of other formalism, e.g., LLinda could simulate the private name passing and the scope extrusion mechanism of the π-calculus [6], they are not readily applicable for the development of mobile agent systems due to the lack of corresponding mobile primitives and a different underlying model for mobile agents.

This conceptual mismatch between those formalisms and existing programming languages and systems makes them hard to be used to develop mobile agent applications.

In this paper, we have given an overview of an integrated formal specification language MobiOZ for mobile agent applications and presented its semantics which separates agent's states with agent's identifiers and captures state changes while the agent is moving around the network.

There are many research issues that remain to be addressed, including enhancement of language features by more powerful communication mechanism such as broadcasting, and verification procedures based on the semantics presented in this paper. We are planning to develop the verification method based on a version of Hennessy-Milner logic based on labelled transition systems presented in this paper.

Acknowledgements

We would like to thank Gabriel Ciobanu and Hugh Anderson for many helpful comments. This work is partially supported by the Academic Research grant *Integrated Formal Methods* from National University of Singapore.

References

1. L. Bettini and R. De Nicola. Translating Strong Mobility into Weak Mobility. In *Proceedings of 5th International Conference on Mobile Agents (MA) 2001*. IEEE, 2001.
2. L. Cardelli. A Language with Distributed Scope. In *Conference Record of POPL'95*, pages 286–297. ACM Press, 1995.
3. L. Cardelli. Wide Area Computation. *ICALP'99*, pages 10–24. 1999.
4. L. Cardelli and A. Gordon. Mobile Ambients. *Foundations of Software Science and Computational Structures*, pages 140–155. Springer-Verlag, 1998.
5. G. Cugola, C. Ghezzi, G. Picco, and G. Vigna. Analyzing Mobile Code Languages. *Mobile Object Systems - Towards the Programmable Internet*, pages 93–111. 1997.
6. R. De Nicola, G. Ferrari, and R. Pugliese. Locality based Linda: programming with explicit localities. *TAPSOFT-FASE'97*, pages 712-726. Springer-Verlag, 1997.
7. R. Duke and G. Rose. *Formal Object Oriented Specification Using Object-Z*. Cornerstones of Computing. Macmillan, March 2000.
8. P. J. M. G.-C. Roman and J. Y. Plun. Mobile unity: reasoning and specification in mobile computing. *ACM Trans. Software Engineering and Methodology*, 6(3):250–282, 1997.
9. D. Lange and M. Oshima. *Programming and Deploying Java Mobile Agents with Aglets*. Addison-Wesley, 1999.
10. B. Mahony and J. S. Dong. Blending Object-Z and Timed CSP: An Introduction to TCOZ. ICSE'98, pages 95–104. IEEE, 1998.
11. R. Milner. *Communicating and mobile systems : the π-calculus*. Cambridge University Press, 1999.
12. G. Picco, A. Murphy, and G.-C. Roman. LIME:Linda Meets Mobility. *ICSE'99*, pages 368–377, IEEE, 1999.
13. J. Riely and M. Hennessy. A typed language for distributed mobile processes (extended abstract). *POPL'98*, pages 378–390, 1998.
14. G. Smith. *The Object-Z Specification Language*. Kluwer Academic Publishers, 2000.
15. K. Taguchi and K. Araki. The State-based CCS Semantics for Concurrent Z Specification. *ICFEM'97*, pages 283–292. IEEE, 1997.
16. J. E. White. Mobile Agents. In J. Bradshaw, editor, *Software Agents*, pages 437–472. MIT Press, 1996.

Z Approach to Semantic Web

Jin Song Dong, Jing Sun, and Hai Wang

School of Computing,
National University of Singapore,
{dongjs,sunjing,wangh}@comp.nus.edu.sg

Abstract. The Semantic Web (SW) service is a web application using Semantic Web techniques which usually involve cooperation between several intelligent agents. The design of SW systems requires precise modelling techniques to capture ontology domain properties and application functionalities. We believe that Z as a specification technique can contribute to the Semantic Web-based system development in many ways. In this paper, we firstly conduct a case study of applying Z to the design of a SW service system (online talk discovery), and then present translation techniques and tools which can extract the SW ontology from the Z model automatically. Furthermore, we discuss how existing Z tools, i.e. Z/EVES, can be used to improve the quality of SW ontology design.

Keywords: Z, Semantic Web

1 Introduction

In recent years, researchers have begun to explore the potential of associating web content with explicit meaning so that the web content becomes more machine-readable and intelligent agents can retrieve and manipulate pertinent information readily. The Semantic Web (SW) [3] proposed by W3C is one of the most promising and accepted approaches. It has been regarded as the next generation of the web. The Semantic Web service is a web application using Semantic Web techniques which usually involve cooperation between several intelligent agents. Some Semantic Web services have been successfully developed recently, e.g. ITTAKLS [2].

The development of Semantic Web systems requires precise modelling techniques to capture ontology domain properties and application functionalities. The Z notation[12] is a formal specification language based on set theory and predicate calculus. We believe that Z as a specification technique can contribute to the Semantic Web-based system development in many ways. In this paper, we take a Semantic Web service example, i.e. the online talk discovery system, and apply Z to the design this Semantic Web service system. This online talk discovery system is a simplified version of the ITTALKS system [2] which is a real life Semantic Web service case study.

The remainder of the paper is organized as follows. Section 2 briefly introduces the Semantic Web. Section 3 formally specifies the functionalities of the Semantic Web service example (Talks discovery system). Section 4 presents the tools which extract the ontology used by the SW service from the Z design model automatically. Section 5 discusses how Z tools can be used to improve the quality of Semantic Web design. Section 6 concludes the paper.

2 Semantic Web Overview

The Semantic Web is a series of technologies proposed by W3C as the next generation web. It extends the current one by giving the web content a well-defined meaning, better enabling computers and people to work in cooperation. HTML, the current Web data standard, is aimed at delivering information to the end user for human-consumption (e.g. display this document). XML is aimed at delivering data to systems that can understand and interpret the information. XML is focused on the syntax (defined by the XML schema or DTD) of a document and it provides essentially a mechanism to declare and use simple data structures. However there is no way for a program to actually understand the knowledge contained in the XML documents.

Resource Description Framework (RDF) [7] is a foundation for processing metadata; it provides interoperability between applications that exchange machine-understandable information on the Web. RDF uses XML to exchange descriptions of Web resources and emphasizes facilities to enable automated processing. The RDF descriptions provide a simple ontology system to support the exchange of knowledge and semantic information on the Web. RDF Schema [4] provide the basic vocabulary to describe RDF vocabularies. RDF Schema can be used to define properties and types of the web resources. Similar to XML Schema which give specific constraints on the structure of an XML document, RDF Schema provide information about the interpretation of the RDF statements. The DARPA Agent Markup Language (DAML) [10] is a semantic markup language based on RDF/RDF-Schema and XML for Web resources. DAML currently combines Ontology Interchange Language (OIL) [5] and features from other ontology systems. It is now called DAML+OIL (DAML for short) and contains richer modeling primitives. DAML+OIL can dramatically improve traditional ad hoc information retrieval because its semantics will improve the quality of retrieval results. Semantic Web is highly distributed, and different parties may have different understanding for the same concept. Ideally, the program must have a way to discover the common meanings from the different understandings. It is central to another important conception in Semantic Web service – ontology. The ontology for a Semantic Web service is a document or file that formally defines the relations among terms. The most typical kind of ontology for the Web has a taxonomy and a set of inference rules. Ontologies can enhance the functioning of the Web in many ways, and RDFS and DAML supply the language to define the ontologies. For example, the following DAML code specifies that a 'talk' (a DAML class) has a property 'talk_place', having only one value 'place' (also a DAML class).

```
<daml:class rdf:ID="talk"> <rdfs:label>Talk</rdfs:label></daml:class>
<daml:class rdf:ID="place"><rdfs:label>Place</rdfs:label></daml:class>
<daml:ObjectProperty rdf:ID="talk_place">
   <rdf:type rdf:resource="http://www.daml.org/2001/03/daml+oil#UniqueProperty"/>
   <rdf:domain rdf:resource="#talk"/><rdf:range rdf:resource="#place"/>
</daml:ObjectProperty>
```

We will use the following notations to summarize the DAML constructs:

Table 1. A Partial Summary of the DAML constructs

Abstract DAML constructs	Description
$daml\_class$	classes
$daml\_subclass[C]$	subclasses of C
$daml\_objectproperty[D \leftrightarrow R]$	relation properties with domain D, range R
$daml\_objectproperty[D \rightarrow R]$	function properties with domain D, range R
$daml\_subproperty[P]$	sub properties of P
$instanceof[C]$	instances of the DAML class C

3 The Talks Discovery System

In this section, an online talks discovery system is used as an example to demonstrate how Z notation can be applied to the Semantic Web service development.

3.1 System Scenario

The Talks Discovery system is a web portal offering access to information about talks, seminars. This web portal can provide not only the talk's information corresponding to the user's profile in terms of his interest and location constraints, but also can further filter the IT related talks based on information about the user's personal schedule, etc.

In the course of operation, the Talks Discovery system discovers that there is an upcoming talk that may interest a registered user based on information in the user's preferences, which have been obtained from his online, DAML-encoded profile. Upon receiving this information, the user's User Agent needs to know more; it consults with its Calendar agent to determine the user's availability, and with the MapQuest agent to find the distance from the user's office to the talk's venue. We assume that a user only wants to attend the talks located within five miles from his office. Finally, after evaluating the information and making this decision, the User Agent will send a notification back to the TALK discovery agent indicating that the user will/will not plan to attend. The completed functionality of the ITTALKS system can be found at http://www.ittalks.org/jsp/Controller.jsp.

3.2 Formal Models of the Talk Discovery System

The system involves four different intelligent agents which communicated interactively. They are the user's Calendar agent, MapQuest agent, user's personal agent, and Talks discovery agent.

Calendar Agent. Firstly, the Date and Time set are defined by the Z given type definitions. As this paper focuses only on demonstrating the approach, we try to make the model simple. Z given type is chosen to define TIME, DATE and some other conceptions. These conceptions can be subdivided into detailed components, e.g. the TIME comprises hour, minute, and second. The more detailed the model is, the more detailed ontology derived automatically from our tool. This tool will be further discussed in the later section.

The *DateTime* was defined as a schema with two attributes date and time.

[TIME, DATE]

$\underline{\quad DateTime \quad\quad\quad\quad\quad\quad}$
$date : Date; \;\; time : Time$

Each user has its own Calendar agent which maintains the user's schedule and supplies some related services.
The *status* defined by the Z free type definition indicates if a person is free or busy.

$status ::= FREE \mid BUSY$

$\underline{\quad Calendar \quad\quad\quad\quad\quad\quad}$
$timetable : DateTime \rightarrow status$

Update is used to update the timetable. The operation *Check_free* is used to check whether a person is available or not for a particular time slot.

$\underline{\quad Update \quad\quad\quad\quad\quad}$
$\Delta Calendar$
$t? : DateTime; \;\; s? : status$
$\overline{timetable' = timetable \oplus \{(t?, s?)\}}$

$\underline{\quad Check\_free \quad\quad\quad\quad}$
$\Xi Calendar$
$dt? : DateTime$
$\overline{timetable(dt?) = FREE}$

MapQuest Agent. MapQuest agent is a third party agent supplying the service for calculating the distance between two places.

Firstly, the *place* is defined as a Z given type. The MapQuest agent contains a set of places in its domain and a database storing the distance between any two places.

[PLACE]

$\underline{\quad MapQuest \quad\quad\quad\quad\quad}$
$places : \mathbb{P}\, PLACE$
$distance : places \times places \rightarrow \mathbb{R}^+$

Operation *Get_dis* will output the distance between two places.

$\underline{\quad Get\_dis \quad\quad\quad\quad\quad}$
ΞMap
$p_1?, p_2? : places$
$dis! : \mathbb{R}^+$
$\overline{distance(p_1?, p_2?) = dis!}$

$\underline{\quad Near \quad\quad\quad\quad\quad}$
$dis? : \mathbb{R}^+$
$\overline{dis? < 5}$

$Check\_near \;\widehat{=}\; Get\_dis \gg Near$

In our system we assume that a user only wants to attend the talks located within five miles from his office. The schema*Near* and *Check_near* will be used to ensure a talk is held within the desired range.

Personal Agent. The personal agent keeps the user's profile including user's name, office location, interesting etc.

[NAME, SUBJECT]

$\begin{array}{|l}\hline \_Person_____\\ name : NAME \\ office : PLACE \\ interests : \mathbb{P}\, SUBJECT \\ \hline \end{array}$

Operation *Get_office* will output the user's office place. The personal agent uses operations *Talks_time* and *Free* to communicate with his calendar agent to check whether the user is free or not.

$\begin{array}{|l}\hline \_Get\_office_____ \\ \Xi Person \\ o! : PLACE \\ \hline o! = office \\ \hline \end{array}$
$\begin{array}{|l}\hline \_Talks\_time_____ \\ tk? : Talk \\ dt! : DateTime \\ \hline tk?.dt = dt! \\ \hline \end{array}$

$Free \mathrel{\hat{=}} Talk\_time \gg Check\_free$

The personal agent use operations *Distance* and *CheckNear* to communicate with the MapQuest agent to ensure the talks will be held nearby.

$\begin{array}{|l}\hline \_Distance_____ \\ tk? : Talk;\ p_1! : Place \\ \hline tk?.place = p_1! \\ \hline \end{array}$

$CheckNear \mathrel{\hat{=}} (Distance \wedge Get\_office[p_2!/o!])$
$\qquad \gg Check\_near$

The personal agent will notify the Talks discovery system if the client will attend the talk.

[NOTIFY]

$\begin{array}{|l}\hline \_Sendnotify_____ \\ no! : NOTIFY \\ \hline \end{array}$

Talks Discovery Agent. Schema *Talk* is defined for a general talk type. *interested_talks* records the interested talks for the users. The Schema *Talks* records a set of talks and users in the database.

$\begin{array}{|l}\hline \_Talk_____ \\ place : PLACE \\ dt : DateTime \\ subject : \mathbb{P}\, SUBJECT \\ \hline \\ \hline later : DateTime \leftrightarrow DateTime \\ \end{array}$

$\begin{array}{|l}\hline interested\_talks : Person \leftrightarrow Talk \\ \_Talks_____ \\ talks : \mathbb{P}_1\, Talk \\ users : \mathbb{P}_1\, Person \\ \hline \end{array}$

The relation *later* determines which *DataTime* happens first. The function *find_nearest* finds the next talk among a set of talks.

$$
\begin{array}{|l}
\textit{find\_nearest} : \mathbb{P}_1\, \textit{Talk} \to \textit{Talk} \\
\hline
\forall\, \textit{tks} : \mathbb{P}_1\, \textit{Talk},\, \textit{tk} : \textit{Talk} \bullet \\
\quad \textit{tk} \in \textit{tks} \land \nexists\, \textit{tk}_1 : \textit{tks} - \{\textit{tk}\} \bullet (\textit{tk}_1.\textit{dt}, \textit{tk}.\textit{dt}) \in \textit{later} \\
\quad \textit{find\_nearest}(\textit{tks}) = \textit{tk}
\end{array}
$$

The operation *Find_interested* will find the upcoming talks in which a user has interest.

$$
\begin{array}{|l}
\textit{Find\_interested} \\
\hline
\Xi\, \textit{Talks} \\
u? : \textit{users};\ \ \textit{tk}! : \textit{talks} \\
\hline
\textit{tk}! = \textit{find\_nearest}(\textit{interested\_talks}(\!|\,\{u?\}\,|\!))
\end{array}
\qquad
\begin{array}{|l}
\textit{Acceptnotify} \\
\hline
\textit{no}? : \textit{NOTIFY}
\end{array}
$$

$\textit{System} \cong (\textit{Find\_interested} \gg (\textit{Free} \land \textit{CheckNear} \land \textit{sendnotify})) \gg \textit{Acceptnotify}$

The number of instances can be created also.

$$
\begin{array}{|l}
\textit{National\_University\_Singapore} : \textit{Place};\ \ \textit{atalk} : \textit{Talk} \\
\hline
\textit{atalk.place} = \textit{National\_University\_Singapore} \\
\ldots
\end{array}
$$

4 Extracting DAML Ontology from the Z Model

It is important to have a thoroughly designed ontology since it will be shared by different agents and it forms the foundation of all agents' service. However designing a clear and consistent ontology is not a trivial job. It is useful to have some tool support in designing the ontology.

In this section, we will demonstrate the development of an XSL [11] program to automatically extract the ontology related domain properties from Z formal models (encoded in ZML format[9]) to DAML. The ontology for the system can be resolved readily from the static parts of Z design documents.

ZML is an XML environment for Z family notations. It encodes the Z documents in XML format so that the Z model can be easily browsed by the Internet Explore 5. For example, in ZML the schema *Get_office* defined n section 3 will be encoded as following:

```
<schemadef layout="simpl" align="left">
  <name>Get_o ffice</name><xi><type>Person</type></xi>
  <decl><name>o?</name><dtype><type>PLACE</type></dtype>
</decl><st/><predicate>o? = office</predicate></schemadef>
```

This XML file can be manually created by any XML editor. A tool to automatically transform the Z model in LaTeX format into XML format is currently under development. The eXtensible Stylesheet Language (XSL) [11] is a stylesheet language to describe rules for matching and transforming XML documents. In our case we transform the ZML to DAML. A set of transformation rules transforming from Z model (in ZML) to DAML ontology are developed in the following presentation.

4.1 Given Type Transformation

The given types in the Z model are directly transformed into DAML classes. This transformation can be expressed as the following rule:

$$\frac{[T]}{T \in daml\_class}$$

For example, given type *TIME* can be transformed into two classes in DAML with *time* and *date* as ID.

```
<daml:class rdf:ID="time"> <rdfs:label>TIME</rdfs:label> </daml:Class>
```

4.2 Z Axiomatic (Function and Relation) Definition Transformation

The transformation from functions and relations in Z to DAML ontology requires several cases.

$$\frac{\begin{array}{|l}R : B \leftrightarrow (\rightarrow, \twoheadrightarrow)C \qquad B, C \in daml\_class \\ \dots \end{array}}{R \in daml\_objectproperty[B \leftrightarrow (\rightarrow, \twoheadrightarrow)C]}$$

The relation R will be transformed into a DAML property with B as the domain class and C as the range class. For total functions we restrict the *daml : cardinality* property to be one and for partial functions we restrict the *daml : maxCardinality* property to be one.

In our Talks Discovery example, the relation *interested_talks* can be transformed into DAML as:

```
<daml:ObjectProperty rdf:ID="interested_talks">
 <rdfs:domain rdf:resource="#person"/><rdfs:range rdf:resource="#talk"/>
</daml:ObjectProperty>
```

4.3 Z Axiomatic (Subset and Constant) Definition Transformation

Subset. In this situation, if N corresponds to a DAML class, then M will be transformed into a DAML subclass of N. If N corresponds to a DAML property, then M will be transformed into a DAML subproperty of N. The transformation rules for the subsets are:

$$\frac{\begin{array}{|l}M : \mathbb{P}\,N \\ \dots\end{array} \quad N \in daml\_class}{M \in daml\_subclass[N]} \qquad \frac{\begin{array}{|l}M : \mathbb{P}\,N \\ \dots\end{array} \quad N \in daml\_objectproperty}{M \in daml\_subclass[N]}$$

Constant. In this situation, X will be transformed into an instance of Y. The following is the transformation rule:

$$\begin{array}{|l}\hline x : Y \hspace{3cm} Y \in daml\_class \\ \hline \dots \\ \hline \end{array}$$

$x \in instantceof[Y]$

For example, the *National_University_Singapore* and *atalk* defined in section 3 can be transformed to

```
<place rdf:ID="National_University_Singapore"/>
<talk rdf:ID="atalk">
  <rdfs:label>atalk</rdfs:label>
  <talk_place  rdf:resource="#National_University_Singapore"/> ...</talk>
```

4.4 Z Schema Transformation

A Z state schema can be transformed into a DAML class. Its attributes are transformed into DAML properties with the schema name as domain DAML class and the Z type declaration as range DAML class. In order to resolve the name conflict between the same attribute names used in different schemas we use the schema name appended with attribute name as the ID for the DAML property.

$$\begin{array}{|l}\hline S \hspace{3cm} T_1, T_2 \in daml\_class \\ \hline X : T_1; \quad Y : \mathbb{P}\, T_2 \\ \hline \dots \\ \hline \end{array}$$

$S \in daml\_class$, $X \in daml\_objectproperty[S \rightarrow T_1]$, $Y \in daml\_objectproperty[S \leftrightarrow T_2]$

For example the *Talk* schema defined in previous section can be transformed to DAML as

```
<daml:classrdf:ID="talk"> <rdfs:label>Talk</rdfs:label></daml:Class>
<daml:ObjectProperty rdf:ID="talk_place">
  <rdf:type rdf:resource=" http://www.daml.org/2001/03/daml+oil#UniqueProperty"/>
  <rdf:domain rdf:resource="#talk"/> <rdf:range rdf:resource="#place"/>
</daml:ObjectProperty>  ...
<daml:ObjectProperty rdf:ID="talk_subject">
  <rdf:domain rdf:resource="#talk"/><rdf:range rdf:resource="#subject"/>
</daml:ObjectProperty>
```

Other transformation rules are omitted as the aim of this paper is to demonstrate the approach rather than providing the complete XSL program design.

5 Improve the Ontology Quality through Z Tools

In the previous section, we discussed a tool which can extract the DAML ontology automatically from the Z model. However if the Z model itself contains some flaws, the inconsistencies will be brought into the ontology also. Fortunately Z has various semi-automatic reasoning and checking tools. A number of tools, including a type checker,

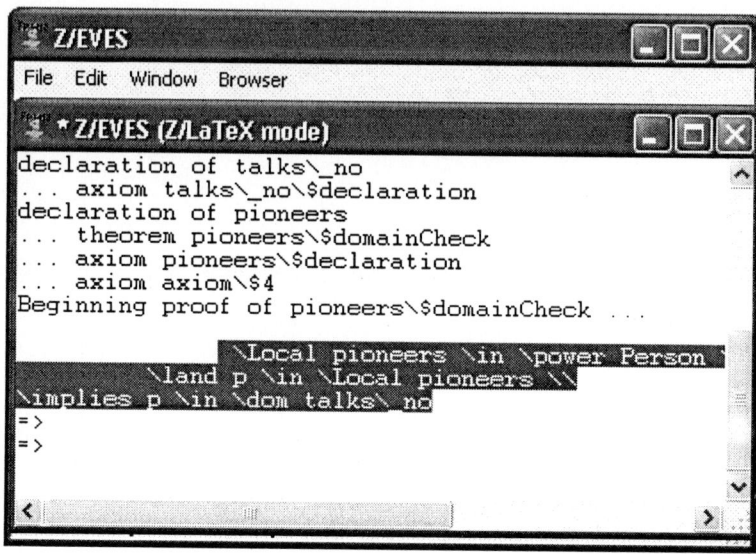

Fig. 1. Domain checking example

model checker, animator and theorem prover for Z, have been successful developed. With assistance from these tools, some inconsistences in the Z model can be detected and removed, so that the quality of the transformed ontology will be improved.

In this paper Z/EVES [8] was used to demonstrate how different kinds of inconsistences can be removed. Z/EVES is an interactive system for composing, checking, and analyzing Z specifications. It supports the analysis of Z specifications in several ways: syntax and type checking, schema expansion, precondition calculation, domain checking, and general theorem proving.

Firstly, we discuss how domain checking can be used to improve the ontology quality. Suppose for each person we also keep the number of talks he gave during last the year. This function can be modelled by a Z relation. Such as

$$| \; talks\_no : Person \nrightarrow \mathbb{N}_1$$

$$| \; pioneers : \mathbb{P} \, Person$$
$$\overline{\forall p : pioneers \bullet talks\_no(p) > 1}$$

We also want to identify a group of frequent speakers who are the pioneers in their areas. We assume that each pioneer gave at least two talks each year.

When the definition of *pioneers* is checked in Z/EVES, the status of the tool shows that it is syntactically and type correct, however it has an unproved goal (see Figure 1):

This means that Z/EVES might be unable to prove the predicates; in this case, this predicate is not true. In fact, the domain checking conditions show that we have forgotten some constraints in the axiom. The condition concerns the well-definedness of the final condition in the axiom, i.e.:

$$\forall p : pioneers \bullet talks\_no(p) > 1$$

In this context, *p* is known only to be a pioneer. However, not every person gives talks. So, this quantification should, in fact, range over only those persons who give at least one talk. (A closer inspection of the definition shows that *talks_on* is a partial function, with an unspecified domain.) In the light of this analysis, we can revise the definition to eliminate these flaws:

$$\begin{array}{|l}
pioneers : \mathbb{P}\, Person \\
\hline
pioneers \subseteq \mathrm{dom}\, talks\_no \land \forall p : pioneers \bullet speaker(p) > 1
\end{array}$$

The ontology extracted from the former error model will be:

```
<daml:class rdf:ID="pioneers">
  <rdfs:subClassOf rdf:resource="#person"/> <rdfs:subClassOf>
</daml:class>
```

After the correction, the DAML ontology we get is:

```
<daml:class rdf:ID="pioneers">
  <rdfs:subClassOf rdf:resource="#person"/>
  <rdfs:subClassOf>
    <daml:Restriction daml:minCardinality="1">
      <daml:onProperty rdf:resource="#talks_no"/>
    </daml:Restriction>
  </rdfs:subClassOf> </daml:class>
```

Note that this kind of error cannot be detected by the current DAML reasoner (i.e. OILEd, http://oiled.man.ac.uk/), therefore the DAML ontology which has been transformed from a (Z/EVES checked) Z model will be unlikely to have this kind of error.

Another kind of inconsistency which the DAML reasoner cannot check but Z/EVES can is illustrated in the following case.

Suppose we divided the talks into two categories *FreeTk* and *TicketTk*. The public can attend the *FreeTk*s freely, while they have to buy a ticket to attend the *TicketTk*. *FreeTk* and *TicketTk* are disjoint. *ftk* is a *FreeTK* and *ttk* is a *TicketTk*.

$$\begin{array}{|l}
FreeTk, TicketTk :: \mathbb{P}\, Talk \\
\hline
FreeTk \cap TicketTk = \emptyset
\end{array}
\qquad
\begin{array}{|l}
ftk : FreeTk \\
ttk : TicketTk
\end{array}$$

A thrifty person will only attend *FreeTk*. Tom and Jerry are two thrifty persons. Tom had attended *ftk* and Jerry had attended *ttk*.

$$\begin{array}{|l}
\underline{Thrifty} \\
attended\_tk : \mathbb{P}\, FreeTk
\end{array}
\qquad
\begin{array}{|l}
Tom, Jerry : Thrifty \\
\hline
Jerry.attended\_tk = \{ftk\} \\
Tom.attended\_tk = \{ttk\}
\end{array}$$

There is an inconsistency in this model. Tom is declared as a thrifty person. At same time Tom also attended a talk – *ttk* which requires buy a ticket. *FreeTk* and *TicketTk* sets are disjoint. This inconsistency cannot be detected by the DAML reasoner. Using Z/EVES the inconsistency can be detected easily at the Z level before transformation to DAML. Suppose we ask Z/EVES to prove the correctness of Jerry and Tom. Jerry is fine, however we get *false* for Tom (see Figure 2).

```
                t \in TicketTk \\
\implies \lnot t \in FreeTk
declaration of ftk
... axiom ftk\$declaration
declaration of ttk
... axiom ttk\$declaration
schema Thrifty
... axiom Thrifty\$declarationPart
Beginning proof of ...
Thrifty[attended\_tk := \{ttk\}]
Which simplifies
with invocation of Person, Thrifty
when rewriting with unitSubset
forward chaining using Person\$declarationPart, Thrifty\$declarationPart,
KnownMember\$declarationPart, knownMember, `[internal items]`
with the assumptions FreeTk\$declaration, tfDJ, ttk\$declaration,
`[internal items]` to ...
false
Proving gives ...
false
*>
```

Fig. 2. Thrifty example

After we study the proving steps the error can be removed.

The inverse transformation (transforming a DAML ontology into a Z model) can be readily achieved through another XSL sheet file. So then the Z tools can be used to improve the quality of the existing ontology. For example, all the flaws in ontology presented in this section could exist in any existing ontology. After transformation of the DAML ontology to Z model and with the assistance from diverse Z tools, these flaws can be detected and removed. The Z can then be transformed back to DAML with an improved quality.

6 Conclusion

In this paper, we demonstrate that Z can capture various requirements of SW services including ontology and service functionalities. The main contribution of this paper is that it develops systematic transformation rules and tools which can project Z models to DAML ontology automatically. Another contribution of this paper is that we demonstrate some ontology related flaws in Z model can be detected and removed with the assistance of Z/EVES so that the transformed DAML ontology from checked Z model will have better quality. One obvious further work is to fully develop the reverse transformation tools from DAML ontology to the Z model then to use Z/EVES tools to detect domain and logical errors that the current DAML reasoner is not able to detect. Transformation from Z operation schemas to DAML-S [1] actions will be another interesting future work.

From a complete different direction, we also recently investigated how RDF and DAML can be used to build a Semantic Web environment for supporting, extending and integrating various formal specification languages [6]. One additional benefit is that RDF query techniques can facilitate formal specification comprehension.

In summary, there is a clear synergy between SW languages and formal specifications. The investigation between those two paradigms will lead great benefits for both areas.

Acknowledgements

We would like to thank Hugh Anderson and anonymous referees for many helpful comments. This work is supported by the Academic Research grant *Integrated Formal Methods* from National University of Singapore and Defence Innovative Research grant *Formal Design Methods and DAML* from Defence Science & Technology Agency (DSTA) Singapore.

References

1. Daml service. http://www.daml.org/services/daml-s/2001/05/.
2. Ittaks homepage. http://www.ittalks.org/jsp/Controller.jsp.
3. T. Berners-Lee, J. Hendler, and O. Lassila. The semantic web. Scientific American, May 2001.
4. D. Brickley and R.V. Guha (editors). Resource description framework (rdf) schema specification 1.0. http://www.w3.org/TR/2000/CR-rdf-schema-20000327/, March, 2000.
5. J. Broekstra, M. Klein, S. Decker, D. Fensel, and I. Horrocks. Adding formal semantics to the web: building on top of rdf schema. In *ECDL Workshop on the Semantic Web: Models, Architectures and Management*, 2000.
6. J. S. Dong, J. Sun, and H. Wang. Semantic web for extending and linking formalisms. In L.-H. Eriksson and P. A. Lindsay, editors, *Proceedings of Formal Methods Europe: FME'02*, Copenhagen, Denmark, July 2002. Springer-Verlag.
7. O. Lassila and R. R. Swick (editors). Resource description framework (rdf) model and syntax specification. http://www.w3.org/TR/1999/REC-rdf-syntax-19990222/, Feb, 1999.
8. Mark Saaltink. The Z/EVES system. In J. P. Bowen, M. G. Hinchey, and D. Till, editors, *ZUM'97: Z Formal Specification Notation*, volume 1212 of *Lecture Notes in Computer Science*, pages 72–85. Springer-Verlag, 1997.
9. J. Sun, J. S. Dong, J. Liu, and H. Wang. Object-Z Web Environment and Projections to UML. In *WWW-10: 10th International World Wide Web Conference*, pages 725–734. ACM Press, May 2001.
10. F. van Harmelen, P. F. Patel-Schneider, and I. Horrocks (editors). Reference description of the daml+oil ontology markup language. Contributors: T. Berners-Lee, D. Brickley, D. Connolly, M. Dean, S. Decker, P. Hayes, J. Heflin, J. Hendler, O. Lassila, D. McGuinness, L. A. Stein. ..., March, 2001.
11. World Wide Web Consortium (W3C). Extensible stylesheet language (xsl). http://www.w3.org/Style/XSL.
12. J. Woodcock and J. Davies. *Using Z: Specification, Refinement, and Proof*. Prentice-Hall International, 1996.

Hardware/Software Partitioning in Verilog*

Shengchao Qin[1],[**], Jifeng He[2],[***], Zongyan Qiu[1], and Naixiao Zhang[1]

[1] School of Mathematical Sciences, Peking University, Beijing, 100871, China
qinshc@pubms.pku.edu.cn, {zyqiu, naixiao}@pku.edu.cn
[2] United Nations University,
International Institute for Software Technology,
UNU/IIST, P.O.Box 3058, Macau
jifeng@iist.unu.edu

Abstract. We propose in this paper an algebraic approach to hardware/software partitioning in Verilog HDL. We explore a collection of algebraic laws for Verilog programs, from which we design a set of syntax-based algebraic rules to conduct hardware/software partitioning. The co-specification language and the target hardware and software description languages are specific subsets of Verilog, which brings forth our successful verification for the correctness of the partitioning process by algebra of Verilog. Facilitated by Verilog's rich features, we have also successfully studied hw/sw partitioning for environment-driven systems.

Keywords: Verilog, algebraic laws, hardware/software co-design, hardware/software partitioning

1 Introduction

The design of a complex control system is ideally decomposed into a progression of related phases. It starts with an investigation of properties and behaviours of the process evolving within its environment, and an analysis of the requirement for its safety performance. From these is derived a specification of the electronic or program-centred components of the system. The project then may go through a series of design phases, ending in a program expressed in a high level language. After translation into a machine code of a chosen computer, it is executed at a high speed by electronic circuity. In order to achieve the time performance required by the customer, additional application-specific hardware devices may be needed to embed the computer into the system which it controls.

Classical circuit design methods resemble the low level machine language programming methods. Selecting individual gates and registers in a circuit like selecting individual machine instruction in a program. State transition diagrams are like flowcharts. These methods may have been adequate for small circuit

---

[*] The work is partially supported by NNSFC under grant Nos. 60173003 and 69983001.
[**] Work as a Research Fellow at Singapore-MIT Alliance, National University of Singapore starting from July 15, 2002. Email: smaqs@nus.edu.sg
[***] On leave from Software Engineering Institute of East China Normal University.

design when they were introduced, but they are not adequate for circuits that perform complicated algorithms. Industry interests in the formal verification of embedded systems are gaining ground since an error in a widely used hardware device can have very bad effect on profits of the enterprise concerned. A method with great potential is to develop a useful collection of proven equations and other theorems, to calculate, manipulate and transform a specification formulae to the product.

Hardware/software co-design is a design technique which delivers computer systems comprising hardware and software components. A critical phase of the co-design process is to partition a specification into hardware and software. This paper proposes a partitioning method whose correctness is verified using algebraic laws developed for the Verilog hardware description language. One of advantages of this approach lies in that it ensures the correctness of the partitioning process. Moreover, it optimises the underlying target architecture, and facilitates the reuse of hardware devices.

The algebraic approach advocated in this paper to verify the correctness of the partitioning process has been successfully employed in the **ProCoS** project. The original **ProCoS** project [6] concentrated almost exclusively on the verification of standard compiler of a high-level programming language based on Occam down to a microprocessor based on Transputer [5]. Sampaio showed how to reduce the compiler design task to program transformation [15]. Towards the end of the first phase of the project, Ian Page *et al* made rapid advance in the development of hardware compilation technique using an Occam-like language targeted towards FPGAs [11], and He Jifeng *et al* provided a formal verification of the hardware compilation scheme within the algebra of Occam programs [4].

Recently, some works have suggested the use of formal methods for the partitioning process [16, 13]. In [16], Silva *et al* provide a formal strategy for carrying out the splitting phase automatically, and present an algebraic proof for its correctness. However, the splitting phase delivers a large number of simple processes, and leaves the hard task of clustering these processes into hardware and software components to the clustering phase and the joining phase. Furthermore, additional channels and local variables introduced in the splitting phase increase the data flow between hardware and software components. In [13], Qin *et al* propose an algebraic approach to partition a specification into hardware and software in one step and as well verify the correctness of the partition process. However, their approach is based on algebraic laws of the high level communicating language Occam, which leaves rather a long distance to go through in hardware/software co-synthesis phase. In this paper, the distance has been shortened by adopting Verilog as the language.

The remainder of this paper is organised as follows. Section 2 introduces Verilog HDL and explores some useful algebraic laws. Section 3 describes our partitioning strategy. The co-specification language and target hardware and software architectures are proposed in section 4. Afterwards, we investigate our partition process in detail in section 5 by designing a collection of proved syntax-based partitioning rules. A simple conclusion is followed in Section 6.

2 Verilog and Its Algebraic Laws

Modern hardware design typically uses a hardware description language (HDL) to express designs at various levels of abstraction. A HDL is a high level programming language with usual programming constructs, such as assignments, conditionals and iterations, and appropriate extensions for real-time, concurrency and data structures suitable for modelling hardware.

Verilog is a HDL that has been standardized and widely used in industry ([9]). Verilog programs can exhibit a rich variety of behaviours, including event-driven computation and shared-variable concurrency. In our hardware/software partitioning process, the non-trivial subset of Verilog we adopt contains the following categories of syntactic elements.

1. A Verilog program can be a sequential process or a program paralleled by several sequential processes, with or without local variable declaration.

$P ::= S \mid P \parallel P \mid var\ x \bullet P$

2. A sequential process in Verilog can be any of the forms as follows.

$S ::= PC$ (primitive command) $\mid S; S$ (sequential composition)
$\mid$ if $b\ S$ else S (conditional) $\mid$ while $b\ S$ (iteration)
$\mid (g\ S) [\!]\ldots[\!] (g\ S)$ (guarded choice) $\mid$ always S (infinite loop)
$\mid$ case $(e)\ (pt\ S)\ldots (pt\ S)$ (switch statement)

where

$PC ::= v := e \mid skip \mid chaos \mid \to \eta_v \mid v := cg\ e$
$g ::= \#\Delta$ (time delay) $\mid eg$ (event control) $\mid \to \eta_v$ (output event)
$cg ::= \#\Delta \mid eg$
$eg ::= @(\eta_v) \mid eg\ or\ eg \mid eg\ and\ eg \mid eg\ and\ \neg eg$
$\eta_v ::= \sim v$ (value change) $\mid \uparrow v$ (value rising) $\mid \downarrow v$ (value falling)

To facilitate algebraic reasoning, the language is enriched with
- assignment event $@(v := e)$
- general guarded choice construct $(g_1\ P_1) [\!]\ldots[\!] (g_n\ P_n)$
- non-deterministic choice $P \sqcap Q$

Although it is reported that Verilog has been much more widely used in industry than VHDL ([1]), the formal semantics of Verilog has not been fully studied. Gordon tries to relate event semantics of Verilog to its trace semantics ([2]). He and Zhu ([7, 19]) explore an operational and a denotational semantics for Verilog and investigate some algebraic laws from them. Zhu, Bowen and He ([17, 18]) establish formal consistency between above-mentioned two presentations. Iyoda and He ([10]) successfully apply simple algebraic laws of Verilog to hardware synthesis process. Recently, He has explored a collection of algebraic laws for Verilog, by which a well-formed Verilog program can be transformed into head normal forms ([3]). In the following, we investigate some algebraic laws for Verilog, which will play a fundamental role in our hardware/software partitioning process.

We have explored a collection of algebraic laws for Verilog programs, which will be useful in later discussions. However, here we have to omit those laws because of page limitation, readers can reach them in our report ([14]).

From the operational semantics of Verilog ([7]), we know the fact that *skip* is not a left zero of sequential composition in general cases, because it might filter some signal. Hereby, the following inequation is obvious.

$$@\uparrow v \neq skip; @\uparrow v$$

The following definition will capture those cases where *skip* is a left zero of sequential composition.

Definition 1 (Event control insensitive).
A process P is event control insensitive if $skip; P = P$. □

Theorem 1. *The following processes are event control insensitive.*
- $x := e$, *skip, chaos, or* $\#(t)$;
- $@(x := e)$, $\rightarrow \eta_v$;
- *if b P else Q, while b Q, case (e) $(pt_1\ S_1)\ldots(pt_n\ S_n)$;*
- $\|_{i \in I}(g_i\ Q_i)$, $v := g\ e$, *where no guards are event controls;*
- $P_1; P_2$, *where P_1 is event control insensitive;*
- $P_1 \sqcap P_2$, $P_1 \parallel P_2$, *where both P_1 and P_2 are event control insensitive;*
- *always S, where S is event control insensitive;*
- *var $v_1,\ldots,v_n \bullet (S_1 \parallel \ldots \parallel S_n)$, where each S_i is either event control insensitive, or only guarded by events with respect to variables in $\{v_1,\ldots,v_n\}$.* □

From those basic algebraic laws mentioned above, we investigate the following lemma, which will be very useful in later discussions.

Lemma 1. *Let $P = (@\eta_u\ P_2)$, $Q = (\rightarrow \eta_u; @\eta_v\ Q_2)$, suppose sequential programs P_1, P_2, Q_1 are event control insensitive, and variables u, v do not occur in P_1 or Q_1, then*

(1). *var $u, v \bullet (P \parallel Q) = var\ u, v \bullet (P_2 \parallel (@\eta_v\ Q_2))$*

(2). *var $u, v \bullet (P \parallel (Q_1; Q)) = var\ u, v \bullet (Q_1; (P \parallel Q))$*

(3). *var $u, v \bullet ((P_1; P) \parallel (Q_1; Q)) = var\ u, v \bullet ((P_1 \parallel Q_1); (P \parallel Q))$* □

Proof. The proof is presented in [12].

We introduce an ordering relation between programs before further investigation.

Definition 2 (Refinement). *Let P, Q be Verilog processes employing the same set of variables, we say Q is a refinement of P, denoted as $P \sqsubseteq Q$, if $P \sqcap Q = P$ is algebraically provable.* □

3   Partitioning Strategy

This section is devoted to introduce our hardware/software partitioning strategy, which can be described in four steps, see Fig. 1.

- Before conducting the partitioning process, the programmer codes the kernel specifcation for the system in our co-specification language, which is a sequential subset of Verilog and will be detailedly explained in next section.

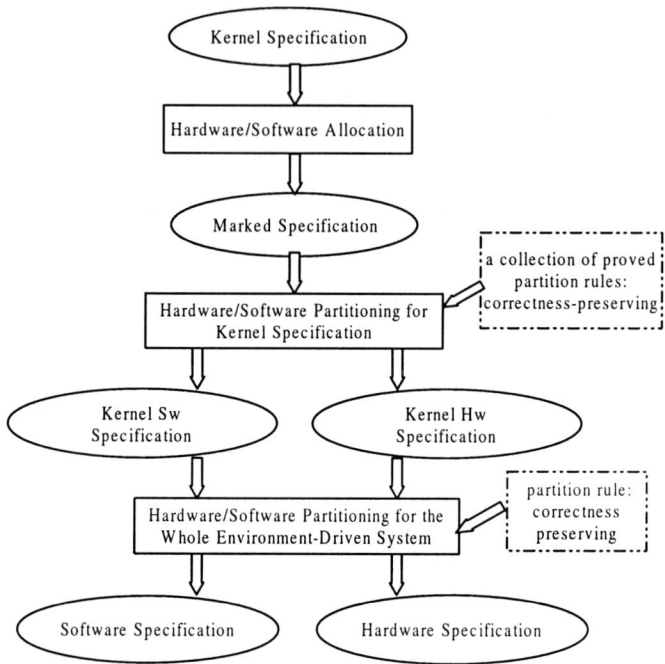

Fig. 1. Hardware/Software Partitioning Strategy

- Then, assisted by program analysis techniques ([13]), the programmer carries out the hardware/software allocation task, i.e., marks out those parts that should be implemented by hardware and divides the variables employed by the kernel specification into two disjoint sets.
- Our hardware/software partitioning algorithm will take such a marked program as input, and deliver as output the corresponding hardware and software kernel specifications. In this step, we design and prove a collection of syntax-based splitting rules, which ensure the correctness of the partitioning process and make computer automatic partitioning possible.
- Finally, hardware/software partitioning results for the whole environment-driven system are derived from the results in the third step.

We successfully propose an algebraic approach to hardware/software partitioning, which ensures the correctness of the hardware/software partitioning process and facilitates the automatic partitioning.

In later sections, we will first investigate our partitioning framework and then explore the algebraic partitioning rules.

4 Hardware/Software Partitioning Framework

In this section, we intend to introduce our hardware/software partitioning framework. We propose our co-specification language and investigate the underlying target hardware/software architectures.

The co-specification language we adopt is a sequential subset of Verilog, which comprises the following syntactic elements.

$S ::= AC$ (primitive command) $\mid S; S$ (sequential composition)
$\mid$ *if* $b\ S$ *else* S (conditional) $\mid S \sqcap S$ (non-deterministic choice)
$\mid$ *while* $b\ S$ (iteration) $\mid (g\ S) \,[\!]\, (g\ S)$ (guarded choice)

where

$AC ::= v := e \mid \rightarrow \eta_v \mid @\eta_v \mid \#\Delta \mid chaos$
$\mid (v := e)_n$ (timing assignment) $\mid \langle S \rangle$ (specific block)

$\eta_v ::= \sim v \mid \uparrow v \mid \downarrow v$

The assignment statement with time constraint $(v := e)_n$ doesn't appear explicitly in Verilog's syntax introduced in section 2, but it is in fact a well-formed Verilog program since

$(v := e)_n = \sqcap_{0 \leq k \leq n} (v := \#k\ e)$

Moreover, the block notation in $\langle S \rangle$ has no semantical meanings.

From the customer's requirements, the programmer can describe the kernel specification for the system to be designed in this co-specification language. After appropriate hardware/software marking and allocation, a marked source program is passed to the partitioning process.

The underlying target hardware and software components from the kernel specification will own specially-chosen forms. We adopt an event-trigger mechanism to synchronise behaviours between hardware and software, and use a shared-variable mechanism to cope with interactions between hardware and software.

The kernel part of the software specification is a member of $CP(r, a)$, a subset of Verilog programs, which is constructed by the following inductive rules.

(1). An event control insensitive process not containing variables r, a;
(2). $\rightarrow \eta_r; C; @\eta_a$, where C is a member of $CP(r, a)$ not mentioning r, a;
(3). $C_1; C_2$, or *if* $b\ C_1$ *else* C_2, or $C_1 \sqcap C_2$, or $(g_1\ C_1) \,[\!]\, (g_2\ C_2)$, where
     $C_1, C_2, g_1, g_2 \in CP(r, a)$;
(4). *while* $b\ C$, where $C \in CP(r, a)$.

We introduce another set $CP_\varepsilon(r, a)$ comprising those processes in $CP(r, a)$ not mentioning variable ε.

As mentioned in last section, our splitting task is divided to two steps. Firstly, we design a collection of algebraic rules to refine any source program S (the kernel specification for the system) to its hardware/software decomposition

$C_0 \parallel D_0$

where the software component C_0 is of the form $(C; \rightarrow \eta_\varepsilon)$, C is a member of $CP_\varepsilon(r, a)$, the special event $\rightarrow \eta_\varepsilon$ is adopted for the purpose of synchronisation between hardware and software, and the hardware component D_0 is subject to the following equation:

$D_0 = \mu X \bullet ((@\eta_r\ M; \rightarrow \eta_a; D_0) \,[\!]\, (@\eta_\varepsilon\ skip))$

where $M =_{df} case\ (id)\ (p_1\ M_1) \ldots (p_n\ M_n)$ is a case construct not containing r, a, ε.

We denote as $DP_\varepsilon(r, a)$ the set of processes with the same form as D_0.

To avoid any possible loss of signals at the moment when the fixed point construct (equation) is expanded, we naturally claim that an abstract event only takes place at the moment when there's no other active events at all.

Secondly, given the kernel specification S of a system, rather than considering its hardware/software partition, we deal with the decomposition for the whole system's specification

$$\Psi_f^s(S) =_{df} always\,(@\eta_s\,S; \to \eta_f)$$

which is driven by the environmental process:

$$Env =_{df} always\,(\to \eta_s; @\eta_f)$$

and derive the partitioning of $\Psi_f^s(S)$ under the environment Env as

$$\Psi_f^s(C) \,\|_{Env}\, D$$

where $P \,\|_{Env}\, Q =_{df} P \,\|\, Env \,\|\, Q$; the software component enjoys the form

$$\Psi_f^s(C) =_{df} always\,(@\eta_s\,C; \to \eta_f)$$

where C is a process from $CP(r, a)$; the hardware component D is of the form:

$$D =_{df} always\,(@\eta_r\,M; \to \eta_a)$$

We denote as $DP(r, a)$ the set of processes of the same form as D.

The following theorem ensures the synchronized termination between the kernel hardware and software specifications.

Theorem 2. *For any C_1, C_2 in $CP_\varepsilon(r, a)$ and D_0 in $DP_\varepsilon(r, a)$, we have*

$$(C_1; C_2; \to \eta_\varepsilon) \,\|\, D_0 \;=\; ((C_1; \to \eta_\varepsilon) \,\|\, D_0); ((C_2; \to \eta_\varepsilon) \,\|\, D_0) \qquad \square$$

Proof. By structural induction on C_1. The detailed proof is presented in [14]. $\square$

The following corollary is directly from theorem 2.

Corollary 1. *Given $C \in CP_\varepsilon(r, a)$ and $D_0 \in DP_\varepsilon(r, a)$, we have*

$$(while\,b\,C; \to \eta_\varepsilon) \,\|\, D_0 \;=\; while\,b\,((C; \to \eta_\varepsilon) \,\|\, D_0) \qquad \square$$

5 Hardware/Software Partitioning

This section specifies our hardware/software partitioning process in detail. As mentioned in section 3, the task is divided to two steps: hardware/software partitioning for kernel specification; decomposition of the whole system's specification. The process will be detailedly investigated in the following two subsections.

5.1 Syntax-Based Splitting Rules for Kernel Specification

This subsection is meant to design program partitioning rules. We explore a set of splitting rules which demonstrate how to construct hardware and software parts of a program construct from those of its constituents. Meanwhile, we show how to split atomic commands.

We introduce a predicate *Split* which plays a vital role in formalising the splitting rules.

Definition 3 (Split). Let $V = \{r, a, \varepsilon, id\}$. Given a program S in the co-specification language, its hardware/software partition $((C; \rightarrow \eta_\varepsilon), D^0)$ is specified by the following predicate:

$Split_V(S, C, D^0) =_{df}$
$(S \sqsubseteq (C; \rightarrow \eta_\varepsilon) \parallel D^0) \wedge (C \in CP_\varepsilon(r, a)) \wedge (D^0 \in DP_\varepsilon(r, a)) \wedge$
$(V \subseteq Var(C; \rightarrow \eta_\varepsilon) \cap Var(D^0)) \wedge (V \cap OccVar(S) = \emptyset)$

where $OccVar(P)$ denotes the set of variables occured in the program P. □

We design two set of syntax-based splitting rules in two different styles: the *bottom-up* style and the *top-down* style. The progammer can choose either of them to conduct hardware/software partitioning.

The Bottom-Up Splitting Rules. The *bottom-up* approach builds the hardware component from a marked program in one step before partitioning, i.e., all services the hardware should provide are integrated at the begining. However, it constructs the software component from those of its constituents using the following rules.

Bottom-Up Rule for Sequential Composition

$$\frac{Split_V(S_i, C_i, D^0), i = 1, 2 \quad Var(S_1) = Var(S_2)}{Split_V(S_1; S_2, \ C_1; C_2, \ D^0)}$$

Proof. $S_1 \ ; \ S_2$ \{; is monotonic\}
$\sqsubseteq ((C_1; \rightarrow \eta_\varepsilon) \parallel D_0); ((C_2; \rightarrow \eta_\varepsilon) \parallel D_0)$ \{theorem 2\}
$= (C_1; \ C_2; \rightarrow \eta_\varepsilon) \parallel D_0$ □

Bottom-Up Rule for Conditional

$$\frac{Split_V(S_i, C_i, D^0), i = 1, 2 \quad Var(S_1) = Var(S_2)}{Split_V(\text{if } b \ S_1 \text{ else } S_2, \ \text{if } b \ C_1 \text{ else } C_2, \ D^0)}$$

Bottom-Up Rule for Non-Deterministic Choice

$$\frac{Split_V(S_i, C_i, D^0), i = 1, 2 \quad Var(S_1) = Var(S_2)}{Split_V(S_1 \sqcap S_2, \ C_1 \sqcap C_2, \ D^0)}$$

Bottom-Up Rule for Guarded Choice

$$\frac{Split_V(S_i, C_i, D^0), i = 1, 2 \quad Var(S_1) = Var(S_2)}{Split_V((g_1 \ S_1) [\!] (g_2 \ S_2), \ (g_1 \ C_1) [\!] (g_2 \ C_2), \ D^0)}$$

Proof. The proofs for the above three rules are presented in [14].

Bottom-Up Rule for Iteration

$$\frac{Split_V(S, \ C, \ D^0)}{Split_V(\text{while } b \ S, \ \text{while } b \ C, \ D^0)}$$

Proof. It's straightforward from corollary 1. □

The Top-Down Splitting Rules. In the *top-down* style, both the hardware and software components of the source program are integrated from those of its constituents.

Before investigating the *top-down* splitting rules, we introduce the notion of *mergable* on hardware components from $DP_\varepsilon(r,a)$.

Definition 4. Let $D^i =_{df} \mu X \bullet ((@\eta_r \ M^i; \to \eta_a; X) \| (@\eta_\varepsilon \ skip))$,
where $M^i =_{df} case \ (id) \ (p_1^i \ M_1^i) \ldots (p_n^i \ M_{n_i}^i)$, for $i = 1, 2$.
D^1 and D^2 are said to be mergable, denoted by $mergable(D^1, D^2)$, if
$\quad Var(D^1) = Var(D^2)$, and
$\quad (p_i^1 = p_j^2)$ **implies** $M_i^1 = M_j^2$, for $1 \leq i \leq n_1$, $1 \leq j \leq n_2$.
In such a case, we define
$\quad D = int(D^1, D^2) =_{df} \mu X \bullet ((@\eta_r \ M; \to \eta_a; X) \| (@\eta_\varepsilon \ skip))$,
where $M =_{df} case \ (id) \ (t_1 \ M_1) \ldots (t_r \ M_r)$,
and $\{t_1, \ldots, t_r\} = \{p_1^1, \ldots, p_{n_1}^1\} \cup \{p_1^2, \ldots, p_{n_2}^2\}$,
and $\{M_1, \ldots, M_r\} = \{M_1^1, \ldots, M_{n_1}^1\} \cup \{M_1^2, \ldots, M_{n_2}^2\}$. □

First of all, we present a basic rule for hardware augmentation, from which and the *bottom-up* rules in the former section we directly obtain the corresponding *top-down* rules in all cases.

Rule for Hardware Augmentation

$$\frac{Split_V(S, \ C, \ D) \quad mergable(D, D')}{Split_V(S, \ C, \ int(D, D'))}$$

Proof. The proof can be reached in [12]. □

Top-Down Rule for Sequential Composition

$$\frac{Split_V(S_i, C_i, D_i) \quad Var(S_1) = Var(S_2) \quad mergable(D_1, D_2)}{Split_V(S_1; S_2, \ C_1; C_2, \ int(D_1, D_2))}$$

Top-down rules for conditional, non-deterministic choice, and guarded choice are omitted here due to page limitation, they are presented in [14]. The top-down rule for iteration enjoys the exact form with its bottom-up rule.

Splitting Atomic Commands. The details for specific blocks' partitioning are similar to discussions in [13].

For the timed assignment $(v := f(x,c))_n$, we only concentrate on the cases where both the hardware and software participate in the update of v.

Case 1: f is a busy function, and x is allocated to hardware.
$\quad Split_B(S = ((v := f(x,c))_n), \ C, \ D)$, where
$\quad C =_{df} ((id := 1)_0; \to \eta_r; @\eta_a; (v := ly)_0)$, and
$\quad D =_{df} \mu X \bullet ((@\eta_r \ case \ (id) \ (1 \ (ly := f(x,c))_n); \to \eta_a; X) \| (@\eta_\varepsilon \ skip))$.
Case 2: f is a busy function, but x is allocated to software.
$\quad Split_B(S = ((v := f(x,c))_n), \ C, \ D)$, where
$\quad C =_{df} ((id := 1)_0; (lx := x)_0; \to \eta_r; @\eta_a; (v := ly)_0)$, and
$\quad D =_{df} \mu X \bullet ((@\eta_r \ case \ (id) \ (1 \ (ly := f(lx,c))_n); \to \eta_a; X) \| (@\eta_\varepsilon \ skip))$.

Case 3: f is not a busy function, but x is allocated to hardware.
$Split_B(S = ((v := f(x,c))_n), C, D)$, where
$C =_{df} ((id := 1)_0; \rightarrow \eta_r; @\eta_a; (v := f(lx,c))_n)$, and
$D =_{df} \mu X \bullet ((@\eta_r \; case \; (id) \; (1 \; (lx := x)_0); \rightarrow \eta_a; X) \mathbin{[\![} (@\eta_\varepsilon \; skip))$.

5.2 Deriving Hw/Sw Partition for an Environment-Driven System

Now we investigate hardware/software partitioning for the whole system. The partitioning process is illustrated in Fig. 2.

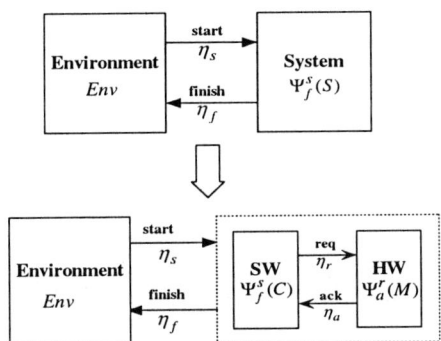

Fig. 2. Hardware/Software Partition for the Whole System

As discussed in sec. 4, suppose the whole system is specified by

$$\Psi_f^s(S) =_{df} always \; (@\eta_s \; S; \rightarrow \eta_f)$$

which is driven by environment process

$$Env =_{df} always \; (\rightarrow \eta_s; @\eta_f)$$

where S is the kernel specification for the system to be designed, and η_s is the start signal, η_f is the finish signal.

For a kernel specification S, suppose we have obtained its hardware/software decomposition as follows by applying those rules in section 5.1:

$Split_V(S, C, D)$
where $V = \{r, a, \varepsilon, id\}$, and $D = \mu X \bullet ((@\eta_r \; M; \rightarrow \eta_a; X) \mathbin{[\![} (@\eta_\varepsilon \; skip))$.

We design the following rule to generate the result for the partition of the whole system.

System Partitioning Rule

$$\frac{Split_V(S, C, D)}{Part(\Psi_f^s(S), \Psi_f^s(C), \Psi_a^r(M))}$$

where $Part(S, C, D) =_{df} ((S \parallel Env) \sqsubseteq (C \parallel D \parallel Env))$
$\Psi_u^v(P) =_{df} always \; (@\eta_v \; P; \rightarrow \eta_u)$
$Env =_{df} always \; (\rightarrow \eta_s; @\eta_f)$

Proof. We define $\{always_n(S)\}$ as follows, for all $n \geq 0$:

$$always_0(S) =_{df} chaos, \quad always_{n+1}(S) =_{df} S; always_n(S)$$

then by law (*always-1*) ([14]), we have

$$always\ S = \bigsqcup_{n \geq 0} always_n(S)$$

Now by continuity of the parallel operator and law (*seq-2*) ([14]), we only need to prove, for all $n \geq 0$,

$$(\Psi_f^s(S)_n \parallel Env_n) \sqsubseteq ((\Psi_f^s(C)_n; \rightarrow \eta_\varepsilon) \parallel D \parallel Env_n)$$

where $\Psi_f^s(P)_n =_{df} always_n(@\eta_s\ P; \rightarrow \eta_f)$
$Env_n =_{df} always_n(\rightarrow \eta_s; @\eta_f)$

The detailed proof is omitted here because of page limitation. Readers can find it in [14]. □

6 Conclusion and Future Work

This paper proposes an algebraic approach to hardware/software partitioning in Verilog algebra. Verilog HDL is a hardware description language widely used by industry. Due to its plentiful language features, Verilog can be either used to capture system specification or adopted to specify subsequent designs of distinct levels of abstraction, including RTL design.

We adopt a sequential imperative subset of Verilog as our co-specification language, and allow it to contain time constraints, so as to describe timing specification. We confine target hardware and software specifications in specially chosen subsets of Verilog, and use Verilog's event-trigger mechanism to synchronise behaviours between them. Whereas, communications between hardware and software is based on Verilog's shared variable mechanism, which will facilitate the subsequent hardware/software co-synthesis, and make it possible to adopt bus techniques to implement interactions between hardware and software.

The partitioning process in this paper is rather different from our former approach in [13], where we only dealt with partitioning for a sequential source program. However, this paper not only develops a collection of splitting rules to partition a source program into hardware and software components, but also discuss hardware/software partitioning for the whole system which takes the source program as its kernel specification. The system is specified by Verilog's *always* constructs and its execution is driven by an environment process. Such systems widely exist in our daily life, embedded systems are of this kind. Developing a partitioning rule for such systmems will be very helpful for us to investigate correctness-preserved design of embedded systems.

As parts of future work, we need to consider optimization and reconfiguration of the hardware specification we generate before hardware synthesis. Meanwhile, in order to introduce this algebraic approach to hardware synthesis, we will have to investigate more helpful algebraic laws for Verilog. He *et al* have made noticeable progress ([3, 10]).

References

1. M. Gordon, "The Semantic Challenge of VERILOG HDL", In *the proc. of Tenth Annual IEEE Symposium on Logic in Computer Science*, IEEE Computer Society Press, pp. 136–145, 1995.
2. M. Gordon, "Relating Event and Trace Semantics of Hardware Description Languages", *The Computer Journal*, pp. 27–36, Vol. 45, No. 1, 2002.
3. He J., "An Algebraic Approach to the Verilog Programming", will appear in the *proc. of Lisbon Workshop*, 2002.
4. He J., I. Page and J. Bowen, "A Provable Hardware Implementation of Occam", *LNCS* 711, pp. 693–703, 1993.
5. He J. and J. Bowen, "Specification, Verification and Prototyping of an Optimised Compiler", *Formal Aspect of Computing* 6, pp. 643–658, 1994.
6. He J. *et al*, "Provably Correct Systems", *LNCS* 863, pp. 288–335, 1994.
7. He J. and Zhu H., "Formalising Verilog", in *the proc. of ICECS 2000*, IEEE Computer Society Press, pp. 412–415, Lebanon, Dec. 2000.
8. C.A.R. Hoare and He J., *Unifying Theories of Programming*, Prentice Hall, 1998.
9. IEEE Computer Society, *IEEE Standard Hardware Description Language Based on the VERILOG Hardware Description Language (IEEE std 1364-1995)*, 1995.
10. J. Iyoda and He J., "Towards an Algebraic Synthesis of Verilog", in *the proc of ERSA'2001*, Las Vegas, USA, 2001.
11. I. Page and W. Luk, "Compiling Occam into FPGAs", in *FPGAs*, eds., W. Moore and W. Luk, pp. 271–283, Abingdon EE&CS books, 1991.
12. Qin S., "An Algebraic Approach to Hardware/Software Partitioning in Hardware/Software Co-Design", Ph.D thesis, School of Mathematical Sciences, Peking University, March, 2002.
13. S. Qin and J. He, "Partitioning Program into Hardware and Software", in *the proc of APSEC 2001*, IEEE Computer Society Press, pp. 309–316, Macau, 4-7 Dec., 2001.
14. Qin S., He J., Qiu Z. and Zhang N., "Hardware/Software Partitioning in Verilog", Research Report 2002-33, School of Mathematical Sciences, http://www.math.pku.edu.cn/printdoc/182.ps.
15. A. Sampaio, *An Algebraic Approach to Compiler Design*, World Scientific, 1997.
16. L. Silva, A. Sampaio and E. Barros, "A Normal Form Reduction Strategy for Hardware/software Partitioning", *Formal Methods Europe (FME) 97, LNCS* 1313, pp. 624–643, 1997.
17. Zhu H., J. Bowen and He J., "From Operational Semantics to Denotational Semantics for Verilog", in *the proc. of CHARME 2001, LNCS* 2144, pp. 449–464.
18. Zhu H., J. Bowen and He J., "Deriving Operational Semantics from Denotational Semantics for Verilog", in *the proc. of APSEC 2001*, IEEE Computer Society Press, pp. 177–184, Macau, 4-7 Dec., 2001.
19. Zhu H. and He J., "A DC-based Semantics for Verilog", in *the proc. of the International Conference on Software: Theory and Practice (ICS2000)*, pp. 421–432, Beijing, Aug. 21-24, 2000.

A Formal Methodology to Specify E-commerce Systems

Adriano Pereira[1], Mark Song[1,2], Gustavo Gorgulho[1],
Wagner Meira Jr.[1], and Sérgio Campos[1]

[1] Department of Computer Science,
Universidade Federal de Minas Gerais,
Caixa Postal 702 - CEP 30.123-970
Belo Horizonte – Minas Gerais – Brazil
Phone Number: 55-31-34995860, Fax: 55-31-34995858
{adrianoc, song, gorgulho, meira, scampos}@dcc.ufmg.br
[2] UNA – União de Negócio e Administração
{mark}@una.br

Abstract. Electronic commerce is an important application that has evolved significantly recently. It gives companies the possibility of reaching an unprecedented number of clients at very low cost. However, electronic commerce systems are complex and difficult to be correctly designed. Currently, most approaches are *ad-hoc*, and frequently lead to expensive, unreliable systems that may take a long time to implement. In this work we propose a methodology that uses formal-method techniques, specifically *symbolic model checking*, to design electronic commerce applications and to automatically verify that these designs satisfy properties such as atomicity, isolation, and consistency. Using the proposed methodology, the designer is able to identify errors early in the design process and correct them before they propagate to later stages. Thus, it is possible to generate more reliable applications, developed faster and at low costs. In order to demonstrate the applicability and feasibility of the technique, we have modeled and verified a virtual store in which multiple buyers compete for product items. The model verified has more than 10^{23} states and verification has been completed in few minutes. For instance, the verification process pointed out a concurrency control error which allowed the same item to be sold twice.

Keywords: electronic commerce, design specification, model checking, formal verification, property patterns

1 Introduction

E-commerce has become a popular application. In general, we can define electronic commerce as the use of the network resources and information technology to ease the execution of central processes performed by an organization.

As new e-commerce services are created, new types of errors appear, some unacceptable. We define error as any unexpected behavior that occurs in a computer program. A typical error that may occur in a site is to allow two users to buy the same item.

However, guaranteeing the correctness of an e-commerce system is not an easy task due to the great amount of scenarios where errors occur, many of them very subtle. Such task is quite hard and laborious if only tests and simulations, common techniques of system validation, are used.

Formal methods consist basically of the use of mathematical techniques to help in the documentation, specification, design, analysis, and certification of computational systems. The use of formal methods, in special model checking, is sufficiently interesting and promising once it consists of a robust and efficient technique to verify the correctness of several system properties, mainly regard to identification of faults in advance.

This paper presents a new methodology to design e-commerce systems applying model checking. The Section 2 defines some important concepts about model checking. In the Section 3, our proposed methodology is explained, and Section 4 shows an example of its use. Section 5 analyzes the related works, and Section 6 presents some conclusions and future work.

2 Model Checking of E-commerce Systems

Most electronic commerce systems can be modeled using a few entities: the products being commercialized such as books or DVDs, the agents that act upon these products such as consumer or seller, and the actions that modify the state of the product such as reserving or selling an item.

Similarly to traditional commercial systems, the main entity of electronic commerce is the product that is transactioned. For each product being commercialized there are one or more items, which are instances of the product. Each item is characterized by its life cycle, which can be represented by a state-transition graph, i.e., the states assumed by the item while being commercialized and the valid transitions between states. Examples of states are *Reserved* or *Sold*. The item's domain is the set of all states the item can be.

The entities that interact with the e-commerce system are called agents. Examples of agents are buyers, sellers and the store manager. The agents perform actions that may change the state of an item, that is, actions correspond to transitions in the life cycle graph. Put an item in the basket or cancel an item's reserve are examples of actions.

Services are sequences of actions on products. While each action is associated with an item and usually comprises simple operations such as allocating an item for future purchase, services handle each product as a whole, performing full transactions. Purchasing a book is an example of a service, which consists of paying for the book, dispatching it, and updating the inventory.

2.1 Business Rules

An e-commerce system can be described by its business rules. A business rule is a norm, denoted property, which specifies the operation of an e-commerce application.

In [4, 5] was developed a system of property specification patterns for finite-state verification tools based in the scope, order and occurrence of an event[1]. Each pattern has a scope, which is the extent of the program execution over which the pattern must hold. There are five basic kinds of scopes, as explained: Global: the entire program execution; Before: the execution up to a given event; After: the execution after a given event; Between: any part of the execution from one given event to another given event; After-until: like between but the designated part of the execution continues even if the second event does not occur.

The scope is defined by specifying a starting and an ending event for the pattern. For state-delimited scopes, the interval in which the property is evaluated is closed at the left and open at the right end. Thus, the scope consists of all states beginning with the starting state and up to but not including the ending state. A list of some patterns, with short descriptions, follows: Absence: a given event does not occur within a scope; Existence: a given event must occur within a scope; Bounded Existence: a given state must occur k times within a scope; Universality: a given event occurs throughout a scope; Precedence: an event P must always be preceded by an event Q within a scope; Response: a event P must always be followed by an event Q within a scope.

In the next subsections we present a brief background on model checking and CTL-formulas.

2.2 Symbolic Model Checking

Ensuring the correctness of the design at its earliest stage is a major challenge in any system development process. Current methods use techniques such as *simulation* and *testing* for design validation. Although effective in the early stages of debugging, their effectiveness drops quickly as the design becomes clear. A serious problem with these techniques is that they explore *some* of the possible behaviors of the system. We may never be sure whether the unexplored execution paths may contain fatal bugs. A very attractive alternative to simulation and testing is the use of *formal verification* approach, which explores exhaustively all possible behaviors of the system.

Symbolic model checking [2] is a formal verification technique by which a desired behavioral property of a system can be verified over a model through exhaustive enumeration of all the states reachable by the application and the behaviors that traverse through them. The system being verified is represented as a *state-transition graph* (the model) and the *properties* (the behaviors) are described as formulas in temporal logic. Labels are associated to the values of the variables in the program, while transitions correspond to steps in the model.

---

[1] In an e-commerce system, an event describes a set of actions.

In the next section we explain our methodology to incrementally design verifiable e-commerce systems.

3 The Formal Specification Methodology

There are many types of e-commerce applications, such as digital library, virtual bookstore, auction sites and others. The difference between them are their nature and their business rules. Some business rules are common, for example: an item should not be sold to more than one customer. On the other hand, there are many other rules specific to the application, as to allow or not the reservation of an item, to provide supply control, or to define priority to transactions executed concurrently.

The proposed methodology, an extension of the *CAFE* methodology [9], consist of a way to design e-commerce systems to apply model checking. *CAFE* methodology explains how to specify an e-commerce system and we consider the user should know some formal language, such as SMV [7], to build the model.

Our methodology is incremental and divided into four major levels. It is relevant to emphasize that these organization were adopted in order to simplify the design specification, but the designer may employ another organization.

The first level, defined as conceptual, embodies the business rules and the definition of the e-commerce system to be designed. As many details the designer specifies, as easier would be to apply the methodology and achieve good results in the verification process.

The second level, called application, models the life cycle of the item that is commercialized, identifying the types of operations (called actions, as we refer to henceforth) that are performed on it and change its state.

The third one, named functional, models the services provided by the system and the concept of multiple items are introduced.

The last level contemplates the components of the system and the user's interaction with them. It completes the scope of the system, modeling its architecture, so we called it the architectural level.

3.1 Properties of an E-commerce System

Properties may be described, for examples, as formulas in CTL [2]. CTL-formulas are built from atomic propositions, boolean connectives and temporal operators.

For example, a rule can describe that an item can only be reserved if it is available. To specify this property, a developer would have to translate this informal requirement into the following CTL-formula: AG ((($item\_state$ = Available) & ($service$ = Reserve) & ($product\_inventory$ > 0) & ($next(product\_inventory)$ = $product\_inventory$ - 1)) $\rightarrow$ AX (($item\_state$ = Reserved))).

As we can see the specification process demands some expertise in formal methods. We contend that acquiring this level of expertise represents a substantial obstacle to the adoption of the methodology. So, to overcome this problem, we suggest to use a *specification pattern system*.

Thinking about an e-commerce application model, we realize that the first important property to verify is completeness. This property guarantees that the model is consistent, by asserting that all states and actions are achieved.

To express this property we can use the property pattern of *Existence*. Additionally it is necessary to define the scope as *after*, considering that "Exists in the Future" means "after current state/event".

Transitivity is a property which defines the next state to be achieved after the occurrence of an event in the current state. It is necessary to check its veracity to guarantee the correct execution of the services that satisfy the business rules.

Most properties to be verified in e-commerce systems relate to transactions. A transaction is an abstraction of an atomic and reliable sequence of operations executed. Transaction processing is important for almost all modern computing environments that support concurrent processing. In an electronic commerce server, a transaction consists of a sequence of actions affecting the existing items, each action potentially modifying the state of the item. One of the most important properties that must be satisfied in this context is guaranteeing that the transactions being executed are consistent, that is, showing that the concurrency control mechanism implemented is correct and that concurrent transactions do not interfere with each other. In other words, we must check that transactions are atomic.

We have verified three types of properties that relate to the consistency of transactions: *Atomicity* - a transaction must be finished or not started, that is, if it does not finish, its effects have to be undone; *Consistency* - the state of the product must remain coherent at all times; *Isolation* - the result of one transaction must not affect the result of another concurrent transaction.

In the next subsections we detail the levels of the formal methodology, using real examples of e-commerce business rules to explain how this properties can be checked.

3.2 Conceptual Level

Formally, we characterize an e-commerce system by a tuple $<P,I,D,Ag,Ac,S>$, where P is the set of products, I is the set of items, D is the set of product domains, Ag is the set of agents, Ac is the set of actions and S is the set of services.

Products are sets of items, that is, $i \in I$ means that $i \in p, p \in P$. The products partition the set of items, that is, every item belongs specifically to a single product. Formally, $I = \bigcup_{\forall p \in P} p$ and $p_i \cap p_j = \emptyset$ for $i \neq j$. Domains are associated with items, that is, each item i is characterized by a domain D_i. Two items of the same product have the same domain, i.e., for all items $i, j \in I$, there is a product p such that if $i \in p$ and $j \in p$, then $D_i = D_j$.

Each action is associated with a transition in the state-transition graph of the item and is defined by a tuple $<a, i, tr> \in Ac$, where $a \in Ag$ is the agent that performs the action, and $i \in I$ is the item over which the action is performed, and $tr \in D_i X D_i$ is the transition associated with the action. In our model, the actions performed on a given item are totally ordered, that is, for each pair of actions x and y, where i_x and i_y are the same, either x has happened before y or y has happened before x. Services are defined by tuples $<p, A>$, where $p \in P$ and $A = a_1, a_2, \ldots$ is a sequence of actions such that if $a_i = (d_1, d_2)$, $a_{i+1} = (d_3, d_4)$ then $d_2 = d_3 \ \forall i, d_i \in D_j$ where D_j is the domain of an item from p.

The items are modeled by their *life cycle graphs*, which represent the state each item can be in during its life cycle in the system. An example of a life cycle graph can be seen in figure 1. States in this graph are possible states for the item such as *Available*, or *Reserved*. Transitions represent the effect of actions such as reserving an item or buying it.

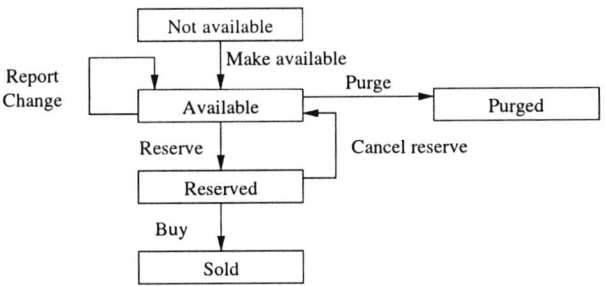

Fig. 1. The life cycle graph of product's item

Each item from I has several attributes, including the associated product, its state, and other characteristics. Finally, the agents are represented by concurrent processes that execute services, which are sequences of transitions on the state-transition graphs.

In this model, each global state represents one state in each product life cycle graph, and transitions model the effects of actions in the system. Therefore, paths in the global graph represent events that can occur in the system. The life cycle of the product is the set of all life cycles of its items.

3.3 Application Level

This level describes the e-commerce system in terms of the life cycle of the items. It is necessary to identify the states of an item, its attributes, the set of actions that could be executed on it and the effects caused by them and the agents that execute these actions. Here we are not interested in the functionalities of the web site and the architecture of them yet.

In this level it is important to verify the completeness property of the e-commerce model. Here, it is important to observe that there are only actions and states. Actions, by definition, are transactional, so the atomicity, consistency and isolation are guaranteed. Transitivity is related to the functionalities, so it will be important only in the next level, where there are services being executed in the model.

To check the completeness property of the business model, we use the CTL-formulas below, where S consists of all the states presented in the application model and A, the universe of actions.

```
EF (state = <S>)        EF (action = <A>)
```

In this level there are agents (Seller and Buyer) that represent the consumer and the supplier of the system. There is an item, which has a set of states. The agents execute actions that could affect the item's state.

3.4 Functional Level

This level introduces the product, composed by zero (the product is not available) or more items. The designer determines the operations the agents can perform, denoted as services. A service is executed on products and its effects might change or not the state of it and its items. The focus of this level is to define clearly how the services are executed and what happened with the product and its items in this case.

In this level it is important to verify the transitivity property of the model. The agents execute services that change the state of the item. This state must be consistent with the life cycle of the item and the related business rule associated with it. An example of transitivity is:

```
AG ((item_state=Not_Available & service=Make_Available) ->
AX (item_state=Available)
```

In this level it is important to verify the atomicity, consistency and isolation properties either. It is essential to check the consistency between the state of the product and its items in a given moment. Moreover, there are agents performing services concurrently, which may cause the system to achieve an invalid state. Therefore the isolation property must be guaranteed.

To become clear, we give some examples of this properties[2]. First we give an example of atomicity. if an item is available and a *Reserve* service is performed by a buyer agent and granted by the server, the item must be reserved in the next state and the inventory must be decremented.

```
AG ((item_state=Available & service=Reserve & product_inventory=1)
-> AX (item_state=Reserved & product_inventory=0))
```

An example of consistency property can be seen as follow:

– If the inventory is zero, then no item should be available.

```
    AG (product_inventory = 0 -> !product_state = Available)
```

---

[2] The actual properties verified are slightly different than the ones presented here, which have been simplified for readability.

An example of isolation property could be: if there are two items available and two buyers reserve these items simultaneously, the inventory must be zero in the next step.

```
AG ((buyer1_service=Reserve & buyer2_service=Reserve
& product_inventory=2) -> AX (product_inventory=0))
```

In this level there are agents that execute services, that could modify the product's state. Some of these services, as a *Reserve* of an instance of the product, change the state of the item either.

It is important to notice that the properties validated in the second level should retain their validity in the third one and so on. The verification of the properties should be incremental as well as the methodology proposed.

3.5 Architectural Level

This level specifies the system in terms of its components and the way they interact with each other. It is important to emphasize that this level encompasses the other ones, completing the specification of the system and describing its architecture.

In this stage, the model is more complex, contemplating the components of the system's architecture. We identify the atomicity properties that should be verified and other consistency and isolation rules. The transactional properties verified in the other levels should be checked again, as the transitivity properties.

We introduce the components of the e-commerce system: the web server, the transaction server and the database. There are agents that submit requests to the web server, which translate them into operations to the transaction server. These operations, named services, are executed by this server, sometimes performing action on the items. This level is important because it enables the designer to get a specification closer to the real implementation he wants to develop.

4 Case Study: An E-commerce Virtual Store

In this section we will present our case study, an e-commerce virtual store, a very useful and popular application. Our goal is to show how the methodology proposed can be used to design more reliable systems. This is a typical electronic commerce application in which most of the aspects that make such applications complex to design are present, such as multiple agents of different types that compete for access to products, products with more than one item and intermediate states for items (for example, one buyer should reserve an item before buying it). We have used the SMV model checker [7] to perform this task.

4.1 Conceptual Level

In the virtual store we modeled, there are six states which correspond to types of pages on the web site: *Home, Browse, Search, Select, Add* and *Pay*. The *Home* page is the initial web page of the site. The *Select* page shows specific information about a product. The *Add* page confirms product reservations and displays the contents of the customer's shop cart. The *Pay* page is loaded after the purchase of the items in the shop cart is completed. The *Search* and *Browse* pages present general information about the products offered by the virtual store. There are still some states that correspond to the administration view of the web site, used by the seller agent to change information about the products (operation *Change*) and modify the its inventory (operation *Make Available*).

The transitions between these pages are associated with actions executed by the agents. An example is the execution of a reserve action by the buyer agent, that causes the transition from *Select* to *Add* if completed with success. Therefore a transition between two web pages is mapped to an action in the life cycle graph of the product's item.

In our virtual store, we have modeled two types of agents. The *Buyer* Agent represents the customers that access the virtual store through WWW to get information about the product and potentially to buy it. The *Seller* Agent represents the product's supplier that will make it available, update its data and potentially sell it. The buyer agent can execute one of the following actions: *Report*, the client requests information about the product; *Reserve/Cancel Reserve*, the client reserves an item or cancel a previous reserve; and *Buy*. The seller agent can execute one of the actions: *Make Available*, when a new item enters the store; *Change* to change its attributes; and *Purge*, when the item is removed from the store.

The life cycle graph of the product's item can be seen in Figure 1. The global model of the virtual store is a collection of life's cycle graphs and additional attributes are represented by variables such as the inventory (the number of product items available). Additional logic is needed to "glue" together the various life cycle graphs. For example, if a reserve is requested for one item but several are available, the store must decide which item will be reserved.

Finally, the agents are modeled as concurrent processes that perform actions. In the model there is one seller agent that represents the administrator of the store and one or more buyer agents that act as the customers. To illustrate how the methodology works in practice, we will present parts of the SMV code for the virtual store.

As defined in the methodology, Section 3.2, conceptual level details the e-commerce system requirements. We list some of the business rules we had identified in our case study:

- If the item is in the state *Not Available* and the action *Make Available* occurs, the next state is *Available*;
- If the item is in the state *Reserved* and the action *Buy* occurs, the next state is *Sold*;
- If the inventory is positive, at least one item must be available;
- The actions *Reserve* and *Cancel Reserve* must be atomic;
- And if there are agents executing concurrently, their actions must be isolated.

4.2 Application Level

A module in SMV consists of a number of variables and their assignments. The main module consists of the parallel composition of each module. This is accomplished by instantiating each module in the main module shown as follow:

```
MODULE main

VAR ba1: buyer_agent();
    ba2: buyer_agent();
    sa1: seller_agent();
    it1: item();
```

As described in Section 3.3, the first important property to be verified is completeness. In this case study, we can do this through the specification written in CTL formulas:

```
EF (it1.state = Not_Available)
                ...
EF (it1.state = Purged)
EF (ba1.action = Buy)
EF (ba2.action = Buy)
EF (sa1.action = Make_Available)
```

These specifications should be consistent with the item's life cycle graph, as illustrated by Figure 1. In our model all of them were verified as *true*, certifying its completeness.

4.3 Functional Level

Continuing the process defined by the methodology we add new modules to the model, which represents the product and its items. Here, we are interested in verify some business rules related to services.

Initially, as described in Section 3.4, we have to check the transitivity properties of the model. We can perform this using the following CTL formulas:

```
AG(state = Available & service = Purge) -> AX(state = Purged)
                ...
AG(state = Available & service = Reserve) -> AX(state = Reserved)
AG(state = Reserved & service = Buy) -> AX(state = Sold)
```

Here, we explain some transactional properties, beginning with atomicity. if an item is available and a reserve action is performed by a buyer, the item must be reserved in the next state and the state must be consistent with this or the service is not executed and the state is not modified.

```
AG ((state = Available & service = Reserve & inventory = v) ->
AX ((state = Available & inventory = v) |
    (state = Reserved & inventory = v-1)))
```

Note that the variable *inventory* partakes of the proposition added to this formula to verify this business rule.

The next formulas illustrate some consistency properties of the virtual store modeled.

The inventory should not be negative:

`AG !(inventory < 0)`

If the inventory is positive, at least one item must be available:

`AG ((inventory > 0) -> (product_state = Available))`

Finally we present examples of isolation.

If there are two buyer agents, one reserving the item and the other canceling his/her reservation, the inventory must be kept consistent after the execution of both services:

`AG ((buyer1_service = Reserve & buyer2_service = Cancel_Reserve & inventory = v) -> AX (inventory = v))`

In the case of *inventory = 0*, the reservation service can not be preceded by the cancellation service. So, to solve this problem we decide to give priority to the buyer agent that wants to cancel the reservation.

In a similar way, we specified all the other business rules and verify their veracity.

4.4 Architectural Level

In this stage we added new modules to represent the e-commerce system as real as possible. So we include the web server, transaction server and database server in the model, adapting the specifications to it. Thus, the properties are related to requests, instead of services.

In this level we do not identify new properties since all the business rules were verified in the previous level.

The complete model has more than 10^{23} states with more than 10^{14} reachable states, used about 17MB of memory, and verification has been completed in just nine minutes for all properties.

5 Related Work

Formal analysis and verification of electronic commerce systems have not been studied in detail until recently. Most work such as [6, 1, 3, 10] concentrates on verifying properties of specific protocols and do not address how these techniques can assist in the design of new systems. Moreover, these techniques seem to be less efficient than ours, ranging from theorem proving techniques [6, 1] which are traditionally less efficient (even though more expressive), to model checking [3, 10]. But even these works tend to be able to verify only smaller systems consuming much higher resources than our method.

6 Conclusions and Future Work

In this paper we propose a methodology to specify e-commerce systems. This technique can increase the efficiency of the design of electronic commerce applications. We use formal methods not only to formalize the specification of the system but also to automatically verify properties that it must satisfy. This technique can lead to more reliable, less expensive applications that are developed significantly faster. We have modeled and verified a virtual store to demonstrate how the method works. As a result of our case study, we were able to detect a serious error, that violated the isolation property, causing the same item to be sold twice. It occurred because two buyer agents tried to acquire the product at the same time and there was only one item available. During this verification we have precisely identified both errors and their causes that would have been difficult to find out otherwise.

The proposed method can be applied in general e-commerce systems, where the business rules can be modeled by state transitions of the items on sale. As the method is based on CTL-formulae, the business rules should be represented by them, what is considered a limitation of the method.

We are currently studying other features of electronic commerce systems that we have not yet formalized, as well as the possibility of generating the actual code that will implement the system from its specification.

References

1. BOLIGNANO. Towards the formal verification of electronic commerce protocols. In *PCSFW: Proceedings of The 10th Computer Security Foundations Workshop* (1997), IEEE Computer Society Press.
2. CLARKE, E. M., GRUMBERG, O., AND PELED, D. A. *Model Checking*. The MIT Press, Cambridge, Massachusetts, 1999.
3. DEPARTMENT, S. L. Model checking the secure electronic transaction (set) protocol. In *Proceedings of the 7th International Symposium on Modeling, Analysis and Simulation of Computer and Telecommunication Systems* (1998).
4. DWYER, M. B., AVRUNIN, G. S., AND CORBETT, J. C. Property specification patterns for finite-state verification. In *2nd Workshop on Formal Methods in Software Practice* (March 1998).
5. DWYER, M. B., AVRUNIN, G. S., AND CORBETT, J. C. Patterns in property specifications for finite-state verification. In *21st International Conference on Software Engineering* (May 1999).
6. GURGENS, S., LOPEZ, J., AND PERALTA, R. Efficient detection of failure modes in electronic commerce protocols. In *DEXA Workshop* (1999), pp. 850–857.
7. MCMILLAN, K. L. *Symbolic Model Checking: An Approach to the State Explosion Problem*. PhD thesis, Pittsburgh, PA, 1992.
8. MCMILLAN, K. L. *Symbolic Model Checking*. Kluwer Academic Publishers, Norwell Massachusetts, 1993.
9. MEIRA JR., W., MURTA, C. D., CAMPOS, S. V. A., AND NETO, D. O. G. *Sistemas de Comercio Eletronico, Projeto e Desenvolvimento*. Campus, 2002.
10. WANG, W., HIDVÉGI, Z., BAILEY, A., AND WHINSTON, A. E-process design and assurance using model checking. In *IEEE Computer* (Oct. 2000).

Model-Based Specification Animation Using Testgraphs

Tim Miller and Paul Strooper

School of Information Technology and Electrical Engineering,
Software Verification Research Centre,
The University of Queensland,
Brisbane, Qld 4072, Australia
`timothym@svrc.uq.edu.au`
`pstroop@itee.uq.edu.au`

Abstract. This paper presents a framework for systematically animating specifications using *testgraphs*: directed graphs that partially model the specification being animated. Sequences for the animation are derived by traversing the testgraph. The framework provides a testgraph editor that allows users to edit testgraphs and supports automated testgraph traversal. Experience with the framework so far indicates that it can be used to effectively animate small to medium-sized specifications and that it can reveal a significant number of problems in these specifications.

1 Introduction

Specification animation allows users to pose questions about the specification that can be answered quickly and automatically. While results obtained via animation are specific to certain cases, as opposed to results gained from techniques such as theorem proving and model checking, animation requires less expertise and can detect many types of errors in specifications. This gives specification designers a way to test that their specifications behave as intended, but is also useful for demonstrating the behaviour of the specification to end users, who typically have little-to-no knowledge of formal notations and specifications, and, as a result, cannot determine the behaviour of a specification using manual analysis.

Much like testing, performing ad-hoc animation does not give a high-level of assurance. If we try to find errors in a specification using only a small number of cases, we have to ensure that the cases selected adequately cover the specification. Most current literature on animation describes only tools and methods for execution or interpretation of specifications, or simply mentions that animation has been used, with little or no description on how and why specific cases were selected.

In earlier work [13] we present a method for systematically animating specifications. We document the process using an animation plan, and use the specification to generate animation inputs. This approach was completely manual, and took significant time and effort. In this paper, we use the idea of animation using a *testgraph* [9]: a directed graph that partially models the possible states and transitions of a specification. Sequences are derived from the testgraph by traversing the testgraph repeatedly from the start node and cases for animation are generated from these sequences. This provides a systematic approach to animation that is partially automated and repeatable. Testing using graphs and finite state machines is not a new concept, but, to our knowledge, it has never been applied to animation. Experience so far with this framework indicates it can be used to effectively animate small to medium-sized specifications and can reveal a signifcant number of problems in these specification.

After reviewing related work in Section 2, we discuss background on the specification language and animation tool used in this work. We then present a method for animation using testgraphs in Section 4, and a framework with tool support for this method in Section 5. We then conclude the paper.

2 Related Work

In this section, we present related work on animation and testing, especially testing using finite state machines (FSMs) and graphs.

2.1 Animation

There are several animation tools that automatically execute or interpret specifications. PiZA [8] is an animator for Z. PiZA translates specifications into Prolog to generate output variables. PiZA provides a facility to embed Prolog statements within the Z specifications and make calls to Prolog from the specifications. The B-Model animator [18] is the animator used in the B formal development process [17]. It is used to animate specifications written in B's model-oriented specification language. The Software Cost Reduction (SCR) toolset [7] contains an animator that is used to test specifications. The IFAD VDM++ Toolbox [10], used for development from the object-oriented extension of VDM, contains an interpreter. This interpreter is used to test specifications, and contains a coverage tool that measures what percentage of specification statements are exercised for each operation during a trace.

Pipedream [12] is another animator for the Z specification language. Pipedream transforms the specification into first-order logic to determine predicates and finite sets, which help Pipedream establish which specifications are executable. Kazmierczak et al. [12] outline an approach for specification animation using Pipedream containing three steps: performing an initialisation check; verifying the preconditions of schemas; and performing a simple reachability property.

2.2 Testing Using Graphs and Finite State Machines

Hoffman and Strooper [9] generate test cases for C++ classes by automatically traversing a *testgraph*, a directed graph that partially models the states and transitions of the class-under-test, using *Classbench*. Later work by Murray et al. [15] and Carrington et al. [3] describe generating Classbench testgraphs from FSMs. States for these FSMs are derived by using the *Test Template Framework* [16] to specify sets of test cases, and extracting pre- and post-states from these test cases. Transitions are then drawn between each node if possible, and the FSM is converted into testgraph. We build on this work by using testgraphs to sequence animation, but rather than derive testgraphs from FSMs, the user can simply generate the testgraph manually. Relying on the specification do generate the testgraph does not make as much sense in our application, because we want to use the testgraph to determine the correctness of the specification.

Dick and Faivre [4] also generate test sequences by retrieving the pre- and post-states from test cases generated by partitioning schemas into *disjunctive normal form* (DNF), and using them as the states of FSMs. A transition is created between two states if the two states can be related via an operation. The FSA is then traversed, with every branch executed at least once.

Bosman and Schmidt [1] use FSMs to test object-oriented programs. Two state machines are developed. One is the state machine for the specification, called the *design FSM*, and the other is the state machine for the implementation, called the *representation FSM*. If two state machines behave identical for all possible input sequences, then they are considered identical.

Callahan et al. [2] have also used model checking to drive testing. They use the counter-example feature found in model checkers to derive sequences for testing. They apply slight syntactical changes to specifications to create mutants that purposely force the model-checker to find a counter-example of a property, and then use the paths in these counter examples to derive FSMs for driving the testing process.

3 Background

In this section, we present the example used throughout this paper, and introduce the Possum animation tool [5, 6] used in this work.

3.1 Example – IntSet

The example is an integer set called *IntSet*. The specification is shown in Figure 1.

The *IntSet* specification is written in Sum [11], a modular extension to Z, and like all Sum specifications, contains a state schema, an initialisation schema, and zero or more operation schemas. The state schema consists of a state variable *intset* (a power set of integers), and a state invariant, which restricts the *intset* to a maximum size of 10, defined by the constant *maxsize*. The initialisation schema is used to set the initial state of the specification, and in this example, it sets *intset* to be empty.

Sum uses explicit preconditions in operation schemas, denoted using the *pre* keyword, and also explicitly defines which state variables can be changed by using the *changes_only* function, which takes, as its sole argument, a set of state variables that are allowed to change for the operation. Like Z, input and output variables are decorated using ? and ! respectively, and post-state variables are primed ('). The *init* schema and all operation schemas automatically include the state schema in their declarations.

The four operation schemas in the *IntSet* specification are: *add*, which adds a particular integer to the set if that integer is not already in the set and the set is not full; *remove*, which removes a particular integer from the set provided it is in the set; *isMember*, which returns a boolean indicating whether a particular integer is in the set; and *size*, which returns the size of the set.

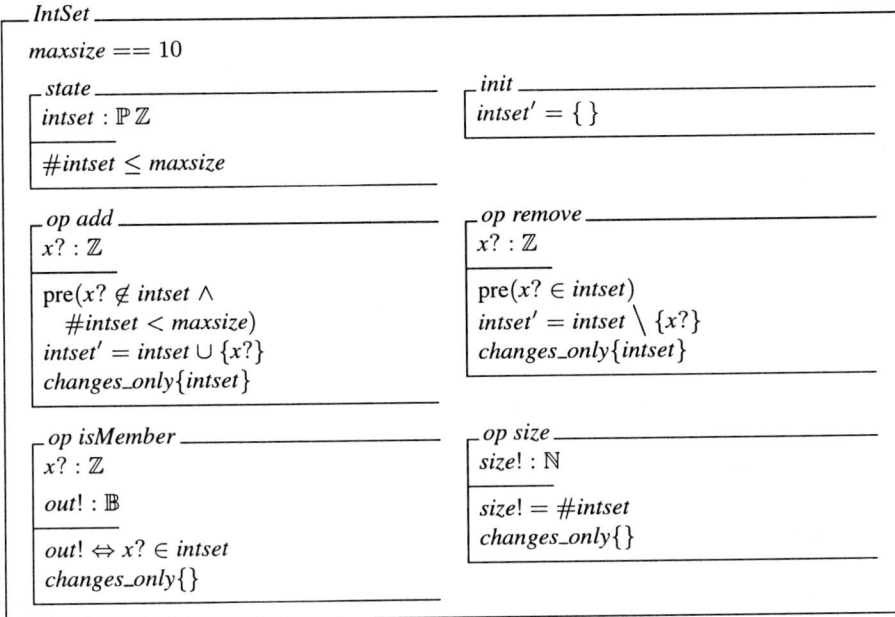

Fig. 1. Sum Specification of *IntSet*

3.2 Possum

Possum is an animator for Z and Z-like specification languages, including Sum. Possum interprets queries made in Sum and responds with simplifications of those queries. A specification can be animated by stepping through operations, and Possum will update the state after each operation. The example below shows a query sent to Possum for the *add* operation in *IntSet* with the value 3 substituted for the input $x?$. Let us assume that the value of the state variable *intset* before the query is $\{1\}$:

$$\text{add } \{3/\text{x?}\}$$

Possum returns with:

$$[\text{intset} := \{1\}, \text{intset}' := \{1, 3\}]$$

This means that the value of the state variable *intset* has been updated to $\{1, 3\}$. Possum also displays any bindings for any variables that it instantiates, but the *add* operation has none other than *intset* and *intset'*.

Possum supports plug-in user interfaces for specifications written in Tcl/Tk, which allows people not familiar with the specification language to interact with the specification through a user interface.

4 Animation Using Testgraphs

In this section, we discuss using testgraphs to perform animation. We use testgraphs because they are straightforward to derive, and deriving cases from testgraphs can be done quickly and automatically. Testgraphs give us a planned, documented, and repeatable approach to animation that allows us to analyse the specification as a whole instead of animating each of the operations in isolation.

4.1 Deriving a Testgraph

A *testgraph* is a directed graph that partially models the states and transitions of the specification being animated. Each node in the testgraph represents a possible state that the specification can reach, and each arc represents a transition (a sequences of calls to operations) that moves the specification from one state to another. One state in the testgraph is selected as the start node, and this node represents the initial state.

Using animation, it is infeasible to check the entire state space of specifications, except for specifications with very small state spaces. If we look at the *IntSet* example, which is a small specification by industry standards, the size of the state space is infinite. Therefore, we select a subset of the state space as nodes for our testgraph. In the context of animation, the state space contains all states that *can* be reached; the testgraph nodes are the set of states that *will* be reached during animation.

The state of a specification provides important information about the selection of states for animation. For example, the *add* operation in *IntSet* will behave differently when the set is full (has *maxsize* elements in it) to when it is not full.

Standard testing practice advocates many methods for selecting special state values using rules such as *the interval rule*. For the *IntSet* example, we select our states based on the size of the set, and include four states: an empty set, a set that is half-full containing only odd numbers, a set that is half-full containing only even numbers, and a set that is full containing both even and odd numbers.

Once we have our testgraph nodes, we derive arcs for the testgraph to be used as transitions during animation. We require each node to have at least one arc leading in to it, except the start node, otherwise the node will be unreachable.

Figure 2 shows the testgraph for the *IntSet* specification. Here, we have four nodes representing the states derived above: *EMPTY*, *ODD*, *EVEN*, and *ALL*. *EMPTY* is the start node and this is indicated by the node being shaded. The five arcs on the testgraph change the state of *IntSet* from one state to another. For example, the *ADDODD* arc represents a transition that adds 1, 3, 5, 7 and 9 to the set. This takes us from *EMPTY* to *ODD*.

4.2 Traversing the Testgraph

We specify operations for our specification that make the transitions defined in the testgraph using the arc labels as the name for the operations. For example, the *ADDODD* transition in the *IntSet* testgraph is shown in Figure 3, where $\S$ represents the sequential composition of operations by identifying the post-state of the first call as the pre-state of the next.

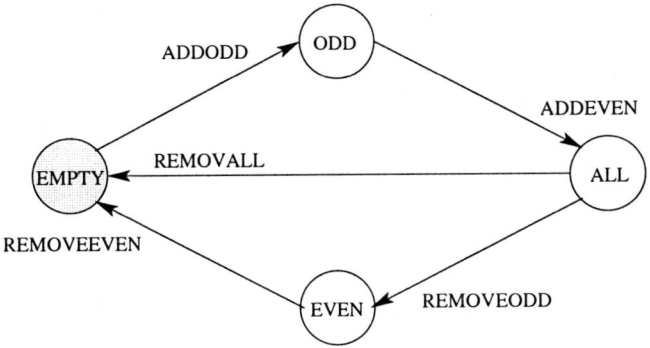

Fig. 2. Testgraph for *IntSet*

$$ADDODD == add\{1/x?\} \mathbin{\raise0.5ex\hbox{$\scriptscriptstyle\circ$}\kern-0.5em\lower0.5ex\hbox{$\scriptscriptstyle\circ$}} add\{3/x?\} \mathbin{\raise0.5ex\hbox{$\scriptscriptstyle\circ$}\kern-0.5em\lower0.5ex\hbox{$\scriptscriptstyle\circ$}} add\{5/x?\} \mathbin{\raise0.5ex\hbox{$\scriptscriptstyle\circ$}\kern-0.5em\lower0.5ex\hbox{$\scriptscriptstyle\circ$}} add\{7/x?\} \mathbin{\raise0.5ex\hbox{$\scriptscriptstyle\circ$}\kern-0.5em\lower0.5ex\hbox{$\scriptscriptstyle\circ$}} add\{9/x?\}$$

Fig. 3. *ADDODD* operation for *IntSet*

We generate our animation sequences by traversing the testgraph to achieve *arc* coverage. The other two types of coverage considered were *node* and *path* coverage. Node coverage does not traverse every transition in a graph, and path coverage is infeasible for graphs with a cycle. Arc coverage traverses every arc, visits every node (provided all testgraph nodes and arcs are reachable from the start node), and is straightforward to achieve.

4.3 Checking States and Operations

Once the testgraph has proceeded to a new node, we want to check properties of the current state of the specification, e.g., that after the transition *ADDODD* from *EMPTY* to *ODD*, *intset* = $\{1, 3, 5, 7, 9\}$, and the *size* operation returns *size*! = 5.

There are two ways to do this: manually using the standard Possum interface, or partially automated using *CHECK* schemas.

The manual approach involves checking the current value of the state is correct for each node, and manually invoking the operations that we wish to check. For example, after the *ADDODD* transition, we would check that the new value of *intset* is $\{1, 3, 5, 7, 9\}$. We would then invoke the *size* operation, expecting *size*! = 5 to be returned, and invoke the *isMember* operation for at least two values, one that returns true and one that returns false.

For the partially automated approach, we define schemas that automatically check the properties for the current state of the specification. For example, the *CHECK_ODD* schema, shown in Figure 4, is used to check: that for the *isMember* operation, every element that returns true is in the *intset* state variable, and vice versa[1]; that the *size* op-

---
[1] Although the set $\mathbb{Z}$ is infinite, Possum has a maximum bound for this that can be changed by the user

eration returns $size! = 5$ and does not change the state, and that $intset = \{1, 3, 5, 7, 9\}$. In this schema, the variable $tgf\_report!$[2] is a finite set of MSG, where MSG is a previously declared set containing the four possible error messages: $ISMEM\_TRUE\_ERR$, $ISMEM\_FALSE\_ERR$, $SIZE\_ERR$, and $STATE\_ERR$. These error messages are defined as abbreviations

---

op CHECK_ODD

$tgf\_report! : \mathbb{F} \, MSG$

$(intset \neq \{isMember\{state.intset/intset, \text{true}/out!\} \bullet x?\}) \Leftrightarrow$
    $ISMEM\_TRUE\_ERR \in tgf\_report!$
$(\mathbb{Z} \setminus intset \neq \{isMember\{state.intset/intset, \text{false}/out!\} \bullet x?\}) \Leftrightarrow$
    $ISMEM\_FALSE\_ERR \in tgf\_report!$
$(\exists s : \mathbb{N}; \, t : \mathbb{P}\mathbb{Z} \mid size\{s/size!, t/intset'\} \bullet s \neq 5 \vee t \neq intset) \Leftrightarrow$
    $SIZE\_ERR \in tgf\_report!$
$intset \neq \{1, 3, 5, 7, 9\} \Leftrightarrow STATE\_ERR \in tgf\_report!$

Fig. 4. Schema $CHECK\_ODD$ for $IntSet$

To use the $CHECK\_ODD$ operation to check the ODD state, we simply run the operation by typing $CHECK\_ODD$ at the Possum prompt.

If a node has been visited previously in the traversal, we need not perform a check like the one above, but instead check that the current value of the state is the same as the previous visit. Possum makes this possible because it displays bindings for variables associated with a specification. If the states are the same, our checks will not find anything different. If not, we have uncovered a problem in our specification or our testgraph. The time and effort saved by checking whether the current state has been visited depends on how long the checks take to perform.

5 Tool Support

In this section, we describe tool support for the method outlined in Section 4. Applying this method manually is time-consuming.

The tool described in this section, called the *Possum Testgraph Framework*, is a tool we have plugged into Possum to allow us to edit, save, and restore testgraphs. It also has options for partial automation of testgraph traversal and report compilation.

5.1 Constructing a Testgraph

The first step is to construct a testgraph. When opened, the editor presents the user with a blank canvas on which the user can design their testgraph.

---

[2] We use the prefix $tgf\_$, which stands for *testgraph*, to prevent variable name clashes.

The user can add nodes to the canvas, and add a directed arc between any two nodes, provided there is not already an arc with the same source and destination nodes. An arc can be removed from between two nodes, and nodes can be removed. Removing a node also removes any arcs that have that node as the source or destination node. Users can also select one node to be the start node of the testgraph.

The default labels of nodes placed on the graph are determined by the order they are added. However, the user can change the label to any string not containing spaces.

Users can also associate a schema with a node. This schema is invoked during the traversal of the testgraph when the user wishes to perform a check on a state.

By default, arcs do not have a label. They are uniquely identified by the source and destination nodes. However, users can add labels to arcs. An arc label is also the name of the transition schema associated with that arc.

Testgraphs can be saved to disk and opened again at a later time. The user also has the option of clearing the canvas and starting a new testgraph.

5.2 Generating Paths

As discussed in Section 4, we traverse the testgraph to achieve arc coverage. We use the testgraph framework to automatically generate a sequence of paths that achieve arc coverage.

The path generation algorithm performs a depth-first search. It starts at the start node, and adds each node to the current path until a node that is already in the path is reached, or there are no more nodes leading from the current node. If there are unreachable nodes or arcs, the path generation algorithm ignores these.

There are two paths generated for the *IntSet* example:

$$< EMPTY, ODD, FULL, EVEN, EMPTY >$$
$$< EMPTY, ODD, FULL, EMPTY >$$

The framework allows the user to save paths that have been generated, and open them again at a later time. This is for three reasons:

- The user can see the paths that have been generated by the algorithm.
- The user can remove some of the paths by editing the file the paths are saved in, thus reducing animation time.
- The user can manually generate paths, save them in a file, and open them for use in the framework.

The file format is simple, with each path being a sequence of node labels in the order they are visited, separated by a space. Paths are separated by a line break.

5.3 Traversing the Testgraph

There are three ways that the framework allows users to traverse the testgraph: manual traversal, partially automated traversal, and fully automated traversal. Whichever method is used, the current node and arc are highlighted in the testgraph during the traversal. The user can switch between any of the traversal methods during a session.

Manually Traversing the Testgraph: The user can manually traverse an arc in the testgraph by right-clicking on that arc, and selecting *"Traverse Arc"* from the menu. If the source node of the selected arc is not the current state, an error message is displayed to the user. If the source node is the current state, the arc is traversed, the transition associated with that arc is sent to Possum, and the current node is updated to the destination node. The tool waits for Possum to complete the transition before sending the schema associated with the destination node to Possum.

Stepping Through the Testgraph: The user can also choose to step through the paths generated by the testgraph framework. By this, we mean traverse one arc at a time. They can do this by holding *Shift* and clicking the middle mouse button, or by selecting this option from a menu. The next arc is traversed, sending the transition associated with the arc to Possum and updating the current node to the destination node. The tool waits for Possum to complete the transition before sending the schema associated with the destination node to Possum.

Automatically Traversing the Testgraph: Automatically traversing the graph uses the paths generated by the framework, but unlike stepping through the testgraph, no user interaction is required. The user simply selects, from the *Animate* menu in the menu bar, the option *"Traverse All Paths"*. The framework traverses the first arc, sends the transition to Possum, updates the current node to be the destination node, and waits for Possum to perform the transition before sending the operation associated with the destination node to Possum. It then waits for Possum to finish running the operation, and performs the next transition in the path. This continues until all arcs in all paths have been traversed.

5.4 Report Generation

The check operations discussed in Section 4, such as *CHECK_ODD*, report problems using a variable called *tgf_report*!, which is a set containing error and warning messages. During animation, the testgraph framework reads the value of this variable every time it changes, and records its contents, along with the current transition, destination and source nodes. The result is a report containing all messages generated and where they occurred.

For example, if after the transition *ADDODD* from the *EMPTY* to *ODD* nodes, the *CHECK_ODD* operation returned an error indicating that the *size* operation returned an incorrect value, the report would include:

```
Transition: (ADDODD, EMPTY |--> ODD); CHECK_ODD returned:
Error: operation 'size' returning unexpected value for 'size!'.
```

After sending a transition or check to Possum during traversal, the traversal algorithm will wait until the value of *tgf_report*! is read back from Possum. Therefore, if a transition fails, the traversal will not continue. To recover from this, we define the *ADDODD* operation in Figure 3 as an auxiliary operation, *ADDODD_AUX* which we then use to

```
┌─ op ADDODD ─────────────────────────────────
│ tgf_report! : 𝔽 ADDODD_FAIL
│ ┌─────────────────────────────────────────
│ │ if ∃ state' • ADDODD_AUX then
│ │     ADDODD_AUX ∧ tgf_report! = {}
│ │ else
│ │     tgf_report! = {ADDODD_FAIL}
│ │ fi
└─────────────────────────────────────────────
```

Fig. 5. Updated *ADDODD* Operation for *IntSet*

define an updated *ADDODD*, shown in Figure 5. The new *ADDODD* operation first checks to see if the transition can be made. If so, the transition is made and *tgf_report*! is set to empty. If not, the error message *ADDODD_FAIL*, which is a previously declared abbreviation for the string: *"Error: Transition ADDODD failed unexpectedly"*, is included in the report variable, *tgf_report*!.

The user can view the report at any point during or after traversal. The report is displayed in a new window.

Once the user has run the traversal, new additions to the report generated during subsequent traversals are appended to the end. The user can clear the report or save it to a text file.

5.5 Advanced Features

Regression Animation: The testgraph framework gives the user the option to perform *regression animation*: where results from previous runs are used to check the results of new runs. When a node is visited for the first time, the tool records the value of the state at that node. A check is performed on the value of the state against this recorded value for subsequent visits to that node.

For this to happen, the user has to define a operation in the specification called *retrieve*, which retrieves the value of the state for the specification being animated. Figure 6 shows the *retrieve* function for *IntSet*.

When a testgraph is saved, the value of the state at each node will also be saved. When the testgraph is opened, these values will be loaded and associated with their respective nodes, and on subsequent runs, these values are compared to their respective values at each node. If there is a difference, an error is added to the report.

The user can turn the regression checking on and off. By default, this option is off.

```
┌─ op retrieve ───────────────────────────────
│ tgf_state! : ℙ ℤ
│ ┌─────────────────────────────────────────
│ │ tgf_state! = intset
│ │ changes_only{}
└─────────────────────────────────────────────
```

Fig. 6. *retrieve* function for *IntSet*

Memoisation: As discussed in Section 4, once a node has been visited and the state associated with that node checked, it is not necessary to check the state on subsequent visits to that node if the state is the same as on previous visits. Therefore, the framework has an option to not check the state of a node that has been previously visited. Instead, it records the state of the specification at each node the first time the node is visited, and checks the states are equal on subsequent visits. If the states are the same, the check is not performed. This is called *memoisation*: where the results of a previous calculation are transparently saved and reused to reduce calculation time. This technique is also used in functional and logical programming languages to improve efficiency of programs. If the states are different, an error is added to the report informing the user.

Memoisation and regression animation are similar, but neither subsumes the other because regression animation will check if the current value of the state at a node is the same as a previous value at that node, but will still perform the check. Like regression animation, memoisation requires a *retrieve* function to get the current value of the state.

The user can turn the memoisation on and off. By default, this option is on.

5.6 Experience

As well as the *IntSet* example, we have used our framework to check several other specifications, including two larger case studies. These case studies show that the method scales to medium-sized specifications, and can uncover a significant amount of errors in these specifications. For brevity, a discussion of these is not included here, but is available in an expanded version of this paper [14].

6 Conclusions and Future Work

Specification animation can be used to check properties and the behaviour of specifications. While not offering the same assurance as proofs, animation can increase our confidence in the correctness of a specification.

In this paper, we presented a framework for animation using testgraphs: directed graphs that model a subset of the states and transitions of the specification being animated. Sequences for animation are derived by traversing the testgraph. We presented tool support to help users construct testgraphs and automate their traversal. This framework was explained using a small example of an integer set, and we also discussed the application of this method on two non-trivial specifications. The results from these case studies were promising, because they took little effort and time, and uncovered several significant problems in both case studies.

Plans for future work in this area are to investigate more generic, specification-independent properties to be checked on specifications.

References

1. O. Bosman and H. W. Schmidt. Object test coverage using finite state machines. In *Proceedings of TOOLS Pacific '95*, pages 171–178, Melbourne, Australia, 1995.
2. J. Callahan, Easterbrook. S., and T. Montgomery. Generating test oracles via model checking. TR NASA-IVV-98-015, NASA / West Virginia University Software Research Laboratory, 1998.
3. D. Carrington, I. MacColl, J. McDonald, L. Murray, and P. Strooper. From Object-Z specifications to Classbench test suites. *Journal on Software Testing, Verification and Reliability*, 10(2):111–137, 2000.
4. J. Dick and A. Faivre. Automating the generation and sequencing of test cases from model-based specifications. In *Formal Methods Europe (FME'93)*, pages 268–284, 1993.
5. D. Hazel, P. Strooper, and O. Traynor. Possum: An animator for the Sum specification language. In *Proc. Asia-Pacific Soft. Eng. Conf. and Int. Comp. Sci. Conf.*, pages 42–51. IEEE Computer Society, 1997.
6. D. Hazel, P. Strooper, and O. Traynor. Requirements engineering and verification using specification animation. In *Proc. 13th IEEE Int. Conf. on Automated Soft. Eng.*, pages 302–305. IEEE Computer Society, 1998.
7. C. Heitmeyer, J. Kirby, B. Labaw, and R. Bharadwaj. SCR*: A toolset for specifying and analysing software requirements. In *Comp-Aided Verif. 10th Annual Conf*, 1998.
8. M. Hewitt, C. O'Halloran, and C. Sennett. Experiences with PiZA, an animator for Z. In *ZUM'97: The Z Formal Specification Notation*, volume 1212 of *LNCS*, pages 37–51, 1996.
9. D. M. Hoffman and P. A. Strooper. ClassBench: A methodology and framework for automated class testing. In D. C. Kung, P. Hsia, and J. Gao, editors, *Testing Object-Oriented Software*, pages 152–176. IEEE Computer Society, 1998.
10. IFAD. Features of VDM tools. http://www.ifad.dk/products/vdmtools/features.htm.
11. E. Kazmierczak, P. Kearney, O. Traynor, and L. Wang. A modular extension to Z for specification, reasoning and refinement. TR 95-15, SVRC, University of Queensland, Australia, February 1995.
12. E. Kazmierczak, M. Winikoff, and P. Dart. Verifying model oriented specifications through animation. In *Proc. Asia-Pacific Soft. Eng. Conf.*, pages 254–261, 1998.
13. T. Miller and P. Strooper. Animation can show only the presence of errors, never their absence. In *Proc. Aust. Soft. Eng. Conf (ASWEC 2001)*. Aust. Comp. Soc., 2001.
14. T. Miller and P. Strooper. Model-based specification animation using testgraphs. TR 02-15, SVRC, The University of Queensland, Australia, 2002. http://www.svrc.uq.edu.au/Publications/2002/svrc2002-015.html.
15. L. Murray, D. Carrington, I. MacColl, J. McDonald, and P. Strooper. Formal derivation of finite state machines for class testing. In *ZUM'98: The Z Formal Specification Notation*, volume 1493 of *LNCS*, pages 42–59. Springer Verlag, 1998.
16. P. Stocks and D. Carrington. A framework for specification-based testing. *IEEE Transactions on Soft. Eng.*, 22(11):777–793, 1996.
17. H. Treharne, B. Ormsby, J. Draper, and T. Boyce. Evaluating the B-Method on an avionics example. In *Proc. DASIA Conference*, pages 89–97, 1996.
18. H. Waeselynck and S. Behnia. B-Model animation for external verification. In *Proc. Conf. for Formal Eng. Methods*. IEEE Computer Society, 1998.

An Abstract Model for Scheduling Real-Time Programs

Alvaro E. Arenas

Laboratorio de Computo Especializado, Universidad Autónoma de Bucaramanga,
Calle 48 No 39 - 234, Bucaramanga, Colombia
aearenas@bumanga.unab.edu.co

Abstract. The main contribution of this paper is to devise a technique that allows one to study the implementation of the same program under different schedulers using high-level abstractions such as algebraic laws and simple methods. We apply the techniques presented in Hoare and He's *Unifying Theories of Programming* in order to develop an abstract model for scheduling real-time programs into a uniprocessor machine. We illustrate the applicability of the model by instancing it with two types of schedulers: a round-robin scheduler, employed when the participating parallel processes do not include deadline constraints, and a priority-based scheduler, used when each participating process is periodic and possesses an associated deadline.

Keywords: Real-time Programming; Program Verification; Scheduling.

1 Introduction

Safety-critical computer systems must be engineered to the highest quality in order to anticipate potential faults and to reduce the possibility of erroneous and unexpected behaviour. Correctness of system properties must then be guaranteed at all levels, from specification to low-level implementation into a target machine.

This paper shows a way of reasoning about correctness of schedulers using high-level abstractions such as algebraic laws. We apply the techniques presented in Hoare and He's *Unifying Theories of Programming* [5] to develop an abstract model for scheduling real-time programs. The applicability of the model is illustrated by instancing it with cyclic and fixed-priority schedulers. The results reported here are part of research aiming to integrate issues of compilation and scheduling of real-time programs within a single framework [1].

Section 2 presents the source programming language and describes its main algebraic laws. Next, section 3 introduces the target language and develops some properties of machine-level programs. We assume that source programs are correctly compiled into the target language. In section 4 we develop our abstract model of scheduling. We then illustrate in section 5 the application of the model to a round-robin scheduler. Following, section 6 presents the application to a fixed priority scheduler with pre-emption. Finally, section 7 gathers some concluding remarks and discusses possible extensions to our work.

2 The Source Language

Our real-time language is a small imperative language with real-time constructors such as deadline and delay, and primitives for asynchronous communication via communication queues. A program (α, P) consists of an *alphabet* α that specifies the way in which that program can interact with the external world, and of a *process description* P describing the behaviour of that program. Alphabet α is represented by a triplet indicating the names of input queues, output queues and program variables of P. In general, process P has the following structure:

$$P ::= \perp \ | \ II \ | \ \overline{x} := \overline{e} \ | \ s\,!\,e \ | \ s\,?\,x \ | \ \Delta d \ | \ [d]P$$
$$| \ P;P \ | \ P \sqcap P \ | \ P \trianglelefteq b \trianglerighteq P \ | \ \mathtt{while}(b, P) \ | \ [P \triangleright_d^s P] \ | \ P \parallel P$$

where $\overline{x}$ is a list of variables, x is a variable, s is a queue, $\overline{e}$ is a list of expressions, e is an expression, b is a Boolean expression, and d is a time expression.

The chaotic process $\perp$ defines an arbitrary behaviour, which is beyond control. The skip process II does nothing, terminating immediately. The multiple assignment $\overline{x} := \overline{e}$, where $\overline{x}$ is a list of distinct variables and $\overline{e}$ an equal-length list of expressions, evaluates the components of $\overline{e}$ and stores these results simultaneously into list $\overline{x}$, preserving the original ordering of the elements. We assume here that the evaluation of an expression always delivers a result and does not change the value of any variable, i.e. no *side-effect* is allowed. The output $s\,!\,e$ stores the value of the expression e into the output queue s, leaving all program variables unchanged. The input $s\,?\,x$ takes the oldest message from queue s and stores it into variable x. If the queue is empty, the process is blocked until a message arrives. We adopt the realistic premise that all communicating processes take time, the amount of time consumed by the instruction not being specified.

Composition $P;Q$ represents a process that executes P first and, at termination of P, starts with the execution of Q. It is assumed that there is no delay associated with the transfer of control from P to Q. Process $P \sqcap Q$ represents the non-deterministic choice between the participating processes. The conditional $P \trianglelefteq b \trianglerighteq Q$ represents a choice between alternatives P and Q in accordance with the value of Boolean expression b; it behaves like P if b is true, and like Q if b is false. It is assumed that some arbitrary time is spent in the evaluation of the guard b. The iteration $\mathtt{while}(b, P)$ executes process P while condition b is true, and terminates when the condition is false. It is also assumed that some time is spent in each iteration evaluating expression b.

The delay process Δd is guaranteed to wait for a minimum of d time units before terminating. The process $[d]P$ behaves as P and its execution does not take more than d time units. The timeout process $[P \triangleright_d^s Q]$ monitors input queue s for d time units; if there is a message in s during that time, it executes process P, otherwise it executes process Q. Parallel composition $P \parallel Q$ describes the concurrent execution of processes P and Q. Each process has its own program state, which is inaccessible to its partner, and interacts with its partner and the external world via communication through shared queues.

In previous work [2], we have given a specification-oriented semantics to our language and derived its main algebraic laws. The semantic is constructed by following the predicative approach described in [5], where a process is modelled as a predicate that describes all the *observations* that it can generate. In [1], we have proposed notation $P \equiv Q$ to denote that processes P and Q are semantically equivalent and proved that all derived laws are sound with respect to the model. Further, we use ordering relation $P \sqsubseteq Q$ to indicate that Q is at least as deterministic as P. It is defined in terms of non-deterministic choice as $P \sqsubseteq Q \,\hat{=}\, (P \sqcap Q) \equiv P$.

In order to reason about the source language, we extended it with specification constructors. The miracle program, denoted by $\top$, stands for a product that can never be used because its conditions of use are impossible to satisfy. The conditional process $(P \triangleleft b \triangleright Q)$ selects one alternative depending on the value of expression b; if b is true, it acts like process P, otherwise it behaves like Q. It differs from the conditional of our programming language in that it is assumed that the evaluation of b does not take time. The assumption of b, denoted by $b^\top$, can be regarded as a miracle test: it behaves like II if b is true; otherwise it behaves like $\top$. By contrast, the assertion of b, denoted by $b_\bot$, also behaves like II if b is true, otherwise it fails, behaving like $\bot$. The idle process Δ represents a process that may terminate at any arbitrary time without changing any variable or communication queue. As usual, iteration $b * P$ can be defined as the least fixed point of the recursive equation $F(X) = ((P;\ X) \triangleleft b \triangleright II)$. The declaration **var** x introduces a new program variable x and permits x to be used in the portion of the program that follows it. The complementary operation, **end** x, terminates the region of permitted use for variable x. The following are typical example of the derived algebraic laws and the use of specification constructors.

Law 1. *(Some Algebraic Laws)*
(1) $P;\ II \equiv II;\ P \equiv P$ 　　　　　　　　(2) $x := e;\ s!f(x) \equiv x := e;\ s!f(e)$
(3) $b^\top;\ (P \triangleleft b \triangleright Q) \equiv b^\top;\ P$ 　　　　　(4) **var** $v;\ \Delta \sqsubseteq$ **var** $v;\ x := e$
(5) $b^\top;\ b * P \equiv b^\top;\ P;\ b * P$ 　　　　(6) $(\neg b)^\top;\ b * P \equiv (\neg b)^\top$
(7) Let $P = (a;\ P_0),\ a \in \{x := e, s!e, ((s \neq \langle\rangle)^\top;\ s?x)\},\ Q = (b;\ Q_0)$,
　　$b \in \{y := f, t!f, ((t \neq \langle\rangle)^\top;\ t?y)\}$. Then $P \parallel Q \equiv (a;\ (P_0 \parallel Q) \sqcap b;\ (P \parallel Q_0))$

3 The Target Language

We suppose there is a step previous to the scheduling process consisting in the compilation of a source program into a target program. We illustrate such a compilation process in [3]. Here we describe the main characteristic of the target language. Our target machine has a simple architecture, consisting of the following components: a store for instructions $m : Addr \to Instr$ modelled as a function from the set of addresses to the set of machine instructions; a program counter $pc : Addr$ that points to the current instruction; and a data stack $st : seq.\mathbb{Z}$ used to hold temporary values. The target language is an *intermediate-representation* language close to the final machine code. The full set of instructions is presented elsewhere [3], the following are examples of target instructions. Symbol $\mathbin{+\mkern-10mu+}$ is used to denote concatenation of sequences; $\#st$ stands for the size of sequence st; **last**.st denotes the last element of st; and **front**.st corresponds to the sequence obtained from eliminating last element of *st*.

$$\begin{aligned}
\texttt{LD}(x) &\mathrel{\hat{=}} pc, st := pc + 1, st \mathbin{+\!\!+} \langle x \rangle \\
\texttt{ST}(x) &\mathrel{\hat{=}} (\#st \geq 1)^\top; \; pc, st, x := pc + 1, \texttt{front}.st, \texttt{last}.st \\
\texttt{OUT}(s) &\mathrel{\hat{=}} (\#st \geq 1)^\top; \; s\,!\,\texttt{last}.st; \; pc, st := pc + 1, \texttt{front}.st \\
\texttt{IN}(s) &\mathrel{\hat{=}} (s \neq \langle\rangle)^\top; \; \texttt{var}\, x; \; s\,?\,x; \; pc, st := pc + 1, st \mathbin{+\!\!+} \langle x \rangle; \; \texttt{end}\, x
\end{aligned}$$

Execution of a target program is modelled by the repetition of a set of target instructions. To formalise such concept, we borrow some elements from [5].

Definition 1. *(Labelled Instruction) Let* INSTR : *Instr be a target instruction and* l : Addr *a machine location. Labelled instruction* l : INSTR *expresses that instruction* INSTR *is executed when the program counter has value* l. *It is defined as* l : INSTR $\mathrel{\hat{=}}$ (INSTR $\triangleleft pc = l \triangleright II$).

Labelled instructions are used to model the possible actions during the execution of a target program.

Definition 2. *(Assembly and Continuation Set) Let* C *be a machine program consisting only of labelled instruction* l : INSTR. *Then,* C *is an assembly program with continuation set* $L.C = \{l\}$. *Let* C *and* D *be assembly programs with disjoint continuation sets* $L.C$ *and* $L.D$ *respectively. The assembly program* $(C \,[\!]\, D)$ *and its continuation set are defined as follows:*

$$C \,[\!]\, D \mathrel{\hat{=}} (C \triangleleft pc \in L.C \triangleright D) \triangleleft (pc \in L.C \cup L.D) \triangleright II$$
$$L.(C\,[\!]\,D) \mathrel{\hat{=}} L.C \cup L.D \;.$$

Execution of an assembly program is modelled as a loop which iterates the program as long as the program counter remains within the continuation set.

Definition 3. *(Execution and Target Code) Let* C *be an assembly program. The execution of* C *is defined as* $C^* \mathrel{\hat{=}} (pc \in L.C) * C$. *The evaluation of the guard in the loop does not consume time. All execution time overheads are accounted for in the machine instructions. Notation* $\langle a, C, z \rangle$ *denote target code* $\texttt{var}\, pc, st; \; (pc = a)^\top; \; C^*; \; (pc = z)_\bot; \; \texttt{end}\, pc, st$. *Declaration* $\texttt{var}\, pc, st$ *introduces the machine components; assumption* $(pc = a)^\top$ *expresses that program counter* pc *should be positioned at location* a *at the beginning of execution of* C; *and assertion* $(pc = z)_\bot$ *states the obligation to terminate with program counter* pc *positioned at location* z.

4   An Abstract Model for Scheduling

Let $\langle a_i, C_i, z_i \rangle$ be a collection of target codes working on machine components pc_i and st_i, for $i = 1, \cdots, n$; and $C = ([D_1]\,C_1^* \parallel [D_2]\,C_2^* \parallel \cdots \parallel [D_n]\,C_n^*)$ be a parallel program where execution of each participating process C_i has an associated deadline D_i. In this section we define an abstract model in which the implementation of C into a uniprocessor machine is represented as transformation $\Psi(C)$ and derive conditions to guarantee the validity of such a transformation.

Let us assume that the continuation set of the participating processes in C is pairwise disjoint. Process C_i is executed when its program counter belongs to the valid set of locations, i.e. $pc_i \in L.C_i$, and the processor has been allocated to it by the scheduler. To represent allocation, integer variable $id : \mathbb{Z}$ is employed. Variable id has value i when the processor has been allocated to process C_i; it has a value different from i when C_i is positioned out of its continuation set. The above restrictions can be summarised in the predicate $\mathcal{I}$, which can be seen as an invariant on id: $\mathcal{I} \stackrel{\wedge}{=} \bigwedge_{i=1}^{n} (id = i \Rightarrow pc_i \in L.C_i) \wedge (id \notin [1,n] \Rightarrow \bigwedge_{i=1}^{n} pc_i \notin L.C_i)$.

The effect of scheduling process C_i is then represented by a transformation $\Psi^i(C_i)$ in which each labelled instruction l : INSTR of C_i is transformed by strengthening its guard by the condition $(id = i)$ and by executing a piece of code, called $CHANGE_\Psi$, at the end of instruction INSTR. Code $CHANGE_\Psi$ performs the allocation of the processor according to the defined policy.

Definition 4. *(Transformation Ψ^i)*
$\Psi^i(l : \text{INSTR}) = (\text{INSTR}; CHANGE_\Psi) \triangleleft pc_i = l \wedge id = i \triangleright II$
$\Psi^i(C \,[\!]\, D) = (\Psi^i(C) \,[\!]\, \Psi^i(D))$.

For simplicity, we assume that scheduling instructions, i.e. the instructions of code $CHANGE_\Psi$, are instantaneous. Their execution time is included in the duration of the associated machine instructions.

The implementation of program C into a uniprocessor machine is represented by a loop that iterates while the processor is allocated to any of the processes. It proves to be useful to include in the loop the case when the processor is idle because no process is active. Such a condition is represented by condition $IdleCond$, that has the property $IdleCond \Rightarrow id \notin [1,n]$. Action $IDLE$ is executed when $IdleCond$ holds; it is defined as $IDLE \stackrel{\wedge}{=} ([1]\Delta \triangleleft IdleCond \triangleright II)$. The loop implementing program C is then defined as:

$$\Psi(C) \stackrel{\wedge}{=} c * ((\,[\!]_{i=1}^{n} \Psi^i(C_i)) \,[\!]\, IDLE) \text{ where } c = ((\bigvee_{i=1}^{n} id = i) \vee IdleCond).$$

To verify that $\Psi(C)$ correctly implements C requires proof that the timing and computational requirements of C are respected by $\Psi(C)$. Such requirements are represented in properties (1) and (2) below.

- Let $\mathcal{T}_\Psi(C_i)$ denote the time spent executing process C_i in $\Psi(C)$. If each process C_i^* in C has an associated deadline D_i, then we have the obligation to prove that implementation $\Psi(C)$ respects those timing constraints, i.e.

$$\mathcal{T}_\Psi(C_i) \leq D_i \quad \text{for } i = 1, \cdots, n. \tag{1}$$

- Let $(\,\|_{i=1}^{n}\, C_i^*)$ denote the parallel execution of the target processes in C, without considering their timing constraints. The fact that the computational behaviour of C is respected by $\Psi(C)$ is represented as follows:

$$(\,\|_{i=1}^{n}\, C_i^*)_{+(id, \mathcal{I})} \sqsubseteq (\bigvee_{i=1}^{n} id = i) * (\,[\!]_{i=1}^{n} \Psi^i(C_i)). \tag{2}$$

Refinement requires that both programs have the same alphabet, hence we use notation $(\,\|_{i=1}^{n}\, C_i^*)_{+(id, \mathcal{I})}$ to indicate that alphabet of $(\,\|_{i=1}^{n}\, C_i^*)$ has been extended with variable id, and invariant $\mathcal{I}$ holds. In general, for program variable v and predicate $\mathcal{V}$ on v, alphabet extension $P_{+(v,\mathcal{V})}$ can be defined as $\mathcal{V}^\top$; P; $\mathcal{V}_\perp$.

We close this part by showing that if the application of transformation Ψ to each machine instruction of C_i is an improvement, then refinement (2) holds directly.

Theorem 1. *(Computational Behaviour)* Let l : INSTR *be an instruction of target process* C_i. *If the refinement* $(\Psi^i(\text{INSTR}); \mathcal{I}^\top) \sqsupseteq \text{INSTR}$ *holds then property (2) is valid.*

Proof. Let $F(X) = ((\overset{n}{\underset{i=1}{[]}}\, \Psi^i(C_i)); X \triangleleft (\overset{n}{\underset{i=1}{\bigvee}}\, id_i = i) \triangleright II)$. The right hand side of property (2) is equivalent to $\mu X \bullet F(X)$. Since each instruction of C_i takes time, function F is time guarded for variable X and the fixed point is unique. We exploit this situation, and use the strategy of proving that $(\overset{n}{\underset{i=1}{\|}}\, C_i^*)_{+(id,\mathcal{I})}$ is a pre-fixed point of function F. Let us begin with the case when arbitrary process C_j is active and has been chosen by the scheduler to be executed. Let $ASS \,\widehat{=}\, (pc_j = l \land id = j \land m[l] = \text{INSTR})$. Then

$F((\overset{n}{\underset{i=1}{\|}}\, C_i^*)_{+(id,\mathcal{I})})$

$\equiv$ Definition of F

$((\overset{n}{\underset{i=1}{[]}}\, \Psi^i(C_i)); (\overset{n}{\underset{i=1}{\|}}\, C_i^*)_{+(id,\mathcal{I})}) \triangleleft (\overset{n}{\underset{i=1}{\bigvee}}\, id_i = i) \triangleright II$

$\equiv$ ASS and elimination of conditional, Law 1(3)

$\Psi^j(C_j); (\overset{n}{\underset{i=1}{\|}}\, C_i^*)_{+(id,\mathcal{I})}$

$\equiv$ Definition of assembly, Def. 2, and elimination of conditional, Law 1(3)

$\Psi^j(\text{INSTR}); (\overset{n}{\underset{i=1}{\|}}\, C_i^*)_{+(id,\mathcal{I})}$

$\sqsupseteq$ Definition of alphabet extension and assumption $(\Psi^i(\text{INSTR}); \mathcal{I}^\top) \sqsupseteq \text{INSTR}$

$\text{INSTR}; (\overset{n}{\underset{i=1}{\|}}\, C_i^*); \mathcal{I}_\perp$

$\sqsupseteq$ Expansion law 1(7)

$((\overset{j-1}{\underset{i=1}{\|}}\, C_i^*) \| (\text{INSTR}; C_j^*) \| (\overset{n}{\underset{i=j+1}{\|}}\, C_i^*)); \mathcal{I}_\perp$

$\equiv$ Unfolding the loop, Law 1(5)

$((\overset{j-1}{\underset{i=1}{\|}}\, C_i^*) \| (C_j^*) \| (\overset{n}{\underset{i=j+1}{\|}}\, C_i^*)); \mathcal{I}_\perp$

$\equiv$ ASS implies predicate $\mathcal{I}$ and definition of alphabet extension

$(\overset{n}{\underset{i=1}{\|}}\, C_i^*)_{+(\{id\},\mathcal{I})}$

The case when all programs have finished their execution, i.e. $\overset{n}{\underset{i=1}{\bigwedge}}\, pc_i \notin L.C_i$, follows in a straightforward manner, since both sides of the refinement reduce to skip.   □

5 Cyclic Scheduling

Let $C = (C_1^* \parallel C_2^* \parallel \cdots \parallel C_n^*)$ be the parallel program to be implemented, where each C_i represents a target process that is neither periodic nor has an associated deadline. Here we apply the technique presented previously to prove the implementation of C into a uniprocessor machine using a *round robin scheduler*. In this model, the execution in the single-processor machine is represented by an interleaving of the instructions executed by the participating processes. The interleaving is represented by executing piece of code $CHANGE_\Psi$ after a communication instruction (machine instructions IN and OUT) and after the last instruction of C_i. Code $CHANGE_\Psi$ is defined as follows.

Definition 5. *($CHANGE_\Psi$)*

$CHANGE_\Psi \;\hat{=}\; (id \in [1,n])^\top;\ \textbf{var}\ A;$
$\qquad\qquad A := \{k \mid 1 \le k \le n+1 \;\wedge\;$
$\qquad\qquad\qquad (\exists j \bullet j = (id+k) \bmod (n+1) \wedge j \ne 0 \wedge pc_j \in L.C_j)\};$
$\qquad\qquad ((id := (id + \min(A)) \bmod (n+1)) \lhd A \ne \emptyset \rhd id := -1);\ \textbf{end}\ A\ .$

Code $CHANGE_\Psi$ assumes initially that variable id has a value in the interval of 1 to n. It then stores in temporal variable A the set of distances between id and the identifier of other active processes, in such a way that the cyclic order is maintained. Finally, it updates id with the identifier of the closest active process.

For target program $\langle a, C_i, z \rangle$, the effect of scheduling process C_i is represented by a transformation $\Psi_z^i(C_i)$. We rewrite definition 4 in the following way.

Definition 6. *(Transformation Ψ_z^i)*

$\Psi_z^i(l\!:\!\texttt{INSTR}) = (\texttt{INSTR};\ CHANGE_\Psi) \lhd pc_i=l \wedge id=i \rhd II$
$\qquad\qquad\qquad$ if $\texttt{INSTR} \in \{\texttt{IN}(s), \texttt{OUT}(s)\}$ or $l:\texttt{INSTR} \equiv (l:\texttt{INSTR};\ (pc_i = z)_\bot)$
$\qquad\qquad = \texttt{INSTR} \lhd pc_i = l \wedge id = i \rhd II \qquad\qquad\qquad\qquad\qquad\text{otherwise}$
$\Psi_z^i(C\ [\!]\ D)\ = (\Psi_z^i(C)\ [\!]\ \Psi_z^i(D))\ .$

Following the abstract model, implementation of C in the single-processor machine is denoted by $\Psi(C)$. Execution of C finishes when all processes C_i terminate their execution; thus, it is not necessary to model in $\Psi(C)$ the idle case in which the processor is not executing processes, and $IdleCond$ is defined to be false. Implementation $\Psi(C)$ for the case of the cyclic scheduler is then defined as follows: $\Psi(C) \;\hat{=}\; (\bigvee_{i=1}^{n} id = i) * (\prod_{i=1}^{n} \Psi_{z_i}^i(C_i))$.

Correctness of $\Psi(C)$ requires verification that the timing and computational constraints hold, i.e. to prove that equation (1) and refinement (2) are valid. Equation (1) follows trivially, since there are not timing constraints associated with processes in C. To prove refinement (2), we utilise theorem 1 and show that the application of transformation Ψ_z^i to a machine instruction is an improvement on the original instruction.

As all assignments in $CHANGE_\Psi$ are instantaneous, execution of $CHANGE_\Psi$ is a refinement of skip.

Lemma 1. *If $id \in [1,n]$ then $(CHANGE_\Psi;\ \mathcal{I}^\top) \sqsupseteq II$* ☐

Proof of refinement (2) follows directly from the next theorem. Application of Ψ_z^i to a machine instruction is an improvement on the original instruction.

Theorem 2. $\Psi_z^i(l : \text{INSTR}); \mathcal{I}^\top \sqsupseteq l : \text{INSTR}$

Proof. The case for instructions that do not execute code $CHANGE_\Psi$ follows directly from the definition of transformation Ψ_z^i. We illustrate the case when $pc_i = l$, $id = i$, $m_i[l] = \text{INSTR}$, and code $CHANGE_\Psi$ is executed after INSTR.

$\Psi_z^i(l : \text{INSTR}); \mathcal{I}^\top$

$\equiv$ Definition of Ψ_i^z, Def. 6

$((\text{INSTR}; CHANGE_\Psi) \triangleleft pc_i = l \wedge id = i \triangleright II); \mathcal{I}^\top$

$\equiv$ Assumption $pc_i = l$ and $id = i$

$(\text{INSTR}; CHANGE_\Psi); \mathcal{I}^\top$

$\sqsupseteq$ Associativity of sequential composition and Lemma 1

$\text{INSTR}; II$

$\equiv$ II unit of sequential composition, Law 1(1), assumption $pc_i = l$ and $id = i$

$\text{INSTR} \triangleleft pc_i = l \triangleright II$

$\equiv$ Definition of labelled instruction, Def. 1

$l : \text{INSTR}$

   □

6 Fixed Priority Scheduling with Pre-emption

Let $C = (\overline{C_1} \parallel \overline{C_2} \parallel \cdots \parallel \overline{C_n})$ be a parallel program where each $\overline{C_i} = [D_i] C_i^*$ is a process with deadline D_i and period T_i. Here we show how to apply the technique presented in section 4 to validate the implementation of C.

In general, in priority-based scheduling schemes processes are assigned priorities such that, at all times, the process with the highest priority is executing (if it is not delayed or otherwise suspended). A scheduling scheme will therefore involve a priority assignment algorithm and a schedulability test, i.e. a means of confirming that the temporal requirements of the system are satisfied [4]. We have selected the *deadline monotonic priority ordering* [7] as our method for priority assignment. In this ordering, the fixed priority of a process is inversely related to its deadline: if $D_i < D_j$ then process C_i has higher priority than C_j. As the parallel operator is commutative and associative, we reorganise processes in C such that if $i < j$ then C_i has higher priority than C_j. Regarding schedulability tests, we have chosen the *worst-case response time* analysis [6]. The worst-case response time of process C_i, denoted by R_i, is defined to be the longest time between the invocation of C_i and its subsequent completion. We assume that the set of processes C_is in C has passed the worst-case response time test, i.e. $R_i \leq D_i$ for $i = 1, \cdots, n$, and use a model of cooperative scheduling [4], in which each machine instruction is considered an atomic action and pre-emption is deferred at the end of executing an instruction.

Code $CHANGE_\Psi$ states the scheduling policy that the processor is always executing the active process with the highest priority. In order to implement such a policy, the following elements are included:

- Integer variable *clock* represents the clock of the system. For simplicity, it is assumed that *clock* is equal to zero when the execution of the system begins.
- Integer variables inv_i and com_i representing the number of invocations and completions of each process C_i respectively. A natural requirement for the system is that each invocation of a process is completed before its next invocation, i.e. $\bigwedge_{i=1}^{n}(inv_i \geq com_i \geq inv_i - 1)$. That requirement holds under the restriction that the deadline of executing a process is less than its period, i.e. $D_i < T_i$. Process C_i is active when condition $inv_i > com_i$ holds; further, it is the highest-priority active process if condition $(inv_i > com_i \wedge \bigwedge_{j=1}^{i-1} \neg (inv_j > com_j))$ is true.
- Following Liu and Joseph [8], to verify that the implementation of C satisfies its real-time constraints, timers Ta_i and Tc_i are included for each process C_i. Timer Ta_i records the time that has elapsed since the last invocation of C_i. Timer Tc_i records the time spent in executing proper instructions of C_i.
- Pre-emption cannot happen in the middle of the execution of a machine instruction; therefore, it is necessary to record those processes that were activated during the execution of an instruction, as well as the time of activation. These values will be used to update the corresponding variables once the execution of the instruction finishes. Auxiliary variable $newact_i$ is true if process C_i was released during the execution of a machine instruction, and t_i records the value of the clock at the moment of the activation.

As initial condition, it is assumed that the system starts execution at time zero, and at that time all participating processes are active. Condition *INIT* represents such situation.

$$INIT \mathrel{\hat{=}} clock = 0 \wedge id = 1 \wedge \bigwedge_{i=1}^{n}(inv_i = 1 \wedge com_i = 0 \wedge pc_i = a_i \wedge \neg newact_i \wedge Ta_i = 0 \wedge Tc_i = 0).$$

Processes are released by the system according to their period. Condition *TRIGGER* represents the release of processes.

$$TRIGGER \mathrel{\hat{=}} \bigwedge_{i=1}^{n}(clock \bmod T_i) = 0 \Rightarrow$$

$$(inv_i, newact_i, Ta_i, Tc_i := inv_i + 1, false, 0, 0 \; \triangleleft \; \bigvee_{j=1}^{n} \neg (inv_j > com_j) \; \triangleright$$

$$inv_i, newact_i, t_i := inv_i + 1, true, clock).$$

If the processor was idle ($\bigvee_{j=1}^{n} \neg (inv_j > com_j)$), we activate the ready processes immediately; otherwise, the activation is deferred until the end of the current machine instruction.

Let us now define code $CHANGE_\Psi$, which is attached to each machine instruction and performs the actions associated with the scheduler: update the timers, activate new processes and achieve pre-emption.

Definition 7. *($CHANGE_\Psi$) Code $CHANGE_\Psi(i, a, z, \mathtt{INSTR})$ where i denotes the identifier of a process C_i, a stands for the initial location of process C_i, z*

corresponds to the final location of C_i, and INSTR denotes a machine instruction of C_i, is defined as follows.

$CHANGE_\Psi(i, a, z, \text{INSTR}) \;\hat{=}$

$\quad Tc_i := Tc_i + \mathcal{T}(\text{INSTR});$ \hfill (Update Tc_i)

$\quad (\bigwedge_{j=1}^{n} newact_j \Rightarrow (newact_j, Ta_j, Tc_j := false, clock - t_j, 0));$ \hfill (New processes)

$\quad (\bigwedge_{j=1}^{n} (inv_j > com_j \land \neg\, newact_j) \Rightarrow Ta_j := Ta_j + \mathcal{T}(\text{INSTR}));$ \hfill (Update Ta)

$\quad (com_i, pc_i := com_i + 1, a \triangleleft pc_i = z \triangleright II);$ \hfill (End of execution of C_i)

$\quad id := \min\{j \in [1, n] \mid inv_j > com_j \land \bigwedge_{k=1}^{j-1} \neg\,(inv_k > com_k)\}$ \hfill (Pre-emption)

$\qquad\qquad\qquad\qquad\qquad \triangleleft \bigvee_{j=1}^{n} inv_j > com_j \triangleright II$

Let us explain the above definition. Timer Tc_i counts the time spent executing instructions of C_i, hence it is incremented by the duration of INSTR. In case a new process C_j was activated during the execution of INSTR, timer Ta_j should count the fraction of time its activation has been deferred. In case other processes C_j are active, timer Ta_j is incremented by the duration of instruction INSTR. If execution of C_i finishes, the counter com_i is incremented and the program counter is located to the initial position, so that it will be ready for the next invocation. Finally, variable id is updated with the identifier of the active process with the highest priority.

For target program $\langle a, C_i, z \rangle$, the effect of scheduling process C_i is represented by a transformation $\Psi^i_{(a,z)}$ in which the guard of each instruction $l : \text{INSTR}$ of C_i is strengthened by the condition $(id = i)$, as is the case in the abstract model, and code $CHANGE_\Psi(i, a, z, \text{INSTR})$ is executed at the end of INSTR. We rewrite definition 4 as follows.

Definition 8. *(Transformation $\Psi^i_{(a,z)}$)*

$\Psi^i_{(a,z)}(l : \text{INSTR}) = (\text{INSTR}; CHANGE_\Psi(i,a,z,\text{INSTR})) \triangleleft pc_i{=}l \land id{=}i \triangleright II$

$\Psi^i_{(a,z)}(C \,[]\, D) \;\;= (\Psi^i_{(a,z)}(C) \,[]\, \Psi^i_{(a,z)}(D)).$

Following the abstract model, implementation of C in the single-processor machine is denoted by $\Psi(C)$. The processor is idle when no process is active; thus, $IdleCond$ is defined as $id \notin [1, n]$. As a result, the guard of loop $\Psi(C)$ is reduced to true. Implementation $\Psi(C)$ for the case of the pre-emptive fixed-priority scheduler is defined as follows: $\Psi(C) \;\hat{=}\; INIT^\top; true*((\,[]_{i=1}^{n} \Psi^i_{(a_i,z_i)}(C_i)) \,[]\, IDLE)$. Correctness of $\Psi(C)$ requires verification that the timing constraints and the computational behaviour of C, equation (1) and refinement (2), are preserved.

6.1 Verifying Computational Behaviour

In order to prove that $\Psi(C)$ preserves the computational behaviour of C, we resort to theorem 1 and simply show that application of $\Psi^i_{(a,z)}$ to a machine instruction of C_i is an improvement on such an instruction. Let us define the auxiliary

variables $\bar{v}$ introduced in the implementation of C and its associated invariant: $\bar{v} \triangleq \{inv, com, clock, Ta, Tc, newact, t\}$ and $\mathcal{V} \triangleq \bigwedge_{i=1}^{n}(inv_i \geq com_i \geq inv_i - 1)$.
The following theorem illustrates that any labelled instruction of process C_i is improved by the application of transformation $\Psi^i_{(a,z)}$.

Theorem 3. $\Psi^i_{(a,z)}(l : \text{INSTR}); \; (\mathcal{I} \wedge \mathcal{V})^\top \sqsupseteq l : \text{INSTR}$.

Proof. The proof follows lines similar to those of proof of theorem 2, since all instructions in $CHANGE_{\Psi}$ are instantaneous. □

6.2 Verifying Timing Constraints

To verify timing constraints, we follow an approach presented previously [8], which relies on the value of timers Ta_i and Tc_i to determine the duration of process C_i. The time spent executing process C_i in $\Psi(C)$ corresponds to the value of timer Ta_i after executing last instruction of C_i; hence, proving equation (1) is equivalent to prove that timer Ta_i is less than the deadline associated to process C_i. As all processes share a common release, it can be shown from general scheduling theory that if all processes meet their first deadline then they will meet all future ones. As a result, we concentrate our attention to the case $com_i = 0$ and $inv_i > com_i$. Assume that all processes with higher priorities than C_i, i.e. processes C_j for $j = 1, \cdots, i-1$, have met their deadline so far. In the worst case, the time spent on executing processes of higher priority than C_i is given by the formula: $Comphp_i \triangleq \sum_{j=1}^{i-1} com_j * \mathcal{T}(C_j) + \sum_{j=1}^{i-1}(inv_j - com_j) * Tc_j$, where $\mathcal{T}(C_i)$ denotes the worst-case execution time of process C_i^*. The next lemma summarises the main properties of Ta_i and Tc_i.

Lemma 2. *(1)* $Tc_i \leq \mathcal{T}(C_i)$.
(2) If $com_i = 0$ *and* $inv_i > com_i$ *then* $Ta_i = Comphp_i + Tc_i$.
(3) If $com_i = 0$ *and* $inv_i > com_i$, *then* $Comphp_i + \mathcal{T}(C_i) \leq R_i$ □

We close this section by proving property (1), i.e. the time spent executing arbitrary process C_i is less than its associated deadline.

Theorem 4. *(Timing Constraints)* Let $C = (\overline{C_1} \parallel \overline{C_2} \parallel \cdots \parallel \overline{C_n})$ be a parallel target program where each process $\overline{C_i} = [D_i]C_i^*$ has associated deadline D_i and period T_i, such that $D_i < T_i$. If the set of processes in C passes the worst-case response analysis, i.e. $R_i \leq D_i$, then the following property holds for implementation $\Psi(C)$: $inv_i > com_i \Rightarrow Ta_i \leq D_i$ for $i = 1, \cdots, n$.

Proof.
$\quad com_i = 0 \wedge inv_i > com_i$
$\Rightarrow$ $\hfill$ Lemma 2
$\quad (Ta_i \leq Comphp_i + \mathcal{T}(C_i)) \wedge (Comphp_i + \mathcal{T}(C_i) \leq R_i)$
$\Rightarrow$ $\hfill$ Transitivity of $\leq$ relation
$\quad Ta_i \leq R_i$
$\Rightarrow$ $\hfill$ Assumption $R_i \leq D_i$
$\quad Ta_i \leq D_i$
$\hfill$ □

7 Conclusion

The results presented here are part of an experiment to determine whether reasoning about subtle timing properties of schedulers can be carried out using algebraic laws and simple methods [1]. We feel the experiment has been successful: it has been shown that having a high-level of abstraction while reasoning about schedulers enables one to model different types of schedulers and to investigate their effect on different programs.

The potential of our model for scheduling has been illustrated by instancing it with two types of schedulers: a round-robin scheduler and a fixed-priority scheduler. In both cases, we have derived and verified properties that guarantee the correctness of the implementation. In the case of the round-robin scheduler, we have verified that the implementation preserves the computational behaviour of the parallel program. In the case of the fixed-priority scheduler, we have verified that the implementation preserves the computational behaviour as well as the timing constraints of the parallel program.

There are some limitations to our experiment; the programs analysed have some restrictions on their structure such as not having deadlines (cyclic scheduler) or being periodic (priority-based scheduler). Intended future work includes studying more general forms of scheduling such as dynamic schedulers.

Acknowledgments

The author would like to thank Jeff Sanders for helpful comments and stimulating discussions. This work was partially funded by Colciencias-BID.

References

1. A. E. Arenas. *Implementation of an Asynchronous Real-Time Programming Language*. D.Phil Thesis, Oxford University Computing Laboratory, 2000.
2. A. E. Arenas. A Specification-Oriented Semantics for Asynchronous Real-Time Programming. In *Proceedings of CLEI'2001, XXVII Conferencia Latinoamericana de Informática*, 2001.
3. A. E. Arenas. An Algebraic Approach for Compiling Real-Time Programs. In *Third Workshop on Models for Time-Critical Systems, Electronic Notes in Theoretical Computer Science*. Elsevier, 2002.
4. A. Burns and A. J. Wellings. *Real-Time Systems and Programming Languages*. Addison-Wesley, 1997.
5. C. A. R. Hoare and He Jifeng. *Unifying Theories of Programming*. Prentice Hall Series in Computer Science, 1998.
6. M. Joseph and P. Pandya. Finding Response Times in a Real-Time System. *The Computer Journal*, 29(5):390–395, 1986.
7. J. Y. T. Leung and J. Whitehead. On the Complexity of Fixed-Priority Scheduling of Periodic, Real-Time Tasks. *Performance Evaluation North Holland*, 2:237–250, 1982.
8. Z. Liu and M. Joseph. Verification, Refinement and Scheduling of Real-Time Programs. *Theoretical Computer Science*, 253(1), 2001.

A Specification and Validation Technique Based on STATEMATE and FNLOG

Olfa Mosbahi, Leila Jemni, Samir Ben Ahmed, and Jacques Jaray

Département des Sciences de l'Informatique, Faculté des Sciences de Tunis,
Campus Universitaire, 1060 le Belvédère Tunis Tunisie.
olfa.mosbahi@fst.rnu.tn, leila.jemni@fsegt.rnu.tn,
samir.benahmed@fst.rnu.tn, jacques.jaray@loria.fr

Abstract. The paper presents a specification technique borrowing features from two classes of specification methods, formal and semi-formal ones. Each of the above methods have been proved to be useful in the development of real-time and critical systems and widely reported in different papers [1], [2]. Formal methods are based on mathematical notations and axiomatic which induce verification and validation. Semi-formal methods are, in the other hand, graphic, structural and user-friendly. Each method is applied on a suitable case study, that we regret some missing features we could found in the other class. This remark has motivated our work. We are interested in the integration of formal and semi-formal methods in order to lay out a specification approach which combines the advantages of theses two classes of methods. The proposed technique is based on the integration of the semi-formal method STATEMATE [3] and the temporal logic FNLOG [7]. This choice is justified by the fact that FNLOG is formal, deals with quantitative temporal properties and that these two approaches have a compatibility which simplifies their integration [7]. The proposed integration approach uses the notations of STATEMATE and FNLOG, defines a various transformations rules of a STATEMATE specification towards FNLOG and extends the axiomatic of the temporal logic FNLOG by new lemmas to deal with duration properties. The paper presents the various steps of our integration approach.

Key words. Formal methods, Integration, Real-time Systems, Semi-formal methods, Specification, Temporal logic, Validation, Verification.

1 Introduction

Critical real-time systems are complex and require a high level of safety and reliability. To reduce this complexity and to reach a necessary degree of reliability and safety, it would be quite interesting to lay out a specification approach which simplifies the requirement description, deals with mathematical notations inducing verification and validation, and allows the description of quantitative temporal properties. Thus, it comes the idea of integrating formal [1], [5] and semi-formal approaches in order to lay out a specification approach which combines the advantages of these two classes of methods. Semi formal methods are graphic, structural and user-friendly ; Formal methods are based on mathematical notations and axiomatic inducing proofs. In this paper, we propose a specification technique integrating STATEMATE [3] as a semi-formal method and the temporal logic FNLOG [7] as a formal one. Several reasons justifies the choice of these methods. STATEMATE [3] is a graphic formalism; covers the various aspects of a complex system. The temporal logic FNLOG [7] provides a requirement specification language that allows a concise expression of properties about quantitative properties. The proposed specification and validation approach introduces an integration method using STATEMATE and FNLOG notations and proposes transformation rules, and an extention of FNLOG axiomatic to reason about duration properties.

2 General View of the Proposed Specification and Validation Method

The proposed integration method [6] comprises mainly five great steps (Fig.1.):

Step 1. Description of Requirements

This step consists on the description of system requirements by using FNLOG notation [7].They are liveness and safety properties specified by the system user.

Step 2. Specification with STATEMATE

This specification reduce system complexity which is broken up into a hierarchy of activities, control and primitives activities, with statecharts and activity-charts.

Development of the Context Diagram. which consists on the main activity, some external processes and flows of information connecting the system to its environment.

Decomposition of the System with Activity-charts. The context diagram is broken up into a series of activities and date-store as well as control activity.

Specification with Statecharts. The control activities are associated with statecharts which describe the behavior of their main activity.

Step 3. Transformation of STATEMATE Primitives to FNLOG

In this step we have proposed some transformations rules from Statecharts and Activity-charts specifications to logical formulae in FNLOG.

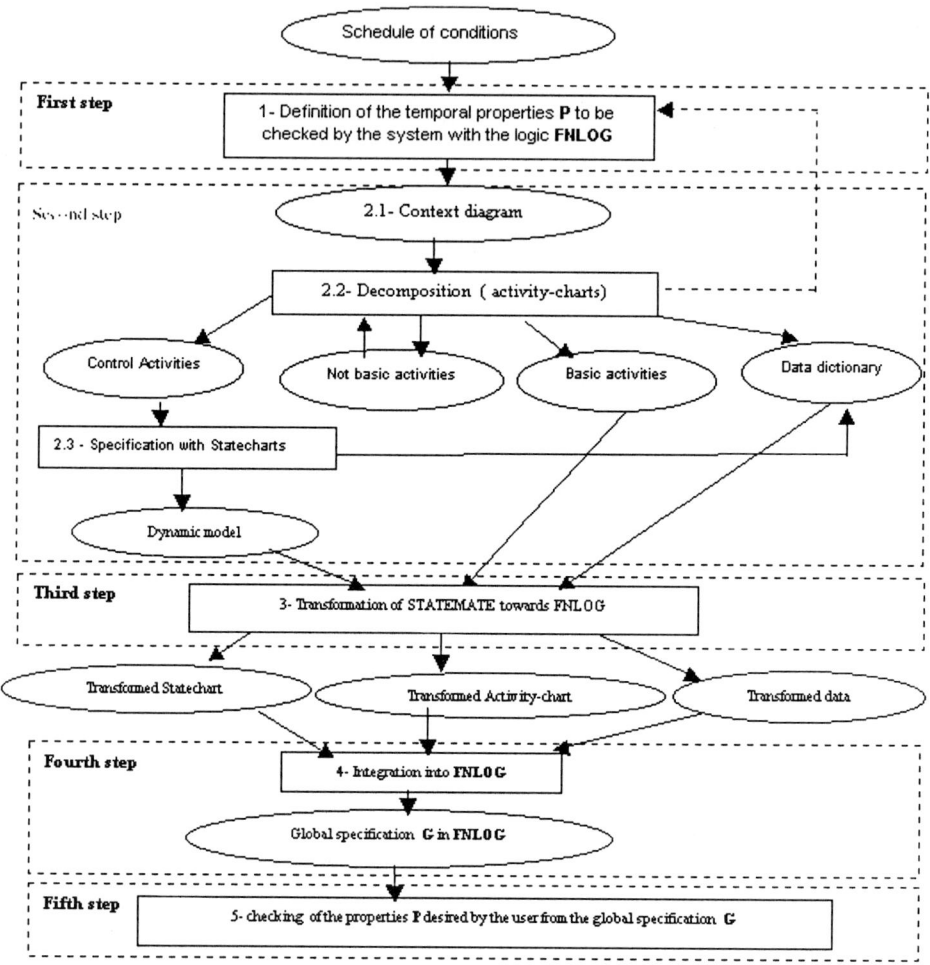

Fig. 1. Method of integration proposed using STATEMATE and FNLOG

Transformation from Statechart to FNLOG. The transformation of a Statecharts specification to an FNLOG specification is based on primitive's and on composition's transformations given in Table 1.

Table. 1. Transformation of statechart's primitives and structures to logic FNLOG

Statecharts	FNLOG
A state	An activity
An action	An event
An event	An event
Duration of an activity	Duration of an activity
Basic statecharts	Functions FNLOG
OR of two statecharts	Disjunction of two specifications FNLOG
AND of two statecharts	Conjunction of two specifications FNLOG

a- The event Timeout tm (E, T): This expression defines a new event which will be generated T units of time after the last occurrence of the event E.

b- The action Scheduled Sc! (G, T): This expression defines the execution of the action G, T units of time after the execution of the primitive Sc.

The transformation of these expressions is given in Fig. 2.

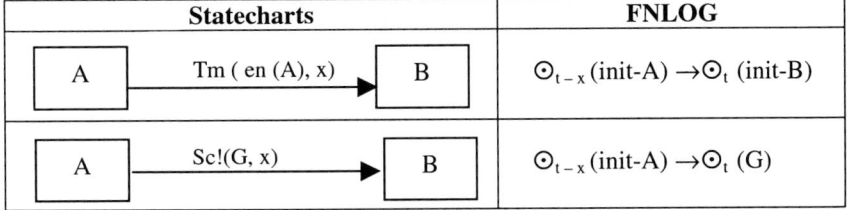

Fig. 2. Transformation of time expressions from statecharts to FNLOG

Transformation of the activity-charts to FNLOG. The transformation of the activity-chart elements is illustrated in Table 2.

Table 2. Transformation of the activity-chart to FNLOG

Activity-charts	FNLOG
An event	An event
A data	An expression of a number
An activity	An activity
A condition	A boolean expression

Step 4. Composition in FNLOG

It's the conjunction of FNLOG formulae found at each level of the decomposition obtained at the steps 2 and 3.

Step 5. Validation

The fifth step consists on proving that the behavior specification found in the fourth step implies the system's requirements specified in the first step. These requirements are in general safety or liveness properties depending on time consideration [4]. However a problem holds in the verification of such duration properties with the existing axiomatic. To simplify such verification, we extend the FNLOG axiomatic [7] by introducing two new lemmas presented in the following :

Lemma 1. Duration over state sequence. The duration of an interval associated to a state sequence is the total length of the sub-intervals associated to each state.

We consider in Fig.3.three consecutive states A, B and C. A is followed by B and B is followed by C. A lasts x time units and B lasts y time units. The duration from the begenning of A to the begenning of C is x+y.

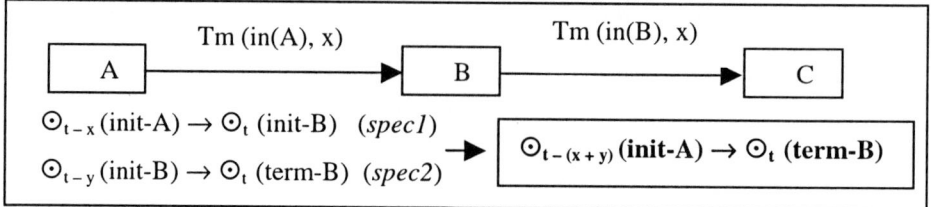

Fig. 3. Lemma 1.

Lemma 2. Atteignability. If a property ϕ holds in an interval [t-k, t] with t > k, then it holds also in the interval [t-j, t]with j ≥ k.

$$\diamondsuit_t^{t-k}(\phi) \Rightarrow \diamondsuit_t^{t-j}(\phi) \quad \forall \ j \geq k$$

3 Conclusion

In this paper, a new technique for the specification and the validation of real-time and critical systems integrating the STATEMATE method [3] and the FNLOG logic [7] has been proposed. The most distinctive characteristic of our approach is the simple way of specifying real-time system's behavior dealing with functional and behavioral aspects. Also, the use of FNLOG has allowed the validation of specification in STATEMATE. We have illustrate our appraoch through an industrial example : a version of a computer controlled gas burner [6]. In order to develop formal technique for specifying and verifying real-time systems integrating STATEMATE and FNLOG, we have extended FNLOG axiomatic to reason about duration properties and proposed a transformation rules from STATEMATE to FNLOG [7].

References

[1] E.M.Clarke and J.M.Wing, *Formal Methods : state of the art and Future Directions*, ACMcomputing survey, Vol. 28, N0 4, P 626-643, décembre 1996.
[2] B.Cohen, *A brief history of formal methods*, FACS Europe, Vol. 1, N0 3, 1994.
[3] D. Harel, *Modeling Reactive systems with Statecharts: The statemate approach*, McGraw-Hill, USA, 1997.
[4] T.A.Henzinger, Z.Manna and A.Pnueli, *Temporal Proof Methodologies for Real-Time Systems*, 18 th Ann. Syym on Principales of Programming Languages, P 353-366, ACM Press, 1991.
[5] F.Jahanian and A.K.-L.Mok, *Safety analysis of timing properties in Real-time systems*, I.E.E.E Trans. On soft. Eng., Vol. 12, N0 9, P 890-904, 1986.
[6] O.Mosbahi, Une technique de spécification et de validation basée sur la méthode STATEMATE et la logique FNLOG, mémoire de D.E.A en informatique, FST, Tunis, Tunisie, 2002.
[7] A.Sowmya and S.Ramesh, *A Semantics-Preserving Transformation of statecharts to FNLOG*, Proc.14 th. IFAC Workshop Distributed Computer Control systems, Seoul, Korea, 1977.

Formal Representation and Analysis of Batch Stock Trading Systems by Logical Petri Net Workflows

Yuyue Du[1,2,3] and Changjun Jiang[1]

[1] Tongji University, Department of Computer Science & Engineering,
Shanghai 200092,, P.R.China
yydu001@163.com, cjjiang@online.sh.cn
[2] Liaocheng University, Department of Computer Science, Liaocheng 252059, P.R.China
[3] Lab. of Computer Science, ISCAS, Beijing 100080, P.R.China

Abstract. This paper focuses on mitigating efficiently the problem of state explosion in Petri net models. A new modeling and analyzing method, logical Petri net workflows (LPNW), of the real-time systems with batch data process procedures is presented based on Petri net and workflow techniques. The use of LPNWs is illustrated by a useful example of a batch stock trading system. The properties and functional correctness of the modeled system are analyzed and verified formally on the basis of temporal logic. It has been sufficiently shown that this approach can avoid the problem of state explosion to a certain extent. Finally, further research work is proposed.

1 Introduction

Today's information, products and services are typically created in business processes, and workflow technology can be used for enhancing the flexibility and efficiency of these processes. Perhaps the most significant development in this direction is Internet-based Stock Trade Systems. However, stock trade procedures must formally be modeled and specified to verify their correctness, fairness and completeness [3]. To date, no generic tool can be used to model and verify the real-time systems in which data are processed in batches. Therefore, a formal method, logical Petri nets workflows (LPNW), is presented based on Petri nets [4,5] and workflows [1,2] in this paper. Its use is illustrated with a useful example of formal representation and analysis of the stock trade system with the function of processing batch orders.

2 Logical Petri Net Workflows

Formally, a Petri net is a triple PN=(P, T; F), where P is a finite set of places, T a finite set of transitions, and P∩T=∅, F⊆(P×T)∪(T×P) a set of arcs. The distribution of tokens over places is called a marking, M, of the PN. We use •t to denote the set of input places for a transition t. The notations t•, •P and P• have similar meanings.

Definition 1[1]. A Petri net PN=(P,T,F) is a workflow net if and only if PN has a source place i: •i=∅ and a sink place o: o•=∅; if we add a transition t* to PN which connects place o with i, then the resulting Petri net is strongly connected.

In workflow nets [1,2], there are three kinds of task dependencies: control-flow dependencies, value dependencies and external dependencies. In batch stock trading systems, we use delay time to represent the wait time for receiving data from other entities. A workflow net is constructed by several basic building blocks: AND-split, AND-join, OR-split and OR-join [1]. A delay transition is said to be enabled only if its each input place has an available token. An enabled delay transition may fire only after its delay time ends. Fig.1 (a) depicts that $t\tau$ can start to execute only after 8 time units from the time which first token arrives in p1.

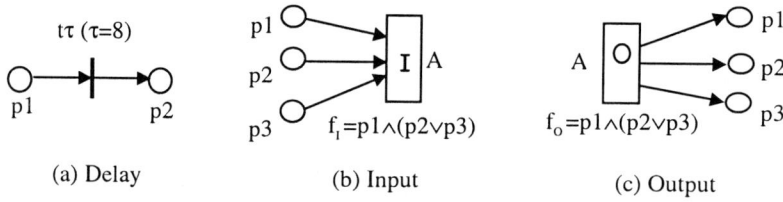

(a) Delay   (b) Input   (c) Output

Fig. 1. PN model examples of delay and logical input/output transitions

A logical input transition is enabled only if the available tokens of its all input places satisfy a given logical expression, and there exists no token in its all input places after it fires. The notation f_i (f_o) is used to denote the logical expression of a logical input (output) transition. Logical input or output transitions are represented graphically by the rectangles in which mark "I" or "O" is embedded, respectively. Fig.1(b) means that task A is enabled only if p1 has at least one token and p2 or p3 has at least one token. The enabling conditions of logical output transitions are the same as ones of the transitions in classical Petri nets. The output places of a logical output transition must satisfy its logical expression f_o and depends on new generated values when firing it. The output of logical output transitions is non-determinate in static structures. Fig.1(c) denotes that one token is generated in p1, and there is one token in one of p2 and p3, or in each of them, after executing task A.

Note that logical input and output transitions cannot be generally expressed in classical Petri nets, but they can be modeled in the Petri nets with inhibitor arcs, in which many additional places and transitions must be appended and the weight of arcs may not equal to 1. Consequently, logical transitions can be used to mitigate the problem of state explosion.

Definition 2. A Logical Petri Net (LPN) is a 9-tuple LPN=(P, TD, TI, TO, F, dt, I, O, M), where P is a set of places; TD is a set of delay transitions; TI is a set of logical input transitions; TO is a set of logical output transitions, and P, TD, TI and TO are disjunct sets; $F \subseteq (P\times(TD \cup TI\cup TO))\cup((TD \cup TI \cup TO) \times P)$ is a set of arcs; dt is a function such that $\forall t\in TD$, $dt(t)\in R$, which denotes the delay time of t; I is a mapping function such that $t\in TI$, $I(t)$ is a logical input expression f_i, while O is a mapping function such that $\forall t \in TO$, O(t) is a logical output expression f_o; M is a marking function.

The LPN representations of delay transitions, logical input and output transitions are shown in Fig.1.

Definition 3. Firing rules of the transitions in LPNs

(1) $\forall t \in TD$, $dt(t)=\tau$, t is said to be enabled if $\forall p \in \bullet t$; $M(p)=1$; t is said to be firable if its enabled time is equal to τ, and firing t results in a new marking M': $\forall p \in \bullet t$: $M'(p)=M(p)-1$; $\forall p \in t\bullet$: $M'(p)=M(p)+1$.

(2) $\forall t \in TI$, $I(t)=f_I$, t is said to be enabled if $f_I|_M = \cdot T\cdot$, i.e. all input places of t satisfy the logical input expression f_I at M; if t is enabled, it can fire, and firing t generates a new marking M': $\forall p \in \bullet t$: $M'(p)=0$; $\forall p \in t\bullet$: $M'(p)=M(p)+1$.

(3) $\forall t \in TO$, $O(t)=f_o$, t is said to be enabled if $\forall p \in \bullet t$, $M(p)=1$; if t is enabled, it can fire, and generates a new marking M': $\forall p \in \bullet t$: $M'(p)=M(p)-1$; for $t\bullet$, $f_o|_{M'} = \cdot T\cdot$.

Definition 4. A LPN is called a LPN workflow net (LPNW) if and only if

(1) The LPN is a workflow net.

(2) The sets of the input and output places of each transition include a control place respectively.

3 LPNW of the Batch Stock Trading System

A stock market involves three types of parties: users (buyers and sellers), brokers and a stock exchange. Brokers communicate with the exchange, while users communicate with the broker committed. We assumed here that the communication system is reliable and robust. In the exchange, there are a secure processor and a number of trading processors. The secure processor accepts each order and records its coming time. It will then transfer the order to a corresponding trading processor, where the order is matched with a fit order. The secure processor will send in time the trading results or revoked orders to corresponding users. Suppose that the secure processor communicates with all (or a group) brokers or all (or a group) trading processors in a time slice. That is, the coming orders from all brokers are accepted in a time slice, and they will be assigned to corresponding trading processors in the other time slice.

Assume that there are n brokers and m trading processors in the batch stock trading system. For the sake of analysis convenience, if a place has more than one order, they will be taken as one token. To save space, the LPNW of the secure processor is only given and analyzed in this paper. An interorganizational LPNW consists of n broker LPNWs, a secure processor LPNW, and m trading processor LPNWs. When they are combined, only one of the same places is reserved.

Once accepting the valid orders and recording their coming time, the secure processor will assign them to corresponding trading processors. And it will send the trading results from each trading processor to corresponding brokers. The LPNW of the secure processor processing system is shown in Fig.2. Task get-order is used to receive all valid orders from n brokers, while task assign-order is used to assign received orders to corresponding trading processors. Task get-result intends to take all trading results from m trading processors, but if there is no trading result here, then the secure processor cannot wait for a long time. Thus, a delay transition is added.

Task send-result will assign accepted trading results to corresponding brokers. PRi-order (1≤i≤m) deposits the valid orders to be processed on trading processor (i), while PRi-result (1≤i≤m) deposits matched results and revoked orders.

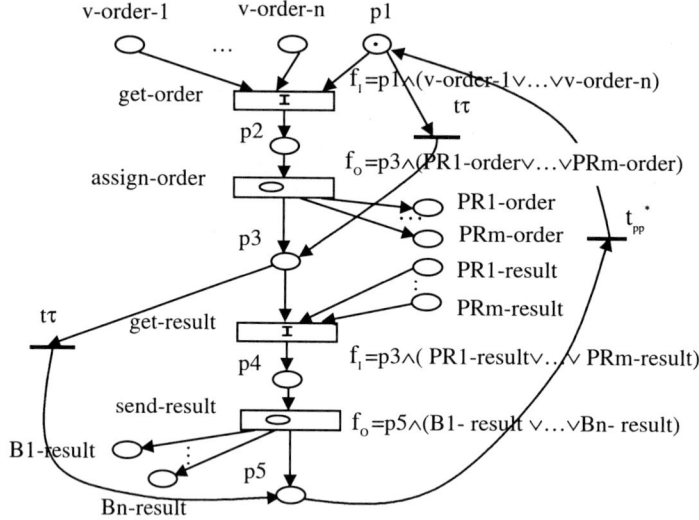

Fig. 2. LPNW of the secure processor processing system

4 Properties Analysis Based on LPNW

In this section, we analyze main properties of the batch stock trading system. The value dependencies between LPNWs are transferred through their common places. These common places are called interface places, while the other places are called inner places. Temporal formula semantics of LPNWs is similar to that of PNs in [3].

Let M be a reachable marking in a LPNW, α a firing sequence at M, f and g LPNW formulae. $\alpha = \beta_i \gamma_i$, β_i is the prefix of α with length i, and γ_i is the postfix of α excluding β_i, and <M, α>|=f means that f is satisfied by the pair of M and α. <M, α>|=p iff there is at least one token in place p at M. <M, α>|=t iff transition t fires, t∈TD∪TI∪TO. <M, α>|=f∨g iff <M, α>|=f or <M, α>|=g. <M, α>|=f∧g iff <M, α>|=f and <M, α>|=g. <M, α>|= f⇒g iff <M, α>|=f implies <M, α>|=g. <M, α>|=○f iff $\alpha \neq \lambda$ and <M_1,γ_1>|=f. <M, α>|=□f iff < M_i,γ_i >|=f for every i: 0≤i≤ |α|. <M, α>|=◊f iff <M_i,γ_i>|=f for some i: 0≤i≤|α|.

Definition 5. A LPNW is pseudo-live if and only if for ∀t∈ TD∪TO∪TI, when •t includes only inner places, t is live; while •t includes interface places, if one token is generated in some or all of the interface places, t can become live.

In fact, if a LPNW is pseudo-live and there exists no value dependency between it and the other LPNWs, the LPNW is live. The following lemma and theorems can be formally verified based on the net construction in Fig.2 and the temporal inference rules in [3], but their proofs are omitted due to the restriction of the size of this paper.

Theorem 1. The LPNW shown in Fig.2 is pseudo-live.

Theorem 2. The interorganizational LPNW of the batch stock trading system is constructive live.

Lemma 1. (If accepting valid orders from brokers, the secure processor will send eventually them to corresponding trading processors.) Let M be a marking reachable of the LPNW from M_0 in Fig.2, for any firing sequence α from M, we have

$<M, \alpha>|= \Box(\text{v-order-1} \vee ... \vee \text{v-order-n} \Rightarrow \Diamond(\text{PR1-order} \vee ... \vee \text{PRm-order}))$

Theorem 3. (All orders sent by customers will be processed eventually.) Let M be a marking reachable of the LPNW from M_0, then for any firing sequence α, we have

$<M,\alpha>|= \Box(\text{v-order-1} \vee ... \vee \text{v-order-n} \Rightarrow \Diamond(\text{B1-result} \vee ... \vee \text{Bn-result}))$

Theorem 4. The functional requirements of the batch stock trading system can be satisfied by the dynamic behaviors of the interorganizational LPNW.

Future work will concern theoretical properties of the method by using, for example, workflow analysis techniques, reachable graph and value-passing dependencies.

Acknowledgements

This work is supported by the projects of National Natural Science Foundation (No.60125205, 69973029, 69933020); National Key Basic Science Foundation of P.R. China (973 Plan, G1998030604); Open Project of Laboratory of Computer Science, Institute of Software, Chinese Academy of Sciences (SYSKF0205); Excellent Ph.D Paper Author Foundation of China (199934); TRAPOYT and Shanghai Science & Technology Foundation.

References

1. van der Aalst, W.M.P.: The application of Petri nets to workflow management. The Journal of Circuits, Systems and Computers 1 (1998) 21-66
2. Adam, N.R.,Atluri,V., Huang,W.K.: Modeling and analysis of workflow using Petri nets. Journal of Intelligent Information Systems 2 (1998) 131-158
3. Du,Y.Y., Jiang,C.J.: Formal analysis of an online stock trading system by temporal Petri nets. In: Williams,A.D.(ed.): Int. Conference on Computer Networks and Mobile Computing, IEEE Computer Society Press, Beijing, China (2001) 197-202
4. Murata,T.: Petri nets: properties, analysis and applications. Proceedings of the IEEE 4 (1989) 541-580
5. Wang,J.C.,Deng,Y., Xu,G.: Reachability analysis of real-time systems using time Petri nets. IEEE Transactions on Systems, Man, and Cybernetics-Part B: Cybernetics 5 (2000) 725-736

A Calculus for Mobile Network Systems

Jinfeng Huang[1], Ad Verschueren[2], Henri Aalderink[3], and Johan Lukkien[4]

[1] Eindhoven Univ. of Tech., EESI, 5600MB Eindhoven, The Netherlands
J.Huang@tue.nl
[2] Eindhoven Univ. of Tech., Electrical Engineering Depart
[3] TNO Industrial Tech., 5600HE Eindhoven, The Netherlands
[4] Eindhoven Univ. of Tech., Mathematics and Computer Science Depart

Abstract. The rapidly increasing demand for ubiquitous communication has led to the widespread use of wireless networks. These systems consist of a group of independently executing components which may migrate through some space during the course of the computation, and the connectivity between the components changes with their migration [5,6]. The support for this physical-distribution-constrained communication paradigm cannot be explicitly seen in the communication model of the π-calculus [7]. In this paper, we first analyze the communication features of mobile network systems. Sequentially, we propose a two-layer connection model for the communication between components in mobile network systems. Finally, an extension of the π-calculus, entity calculus is introduced.

1 Introduction

Process algebras, such as CCS [3] and its successor the π-calculus [4], have shown to be very effective for verifying interactive systems such as wired communication systems and mobile agent systems at the system level, and the formal languages based on these algebras have gained great success in modelling such systems.

In mobile network systems (later referred as MNS), the physical location (or other physical states such as power strength) of processes may affect the interaction results between processes. It is technically difficult to model the dynamic physical distribution of processes in the π-calculus. Furthermore, the verification of the π-calculus based models often neglects the physical distribution effect, which is an important feature of MNS. Most of the properties of MNS, such as the presence of deadlock states, are relevant to the resource allocation strategy of systems, and the dynamic physical distribution is one of the most important factors that lead to resource reallocation.

Mobility of concurrent distributed systems has received much attention in the last ten years, and several calculi based on the π-calculus have been proposed to model the physical distribution properties. The πF calculus [1][2] derived from the π-calculus is more closely related to our work. The authors, Ando et al, define a field concept which is a set of locality constraints on communications; they also model the environment independently.

The motivation of our work is to incorporate the dynamic physical distribution into the calculus, which allows the designer to have the capability of

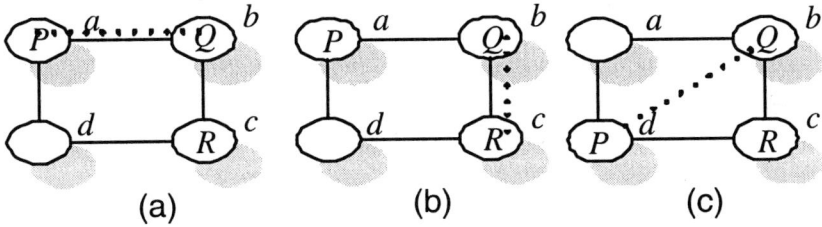

Fig. 1. Two kinds of Mobility
$P \stackrel{def}{=} \overline{\alpha}\langle\beta\rangle.0;\ Q \stackrel{def}{=} \alpha(y).\overline{y}\langle t\rangle.0;\ R \stackrel{def}{=} \beta(x).0$

verifying system characteristics such as the absence of a deadlock in the scope of different dynamic distributions.

The content of this paper is organized as follows. In section 2, we analyze the mobility issue in MNS; the entity calculus is introduced in section 3. Finally, we summarize the work.

2 Mobility in Mobile Network Systems

MNS are composed of a group of independently executing components which may migrate through some space during the course of computation. The connectivity between the components may change with their migration [5][6]. Every component in MNS may exhibit two behaviors: one is migration in some space, the other is independent computation and synchronous communication.

In Fig 1, there are four physical locations: a, b, c, d. The solid lines represent physical signal reachability between physical locations and the dotted lines stand for the logical synchronous relation between processes. In this case, process P sends a new port name β to process Q, then Q uses the new port to send a name t to process R. After two synchronization, all of processes successfully terminate and reach the state 0.

Logical Mobility: After P sends β to Q, the logical topology of the processes is changed from Fig 1(a) to Fig 1(b), and their physical distribution remains unchanged.

Physical Mobility: After process Q moves from a to b, the physical distribution of processes is changed from Fig 1(a) to Fig 1(c). However, their logic topology may not be changed.

3 The Entity Calculus

In this section, we give an informal explanation of our formalization and then follows its syntax and its operational semantics. Our formalization is based on the standard π-calculus, while the physical distribution is added as an extension.

A basic entity consists of two components: a group of processes and an external state. For example, $\{P, q\}$ is a basic entity representation where P is a process or a group of processes, and q is its physical state. They are bounded by a pair of braces.

In entity calculus, the physical space is defined as $Sact$, which includes all possible physical states. $Cset$ is used to express the relation between physical states. For example, in Fig 1, $Cset$ is specified as follows:
$$Cset = \{(a,b), (b,a), (b,c), (c,b), (c,d), (d,c), (a,d), (d,a), (a,a), (b,b),$$
$$(c,c), (d,d)\}.$$

In the calculus, parallelism of two granularity levels is treated. Entities concurrently run and synchronize through physical-state-constrained communication. Inside the entity, processes are carried out in parallel and synchronized through communication channels. The processes bound in an entity share the same physical state. Unlike other process calculi, we treat physical state actions as observable actions. The physical state actions change their physical states, which put constraints on their synchronization . These constraints are mainly caused by the fact that physical communication signals, being the carrier of logical messages, can not be exchanged between all of the physical states in the physical space.

Syntax of the Entity Calculus: The process-layer syntax is the same as that of the standard π-calculus except that the action set $Pact$ is extended with physical state actions. In entity calculus, we partition the action set into three independent action sets: physical state action set $Sact$, send action set $Csact$ and receive action set $Cract$.

The entity-layer syntax is given as follows:

1. Entity action: $\mu ::= \alpha(\widetilde{x})@\widehat{\beta} \mid \overline{\alpha}\langle\widetilde{x}\rangle@\widehat{\beta} \mid \tau@\widehat{\beta} \mid \widehat{\alpha}@\widehat{\beta} \mid \varepsilon$. The parallel actions at the entity layer are represented by $\alpha(\widetilde{x})@\widehat{\beta}$, $\overline{\alpha}\langle\widetilde{x}\rangle@\widehat{\beta}$, $\tau@\widehat{\beta}$, $\widehat{\alpha}@\widehat{\beta}$ and ε, where $\overline{\alpha}\langle\widetilde{x}\rangle$ sends a message with a value list $\widetilde{x}$ and $\alpha(\widetilde{x})$ receives a message with a parameter list $\widetilde{x}$. $\widehat{\beta}$ represents the external state of a basic entity. ε is an internal action between entities. $\tau@\widehat{\beta}$ and ε are two different unobservable actions of entity. The former represents the internal action in one basic entity and cannot be observed at the process layer. The latter represents the internal action between two different basic entities.
2. Entity: $A ::= \{P,p\} \mid A|_e B \mid (x)B$. $|_e$ is an entity parallel operator, and $|_p$ is a process parallel operator. $(x)B$ makes action name x local to entity B.
3. Constraint set $Cset$: $Cset \subseteq Sact \times Sact$.

Structure Congruence: Two parallel elements, process and entity, are defined in the syntax of the entity calculus. Accordingly, the process-layer structure congruence ($\equiv_p$) and the entity-layer structure congruence ($\equiv_e$) are defined. Again, the process-layer structure congruence is the same as that of the standard π-calculus. The smallest entity-layer structure congruence is given as follows: [1]

(1) $A|_e B \equiv_e B|_e A$, $(A|_e B)|_e C \equiv_e A|_e(B|_e C)$, $A|_e\{NIL,p\} \equiv_e A$;
(2) $(x)(y)A \equiv_e (y)(x)A$, $(x)(A|_e B) \equiv_e A|_e(x)B$ $if x \notin fn(A)$[2],

---
[1] In the entity calculus, the restrictions only take effects on send names and receive names.
[2] $fn(A)$ represents all the free send and receive names of entity A.

$(x)\{P,\widehat{\beta}\} \equiv_e \{(x)P,\widehat{\beta}\}$ where $\widehat{\beta} \in Sact$;
(3) $\{P,\widehat{\beta}\} \equiv_e \{Q,\widehat{\beta}\}$ where $P \equiv_p Q$ and $\widehat{\beta} \in Sact$.

The last structure congruence shows the relation between the process-layer congruence and the entity-layer congruence.

Operational Semantics: Similar to the syntax of the entity calculus, the operational rules of the entity calculus are also classified into two layers. The process-layer operational rules are basically the same as those of the standard π-calculus, while three additional rules, $r1$, $r2$, and $r3$, are introduced to express the relation of process transitions and entity transitions.

$$r1: \frac{P \xrightarrow{\eta} P'; \eta \in Csact \cup \tau}{\{P,\widehat{\beta}\} \xrightarrow{\eta@\widehat{\beta}} \{P',\widehat{\beta}\}}; r2: \frac{P \xrightarrow{\eta} P'; \eta \in Cract}{\{P,\widehat{\beta}\} \xrightarrow{\eta@\widehat{\beta}} \{P+P',\widehat{\beta}\}}; r3: \frac{P \xrightarrow{\eta} P'; \eta \in Sact}{\{P,\widehat{\beta}\} \xrightarrow{\eta@\widehat{\beta}} \{P',\eta\}}$$

$r2$ denotes that there is a non-determination inside an entity when it issues a receive action. The selected branch is determined by its physical state and its peer's physical state, not by itself alone (see rules $eCOMM1$ and $eCOMM2$).

The entity-layer operational rules are given as follows:[3]

$$eLPAR: \frac{A \xrightarrow{\mu} A'}{A|_e B \xrightarrow{\mu} A'|_e B}; \quad ePAR: \frac{A|_e B \xrightarrow{\mu} C}{B|_e A \xrightarrow{\mu} C}; \quad eRES: \frac{A \xrightarrow{\eta@\widehat{\beta}} A'; x \neq \eta}{(x)A \xrightarrow{\eta@\widehat{\beta}} (x)A'}$$

$$eCOMM1: \frac{A \xrightarrow{\overline{\alpha}@\widehat{\beta}} A'; \{P,\widehat{\beta}\} \xrightarrow{\alpha@\widehat{\gamma}} \{P'+P,\widehat{\beta}\}}{A|_e \{P,\widehat{\beta}\} \xrightarrow{\varepsilon} A'|_e \{P',\widehat{\beta}\}} \text{ if } (\widehat{\beta},\widehat{\gamma}) \in Cset$$

$$eCOMM2: \frac{A \xrightarrow{\overline{\alpha}@\widehat{\beta}} A'; \{P,\widehat{\beta}\} \xrightarrow{\alpha@\widehat{\gamma}} \{P'+P,\widehat{\beta}\}}{A|_e \{P,\widehat{\beta}\} \xrightarrow{\varepsilon} A'|_e \{P,\widehat{\beta}\}} \text{ if } (\widehat{\beta},\widehat{\gamma}) \notin Cset$$

Rules $eCOMM1$, $eCOMM2$ together with $ePAR$ describe the physical-state-constrained communication. The result of synchronization depends on their physical states. If the physical signal can be transferred between two physical states, the process in the receive entity goes into the next state. Otherwise, the process remains in its original state.

Now, let us check the interaction between processes considering their dynamic physical distribution in Fig 1. The physical movement between location d and a is specified by process P_m ($P_m \stackrel{def}{=} d.a.P_m$).

The system is represented as the following:

$System \stackrel{def}{=} \{P|_p P_m, a\}|_e \{Q,b\}|_e \{R,c\}$.

The deduction of the system is given as the following.

---
[3] We can use rules $eLPAR$, $eCOMM1$, $eCOMM2$ together with $ePAR$ to deduce their symmetrical rules. For example: $eLPAR$ together with $ePAR$ deduces to rule

$eRPAR: \frac{A \xrightarrow{\mu} A'}{B|_e A \xrightarrow{\mu} A'|_e B}$.

$$System \stackrel{def}{=} \{\overline{\alpha}\langle\beta\rangle.0|_p d.a.P_m, a\}|_e \{\alpha(y).\overline{y}\langle t\rangle.0, b\}|_e \{\beta(x).0, c\}$$
$$\stackrel{d@a}{\rightarrow} \{\overline{\alpha}\langle\beta\rangle.0|_p a.P_m, d\}|_e \{\alpha(y).\overline{y}\langle t\rangle.0, b\}|_e \{\beta(x).0, c\}$$
$$\stackrel{\varepsilon}{\rightarrow} \{0|_p a.P_m, d\}|_e \{\alpha(y).\overline{y}\langle t\rangle.0, b\}|_e \{\beta(x).0, c\}$$

At first, P moves from location a to d; then P tries to synchronize with Q at action α. Using rule $eCOMM2$, P issues a send action and goes into terminate state, but Q does not receive the new port name from P. At present, both Q and R are waiting for receiving a message, thus the system goes into a deadlock state.

In this example, we demonstrate that a mobile network system may exhibit different behaviors according to its physical distribution. The main motivation of the entity calculus is trying to reason about this situation, and provide a mathematic framework for mobile network system modelling and verification.

4 Conclusion

In this paper, we proposed a concurrent calculus, entity calculus, for formalizing MNS. In the entity calculus, an entity represents a group of processes that share the same external state. In this way, the physical-distribution-constrained communication paradigm can be more easily modelled in the entity calculus than in the π- calculus.

Acknowledgments

Here I would like to express my gratitude to Jeroen Voeten and Ana Sokolova for their helpful comments on an earlier draft of this paper.

This research has been sponsored through the PROGRESS organization by STW, Philips and TNO.

References

1. Ando, T.; Takahashi, K.; Kato, Y.; Shiratori, N.: A Concurrent Calculus with Geographical Constraints. IEICE TRANS.FUNDAMENTALS, VOL.E81-A, NO.4, (1998).
2. Ando, T.; Takahashi, K.; Kato, Y.; Shiratori, N.: Maintenance of mobile system ambients using a process calculus. Computer Networks 32(2): 229-256 (2000)
3. Milner, R.: Communication and Concurrency. International Series in Computer Science, Prentice Hall (1989)
4. Milner, R.: Communicating and mobile systems: the π-calculus. Cambridge University Press (1999)
5. Roman, G.-C.; McCann, P.J.: A Notation and Logic for Mobile Computing. Formal Methods in System Design, 1-22. Kluwer Academic Publishers (1999)
6. Roman, G.-C.; Picco, G.; Murphy, A.: Software Engineering for Mobility: A Roadmap. Future of Software Engineering, 241-258. In Finkelstein, A, Editor. ACM Press (2000)
7. Sangiorgi, D.: Locality and Non-interleaving Sematics in claculi for mobile processes. International Conference on Theoretical Aspects of Computer Software (TACS'94), Japan (1994)

Modelling Real-Time Systems with Continuous-Time Temporal Logic*

Guangyuan Li and Zhisong Tang

Key Laboratory of Computer Science, Institute of Software,
The Chinese Academy of Sciences, Beijing, 100080, P.R. of China
{ligy, cst}@ios.ac.cn
http://lcs.ios.ac.cn

Abstract. LTLC is a continuous-time linear temporal logic for the specification of real-time systems. It can express both the properties and the implementations of real-time systems. With LTLC, real-time systems can be described at many levels of abstraction, from high-level requirement specifications to low-level implementation models, and the conformance between different descriptions can be expressed by logical implication. This paper will describe how LTLC is used to represent and reason about real-time systems.

1 Introduction

In order to specify real-time systems, many temporal logics, such as Timed Computation Tree Logic [1], Metric Interval Temporal Logic[2] and Real-Time Temporal Logic[4], have been proposed. Though these logics are good at specifying properties of real-time systems, they are not suited to describing the implementations of such systems. They lack the ability to describe the dynamic change in the state of real-time systems.

LTLC [3] is a linear temporal logic with continuous semantics for the specification of real-time systems. It provides a unified logic framework for the specification, refinement, composition and verification of real-time systems. With LTLC, systems can be described at many levels of abstraction, from high-level requirement specifications to low-level implementation models. The refinement relation between two different systems can be expressed by logical implication and the parallel composition of systems can be reduced to logical conjunction. This paper will give a brief introduction to LTLC and describe how it is used to represent and reason about real-time systems.

---

* Supported by the National High Technology Development 863 Program of China under Grant No.2001AA113200; the National Natural Science Foundation of China under Grant No.60073020.

2 LTLC: Syntax and Semantics

Definition 1. *Let $\mathcal{B}$ be a set of boolean variables, and $\mathcal{C}$ be a set of clock variables disjoint with $\mathcal{B}$. The set $\Phi_{\mathcal{B},\mathcal{C}}$ of formulas of LTLC are defined inductively as follows:*

$$\varphi ::= p \mid p' \mid (c=m) \mid (c \leq m)(c'=0) \mid (c'=c) \mid \mid (\neg\varphi) \mid (\varphi_1 \wedge \varphi_2) \mid (\Box\varphi) \mid (\Box_{(0,1]}\varphi) \mid (\exists p.\,\varphi) \mid (\exists c.\,\varphi)$$

where $p \in \mathcal{B}$, $c \in \mathcal{C}$, and m is a nonnegative integer constant.

In LTLC, we use the set $\mathcal{R}^+$ of the nonnegative real numbers as time domain. Each variable in $\mathcal{B} \bigcup \mathcal{C}$ is interpreted by a function defined on $\mathcal{R}^+$.

Definition 2. *$f : \mathcal{R}^+ \mapsto \{0,1\}$ is called a boolean-valued step function if there exists an unbounded increasing sequence $a_0 = 0 < a_1 < a_2 < \ldots < a_n < \ldots$ such that f is constant on every interval $(a_i, a_{i+1}]$.*

Definition 3. *$f : \mathcal{R}^+ \mapsto \mathcal{R}^+$ is called a clock function if there exists an unbounded increasing sequence $a_0 = 0 < a_1 < a_2 < \ldots < a_n < \ldots$ such that*

$$(f(0){=}0) \wedge ((a_i < t \leq a_{i+1}) \Rightarrow (f(t){=}t{-}a_i)),$$

or there exists a finite sequence $a_0 = 0 < a_1 < a_2 < \ldots < a_n$ such that

$$(f(0){=}0) \wedge ((a_i < t \leq a_{i+1}) \Rightarrow (f(t){=}t{-}a_i)) \wedge ((t > a_n) \Rightarrow (f(t){=}t{-}a_n)).$$

Definition 4. *Let f be a boolean-valued step function or a clock function, a new function f' associated with f is defined by $f'(t) ::= \lim_{t_1 \to t+} f(t_1)$ for every $t \in \mathcal{R}^+$, where $\lim_{t_1 \to t+} f(t_1)$ denotes the limit from the right of f at the point t.*

Definition 5. *An interpretation over $\mathcal{B} \bigcup \mathcal{C}$ is a mapping σ defined on $\mathcal{B} \bigcup \mathcal{C}$, satisfying the following conditions.*
  1. *For every $p \in \mathcal{B}$, σ assigns a boolean-valued step function f_p to p.*
  2. *For every $c \in \mathcal{C}$, σ assigns a clock function f_c to c.*

Definition 6. *Let $\varphi \in \Phi_{\mathcal{B},\mathcal{C}}$ and σ be an interpretation over $\mathcal{B} \bigcup \mathcal{C}$. For each $t_0 \in \mathcal{R}^+$, the satisfaction relation $(\sigma, t_0) \models \varphi$ is defined inductively as follows:*

1. $(\sigma, t_0) \models p$ iff $f_p(t_0) = 1$.
2. $(\sigma, t_0) \models p'$ iff $f'_p(t_0) = 1$.
3. $(\sigma, t_0) \models (c{=}m)$ iff $f_c(t_0) = m$.
4. $(\sigma, t_0) \models (c{\leq}m)$ iff $f_c(t_0) \leq m$.
5. $(\sigma, t_0) \models (c'{=}0)$ iff $f'_c(t_0) = 0$.
6. $(\sigma, t_0) \models (c'{=}c)$ iff $f'_c(t_0) = f_c(t_0)$.
7. $(\sigma, t_0) \models (\neg\varphi)$ iff $(\sigma, t_0) \not\models \varphi$.
8. $(\sigma, t_0) \models (\varphi_1 \wedge \varphi_2)$ iff $(\sigma, t_0) \models \varphi_1$ and $(\sigma, t_0) \models \varphi_2$.
9. $(\sigma, t_0) \models (\Box\varphi)$ iff for all $t_1 \geq t_0$, $(\sigma, t_1) \models \varphi$.
10. $(\sigma, t_0) \models (\Box_{(0,1]}\varphi)$ iff for all $t_1 \in (t_0, t_0+1]$, $(\sigma, t_1) \models \varphi$.

11. $(\sigma, t_0) \models (\exists p.\varphi)$ iff there exists a boolean-valued step function g such that $(\sigma[g/p], t_0) \models \varphi$.
12. $(\sigma, t_0) \models (\exists c.\varphi)$ iff there exists a clock function h such that $(\sigma[h/c], t_0) \models \varphi$.

where f'_p is the function associated with f_p, and $\sigma[g/p]$ is an interpretation which maps p to g and agrees with σ on all variables distinct from p.

If $(\sigma, 0) \models \varphi$, we say σ is a model of φ. If every model of φ is also a model of ψ, we say ψ is a logical consequence of φ, denoted by $\varphi \models \psi$.

Notation 1. A state formula is an LTLC formula defined by the grammar $\varphi ::= p \,|\, (c \le m) \,|\, (c = m) \,|\, (\neg \varphi) \,|\, (\varphi_1 \wedge \varphi_2)$. An action formula is an LTLC formula defined by the grammar $\varphi ::= p' \,|\, (\neg p') \,|\, (c' = 0) \,|\, (c' = c) \,|\, (\varphi_1 \wedge \varphi_2)$.

3 Representing Real-Time Systems with LTLC

Real-time systems are modeled by *timed modules* in this paper. A timed module represents a real-time system that interacts with an environment. The variables of a timed module M can be divided into three pairwise disjoint sets: the set $priv(M)$ of *private variables*, the set $read(M)$ of read variables and the set $write(M)$ of write variables. We refer to $ctr(M) = priv(M) \cup write(M)$ as the controlled variables, to $obs(M) = write(M) \cup read(M)$ as the observable variables. Each *private variable* can be read and modified by the module, and neither read nor modified by the environment. Each *write variable* can be read by both the module and the environment, and modified by the module only. Each *read variable* can be read by both the module and the environment, and modified by the environment only. Every variable in timed modules has a type. *boolean, clock* and finite enumerating sets are frequently used types in timed modules. As an enumerated variable can be encoded by several boolean variables, it suffices to consider only boolean variables and clock variables in our definitions for timed modules.

A timed module has a finite set of locations. The module can either delay in a location for some time or jump from one location to another location. Boolean variables are used in timed modules to encode the location information and clock variables express the timing constraints. Variables are updated by transitions. A timed module has two kinds of transitions: jump transitions and delay transitions. A jump transition is instantaneous, it switches the module from one location to another location, in zero time. A delay transition has a positive duration. During the period, the values of all controlled boolean variables remain unchanged, and the values of all controlled clock variables increase continuously at the rate 1.

A jump transition can be written as a guarded command '$guard \longrightarrow assign$', where '$guard$' is a state formula and '$assign$' is an action formula(see Notation 1). '$guard$' expresses the enabling condition of the transition and '$assign$' updates the values of all controlled variables. A delay transition can be written in the form '$location \longrightarrow invariant$', where '$invariant$' is a state formula, and '$location$' is a state formula without any clock variables.

```
module      Controller
read        req : boolean
write       light : { red, green }
private     pc : { 1, 2, 3 };   c : clock
init        pc = 1 ∧ light = red ∧ c = 0
jump
    pc=1 ∧ c=1 ∧ req   ⟶  pc' =2 ∧ light' = light ∧ c' =0;
    pc=1 ∧ c=1 ∧ ¬req  ⟶  pc' =pc ∧ light' = light ∧ c' =0;
    pc=2 ∧ c=1         ⟶  pc' =3 ∧ light' = green ∧ c' =0;
    pc=3 ∧ c=2         ⟶  pc' =1 ∧ light' = red ∧ c' =0
delay
    pc=1 ⟶ c≤1;
    pc=2 ⟶ c≤1;
    pc=3 ⟶ c≤2
```

Fig. 1. The timed module *Controller*

Example 1. A traffic-light is set by a road. Normally the light is red. If you want to cross the road, you should make a request by pressing a designated button. After some delay, the light will turn to green and you can cross the road. The timed module *Controller* of Fig. 1 models such a light controller. It has three locations. In location 1 ($pc=1$), the light is red and the controller is waiting for a request. It checks whether these is an available request every one minute. Once a request is found, the controller switches to location 2. After one minute delay in location 2, the controller changes to location 3 and the light turns to green at the same time. The state of being green lasts 2 minutes, and then the controller turn back to location 1. Fig. 2 is a graphic representation of the timed module *Controller*.

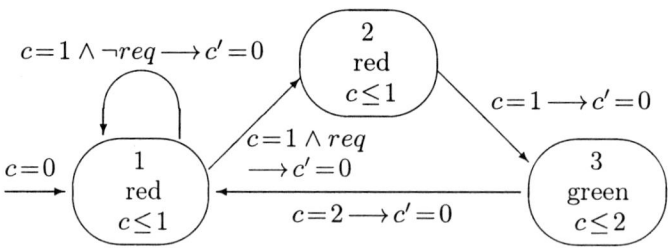

Fig. 2. A graphic representation of the module *Controller*

Notation 2. For a boolean variable p, we write $p'=p$ for the formula $(p' \wedge p) \vee (\neg p' \wedge \neg p)$. For a set V of variables, we write $(V'=V)$ for the formula $\bigwedge_{v \in V}(v'=v)$. Let $\alpha := guard \longrightarrow assign$ be a jump transition, and $\beta := loc \longrightarrow invar$ be a delay transition. We use $\mathrm{TLF}(\alpha)$ to denote the formula '$guard \wedge assign$' and use $\mathrm{TLF}(\beta)$ to denote the formula '$loc \wedge invar$'.

Definition 7. Let M be a timed module. Suppose $<v_0, v_1, v_2, \ldots, v_{m-1}>$ is an enumeration of all variables in $priv(M)$, $<\alpha_0, \alpha_1, a_2, \ldots, \alpha_{n-1}>$ an enumeration of all jump transitions of M, and $<\beta_0, \beta_1, \beta_2, \ldots, \beta_{l-1}>$ an enumeration of all delay transitions of M. Define the formula
$$\exists v_0 \exists v_1 \ldots \exists v_{m-1}(init \wedge (\Box(V_c' = V_c \vee \bigvee_{j<n} TLF(\alpha_j))) \wedge \Box \bigvee_{k<l} TLF(\beta_k)),$$
to be the temporal formula associated with M (denoted by $TLF(M)$), where 'init' is the initial condition of M, and V_c is the set of $ctr(M)$.

We define the semantics of a timed module M by that of the temporal formula $TLF(M)$, and regard the models of $TLF(M)$ as the models of M. If $TLF(M) \models \varphi$ holds for a formula φ, we say φ is a property of M, denoted by $M \models \varphi$.

For the timed module $Controller$ of Fig.1, $TLF(Controller)$ is $\exists pc. \exists c.((pc = 1 \wedge light = red \wedge c = 0) \wedge (\Box((pc' = pc \wedge light' = light \wedge c' = c) \vee (pc = 1 \wedge c = 1 \wedge req \wedge pc' = 2 \wedge light' = light \wedge c' = 0) \vee (pc = 1 \wedge c = 1 \wedge \neg req \wedge pc' = pc \wedge light' = light \wedge c' = 0) \vee (pc = 2 \wedge c = 1 \wedge pc' = 3 \wedge light' = green \wedge c' = 0) \vee (pc = 3 \wedge c = 2 \wedge pc' = 1 \wedge light' = red \wedge c' = 0))) \wedge \Box((pc = 1 \wedge c \leq 1) \vee (pc = 2 \wedge c \leq 1) \vee (pc = 3 \wedge c \leq 2)))$.

From Definition 6, we can prove that $TLF(Controller) \models \Box((light = green) \Rightarrow \Diamond_{(0,2]}(light = red))$. So $\Box((light = green) \Rightarrow \Diamond_{(0,2]}(light = red))$ is a property of the module $Controller$, where $\Diamond_{(0,2]}$ is the abbreviation for $\neg \Box_{(0,1]} \Box_{(0,1]} \neg$.

Definition 8 (Refinement and equivalence). Let M_1 and M_2 be two timed modules, and $obs(M_1) = obs(M_2)$. If $TLF(M_1) \models TLF(M_2)$, we say that M_1 refines M_2. M_1 and M_2 are called equivalent if each of them refines the other.

Two modules M_1 and M_2 are said to be compatible if $write(M_1) \cap write(M_2) = \emptyset$ and for every $v \in obs(M_1) \cap obs(M_2)$, v shares same type in M_1 and M_2. $M_1, M_2, \ldots, M_n$ are said to be compatible if they are pairwise compatible.

Definition 9 (Parallel composition). If timed modules $M_1, M_2, \ldots, M_n$ are compatible, we use $[M_1 \parallel M_2 \parallel \ldots \parallel M_n]$ to denote their parallel composition. Its semantics is defined by the temporal formula $TLF(M_1) \wedge TLF(M_2) \wedge \ldots \wedge TLF(M_n)$. If $TLF(M_1) \wedge TLF(M_2) \wedge \ldots \wedge TLF(M_n) \models \varphi$ for a formula φ, we say φ is a property of $[M_1 \parallel M_2 \parallel \ldots \parallel M_n]$.

4 Conclusion

This paper presents a unified logic framework for expressing and reasoning about real-time systems. Real-time systems and their properties are represented in the same logic, so the assertion that a system meets a specified property and the assertion that one real-time system refines another are both expressed by logical implication.

As future work, we will develop both deductive and algorithmic approaches to the verification of real-time systems with LTLC.

References

1. R. Alur, C. Courcoubetis, and D.L. Dill. Model-Checking in Dense Real-Time. Information and Computation, 104:2-34, 1993.
2. R. Alur, T. Feder, T.A. Henzinger. The Benefits of Relaxing Punctuality. Journal of the ACM, 43:116-146, 1996.
3. Li Guangyuan. LTLC: A Continuous-time Temporal Logic for Real-time and Hybrid Systems(in Chinese). PhD Thesis, Institute of Software, Chinese Academy of Sciences, March, 2001.
4. J.S. Ostroff. Temporal logic for real-time systems. Research Studies Press Limited, Taunton, 1989.

On Concept-Based Definition of Domain-Specific Languages [*]

Ying Liu and Naixiao Zhang

Department of Informatics, School of Mathematical Sciences,
Peking University
alice_liu@math.pku.edu.cn
znx@pku.edu.cn

Abstract. This paper provides a new method of developing domain-specific languages(DSLs). A DSL is composed of concepts, including common language concepts and domain concepts. From the functionality point of view, concepts can be divided into two kinds: element concepts and complement concepts. Element concepts capture the basic functions of a DSL, and complement concepts define some auxiliary functions for a DSL. Because extended *attribute grammar* and *evolving algebra* are used to specify the semantics of element concepts, the descriptions are formal, yet easily understood. Transformation rules are used to specify the semantics of complement concepts. In order to improve the reusability, element and complement concepts are defined at a high abstract level, and they are defined as some independent components. The definition of a new DSL follows two steps: defining element and complement concepts separately; instantiating concepts and assembling them. Based on the above idea, a DSLs development language ($\mathcal{DD}$) is defined.

Keywords: Domain-Specific Languages, Evolving Algebra, Attribute Grammar, Language Concept, Reuse, Static Semantics, Dynamic Semantics

1 Introduction

DSLs[1] provide a higher level of abstraction concepts and methods for users to solve domain problems. With the development of computer industry, more and more DSLs are required. Therefore, the development method for DSLs has become an important research topic. In this paper, the concept-based method introduced in this paper supports specifying DSLs at a higher level of abstraction. It makes the development of DSLs more easily because it supports modular definition of DSLs, provides good reuse mechanism, and guarantees automatic implementation of compiler or interpreter from specification.

We have provided a framework in [2] for developing DSLs. The idea of component-based DSLs development method has been put forward there. Several instances proved that the development efficiency of DSLs can be improved

---

[*] This paper was supported by the National Natural Science Foundation of China under Grant. No. 69983001.

significantly using this method. However, the partition approach of components is mainly for imperative paradigm languages. In order to make this idea applicable for more paradigm languages, we develop the partition approach of language components by combining object-oriented idea with language composition feature. So the concept-based method is put forward. This method proposes that a DSL should be the composition of its concepts. In addition, we change the method of specifying semantics of DSLs in the new method. *Evolving algebra*(EA)[7][8] and *attribute grammar*(AG)[10] make language specifications formal, yet easily understood.

Any language is composed of many concepts. Once all the concepts of a language are defined clearly, the language is defined clearly. From the functionality point of view, language concepts can be divided into two kinds: element concepts and complement concepts. Element concepts, such as *statement, branch statement, expression*, or *function*, are generally used to describe the corresponding structures of a language. They capture the basic functions of a DSL. Each element concept is encapsulated with GARMENT[5] which is a mechanism for abstraction and encapsulation of languages. Each element concept generally has a syntax structure which is specified with abstract syntax. The semantics of an element concept can be divided into static semantics and dynamic semantics. *Extended attribute grammar* is used to specify the static semantics, and *extended evolving algebra* is used to specify the dynamic semantics. Complement concepts, such as *side effect, scope rule, alias rule*, or *call by reference*, often act as the auxiliary definition of static or dynamic features of language. Some domain concepts in DSLs can also be regarded as complement concepts. This idea is similar to [3]. It is necessary to stress that a complement concept must be correlative to some element concepts. For example, *scope rule* is a complement concept, this concept is used to describe whether a *variable* has been defined in a *block* or not. This *block* may be a *declaration statement* or a *function definition*. *Variable, block, declaration statement, and function definition* are all element concepts. Each complement concept is defined as an independent component. It can be reused by many element concepts or DSLs.

Many element concepts have some relations with the other concepts, for example, *statement* is an element concept which is correlative to *assignment statement, switch statement, etc.* which are all element concepts. It is too complex to define an complex concept from scratch. On the other hand, many element concepts are constructed on the basis of many other basic element concepts. Those basic element concepts can be reused by many complex element concepts if they are defined as independent components. This problem was put forward by Strachey in the 1960s[4]. In order to improve the reusability of concepts, element and complement concepts are specified at a higher abstract level. They are allowed to have formal parameters which are used to indicate all the correlative element concepts. If the specification of a concept has parameters, this concept is called an *abstract concept*. While defining a new DSL, developers need to replace these formal parameters with actual parameters. If all the formal parameters of a concept are replaced with actual parameters, a *concrete concept* of a DSL is gotten. This *concrete concept* is called an *instance* of the abstract concept. The process of replacing the formal parameters with actual parameters is called an *instantiating process*.

Based on the above idea, we designed a DSLs development language which is called $\mathcal{DD}$. This paper is structured as follows. Section 2 introduces how to specify element concepts including their syntax and semantics. Because both *evolving algebra* and *attribute grammar* can be regarded as state transition system(STS), the general notion of STSs composition is introduced in section 2. In section 3, we introduce how to specify complement concepts using $\mathcal{DD}$. In section 4, we introduce how to define a new DSL using $\mathcal{DD}$. Finally, we will discuss the related and future work.

2 Element Concept

GARMENT is used to encapsulate element concepts in $\mathcal{DD}$. If an element concept is specified with GARMENT, its specification is called a *garment*. Every *garment* is an independent component, and it can be reused by the other *garments* or DSLs. The syntax structure of an element concept is specified with an abstract syntax structure. While this *garment* is instantiated, its abstract syntax can be replaced with a concrete syntax structure.

The specification method of semantics is expected to satisfy four conditions: the descriptions of semantics are formal; specification notations are easy to be used and understood; the specification file is intuitive and easy to be read; compiler or interpreter can be generated automatically from the specification. The semantics of an element concept can be divided into static semantics and dynamic semantics. Although there is no common idea what is static semantics and what is dynamic semantics. Most experts believe that what can be gotten through static analyzing are static semantics, i.e. compiler-time behavior[16]. For example, static typing rules, scope rules, and static evaluation are all static semantics. *Attribute grammar* is used to specify the static semantics of element concepts. Because $\mathcal{DD}$ supports modular definition of element concepts, we extend *attribute grammar* with modular and parameterized mechanism. The program states change dynamically, then the state transitions are regarded as the dynamic semantics. *Evolving algebra* is used to specify dynamic semantics of element concepts. *Evolving algebra* is also extended with parameterized and modular mechanism.

2.1 Dynamic Semantics

EA has been successfully used to model the dynamic semantics of many high level programming languages, such as C, C++, Java, Prolog, and Occam. EA is chosen to specify the dynamic semantics of element concepts.

Evolving algebras are *state transition systems* whose states are static algebras, i.e. first-order interpretations over a vocabulary or signature. Formally, the definition of EA is given as follows:

Definition 1. (Evolving Algebra:)[9] an EA is a quadruple $<\sigma, S, T, I_0>$, where σ is a signature or vocabulary, i.e. a finite set of function names with associated arity, S is a nonempty set, called the superuniverse, T is a finite set of transition rules and $I_0 : \sigma \to \bigcup_{n \geq 0}(S^n \to S)$ is the initial interpretation of functions in σ, i.e. I_0 maps every function name of arity n to an interpretation function $I_0(f) : S^n \to S$.

The transformation rule in EA has the form

$$if\ t_0\ then\ f(t_1,\ldots,t_r) := t_{r+1}\ endif$$

where $t_0, f(t_1,\ldots,t_r)$, and t_{r+1} are closed terms(i.e. terms containing no free variables) in the signature σ.

A state is a static algebra. A static algebra $\mathcal{A} = (A, S)$ over a signature σ consists of a non-empty set S, superuniverse, and an interpretation A of the function symbols, $A(f) : S^{(n)} \to S$.

Goos has pointed out that abstract state machine(ASM) is a STS[15]. Gurevich had pointed out that an EA is a ASM[7]. Then an EA is a STS. STS is a triple $\mathcal{S} = (\mathcal{Q}, \mathcal{I}, \to)$, where Q denotes the set of states, I denotes the initial state, and $\to$ denotes the set of transformation rules of this STS. While describing a *garment*, it is allowed to have parameters. Then, what is *parameterized STS* and how to compose STSs are discussed here. In [15], the basic definition of parameterized STS has been given. In that paper, a STS is represented with a directed graph G=(V,E) with $V = S_1, \ldots, S_k \cup I, T_{k+1}, \ldots, T_m$, each edge (S_i, S_j) and (S_i, T_j) is associated with a subset $F_{i,j}$ of final states of S_i. Because a *garment* is an independent module, a *garment* is regarded as a modular STS. Here, we discuss STSs composition and parameterized STS in a more general way.

STSs Composition: Let $S_1 = (Q_1, I_1, \to_1), \ldots, S_k = (Q_k, I_k, \to_k)$ are k STSs. $S = S_1 \uplus \ldots \uplus S_k$ is called the compositions of $S_1, \ldots, S_k$, iff the following condition are satisfied:

There is no conflict among any two STSs' rules. Conversely, if one of the conditions is satisfied, these two STSs have conflict:

- equal rules: $\to_i \cap \to_j \neq \phi$, where $1 \leq i \leq j \leq k$;
- equal guard conditions: Suppose $R \in \to_i$, and the guard condition of R is $g(R)$, and $R' \in \to_j$ $(1 \leq i \leq j \leq k)$, and the guard condition of R' is $g(R')$, then $g(R)=g(R')$.

Then the STSs composition S can be gotten according to the following rules which compute any two STSs compositions. Suppose S_i and S_j are any two STSs in the above k STSs, then the STSs composition of S_i and $S_j (1 \leq i \leq j \leq k)$ is $S = S_i \uplus S_j = (Q, I, \to)$:

- if $Q_i \cap Q_j = \phi$, then $Q = Q_i \cup Q_j$, $I = I_i \cup I_j$, and $\to = \to_i \cup \to_j$;
- if $(Q_i \cap Q_j \neq \phi)$ and $(Q_i \cap I_j \neq \phi)$, then $Q = Q_i \cup Q_j$, $I = (I_i \cup I_j) - (I_j \cap Q_i)$, and $\to = \to_i \cup \to_j$;

- if $(Q_i \cap Q_j \neq \phi)$ and $(Q_j \cap I_i \neq \phi)$, then $Q = Q_i \cup Q_j$, $I = (I_i \cup I_j) - (I_i \cap Q_j)$, and $\to = \to_i \cup \to_j$;
- if $(Q_i \cap Q_j \neq \phi)$ and $(Q_i \cap I_j = \phi)$, or $(Q_i \cap Q_j \neq \phi)$ and $(Q_j \cap I_i = \phi)$ then $Q = Q_i \cup Q_j$, $I = I_i \cup I_j$, and $\to = \to_i \cup \to_j$;

parameterized STS: A parameterized STS is denoted by $S[X_1 : T_1, \ldots, X_n : T_n]$, the parameters $X_1, \ldots, X_n$ are instantiated to $S_1, \ldots, S_n$. Suppose that S includes some basic garments, $S'_1, \ldots, S'_k$, then an instance of the parameterized STS is denoted by $[S'_1, \ldots, S'_k][S_1, \ldots, S_n]$. This parameterized STS may have the following three situations:

- **better-defined:** If we can get a STSs composition from $S_1, \ldots, S_n, S'_1, \ldots, S'_k$, then the parameterized STS is **better-defined**.
- **well-defined:** We can not get a composition STS directly, however, we can get the isomorphism STSs $S''_1, \ldots, S''_n$ for $S_1, \ldots, S_n$ separately. Then the STSs composition of $S''_1, \ldots, S''_n, S'_1, \ldots, S'_k$ can be gotten. We say that this parameterized STS is **well-defined**.
- **badly-defined:** Whatever we do for the parameters, we can not get the composition STS, this parameterized STS is called **badly-defined**.

While designing a language using parameterized STS, we must check whether it is **well-defined** or **better-defined**. If it is a **badly-defined**, the definition of parameterized garment is not right.

The following is an example which specifies the dynamic semantics of *regular expression rule*, 'RegRule', of LEX[14] using EA:

```
RegRule::= RegExpr Action // This is the abstract syntax of RE
//The following is the dynamic semantics of RE
  if TaskType(CurTask)==RegExp Then{
    CurNfa(CurTask)=AddNfa(CurNfa,(GenState(CurState),GenState
                    (GenState(CurState)),ExprSymbol(CurTask)))
    ReportNfa(LeftTask(CurTask))=CurNfa(CurTask)
    CurState=GenState(GenState(CurState))
    PreState(CurTask)=GenState(CurState)
    PostState(CurTask)=GenState(GenState(CurState))
    StateContent(GenState(GenState(CurState)))=Content(CurState)
    PreState(LeftChild(CurTask))=PreState(CurTask)
    PostState(LeftChild(CurTask))=PostState(CurTask)
    CurTask=NextTask(CurTask) }
```

In this example, the program execution is modeled by the evolution of nine dynamic functions: 'CurTask', 'CurState', 'PreSate', 'PostState', 'StateContent', 'AddNfa', 'DeleteNfa', 'ReportNfa', and 'CurNfa'. 'CurTask' points to the part of the program text currently in execution and may be seen as an abstract program counter. 'CurState' records the current state in order to generate different state for later use. 'PreState' and 'PostState' are used to record two states in current NFA(Nondeterministic Finite Automaton) which will be used in later computing.

'AddNfa' is used to add a new Nfa to the current NFA lists. 'DeleteNfa' is used to delete a NFA from the NFA lists. 'ReportNfa' passes the current NFA to its children of 'CurTask'. 'CurNfa' points to the current NFA list.

2.2 Static Semantics

An *attribute grammar* is a quadruple AG=<G,A,R,P>, where G specifies the syntax of the target language, A is a set of attribute symbols, R is a set of attribute rules, and P is a set of functions self-defined by users. In order to support the definition of *garments*, we extend AG with modular and parameterized mechanism which is called *modular and parameterized attribute grammar(MPAG)*. MPAG is used to specify the static semantics of a *garment*, i.e. each element concept includes a *MPAG module*. This decomposition approach of attribute grammar modules is different from the others, such as nonterminal method[11], attribute method[12], and semantic aspect method[13].

If a *MPAG module* has no parameter, it is called an *attribute grammar module(AGM)*. An AGM is also a quadruple:$< G_M, A_M, R_M, P_M >$, where G_M denotes the abstract syntax structure of this module which is expressed with a product, A_M denotes attribute symbols which are used in the module, R_M denotes attribute rules, and P_M denotes the functions used in the attribute rules of this module. Compared with *attribute grammar*, attribute grammar module is one part of *attribute grammar*. Their expression format is the same. However, some attribute symbols used in an attribute grammar module may not be defined in this module but in another module. Several attribute grammar modules can compose an attribute grammar if some conditions are satisfied. Suppose there are k attribute grammar modules, $< G_i, A_i, R_i, P_i >$, i=1,2,...,k. If the following conditions can be satisfied, these attribute grammar modules can compose an *attribute grammar*, denoted by AG_i:

1. There is no conflict among P_is. Let f_1 be a function of P_i and f_2 be a function of P_j, P_i and P_j have conflict if f_1 and f_2 have the same function head but the different function body.
2. There is no conflict among R_is. Let r_1 be an attribute rule of R_i and r_2 be an attribute rule of R_j, R_i and R_j have conflict if r_1 and r_2 have the same left side but the different right side. For example, $mapL\_declare.symbols = right_1$ and $mapL\_declare.symbols = right_2$ have the same left side but the different right side.
3. There is no cycle among the dependent relations of attributes.

We call these conditions *composition conditions*. If the above conditions are satisfied, then $AG_i = < Concrete(\cup G_i), \cup A_i, \cup R_i, \cup P_i >$, i=1,2,...,k, where $\cup G_i$ denotes to joint all the abstract syntax products of these k attribute grammar modules, *Concrete* is an injection from some abstract syntax products to some concrete syntax products, and $Concrete(\cup G_i)$ denotes all the concrete syntax products corresponding to $\cup G_i$, $\cup A_i$ denotes to joint all the attribute symbols, $\cup R_i$ denotes to joint all the attribute rules, and $\cup P_i$ denotes to joint all the functions self-defined by users.

A MPAG is a pair: $< MAG, [X_1, X_2, \ldots, X_k] >$, where $X_1, X_2, \ldots, X_k$ are parameters of this MAG. In fact, each parameter is a variable of an attribute grammar module. When these parameters are replaced by some attribute grammar modules, a new attribute grammar module is the composition of MAG and these attribute grammar modules. Therefore if a parameterized attribute grammar is *well-defined*, the above *composition conditions* must be satisfied.

The following is an AGM of 'RegRule'. Before giving the attribute rules, we must define all the attribute. Attributes can be divided into two kinds: input attributes and output attributes. We use the notation ' $>$ ' to denote the input attributes, and ' $<$ ' to denote the output attributes.

```
SYNTAX:   RegRule::= RegExpr Action //abstract syntax
ATTRSYM:  RegRule: Content<, ..., NextTask<; Action: Content>, ...
          RegExpr: ExprSymbol>, tag>, ...
ATTRULE:  RegRule.content= Action.content
          RegRule.NextTask=RegExpr.tag
          ...
```

where, 'RegExpr' and 'Action' in this module are two parameters of this module, and they include corresponding AGMs. When these two parameters are replaced with some actual parameters, a new AGM is the composition of two AGMs of these two actual parameters and the AGM of 'RegRule'.

Here, we state that an *attribute grammar* is a STS[15]. An EA is also a STS. Two different methods are unified to a single theory so that we can discuss all the problems under a unified theory foundation, which is another reason that we use *attribute grammar* to specify the static semantics of DSL. A STS is a triple $S = (Q, I, \rightarrow)$. Although MPAG is used to specify the static semantics of element concepts, we have stated that the composition of MPAG modules is an AG. Here, we only need to discuss that an AG is a STS.

Remark: The set of values of all the attributes are regarded as a state, and it is denoted by S. Δ and Δ' denote the sets of states. If attribute rules $\mathcal{R}$ acts on a state Δ, we use the following equation to express it: $\Delta' = \Delta_\mathcal{R}$. A set of the initial values of attributes is regarded as the initial state of STS, denoted by S_0. Furthermore, attribute rules can act on the states iteratively, and the set of states can be gotten. We can used the following pseudo-code to define the set of states Q of AG:

$$Q =;$$
$$\Delta = S_0;$$
$$while\ \Delta \not\subseteq Q\ do$$
$$\quad \Delta' =;$$
$$\quad for\ S \in \Delta\ do$$
$$\quad\quad if\ S \notin Q\ then$$
$$\quad\quad\quad \Delta' = \Delta' \cup S_R;$$
$$\quad\quad endif$$
$$\quad endfor$$
$$\quad Q = Q \cup \Delta$$
$$\quad \Delta = \Delta'$$
$$endwhile$$

Then an AG is equal to a STS, denoted by $(Q, S_0, \mathcal{R})$.

Finally, we give the syntax of GARMENT of $\mathcal{DD}$ as follows:

```
GARMENT name(a:T1,....,a:Tn)[EXTEND garment_name]
[IMPORT file1,...]{ <abstract syntax>
                    <attribute rule definitions>
                    <EA rule definitions>  }
```

where, EXTEND clause means that a *garment* can inherit the content of the other *garment*. Because a *garment* has to describe its corresponding syntax structure, multi-inheritance may lead to syntax definition conflict. $\mathcal{DD}$ language doesn't allow multi-inheritance, i.e. every *garment* is only allowed to inherit a *garment* at most. Some self-defined functions and external functions used in attribute rules or EA rules are defined in file1,.... The name of these files are declared by IMPORT clause.

3 Complement Concept

Complement concepts are specified with ATTRIBUTE in $\mathcal{DD}$. If a complement concept is specified with ATTRIBUTE, the specification is called an *attribute*. Most of specification methods don't abstract complement concepts from general concepts. We believe that the following two reasons require us to provide a formal method to specify complement concepts independently.

- An *attribute* may be reused by different languages. If we mix some *attributes* with some *garments*, these *attributes* can not be reused by the other languages.
- Some *attributes* are relevant to many *garments*. If we specify the *attributes* independently, these *attributes* can be reused by many *garments*.

In fact, this idea is similar to aspect-oriented programming[17].

We use transformation rules to specify the semantics of complement concepts. This method is general in aspect-oriented programming. The following is the syntax of ATTRIBUTE:

```
ATTRIBUTE name(s1:T1,...,sm:Tm)[EXTEND name]
IMPORT [file1,...]{ <symbol, function, and block definitions>
                    <transformation rules> }
```

The meanings of EXTEND and IMPORT clauses are the same as those of GARMENT. Its parameters are *garment* names. 'Transformation rules' are the main part of an ATTRIBUTE body. Complement concepts must have relations with some element concepts. How to weave them is an important topic. We use transformation rules to insert some actions into some *garments*. The insert point is expressed with a pair: ρ=(garment_name, mark), where *garment_name* is the name of *garment* that the *attribute* will weave, and *mark* points out in which position some action will be inserted. All the specifications which will be inserted into the other *garments* are defined as some blocks. Transformation rules only need to refer to some block names. The syntax of transformation rules are given as follows written in extended BNF(Backus-Naur Form):

```
TransRule::=AddRule|UpdateRule|ChoiceRule
AddRule::= 'ADD_Voc'AddPos BlockName
AddPos:: = '(' Name Unit ')'
Unit ::= 'ATTSYM'|'ATTRRULE'|'SUNIVERSE'|'DUNIVERSE'|'SFUNCTION'
         |'DFUNCTION' | 'EARULE'
UpdateRule ::= 'Modi_Rule' ModiPos AddList
ModiPos::= '('Name UnitAttrRule|EARule ')'
ChoiceRule::='if' ExtendGua 'then'TransRule
ExtendGua::= QualityTerm | LogQualityTerm
QualTerm::=Quality* {':'}? Term
Quality::='EX' Name | 'EN' Name
LogQualityTerm ::= QualityTerm LogSym QualTerm
```

The following is an example about *match conflict* of LEX. When the scanner matches the read character to the DFA(Deterministic Finite Automaton), a match conflict may appear, i.e. two states can match a single character. How to solve this problem is one of the *attributes* of scanner. Some scanners may adopt *first-come-first-match* strategy, the others may adopt *look-advance* approach. These two different strategies can be defined as two different *attributes*. The following is for *look-advance* strategy:

```
ATTRIBUTE match_conflict(Prog p){
  SUNIVERSE: dfa, char
  SFUNCTION: match:dfa*char->BOOL; advance:char*dfa->dfa;
  EARULE: MATCH: if !match(char,dfa) then read(ch);match(ch,dfa);}
  RULES:
```

$$\text{if } \exists f : SFUNCTION.(f == match) \wedge (f \in EARULE) \text{ then}$$
$$\textbf{Modi\_Rule}\ \ (p, match), MATCH\ \ \}$$

4 Defining DSLs Using $\mathcal{DD}$

$\mathcal{DD}$ provides a *language definition function* to instantiate concepts and assemble them. The following is the syntax of it.

```
LANGUAGE name [IMPORT file1,...]{DECL:< variable declaration>
                                 CONSTRUCT:<construct statements>}
```

The meaning of IMPORT is the same as that of GARMENT. All the variables used in this function should be declared in DECL.

Instantiated concepts are assembled by language construct statements provided by $\mathcal{DD}$. Here, we introduce the expressions: instantiating *garment* and *attribute*, weaving *garment* and *attribute*, and variable.

- **instantiating garment:** It is similar to the expression of function call. While instantiating a *garment*, users need to provide some actual parameters if the *garment* includes parameters; for example, *simp_assign(mapl_var, mapl_expr)* is an **instantiating garment** expression, where *mapl_var* and *mapl_expr* are *garment instances*. If the abstract syntax needs to be replaced by a concrete syntax, the **instantiating garment** should include the concrete syntax, for example, *simp_assign(mapl_var, mapl_expr)[mapl_var'::=' mapl_expr]*.
- **weaving garment and attribute:** Suppose that attribute A needs to weave *garment* G, then we use $A * G$ to denote their weaving expression.
- **variable:** Variables must be declared before they are used. The types of variables are *garments* or *attributes*, for example, there is a variable declaration x:*Element*, then the type of variable x is *Element*. The name of *language definition function* is a variable used in this function, and this name is the name of a DSL which is defined by this function.

There are two kinds of statements in *language definition function*, declaration statement and assignment statement.

- **garment declaration statement:** Declaration statements are used to declare the variables which will be used in *language definition function*.
- **assignment statement:** In assignment statement, the left side is a variable, and the right side is a language construct expressions. We must stress that the variables except for the name of the DSL can be assigned more times. The name of the DSL as a variable can only be assigned one time.

Let's look at the following example which is a language definition function of LEX.

```
LANGUAGE LEX IMPORT lex_gar.ddl,lex_attr.ddl{
DECL:lex_decl:Decl_Section; lex_rule:Rule_Section; lex_prog:Prog_
     Section; lex_math:math_conflict; temp_lex:Prog;....
CONSTRUCT:            ......
             lex_decl= Decl_Section(...)
             temp_lex = Prog(lex_decl, lex_rule, lex_prog)
             lex_match = match_conflict(temp_lex)
             LEX = temp_lex * lex_match }
```

5 Related and Future Work

In this paper, we have introduced how to develop a DSL using the concept-based method. We propose to compose a DSL with many *garments* and *attributes* which corresponds to element concepts and complement concepts of the DSL. In order to improve the reusability of concepts, they are specified at a high abstract level using $\mathcal{DD}$. *Garments* and *attributes* are allowed to have parameters. While defining a new DSL, users need to follow two steps: the first step is to find or define all the *garments* and *attributes* which are relative to all the concepts of the new DSL; the second step is to create *garment instances* by *instantiating garments* and assembling them. This process is similar to the product line of industry. Every step can be done by different people. Domain experts and language experts can take part in the development DSLs together.

Language development meta-tools are ubiquitous, such as Eli[18], ASF+SDF[20], Montage[6], LDA[19], but rarely do they address a composition of concepts such as those addressed in this paper. Compared to them, the concept-based method improves the reusability of DSL development significantly.

There are still some problems that are worth studying for the concept-based DSLs development method: first, it is very important to prove that the concept-based method is appropriate for many DSLs through experiments. We have developed three DSLs, LEX, *mapL*[21] which is a map langauge, and XML[22] which is a markup language; secondly, the weaving technique of *attributes* and *garments* must guarantee that the original semantics of the *garments* don't be destroyed while weaving them; thirdly, how to implement the definition of language polymorphism is a worthy topic.

References

1. A. van Deursen, P. Klint, and J. Visser: Domain-Specific Languages – An Annotated Bibliography. (2000)ACM SIGPLAN Notices.
2. Zhang Naixiao, Liu Ying: A Component-based Framework and Reusability in Garment. Proceedings of the Asia-Pacific Software Engineering Conference APSEC-(2001)411–418. Published in 2001 by the IEEE Computer Society.
3. Maja D'Hondt and Theo D'Hondt: Is Domain Knowledge an Aspect? Position papers of the AOP workshop at ECOOP'99. http://trese.cs.utwente.nl/aop-ecoop99
4. Christopher Strachey: Fundamental Concepts in Programming Languages. Higher-order and Symbolic Computation,13(2000):11–49.
5. Zhang Naixiao, Zheng Hongjun, Qiu Zongyan: Garment - A Mechanism for Abstraction and Encapsulation of Languages. ACM SIGPLAN Notices, Vol. 32, No. 6, (1997):53-60.
6. Philipp W. Kutter, Alfonso Pierantonio: Montages Specifications of Realistic Programming Languages. Journal of Universal Computer Science, Vol.3 No.5(1997), 416–442.
7. Y. Gurevich: May 1997 Draft of the ASM Guide. Department Technical Report CSE-TR-336-97, University of Michigan,(1997).
8. Y. Gurevich: Evovling Algebras 1993: Lipari Guide. In E. Börger, editor, Specification and Validation Methods, Oxford University Press, (1995):9-36.
9. Stephan Diehl: Transformation of Evolving Algebras. Proceedings of the VIII Conference on Logic and Computer Science LIRA'97. VoviSad,Yugoslavi, September 1-4,(1997):51–57.
10. Jukka Paakki: Attribute grammar paradigms – a high-level mathodology in language implementation. ACM Computing Surveys. Vol.27, No.2, (1995)196-255.
11. Koskimies, K. : Object-orientation in attribute grammars. In attribute grammars, Applications and System. Lecture Notes in Computer Science, vol. 545(1991). Springer-Verlag, New York, 297-329.

12. Dueck, G.D.P. and Cormack, G. V.: Modular attribute grammars. Comput. J.33,2, (1990)164-172.
13. Farrow, R. : Attribute grammars and data-flow languages. In Proceedings of the ACM SIGPLAN'83 Symposium on Programming Language Issues in Software Systems. ACM SIGPLAN Notice. 18. 6, (1983)28-40.
14. John R. Levine, Tony Mason, Doug Brown: Lex & Yacc 2nd/updated edition (October 1992) O'Reilly & Associates ISBN: 1565920007.
15. Gerhard Goos, Andreas Heberle, Welf Löwe, and Wolf Zimmerman: On Modular Definitions and Implementations of Programming Languages. In Y. Gurevich, P. Kutter, M. Odersky, and L. Thiele, eds., "Abstract State Machines – ASM 2000", International Workshop on Abstract State Machines, Monte Verita, Switzerland, Local Proceedings, TIK-Report 87, Swiss Federal Institute of Technology (ETH) Zurich, March (2000):174–208.
16. Robert Milne: From Language Concepts to Implemantation Concepts. Hihger-Order and Symbolic Computations,13(2000):77-81.
17. Ralf Lämmel: Declarative aspect-oriented programming. Proceedings PEPM'99, 1999 ACM SIGPLAN Workshop on Partial Evaluation and Semantics-Based Program Manipulation PEPM'99(1999), San Antonio (Texas), BRICS Notes Series NS-99-1.
18. The Eli Home Page: http://www.cs.colorado.edu/ eliuser/ExplainEli.html.
19. Peter Pfahler, Uwe Kastens: Language Design and Implementation by Selection. Proc. 1st ACM-SIGPLAN Workshop on Domain-Specific-Languages, DSL '97, Paris, France, January 18, 1997.
20. M.G.J. van den Brand, A. van Deursen, J. Heering, H.A. de Jong, M. de Jonge, T. Kuipers, P. Klint, L. Moonen, P.A. Olivier, J. Scheerder, J.J. Vinju, E. Visser, and J. Visser: "The ASF+SDF Meta-Environment. a Component-Based Language Development Environment," in Compiler Construction 2001 (CC'01), (R. Wilhelm, ed.), pp. 365–370, 2001.
21. Randy M. Kaplan: Constructing Language Processors for Little Languages. John Wiley & Sons, Inc, 1994.
22. XML document: http://www.w3.org/TR/2000/REC-xml-20001006.

Formal Specification of Evolutionary Software Agents

Hong Zhu

Dept. of Computing, Oxford Brookes Univ., Wheatley Campus, Oxford OX33 1HX, UK
hzhu@brookes.ac.uk

Abstract. How to specify agent's intelligent behaviour is a challenging open problem in the development of agent-based systems. This paper presents a case study of developing the formal specification of the evolutionary multi-agent ecosystem Amalthaea developed at MIT Media Lab. A diagrammatic notation is used for the development of agent models and to derive a formal specification of the system in SLABS, which is a formal specification language for agent-based systems.

1 Introduction

Agent technology is widely perceived to be a viable solution for large-scale industrial and commercial applications in the Internet environment [1~4]. However, it has been recognised that the lack of rigour is one of the major factors hampering the wide-scale adoption of agent technology [5]. How to specify, test and verify the intelligent behaviours of agent-based systems remains an open problem.

Much work has been done on formal modelling of agents' rational behaviour by logic systems and game theories, c.f. [6~11]. On the other hand, research work has also been reported in the literature about the development processes and methods for engineering agent-based systems by utilising diagrammatic notations, e.g. [12~16]. Unfortunately, there is a big gap between these two approaches. In this paper, we investigate how descriptions of multi-agent systems in a simple diagrammatic notation can be used to derive formal specifications of multi-agent systems.

The paper is organised as follows. Section 2 gives the background of the paper by a brief review of the formal specification language SLABS [17~19] and a methodology and a diagrammatic notation [20] for agent-oriented software system analysis, design and modelling. Section 3 presents the case study of an evolutionary multi-agent ecosystem called Amalthaea, which is developed in MIT's Media Lab [21]. Section 4 concludes the paper with discussions of related works and further work.

2 Review of the Language and Methodology

SLABS is a model-based formal specification language designed for engineering multi-agent systems [17, 18]. This section briefly reviews the main features of the language and a methodology of developing formal specifications in SLABS.

2.1 The Underlying Model

In our model, agents are defined as encapsulations of data, operations and behaviours that situate in their designated environments. Here, data represents an agent's state. Operations are the actions that an agent can take. Behaviour is a collection of sequences of state changes and operations performed by the agent in the context of its environment. By encapsulation, we mean that an agent's state can only be changed by the agent itself. Moreover, an agent has its own rules that govern its behaviour in its designated environment. Constructively, agents are active computational entities with a structure comprising the following elements.

1. *Name*, which is the agent's identity.
2. *Environment description*, which indicates what the agent interacts with.
3. *State,* which consists of a set of variables and is divided into two parts: the visible state and internal state.
4. *Actions,* which are the atomic actions that the agent can take. Each action has a name and may have parameters.
5. *Behaviour rules*, which determine the behaviour of the agent.

Agents constructively defined above have a number of features. First, they are autonomous in the sense of [22]. Second, they are communicative and social, yet it is independent of any particular agent communication language or protocol. Third, agents are situated in their designated environments. It requires an explicit and clear specification of the boundary and interface between an agent and its environment as well as the effects of the environment on the agent's behaviour. Fourth, as argued in [18], our definition implies that objects are special cases of agents in a degenerate form, while agents may be not objects. Finally, various agent models can be naturally defined in our model. Using the SLABS language, we have formally specified examples of personal assistants [17], ants, learning agents [18], communication protocols [19], etc. In this paper, we will also demonstrate how an evolutionary multi-agent ecosystem can be formally specified in SLABS. A formal definition of the model can be found in [18].

The notion of caste plays an important role in our model. It is a natural evolution of the key notion of class in object-oriented paradigm. Here, a caste is a template of agents as class is a template of objects. Similarly, agents are instances of castes just as objects are instances of classes. The agents of a caste, thus, have common structural and behavioural characteristics. Castes also have inheritance relations between them. However, there are a number of significant differences between classes and castes; hence, they deserve a new name. Readers are referred to [19] for more details about the notion of caste and its role in the development of multi-agent systems.

2.2 The SLABS Language

The specification of a multi-agent system in SLABS consists of a set of specifications of agents and castes. The main body of an agent/caste specification in SLABS contains a description of the structure of its states and actions, a description of its behaviour, and a description of its environment. The following gives the graphic form of specifications of castes and agents. Their syntax in EBNF can be found in [18].

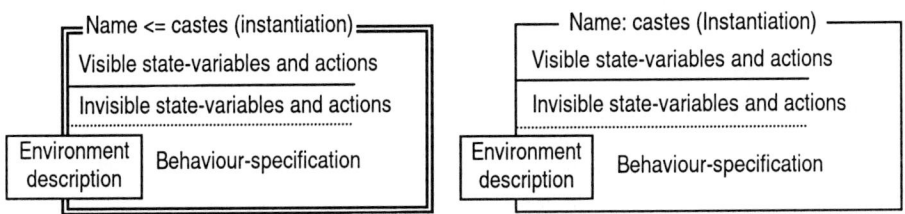

The SLABS language enables software engineers to explicitly specify the environment of an agent as a subset of the agents in the system that may influence its behaviour. Environment description can be in three forms: (a) *an agent-name*, which indicates an agent is in its environment, (a) *All: caste-name*, which means all agents of the caste are in the environment, (3) *variable: caste-name*, which is a parameter of the caste. When it is instantiated, it represents an agent in the environment.

Agents behave in real-time concurrently and autonomously. An agent's behaviour is an events sequence indexed by the time. The state space of an agent is described by a set of variables with keyword VAR. The set of actions is described by a set of identifiers with keyword ACTION, which may have some parameters. The global state of a multi-agent system at any time consists of the states and actions of all agents in the system. However, each agent can only view the externally visible states and actions of the agents in its environment explicitly specified in its description. Because an agent's view is only a part of the global state, two different global states may become equivalent from its view. Although an agent may not be able to distinguish two global states, the histories of the runs leading to states may be different. The SLABS language provides language facilities to express an agent's view of the current state as well as the history of the run of the system so that intelligent behaviours such as learning and evolution can be easily specified. A pattern describes the behaviour of an agent in the environment by a sequence of observable state changes and actions. Scenarios describe global situations of the whole system. Table 1 and 2 below give the formats and the meanings of patterns and scenarios, respectively.

An agent's behaviour is defined by a set of rules that describe its responses in various scenarios. A rule has the following structure.

Behaviour-rule ::= [<rule-name>] pattern|[prob]–>event, [*if* Scenario] [*where* pre-cond] ;

Table 1. Meanings of the patterns

Pattern	Meaning
$	The *wild card*, which matches with all actions
~	The *silence* event
Action variable	It matches an action
$P \wedge k$	A sequence of k events that match pattern P
! *Predicate*	The state of the agent satisfies the predicate
Act $(a_1, a_2, ...a_k)$	An action *Act* that takes place with parameters match $(a_1, a_2, ...a_k)$
$[p_1, ..., p_n]$	The previous sequence of events match the patterns $p_1, ..., p_n$

Table 2. Semantics of scenario descriptions

Scenario	Meaning
A: P	The situation when agent A's behaviour matches pattern P
$\forall X \in C: P$	The situation when the behaviours of all agents in caste C match pattern P
$\exists_{[m]} X \in C: P$	The situation when there exists at least m agents in caste C whose behaviour matches pattern P where the default value of the optional expression m is 1
$\mu X \in C: P$	The number of agents in caste C whose behaviour matches pattern P
$S_1 \& S_2$	The situation when both scenario S_1 and scenario S_2 are true
$S_1 \vee S_2$	The situation when either scenario S_1 or scenario S_2 or both are true
$\neg S$	The situation when scenario S is not true

In a behaviour rule, the pattern on the left-hand-side of the –> symbol describes the pattern of the agent's previous behaviour. The scenario describes the situation in the environment, which are the behaviours of the agents in the environment. The where-clause is the pre-condition of the action. The event on the right-hand-side of –> symbol is the action to be taken when the scenario happens and if the pre-condition is satisfied. The agent may have a non-deterministic behaviour. The expression prob in a behaviour rule is an expression that defines the probability for the agent to take the specified action in the scenario. SLABS also allows the specification of non-deterministic behaviour without giving the probability distribution. In such cases, the probability expression is omitted. It means that the probability is greater than 0 and less than 1. For example, the following behaviour rule of search engines states that if there is an agent A in the environment that calls for search the Web with a set of keywords, it will return a set of urls that matches the keywords.

[$]|–> Search_Result(keywords, urls); if ∃A:[Search(Self, keywords)]

2.3 The Development Process

In [20], we proposed a process for developing formal specifications of multi-agent systems and devised a simple diagrammatic notation to support the process. As shown in Fig 1, the process is an iteration of the following activities.

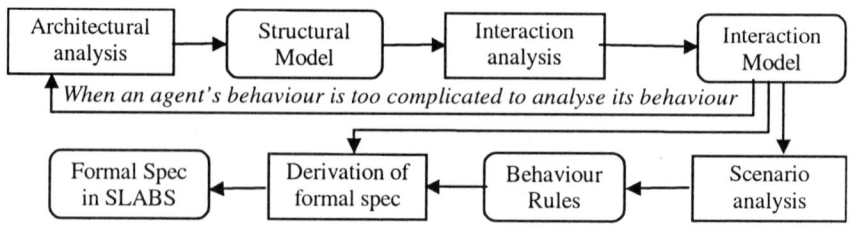

Fig. 1. Process of developing formal specifications in SLABS

- *Architectural analysis.* Its main purpose is to define the overall structure of the system. It is achieved by identifying the agents and castes and their inter-relationships in terms of how agents influence each other.
- *Interaction analysis.* It aims to further clarify the interactions between the agents by identifying the visible actions and states of each agent or a caste of agents.
- *Scenario analysis.* It is applied to each agent or each caste of agents to identify the typical scenarios that the agent will deal with and its designed behaviour in such a scenario. The result of scenario analysis is a set of behaviour rules that characterize the dynamic behaviour of the agent or the caste of agents.
- *Iteration and refinement.* When an agent's behaviour is too complicated to express in terms of the scenarios in the environment and the events that the agent responds to, the internal structure of the agent is analysed. An iteration of the process of architectural analysis and interaction analysis starts and continues until scenario analysis can be successfully applied to the agents.
- *Derivation of formal specification.* The formal specification of the multi-agent system is derived based on the results of above analysis.

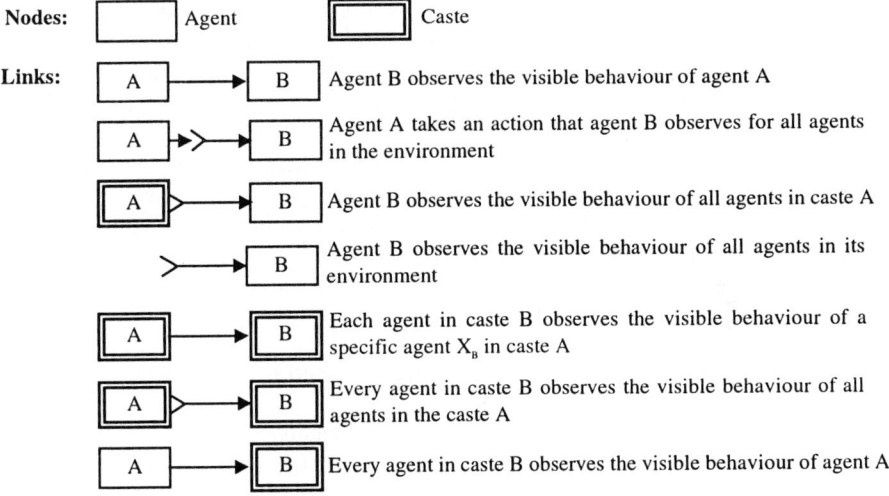

Fig. 2. Notation of agent diagram

2.4 Diagrammatic Representation of Agent Models

An architectural model of a multi-agent system can be built and represented in a simple diagrammatic notation given in Fig 2.

There are two types of nodes in an agent diagram. An *agent node* represents an agent in the system. A *caste node* represents a set of agents in a caste. A link from node A to node B represents that the visible behaviour of agent/caste A is observed by agent/caste B. Therefore, agent/caste A influences agent/caste B. An agent may have an 'open end arrow' from a caste to an agent. It means that all the agents in the caste may influence the agent. If an 'open end arrow' that points to the agent connects to no caste, it means that all agents in the environment influents its behaviour.

An agent or caste in an agent diagram may itself be a complicated multi-agent system. In such a case, a lower level diagram is drawn for the node that represents the agent. Fig 3 shows an example of lower level diagrams for a node AgentX, where agents E_1, and E_2 and caste C_1 are the

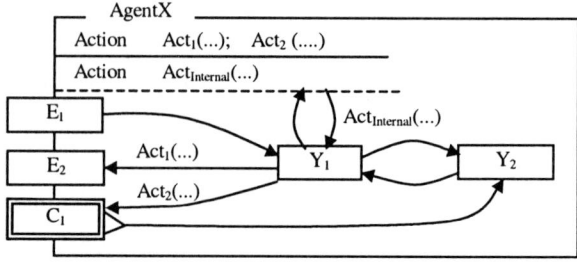

Fig. 3. Lower level agent diagram for a node

agents and castes in the environment that interact with AgentX. Y_1 and Y_2 are the component agents internal to the AgentX.

3 Case Study: Amalthaea

Amalthaea is an evolutionary multi-agent ecosystem developed at MIT Media Laboratory [21]. Its main purpose was to assist its users in finding interesting information on the web. There are two species of agents in the system: *information filtering agents* (IFA) that model and monitor the interests of the user, and *information discovery agents* (IDA) that model the information sources. These agents evolve, compete and collaborate in a market-like ecosystem. Agents that are useful to the user or other agents reproduce while low-performing agents are destroyed. The evolution of the system enables it to keep track of the changing interests of the user. In this section, we apply the methodology described in the previous section to develop a formal specification of Amalthaea in SLABS.

3.1 System's Architecture and Interactions between the Agents

Amalthaea [21] is composed of the following components.
- *User Interface*, where the user is presented with the retrieved information and gives feedback on its relevance;
- *The Ecosystem*, which consists of IDA and IFA agents;
- *The WWW search engines* for retrieving documents;
- *WKV Generator*, which extracts keywords from retrieved documents and generates the weighted keyword vectors;
- A *Database* of the retrieved documents.

These components plus the user are the agents of system. The visible states and actions of the agents are determined by how information flows in the system. For example, the user browses the information presented on the interface and gives a rating for each item. The only visible action of the user is 'rate on a digest'. The analysis of the interactions between the agents can be represented on the diagram by annotating the links with the actions that an agent / caste is interested in. Fig 4 is the result of the architectural and interaction analysis of Amalthaea.

Formal Specification of Evolutionary Software Agents   255

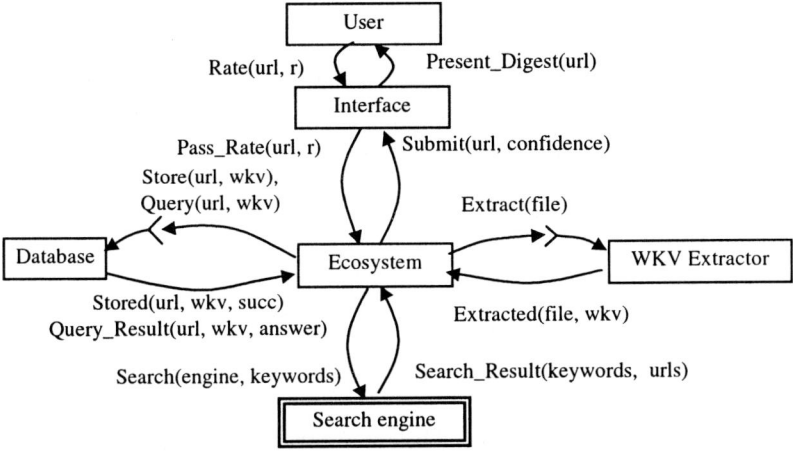

Fig. 4. Agent diagram with observable actions

The visible actions and states of the agents / castes can be derived directly from such a diagram. For example, the Interface should have two visible actions: *Pass_Rate(url, r)* and *Present_Digest(url)* according to the diagram.

3.2   Scenario Analysis and Description of Behaviour

Agent and castes of simple behaviour can be easily described via scenario analysis. In Amalthaea, the Search Engines is a caste that consists of a number of search engines, which have a common simple behaviour. Whenever a search engine receives a search request, it performs the Internet search and returns a set of URLs as search results. This can be specified by the following rule.

   [$] |–> [Search_Result(keywords, urls)]; if ∃A: [Search(Self, keywords)]

Together with the information contained in Fig. 4, we can derive the following specification of the caste of Search Engines.

```
╔═══ Search Engines ═══════════════════════════════════════════════╗
║     Action         Search_Result (K:Keywords, urls: set of URL)  ║
║─────────────────────────────────────────────────────────────────║
║   All   [$] |–> Search_Result(keywords, urls);  if ∃A: [Search( Self, keywords)] ║
╚══════════════════════════════════════════════════════════════════╝
```

The Database, User, Interface and WKV generator are also simple agents. Their formal specifications can be derived similarly.

```
┌─── User ─────────────────────────────────────────────────────────┐
│   Action Rate(url: URL, r: {1, 2, 3, 4, 5})                      │
│ Interface  [$] |–> Rate(url, r); if Interface: [$, Present_Digest(url), $^k ‖ N>k≥0 ] │
└──────────────────────────────────────────────────────────────────┘
```

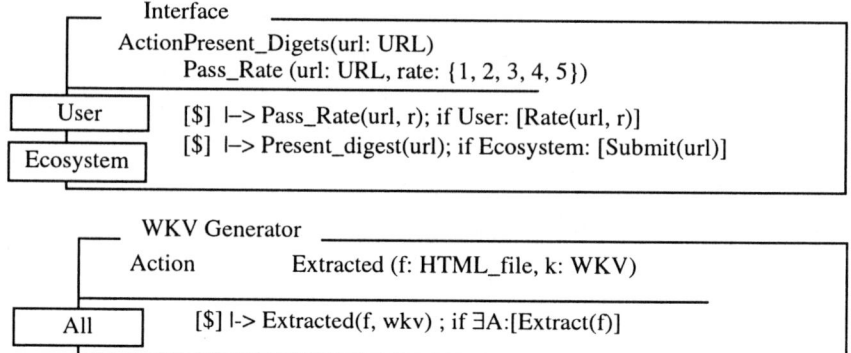

3.3 Decomposition and Analysis of Internal Structure

The Ecosystem in Amalthaea has complicated behaviours that cannot be described straightforwardly as above. It is therefore decomposed and analysed for its internal structure. The Ecosystem contains two types of agents: *IFAs* and *IDAs*. IFAs select the information proposed by IDAs and submit it to the interface. IDAs search the Internet by interacting with the search engines, database and WKV generator. The Interface passes user's rating to the Ecosystem, which takes an internal action of assigning credits to the agents who discovered, selected and submitted the information to the Interface. All the agents in the Ecosystem must also pay a fixed amount of rent for each fixed period of time. Hence, we have the refined description of the Ecosystem in Fig 5.

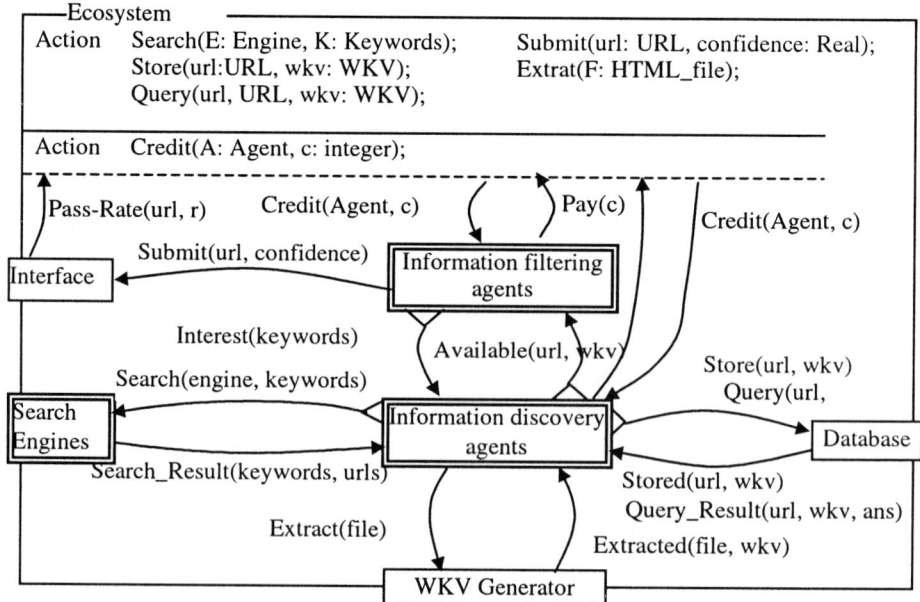

Fig. 5. Agent diagram of the Ecosystem

Formal Specification of Evolutionary Software Agents   257

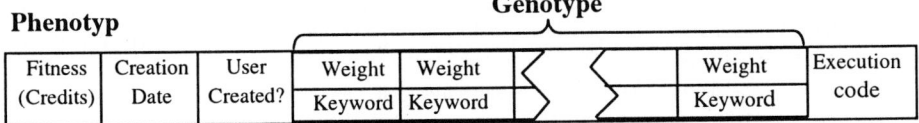

Fig. 6. The phenotype of information filtering agents

Each IFA only selects a specific type of documents that is determined by its 'phenotype'; see Fig 6. Therefore, an IFA has four internal state variables: (1) the fitness, (2) creation date, (3) the tag for if it is user created, and (4) the genotype in the form of a weighted keyword vector.

The following four scenarios trigger the behaviour of IFA.
- *Scenario 1*: when the Ecosystem credits the agent.
- *Scenario 2*: when it is the time to pay the rent.
- *Scenario 3*: when a user's interests in a topic are announced.
- *Scenario 4*: when an IDA retrieved some information.

```
┌═══════ Information Filtering Agents ═══════
│ Action   Recommend(Title, URL); Request(keywords); Pay Rental (Natural)
│ Var      Fitness: Integer; Creation Date: Date; User Created: Bool;
│          Genotype: WKV
│ ─────────────────────────────────────────────
│ [!(fitness=x) ] |-> !(fitness = x+c); if Ecosystem: [credit(self, c)]
│ [!(fitness=x) ] |-> t: pay(c) !(fitness = x-c); where pay_time(t)
│ [$] |-> Interest(keys(Self.genotype));
│ [Interest(keywords)] |-> Submit(url, confidence);
│     if ∃A∈ IDA: [Available(urls, wkv)]
│     where confidence=Distance(genotype, wkv) and confidence > threshold
```

All: IDA
Ecosystem
Interface

```
┌═══════ Information Discovery Agents ═══════
│ Action  Search(engine:Search Engine, keywords: set of keywords, max, min: Natural)
│         Pay (rent: Natural); Extract(f: HTML_file); Query(url: URL, wkv: WKV)
│         Store(url: URL, wkv: WKV); Available(url: URL, wkv: WKV)
│ ─────────────────────────────────────────────
│ Var  Fitness: Integer; Creation Date: Date; SearchEngine: Search Engines
│      NumberOfkKeywords, MinimumHits, MaximunHits: Natural
│ ─────────────────────────────────────────────
│ [!(fitness=x) ] |-> !(fitness = x+c); if Ecosystem: credit(Self, c)
│ [!(fitness=x) ] |-> t: pay(c) !(fitness = x-c); where pay_time(t)
│ [$] |-> search(Self.SearchEngine, keywords, Self.minimum_hit,
│      Self.maximum_hit);
│      if ∃A: [Interest(keywords)], where Good_Track_Record(A)=true
│ [search(Engine, keywords, min, max) ]
│ |-> Forall file ∈ {f at u | u ∈ urls}. Extract(file);
│      if Engine:[Search_Result(keyword, urls)]
│ [Extract(file)] |-> Query(url, wkv); if WKV Generator : [Extracted(file, wkv)]
│ [Query(url, wkv)] |-> Available(url, wkv);
│      if DataBase:[Query_Result(url, wkv, 'no')]
```

All: IFA
Ecosystem
E: Search Engines
Database
WKV Generator

For each scenario, the behaviour of an IFA can be specified by rules. For example, in Scenario 1, when the Ecosystem credits an agent, it increases the fitness by the amount of the credit assigned. Therefore, the rule is as follows.

[!(fitness=x)] |–> !(fitness = x+c); if Ecosystem: [credit(self, c)]

The specifications of IFAs and IDAs are given in the diagram above.

The credit of an agent serves as the fitness function. The higher the fitness of an agent, the more chances it has to survive and produce offspring. In the analysis of the behaviour of the Ecosystem, the following scenarios are identified.

- *Scenario 1*: when the user's rating on a presented digest is passed to the Ecosystem.
- *Scenario 2*: when it is the time for the agents to pay.

In scenario 1, the system credits the IFA that proposed the item and the IDA that retrieved it. Let *Credit_IFA:Rate×Confidence→N* and *Credit_IDA: Rate×Confidence →N* be functions that calculate the amount of the credit to be given to the IFA and IDA, respectively. Then, we have the following rule.

[$] |–> (Credit(A, c1), Credit(B, c2)) ;
   if Interface: [Pass_rate(url, r)] & A: [$, Submit(url, confidence), $^k] & B: [Available(url, wkv), $^k'],
   where c1=Credit_IFA(r, confidence) and c2=Credit_IDA(r)

In scenario 2, the Ecosystem evolves by purging bad agents and producing new offspring. The overall fitness is measured according to the percentage of positive feedbacks from the user in the past N ratings. It decides the numbers of agents to be purged and new agents to be produced. Only the best agents of the whole population are allowed to produce offspring, while the worst are purged. Let *NPurges* (*ratings*) be the number of agents to be purged. We have the following rule.

[!(A∈ IFA∪IDA)] |–> Purge(A) !(A∉ IFA∪IDA) ;
   if ∀X:IFA:[Pay(c)] and ∀Y:IDA:[Pay(c)] and Interface:[Pass_rating(r_n)^N]
   where A∈ PurgeSet & PurgeSet⊆{X| X∈ IFA or X∈ IDA} &
     ∀X∈ PurgeSet.∀Y∉ PurgeSet. (X.fitness≤Y.Fitness} & ||PurgeSet|| = NPurges($<r_n>_{n=1,...,N}$)

where *Purge* is an internal action that removes an agent from the system.

```
┌─ Ecosystem ─────────────────────────────────────────────────────
│   Action  Search(E: Engine, K: Keywords);   Submit(url: URL, confidence: Real)
│           Store(url:URL, wkv: WKV);         Extract_WKV(F:HTML_file);
│           Query(url, URL, wkv: WKV)
│   ─────────────────────────────────────────────────────────────
│   Var     IFA: Caste Information_Filtering_Agents;
│           IDA: Caste Information_Discovery_Agents
│   Action  Credit(A: Agent, c: Integer);  Purge(A: Agent);  Generate(A: Agent)
│   ─ ─ ─ ─ ─ ─ ─ ─ ─ ─ ─ ─ ─ ─ ─ ─ ─ ─ ─ ─ ─ ─ ─ ─ ─ ─ ─ ─ ─ ─
│   [$] |-> (Credit(A, c1), Credit(B, c2)) ;
│     if Interface: [Pass_rating( url, r)] & A: [$, Submit(url, confidence), $^k]
│                 & B: [Available(url, wkv), $^k'],
│     where c1=Credit_IFA(r, confidence) and c2=Credit_IDA(r, confidence)
│   [!(A∈ IFA∪IDA)] |-> Purge(A) !(A∉ IFA∪IDA) ;
│     if ∀X:IFA:[Pay(c)] & ∀Y:IDA:[Pay(c)] & Interface:[Pass_rating($r_n$)^N]
│     where A∈ PurgeSet and PurgeSet⊆{X| X∈ IFA or X∈ IDA}
│            and ∀X∈ PurgeSet.∀Y∉ PurgeSet. (X.fitness≤Y.Fitness}
│            and ||PurgeSet|| = NPurges($<r_n>_{n=1,...,N}$)
│   [!(A∉ IFA∪IDA)] |-> Generate(A) !(A∈ IFA∪IDA) ;
│     if ∀X:IFA:[Pay(c)] & ∀Y:IDA:[Pay(c)] & Interface:[Pass_rating($r_n$)^N]
│     where A∈ NewAgentSet & NewAgentSetSpec
└─────────────────────────────────────────────────────────────────
```

Connections (left side): Interface; All: Search Engines; Database; WKV Generator

Similarly, we have the following rule for producing offspring.

[!(A∉IFA∪IDA)] |—> Generate(A) !(A∈IFA∪IDA) ;
    if ∀X:IFA:[Pay(c)] & ∀Y:IDA:[Pay(c)] & Interface:[Pass_rating(r_n)^N], where A∈ NewAgentSet

where *Generate* is an internal action that adds an agent to the system. Therefore, we have the above specification of the ecosystem.

This completes the specification of Amalthaea system.

4 Conclusion

In this paper, we presented a case study of developing a formal specification of a non-trivial evolutionary multi-agent system, which has a number of attractive features of its own. The result of the case study was satisfactory. A complete formal specification of the system is obtained with a reasonable effort through a smooth process.

Existing work on agent-oriented software development methodology has been focused on process models for analysis and design of agent-based systems using diagrammatic notations. Little work has been reported that enable software engineers to use formal logic and other formalisms that have been investigated in the literature for agent technology. Few complete formal specifications of non-trivial multi-agent systems are reported in the literature. It is unclear about how to use formal modal logic systems of BDI such as [8] and game theories [9] to express the behaviours of evolutionary ecosystems, which involves purging existing agents and producing offspring of existing agents.

The case study clearly demonstrated a number of advantages of the language SLABS and the methodology for developing formal specifications in SLABS in comparison with formal specification in general purpose languages such as Z [23~25]. Firstly, the language is expressive and suitable for the formal specification of multi-agent systems. The evolution process as well as other intelligent behaviour of the system can be clearly and naturally described. Second, the model of the system represented in the diagrammatic notation greatly helped to understand the system's behaviour, especially how agents communicate with each other. This model can be naturally transformed into the overall structure of the formal specification, which, from our previous experience, is one of the most difficult tasks in developing formal specifications without such a model. Third, the process naturally bridges the gap between informal and formal notations.

We are further investigating how tools can be developed to automate the transformation from the diagrammatic notation to formal specification in SLABS in the way that structured requirements definitions are translated into formal specifications in Z [26, 27]. We are also investigating how scenarios analysis can be graphically represented in a diagrammatic notation.

References

1. Jennings, N.R., Wooldridge, M.J. (eds.): Agent Technology: Foundations, Applications, And Markets. Springer, Berlin Heidelberg New York (1998)
2. Huhns, M., Singh, M.P. (eds.): Readings in Agents. Morgan Kaufmann, San Francisco (1997)

3. Jennings, N. R.: On agent-based software engineering. Artificial Intelligence 117, (2000) 277~296.
4. Lange, D. B.: Mobile Objects and mobile agents: The future of distributed computing? In: Proc. of The European Conference on Object-Oriented Programming, (1998)
5. Brazier, F.M.T., Dunin-Keplicz, B.M., Jennings, N.R., Treur, J.: DESIRE: Modelling Multi-Agent Systems in a Compositional Formal Framework. Int. J. of Cooperative Information Systems 1(6) (1997) 67~94
6. Rao, A.S., Georgreff, M.P.: Modeling Rational Agents within a BDI-Architecture. In: Proc. of the International Conference on Principles of Knowledge Representation and Reasoning (1991) 473~484.
7. Singh, M.P.: Semantic Considerations on Some Primitives for Agent Specification. In: Wooldridge, M., Muller, J., Tambe, M. (eds): Intelligent Agents. LNAI, Vol. 1037. Springer (1996) 49~64
8. Wooldridge, M.: Reasoning About Rational Agents. The MIT Press (2000)
9. Ambroszkiewicz, S., Komar, J.: A Model of BDI-Agent in Game-Theoretic Framework. In: [10] (1999) 8~19
10. Myer, J-J., Schobbens, P-Y. (eds.): Formal Models of Agents - ESPRIT Project ModelAge Final Workshop Selected Papers. LNAI, Vol. 1760. Springer (1999)
11. Wooldridge, M.J. and Jennings, N.R.: Agent Theories, Architectures, and Languages: A Survey. In: Intelligent Agents. LNAI, Vol. 890. Springer-Verlag (1995) 1~32
12. Kinny, D., Georgeff, M., Rao, A.: A Methodology and Modelling Technology for Systems of BDI Agents. In: Agents Breaking Away: Proc. of MAAMAW'96. LNAI, Vol. 1038. Spriger-Verlag (1996)
13. Moulin, B., Brassard, M.: A Scenario-Based Design Method and An Environment for the Development of Multiagent Systems. In: Lukose, D. and Zhang C. (eds.): First Australian Workshop on Distributed Artificial Intelligence. LNAI, Vol. 1087. Springer-Verlag (1996) 216~231
14. Wooldridge, M., Jennings, N., Kinny, D.: A Methodology for Agent-Oriented Analysis and Design. In: Proc. of ACM Third International Conference on Autonomous Agents, Seattle, WA, USA (1999) 69~76
15. Iglesias, C.A., Garijo, M., Gonzalez, J.C.: A Survey of Agent-Oriented Methodologies. In: Muller, J. P., Singh, M. P., Rao, A., (eds.): Intelligent Agents V. LNAI, Vol. 1555. Springer, Berlin (1999) 317~330
16. Bauer, B., Muller, J.P., and Odell, J.: Agent UML: a Formalism for Specifying Multiagent Software Systems. In: Ciancarini, P. and Wooldridge, M. (Eds.): Agent-Oriented Software Engineering. LNCS, Vol. 1957. Springer (2001) 91~103
17. Zhu, H.: Formal Specification of Agent Behaviour through Environment Scenarios. In: Proc. of FAABS 2000. LNCS, Vol. 1871. Springer (2001) 263~277
18. Zhu, H.: SLABS: A Formal Specification Language for Agent-Based Systems. Int. J. of Software Engineering and Knowledge Engineering 11(5) (2001) 529~558
19. Zhu, H.: The Role of Caste in Formal Specification of MAS. In: Proc. of PRIMA'2001. LNCS Vol. 2132. Springer (2001) 1~15
20. Zhu, H.: Developing formal specifications of MAS in SLABS, to appear in Proc. of AOIS"2002.
21. Moukas, A.: Amalthaea: Information Discovery and Filtering Using a Multi-Agent Evolving Ecosystem. Journal of Applied Artificial Intelligence 11(5) (1997) 437~457
22. Jennings, N.R.: Agent-Oriented Software Engineering. In: Garijo, F.J., Boman, M. (eds.): Multi-Agent System Engineering, LNAI 1647. Springer, (1999) 1~7
23. Spivey, J.M.: The Z Notation: A Reference Manual. 2nd edn. Prentice Hall (1992)
24. D'Inverno, M., Kinny, D., Luck M. and Wooldridge, M.: A formal specification of dMARS in Singh, M. P. Rao, A. and Wooldridge, M. (eds.): Intelligent Agents IV: Agent Theories, Architectures, and Languages. LNAI Vol. 1365. Springer (1998) 155~176

25. Luck, M. and d'Inverno, M.: A formal framework for agency and autonomy in Proc. of First International Conference on Multi-agent Systems. AAAI Press/MIT Press (1995) 254~260,
26. Jin, L., Zhu, H.: Automatic Generation of Formal Specification from Requirements Definition. In: Proc. of IEEE 1st Int. Conf. on Formal Engineering Methods, Hiroshima, Japan (1997) 243~251
27. Zhu, H., Jin, L.: Scenario Analysis in an Automated Tool for Requirements Engineering. J. of Requirements Engineering 5(1) (2000) 2~22

Detecting Deadlock in Ada Rendezvous Flow Structure Based on Process Algebra*

Yuan Liu[1], Baowen Xu[1,2], and Zhenqiang Chen[1]

[1] Department of Computer Science and Engineering, Southeast University, China
{liuyuan, bwxu, chenzq}@seu.edu.cn
[2] State Key Laboratory of Software Engineering, Wuhan University, China

Abstract. Many approaches have been presented to detect deadlock of Ada concurrent programs. Most of them adopt some kind of flow structure or Petri nets. In this paper, we express Ada rendezvous flow structure using process algebra. Through the deduction of process algebra expressions with equivalence, information about communications among processes can be obtained. Together with the help of communication dependence analysis, the paper proposes a static approach to detect deadlock in Ada rendezvous flow structure.

1 Introduction

Ada is a programming language designed to support the construction of long-lived, highly reliable software systems, includes a complete facility for the support of concurrent programming[11], but some particular problems should be well handled during design concurrent programs, among which deadlock prevention is of great importance.

A deadlock is a blocked situation that a group of processes mutually wait on each other, competing for resources. In Ada concurrent programs, a deadlock occurs when a group of entry calls(caller for short) and accept statements(acceptor for short) wait on each other so that no one can go any further.

Up to now, many static approaches have been proposed to detect deadlock in Ada concurrent programs, which mainly base on certain flow structure or Petri net. When adopting flow structure[4], some certain kind of condensed flow structures(or similar structures, in which nodes represent synchronization and directed edges represent control flow) are extracted from codes to represent the programs[13]. Based on these flow structures, many techniques[12] have been presented to simplify or abstract those flow structure, so as to make detection possible and easier. Those methods using Petri net [14], usually modify or add some new behaviors or properties to the

---

* This work is supported in part by the National Natural Science Foundation of China (NSFC) (60073012), Natural Science Foundation of Jiangsu, China (BK2001004), Opening Foundation of State Key Laboratory of Software Engineering in Wuhan University, and Foundation of State Key Laboratory for Novel Software Technology in Nanjing University.

basic Petri net so as to satisfy their actual demands, which brings out a great variety of different Petri net structures(or similar). These Petri net models[8, 9] extract properties and abstract behaviors from programs, therefore deadlock detection can be achieved according to the flow of resources. In static deadlock detection, some common methods based on Petri net are often used, such as using invariants, relying on reachability analysis, making use of extended Petri nets and carrying reduction transforms. Though Petri nets are intuitive, all of them rely on states enumeration and few adopting approximation methods, which will certainly lead to state explosion[15]. Similarly, quite a large number of methods based on flow structure rely on state enumeration too, so certain measures also should be taken to avoid state explosion. Many different techniques have been proposed to combat state explosion are state reduction, such as symbolic model checking, compositional techniques, abstraction, data flow analysis and integer programming[7].

Though many approaches have been proposed, each of them has its strong point but none does perfectly well and many things are to be handled in future. However all these ideas are helpful to further researches. Here in this paper, we use process algebra to express Ada rendezvous flow structure and propose how to carry out static deadlock detection and reachability analysis. Section 2 briefly introduces process algebra. Section 3 presents an ACP description of Ada rendezvous and Section 4 presents how to transform Ada rendezvous flow structure into ACP expressions, based on which Section 5 proposes a static deadlock detecting approach. A case study is presented in Section 6. And conclusion remarks are given in the last section.

2 Preliminaries

Process algebra can be seen as a worthy descendant of "classical" automata theory [1]. The crucial difference is that classical automata theory can only describe the execution trace of a single automata but has no ability of handling communication system[3]. Process algebra has strong ability of representing and analyzing concurrent system using algebraic structures. It is of great value of modeling and analyzing concurrent system and has proven its value in various application domains[2].

CCS, CSP and ACP are the three most famous theories in process algebra, among which ACP is of the most simple and convenient. It can clearly describe finite states communication automata, simplify process composition and conveniently hide internal details. So we make use of ACP as a powerful tool of detecting deadlock. As preliminary notations, process algebra and ACP[1] are briefly introduced as follow.

A process algebra consists of a set of actions(events), symbols, operators and axioms describing operators' properties. BPA(Basic Process Algebra) is the kernel of all theories of process algebra. The basic unit in BPA is atomic action, which is an undividable action or event. A process is obtained by using two most basic operators:
1) · denotes sequential combination; a · b is a process that first executes a then b;
   · satisfies associativity;
2) + denotes alternative composition; a + b is a process that executes either a or b but not both;

\+ satisfies commutativity, associativity, idempotency and right distributivity with A binary relation $\xrightarrow{a}$ and unary relation $\xrightarrow{a} \sqrt{}$ are defined:

$T \xrightarrow{a} S$ denotes T can turn into S after action a is executed;

$T \xrightarrow{a} \sqrt{}$ denotes after action a, T can terminate successfully.

After two important constants δ and ε are introduced, BPA is extended to BPA_δ and BPA_ε respectively. δ represents deadlock and ε represents empty process.

Extended from BPA, ACP has strong ability of describing concurrent system. In ACP, three operators are introduced: ||, the merge operator, ||_, the left merge operator and |, the communication operator. x||y denotes a process that executes process x and y concurrently. x||_y is similar to x||y, but with a restriction that the first step must start from process x. x|y denotes process x and process y communicate with each other.

There are two important operators, ∂_H and τ_I. ∂_H is called encapsulation operator and τ_I is called abstraction operator. Among the two, ∂_H has been considered as an indispensable operator in process algebra. This encapsulation operator renames all actions from H in its argument into δ, while the abstraction operator renames all actions from I in its argument into τ, where τ is called silent step denoting an internal action.

3 ACP Description of Ada Rendezvous

Task is the basic concurrent unit in Ada, and rendezvous is the basic concurrency. In rendezvous, the point when rendezvous begins and the point when rendezvous ends are two synchronization points. As shown in Fig.1(a), this rendezvous is denoted by M. A is the state of entry call, E is the state of acceptance. R and R' are two successful states of synchronization, each corresponding to a synchronization point, i.e., r and r'.

In Fig.1(a), each edge is an atomic action. Those control edges leading to the synchronization points are modified a little. Each of them is attached by another atomic action $\gamma_{s,r}$[10]. This kind of atomic action is called communication atomic action, CA for short. We refer other atomic actions as common atomic actions. The purpose of adding CAs is to distinguish synchronization edges from those common edges. These CAs act as agents of their synchronization edges, taking over communication control from their synchronization edges. After synchronization, the life span of a CA terminates successfully. Thus Fig.1(a) is extended to Fig.1(b), in which before synchronization point r and r•, several CAs are appended after synchronization edge m, a, w and e.

In Fig.1(b), A and E execute concurrently, which can be denoted by A||E. $\gamma_{m,r}$ and $\gamma_{a,r}$ communicate each other in synchronization point r, followed by $\gamma_{w,r}$ and $\gamma_{w,r}$ communicating each other in synchronization point r•. The behavior of each control edge can be regarded as following:

$$\lambda \xrightarrow{l} \lambda',$$

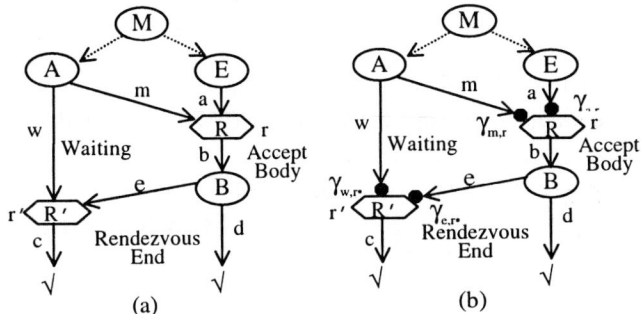

Fig. 1. Control Flow of Ada Rendezvous

which denotes that through action t(non-atomic actions are allowed), state λ turns into state λ' by executing action t. The corresponding process algebra expression is:
$$\lambda = t\lambda',$$
in which λ is called an *action chain*(*chain* in short) in this paper, and so is λ', which stands for a new chain after the execution of t by chain λ.

Thus the control flow of Ada rendezvous can be described by using ACP:

$M = \tau_I(\partial_H(A\|E))$, $A = (m\gamma_{m,r})\|(w\gamma_{w,r'})$, $E = a\gamma_{a,r}$, $R = bB$, $B = (e\gamma_{e,r'})\|d$, $R' = c$

where, $H = \{\gamma_{m,r}, \gamma_{a,r}, \gamma_{w,r'}, \gamma_{e,r'}\}$, $\gamma_{m,r}|\gamma_{a,r} = R$, $\gamma_{w,r'}|\gamma_{e,r'} = R'$, $I = \{w\}$.

Among $\gamma_{m,r}$, $\gamma_{a,r}$, $\gamma_{w,r'}$ and $\gamma_{e,r'}$, only $\gamma_{m,r}|\gamma_{a,r}$ and $\gamma_{w,r'}|\gamma_{e,r'}$ can carry on; other combinations will lead to δ. For these two communication pairs, we have $\gamma_{m,r}|\gamma_{a,r} = R$ and $\gamma_{w,r'}|\gamma_{e,r'} = R\bullet$. In communication, those CAs that occur alone mean no communication can be obtained. So these four CAs are put into the set H of encapsulation operator ∂_H, which therefore can be renamed to δ during rendezvous through encapsulation operation. As a matter of fact, action w is just an internal action in Ada rendezvous, which should be totally hidden. So the set I in abstraction operator τ_I should include action w so that w can be removed by abstraction operation. Axioms and operations of ACP can be applied to deduce the expressions we have got above. Each step of deduction is an equivalence. The deduction is shown as below(some steps skipped to save space).

$M = \tau_I(\partial_H(A\|E))$
$= \tau_I(\partial_H(((m(\gamma_{m,r}\|(a\gamma_{a,r})) + a(\gamma_{a,r}\|(m\gamma_{m,r})))\|(w\gamma_{w,r'})))$
$= \tau_I(\partial_H(((m(\gamma_{m,r}a\gamma_{a,r} + a(\gamma_{a,r}\gamma_{m,r} + \gamma_{m,r}\gamma_{a,r} + R))$
$\quad + a(\gamma_{a,r}m\gamma_{m,r} + m(\gamma_{m,r}\gamma_{a,r} + \gamma_{a,r}\gamma_{m,r} + R)))\|(w\gamma_{w,r'})))$
$= \ldots$
$= \tau_I((a\|m)(b(((e\|w)c)\|d) + wb((ec)\|d)) + ((m\|w)a + (a\|w)m)(b((ec)\|d)))$
$= (a\|m)b((ec)\|d)$

Through strict deduction with equivalence, Ada rendezvous can be represented by process algebra expressions. If omitting the message returned to entry call, further abstraction can be made by appending action e to set I, i.e. I = $\{w,e\}$, thus we get M = $(a\|m)b(c\|d)$. Thus, by using abstraction operation, some details in rendezvous can be omitted. From the ACP viewpoint, rendezvous can be regarded as the following sequential composition: *synchronization of entry call and accept statement · execution of accept statement body · concurrent execution of codes belong to caller and caller after rendezvous*. In this kind of simplified rendezvous, only one synchronization is needed with only a pair of CAs. We classify these CAs as two kinds, one is communication atomic action of entry call(CAC for short, denoted by γ) and another is communication atomic action of accept statement(CAA for short, denoted by $\gamma^{\#}$).

4 ACP Description of Ada Rendezvous Flow Structure

From the simplified model of rendezvous above, rendezvous can be treated as a synchronization between entry call and accept statement. In Ada concurrent programs, we only concern about those rendezvous. Thus rendezvous flow structure is extracted from Ada concurrent programs, only consisting of callers, acceptors and their rendezvous. Similarly each edge leading to a rendezvous is attached by the communication atomic action $\gamma_{s,r}$ (Fig.2).

```
task body P1 is    task body P2 is
begin              begin
  Fork1.Pick;        Fork2.Pick;
  Fork2.Pick;        Fork1.Pick;
end P1;            end P2;

task body Fork1 is task body Fork2 is
begin              begin
  accept Pick;       accept Pick;
end Fork1;         end Fork2;

        (a)
```

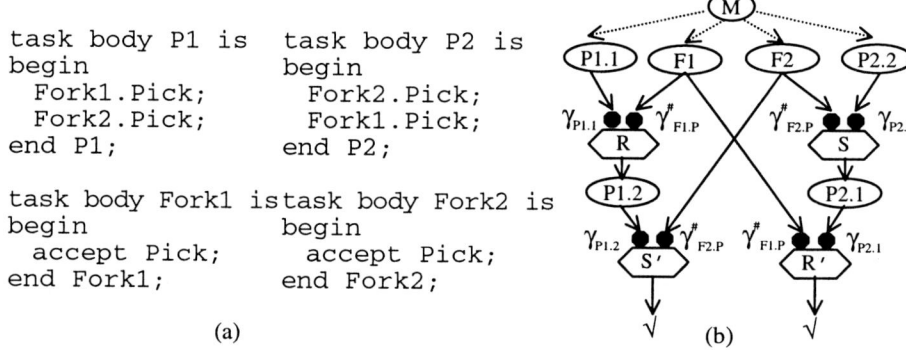

Fig. 2. Ada Rendezvous Flow Structure

In Fig.2, there are four task bodies and Fig.2(b) is the corresponding rendezvous flow structure. In Fig.2(b), P1.1 is a caller representing *Fork1.Pick* in task P1; P1.2, P2.1 and P2.2 are similar. And F1 is an acceptor represents *accept pick* in Fork1; F2 is similar. The corresponding CAs of these caller and acceptors are $\gamma_{P1.1}$, $\gamma^{\#}_{F1.P}$, etc. Those control edges come out of the same caller or acceptor are of alternative relationship.

Still we adopt the notion of action chain described above. The initial state M of Ada rendezvous flow structure is the initial chain λ. Rules of transforming rendezvous flow structure into ACP expressions are shown as below.

1. $\lambda_0, \ldots, \lambda_n$ are concurrent chains:
   $\lambda = \lambda_0 \| \ldots \| \lambda_n$
2. Chain starts from a conditional statement:
   $\lambda = (\lambda_1 + \ldots + \lambda_n) \cdot \lambda'$
3. Chain starts from loop statement with or without control condition respectively:
   $\lambda = \text{LoopBody}_\lambda \cdot \lambda'$; $\lambda = \text{LoopBody}_\lambda \cdot \lambda' + \lambda'$
4. Entry call and accept statements; Chain T starts from $\gamma_{\lambda,E}$, which is a CAC; chain λ starts from $\gamma^{\#}_{\lambda,E}$, which is a CAA:
   $\lambda = \text{Call}_E \cdot \gamma_{\lambda,E}$; $\lambda = \text{Accept}_E \cdot \gamma^{\#}_{\lambda,E}$

5. Chain λ starts from a select statement:
   $\lambda = (\lambda_1 + \ldots + \lambda_n) \cdot \lambda'$
6. Chain terminates successfully:
   $\lambda = \sqrt{}$
   No subsequent chains behind and λ consists only common atomic actions. According to the hierarchical operating process, $\sqrt{}$ occurs only when a root branch terminates successfully.
7. Terminate statement, which is an abnormal termination:
   $\lambda = \delta$
8. Execution of ATC(Asynchronous Transfer of Control) has four possibilities:
   i. Only triggering alternative is executed;
   ii. Triggering alternative is not triggered until abortable part is executed;
   iii. While abortable part is executing, triggering alternative is triggered. Abortable part aborts immediately, and triggering alternative is executed. To transform this to process algebra expression, a substitution operation $\lambda_2(s, \lambda_1)$ is defined, in which λ_2 aborts after its s-1 action has been executed and then triggering alternative is executed.
   iv. Abortable part is executed, attempting to terminate triggering alternative which is waiting for rendezvous, but failed. Thus triggering alternative is executed too.
   $\lambda = (\lambda_1 + \lambda_2 + \lambda_2(s, \lambda_1) + \lambda_2 \cdot \lambda_1) \cdot \lambda'$
   Where λ_1 is triggering alternative and λ_2 is abortable part, and the four alternatives correspond to those above.
9. Communication of rendezvous; body of accept statement is first executed, then corresponding paths after rendezvous are executed concurrently:
   $\gamma_{C,E} \, | \gamma^{\#}_{A,E} = \text{AcceptBody}_E \cdot \text{ (C||A)}$

Similarly, all the CAs are put into the set H of encapsulation operator ∂_H, which will be renamed to δ by encapsulation operation. So the whole rendezvous flow structure can be denoted by: $M = \partial_H(\lambda)$, where H contains all the CAs during transformation.

We take Fig.2 as an example to transform Fig.2(b) into ACP expressions. The result is shown in Fig.3.

$M = \partial_H(P1.1 \cdot \gamma_{P1.1} \parallel F1 \cdot \gamma^{\#}_{F1.P} \parallel P2.2 \cdot \gamma_{P2.2} \parallel F2 \cdot \gamma^{\#}_{F2.P})$;

$\gamma_{P1.1} \, | \, \gamma^{\#}_{F1.P} = R$; $\gamma_{P2.2} \, | \, \gamma^{\#}_{F2.P} = S$;

$R = P1.2 \cdot \gamma_{P1.2}$; $S = P2.1 \cdot \gamma_{P2.1}$;

$\gamma_{P1.2} \, | \, \gamma^{\#}_{F2.P} = S'$; $\gamma_{P2.1} \, | \, \gamma^{\#}_{F1.P} = R'$;

$S' = \sqrt{}$; $R' = \sqrt{}$;

where $H = \{\gamma_{P1.1}, \gamma_{P2.2}, \gamma_{P1.2}, \gamma_{P2.1}, \gamma^{\#}_{F1.P}, \gamma^{\#}_{F2.P}\}$.

Fig. 3. ACP Expressions of Fig.2(b)

5 Deadlock Detection in Ada Rendezvous Flow Structure

The occurrence of a deadlock requires the following four premises: mutual exclusion, hold and request, non deprivable and forming a circular waiting on resources[6]. In Ada rendezvous flow structure, detecting the deadlock cycle is of major concern.

From the ACP viewpoint, different kinds of CAs can successfully shake hand and therefore turn into a new state if these two CAs require each other for sure, otherwise a dead communication occurs. The attempt of communicating between the same kind of CACs will certainly lead to a dead communication, which denotes each of these two demands for its own CAA but fails and thus has to wait. The attempt of communicating between the same kind of CAAs act just the same, each demands for a CAC for its own. What we should discover and analyze in our deadlock detection are just the behaviors of communication between these CAs.

5.1 Basic Definitions

Definition 1. For every CAC and CAA occurs in rendezvous flow structure, its *Dependence_Set* is defined. Suppose C_1 is a CA in a chain $Chain_1$, $Chain_1$ is checked upwards until a set of CAs is obtained(supposed to be $\{C_i\}$), then C_1 depends on C_i and all the CAs that could successfully communicate with C_i. According to transitivity, *Dependence_Set* of C_1 can be easily obtained.

Based on *Dependence_Set*, notations of *predecessor* and *successor* are defined as:
Definition 2. Let γ_1 and γ_2 be two CAs. If γ_1 is in the dependence set of γ_2, then γ_2 is a *successor* of γ_1, denoted by $\gamma_2 < \gamma_1$, and γ_1 is a *predecessor* of γ_2, denoted by $\gamma_1 > \gamma_2$, and $\gamma_1 <> \gamma_2$ denotes that neither γ_1 nor γ_2 are the predecessor of each other. Let C_1 and C_2 be two chains containing CAs. If the first CA in C_2 is the successor of the one in C_1, then C_2 is the *successor* of C_1, and C_1 is the *predecessor* of C_2, which have the same notations as above. Let Chain be a chain containing CAs and let γ be a CA. If the first CA in Chain is the successor(predecessor) of γ, then Chain is the *successor(predecessor)* of γ, and γ is the *predecessor(successor)* of Chain, which have the same notations as above.

In an Ada rendezvous flow structure, if several callers and acceptors wait on each other in a cycle, a deadlock cycle is formed and deadlock will possibly occur. So these callers and acceptors must be found out first.

Definition 3. A *Deadlock Cycle* occurs when one of the following three holds:
(a) Given a set of chain P(I) containing $\gamma_{P(I),E(I)}$ and a set of chain Q(J) containing $\gamma^{\#}_{Q(I),A(I)}$, where I = [0,n-1].

If $\forall\ I \in [0,n-1]\ (\gamma_{P(I),E(I)} < \gamma^{\#}_{Q(I),A(I)})$, where A(I) = E((I+1) mod n)(or E(I) = A((I+1) mod n)), and $!\ \exists\ I,J \in [0,n-1]\ (\gamma^{\#}_{Q(I),A(I)} <> \gamma^{\#}_{Q(J),A(J)})$, $!\ \exists\ I,J \in [0,n-1]\ (\gamma_{P(I),E(I)} <> \gamma_{P(J),E(J)})$, then these $\gamma^{\#}_{Q(I),A(I)}$ and $\gamma_{P(I),E(I)}$ form a *Deadlock Cycle*.

(b) Given a set of chain P(I) containing $\gamma_{P(I),E(I)}$ and a set of chain Q(J) containing $\gamma^{\#}_{Q(I),A(I)}$, where I = [0,n-1].

If $\forall\ I \in [0,n-1]\ (\gamma_{P(I),E(I)} > \gamma^{\#}_{Q(I),A(I)})$,

where $A(I) = E((I+1) \bmod n)$ (or $E(I) = A((I+1) \bmod n)$),
and $!\exists I,J \in [0,n-1]$ ($\gamma^{\#}_{Q(I),A(I)} <> \gamma^{\#}_{Q(J),A(J)}$), $!\exists I,J \in [0,n-1]$ ($\gamma_{P(I),E(I)} <> \gamma_{P(J),E(J)}$),
then these $\gamma_{P(I),E(I)}$ and $\gamma^{\#}_{Q(I),A(I)}$ form a *Deadlock Cycle*.

(c) Given $\gamma_{P(0),E(0)}$, $\gamma^{\#}_{Q(0),A(0)}$, $\gamma_{P(1),E(1)}$ and $\gamma^{\#}_{Q(1),A(1)}$,
if $\gamma_{P(0),E(0)} > \gamma_{P(1),E(1)}$, $\gamma^{\#}_{Q(0),A(0)} > \gamma^{\#}_{Q(1),A(1)}$, where $E(0) = A(1)$ and $E(1) = A(0)$,
and $\gamma_{P(0),E(0)} <> \gamma^{\#}_{Q(0),A(0)}$, $\gamma_{P(1),E(1)} <> \gamma^{\#}_{Q(1),A(1)}$,
then $\gamma_{P(0),E(0)}$, $\gamma^{\#}_{Q(0),A(0)}$, $\gamma_{P(1),E(1)}$ and $\gamma^{\#}_{Q(1),A(1)}$ form a *Deadlock Cycle*.

Definition 4. In concurrent programs, a deadlock which may occur in some paths is called a *Partial Deadlock*, the corresponding deadlock cycle is called a *Partial Deadlock Cycle*. A deadlock which occurs in all paths is called a *Complete Deadlock*, the corresponding deadlock cycle is called a *Complete Deadlock Cycle*.

If all the $\gamma^{\#}_{Q(I),A(I)}$ in Definition 3(a) have never been matched, then a complete deadlock cycle is formed(Fig.4(a)). In Definition 3(b), the CAC is the predecessor of the CAA in each pair of $\gamma_{P(I),E(I)}$ and $\gamma^{\#}_{Q(I),A(I)}$, thus the deadlock cycle defined in Definition 3(b) is a complete deadlock cycle. In Definition 3(c), if the two $\gamma^{\#}_{Q(0),A(0)}$ have never been matched, then $\gamma_{P(0),E(0)}$, $\gamma^{\#}_{Q(0),A(0)}$, $\gamma_{P(1),E(1)}$ and $\gamma^{\#}_{Q(1),A(1)}$ form a complete deadlock cycle(Fig.4(c)). In the following of this paper, detection of complete deadlock cycles and partial deadlock cycles are presented.

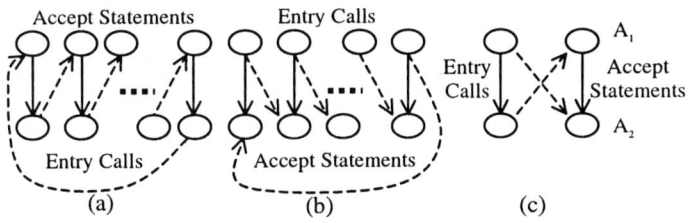

Fig. 4. Complete Deadlock Cycles

5.2 Detection of Complete Deadlock Cycles

In order to detect complete deadlock cycles in rendezvous flow structure, the whole rendezvous flow structure must be scanned first. In this paper, we take the whole scan as a complete execution path simulation concurrently. From root task, all concurrent *root branches*(branches start from root are called *root branches*) start the scan together, each of which does not stop until meet a rendezvous. When the scan stops in all branches, either meeting a rendezvous or coming to an end of root branches, all the entry calls and accept statements when met during scan are checked. Every possible rendezvous that could carry on so far are listed out, which make corresponding paths possible to continue next step of scan. Those entry calls and accept statements that cannot find their match are suspended and cannot continue next step of scan, waiting for further match. After this, the next step of scan proceeds if possible. Thus step by step, until all the root branches come to an end or cannot go ahead any further.

Definition 5. Such a step of operation as *scan concurrently→scan stops→match entry calls and accept statements* is called a layer of *Hierarchical Operating*. Such a whole process of scanning and matching is called *Hierarchical Operating Process*. A set consists of all newly occurred CAs during a single step is called *Hierarchical Operating Space*.

During hierarchical operating process on Ada rendezvous flow structure, we can obtain the following sets easily.
- *Call_Record*(CAA) is a set that consists of all CACs that match this CAAs.
- *Uncalled_CAA* is a set that consists of all those CAAs that occur without having been matched.
- *Nonoccurred_CAA* is a set that consists of all the CAAs waited by some CACs but not occur.
- *Unaccepted_CAC* is a set that consists of all the CACs that have not been matched. This set can be generated from *Nonoccurred_CAA*. To make reduction easier, rename all the CAAs and CACs in the sets above into δ.

According to the CAAs in *Uncalled_CAA* and *Nonoccurred_CAA*, three kinds of deadlock can be detected(shown in Fig.4, in which solid arrows denote dependence relation and dotted arrows denote entry call).

1. Deadlock caused only by CAAs in *Uncalled_CAA*. For every CAA in *Uncalled_CAA*, get those corresponding CACs by looking into Call_Record(CAA). Then in these CAAs and CACs, find out all the deadlock cycles similar to Fig.4(a). A deadlock cycle consists of only a CAA and a CAC is the simplest one.
2. Deadlock caused only by CAAs in *Nonoccurred_CAA*. The way of detecting this kind of deadlock cycles are similar to that above.
3. Deadlock caused by both. A_1 is an element in *Uncalled_CAA*, and A_2 is an element in *Nonoccurred_CAA*. $\forall\ A_1, A_2$ ($A_1 \in$ *Uncalled_CAA*, $A_2 \in$ *Nonoccurred_CAA* and $A_2 < A_1$), for each pair of such A_1 and A_2, find out all the deadlock cycles similar to Fig.4(c) in $\{A_1, A_2, Call\_Record(A_1), Call\_Record(A_2)\}$.

5.3 Detection of Partial Deadlock Cycles

To detect partial deadlock cycles, three theorems are presented as below.

Theorem 1. During deduction,
1) If $\gamma_{P(i),E(i)}|\gamma_{P(j),E(j)}$ occurs, then $\gamma_{P(i),E(i)} <> \gamma_{P(j),E(j)}$;
2) If $\gamma_{P(i),E(i)}|\gamma^{\#}_{P(j),E(j)}$ occurs, then $\gamma_{P(i),E(i)} <> \gamma^{\#}_{P(j),E(j)}$;
3) If $\gamma^{\#}_{P(i),E(i)}|\gamma^{\#}_{P(j),E(j)}$ occurs, then $\gamma^{\#}_{P(i),E(i)} <> \gamma^{\#}_{P(j),E(j)}$.

Proof: Suppose $\gamma_{P(i),E(i)} > \gamma_{P(j),E(j)}$. In one particular path during deduction of process algebra expressions, a successor $\gamma_{P(j),E(j)}$ cannot occur until its predecessor $\gamma_{P(i),E(i)}$ have successfully communicated with a certain CAA. $\gamma_{P(i),E(i)}$ certainly cannot communicate with its successor. So $\gamma_{P(i),E(i)} > \gamma_{P(j),E(j)}$ does not hold. Therefore if $\gamma_{P(i),E(i)}|\gamma_{P(j),E(j)}$ occurs during deduction, $\gamma_{P(i),E(i)} <> \gamma_{P(j),E(j)}$ holds. The rest can be proved as the same.

Theorem 2. During deduction, there must be a deadlock cycle if
1) $\gamma_{P(I),E(I)}|\gamma_{P((I+1) \bmod n),E((I+1) \bmod n)}$ occurs, where $I = [0,n-1]$, $n>1$;
2) $\forall\ I \in [0,n-1]\ (\exists\ \gamma^{\#}_{T(I),E((I+1) \bmod n)}\ (\gamma^{\#}_{T(I),E((I+1) \bmod n)} > P(I))$
or $\exists\ \gamma^{\#}_{T(I),E((I-1) \bmod n)}\ (\gamma^{\#}_{T(I),E((I-1) \bmod n)} > P(I)))$.

Proof: According to Theorem 1, we have $\forall\ I \in [0,n-1]\ (\gamma_{P(I),E(I)} <> \gamma_{P((I+1) \bmod n),E((I+1) \bmod n)})$. Premise 2 indicates that a CAA required by a CAC is the predecessor of one of the CAC's neighbour, i.e. $\gamma^{\#}_{P'(n),E(n)} > \gamma_{P((I+1) \bmod n),E(I)}$ or $\gamma^{\#}_{P'(n),E(n)} > \gamma_{P((I-1) \bmod n),E(I)}$. And since $\gamma_{P(1),E(1)}, \ldots, \gamma_{P(n),E(n)}$ have already occur, their corresponding predecessors $\gamma^{\#}_{P'(1),E(1)}, \ldots, \gamma^{\#}_{P'(n),E(n)}$ have been remove, which means the resource required by each $\gamma_{P(I),E(I)}$ is held by one of its neighbours.

When $n = 2$ (According to "$I = [0,n-1]$, $n>1$", n is greater than 1). According to the premises, we have $\gamma^{\#}_{P\cdot(0),E(0)} > \gamma_{P(1),E(1)}$ and $\gamma^{\#}_{P\cdot(1),E(1)} > \gamma_{P(0),E(0)}$. Apparently $\gamma^{\#}_{P\cdot(0),E(0)}$, $\gamma_{P(1),E(1)}$, $\gamma^{\#}_{P\cdot(1),E(1)}$ and $\gamma_{P(0),E(0)}$ form a deadlock cycle according to Definition 3(a).

When $n > 2$. Suppose both $\gamma^{\#}_{P\cdot(0),E(0)}$ and $\gamma^{\#}_{P\cdot(2),E(2)}$ are predecessors of $\gamma_{P(1),E(1)}$. So either $\gamma_{P(0),E(0)}$ or $\gamma_{P(2),E(2)}$ is the successor of $\gamma^{\#}_{P\cdot(1),E(1)}$. Thus we get a deadlock cycle consists either of $\{\gamma_{P(1),E(1)}, \gamma^{\#}_{P\cdot(0),E(0)}, \gamma_{P(0),E(0)}, \gamma^{\#}_{P\cdot(1),E(1)}\}$ or $\{\gamma_{P(2),E(2)}, \gamma^{\#}_{P\cdot(1),E(1)}, \gamma_{P(1),E(1)}, \gamma^{\#}_{P\cdot(2),E(2)}\}$. So $\gamma_{P(i),E(i)}$ cannot be a successor both of $\gamma^{\#}_{P\cdot((i-1) \bmod n),E((i-1) \bmod n)}$ and $\gamma^{\#}_{P\cdot((i+1) \bmod n),E((i+1) \bmod n)}$, but of only one. Therefore, we have $\forall\ I \in [0,n-1]\ \exists T(I)\ (\gamma_{P(I),E(I)} < \gamma^{\#}_{T(I),E((I+1) \bmod n)})$ or $\forall\ I \in [0,n-1]\ \exists T(I)\ (\gamma_{P(I),E(I)} < \gamma^{\#}_{T(I),E((I+1) \bmod n)})$, which denotes each $\gamma_{P(I),E(I)}$ holds the resource requested by one of its neighbours. Therefore no one can carry on the rendezvous.

Suppose $\gamma_{P(I),E(I)} > \gamma_{P(J),E(J)}$. We assume might as well that there are no other partial order in $\gamma_{P(1),E(1)}, \ldots, \gamma_{P(n),E(n)}$, where $0<I<J<n-1$, and that $\gamma_{P(J),E(J)}$ holds the resource of $\gamma_{P(J+1),E(J+1)}$ which is one of its neighbour. Because $\gamma_{P(I),E(I)}$ is the predecessor of $\gamma_{P(J),E(J)}$, so $\gamma_{P(I),E(I)}$ holds the resource $\gamma_{P(J+1),E(J+1)}$. Therefore $\gamma_{P(0),E(0)}, \ldots, \gamma_{P(I),E(I)}, \gamma_{P(J+1),E(J+1)}, \ldots, \gamma_{P(n-1),E(n-1)}$ form a deadlock cycle according to Definition 3(a). As a result there must be a deadlock cycle similar to Fig.4(a).

If the second premise in Theorem 2 changes to $\forall\ I \in [0,n-1]\ (\exists\gamma^{\#}_{T(I),E((I+1) \bmod n)}\ (\gamma^{\#}_{T(I),E((I+1) \bmod n)} < P(I))$ or $\exists\gamma^{\#}_{T(I),E((I-1) \bmod n)}\ (\gamma^{\#}_{T(I),E((I-1) \bmod n)} < P(I)))$, a deadlock cycle can be formed like Fig.4(b). Since Fig.4(b) represents a complete deadlock cycle, it is not necessary to consider this in Theorem 2.

Theorem 3. During deduction, there must be a deadlock cycle if
1) $\gamma^{\#}_{P(I),E(I)}|\gamma^{\#}_{P((I+1) \bmod n),E((I+1) \bmod n)}$ occurs, where $I = [0,n-1]$, $n>1$;
2) If $\forall\ I \in [0,n-1]\ (\exists\gamma_{T(I),E((I+1) \bmod n)}\ (\gamma_{T(I),E((I+1) \bmod n)} < P(I))$
or $\exists\gamma_{T(I),E((I-1) \bmod n)}\ (\gamma_{T(I),E((I-1) \bmod n)} < P(I)))$.

The proof of Theorem 3 is similar to the one of Theorem 2.

As a mater of fact, Theorem 3 shows the same as Theorem 2, except for a different premise. According to Theorem 2 and Theorem 3, only $\gamma_{P(i),E(i)}|\gamma_{P(j),E(j)}$ or $\gamma^{\#}_{P(I),E(I)}|\gamma^{\#}_{P(J),E(J)}$ occurred in deduction should be checked. Checking either $\gamma_{P(i),E(i)}|\gamma_{P(j),E(j)}$ or $\gamma^{\#}_{P(I),E(I)}|\gamma^{\#}_{P(J),E(J)}$ will finally obtain the same deadlock cycles.

Theorem 2 and 3 are the basic foundation we use to detect partial deadlock cycles. After we have got process algebra expressions transformed from Ada rendezvous flow structure, deduction with equivalence is carried out by applying axioms of ACP.
1. Before deduction:
   - *DCS*(Dead Communication Set) is defined and initiated with $\emptyset$;

- *RS*(Reachability Set) is defined and initiated with $\emptyset$;
- Because a successful termination of a task does not have an influence on others, and this task does not communicate with others any more, we modify and extend the property of $\sqrt{}$. A new successful termination, $\sqrt{\#}$, is defined in concurrent programs, which obeys:

$$x \cdot \sqrt{\#} = x ; \qquad \sqrt{\#} \cdot x = x; \qquad x + \sqrt{\#} = x; \qquad x \mid \sqrt{\#} = \delta$$

2. During deduction:
   - For every $\gamma_{P(i),E(i)} \mid \gamma_{P(j),E(j)}$, check *Dependence_Set* of $\gamma_{P(i),E(i)}$ and $\gamma_{P(j),E(j)}$. If $\exists \gamma^{\#}_{T(i),E(j)}$ ($\gamma^{\#}_{T(i),E(j)} > \gamma_{P(i),E(i)}$) or $\exists \gamma^{\#}_{T(j),E(i)}$ ($\gamma^{\#}_{T(j),E(i)} > \gamma_{P(j),E(j)}$), then put them into *DCS*. Put every $\gamma_{P(i),E(i)} \mid \gamma^{\#}_{P(j),E(j)}$ unable to communicate successfully into *DCS*;
   - When a $\sqrt{\#}$ occurs, denoting a root branch terminates successfully, put the corresponding task into *RS*;
3. After deduction:
   - Among all the $\gamma_{P(i),E(i)} \mid \gamma_{P(j),E(j)}$ in *DCS*, find out all the cycles like $\{\gamma_{P(i),E(i)} \mid \gamma_{P(j),E(j)}, \gamma_{P(j),E(j)} \mid \gamma_{P(k),E(k)}, \gamma_{P(k),E(k)} \mid \ldots, \ldots \mid \gamma_{P(i),E(i)}\}$, in which those CACs forms a partial deadlock cycle.
   - Among all the $\gamma_{P(i),E(i)} \mid \gamma^{\#}_{P(j),E(j)}$ in *DCS*, find out all the cycle like $\{\gamma_{P(i),E(i)} \mid \gamma^{\#}_{P(j),E(j)}, \gamma_{P(k),E(j)} \mid \gamma^{\#}_{P(l),E(i)}\}$, if $\gamma_{P(i),E(i)} > \gamma_{P(k),E(j)}$ and $\gamma^{\#}_{P(j),E(j)} > \gamma^{\#}_{P(l),E(i)}$, or if $\gamma_{P(i),E(i)} < \gamma_{P(k),E(j)}$ and $\gamma^{\#}_{P(j),E(j)} < \gamma^{\#}_{P(l),E(i)}$, then such $\{\gamma_{P(i),E(i)}, \gamma^{\#}_{P(j),E(j)}, \gamma_{P(k),E(j)}, \gamma^{\#}_{P(l),E(i)}\}$ forms a partial deadlock cycle.

Detection of complete deadlock cycles and partial deadlock cycles has been carried out. The set *RS* contains all the reachable tasks. If $RS = \emptyset$, then the whole concurrent programs is in a deadlock, otherwise, it the whole system is reachable.

6 Case Study

In fact Fig.2 presents a simplified Dining Philosophers Problem[7]. In Dining Philosophers Problem, several philosophers sit around a table, thinking or dining. There is a fork in the middle of every two philosophers who are neighbours. Before dining, a philosopher must get both forks in his right hand and his left hand. And after having had dinner, he must put the two forks back for others use. In Fig.2, there are only two philosophers and forks need not be put back.

We apply the approach proposed in 5.2 and 5.3 to the ACP expressions shown in Fig.3 so as to detect deadlocks in this simplified Dining Philosophers Problem. The result is shown as below.

$$Uncalled\_CAA = \emptyset; \qquad Nonoccurred\_CAA = \emptyset$$

which denotes that there is no complete deadlock cycle in this concurrent programs.

$$RS = \{ P1, Fork1, P2, Fork2 \}; \qquad Partial\_Deadlock\_Set = \{\{\gamma_{P1.2}, \gamma_{P2.1}\}\};$$

where $\{\gamma_{P1.2}, \gamma_{P2.1}\}$ is a partial deadlock cycle. It denotes that sometimes a deadlock may occurs, iff each philosopher takes a fork.

7 Conclusions

In this paper, an approach is proposed to transform Ada rendezvous flow structure into ACP expressions. Through deduction with equivalence on these expressions, all possible execution path can be simulated, in which dead communications are extracted. Among these dead communications, deadlock cycles can be easily found out with the help of dependence analysis between communications. At the same time, all reachable paths can be obtained through deduction. Compared to some approaches based on Petri net and flow structure, using process algebra expressions to represent Ada concurrent programs is more formal and compact. Furthermore, detecting deadlock cycles by analyzing dead communications in deduction is simple and accurate.

Further research is required to combat state explosion, because deduction on process algebra expressions costs quite a lot though it can be totally done automatically by applying axioms. Since ACP has strong ability of simplifying process composition and of hiding internal details, we have much prospect of doing this well. Moreover, dependence analysis can also be applied to reduce states in large amount, to which we have made great efforts[5].

References

1. J.C.M. Baeten, W.P. Weijland. *Process Algebra.* Cambridge University Press, Cambridge, United Kingdom, 1990.
2. J.C.M. Baeten, editor. Applications of Process Algebra. Cambridge University Press, Cambridge, United Kingdom, 1990.
3. J. A. Bergstra, J. W. Klop, Process Algebra for Synchronous Communication. *Information and Control,* 60:109-137, 1984.
4. J. Blieberger, B. Burgstaller, B. Scholz. Symbolic Data Flow Analysis for Detecting Deadlocks in Ada Tasking Programs. *In Proc. of the Ada-Europe International Conference on Reliable Software Technologies,* Potsdam, Germany, June 2000. Springer.
5. Zhenqiang Chen Baowen Xu. Slicing Concurrent Java Programs. *ACM SIGPLAN Notices,* 2001, 36(4): 41-47.
6. J. Cheng, K. Ushijima. Analyzing Ada Tasking Deadlocks and Livelocks Using Extended Petri Nets. In *Lecture Notes in Computer Science #499,* pp 125-146, Springer-Verlag, 1991.
7. James C. Corbett, Evaluating Deadlock Detection Methods for Concurrent Software. *IEEE Transactions on Software Engineering,* 1996, 22(3): 161-180.
8. Matthew B. Dwyer, Kari A. Nies, Lori A. Clarke. Compact Petri Net Representation for Concurrent Programs. ICSE, 1994.
9. R. Gedela, S. Shatz, H. Xu. Former Modeling of Synchronization Methods for Concurrent Objects in Ada 95. *Proceedings of the ACM Annual International Conference on Ada* (SIGAda-99), Redondo Beach, Calif., Oct. 1999, pp. 211-220.
10. A.H.M ter Hofstede. Task Structure Semantics through Process Algebra. *Software Engineering Journal,* 8(1):14-20, January 1993.

11. ISO/IEC 8652:1995(E). Ada Reference Manual-Language and Standard Libraries.
12. Douglas L. Long, Lori A. Clarke. Task Interaction Graphs for Concurrency Analysis. In *Proceedings of the 11th ICSE*, pp 44-52, Pittsburgh, May 1989.
13. Stephen P. Masticola, Static Detection of Deadlocks in Polynomial Time. A dissertation submitted to the Graduate School-New Brunswick Rutgers, The State University of New Jersey, May, 1993.
14. J. L. Peterson. *Petri Net Theory and the Modeling of Systems.* Prentice Hall, Englewood Cliffs, N.J., 1981, ISBN 0-13661-983-5.
15. R.N. Taylor. Complexity of Analyzing the Synchronization Structure of Concurrent Programs. *Acta Informatica*, 19:57-84, 1983.

Formal Analysis
of Real-Time Systems with SAM *

Huiqun Yu[1,2], Xudong He[1], Yi Deng[1], and Lian Mo[1]

[1] School of Computer Science,
Florida International University,
Miami, FL 33199, USA
{yhq|hex|deng|lmo01}@cs.fiu.edu

[2] Department of Computer Science and Engineering,
East China University of Science and Technology,
Shanghai 200237, China

Abstract. The Software Architecture Model (SAM) is a general software architecture model based on a dual formalism combining Petri nets and temporal logic. This paper proposes a formal method for modeling and analyzing real-time systems with SAM. A high level Petri net and a linear time temporal logic are used as the theoretical basis for SAM. Behaviors of real-time systems are modeled by Petri nets, while their properties are specified by temporal logic. By translating Petri nets into clocked transition systems, we can apply the Stanford Temporal Prover to automating the analysis of real-time systems. A case study of interactive multimedia documents demonstrates our approach to modeling and analyzing real-time systems with SAM.

Keywords: Real-time system, SAM, Petri net, temporal logic, model, analysis

1 Introduction

SAM is a general software architecture model for developing and analyzing software architecture specifications. The theoretical basis of SAM is a combination of two complementary formal notions: Petri nets [Mur89] and temporal logic [Pnu77], with the choice of Petri nets and temporal logic open. In [WHD99], Time Petri Nets (TPNs) and Real-Time Computation Tree Logic (RTCTL) are used, while in [HD02], Predicate Transition Nets (PrTNs) and a first order linear time temporal logic (LTL) are used. Other kind of Petri nets [Tro95] and/or temporal logic [Eme90] can also be used. In the SAM framework, Petri nets are used to define the behavior models of systems and temporal logic is used to specify system properties (or constraints). The sound mathematical foundation of SAM can help to detect and eliminate design errors early in the development cycle, avoid costly fixes at the implementation stage.

---

* Supported in part by the NSF under grants HDR-9707076 and CCR-0098120, and by NASA under grant NAG 2-1440.

Several earlier works dealt with real-time system modeling and analysis based on Petri nets [MF76,CR83,LS87], but few built tools to support the analysis process. This paper shows how to model and analyze real-time systems in the SAM framework. Our work differs from [BD91] in that we use high-level Petri nets and a first-order temporal logic as our formal foundations. In addition, we formalize and automate analysis process, which is believed to be vital for practical use of formal methods [CW96].

The rest of the paper is organized as follows: Section 2 gives a brief introduction to SAM and its application in modeling and specification of real-time systems. Section 3 proposes our analysis method. Section 4 presents a detailed case study which shows how to apply our method to formally modeling interactive multimedia documents and analyzing their consistency. Section 5 is the conclusion.

2 Real-Time Modeling in SAM

2.1 The SAM Specification Structure

In SAM, a software architecture is defined by a hierarchical set of compositions in which each composition consists of a set of components, a set of connectors and a set of constraints to be satisfied by the interacting components. Basically, behaviors of components and connectors are modeled by Petri nets, while their properties (or constraints) are specified by temporal logic formulas. The interfaces of components and connectors are *ports*. Figure 1 shows a graphical view of a SAM architecture model, where the higher level component $A3$ is decomposed into a lower level sub-architecture.

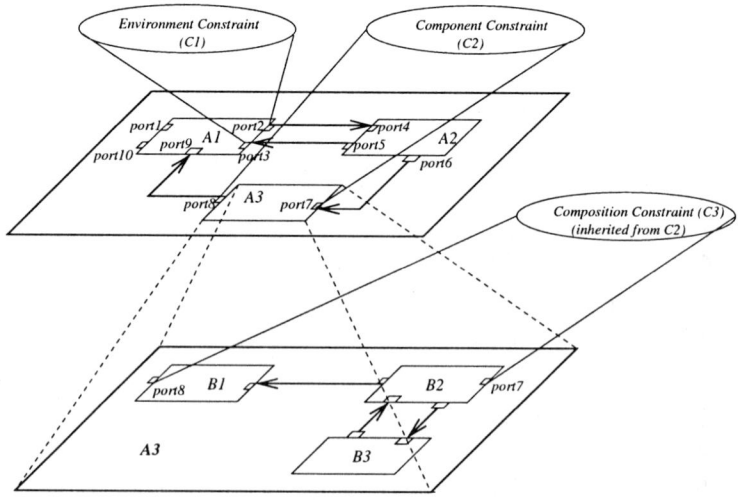

Fig. 1. A SAM architecture model

Several correctness criteria of SAM models are identified in [HD02]. One basic criterion is *element correctness* which requires the property specification S to hold in the corresponding behavior model B, i.e. $B \models S$.

2.2 PrTNs and Behavior Modeling

A *PrTN* is defined with an underlying first-order language $\mathcal{L}_P$ with typed domains. The logic contains ordinary symbols for variables, constants, functions, predicates, logic connectives, and quantifiers. The set of variables V is partitioned into two disjoint sets: D (the set of discrete variables) and C (the set of clock variables). One of the clock variables T is designated as the *master clock*. The sets of terms and well-formed formulas of $\mathcal{L}_P$ are denoted by *Term* and *Wff*. Let Ms denote multi-set of terms of the special forms $\{k_1 a_1, \ldots, k_n a_n\}$, where $k_i \in Nat$ and a_i is a ground term.

A PrTN in $\mathcal{L}_P$ is a tuple $\pi = (P, Tr, F, L, R, m_0)$, where

- P: a finite set of places;
- Tr: a finite set of transitions ;
- $F \subseteq P \times Tr \cup Tr \times P$: the set of arcs;
- $L : F \to Ms$: labels;
- $R : Tr \to Wff$: transition constraints. We assume that R contain both functional constraint R_F and real-time constraint R_T. In particular, a real-time constraint for transition t is a realtion of the form $c_t \in [\ell, u]$, where c_t is a local clock associated with transition t, ℓ is called the *earliest firing time* (EFT) for t, and u the *latest firing time* (LFT).
- m_0: the initial marking.

Remarks:

- As far as real-time specification is concerned, a PrTN is similar to a TPN. A real-time constraint R_T in a PrTN is the counterpart of *static interval marking* (SIM) in TPN [BD91]. Consequently, they share similar real-time semantics.
- PrTNs allow for complex data structures. In particular, we require that each token in a PrTN contain a time stamp (global time).

Graphical Notations: A real-time constraint for transition t is generally represented by a time interval $[\ell, u]$. For simplicity, we use several graphical notations as defined in Table 1.

Table 1. Several graphical notations

Description	Instantaneous	Acurate time	Lower bounded	Upper bounded
Notation	▯ t	a ▯ t	>=a ▯ t	<=a ▯ t
Meaning	$l = u = 0$	$l = u = a$	$l = a, u = \infty$	$l = 0, u = a$

A general form for a state S of a PrTN can be defined as a pair $S = (m, I)$ consisting of:

- a marking m;
- a firing interval set I which is a vector of possible firing times. The number of entries in this vector is given by the number of transitions enabled by marking m.

Given a marking m, a transition $t \in Tr$ is *enabled* if the following condition is satisfied : $\forall p \in P.(L(p,t) \subseteq m(p)) \wedge R_F(t)$.

A transition t is *firable* from state $S = (m, I)$ at time $\tau + \theta$ if both of the following conditions hold:

- t is enabled by marking at time τ: $\forall p \in P.(L(p,t) \subseteq m(p)) \wedge R_F(t)$
- the relative firing time θ is not smaller than EFT of t and not greater than the smallest of the LFT's of all the transitions enabled by the marking M.

Let us assume transition t be firable at time $c + \theta$ from state $S = (m, I)$. Then the state $S' = (m', I')$ *reached from* S *by firing* t *at the relative time* θ can be computed as follows.

- m' defined by $m'(p) = m(p) - L(p,t) + L(t,p)$, for all $p \in P$. We call m' the t-successor of m, denoted by mtm'. [1]
- I' is computed in three steps:
  - Remove from the expression of I the intervals that are related to the transitions disabled when t is fired.
  - Shift of the value θ towards the origin of times all remaining firing intervals, i.e., the intervals that remain enabled and so remain in I, and truncate them, when necessary, to nonnegative values.
  - Introduce in the domain the time interval of new transitions enabled.

The behavior "transition t is firable from state S at time c and its firing leads to state S'" is denoted as:
$$S \xrightarrow{(t,c)} S'.$$

A *firing schedule* is a sequence of pairs
$$(t_1, c_1) \bullet (t_2, c_2) \bullet \ldots \bullet (t_n, c_n) \ldots$$
in which $t_1, t_2, \ldots, t_n, \ldots$ are transitions and $c_1, c_2, \ldots, c_n, \ldots$ are times. This firing schedule is *feasible* from a state (m_0, I_0) iff there exist states $(m_1, I_1), (m_2, I_2), \ldots, (m_n, I_n), \ldots$ such that:
$$(m_0, I_0) \xrightarrow{(t_1, c_1)} (m_1, I_1) \xrightarrow{(t_2, c_2)} (m_2, I_2) \ldots \xrightarrow{(t_n, c_n)} (m_n, I_n) \ldots.$$

A *run* of a PrTN is a sequence of observations $(m_0, c_0), (m_1, c_1), (m_2, c_2), \ldots$ in the above firing sequence. We define the *computation* of π, denoted by $Comp(\pi)$, to be the set of all possible runs.

---

[1] Note that multiple non-conflicting transitions are capable of being fired simultaneously. In this case, m' equals to the final marking by arranging transitions to be fired one by one.

2.3 LTL and Property Specification

The requirement specification language is LTL. A *temporal formula* in LTL is constructed out of state formulas to which we apply the boolean connectives and temporal operators. Future temporal operators include $\Box$ (always), $\mathcal{W}$ (wait-for), $\Diamond$ (eventually), $\bigcirc$ (next), and $\mathcal{U}$ (until). Past operators include $\ominus$ (previously), $\boxminus$ (so-far), $\diamondsuit$ (once), and $\mathcal{S}$ (since). We write $p \Rightarrow q$ as an abbreviation of $\Box(p \rightarrow q)$. A *past formula* is one that contains no future temporal operators.

A *model* for a temporal formula p is an infinite sequence of states $\sigma : s_0, s_1, \ldots$, where each state s_j provides an interpretation for the variables mentioned in p. The semantics of a temporal formula p in a given model σ and position j is denoted by $(\sigma, j) \models p$. We define:

- For a state formula p, $(\sigma, j) \models p \Leftrightarrow s_j \models p$
- $(\sigma, j) \models \neg p \Leftrightarrow (\sigma, j) \not\models p$
- $(\sigma, j) \models p \vee q \Leftrightarrow (\sigma, j) \models p$ or $(\sigma, j) \models q$
- $(\sigma, j) \models \Box p \Leftrightarrow (\sigma, i) \models p$ for all $i \geq j$
- $(\sigma, j) \models \Diamond p \Leftrightarrow (\sigma, i) \models p$ for some $i \geq j$

These are all the LTL operators we will use in this paper. The interested reader is referred to [MP92,MP95] for detailed presentation of temporal logic.

Two important classes of properties are: *safety* and *response*.

- Safety properties are those that can be expressed by a formula $\Box \psi$, for some past formula ψ.
- Response properties are those that can be expressed by a formula $p \Rightarrow \Diamond q$, for some past formula p and q.

Since clocks are explicit variables in PrTNs, temporal formulas may freely refer to them. This includes, in particular, the master clock T, allowing the natural expression of time-dependent properties. For example, $\Box(\ell \leq T \wedge T \leq u \rightarrow p)$ states that p holds over the time interval $[\ell, u]$.

One interesting point is that many useful specifications which are progress properties in their untimed version correspond to safety properties when a time bound is added [MP96]. For example, showing that a system reaches and maintains p within time δ is expressed as the invariance $\Box(T \geq \delta \rightarrow p)$.

A model $\sigma : s_0, s_1, \ldots$ satisfies a temporal formula if $(\sigma, 0) \models p$. A temporal formula p that is *valid* over a program P specifies a property of P, i.e., states a condition that is satisfied by all computations of P.

Since LTL is an extension of first-order logic, the deductive system for LTL includes axioms and rules from first-order logic, as well as those axioms and rules specific to temporal operators. Typical rules include:

- Modus ponens: $p, p \rightarrow q \vdash q$
- Chain: $p \rightarrow \Diamond q, q \rightarrow \Diamond r \vdash p \rightarrow \Diamond r$

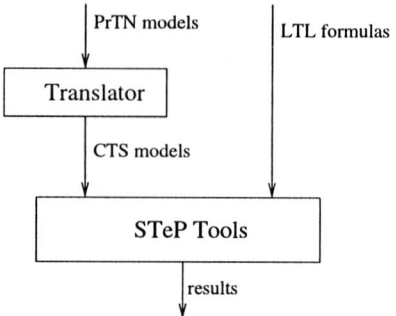

Fig. 2. A formal analysis method

3 Formal Analysis of SAM Models

3.1 A Formal Analysis Method

Our analysis method is illustrated in Figure 2, which is based on the Stanford Temporal Prover (STeP) [MAB+94]. PrTNs are systematically translated into CTSs. The latter becomes one input to STeP tools. The correctness of LTL formulas against CTSs is verified either by deductive proof, or by model checking.

The basic verification rule for safety properties is B-INV:

$$\frac{\Theta \to p, \quad \{p\}\mathcal{T}\{p\}}{\Box p}$$

A verification session in STeP begins by loading a program or transition system that describes the system of interest and entering a temporal-logic formula that expresses one or more properties to be proved. The formula becomes the root goal of a proof tree. Verification can be performed by the model checker or by deductive means. The most common route to proceed proof is to apply a verification rule, which generates the first level of subgoals of the proof tree. If all subgoals are established automatically by the Simplifier, the proof is finished. For those verification conditions that are not proved automatically, an interactive Gentzen-style theorem prover is usually invoked.

3.2 Clocked Transition Systems

A CTS is an extension of transitions systems to account for continuous real-time. The basic idea is to add explicit real-valued clock variables to the system, which measure the passing of time. Formally, a CTS $\mathcal{S} = (V, \Theta, \mathcal{T}, \Pi)$ consists of:
- V: A finite set of *system variables*, partitioned into a set D of discrete variables and a set C of real-valued clock variables. We define a *state* s to be a type-consistent interpretation of V. The set of all state is denoted by Σ.
- Θ: The *initial condition*, a satisfiable assertion characterizing the possible initial states. We require that Θ implies $T = 0$.

- $\mathcal{T}$: A finite set of *transitions*. Each transition $\tau \in \mathcal{T}$ is a function

$$\tau : \Sigma \to 2^\Sigma,$$

  mapping each state $s \in \Sigma$ into a (possibly empty) set of states $\tau(s) \subseteq \Sigma$. Each state in $\tau(s)$ is called a τ- *successor* of s.
  We say that the transition τ is *enabled* on the state s if $\tau(s) \neq \emptyset$. Otherwise, we say that τ is *disabled* on s.
- Π: The *time-progress condition*. This is an assertion over V, used to specify a global restriction on the progress of time.

To account for the passage of time, a *tick* transition is added to the set of transitions. The transition relation for *tick* is given by

$$\rho_{tick} : \exists \Delta. \begin{pmatrix} \Delta > 0 \land \forall t \in [0, \Delta].\Pi(D, C+t) \\ \land \\ D' = D \land C' = C + \Delta \end{pmatrix}$$

where $C' = C + \Delta$ stands for $\land_{c \in C}(c' = c + \Delta)$. Thus, *tick* preserves the values of all discrete variables and uniformly increments all clocks by an amount Δ that satisfies the global time-progress condition Π. We denote the set $\mathcal{T} \cup \{tick\}$ by $\mathcal{T}_T$.

A *run* of a CTS $\mathcal{S} : (V, \Theta, \mathcal{T}, \Pi)$ is an infinite sequence of states $\sigma : s_0, s_1, \ldots$ such that (1) $s_0 \models \Theta$ and (2) for each $j \geq 0$ there is some $\tau \in \mathcal{T}_T$ such that $s_{j+1} \in \tau(s_j)$. In this case we say that τ is taken at s_j. A state s is *reachable* if it appears in some run of $\mathcal{T}$. A run is a *computation* if it satisfies *time divergence*, that is, the value of T increases beyond any bound. $Comp(\mathcal{S})$ is the set of all the computations of $\mathcal{S}$.

3.3 From PrTNs to CTSs

We adopt the idea from [MP96] to associate lower and upper time bounds with transitions. A lower bound ℓ on transition τ is enforced by associating a clock c_τ and adding the condition $c_\tau \geq \ell$ to τ's enabling condition. When the enabling condition for τ first becomes true, c_τ is reset to 0. Upper bounds appear as constraints on Π: if u is the upper bound on τ, then $c_\tau \leq u$ appears as a conjunct in Π.

Given a PrTN $\pi = (P, Tr, F, L, R, m_0)$ as defined in section 2.2, we define a corresponding CTS by $\mathcal{S} = (V, \Theta, \mathcal{T}, \Pi)$, where

- The set of local variables: $V = \{v_p \mid p \in P\} \cup \{c_t \mid t \in Tr\} \cup \{T\}$.
- Initial conditions:

$$\Theta = \bigwedge_{p \in P}(v_p = m_0(p)) \bigwedge_{t \in Tr}(c_t = 0) \land (T = 0)$$

- For every transition $t \in Tr$, there is a corresponding transition τ_t, whose transition relation is defined as $\rho_{\tau_t} \stackrel{def}{=} en(\tau_t) \to f(\tau_t)$, where

$$en(\tau_t) = R_F(t) \wedge \bigwedge_{p \in P} (v_p \supseteq L(p,t))$$

$$f(\tau_t) = \bigwedge_{p \in P} (v'_p = v_p - L(p,t) + L(t,p))$$

The set of all possible transitions $\mathcal{T} = \{\tau_t \mid t \in Tr\}$
- For the special transition *tick*: the transition relation is the same as in section 3.2.
- The time-progress condition Π is: $\bigwedge_{t \in Tr}(c_t \leq u_t)$

Theorem 1 (Soundness of the transformation). *Given a PrTN π, suppose $\mathcal{S}_\pi = (V, \Theta, \mathcal{T}, \Pi)$ be the CTS obtained from π using the above transformation rules.*

- *For any run $\sigma = (m_0, c_0), (m_1, c_1), (m_2, c_2), \ldots \in Comp(\pi)$, $\forall i \in Nat$, there exists a mapping s_i from V to the correspondence domain such that $\forall v_p \in V. s_i(v_p) = m_i(p), s_i(T) = c_i$, and $\sigma' = s_0, s_1, s_2, \ldots \in Comp(\mathcal{S}_\pi)$.*
- *For any state sequence $\sigma = s_0, s_1, s_2, \ldots \in Comp(\mathcal{S}_\pi)$, $\forall p \in P, i \in Nat$, let $m_i(p) = s_i(v_p), c_i = s_i(T)$, then $\sigma' = (m_0, c_0), (m_1, c_1), (m_2, c_2), \ldots \in Comp(\pi)$.*

Proof:
(1) Suppose $\sigma = (m_0, c_0), (m_1, c_1), (m_2, c_2), \ldots \in Comp(\pi)$. Let the corresponding transition sequence be $t_0 t_1 t_2 \ldots$. By definition, the following predicate holds:
$\forall i \in Nat, \forall p \in P.(m_i(p) \supseteq L(p,t)) \wedge R_F(t_i)) \wedge (m_{i+1} = m_i(p) - L(p,t) + L(t,p))$
$\forall v_p \in D, c \in C$, let $s_0(v_p) = m_0(p), s_0(c) = 0$, we get $s_0 \models \Theta$. For each $i \in Nat$, $(s_i, s_{i+1}) \models \tau_{t_i}$ holds. Consequently, $s_0, s_1, s_2 \ldots$ is a run of $\mathcal{S}_\pi$. Therefore $\sigma' = s_0, s_1, s_2, \ldots \in Comp(\mathcal{S}_\pi)$.

(2) Suppose $\sigma = s_0, s_1, s_2, \ldots \in Comp(\mathcal{S}_\pi)$. Let the corresponding transition sequence be $\tau_{t_0} \tau_{t_1} \tau_{t_2}, \ldots$. So $(m_i, c_i) \in [(m_0, c_0) >$ [2] follows from the definition of m_i, c_i, and τ_t. Consequently, $\sigma' = (m_0, c_0), (m_1, c_1), (m_2, c_2), \ldots \in Comp(\pi)$.
□

4 An Example: Consistency of SMIL Documents

SMIL is the W3C format for multimedia synchronization on the web [Rec98]. It uses the XML to define a set of markup tags to associate timing and positioning relationships between multimedia objects, such as audio, video, image and text.

---
[2] The notation $(m_i, c_i) \in [(m_0, c_0) >$ denotes that (m_i, c_i) is reachable from the initial observation (m_0, c_0).

One important issue about specification of temporal constraints of an interactive multimedia document is how to meet the user's QoS requirements. In the case of SMIL, the tag *switch* is applied to express the user's preferences concerning bit-rate transmission capabilities, preferred language, size of screen, alternative media presentation, etc.. However, the satisfaction of user's QoS requirements may lead to unexpected bad timing constraints. By defining formal semantics for SMIL, we can verify the correctness of a SMIL document against its specification.

Consider the following SMIL document.

```
< id=''par01'' >
  < seq id=''seq01'' >
    < Img1 dur = '5s'.../ >
    < switch >
      < Audio dur = '20s'.../ >
      < Txt dur = '3s'.../ >
    < /switch >
  < /seq >

  < seq id=''seq02'' end=''id(seq01)(end)'' >
    < Video dur = '10s'.../ >
    < Img2 .../ >
  < /seq >
< /par >
```

It consists of a sequence of a video clip (*Video*) followed by an image (*Img2*). This sequence (*Seq02*) must be presented simultaneously with another sequence (*Seq01*) which consists of an image (*Img1*) followed by some related information. This information corresponds to an element of the SMIL operator *switch*, such as an audio segment (*Audio*) or a text (*Txt*). The end of presentation of *Img2* is determined by the end of the sequential presentation of *Img1* and the element chosen in the *switch* operator.

The above SMIL document can be formally modeled by a PrTN in Figure 3.

By applying the translation rules, we can obtain a corresponding CTS $S = (V, \Theta, \mathcal{T}, \Pi)$ from the PrTN in Figure 3, where

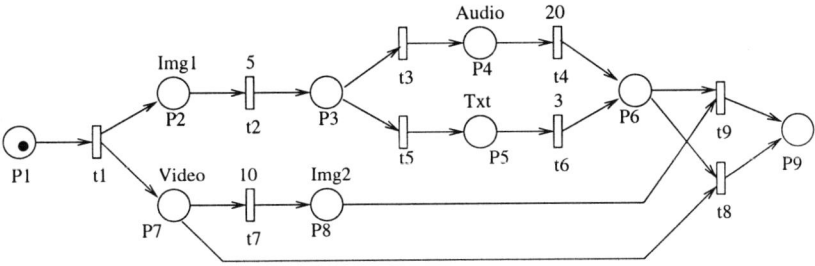

Fig. 3. A PrTN for the SMIL document

- $V = \{v_{p_1}, \ldots, v_{p_9}, c_{t_1}, \ldots, c_{t_9}, T\}$
- $\Theta = ((v_{p_1} = 1) \bigwedge_{x \neq v_{p_1}} (x = 0))$
- $T = \{t_1, t_2, \ldots, t_9\}$
- $\Pi = \bigwedge_{t \in Tr}(c_t \leq u_t)$

The CTS in STeP script is as follows.

```
Clocked Transition System % A CTS for the SMIL document
out p:array [1..9] of int
   where (p[1]=1) /\ Forall i:[2..9]. (p[i]=0)
clock c1,c2,c3,c4,c5,c6,c7,c8,c9
   where c1=0 /\ c2 =0 /\ c3=0 /\ c4 =0 /\ c5=0 /\ c6=0
      /\ c7=0 /\ c8 =0 /\ c9=0
Progress
     (p[2]=1 --> c2 <= 5) /\ (p[4]=1 --> c4 <= 20)
  /\ (p[5]=1 --> c6 <= 3) /\ (p[7]=1 --> c7 <= 10)
Transition t1: enable p[1]=1
               assign (p[1],p[2],p[7],c2,c7) := (0,1,1,0,0)
Transition t2: enable p[2]=1 /\c2>=5
               assign (p[2],p[3]) := (0,1)
Transition t3: enable p[3]=1
               assign (p[3],p[4],c4) := (0,1,0)
Transition t4: enable p[4]=1 /\c4>=20
               assign (p[4],p[6]) := (0,1)
Transition t5: enable p[3]=1
               assign (p[3],p[5],c6) := (0,1,0)
Transition t6: enable p[5]=1 /\c6>=3
               assign (p[5],p[6]) := (0,1)
Transition t7: enable p[7]=1 /\c7>=10
               assign (p[7],p[8]) := (0,1)
Transition t8: p[6]=1 /\ p[7]=1
               assign (p[6],p[7],p[9]) := (0,0,1)
Transition t9: enable p[6]=1 /\ p[8]=1
               assign (p[6],p[8],p[9]) := (0,0,1)
```

One real-time requirement of the SMIL document is consistency between the two media sequences, i.e.,

Once the two media sequences start to play, they will coincide within 25 time units.

This property can be formally expressed by the following LTL formula:
   [] (T >= 25 --> p[9]=1).

This property is inductive, that is, it is preserved by all transitions. It is proved automatically using rule B-INV and automatic simplification procedures, which is shown in Figure 4.

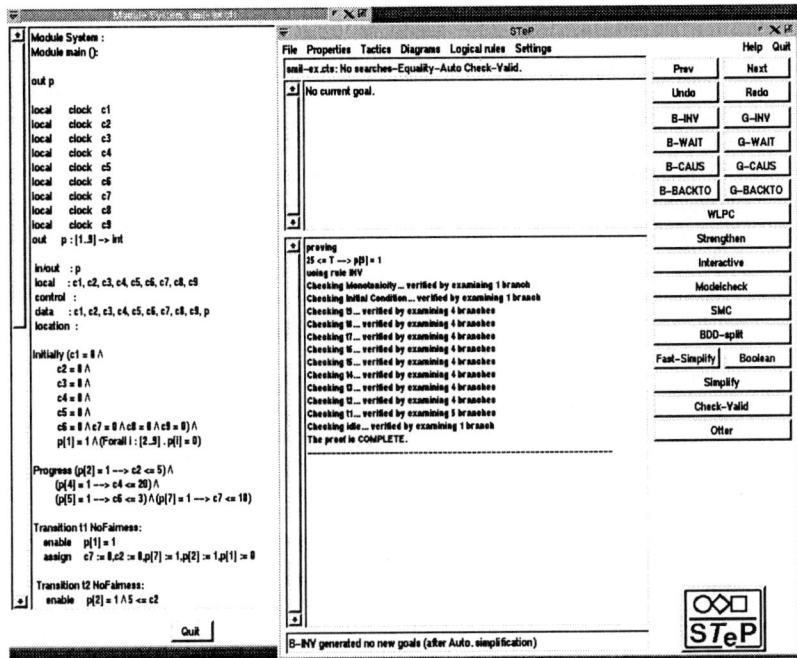

Fig. 4. A snapshot of the verification session

5 Conclusion

This paper proposes a formal method for modeling and analyzing real-time systems with SAM. PrTN and LTL are used as the theoretical basis for SAM. Behaviors of real-time systems are modeled by PrTNs, while their properties are specified by LTL. PrTNs have expressive power to model real-time behaviors and complex data structures. By using explicit clock variables in PrTNs, ordinary temporal logic like LTL is capable of specifying real-time properties, which eliminates the need of other specification languages. PrTNs are systematically translated into CTSs. Consequently, we can resort to STeP tools for automating the analysis process.

Our method differs from that in [SC00] for analysis of interactive multimedia documents. In [SC00], interactive multimedia documents are translated into RT-LOTOS specifications [CSLO00], and reachability analysis is performed on the transformed specifications. Instead, we use high-level Petri nets and first-order temporal logic as our formal foundations, and base our method on STeP, where deductive proof or model checking or the combination allow for the verification of a broader class of systems.

Interesting research topics include compositional verification methods and tools for real-time systems with SAM, application of SAM to modeling and design of industrial scale real-time systems.

References

[BD91] B. Berthomieu and M. Diaz. Modeling and verification of time dependent systems using Time Petri nets. *IEEE Transactions on Software Engineering*, 17(3):259–273, 1991.

[CR83] J.E. Coolahan,Jr. and N. Roussopoulos. Timing requirements for time-driven systems using augmented Petri nets. *IEEE Transactions on Software Engineering*, 9(5):603–616, 1983.

[CSLO00] J.P. Courtiat, C.A.S. Santos, C. Lohr, and B. Outtaj. Experience with RT-LOTOS, a temporal extension of the LOTOS formal description technique. *Computer Communications*, 23(12):1104–1123, 2000.

[CW96] E.M. Clarke and J.M. Wing. Formal methods: state of the art and future directions. *ACM Computing Surveys*, 28(4):626–643, 1996.

[Eme90] E.A. Emerson. Temporal and modal logic. In J. van Leeuwen, editor, *Handbook of Theoretical Computer Science*, chapter 16. Elsevier Science Publisher B.V., 1990.

[HD02] X. He and Y. Deng. A framework for developing and analyzing software architecture specifications in SAM. *The Computer Journal*, 45(1):111–128, 2002.

[LS87] N.G. Leveson and J.L. Stolzy. Safety analysis using Petri nets. *IEEE Transactions on Software Engineering*, 13(3):386–397, 1987.

[MAB+94] Z. Manna, A. Anuchitanukul, N. Bjørner, A. Browne, E. Chang, M. Colón, L. de Alaro, H. Devarajan, H. Sipma, and M. Uribe. STeP: the Stanford Temporal Prover. Technical Report STAN-CS-TR-94-1518, Department of Computer Science, Stanford University, June 1994.

[MF76] P. Merlin and D.J. Faber. Recoverability of communication protocols. *IEEE Transactions on Communications*, COM-24(9):1036–1043, 1976.

[MP92] Z. Manna and A. Pnueli. *The Temporal Logic of Reactive and Concurrent Systems: Specification*. Springer-Verlag, 1992.

[MP95] Z. Manna and A. Pnueli. *Temporal Verification of Reactive Systems: Safety*. Springer-Verlag, 1995.

[MP96] Z. Manna and A. Pnueli. Clocked transition systems. Technical Report STAN-CS-TR-96-1566, Computer Science Department, Stanford University, 1996.

[Mur89] T. Murata. Petri nets properties, analysis and applications. *Proceedings of the IEEE*, 77(4):27–60, 1989.

[Pnu77] A. Pnueli. The temporal logic of programs. In *18th Ann. IEEE Symp. on Foundations of Computer Science*, pages 46–57, 1977.

[Rec98] W3C Recommendation. *Synchronized Multimedia Integration Language (SMIL) 1.0 Specification*. http://www.w3.org/TR/REC-smil, 1998.

[SC00] P.N.M. Sampaio and J.P. Courtiat. A formal approach for the presentation of interactive multimedia documents. In *Proceedings Proceedings of the 7th ACM International Conference on Multimedia (Part 1)*, pages 435–438, 2000.

[Tro95] M. Trompedeller. *A Classification of Petri Nets*. http://www.daimi.dk/PetriNets/classification, 1995.

[WHD99] J. Wang, X. He, and Y. Deng. Introducing software architecture specification and analysis in SAM through an example. *Information and Software Technology*, 41:451–467, 1999.

Tool Support for Visualizing CSP in UML

Muan Yong Ng and Michael Butler

Department of Electronics and Computer Science,
University Of Southampton,
Southampton, SO17 1BJ, United Kingdom.
Phone: +44-(0)2380-593123
Fax: +44-(0)2380-593045
{myn00r,mjb}@ecs.soton.ac.uk

Abstract. In this paper, we propose an approach to translating UML to CSP that allows one to utilize both UML and CSP in a system design. To do so, we divide the visualization task based on three aspects of CSP: (i) the dynamics behavior, (ii) the static architecture, and (iii) the refinement assertions. In doing so we are able to visualize CSP via UML in a hierarchical manner which enhances understanding in the design process. In a way, we also provide a formal verification for the UML diagrams using CSP, since there are model checkers like FDR available. We have adopted the use of UML state diagram and class diagram for our work. In addition, we have outlined a prototyped tool that translates these diagrams to CSP that could be model-checked in FDR.

Keywords: state diagram, class diagram, CSP, UML

1 Introduction

UML (stands for *Unified Modelling Language*) [9] is a graphical modelling language comprising a collection of graphical notations(diagrams) illustrating different aspect of a software system. It has an extensively structured set of constructs but lacks a comprehensive static or behavioral semantics. CSP (Communicating Sequential Process) [1], on the other hand, is a notation for describing mainly concurrent system with components interacting with one another. It has a well-defined behavioral semantics supported by model checkers such as FDR [5]. To combine the different potential offered by the two in a design process, we propose an approach to translating UML diagrams to CSP. To do so, we use the UML state diagrams to visualize the CSP dynamic behavior such as event occurrence and state transitions. At the same time, we adopt the class diagram to show the static relationships between different CSP processes. To complete the CSP visualization in UML, we have also defined a method to model refinement relationship in the class diagram. In addition, we have developed an automated tool (built into UML Rational Rose) that will translate the UML diagrams into CSP notation, and the outcome could be analyzed by the FDR model-checker.

There are three main contributions in this paper. Firstly, we demonstrate the usefulness of incorporating graphical modelling language in the system design that uses CSP notation. Secondly, the mapping of the UML diagrams to

CSP allows correctness checking on the diagrams using CSP model checkers like FDR. Thirdly, the automated translation of UML diagrams to CSP provides a graphical interface to work with CSP, and this could be useful for CSP novices.

The paper is structured as follows. We start by giving a brief introduction to the CSP notation and UML diagrams in section 2 and 3 respectively. In Section 4, we define the approach used to translate UML to CSP. We then demonstrate in section 5 how we apply the translation rules on a case study. We end with a conclusion in section 6.

2 CSP

CSP (Communicating Sequential Processes) [1] is a notation for describing concurrent system whose component, which are called **processes**, interact with each other and the environment by communication. A process can be thought of as an independent entity which has interfaces through which the process interact with the external environment. A process is defined in terms of **events**, which are the basic elements of CSP. The occurrence of an event is assumed to be instantaneous. A single event may contain more than one piece of information, in this case it is called a **compound event**. A dot operator "." separates each piece of information in a compound event. For example, $gate.open$ is a compound event with $gate$ being the entity and $open$ being the kind of action associated with the entity.

The CSP process $a \rightarrow P$ will execute event a and then behave as process P. There are two generic CSP processes: $STOP$ and $SKIP$, which represent deadlock and successful termination respectively. When $STOP$ is executed, the system comes to a halt and it does not terminate and hence, we have a deadlock. $SKIP$, on the other hand, denotes successful termination and is identified as $\sqrt{} \rightarrow STOP$. $\sqrt{}$ is a special event in CSP that represents the act of terminating successfully. Also, given $\sum$ as a set of all possible external events, $\sqrt{} \notin \sum$.

In the following, we list out the subset of CSP that is considered in our work and discuss briefly the semantic for each one of them.

- **Parallel.** $P_X \|_Y Q$ means P is in parallel with Q over events $X \cap Y$.
- **Interleave** $P_X \|\|_Y Q$ means P interleaves with Q and there is no synchronization between their events.
- **Boolean Guard.** $B \& P$ is a Boolean guard where B is a Boolean expression such that if B is true then process P will be executed.
- **Choice.** There are two types of choices: external choice ($\Box$) and internal choice ($\sqcap$) whereby the choice is made by the environment in the former and by the process in the later.
- **Event Hiding.** In the process $Q = P \backslash S$, the execution of events in set S for process P is hidden and become internal for process Q. This is useful when a collection of processes has been combined into a system, and certain communications between the components need to be insulated and hidden from others.

- **Refinement.** Refinement is a relationship between two processes such that if the behavior of B is a subset of the behavior of A, then we say B is a refinement of A and this is expressed as $A \sqsubseteq B$ (pronounced A refined by B). The behavior of a CSP process is usually defined in terms of its trace, failure and divergence behavior [1]. Hence, we may have trace, failure or failure-divergence refinement which is stated as $A \sqsubseteq_T B$, $A \sqsubseteq_F B$ or $A \sqsubseteq_{FD} B$.
- **Indexing.** Some operators can be used in replicated versions with the use of index, e.g.
  - $||x : X@P(x)$ is an **indexed parallel** composition of all processes $P(x)$
  - $|||y : Y@P(y)$ is an **indexed interleaving** composition of all processes $P(y)$, and so on.

FDR (stands for *Failure Divergence Refinement*) is a model checker for CSP. It allows concrete design description to be compared with abstract specification in order to check if the refinement properties (mentioned above) are satisfied. If the properties are not satisfied (thus the refinement check fails), FDR will generate counter example that could be used to pin point the fault.

3 UML

3.1 State Diagrams

The UML state diagram semantics and notations are substantially those of Harel's Statechart [2] except that it is an object-based variant of Harel's. A State diagram is used to describe the dynamic aspect of a system that includes the system control and timing. It specifies the **states**, which the system resides in, and the **transitions** between the states and how the system responds to various **trigger** events that cause the transition. The basic semantics of state diagrams say that a described system is always in *one* of a finite set of states. A state is a situation during the life of the model element, in which it performs some actions, satisfy some conditions, or wait for some events to occur. States take time. However, the semantics allow the modelling of states being passed either instantaneously or not instantaneously. When a trigger occurs, it will prompt the system to perform an action, which could be taking a transition, changing a variable value or generating a signal. Most often we find **events** being the triggers for the transitions. Events in state diagrams are treated as instantaneous occurrence. Suppose we have a simple cassette player mechanism that may reside in one of the two states: *PAUSE* and *PLAYING*. As shown in Figure 1, when state *PAUSE* is active, if event *play* occurs, it triggers the action *turn_on_player* and also a transition that brings the system to state *PLAYING*. At state *PLAYING*, the event *pause* triggers an opposite transition that brings the system back to the state *PAUSE*. For a state with more than one outgoing transition, only one transition can be fired at the point of exiting the state. The syntax for a transition label has three parts, all of which are optional: *Event [Guard] / Action*. A *guard* is a logical condition and a guarded transition may only occur if the guard resolves to "true".

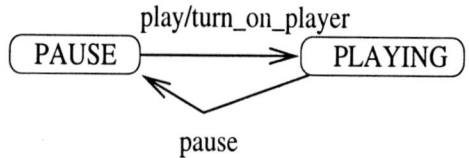

Fig. 1. A state diagram with two states.

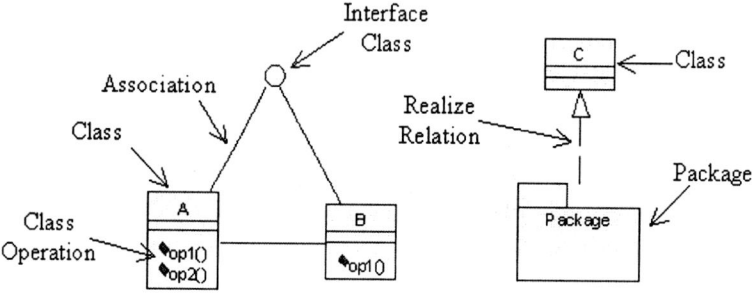

Fig. 2. Elements in a class diagram

3.2 Class Diagram

In the UML context, class diagrams are used to describe the types of objects in the system and the various kinds of static relationships that exist among them. Figure 2 shows the the various graphical representations of different elements in a class diagram that we make use of. The main entity in a class diagram is the **class**. Each class has its own operations. **An Interface Class** is a variation of the normal class. It is a class that acts as a template for other classes and no instances of it can be created. **Package**, on the other hand, is a general purpose model element that organize other elements such as classes into a group. The principal kind of static relationship between classes is the **Association**. Each association has two ends with each end being attached to one of the classes in the association. Another type of relationship that exists between two entities is the **Realize Relationship**. It is a dotted arrow line showing a class realizing the operations offered by the other entity (pointed by the arrow head).

4 Our Approach

We divide our task into three main aspects. We first define in Section 4.1 the method used to model the dynamic behaviour of individual CSP processes where state transitions and event occurrence are involved. In section 4.2, we propose an approach to model the CSP static structure that is concerned with the relationship between individual processes. We then illustrate how we visualize the CSP refinement assertion in section 4.3.

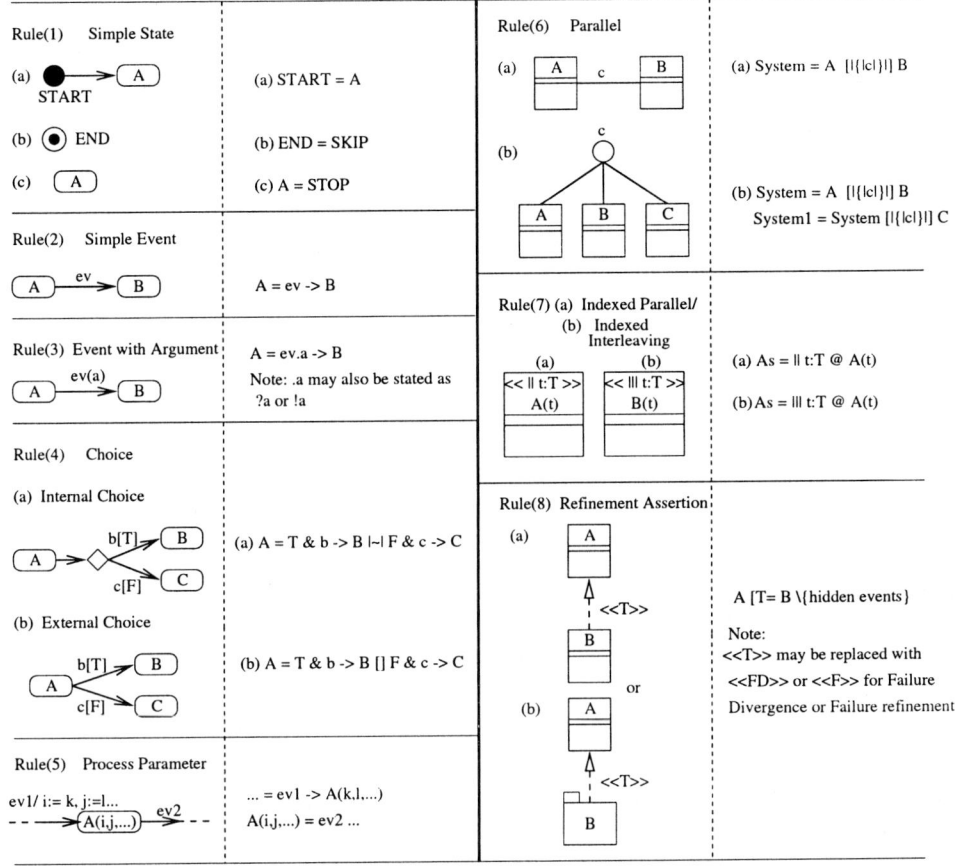

Fig. 3. Mapping rules from UML to CSP

4.1 Visualizing the Dynamic Behavior of CSP

In the object-oriented context of UML, *start* state signifies the creation of an object and the beginning of the object lifetime, whereas *end* state signifies the termination of the object lifetime. We map each UML state to a CSP process, such that the *start* state represents the start process in CSP, the *end* state represents the termination process - SKIP. For a normal state with no outgoing transition, it denotes a deadlock and hence we equate it with STOP. These mapping are summarized as Rule(1) in Figure 3. Note that all the CSP expressions found in Figure 3 are expressed in ASCII form as supported by FDR.

Next, we move on to consider the CSP **external events**. For CSP, given $Q = a \rightarrow P$, with Q and P being the CSP processes and a as the external event, when a is offered by the environment, the system being modelled will react and pass on the control from Q to P. Similar concept can be found in state diagrams. In the state diagrams context, transitions are triggered by stimuli generated by the environment and these external stimuli could be events or changes to the data values. Once the system detects such inputs, it will react by making a transition from one state to another, i.e. exit from the source state and enter the destination state. Intuitively, we obtain another mapping rule such that any external event in CSP that causes the passing of the system control from one process to the next is represented as a trigger event in State diagrams that causes a transition from one state to another.(Rule(2) in Figure 3).

In addition to simple events, we might have other information attached to an event to get a **compound event** such as $a.x$, $a?x$ or $a!x$. In UML, the notation for the event label may include a list of parameters separated by commas such that the format will be *event-name(parameter-name,...)*. We can represent the CSP event information using the UML event parameter list in which case $a.x$ will be written as $a(x)$, $a?x$ as $a(?x)$ and $a!x$ as $a(!x)$. The same mapping rule is applied to multiple-part compound event,e.g. $a.x?y$ is represented as $a(x?y)$ in UML.(see Rule(3) in Figure 3)

There are two types of **choice** representation in UML: a choice state (represented as a diamond shape) or a normal state with more than one outgoing transition. Every transition out of these states represents a branch for the choice and it may have an attached guard. If more than one of the guards are evaluated to true, an arbitrary branch is chosen. Conversely if none of the guards are evaluated true, the design is considered ill-formed. The two representations can be distinguished in that for the choice state, the decision on which branch to take depends on the prior actions in the same execution step[1]. Because of this, it is also called a *dynamic conditional branch*. In contrast, a normal state with more than one outgoing transition denotes a *static conditional branch*- where the choice of branch depends on the trigger event that occurs upon exiting from the current state. We can apply these notions to the representation of CSP choice in UML and obtain the mapping Rule(4) in Figure 3. A CSP internal choice is represented using a choice state(Rule(4a)) while a CSP external choice is represented with a normal state with more than one outgoing transition (Rule(4b)). For simplicity, we only consider boolean guard expression for CSP choice construct.

Often in CSP we wish to call a process with expressions substituted for **process parameters**. To model this in UML, we use the action in state diagrams. Referring to Rule(5) in Figure 3, the action label specifies the substitution of the parameter i with the new value k, j with the new value l and so on in the call to process A. The process A must have adequate number of process arguments to receive the substituted parameters.

4.2 Visualizing the Static Structure of CSP

So far, we have illustrated how we use the UML state diagrams to model the CSP events occurrence and transitions for a process. Now, we move on to discuss how

---

[1] Based on [2], a system is said to carry out an execution step when it performs all the relevant reactions triggered by a stimulus or a group of stimuli. Both the triggers and the reactions occur within the same step.

we gather these processes and visualize the static relationships between them. To achieve this, we use the class diagram.

The conventional role of UML class diagram provides a structural architecture for classes and model the static associations between them. We adopt this role for our work but treat each **class** as a CSP *process* instead. All the *events* that are involved in a process is listed under the **class operation** compartment.

The **association** that is used to connect two classes together is modelled as a *channel* that serves as an interface between two processes. The association **label** is used to name the common channel. In the case when more than two processes are sharing a common channel, we use a UML interface class which more than two processes may be connected to. (see Rule(6b) of Figure 3).

The diagram for Rule(7) in figure 3 shows the stereotyped class used to represent processes involved in indexed parallel/interleaving. Rule(9) defines the mapping rules for such representation.

4.3 Visualizing CSP Refinement Assertion

In this section, we discuss the final aspect of CSP visualization in UML by looking at the CSP refinement assertion, and we accomplish the task using the class diagram. There are two participants involved in a refinement assertion: the *abstract specification* and the *concrete implementation*. Assuming we have an abstract process A and a concrete process B such that $A \sqsubseteq B$. We use the **realize relationship** to connect B to A with the arrow pointing to A as in Rule(8a) figure 3. In the case where there is more than one process involves in the implementation, we group the processes (i.e. classes) into a package as shown in Rule8(b). Note the label $\langle\langle T \rangle\rangle$ beside the dotted line. It represents a *trace* refinement. Similarly, we can model the failure-divergence or failure refinement using $\langle\langle FD \rangle\rangle$ or $\langle\langle F \rangle\rangle$ respectively. The hidden events are generated automatically by the tool by comparing the events in the specification with the events in the implementation.

5 Case Study: The Lift System

In this section, we demonstrate how to apply the methods developed in section 4 on a case study.

The case study is based on a lift system that serves four floors in a building. There is a door at each of the four floors. When the lift arrives at a floor, both the lift and the floor door will open. Passengers then enter the lift and press a button corresponding to the floor they wish to go. The lift and the floor door close before the lift moves to the next destination floor. During the course of the lift moving, an emergency button can be pressed and the lift will come to a stop. The lift will remain at halt until the button is released. For simplicity, we do not include the mechanism for requesting the lift.

5.1 Dynamic Behavior View

First of all, we define the dynamic behavior of the system using state diagrams. We identify three main entities in the system: the lift, the floor door (where there are four of them) and the emergency button. For each of these entities, we develop a state diagram to model their dynamic behavior. Figure 4 shows the state diagrams for the entities.

We begin by looking at Figure 4(a) for the lift entity. We define five states : *LIFT, STOPP, BOARDING, COMPLETE* and *CLOSED* which the lift goes through. The whole process begins at state *LIFT*. Using Rule(1a) (in figure 3), we get

$$Start2 = LIFT(i)$$

When the event *liftStop.i* occurs, that is when the lift stops at the ith floor, it triggers the system to transit to state *STOPP(i)*. Notice that here we use a process parameter at the state name to receive the argument from the event. Based on Rule(3), we obtain

$$LIFT(i) = liftStop.i \rightarrow STOPP(i).$$

Applying the same rule to states *STOPP(i)*, *BOARDING(i)* and *COMPLETE(i,k)* we get

$$STOPP(i) = liftOpen.i \rightarrow BOARDING(i).$$

$$BOARDING(i) = liftClose.i \rightarrow COMPLETE(i,k).$$

$$COMPLETE(i,k) = liftClose.i \rightarrow CLOSED(i,k).$$

While the system is in state *BOARDING(i)*, it waits for the passenger to press any button, *k*, except the current floor *i* such that *k:diff(FLOOR,{i})* where *FLOOR* = {1..4}.

At state *CLOSED(i,k)*, when event *liftMove* takes place, it not only triggers a transition from *CLOSED(i,k)* to *LIFT(i)*, but at the same time it also triggers an action *i := k* that will substitute *i* with *k*. In this case, using Rule(5), we have

$$CLOSED(i,k) = liftMove \rightarrow LIFT(k)$$

whereby we now call process *LIFT()* with its parameter substituted with *k*.

We do the same for the floor door (see figure 4(b)). Bear in mind that there is more than one floor door involved in the system, and hence *i* in *DOOR(i)* refers to a specific door in the system. Due to space problems we will not list out the CSP for the floor door. As for the emergency button in figure 4(c), we name the states as *X*, *ACTIVE* and *HALT*. The process begins at state *X*. Using Rule(1a), we obtain

$$Start5 = X$$

Once the lift starts moving, the system transits to state *ACTIVE*. Rule(2) then gives

$$X = (liftMove \rightarrow ACTIVE)$$

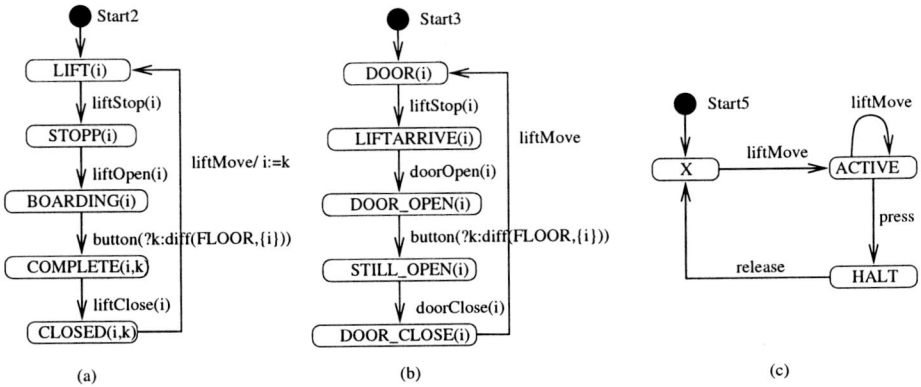

Fig. 4. State diagram for (a) lift (b) floor door and (c) emergency button

The system will remain at this state as long as the lift is moving, i.e. event *liftMove* is offered by the environment continuously. At the point when the emergency button is pressed, i.e. event *press* takes place, and the system comes to a *HALT*. Hence, we can say that at state *ACTIVE* there are two events that could possibly occur, and these depend on the environment, i.e. whether the button is pressed. This is expressed in CSP using Rule(4b) as

$$ACTIVE = press \rightarrow HALT \,\square\, liftMove \rightarrow ACTIVE$$

The only way out from state *HALT* is the transition that is triggered by event *release*. Therefore, when the emergency button is released, the system goes back to state X, and the whole process is repeated.

$$HALT = release \rightarrow X$$

5.2 Static Structure View

In the previous section, we have defined three state diagrams that illustrate three main processes for the lift, the floor door and the emergency button. Now, we need to combine these individual processes and put them in parallel in order to produce a complete concrete design. We achieve this using the method we developed in section 4.2. As shown in figure 5, we have three classes representing the three main processes: *LIFT(1)*, *DOOR(i)* and X. Notice the for process *DOOR(i)*, it is stereotyped as $\langle\!\langle\, |||i{:}FLOOR\, \rangle\!\rangle$. Since $FLOOR = \{1..4\}$, it indicates that there are four copies of processes DOOR(i) interleave with one another. Translating the class into CSP using Rule(7b) we get

$$DOORs = |||i : FLOOR\, @\, DOOR(i)$$

Figure 5 is interpreted as follows : *DOORs* is in parallel with *LIFT(1)* and they synchronize via the common channels *liftMove, liftStop* and *button*. They

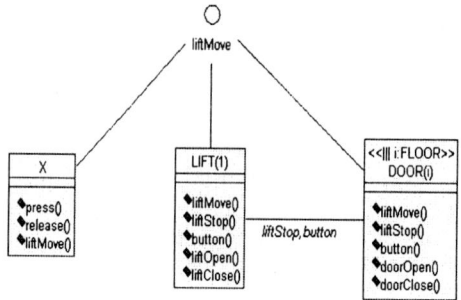

Fig. 5. The static behaviour of CSP processes

in turn are in parallel with X (since X is in parallel with both $LIFT(i)$ and $DOORs$) via the common channel liftMove. Applying Rule(6b), we get

$$System1 = DOORs \underset{\{|liftMove, liftStop, button|\}}{||} LIFT(1)$$

$$System = System1 \underset{\{|liftMove|\}}{||} X$$

5.3 Refinement View

All the three classes defined in section 5.2 is grouped under a package named *System* as shown in figure 6. The package forms the concrete design for the system, and this is used to refine the abstract specification *SPEC(1)*. A refinement assertion (shown below) is generated (using Rule(8b) found in figure 3).

assert $SPEC(1) \sqsubseteq_T System \setminus \{|press, release, doorOpen, doorClose, liftOpen, liftClose|\}$

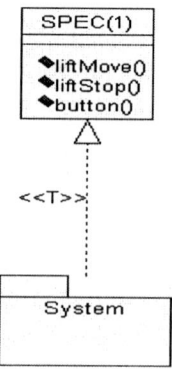

Fig. 6. The refinement assertion

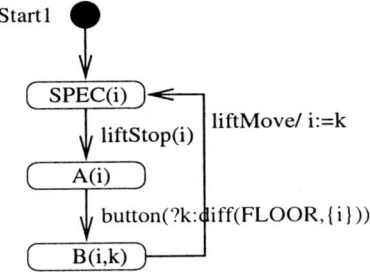

Fig. 7. Modeling the abstract behaviour of the System.

To define the abstract specification, we specify the basic requirements such that when the lift is in floor i, the next destination floor will depend on the button being pressed. The requirement is modelled via the state diagram found in figure 7. Using Rule(1a & 3) to map the state diagram to CSP we obtain

$$START1 = SPEC(i)$$
$$SPEC(i) = liftStop.i \rightarrow A(i)$$
$$A(i) = button?k:diff(FLOOR,\{i\}) \rightarrow B(i,k)$$
$$B(i,k) = liftMove \rightarrow SPEC(k)$$

5.4 The Overview

Figure 8 put together all the diagrams we have developed so far and present an architectural structure showing how the lift system in modeled in UML.

6 Conclusion

In this paper, we have proposed a set of mapping rules that could be used to visualize CSP in UML using state diagrams and class diagrams. We have used the state diagrams to model the dynamic behaviors of a system which is made up of different CSP processes, and the class diagram to visualize the static relationships between the CSP processes and also the refinement assertion. The diagrams are then combined to give a complete representation of CSP in UML. Meanwhile, a prototype tool has also been developed based on the mapping rules that will automatically translate the UML diagrams to CSP that is accepted by FDR.

Closely related to our work is that of [6] which involves Activity Graph and CSP. The work takes a different appproach which defines a formal semantics for activity graph and then compares it with CSP, whereas we concentrate on giving a full representation of CSP in UML, and emphasizes on providing a graphical support towards CSP. [7] presented a mapping between Hoare's CSP

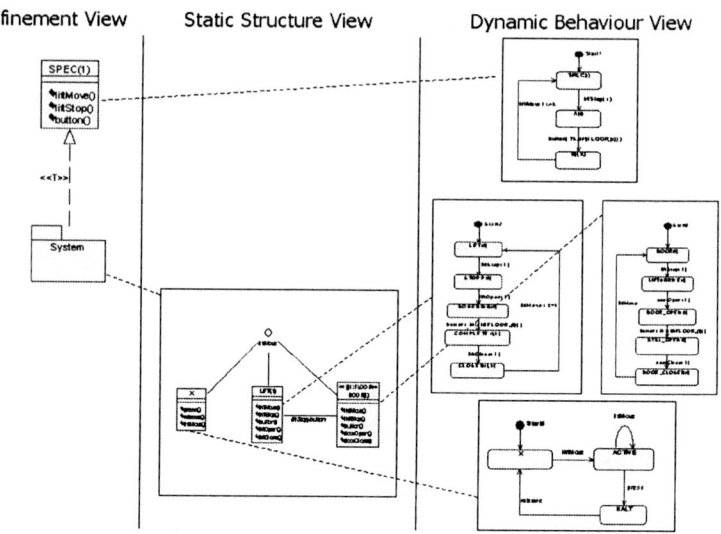

Fig. 8. An overview of the lift system in UML.

and a subset of Role Activity Diagrams(RADs) but it does not support the CSP refinement construct. Other related work includes [8] which emphasizes on specifying and analyzing behavioral constraints in UML and using CSP as the semantic domain for formulating the consistency constraint.

We have not covered all the CSP constructs in our visualization and we hope to pursue this in near future. We also plan to extend our work by looking at the composite states in the State diagrams.

References

1. A.W.Roscoe. The Theory and Practice of Concurrency. Prentice Hall. 1998.
2. David Harel and Michal Politi. Modeling Reactive Systems with State diagrams. Computing McGraw-Hill. 1988. ISBN 0-07-026205-5.
3. OMG Unified Modeling Language Specifictaion, Version 1.3 June 1999. http://www.rational.com/uml/resources/documentation/post.pdf
4. Mark Priestly. Practical Object_Oriented Design with UML. MacGraw Hill. 2000.
5. Formal Systems Website. http://www.formal.demon.co.uk/FDR2.html
6. Christie Bolton and Jim Davies. Activity Graphs and Processes. Integrated Formal Methods, 2nd International Conference, IFM 2000 Dagstuhl Castle, Germany, Nov 2000.
7. Geetha Abeysinghe, Keith Phalp. Combining Process Modeling Methods. Information and Software Technology 39 (1997) 107-124.
8. Gregor Engels, Reiko Heckel and Jochen Malte Kuster. Rule-based Specification of Behavioral Consistency based on the UML Meta-Model. 4th International Conference on the Unified Modeling Language:UML 2001. 2001.
9. Martin Fowler and Kendall Scott. UML Distilled. Applying The Standard Object Modeling Language. Addison-Wesley.1997.

Theorem Prover Support for Precondition and Correctness Calculation

Orieta Celiku and Joakim von Wright

Åbo Akademi University and Turku Centre for Computer Science,
Lemminkäisenkatu 14 A, 20520 Turku, Finland
{oceliku,jwright}@abo.fi

Abstract. Tools for automatically extracting the conditions for which a program is correct with respect to a precondition and postcondition can make proving program correctness easier. We build a HOL-based tool that uses weakest preconditions and semantically derived rules to prove correctness theorems with the verification conditions as assumptions. The rules include two new rules for calculating loop preconditions and recursion correctness while taking specification variables into consideration. The programming language has (recursive) procedures, and both demonic and angelic nondeterminism, which can be used to model interaction. Program variables can be of arbitrary types. Programs with procedures are handled modularly, and proved facts about individual procedures are stored in a database available to all programs.

1 Introduction

Hoare logic [10] and Dijkstra's weakest precondition [5] are suitable for reasoning about program correctness but the proofs require a lot of work even for very small programs.

Calculating program correctness amounts to analyzing the program structure and collecting, for each statement, the verification conditions under which the statement is correct with respect to a (given or calculated) precondition and postcondition. Automation requires that loops are annotated with invariants and termination functions, and procedures are annotated with preconditions, postconditions and, if recursive, also with invariants and termination functions. If Hoare-logic rules are used, sequences should be annotated with intermediate assertions.

For correctness tools to be dependable they should be verified or built in a safe way. Regardless of the approach, confidence in proofs is increased if theorem provers are used. The main steps in building a theorem-prover-based tool are:

1. Embedding the programming language of interest into the theorem prover. The embedding can be shallow, meaning that programs are identified with their semantic functions, or deep, meaning that first the language syntax is embedded and then a semantic function is provided.

2. Coming up with a collection of correctness rules. For a deep embedding, the rules are syntactic and should be proved sound with respect to the semantics. For a shallow embedding, the rules should be derived from the semantics by formal proof.
3. Building a verification condition generator. This includes: providing support for annotating programs, implementing transformations that use the correctness rules to automatically calculate program correctness, and providing support for simplifying the verification conditions.

We build a tool for calculating preconditions and (total) correctness, based on the HOL theorem prover [8]. The tool reuses the language embedding from a previous formalization of a programming language [3] and its extension with (recursive) procedures [14]. We extend the embedding with two angelic nondeterministic statements which together with demonic nondeterministic statements can be used to model interactive and game-like systems [1]. The language embedding is shallow and programs are given a weakest precondition predicate transformer semantics. Program variables may have any HOL type.

We introduce new rules for calculating preconditions of loops and recursive statements. The rules are new in the way they take the presence of specification variables into consideration. Specification variables are usually used to refer to the initial values of program variables. Our loop rule makes it possible to use them in loop invariants to refer to the values of the program variables upon entering the loop. This makes loop invariants more intuitive and easier to come up with since they can refer to suc h values regardless of the context the loop is in. For the same reason, proving loop correctness becomes modular. The recursion rule is used to prove correctness of recursive procedures with specification variables and (unbounded) nondeterminism which, to our knowledge, has not been done before.

We implement a verification condition generator that uses weakest preconditions and the above mentioned rules to automatically extract the conditions for the correctness of suitably annotated programs. Programs with procedures are handled in a modular way, by first proving that the body of a procedure satisfies some specification and then adapting this result to derive conclusions about programs that employ the procedure. A database mechanism allows for procedures to be employed even from programs that do not declare them.

An automatic correctness calculator can lessen the burden of proving programs correct. Such a verification tool could be integrated into a software development toolkit along with analysis systems such as [2] which automatically infers useful program invariants. Individual components of the toolkit can be treated as black boxes and their interaction made possible by interfaces such as PROSPER [4]. Alternatively, they can be more tightly coupled. For instance, Heintze et al. [9] describe a framework for low level interaction between analysis and verification tools. In this framework, the verifier has the task of checking give n assertions (inferred by an analyzer), and the analyzer that of inferring (from checked assertions). The modular way we treat procedures and loops makes our tool suitable for either kind of interaction.

2 Related Work

Verification condition generators and the embedding of different programming languages into theorem provers have been going in and out of fashion for a while. Here we concentrate on what we found most relevant to our work; for a detailed overview see Homeier's Ph.D. thesis [11].

Gordon's work [7] on a shallow embedding of a deterministic while-language (as well as constructs from dynamic logic) in HOL has been an inspiration for many other embeddings. Hoare-logic rules are used to prove correctness and a HOL tactic generates verification conditions for programs with annotations.

Homeier [11] performs a HOL deep embedding of a deterministic while-language with procedures and expressions with side effects. A method for proving correctness of recursive procedures, including mutually recursive ones, is implemented. Hoare-logic rules are used to automatically generate verification conditions. A significant limitation of this work is that programs are assumed to work on an initial state where the program variables are assigned explicit values; hence it is impossible to prove correctness assertions for arbitrary initial states. Another limitation is that program variables can only be of natural number type.

Nipkow [16] deeply embeds a small deterministic while-language in the Isabelle proof assistant. Partial correctness is analyzed by calculating the weakest liberal precondition of the statements while generating the corresponding verification conditions. However, the focus is on embedding several semantics for the language following a program semantics textbook, so the language is quite basic, variables are only of natural number type, and there is no treatment of termination or mention of specification variables.

Filliâtre [6] formalizes a language with both functional and imperative features in the Coq system. The language has recursive functional procedures but not mutually recursive ones. Program variables are variables of the logic and hence may have any type. A Coq tactic for proving (total) program correctness is implemented. The need for explicit auxiliary variables is eradicated by use of labels, for example $a@0$ gives the value of a before the statement labeled by 0.

The Refinement Calculator [3] is a HOL based refinement tool. The programming language is shallowly embedded according to a weakest precondition semantics. Program variables may have any HOL type. Laibinis [14] extended the formalization with (recursive) procedures with value and reference parameters. We reuse and extend this formalization.

3 The Correctness/Precondition Calculator

We start with a description of the language embedding from the Refinement Calculator [3]. Then we show how weakest preconditions for basic statements (excluding loops and procedures) are calculated and how program correctness is analyzed. Section 3.3 is a note on correctness of programs with angelic nondeterminism. In Section 3.4 we discuss the new rule for calculating loop preconditions. Procedures, first nonrecursive, and then recursive are treated in Sections ?? and 3.6. Finally, we discuss the issue of simplifying verification conditions.

3.1 Language Embedding

In the Refinement Calculator programs are modeled as predicate transformers (functions from state predicates to state predicates) according to a weakest precondition semantics.

The programming language is shallowly embedded in the HOL logic. The shallow embedding allows the identification of types in the embedded language with types in the HOL logic. Hence, when types are mentioned they refer to HOL types. Function application is written as $f\ x$.

The program state is implemented as a tuple where every component corresponds to the value of a program variable. The state has a polymorphic type Σ that for each program is instantiated to the product of the concrete types of the program variables. The program variables, in fact, are functions from states to values ($\Sigma \to \alpha$, where α can be any HOL type) and correspond to the projection functions of the state. Note that the definitions that follow do not depend on the state implementation – they consider the state as having polymorphic type.

The programming language originally included while statements, blocks with local variables, and demonic nondeterministic statements, but was later extended with (recursive) procedures [14]. We have extended the language with two angelically nondeterministic constructs. All the statements are monotonic predicate transformers (c is monotonic if $p \subseteq q$ implies $c\ p \subseteq c\ q$, where $\subseteq$ means "stronger than," and $c\ p$ is the weakest precondition for c to establish p).

$$
\begin{aligned}
\mathsf{skip}\ q &= q & &skip \\
\{p\}\ q &= p \wedge q & &assertion \\
[p]\ q &= p \Rightarrow q & &guard \\
(x := e)\ q &= q[x := e] & &determ.\ update \\
\{x := x' \mid P\}\ q &= (\exists x'.\ P \wedge q[x := x']) & &angelic\ update \\
[x := x' \mid P]\ q &= (\forall x'.\ P \Rightarrow q[x := x']) & &demonic\ update \\
(c_1; c_2)\ q &= c_1\ (c_2\ q) & &sequence \\
(c_1 \sqcup c_2)\ q &= (c_1\ q) \vee (c_2\ q) & &angelic\ choice \\
(c_1 \sqcap c_2)\ q &= (c_1\ q) \wedge (c_2\ q) & &demonic\ choice \\
\text{if } g \text{ then } c_1 \text{ else } c_2 \text{ fi } q &= (g \wedge (c_1\ q)) \vee (\neg g \wedge (c_2\ q)) & &conditional \\
[\![\mathsf{var}\ y \mid b.\ c]\!]\ q &= (\forall y.\ b \Rightarrow c\ q) & &local\ block
\end{aligned}
$$

Fig. 1. Weakest precondition definition

The weakest precondition for each of the basic statements is defined in Figure 1 following the refinement calculus [1]. skip is the statement that does nothing. The demonic choice is seen as the choice we have no control over, thus both statements should establish the postcondition for the choice to do so. The angelic choice is interpreted as the choice we can affect, hence, if any of the statements establishes the postcondition, so does the angelic choice. The demonic and angelic updates, in which $x := x' \mid P$ describes a state relation that leaves all variables except x unchanged, are interpreted similarly to the choices.

Extralogical parsing is used to translate the syntax used in the definitions into HOL logic syntax. For example, the program skip; $x := x+1$ in the environment with program variables x and y is translated into this HOL term:

```
let x = FST in let y = SND in skip seq assign (λs. (x s + 1, y s))
```

where `FST` and `SND` are tuple projection functions, and `x s` and `y s` give the values of x and y in state `s`.

3.2 Basic Calculations

The calculation of the weakest precondition of programs containing only basic statements with respect to some postcondition is done using the definitions in Figure 1. For example, calculating the weakest precondition of skip; $x := x+1$ with respect to postcondition $x = 1$ gives the following HOL theorem:

```
let x = FST in let y = SND in
    (skip seq assign (λs. (x s + 1, y s))) (λs. x s = 1)
=
let x = FST in let y = SND in (λs. x s + 1 = 1)
```

Note the explicit state abstraction in the predicates: the calculated precondition can be simplified to (λs. x s = 0) which in ordinary syntax would simply be written as $x = 0$.

For all the basic statements the calculation gives the weakest precondition of the statement with respect to the postcondition. However, for loops and procedures we will generally not get the weakest precondition, but something stronger.

We analyze program correctness by calculating weakest preconditions. A total correctness assertion $p \{\!|\, c \,|\!\} q$ is equivalent to $p \subseteq c\ q$. Note that for sequences we can automatically use as intermediate assertion the weakest precondition of the second statement with respect to the postcondition.

Calculating correctness assertions such as

$$x = 0 \ \{\!|\, \text{skip}; x := x + 1 \,|\!\} \ x = 1$$

will always generate a verification condition. Here, this condition would be $\forall x.\ (x = 0) \Rightarrow (x + 1 = 1)$ (the condition no longer has a state argument).

Programs and pre- and postconditions can contain free variables (*global constants*), which are implicitly universally quantified in a correctness assertion. An important special case of such variables is that of *specification variables* (also known as auxiliary or logical variables), which are usually used to refer to the initial values of program variables and make reasoning about arbitrary initial states possible. They may occur free in preconditions, postconditions, and invariants, but cannot be used in program statements. For example, in the following correctness assertion (for a "swapping" assignment) a_0 and b_0 are used to refer to the initial values of a and b:

$$(a = a_0 \land b = b_0) \ \{\!|\, a, b := b, a \,|\!\} \ (a = b_0 \land b = a_0)$$

Specification variables are often indicated by special syntactic conventions, such as zero subscription. Another possibility is to make assertions explicitly dependent on the specification variables in addition to the state [17]. In our framework, they require special treatment only when appearing in loops and procedures.

3.3 Angelic Statements

Angelic and demonic statements can be used together to model interactive systems [1]. Such systems can be thought of as two-player games where one player (the angel) tries to achieve a goal while playing against an opponent (the demon). Proving correctness for such systems means analyzing the goal achievability for the angel (an example is given in Section 4.1).

Angelic statements introduce existential quantifiers or disjunctions in the preconditions. For example, the weakest precondition of skip $\sqcup\, x := x+1$ with respect to $x = 1$ is $x = 0 \lor x = 1$ and both the following hold:

$$x = 0 \ \{\!|\ \text{skip} \sqcup x := x+1\ |\!\}\ x = 1 \qquad x = 1 \ \{\!|\ \text{skip} \sqcup x := x+1\ |\!\}\ x = 1$$

As a result, in order to verify correctness assertions involving angelic nondeterminism a choice between disjuncts must be made (or an existential witness supplied). This typically requires user intervention, which can be seen as describing a winning strategy for the angel.

3.4 Loops

The loop construct is defined in the usual way, as the least fixpoint (in the predicate transformer lattice) of the unfolding function:

$$\text{do}\ g \to c\ \text{od}\ =\ (\mu X.\ \text{if}\ g\ \text{then}\ c; X\ \text{else skip fi})$$

In order to verify correctness of a loop, we need an invariant and a variant. A loop invariant is a precondition of the loop, although not necessarily the weakest precondition. In existing systems based on precondition calculation, the invariant has generally been used as the calculated precondition of the loop [16]. A well chosen invariant may have to refer to specification variables introduced as initial values for one or more program variables. While possible, this can make the annotation of the loop difficult, since the role of the specification variables may not be easy to trace (especially if the loop occurs late in the program text). Another possibility would be to use a "binary invariant," i.e., a relation rather than a predicate (as in VDM [12]).

Our novel solution, which fits well into the classical correctness-based framework, is based on the following (formally proved) generalization of the variant-invariant theorem for loops, where the invariant I has an extra argument:

$$\forall s_0\ x.\ (\lambda s.\ I\ s_0\ s \land g\ s \land (t\ s = x))\ \{\!|\ c\ |\!\}\ (\lambda s.\ I\ s_0\ s \land t\ s < x)$$
$$\Rightarrow$$
$$\forall h.\ (\lambda s.\ I\ (h\ s)\ s \land (\forall s'.\ \neg(g\ s') \land I\ (h\ s)\ s' \Rightarrow q\ s'))\ \subseteq\ (\text{do}\ g \to c\ \text{od})\ q$$

(Here $\subseteq$ indicates that the precondition is not necessarily the weakest one.)

This theorem allows us to introduce specification variables (here s_0, but it can be a tuple of variables) as names for any function (here h) of the initial loop state, and then the invariant may refer to these specification variables. An important advantage is that this makes loop annotation modular – we can annotate the loop without knowing what context it will be used in. Note also that the requirement that the postcondition must hold upon termination here becomes included in the precondition rather than appearing as a separate verification condition.

For example, the following is a correct loop annotation:

var x, y, z : num.
...
do /* invariant $(z + x * y = z1 + x1 * y1) \land y = y1$ variant x init $(x1, y1, z1)$ */
$0 < x \rightarrow x, z := x - 1, z + y$ od

Here the specification variables are introduced using the init-annotation which indicates that $x1, y1, z1$ stand for the values of the program variables x, y, z at the beginning of the loop (independently of whether specification variables are used in the precondition to stand for their initial values).

Given this loop and the postcondition $z = n$ (where n is a free variable), the tool gives (after some simplification) the precondition $z + x * y = n$.

Having the specification variables stand for initial values of program variables means that the function h in the loop theorem is always instantiated to the identity function. It would be possible to allow more complex specification variables (e.g., standing for the sum of two variables) but that would require a more elaborate annotation scheme.

3.5 Procedures and Adaptation

A procedure is a parameterized program statement that can be used in different contexts. Using the procedure requires adapting the procedure body to the program context that calls it: actual parameters should be substituted for formal ones. Moreover, a procedure works on a state of its own (the parameter space). The adaptation also includes a jump from the calling state to the local procedure state and then back again.

We reuse Laibinis's formalization of procedures [14]. Here we omit the details of this formalization and concentrate only on correctness of programs with procedures.

Calls to non-recursive procedures can be handled by unfolding the procedures but this requires the procedure body to be analyzed for each procedure call. We are more interested in the modular way of treating procedures, which also gives us a unified way of treating both recursive and nonrecursive procedures.

For each procedure the tool proves the procedure body correct with respect to the precondition and postcondition that annotate the procedure definition. Once proved, the correctness theorem is stored in a database and for each procedure call it is adapted by substituting the actual parameters for the formal ones, and lifting the precondition and postcondition to the global state.

As an example, consider the procedure $Swap$ defined as:

procedure $Swap$(var a, b : num)
/* pre $a = a_0 \land b = b_0$ post $a = b_0 \land b = a_0$ */
$a, b := b, a$

For a call with actual parameters x and y the following theorem is generated:

$Swap = a, b := b, a \vdash \forall a_0\ b_0.\ (x = a_0 \wedge y = b_0)\ \{\!|\ Swap(x,y)\ |\!\}\ (x = b_0 \wedge y = a_0)$

Note that the procedure name is a free variable, and the procedure definition is included as an assumption of the theorem.

This theorem should be adapted in order to calculate the precondition of $Swap(x, y)$ with respect to some postcondition, e.g., $x > z$, over the state of the calling program.

Procedure Adaptation. The adaptation problem can be described as looking for a rule of the form

$$(p\ \{\!|\ c\ |\!\}\ q) \Rightarrow (?\ \{\!|\ c\ |\!\}\ r)$$

that would enable us to fill in the missing precondition. The rule is said to be *sharp* if it gives the weakest possible precondition, i.e., it is an equivalence. The fact that specification variables can be present makes this problem nontrivial to solve in a mechanized logic, and the problem has attracted quite a lot of attention recently, e.g., [13, 15]. We use the following sharp theorem from [15].

$\forall c\ p\ q.$ monotonic $c \Rightarrow$
$\quad ((\forall m.\ p(m)\ \{\!|\ c\ |\!\}\ q(m)) = (\forall q'\ m.\ (\{p(m)\}; [x := x'\ |\ q(m)])\ q' \subseteq c\ q'))$

m stands for one or more specification variables that may occur free in the pre- and postconditions p and q. The tool identifies specification variables from the procedure annotation using a simple heuristic: any free variable that occurs on the right-hand side of an equality where the left hand side is a program variable is considered to be a specification variable.

$p(m)\ \{\!|\ c\ |\!\}\ q(m)$ matches the procedure correctness theorem, lifted to the calling state, and q' matches the actual postcondition for the procedure call.

Applying the theorem to a call to procedure $Swap$ gives as expected:

$$(Swap(x,y))(x > z) = (y > z)$$

where z can be a program variable of the calling state or a free variable.

3.6 Recursive Procedures

Recursive procedures are often handled by considering the procedure names as a collection of recursively defined constants. In contrast, we reuse the recursion operator μ of the underlying formalization of the refinement calculus. Thus, a recursive procedure is an ordinary procedure of the form $P = (\mu X.S[X])$ and the procedure name is a free variable. Separating procedures and recursion simplifies the treatment of recursive procedures, but since the recursive occurrence of the recursion variable is as an argument to the procedure call operator, the separation is not complete.

Exactly as for loops, we have proved a theorem for correctness of recursion using an invariant and a variant, and specification variables:

$\forall s_0\ x.\ (\lambda s.\ p\ s \wedge (h\ s = s_0) \wedge (t\ s = x))\ \{\!|\ f(\{\lambda s.\ p\ s \wedge t\ s < x\}; [\lambda s\ s'.\ Q\ (h\ s)\ s'])\ |\!\}\ Q\ s_0$
$\Rightarrow$
$\forall s_0.\ (\lambda s.\ p\ s \wedge (h\ s = s_0))\ \{\!|\ \mu f\ |\!\}\ Q\ s_0$

Here the invariant and the variant (t) are expressed in terms of the parameters at the point of the recursive calls and specification variables that are local to the procedure. Instead of having an induction assumption about correctness of the recursive call, the antecedent in this rule has an explicit nondeterministic statement at the recursion point (the argument to the function f) which states that the variant is decreased and the postcondition established, taking into account that specification variables now refer to the values of the program variables at the recursive call.

Exactly as in the loop theorem, the specification variables (s_0 in the theorem) can stand for any function (h) of the initial state. In practice, the heuristic used to identify specification variables restricts them to stand for initial values of program variables.

Observe that procedures are handled in a uniform way, whether they are (unboundedly) nondeterministic or not. With our approach, unbounded nondeterminism is nothing special and can easily be used in procedures since the language includes unbounded nondeterminism in the demonic assignment.

For an example of a recursive procedure, see Section 4.2 (procedure *Add*).

3.7 Simplification

The generated verification conditions are simplified using the basic HOL simplifier. For all but trivial examples, this simplification is not sufficient to discharge all the proof obligations and specialized reasoning about the specific datatypes and program domain is needed. However, there is some specialized simplification that can be performed by exploiting patterns that repeatedly appear in different verification conditions. For example, one of the typical conditions has to do with the loop variant decreasing for each iteration and could take this form:

$$\cdots 0 < x \cdots \Rightarrow \cdots \wedge (x - 1 < x) \wedge \cdots$$

Similarly, demonic and angelic updates give rise to quantified conditions that can be simplified using certain sequences of rewrites and quantifier manipulations. We specialize the general HOL simplifier with some of these patterns in mind.

4 Examples

The first example illustrates game-like programs with angelic and demonic nondeterminism, the second example shows procedures at work, while the third example contains multiple loops and program variables with array types.

4.1 Angelic and Demonic Nondeterminism

In Nim two players take turns in removing one or two matches from a pile (of x matches). The player to remove the last match loses the game. We side with the first player, hence the first player is interpreted as the angel and the other player as the demon. We prove that the angel can win the game, provided that initially $x \text{ MOD } 3 \neq 1$, by making sure that $x \text{ MOD } 3 = 1$ after his turn.

```
var x : num.
¬(x MOD 3 = 1) {|
do /* invariant ¬(x MOD 3 = 1) variant x */
T → [0 < x]; {x := x' | (x' MOD 3 = 1) ∧ (x' = x − 1 ∨ x' = x − 2)};
    {0 < x}; [x := x' | x' = x − 1 ∨ x' := x − 2] od
|} T
```

The guard $[0 < x]$ is interpreted as: check if there are matches before the angel takes the turn and if not terminate miraculously with the angel winning the game. Similarly, the demon wins if the assertion $\{0 < x\}$ fails.

The correctness proof generates one verification condition:

$$\forall x. \, (\neg(x \text{ MOD } 3 = 1) \land 0 < x) \Rightarrow$$
$$(\exists x'. \, (x' \text{ MOD } 3 = 1) \land (x' = x - 1 \lor x' = x - 2) \land 0 < x' \land$$
$$(\forall x''. \, (x'' = x' - 1 \lor x'' = x' - 2) \Rightarrow \neg(x'' \text{ MOD } 3 = 1) \land x'' < x))$$

This verification condition should be read as: provided that the precondition holds and there are matches in the pile there exists a winning strategy for the angel regardless of what the demon chooses. The witness for the existential quantifier gives, in fact, the winning strategy for the angel. If x MOD $3 = 0$ the angel should remove two matches, and if x MOD $3 = 2$ the angel should remove one match. Our specialized simplifier removes quantifiers and the condition that comes from the variant $(x'' < x)$ but the complete proof involves more specialized reasoning about the MOD operator and has to be separately carried out in HOL.

4.2 Nested and Recursive Procedures

This program stores the product of two natural numbers x and y into y.

```
procedure Inc(var a : num)
/* pre a = a₀ post a = a₀ + 1 */
    a := a + 1
procedure Dec(var a : num)
/* pre 0 < a ∧ a = a₀ post a = a₀ − 1 */
    a := a − 1
procedure Add(val a : num var b : num)
/* pre a = a₀ ∧ b = b₀ post b = b₀ + a₀ invariant b = b₀ + (a₀ − a) variant a */
    if 0 < a then Inc(b); Dec(a); Add(a,b) else skip fi
procedure Mult(val a : num var b : num)
/* pre a = a₀ ∧ b = b₀ post b = b₀ * a₀ */
    |[var z : num | z = b.
    b := 0;
    do /* invariant z = Z ∧ (b + a * z = B + A * z) variant a init (Z, A, B) */
    0 < a → Add(z,b); Dec(a) od]|
var x, y : num. Mult(x, y) (y = z)
```

Add is a recursive procedure, so an invariant and variant for the recursion are needed (note that the invariant refers to the specification variables introduced in the precondition).

The calculated precondition is $x * y = z$ and the generated verification conditions are automatically discharged by our specialized simplifier.

4.3 Arrays and Multiple Loops

The following program finds the least number that does not occur in an array $a[0..n-1]$ of natural numbers by first noting in a separate boolean array b which numbers occur in a. Arrays of type α are modeled as functions num $\to \alpha$. Note that the loop annotations are sufficient for the tool to verify correctness:

var i : num; a : num $\to$ num; b : num $\to$ bool.
T {|
$i := 0$;
do /* invariant $i \leq n \land (\forall k.\ k < i \Rightarrow \neg b[k])$ variant $n - i$ */
$i < n \to b := (\lambda k.\ (k = i) \to \mathsf{F} \mid b[k]); i := i + 1$ od;
$i := 0$;
do /* invariant $i \leq n \land (\forall k.\ k < n \Rightarrow (b[k] = (\exists j.\ j < i \land a[j] = k)))$ variant $n-i$ */
$i < n \to b := (\lambda k.\ (k = a[i]) \to \mathsf{T} \mid b[k]); i := i + 1$ od;
$i := 0$;
do /* invariant $i \leq n \land (\forall k.\ k < n \Rightarrow (b[k] = (\exists j.\ j < i \land a[j] = k))) \land$
    $(\forall k.\ k < i \Rightarrow b[k])$ variant $n - i$ */
$i < n \land b[i] \to i := i + 1$ od
|} $i \leq n \land (i < n \Rightarrow (\forall j.\ j < n \Rightarrow \neg (a[j] = i))) \land (\forall k.\ k < i \Rightarrow (\exists j.\ j < n \land a[j] = k))$

Interactive proof is needed to discharge the generated verification conditions.

5 Conclusion

A tool for automatically extracting the conditions for which a program is correct with respect to a pre- and postcondition can mitigate the laborious task of proving program correctness. Although the idea is not new, there are hardly any tools that can handle both realistic languages and realistic program variable types. Specification variables are also handled in varying degrees. The most interesting tool in both respects we found to be Filliâtre's [6]. Homeier's [11] is interesting in that it is the only one to also handle mutually recursive procedures.

Our HOL-based tool automatically generates the conditions for which a program is correct with respect to a pre- and postcondition by using weakest preconditions and semantically derived rules to prove a correctness theorem with the verification conditions as assumptions. Our tool fares well with respect to the complexity of the language and that of the program variable types. Program variables can be of arbitrary types and the language, unlike the other mentioned languages, has angelic and demonic nondeterministic statements, which are suitable for modeling interactive systems.

The two new (semantically derived) rules for calculating preconditions of loops and recursive statements take into consideration the presence of specification variables in the invariants. The recursion rule is used to prove correctness of recursive procedures with specification variables and (unbounded) nondeterminism.

The modular way we treat programs with procedures makes it easier to verify large programs. The fact that loops as well can be handled modularly makes the tool more usable in the sense that we could extract the more difficult parts of the programs and prove them separately.

The soundness of the verification condition generators is an important issue. Nipkow [16] and Homeier [11] prove their verification condition generators sound. Our tool is an unverified HOL/ML-program, but since we use only extension mechanisms that preserve consistency and the result of each precondition/correctness calculation is a HOL theorem, we get soundness for free.

References

1. R. J. Back and J. von Wright. *Refinement Calculus: A Systematic Introduction.* Springer-Verlag, 1998.
2. S. Bensalem, Y. Lakhnech, S. Saidi. Powerful Techniques for the Automatic Generation of Invariants. In *Computer Aided Verification, CAV '96*, LNCS 1102, 1996.
3. M. J. Butler, J. Grundy, T. Långbacka, R. Rukšenas, and J. von Wright. The Refinement Calculator: Proof Support for Program Refinement. In *Proc. FMP'97 - Formal Methods Pacific*, Discrete Mathematics and Theoretical Computer Science, Wellington, New Zealand, July 1997. Springer-Verlag.
4. L. A. Dennis, G. Collins, M. Norrish, R. Boulton, K. Slind, G. Robinson, M. Gordon, and T. Melham, The PROSPER Toolkit. In *Proc. of TACAS 2000*, LNCS 1785, Springer-Verlag.
5. E. W. Dijkstra. *A Discipline of Programming.* Prentice-Hall International, 1976.
6. J. C. Filliâtre. Proof of imperative programs in Type Theory. In *International Workshop, TYPES'98*, Kloster Irsee, Germany. LNCS 1657, Springer-Verlag, 1998.
7. M. Gordon. Mechanizing Programming Logics in Higher Order Logic. In G. Birtwistel and P. Subrahmanyam, editors, *Current Trends in Hardware Verification and Automated Theorem Proving*. Springer-Verlag, 1989.
8. M. J. C. Gordon and T. F. Melham. *Introduction to HOL.* Cambridge University Press, New York, 1993.
9. N. Heintze, J. Jaffar, and R. Voicu. A Framework for Combining Analysis and Verification. In *Proc. of POPL 2000*, pp 26-39, 2000.
10. C. A. R. Hoare. An axiomatic basis for computer programming. *Communications of the ACM*, 12(10):576-583, 1969.
11. P. V. Homeier. Trustworthy Tools for Trustworthy Programs: A Mechanically Verified Verification Condition Generator for the Total Correctness of Procedures. Ph.D. Dissertation, UCLA Computer Science Department, 1995.
12. C. B. Jones. *Systematic Software Development Using VDM.* Prentice-Hall International, 1986.
13. T. Kleymann. Hoare Logic and VDM: Machine-Checked Soundness and Completeness Proofs. Ph.D. Thesis, University of Edinburgh, ECS-LFCS-98-392, FCS, 1998.
14. L. Laibinis. Mechanized Formal Reasoning about Modular Programs. Ph.D. Thesis, Turku Centre for Computer Science Dissertations, 24, Finland, April, 2000.
15. L. Laibinis and J. von Wright. What's in a Specification. In *Proc. International Refinement Workshop and Formal Methods Pacific 1998*, Discrete Mathematics and Theoretical Computer Science, Canberra, Australia, 1998. Springer-Verlag.
16. T. Nipkow. Winskel is (almost) Right: Towards a Mechanized Semantics Textbook. *Formal Aspects of Computing*, 10(2):171-186, 1998.
17. D. von Oheimb. Hoare Logic for Mutual Recursion and Local Variables. In *Foundations of Software Technology and Theoretical Computer Science (FST and TCS)*, Springer LNCS, 1999.

XML-Based Static Type Checking and Dynamic Visualization for TCOZ

Jin Song Dong, Yuan Fang Li, Jing Sun, Jun Sun, and Hai Wang

School of Computing,
National University of Singapore
{dongjs,liyuanfa,sunjing,sunjun,wangh}@comp.nus.edu.sg

Abstract. Timed Communicating Object Z(TCOZ) combines Object-Z's strengths in modelling complex data and state with TCSP's strengths in modeling real-time concurrency. Based on our previous work on the XML environment for TCOZ, this paper firstly demonstrates the development of a type checker for detecting static semantic errors of the TCOZ specification, then illustrates a transformation tool to automatically project TCOZ models into UML statechart diagrams for visualising the dynamic system behaviour.

Keywords: TCOZ tool support, XML/XSL, UML/XMI.

1 Introduction

The main stimulus for the inception of formal specification techniques is to precisely describe software and system requirements so that tools can be applied to perform checking and analysis on the formal requirement models. Various formal notations are often combined for modelling large and complex systems which may have intricate system states and complex concurrent and real-time behavior. Timed Communicating Object Z (TCOZ) [8] builds on the strengths of Object-Z [4, 12] in modeling complex data and state with the strengths of TCSP [10] in modeling process control and real-time interactions. Our previous works on ZML (Z [15] family on the Web through XML) [14, 13] have been focusing on displaying formal specifications on the web and projecting TCOZ models to UML class diagrams. This paper reports on the developments of a type checking and UML statechart visualization tools for TCOZ.
There have been previous works on type checking Z and Object-Z. For example, *Wizard* [5] is a LaTeX-based type checker for Object-Z. Our type checking tool aims to check TCOZ (including Z and Object-Z) specifications with XML as an input format.
UML can be used for visualizing formal specification models. For the purpose of visualizing the static properties of TCOZ specification, we have previously developed a transformation tool from TCOZ to UML class diagram [13]. The second part of this paper aims to develop the techniques and tools for visualizing TCOZ behaviour specifications (mainly TCSP) by transforming TCOZ models into UML statechart diagrams. Brooke and Paige [3] have recently developed a tool-supported graphical notation for TCSP. The difference between Brooke and Paige's approach and ours is that we use existing graphical notations instead of creating new ones.

The remainder of the paper is organized as follows. Section 2 briefly introduces the technical background: the TCOZ notation and XML/XMI. Section 3 provides the overall design of the type checker and outlines type hierarchy and typing rules. Section 4 develops the proper projection rules for transforming TCOZ models to UML statecharts and illustrates the development of the automatic projection tools using JAVA. Section 5 presents a case study of the project, showing the working and output of the type checker and visualization in UML statechart diagrams. Section 6 concludes the paper and comments on possible future work directions.

2 Technical Background

2.1 TCOZ

Timed Communicating Object Z (TCOZ) builds on the strengths of Object-Z and TCSP. The syntactic structure of TCOZ is similar to Object-Z. A TCOZ document consists of a sequence of definitions, including type and constant definitions in the usual Z style. TCOZ varies from Object-Z in the structure of class definitions, which may include CSP channel and process definitions.

In the remainder of this subsection, some important features of TCOZ are briefly introduced. A detailed introduction can be found elsewhere [8]. The formal semantics of TCOZ is also documented in [6].

Active Object
In TCOZ, active objects have their own thread of control, while passive objects are controlled by other objects in a system. An identifier *MAIN* is used to represent the behavior of active objects of a given class. The *MAIN* operation is optional in a class definition. It only appears in a class definition when the objects of that class are active objects.

Interface: Channels, sensors and actuators
Channel is one of the most important concepts in CSP and it is given an independent, first class role in TCOZ. The class state-schema convention (mechanism in Object-Z) is extended to allow the declaration of communication channels. If c is to be used as a communication channel by any of the operations of a class, then it must be declared in the state schema to be the type of **chan**, for example *in, out* in the above example. One thing special about channel is that channels are type heterogeneous and may carry communications of any type. Contrary to the conventions adopted for internal state entities, channels are viewed as shared rather than as encapsulated entities, that is, channels are commonly used to carry information between TCOZ classes.

Complementary to the synchronizing CSP channel mechanism, TCOZ also adopts a nonsynchronizing shared variable mechanism [7]. A declaration of the form $s : X$ *sensor* provides a channel-like interface for using the shared variable s as an input. A declaration of the form $s : X$ *actuator* provides a local-variable-like interface for using the shared variable s as an output.

Network Topology
The syntactic structure of the CSP synchronization operator is convenient only in the case of pipe-line like communication topologies. Expressing more complex communication

topologies generally results in unacceptably complicated expressions. In TCOZ, a graph-based approach is adopted to represent the network topology. For example, consider that processes A and B communicate privately through the interface ab, processes A and C communicate privately through the interface ac, and processes B and C communicate privately through the interface bc.
This network topology of A, B and C may be described by

$$\| (A \xleftrightarrow{ab} B;\ B \xleftrightarrow{bc} C;\ C \xleftrightarrow{ca} A).$$

2.2 XML and XMI

Our previous work [14] has used XML and XML schema to define a standard exchange format for Z-family languages (Z, Object-Z and TCOZ). An XML Schema file was created for describing the structure of the Z-family languages in XML. It defines the contents of all elements, the order and cardinality of sub-elements, and data types of some of the elements.

XMI (XML Metadata Interchange) is an industry standard for storing and sharing object programming and design information, allowing developers of distributed systems to share object models and other metadata over the Internet. Three key industry standards, XML (eXtensible Markup Language), UML (Unified Modelling Language) and MOF (Meta Object Facility), are integrated in XMI. XMI marries the OMG and W3C metadata and modelling technologies [1]. Rational Rose 2001 from OMG which supports XMI can generate UML diagrams once it imports XMI documents, and it can also export XMI documents for any existing UML diagrams as well. This is very useful for our work since we only need to generate the proper XMI from a TCOZ specification in XML format. The syntax definition of XMI for UML is specified in XMI 1.1 RTF UML DTD [1]. This DTD file defines all entities and XMI syntax signatures for UML. An XMI file validated by UML.DTD version 1.3 has the following structure:

```
<?xml version = '1.0' encoding = 'ISO-8859-1' ?>
<XMI xmi.version='1.1' xmlns:UML='//org.omg/UML/1.3'>
    <XMI.header> ... </XMI.header>
    <XMI.content>
        <UML.Model>
            <UML.StateMachine> ... </UML.StateMachine>
        </UML.Model>
        <UML:Diagram> ... </UML:Diagram>
    </XMI.content\>
</XMI>
```

XMI.header contains general information like the UML.DTD version. UML StateMachine is the most important part of *UML.content*, which contains information about Statechart. *UML : Diagram* is used to display the UML diagrams. It contains the exact position of every displayable unit in the UML diagram.

3 Type Checker Design and Typing Rules

3.1 High-Level Design

In order to parse the TCOZ languages in XML format, we need to parse the entire XML file. A compiler approach was taken. A handcrafted[1] front end of a complete compiler was written, which includes modules like the scanner, the symbol table, the expression parser, the predicate parser and other miscellaneous utility modules. This type checker has a handcrafted front end of a compiler. A top-down, or recursive descent approach is taken for two reasons. The first reason is that both DOM and SAX parsers parse an XML file from the root element, which is the top element, down to the bottom elements. The other reason is simplicity; the recursive descent approach is easier to understand and to build. The class diagram of the project is illustrated in Figure 1.

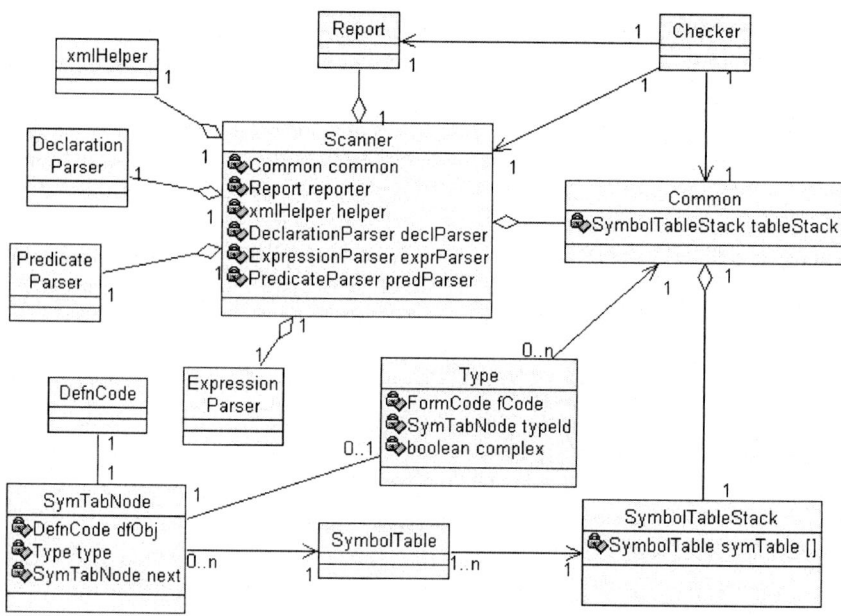

Fig. 1. Class diagram of the project

The two major functionalities of the type checker are to check syntax errors and to check static semantic errors in the TCOZ specifications in XML format. In the normal case, the program works as a 2-pass parser. When a forward declaration is present and recognized by the type checker, the XML document will be parsed again. At startup, the program takes a list of XML files as parameters. For each file, it calls the Xerces XML parser to

---

[1] Except for the Xerces XML Parser, no other parsing packages, utility functions such as Lex, YACC or JavaCC are used.

parse it and look for syntax errors. If there is any syntax error, the parser flags it then skips the file. If there is no syntax error, the program parses the file again, traversing through the structure to check for type errors. Upon encountering a type error, the program flags it, re-synchronizes itself and continues, until it finishes parsing all the files in the list. The TCOZ type checker has been designed in a way to support modularity and reusability. It is organized into Java packages.

3.2 Type Hierarchy and Rules

Figure 2 represents the hierarchy of types defined in the project. A utility class **FormCode** is also constructed. It has a set of constant definitions, each with a unique integer value identifying one of the types. The hierarchy consists of 10 types and their relationships as discussed below.

Type is the super class in the hierarchy and all other types inherit from **Type**, such as **EnumType**, **RecordType**, **RelationType**, and so on. **ClassType** defines a class as a type with inheritances.

Smith has developed type rules for Object-Z classes [11]. For example, given a generic state definition of class $A[X_1, ..., X_n]$, the state schema rule can be defined as follows:

$$[d_1, \Delta d_2 \mid p]$$

$$\frac{A[t_1, ..., t_n] :: STATE = [\uparrow STATE;\ b \odot d_1;\ b \odot d_2;\ \mid b \odot p] \vdash}{A[t_1, ..., t_n] :: \vdash} [\,q\,]$$

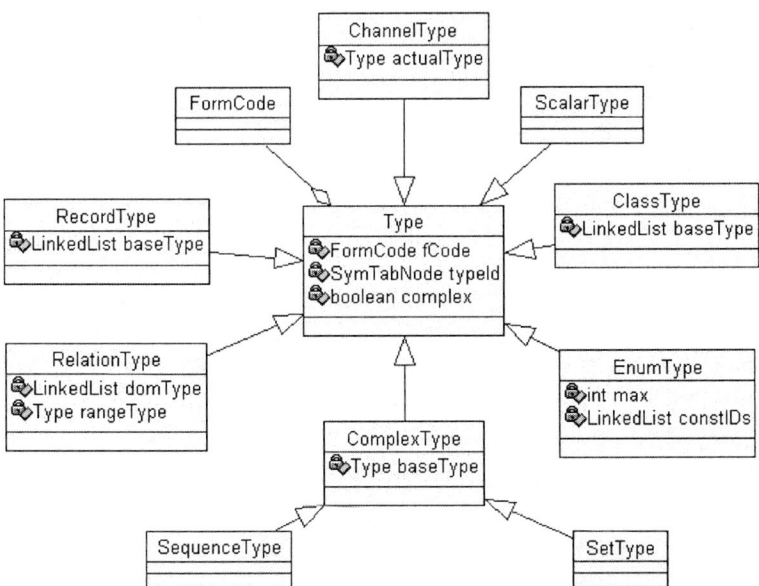

Fig. 2. Class hierarchy of the package TYPING

STATE refers to the state definition of a class, ↑ *STATE* stands for the inherited state definitions from its super classes, and the proviso q is in the form of $q \equiv b = (\!| X_1 \leadsto t_1, ..., X_n \leadsto t_n |\!)$ where t_i is the actual parameter substituted to X_i through substitution operator ⊙. Other type rules for operation schema and inheritance can be found in [11]. We extend Smith's work with extra type rules for additional TCOZ constructs. For example, the **ChannelType** inherits **Type**. Variables declared of **ChannelType** are used for inter-process communications. There are three kinds of channels: channel, sensor and actuator. A simple synchronized communication (Channel) typing rule for a generic network topology definition of classes A, B and AB, can be defined as follows:

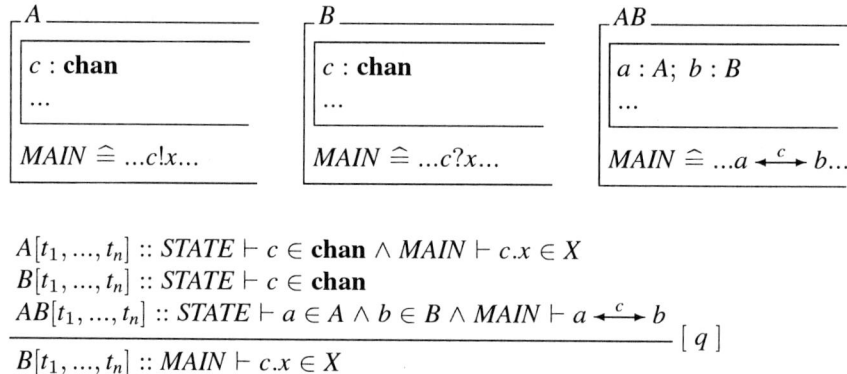

$$\frac{A[t_1,...,t_n] :: STATE \vdash c \in \mathbf{chan} \land MAIN \vdash c.x \in X}{B[t_1,...,t_n] :: STATE \vdash c \in \mathbf{chan}} \\ AB[t_1,...,t_n] :: STATE \vdash a \in A \land b \in B \land MAIN \vdash a \xleftrightarrow{c} b}{B[t_1,...,t_n] :: MAIN \vdash c.x \in X} [q]$$

The above states that if class A and B are communicating through channel c, synchronization will be enforced on the input and outputs, i.e., outputs from A through c will lead to inputs to B. The typing rules for the asynchronous communication (sensor/actuators) can be similarly developed.

RecordType, SetType and **SequenceType** can have no names associated with them; in other words, they can be anonymous types. The special scalar type **dummyType** is used in two ways. Firstly, it is used to signal type errors when parsing predicates, expressions and declarations. If the typing is correct, **boolType** *boolean* (for predicate) or respective data type (for expression and declaration) is returned; or else **dummyType** is returned. Secondly, it is used as the base type for empty sets or sequences, since an empty set can be subset of a set of any type.

Now we have finished the discussion on the development of a type checker for detecting static semantic errors for TCOZ specifications in XML format. Next we will discuss the development of an automatic tool for transforming TCOZ dynamic behaviour models to UML statecharts via XMI.

4 TCOZ to UML Statechart Projection

As a requirement specification of software systems, TCOZ models are precise and elegant but difficult to read and interpret by software engineers without relevant mathematical background. In comparison, the most popular graphical notation, UML, is much easier to understand and widely accepted by the industry. Our key idea for using UML statechart to visualize TCOZ is:

– States of UML Statechart are identified with TCOZ processes (operations) and the state transition links are identified with TCOZ events /guards.

In TCOZ, behavior of a class is specified by the operations as processes. Figure 3 shows the detailed transformation rules from TCOZ behaviour models to UML statecharts.

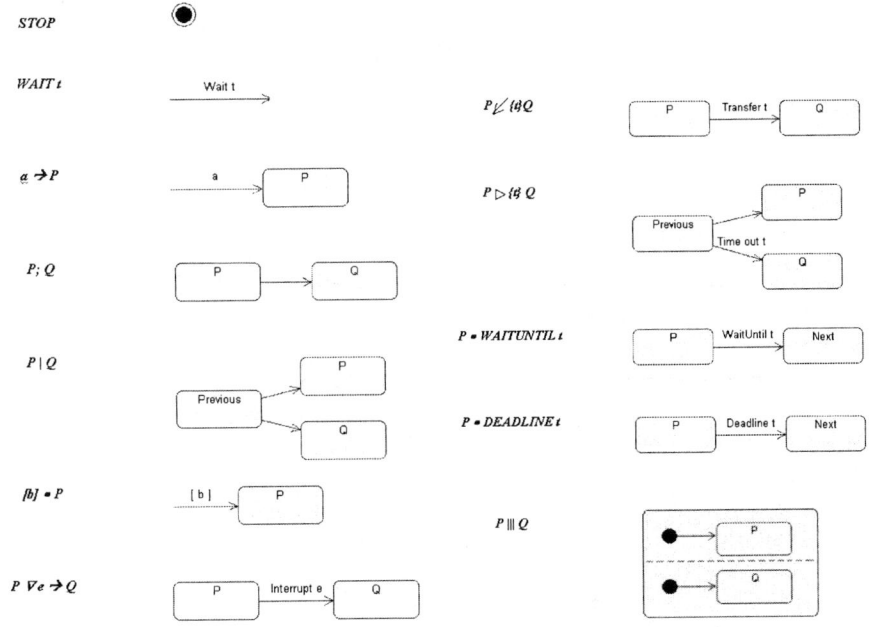

Fig. 3. UML projection rules

The projection rules for automatically translating TCOZ models (in XML) to UML Statecharts (in XMI) is implemented by a JAVA application. The following discusses the algorithm and implementation steps.

Step One: Preparation

At this stage, the XML file is read in and parsed class-by-class, operation-by-operation. A tag named *processexpr* is associated with each operation, which identifies the computational logic of the operation. The *processexpr* follows the grammar defined for TCOZ operation expressions. *processexpr* is divided into 13 types [2]. The activities preformed by the preprocessor are:

– Build up the operation table for each class.

---

[2] For detail information about fully annotated operation expressions, please refer to http://nt-appn.comp.nus.edu.sg/fm/zml/zml.xsd.

- Associate each class with its corresponding super class. One class may have more than one super class and it may invoke operations defined in different super classes.
- Build up the variable table for each class.
- For each operation, identify its *processexpr*. Check whether the operation invokes other operations. If not, mark this operation as a simple operation and generate the proper string representation of this operation. Otherwise, identify the type of the *processexpr*. For each type of *processexpr*, gather the important information for that type. For example, if the type is *networktopology*, identify what are the active objects and what are communication channels. For *processexpr* contained in *processexpr*, do the same recursively.

Step Two: Generation

For each active object, a new XMI file is created with the necessary header information. A top level composite state named 'op' is added to the Statemachine. An initial state (pseudostate) is added to the top-level composite state. A MAIN operation matches to a main state in the Statechart, which is the first state besides the initial state. Starting from the main operation, we syntactically analyze the *processexpr* based on the type information and generate proper states for each operation.

One challenge here is that at some point we may not know which projection rules could be used. For example, if some other operation is invoked by MAIN, shall we model the called operation as a simple state or a composite state? (At this point, we may not be able to find out whether the called operation will consequently invoke other operations.) One simple solution is to model all called operations as composite states and later replace those unnecessary composite states by simple states.

Step Three: Simplification

After the a complete Statechart is generated, the simplification process involves:

- Remove unnecessary simple states. "Unnecessary simple states" means state that are temporarily added into the statechart.
- Remove trivial composite states. "trivial composite state" means composite states that have one or even no substates.

Step Four: Layout

At this stage, we need to calculate the exact positions of all the states, transitions and events/guards in a diagram. The following formulas are used to calculate the width and height of a composite state. Given W the width, H the height, M the number of simple states in the composite state, N the number of composite states in the composite state. *WSimple* is the default width of any simple state. *HSimple* is the default height of any simple state. $W_1, \cdots, W_N$ are width for each composite state in this composite state. $H_1, \cdots, H_N$ is the height for each composite state in this composite state. S is the default horizontal space between states. K is the default vertical space between states. P is the width (or height) of any pseudostate and Q is the width (or height) of any final state.

$$W = max\{(\sqrt{M} + 1) * (WSimple + S), W_1, W_2, \cdots, W_N\} + 4S + P + Q$$
$$H = (\sqrt{M} + 1) * (HSimple + K) + (H_1 + H_2 + \cdots + H_N) + N * K$$

Note that the calculation is done in a bottom-up manner since the size of the outer composite state depends on the size of the inner one. Once we know the width and height, we place simple states at the top ($\sqrt{M}$ simple states per row) and composite states at the bottom (one per row).

5 Case Study: Light Control System

In this section, we firstly present a TCOZ LCS (Light Control System)[3] model. Then we use this model to test our type checker and transformation tool to UML statechart. The LCS system composes of *RoomController* and *RoomDevices*. *RoomController* controls the whole system. *RoomDevices* consists of lights and motion detectors. The TCOZ specification for LCS is given as follows. *Illmination* is an abstract type, *Percent* is defined as *Percent* == $\{0\} \cup 10..100$

─── *Light* ───────────────────────────────────
  dim : *Percent* **actuator**;   *on* : $\mathbb{B}$
  ─────────────────────────────
  TurningOn $\widehat{=}$ *dim* := 100; *on* := *true*
  TurningOff $\widehat{=}$ *dim* := 0; *on* := *false*
──

The *Light* class has two operations, *TurningOn* and *TurningOff*.

─── *ControlledLight* ─────────────────────────
  Light
  ─────────────────────────────
  button, *dimmer* : **chan**
  ─────────────────────────────
  ButtonPushing $\widehat{=}$ *button*?1 $\rightarrow$ ([*dim* > 0] • *TurningOff* $\Box$
    [*dim* = 0] • *TurningOn*)
  DimChange $\widehat{=}$ [*n* : *Percent*] • *dimmer*?*n* $\rightarrow$ ([*on*] • *dim* := *n* $\Box$
    [$\neg$ *on*] • SKIP)
  MAIN $\widehat{=}$ μN • (*ButtonPushing* $\Box$ *DimChange*); *N*
──

The *ControlledLight* is a subclass of *Light*. Two extra operations are defined: *ButtonPushing* and *DimChange*. Any occupant can manually turn on or turn off the light using *ButtonPushing* or the system will automatically adjust the illumination using *DimChange*. For each light, a CSP channel *button* is defined to capture the status of the button. The other channel *dimmer* is used to communicate with the system controller.

---
[3] LCS is an intelligent embedded control system. It can detect the occupation of the building, then turn on or turn off the lights automatically. It is able to adjust illumination in the building according to the outside light level. The full specification model can be found at: http://nt-appn.comp.nus.edu.sg/fm/zml/xml-web/light.xml

The *RoomController* controls both *MotionDetector* (for detecting any movement in the room) and *ControlledLight* by sending proper signals on channel *motion* and *dimmer*. (The *MotionDetector* definition is omitted due to space limitation.)

┌─ *RoomController* ──
│ ┌──
│ │ *dimmer*, *motion* : **chan**
│ │ *odsensor* : *Illumination* **sensor**
│ │ *absenT* : 𝕋
│ │ *olight* : *Illumination*
│ └──
│ ...   [behaviour part is omitted]
└──

5.1 Static Type Checking

Object-Z related type errors can be detected in a similar way as Wizard. The following example illustrates that the type checker spots TCOZ channel-related error and reports it. In the MAIN operation of class *LCS*, processes *m* and *r* (belonging to classes *MotionController* and *RoomController* respectively) communicate via a common channel called *motion*; *r* and *l* (belonging to *ControlledLight*) also communicate via another common channel called *dimmer*. Assuming that in class *RoomController*, the channel *motion* is renamed to *movement* and there is no other change to the specification:

┌─ *RoomController* ──
│ ┌──
│ │ *dimmer* : **chan**
│ │ *movement* : **chan**   [Changed!]
│ │ ...
│ └──
│ ...
└──

As a result, the processes *m* and *r* cannot communicate any more since they no longer share a common channel. This is captured by the type checker as follows.

```
Error!  LCS.xml: 305: Identifier not found Symbol: motion
Location:    SymTabNode: RoomController   >>
    Class Definition [Class Type: RoomController]

Error!  LCS.xml: 305: No common channel defined!
Symbol: motion Location: SymTabNode: Main >> Class Operation
    OF  SymTabNode: LCS >> Class Definition [Class Type: LCS]

LCS.xml parsed 2 times.

2 errors.
```

5.2 Dynamic UML Visualizing

In this subsection we will show how to apply projection techniques and the tool to generate a proper UML statechart from the LCS formal model. For *controlledLight*, we start from the MAIN operation since MAIN is the state that starting state leads to. By mapping the TCOZ notations to a Statechart diagram, a rough statechart is generated as shown in the left part of figure 4. After that, we apply projection rules to operation *DimChange* and *ButtonPushing* and get the final statechart as shown in the righthand side of figure 4.

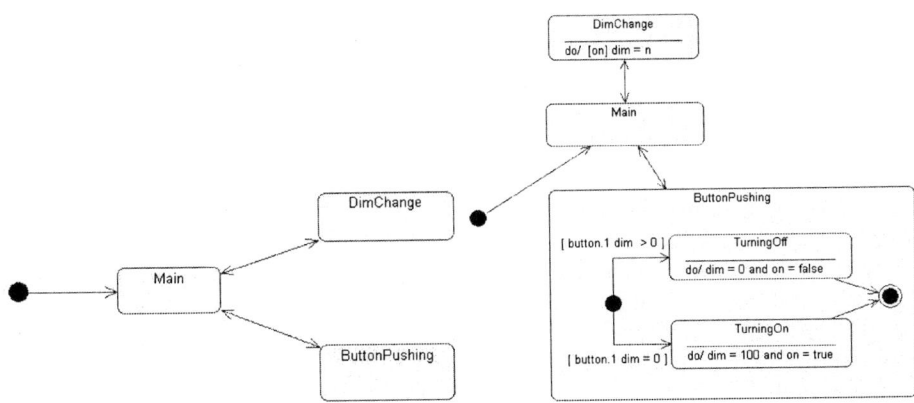

Fig. 4. Statechart for ControlledLight

6 Conclusions

The first contribution of the paper is the development of a syntax and static semantic checker for the TCOZ language in XML format, using a compiler approach. As TCOZ is a super set of Object-Z and Z, the type checker can also be used to type check Object-Z and Z specifications in XML format.

For the purpose of visualizing TCOZ behaviour model, the second part of the paper defined a set of projection rules for transforming a TCOZ model to UML statechart and demonstrated the implementation steps for the tool development.

In summary, this paper presents some 'light-weight' tool support for the TCOZ integrated formal specification technique. One future work on the type checker is to extend its capabilities with the techniques from ESC [9]. Looking at even more 'heave-weight' tools support, i.e. model checking and theorem proving, one further work is to translate TCOZ to timed automata so that tools like UPPAAL [2] can be used to check other TCOZ properties. We are currently also investigating the encoding of TCOZ notation in theorem provers such as HOL/Isabelle for automatic verification.

Acknowledgements

We would like to thank Hugh Anderson for many helpful comments. This work is supported by the Research Grants *Integrated Formal Methods* from National University of Singapore and *Techniques and Tools for Designing Embedded and Hybrid Systems* from Singapore A*STAR Program.

References

1. Xmi: Xml metadata interchange. http://www-4.ibm.com/software/ad/standards/xmi.html, 2000.
2. J. Bengtsson, K. Larsen, F. Larsson, P. Pettersson, and Y. Wang. UPPAAL - a tool suite for automatic verification of real-time systems. In *Hybrid Systems*, pages 232–243, 1995.
3. P. J. Brooke and R. F. Paige. The Design of a Tool-Supported Graphical Notation for Timed CSP. In *Proc. Integrated Formal Methods 2002 (IFM'02)*, pages 299–318, Turku, Finland, May 2002.
4. R. Duke and G. Rose. *Formal Object Oriented Specification Using Object-Z*. Cornerstones of Computing. Macmillan, March 2000.
5. W. Johnston. A type checker for Object-Z. Technical report 96-24, Software Verification Research Centre, School of Information Technology, The University of Queensland, Brisbane 4072. Australia, July 1996.
6. B. Mahony and J. S. Dong. Overview of the semantics of TCOZ. In K. Araki, A. Galloway, and K. Taguchi, editors, *IFM'99: Integrated Formal Methods, York, UK*, pages 66–85. Springer-Verlag, June 1999.
7. B. Mahony and J. S. Dong. Sensors and Actuators in TCOZ. In J. Wing, J. Woodcock, and J. Davies, editors, *FM'99: World Congress on Formal Methods*, Lect. Notes in Comput. Sci., pages 1166–1185, Toulouse, France, September 1999. Springer-Verlag.
8. B. Mahony and J. S. Dong. Timed Communicating Object Z. *IEEE Transactions on Software Engineering*, 26(2):150–177, February 2000.
9. G. Nelson, K. Rustan, M. Leino, J. Saxe, and R. Stata. Extended static checking home page. Available on the Internet from http://www.research.digital.com/SRC/esc/Esc.html., 1996.
10. S. Schneider and J. Davies. A brief history of Timed CSP. *Theoretical Computer Science*, 138, 1995.
11. G. Smith. Extending W for Object-Z. In J. P. Bowen and M. G. Hinchey, editors, *Proceedings of the 9th Annual Z-User Meeting*, pages 276–295. Springer-Verlag, September 1995.
12. G. Smith. *The Object-Z Specification Language*. Advances in Formal Methods. Kluwer Academic Publishers, 2000.
13. J. Sun, J. S. Dong, J. Liu, and H. Wang. A XML/XSL Approach to Visualize and Animate TCOZ. In J. He, Y. Li, and G. Lowe, editors, *The 8th Asia-Pacific Software Engineering Conference (APSEC'01)*, pages 453–460. IEEE Press, 2001.
14. J. Sun, J. S. Dong, J. Liu, and H. Wang. Object-Z Web Environment and Projections to UML. In *WWW-10: 10th International World Wide Web Conference*, pages 725–734. ACM Press, May 2001.
15. J. Woodcock and J. Davies. *Using Z: Specification, Refinement, and Proof*. Prentice-Hall International, 1996.

μ-Chart-Based Specification and Refinement

Doug Goldson[1], Greg Reeve[2], and Steve Reeves[2]

[1] School of Information Technology and Electrical Engineering,
University of Queensland,
Australia
goldson@itee.uq.edu.au
[2] Department of Computer Science,
University of Waikato,
New Zealand
{gregr,stever}@cs.waikato.ac.nz

Abstract. We introduce two new notions of refinement for μ-charts and compare them with the existing notion due to Scholz. The two notions are interesting and important because one gives rise (via a logic) to a calculus for constructing refinements and the other gives rise (via model checking) to a way of checking that refinements hold. Thus we bring together the two competing worlds of model checking and proof.

1 Introduction

μ-Charts are one of many Statechart-like languages: a family of visual languages that are used for designing reactive systems. They are simpler than the original Statecharts [2], which gives them a more comprehensible informal semantics, though just as expressive. Their formal semantics has been given denotationally using automata [10], and logically [4] using the specification language Z [11]. While different aspects, and versions, of μ-Charts have been published [7–9], the definitive account is published in [10]. Characteristic features of μ-Charts are that the output of control signals is *instantaneous* with the input of control signals; that communication on signals (feedback) between charts is *local* (pairwise) rather than global; and that charts may *nondeterministically* choose between state transitions.

The aim of this paper is to report recent work on refinement theories of μ-Charts, but limited space prevents illustration of how refinement can be used in reactive system design; for this, the reader is referred to an extended version of this paper [1]. Section 2 begins by introducing the language of μ-Charts, and the following sections outline two formal models of μ-Charts, the model in Section 3 uses the language CSP [3,5], while the model in Section 4 uses the language Z [11]. Note that both models share an important motivation for their development: the availability of computer tools to assist in their use. In the case of Z the tool is the proof-assistant Z/EVES [6], and for CSP the tool is the model-checker FDR [5]. Noteworthy too is the effect of this language (and tool) selection on practice. The synthetic, proof-oriented Z approach raises the potential for a calculus for constructing μ-Charts, where the analytic, model-checking CSP approach raises the potential for automatic verification of μ-Charts. Familiar tradeoffs to do with the methodology of system design, the ease of use of tools, and the limits of automation make it fit to present these two approaches side by side.

The ongoing work described in this paper can be viewed in two ways: an attempt to strengthen a language of reactive system design by augmenting it with new methods and computer tools; an attempt to reconceptualise the language in terms of new models. The one view does not exclude the other. That the language of μ-Charts is worthy of this attention we take for granted. Both [2] and [10] argue that the visual nature of Statecharts and μ-Charts strongly recommends their use. At the least, it can not be denied that visual languages carry a high value in computer and software engineering.

2 Introduction to μ-Charts

This section gives some background on the language of μ-Charts, but see [10] for the full story. A μ-Chart is either sequential or parallel. A sequential chart is a state machine where a transition in the chart is labelled with a pair, *guard/action*. The transition is conditional on the guard being satisfied and the action is caused by the transition being taken. Each chart has an input interface designating signals that can trigger a transition and an output interface designating signals that the chart can output. A fundamental assumption is that time passes in the control states of a chart, but the transitions between these states occur *instantaneously*. A chart reaction is therefore characterised by the input of a set of signals from the environment and the instantaneous output of a set of signals to the environment. This reaction is called a step or a tick of the clock, but note that this does not mean that the intervals between reactions must be equal.

In order to define large reactive systems, the language has two structuring mechanisms: hierarchic and parallel composition. In a parallel μ-Chart each component chart reacts *synchronously* on a global clock. A feedback mechanism between pairs of charts makes output signals instantaneously available as input signals, which allows component charts to communicate *asynchronously* on signals. While the feedback of signals can cause chain-reactions of input-output behaviour, where it makes sense to talk of micro-steps or micro-ticks, no such micro-behaviour is observable in the environment. In the environment, there is just one reaction/tick.

The states of a sequential chart may not be atomic, but rather one chart may be embedded in another as a sub-chart, using hierarchic composition. However, since [10] shows how to define hierarchic composition using parallel composition, this feature of μ-Charts will be ignored in this paper.

A sequential chart C has an input interface $in.C$ that typically includes all of the signals that may appear in its transition guards and an output interface $out.C$ that includes all of the signals that may appear in its transition actions. A parallel chart $C = C_1 \triangleleft l \triangleright C_2$ has an input interface $in.C = (in.C_1 \cup in.C_2) \setminus l$, which is restricted from feedback signals l, and an output interface $out.C = out.C_1 \cup out.C_2$.

The meaning of a chart is defined by its complete input-output behaviour over time. This abstracts on the control and data states of a chart by defining the chart by its reactions in the environment. In the Scholz model in [10], the meaning of a chart C is $[\![C]\!]_{io}$, where, given $(i, o) \in [\![C]\!]_{io}$, i is an infinite sequence of input events for C and o is an infinite sequence of output events for C. These events are defined by the input and output interfaces of C, where $i \in (\mathbb{P}(in.C))^\infty$ and $o \in (\mathbb{P}(out.C))^\infty$. An element of i is an input event, in the power set of $in.C$, and an element of o is an output event, in the power set of $out.C$. Pairwise elements of i and o are a reaction, i.e. (i_n, o_n) is the reaction of C at clock tick n of a particular run (i, o) of C. Note that the input traces i of a chart C, what the environment is willing to offer, are here defined in terms of the input interface $in.C$ of the chart, what the chart is able to react to from the environment (after fed back signals are removed from consideration).

To make the above ideas concrete we next give some example μ-Charts which illustrate the concrete syntax of charts. Define four simple charts A_1, A_2, B_1 and B_2:

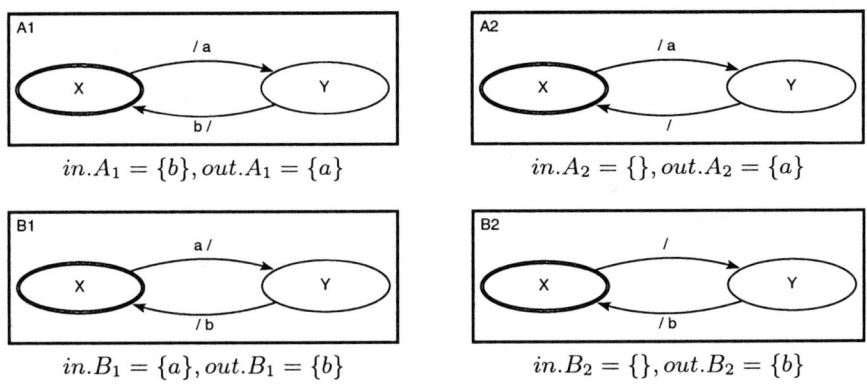

In A_1, the guard of the transition from X to Y is empty, which makes it an unconditional transition. This transition causes the signal a to be output. The transition from Y to X, on the other hand, is conditional on signal b being on the input. This transition causes a change of state, but no output. The other charts can be interpreted in a similar way.

Next define a family of four parallel charts, each with the same interface. Firstly:

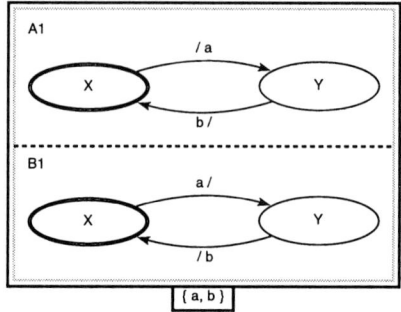

which has interface $in._ = \{\}$, $out._ = \{a, b\}$. In this chart the output a of A_1 and b of B_1 are instantaneously fedback into the component charts. Informally tracing its behaviour, initially, *i.e.* at the beginning of the first tick, both components are in their X states. At the first tick A_1 outputs a which triggers a transition in B_1 so that, at the end of the first tick, both components are in their Y states and a is output. At the second tick B_1 outputs b which triggers a transition in A_1 so that, at the end of the second tick, both components are in their X states and b is output, and so the two components make progress in perfect synchrony. The remaining three parallel charts are[1]: $A_1 \triangleleft \{b\} \triangleright B_2$, $A_2 \triangleleft \{a\} \triangleright B_1$ and $A_2 \triangleleft \{\} \triangleright B_2$. Subsequent sections will formally characterise the behaviour of parallel charts, and argue that these four charts are all equal.

Finally, before discussing formal models, it is important to distinguish two types of μ-Chart model: chaotic and nonchaotic models. Call a chart *responsive* if in every state, every input event (as defined by the input interface) has an enabled transition, and, equivalently, call it *non-responsive* if some input event, say *ie*, does not have an enabled transition in some state, say X. The semantic model is *chaotic* if a chart that is non-responsive behaves chaotically after *ie* is input in X, where chaotic behaviour involves arbitrarily changing control state, changing data state, outputing signals in the output interface, or none of these things. The semantic model is called *nonchaotic* if a chart that is non-responsive does nothing after *ie* is input in X.

To give an example, consider chart A_1 above. Its input interface defines its input events as $\{\{\}, \{b\}\}$, which makes A_1 non-responsive on input event $\{\}$ in state Y. In the chaotic model, A_1 is therefore equal to CA_1:

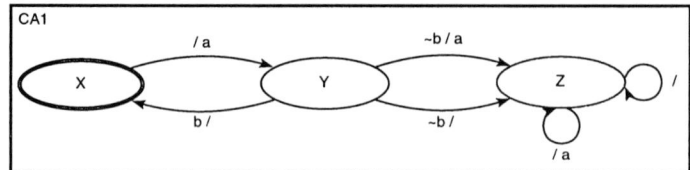

The guard $\sim b$ is true when signal b is not on the input. In words, after $\{\}$ in Y, CA_1 may or may not output a, after which it may or may not output a whether

---

[1] Henceforth we will present parallel charts in their textual form for the sake of brevity.

b is or is not input. Contrariwise, in the nonchaotic model of A_1, after $\{\}$ in Y, A_1 outputs nothing and remains in state Y.

Note that any chart C can be translated into a responsive chart $resp.C$ with the same interface, such that the behaviour of C in the nonchaotic model is equal to the behaviour of $resp.C$ in the chaotic model. The translation is made by adding a *donothing* transition to each state of C, which is a self-loop with command $\sim(g_1 \wedge \ldots \wedge g_n)/$, where g_i are the guards of all other exit transitions on the state. Call this function $resp.C$, the *responsive translation* of C. In this example, $resp.A_1$ is simply:

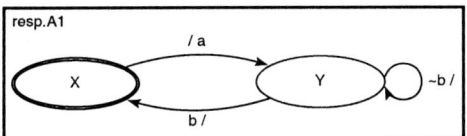

3 The CSP Model

The operational semantics of μ-Charts using the language CSP [3, 5] is the most recent attempt to mathematise μ-Charts; indeed, it is still under development. As befits an operational semantics, it is a nonchaotic model. This section concentrates on showing how a CSP trace semantics of charts can be used to define a new concept of μ-Chart refinement that imitates the Scholz relation in [10]. After introducing the trace semantics, the new chart refinement relation is defined in Section 3.1. Recalling the practical motivation for this work, Section 3.2 ends by showing how a chart refinement can be expressed as a CSP trace refinement, and so automatically tested using the model-checking tool FDR [5].

In the CSP model, the meaning of a chart C is the set of its CSP traces, where an input event x and an (instantaneous) output event y are communicated on two CSP channels *input* and *output* such that a trace of C has the form of paired communications on these channels, which are the only observable CSP events in the model[2]. Schematically, a trace of C looks like

$$\langle input.x_0, output.y_0, input.x_1, output.y_1, \ldots \rangle$$

In this way, a pair of CSP events *input.x* and *output.y* models a single reaction/clock tick/pair of instantaneous chart events x and y in a single trace/run/history of the modelled chart.

Now let function $tr.is.C.os$ designate the translation of chart C where $\mathbb{P}(is)$ is the type of input events on channel *input* and $\mathbb{P}(os)$ is the type of output events on channel *output*. In this way, translating C as $tr.(in.C).C.(out.C)$ makes it agree with the Scholz model of charts, in so far as the chart interface determines the type of its input and output events. In what follows, this translation is abbreviated to $tr.C$, so we have $tr.C =_{def} tr.(in.C).C.(out.C)$.

The traces of a parallel composition of two charts can now be defined in terms of the traces of its component charts:

---

[2] Since CSP traces are finite, this is an important difference to the Scholz model.

Trace definition of $C_1 \triangleleft l \triangleright C_2$:

$\forall s :: \exists t, u :: \forall i :: \exists v, x, y, z ::$

$$s \in traces.(tr.(C_1 \triangleleft l \triangleright C_2))$$

$\Longleftrightarrow$

$(\quad even.i \Rightarrow$
$\quad(\qquad (s.i = input.v \wedge s.(i+1) = output.x \wedge x = y \cup z)$
$\qquad \Longleftrightarrow$
$\qquad (t \in traces.(tr.C_1) \wedge t.i = input.((v \cup (x \cap l)) \cap in.C_1) \wedge t.(i+1) = output.y$
$\qquad \wedge$
$\qquad u \in traces.(tr.C_2) \wedge u.i = input.((v \cup (x \cap l)) \cap in.C_2) \wedge u.(i+1) = output.z)$
$\quad)$
$)$

This definition is intended to correspond to the definition of $[\![C_1 \triangleleft l \triangleright C_2]\!]_{io}$ in the Scholz model. In words, the output event of reaction i, $x = y \cup z$, of $C_1 \triangleleft l \triangleright C_2$ is defined by the output events y of C_1 and z of C_2, where these, in turn, are defined by the instantaneous feedback of x into C_1 and C_2, after x is restricted to the allowable feedback signals l. Further, the input event of C_i must also be restricted to its input interface $in.C_i$.

3.1 Chart Refinement in the CSP Model

The CSP trace semantics of charts gives rise to a concomitant notion of chart refinement, which is defined using the auxiliary function $rest$: function $rest.t.z.w$ restricts trace t to the input signals in z and output signals in w:

$rest.\langle\rangle.z.w = \langle\rangle$
$rest.(\langle input.x, output.y \rangle \frown t).z.w =$
$\quad \langle input.(x \cap z), output.(y \cap w) \rangle \frown rest.t.z.w$

The chart refinement of C_1 by C_2 is now defined:

Trace definition of $\sqsubseteq$:

$C_1 \sqsubseteq C_2 \quad =_{def}$
$\quad in.C_1 \subseteq in.C_2 \wedge out.C_1 \subseteq out.C_2 \wedge$
$\quad \forall t : t \in traces.(tr.C_2) : rest.t.(in.C_1).(out.C_1) \in traces.(tr.C_1)$

In words, C_2 refines C_1 if its interface is not smaller and every trace of C_2, after it is restricted to the interface of C_1, is a trace of C_1.

That the refinement relation is transitive is easily proved [1], so we have:

$\sqsubseteq$ is a transitive relation:

$C_1 \sqsubseteq C_2 \wedge C_2 \sqsubseteq C_3 \Rightarrow C_1 \sqsubseteq C_3$

$\sqsubseteq$ is a compositional relation:

$$l \cap out.C_1 = l \cap out.C_2 \Rightarrow$$
$$C_1 \sqsubseteq C_2 \Rightarrow C_1 \triangleleft l \triangleright C_3 \sqsubseteq C_2 \triangleleft l \triangleright C_3$$

In words, if C_2 refines C_1 then C_2 composed with C_3 refines C_1 composed with C_3, provided that the fedback signals in the output $out.C_2$ are also in the output $out.C_1$.

3.2 Practicalities

The previous section defines a chart refinement $C_1 \sqsubseteq C_2$ in terms of the trace sets of its translating processes $traces.(tr.(in.C_i).C_i.(out.C_i))$:

$$t \in traces.(tr.(in.C_2).C_2.(out.C_2)) \Rightarrow$$
$$rest.t.(in.C_1).(out.C_1) \in traces.(tr.(in.C_1).C_1.(out.C_1))$$

Recall that arguments $in.C_i$ and $out.C_i$ of function tr determine the types of values communicated on channels *input* and *output*, and note that these types may be different in the two translations. But in order for a chart refinement $C_1 \sqsubseteq C_2$ to be automatically tested, it must be expressible as a trace refinement of the translations of C_1 and C_2, and for this, the types of *input* and *output* in each translation must agree.

First note that in the translation $tr.is.C.os$ of C it is possible to make the type of *output*, $\mathbb{P}(os)$, smaller than the type $\mathbb{P}(out.C)$ of C's output events. In such a case, where C can output an event $y \subseteq out.C$ but $y \not\subseteq os$, the value communicated on *output* is simply event $y \cap os$, the event y restricted to signals in the type of *output*.

Automation of chart refinement is now achieved by restricting the input interfaces of C_1 and C_2 to be equal (see [1]):

Automation of $\sqsubseteq$:

$$in.C_1 = in.C_2 \wedge out.C_1 \subseteq out.C_2 \Rightarrow$$
$$tr.(in.C_1).C_1.(out.C_1) \sqsubseteq_T tr.(in.C_1).C_2.(out.C_1) \iff C_1 \sqsubseteq C_2$$

The practical use of this chart refinement is illustrated by returning to the example charts of Section 2. For instance, the equality of $A_1 \triangleleft \{a,b\} \triangleright B_1$ and $A_2 \triangleleft \{\} \triangleright B_2$ is easily tested as a mutual refinement:

$$A_1 \triangleleft \{a,b\} \triangleright B_1 = A_2 \triangleleft \{\} \triangleright B_2$$
$$\iff$$
$$A_1 \triangleleft \{a,b\} \triangleright B_1 \sqsubseteq A_2 \triangleleft \{\} \triangleright B_2 \sqsubseteq A_1 \triangleleft \{a,b\} \triangleright B_1$$
$$\iff \quad \{\text{Interfaces are equal}\}$$
$$tr.(A_1 \triangleleft \{a,b\} \triangleright B_1) \sqsubseteq_T tr.(A_2 \triangleleft \{\} \triangleright B_2) \sqsubseteq_T tr.(A_1 \triangleleft \{a,b\} \triangleright B_1)$$

And while it is possible to characterise the behaviour of a chart C by defining a (usually complex) predicate on its traces, it is easier, more comprehensible, and *testable* to define a specifying chart S and then show that C refines S. In the present case, to understand the behaviour of $A_1 \triangleleft \{a,b\} \triangleright B_1$, define S_1 with an equal interface:

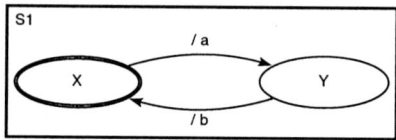

and show that $S_1 = A_1 \triangleleft \{a,b\} \triangleright B_1$. In words, the chart behaves by outputing a, then outputing b and repeating.

A characteristic of a concurrent system is that a simple change to its definition requires a difficult re-analysis of its meaning. For example, reducing the fedback signals in $A_1 \triangleleft \{a,b\} \triangleright B_1$ from $\{a,b\}$ to $\{a\}$ gives chart:

$$A_1 \triangleleft \{a\} \triangleright B_1: in.\_ = \{b\}, \quad out.\_ = \{a,b\}$$

where the simplicity of the equivalent (specifying) chart S_2:

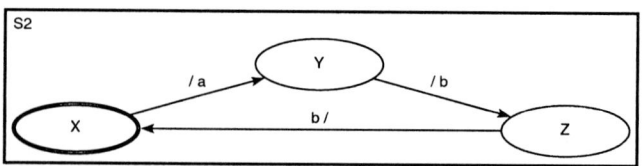

belies the difficulty of understanding $A_1 \triangleleft \{a\} \triangleright B_1$ using pencil and paper operational analysis. In words, this chart behaves by outputing a, then outputing b and then waiting for b on the input before repeating.

4 The Z Model

As an alternative to the CSP approach above, the meaning of a μ-Chart can also be given by the systematic translation of a μ-Chart specification into Z.[3] Our claim is that once translated the behaviour captured by the μ-Chart specification can be investigated and refined using all of the typical Z methods, such as stating and proving critical requirements of the system, animation of the specification, using refinement to guide system design from specification, and showing that refinements hold between specifications at differing levels of abstraction. We thus have two ways to attack the problems arising when specifying reactive or interactive systems: the attractive graphical formalism of charts together with a vocabulary, familiar to engineers, of states and transitions; and the powerful

---

[3] We have developed tools which allow us to draw and edit chart diagrams and translate them automatically into Z.

toolset available for Z together with the alternative view of the system that translation into Z brings.

Here we concentrate on the process of using Z refinement to check refinements between two separate chart specifications. This is in order that we can contrast refinements in the Z model with the original notion of refinement for μ-Charts given by Scholz and likewise with refinements in the CSP model.

Although it is possible to give a Z model with the same interpretation as Scholz's chaotic model, the initial Z model, and the one used here, is a nonchaotic model and therefore gives the same interpretation to charts as the CSP model.

Since we do not have space to describe the translation of μ-Charts into Z, we leave the reader to consult [4]. Suffice to say, the translation requires the description of each sequential chart of the specification (by giving appropriate Z state schemas for each of its states and operation schemas for each of its transitions), and then the combination of these, respecting any chart structure, into a single schema that describes any given step of the system.

4.1 Chart Refinement in the Z Model

We denote the Z translation of a chart C (as introduced above) by $[\![C]\!]$. Our goal in this section is to define the relation $C_1 \sqsubseteq C_2$ in terms of a Z refinement relationship between the corresponding Z models for the respective charts, i.e. in terms of $[\![C_1]\!] \sqsubseteq_Z [\![C_2]\!]$.

First we consider what we mean when we say that a chart C_2 refines another chart C_1. Like Scholz we define the notion of chart refinement in terms of not increasing nondeterminism and not decreasing the interface with which the chart interacts with the environment.

Not increasing nondeterminism requires that the refinement C_2 exhibits no more behaviour than C_1 over the interface of C_1. Not decreasing the interface allows C_2 to exhibit new behaviour outside of the interface of C_1. Therefore C_2 may react to more signals and output more signals than C_1, but when restricted to the interface of C_1, C_2 must do no more than C_1.

In order to define such a refinement relation we introduce a notion of *corresponding configurations*. By definition a configuration X of C_1 corresponds to a configuration Y of C_2 if and only if there exists at least one sequence of inputs such that if C_1 and C_2 start in their initial states and react to this sequence of inputs they will end in configurations X and Y respectively, having given an output sequence that agrees over the intersection of their respective output interfaces. We denote the set of corresponding configurations for charts C_1 and C_2 by $corr(C_1, C_2)$.

The notion of corresponding configurations captures, for the Z model, the dynamic information about charts that is present in a trace semantics. As is to be expected, both the CSP and Z models of charts have to encode essentially the same information but they do it in ways which are natural to them—in the case of CSP this is done in terms of traces and in the case of Z it is done by modelling states and state changes.

$[\![C]\!]$ is, essentially, a relation between inputs, outputs, starting configurations and ending configurations. It is true, which we shall write by saying $[\![C]\!](i, o, c, c')$ holds, if starting in configuration c with input i we end in configuration c' having had output o.

Given this, we can consider refinement for charts. Recall that this is about not increasing nondeterminism, which is to say that C_2 does no more than C_1 (over C_1's interface), i.e. everything that C_2 does, C_1 can do too. This is expressed by saying that if C_2 moves between configurations due to some input, giving some output, then C_1 moves between corresponding configurations given the same input, and giving the same output.

$$C_1 \sqsubseteq C_2 =_{def}$$
$$in.C_1 \subseteq in.C_2 \wedge out.C_1 \subseteq out.C_2 \wedge$$
$$\forall (x,y) \in corr(C_1, C_2); i \subseteq in.C_2; o \subseteq out.C_2;$$
$$v \in conf(C_2) \bullet [\![C_2]\!](i, o, y, v) \Rightarrow \exists u \in conf(C_1) \bullet$$
$$[\![C_1]\!](i \cap in.C_1, o \cap out.C_1, x, u) \wedge (u, v) \in corr(C_1, C_2)$$

where the predicate $conf(C)$ gives the set of all configurations for chart C.

Finally, using the standard definitions of Z refinement, we can show that the following, which relates chart refinement to Z refinement, holds:

$$C_1 \sqsubseteq C_2 \iff$$
$$in.C_1 \subseteq in.C_2 \wedge out.C_1 \subseteq out.C_2 \wedge$$
$$\forall (x,y) \in corr(C_1, C_2); i \subseteq in.C_2; o \subseteq out.C_2; v \in conf(C_2) \bullet$$
$$\exists u \in conf(C_1) \bullet$$
$$[\![C_1]\!](i \cap in.C_1, o \cap out.C_1, x, u) \sqsubseteq_Z [\![C_2]\!](i, o, y, v)$$

As with the CSP definition for $\sqsubseteq$ in Section 3.1 we also have that the relation is transitive and compositional. Proofs for these results and the equivalence above are given in[1] since we do not have space to present them here.

5 Comparing Refinement Relations

The refinement relation $\rightsquigarrow$ on charts described in [10] is defined:

$$C_1 \rightsquigarrow C_2 \quad =_{def}$$
$$in.C_1 \subseteq in.C_2 \wedge out.C_1 \subseteq out.C_2 \wedge$$
$$\forall i : i \in (\mathbb{P}(in.C_2))^\infty : \forall o : o \in (\mathbb{P}(out.C_2))^\infty :$$
$$(i, o) \in [\![C_2]\!]_{io} \Rightarrow (i|in.C_1, o|out.C_1) \in [\![C_1]\!]_{io}$$

where $s|x$ designates the elementwise restriction of infinite sequence s to set x, i.e., the map of $\lambda y.y \cap x$ over s.

Since the refinement relation in both the CSP model and the Z model has been defined to imitate the Scholz notion of refinement, it is tempting to suppose them equivalent. They are not, for the reason that the Scholz model of μ-Charts is chaotic, but the CSP and Z models are not. To give an example of a refinement in the Scholz model that is not a refinement in either the CSP or Z model, take charts A_1 and CA_1 from Section 2 and chart A_3 defined as follows:

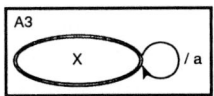

This gives:

$A_1 \rightsquigarrow A_3$
$\quad \iff \quad \{A_1 = CA_1\}$
$CA_1 \rightsquigarrow A_3$
$\quad \iff \quad \{\text{Note 1}\}$
$true$
$\quad \iff \quad \{\text{Note 2}\}$
$A_1 \sqsubseteq A_3$

Note 1: A_3 refines CA_1 in the Scholz model. Both charts are responsive. By inspection of A_3, at every tick A_3 *must* output a. By inspection of CA_1, at every tick CA_1 *may* output a.

Note 2: A_3 does not refine A_1 in either the CSP or the Z model. At every tick A_3 must output a. At the second tick A_1 can not output a.

While a CSP or Z refinement is not equivalent to a Scholz refinement, given that $resp.C$ has the same meaning in the chaotic model as C has in the non-chaotic models, it is equivalent after responsive translation of charts:

$$C_1 \sqsubseteq C_2 \iff resp.C_1 \rightsquigarrow resp.C_2$$

In the example above, this gives:

$A_1 \sqsubseteq A_3$
$\iff$
$resp.A_1 \rightsquigarrow resp.A_3$
$\quad \iff \quad \{resp.A_3 = A_3\}$
$resp.A_1 \rightsquigarrow A_3$
$\quad \iff \quad \{\text{Note}\}$
$false$

Note: A_3 does not refine $resp.A_1$ in the Scholz model. At every tick A_3 must output a. At the second tick $resp.A_1$ can not output a.

6 Conclusions

Two formal models of μ-Charts have been presented, with each giving concomitant notions of refinement. The reasons for developing the models have already been given: to give a better understanding of the complex semantics of μ-Chart models, and to provide automatic assistance in μ-Chart design. An extended version of this paper will appear as [1], to include proofs of results herein and a small example of charts to show the use of refinement in design and the place of computer tools.

As to future work, the operational semantics of μ-Charts using CSP is currently being revised in order to closer align it to a nonchaotic interpretation of the semantics in [10]. After which there is the need to test the two models and tools on some demanding case studies, in order to test their scalability, and where it is hoped that the two complementary approaches will yield a combination that is greater than the sum of its parts.

References

1. D. Goldson, G. Reeve, S. Reeves μ-Chart-based specification and refinement, *SVRC Technical Report 02-21*. 2002. (To appear)
2. D. Harel. Statecharts: A Visual Formalism for Complex Systems, in *Science of Computer Programming.* 8:231-274, 1987.
3. C. A. R. Hoare. *Communicating Sequential Processes*. Prentice Hall, 1985.
4. G. Reeve, S. Reeves. μ-Charts and Z: Hows, Whys and Wherefores, in *Proceedings of IFM2000: The Second International Conference on Integrated Formal Methods*, (eds.) W. Grieskamp, T. Santen, B. Stoddart. pp. 256-276. Springer LNCS 1945, 2000.
5. A. W. Roscoe. *The Theory and Practice of Concurrency*. Prentice Hall, 1998.
6. M. Saaltink. The Z/EVES system. In J. Bowen, M. Hinchey, and D. Till, editors, *Proc. 10th Int. Conf. on the Z Formal Method (ZUM)*, volume 1212 of *Lecture Notes in Computer Science*, pages 72–88. Springer-Verlag, Berlin, April 1997.
7. P. Scholz, J. Philips. Compositional Specification of Embedded Systems with Statecharts, in *TAPSOFT '97: Theory and Practice of Software Development*. (eds.) M. Bidoit, M. Dauchet. pp. 637-651. Springer LNCS 1214, 1997.
8. P. Scholz, J. Philips. Formal Verification of Statecharts with Instantaneous Chain Reactions, in *TACAS '97: Tools and Algorithms for the Construction and Analysis of Systems*. (ed.) E. Brinksma, pp. 224-238. Springer LNCS 1217, 1997.
9. P. Scholz. A Refinement Calculus for Statecharts, in *FASE '98: Fundamental Approaches to Software Engineering*. (ed.) E. Astesiano. pp. 285-301. Springer LNCS 1382, 1998.
10. P. Scholz. *Design of Reactive Systems and their Distributed Implementation with Statecharts*. PhD Thesis, Technical University of Munich. TUM-I9821, 1998. http://www.informatik.tu-muenchen.de/forschung/report/1998/
11. J. M. Spivey. *The Z notation: A reference manual*. Prentice Hall, 1989.

Towards a Refinement Calculus for Concurrent Real-Time Programs

Sibylle Peuker[1] and Ian Hayes[2]

[1] Software Verification Research Centre.
[2] School of Information Technology and Electrical Engineering,
The University of Queensland, Australia
sibylle@svrc.uq.edu.au
ianh@itee.uq.edu.au

Abstract. We define a language and a predicative semantics to model concurrent real-time programs. We consider different communication paradigms between the concurrent components of a program: communication via shared variables and asynchronous message passing (for different models of channels).
The semantics is the basis for a refinement calculus to derive machine-independent concurrent real-time programs from specifications. We give some examples of refinement laws that deal with concurrency.

1 Introduction

The importance of methods for the stepwise refinement of programs was already advocated in [13] and is well-known. Based on the refinement calculus [11, 1], and the real-time refinement calculus for sequential programs [8], we aim at a method for stepwise refinement of concurrent real-time programs.

In a concurrent program, several processes operate concurrently to achieve a common goal. Usually, the processes have to communicate with each other during an execution. The semantics of a concurrent program depends to a high degree on the model of communication.

We define a language that allows one to model different forms of communication: shared variables and asynchronous message passing with arbitrary different models of channels, e.g. blocking channels and infinite FIFO channels.

The real-time language contains a non-implementable specification command (as in [11]), and the likewise non-implementable **deadline** command [4]. Syntax and semantics of the language are a development of the real-time language for sequential programs introduced by Hayes and Utting [8]. We define refinement in a similar way, and most of the refinement laws for sequential programs from [8] hold as well in the concurrent language. Therefore, we concentrate on refinement laws that are crucial and specific for the development of concurrent programs. We give a law for refinement steps that independently refine both sides of a parallel composition and a law that increases the degree of distribution of a program by refining a specification command into two specification commands that run in parallel.

There are other approaches for developing concurrent real-time programs from specifications [12, 10]. The languages used in these approaches differ mainly in their expression of timing constraints. We express deadlines via the **deadline** command which may be placed anywhere in the program. In the Temporal Agent Model (TAM) [12], deadlines are expressed as a constraint on the allowed execution time for a command. Hooman and Roosmalen [10] associate a constant with each atomic command that represents its execution moment (i.e. the time at the moment of execution). The timing constraints for the program must be expressed by assigning constraints on the execution moment of individual commands.

Program derivation and analysis using the **deadline** *command.* Using valid refinement laws, the specification of a program is refined into a final program that only contains implementable commands (such as assignments) and **deadline** commands. Whereas a specification command has to be "refined away" before implementing the program, a **deadline** command is part of the final program. The final program is provably correct but each command of the form **deadline** D "ensures" that its execution takes place before time D. A command providing this cannot be implemented. The final program is implemented using the deadline commands as directives which allow for timing analysis of the program. The implemented program is correct if all deadlines are met and this depends on the concrete machine on which the program is implemented.

Nevertheless, the **deadline** command allows for a timing constraint analysis in three phases such that two of the phases are machine-independent and the third, machine-dependent phase is a check when the properties of the machine are known. Grundon, Hayes, and Fidge describe the first two phases for sequential programs [5]. In the first phase, all timing paths ending with a deadline command are extracted from the control flow graph of the program. Then for each path a timing constraint for the worst case execution time of this path is determined.

Timing path extraction and analysis in concurrent programs is more complex than in sequential programs because whether a deadline is met may depend on several parallel processes. However, a formal discussion of the timing constraint analysis is beyond the scope of this paper. We only discuss the derivation of the final program and give a simple informal example for timing path extraction and analysis.

Structure of the Paper. In Section 2, we give the syntax and semantics of the language to model programs that communicate via shared variables. In Section 3, we extend this language to model programs that communicate via asynchronous message passing. In Section 4, we show the feasibility of the defined language as a basis for a real-time refinement calculus by stating two refinement laws. In Section 5, we illustrate the language, the refinement laws, and the timing constraint analysis by means of a simple example.

2 Language and Meaning

We assume a global time that is accessible for each process. We model time by non-negative real numbers, Time $\triangleq \{r \in \mathbb{R} \mid 0 \leq r\}$. We distinguish four kinds of variables: input variables, output variables, local variables and the distinguished variable τ. The variable τ always stands for the current time. In order to allow non-terminating processes, we allow τ to equal infinity. Hence, we always have $\tau \in \text{Time} \cup \{\infty\}$. All variables except τ are traces over time, i.e. mappings from Time into a set of values. For the purpose of this paper, we assume a universal set of values $\mathcal{V}$ for all variables. $\mathcal{V}$ contains at least the real numbers ($\mathbb{R}$), the natural numbers ($\mathbb{N}$), and the booleans ($\mathbb{B} \mathrel{\widehat{=}} \{\textbf{true}, \textbf{false}\}$). Typing is the option to restrict the set $\mathcal{V}$ for each variable. We omit the possibility of typing because it does not add anything new.

Local variables have a fixed scope inside a process. Local variables and output variables are controlled by the process, i.e. they may only be changed by the process. Input variables are not under the control of the process. An input variable i of a process A may be an output variable for a process B that runs in parallel. Hence i may be changed by B but it changes non-deterministically from the process A's point of view.

Processes are built from the real-time specification command (see below), primitive real-time commands (such as the assignment command), and compound real-time commands (such as the parallel or sequential composition of two commands). We sometimes use the notion *process* as a synonym for command if it is more intuitive, e.g. in the parallel composition of two processes.

The *meaning* of a command is given with respect to an *environment*. An environment $\rho = (in(\rho), out(\rho))$ determines a set $in(\rho)$ (of names) of input variables, and a set $out(\rho)$ (of names) output variables. The environment could be extended to specify the types of the variables but as mentioned before, we omit this possibility in this paper.

Most of the commands have restrictions on the variables involved, e.g. $x : \textbf{read}(i)$ requires that i is an input variable and x is an output variable for the command. To define a meaningful environment for a command, we define for each command C a set $in(C)$ that determines the minimal set of input variables of the environment and a set $out(C)$ that determines the minimal set of output variables of the environment.

An environment ρ is *meaningful* for a command C if it contains at least the input and output variables of C, i.e. $in(C) \subseteq in(\rho)$ and $out(C) \subseteq out(\rho)$. We call a command together with a meaningful environment ρ a *program*.

The meaning of a command C in a meaningful environment ρ is given by a meaning function $\mathcal{M}_\rho$. The meaning function returns a logical formula for each command. Similar to [6, 9], we define refinement for commands C and D in the environment ρ as reverse implication. If ρ is meaningful for both C and D then C is refined by D with respect to ρ (denoted by $C \sqsubseteq_\rho D$) if, and only if, $\mathcal{M}_\rho(D) \Rightarrow \mathcal{M}_\rho(C)$, where $\Rightarrow$ means logical implication for all possible values of the free variables. We write $C \sqsubseteq D$, if the meaningful environments of C and D coincide and $C \sqsubseteq_\rho D$ is valid for all meaningful environments ρ. C and D are *equivalent* (denoted by $C \sqsupseteq\sqsubseteq D$), if and only if, $C \sqsubseteq D$ and $D \sqsubseteq C$.

2.1 The Real-Time Specification Command

The meaning of the primitive real-time commands is based on the meaning of the real-time specification command. The real-time specification command has the form $\infty \vec{x} : [P, \; Q]$. The '$\infty$' indicates that it is possible for the command to not terminate. Given, that the precondition P holds at the start then the command establishes the postcondition Q. During the execution the variables $\vec{x}$ (the frame of the command) may be changed. All other output variables remain stable.

Definition 1 (stable). *Given a variable v and a non-empty subset $S \subseteq \text{Time}$, let the image set of S with respect to v be denoted by $v(\!|\, S \,|\!)$, then we define $\text{stable}(v, S) \stackrel{\frown}{=} (\exists\, x \bullet v(\!|\, S \,|\!) = \{x\})$.*

Convention: τ_0 stands for the starting time of a command, and for each time-traced variable x in a real-time command, x_0 stands for $x(\tau_0)$, the initial value of x, and the unsubscripted form x stands for $x(\tau)$, the final value of x. We extend this to predicates, i.e. P_0 is the predicate P with all occurrences of free variables replaced by their zero-subscripted forms. Furthermore, for a vector $\vec{x}$ we use $\vec{x}$ as well to denote the set of all variables of the vector. It is always clear from the context if we mean the vector or the set of all variables of the vector.

Definition 2 (real-time specification). *Given an environment, ρ, a frame, $\vec{x}$ that is a vector of distinct variables that are contained in $out(\rho)$, a predicate P without initial (zero-subscripted) variables, and a predicate Q that may involve initial variables, the meaning of a possibly nonterminating real-time specification command is defined by the following.*

$$\mathcal{M}_\rho\left(\infty \vec{x}\colon\ [P,\ Q]\right) \stackrel{\frown}{=} \begin{array}{l} \tau_0 \leq \tau \wedge ((\tau_0 < \infty \wedge P_0) \\ \Rightarrow Q \wedge \text{stable}(out(\rho) \setminus \vec{x}, [\tau_0 \ldots \tau])) \end{array}$$

where '\' denotes set difference.

By $\tau_0 \leq \tau$, we assume that time never runs backwards. Because the variables $\vec{x}$ may be changed by the program, we require in the definition that all variables of $\vec{x}$ are output variables of the environment (abbreviated by $\vec{x} \subseteq out(\rho)$). For all other variables occurring free in P and Q, the command does not determine if they are inputs or outputs of the command. This is determined by the environment. If the frame is empty, no output variable may be changed by the command but there may still be input variables that are changed by other commands that run in parallel.

Command C	$in(C)$	$out(C)$	Meaning $\mathcal{M}_\rho(C)$
$\infty \vec{x}\colon\ [P,\ Q]$	$\varnothing$	$\vec{x}$	see Def 2
$\vec{x}\colon\ [P,\ Q]$	$\varnothing$	$\vec{x}$	$\mathcal{M}_\rho\left(\infty \vec{x}\colon\ [P,\ Q \wedge \tau < \infty]\right)$
$\infty \vec{x}\colon\ [P]$	$\varnothing$	$\varnothing$	$\mathcal{M}_\rho\left(\infty \vec{x}\colon\ [\textbf{true},\ P]\right)$
$\{P\}$	$\varnothing$	$\varnothing$	$\mathcal{M}_\rho\left([P,\ \tau_0 = \tau]\right)$

Fig. 1. Real-time specification commands

Fig. 1 lists some abbreviations for special cases of the real-time specification command together with their minimal meaningful environments and their meanings. We consider the *terminating* specification command $\vec{x}\colon\ [P,\ Q]$, the specification command with the valid precondition $\infty \vec{x}\colon\ [P]$, and the assertion $\{P\}$. The coercion $[P]$ is the special case of the terminating specification command with an empty frame.

2.2 Primitive Real-Time Commands

Fig. 2 lists the primitive real-time commands of the language together with their minimal meaningful environments and their meaning. Their informal meanings are explained as

Command C	$in(C)$	$out(C)$	Meaning $\mathcal{M}_\rho(C)$
skip	∅	∅	$\mathcal{M}_\rho\left(\left[\tau_0 = \tau\right]\right)$
idle	∅	∅	$\mathcal{M}_\rho\left(\left[\tau_0 \leq \tau\right]\right)$
∞idle	∅	∅	$\mathcal{M}_\rho\left(\infty\left[\tau_0 \leq \tau\right]\right)$
$\vec{x} := \vec{E}$	∅	$\vec{x} \cup \mathit{free}(\vec{E})$	$\mathcal{M}_\rho\left(\vec{x}\colon \left[\mathit{def}(\vec{E}),\ \vec{x} = \vec{E}\,[\vec{x}_0/\vec{x}]\right]\right)$
$v : \mathbf{read}(i)$	$\{i\}$	$\{v\}$	$\mathcal{M}_\rho\left(v\colon \left[v \in i(\!(\tau_0 \ldots \tau]\!)\right]\right)$
$t : \mathbf{gettime}$	∅	$\{t\}$	$\mathcal{M}_\rho\left(t\colon \left[\tau_0 \leq t \leq \tau\right]\right)$
deadline D	∅	$\mathit{free}(D)$	$\mathcal{M}_\rho\left(\left[\tau_0 = \tau \leq D\right]\right)$
delay until D	∅	$\mathit{free}(D)$	$\mathcal{M}_\rho\left(\left[D \leq \tau\right]\right)$

Fig. 2. Primitive real-time commands

follows: **skip** does nothing and takes no time; **idle** does nothing and may take a finite amount of time; **∞idle** does nothing and may or may not terminate; the assignment command $\vec{x} := \vec{E}$ changes the value of $\vec{x}$ to the value of the expression $\vec{E}$; the command $v : \mathbf{read}(i)$ reads the input variable i into the output variable v; the command $t : \mathbf{gettime}$ assigns the current time to t; the command **deadline** D takes no time and finishes before D; the command **delay until** D delays the execution of the program until D.

The expressions used in the commands are assumed to be idle-stable, that is, their value does not change over time provided all the variables under the control of the program are stable. This is guaranteed if the expression does not refer to τ or to the value of external inputs (but this is not a necessary condition).

Definition 3 (idle-stable). *Given variables ρ, an expression E is* idle-stable *provided that* $\tau_0 \leq \tau \wedge \mathit{stable}(\mathit{out}(\rho), [\tau_0 \ldots \tau]) \Rightarrow E\,[\tau_0/\tau] = E$.

In Fig. 2, we assume that D is an idle-stable, time-valued expression; $\vec{E}$ is a vector of idle-stable expressions of the same length as $\vec{x}$; and $\mathit{def}(\vec{E})$ is a boolean valued expression that is true if $\vec{E}$ is well-defined, e.g. that there is no division by zero; v is an output variable; i is an input variable; t is a time-valued variable; and ρ is a meaningful environment for the command.

In the traditional untimed refinement calculus [1] the assertion $\{\mathbf{true}\}$ and the coercion $[\mathbf{true}]$ are both equivalent to the **skip** command. In our setting, $\{\mathbf{true}\}$ takes no time and is equivalent to the **skip** command whereas $[\mathbf{true}]$ may take a finite amount of time and is therefore equivalent to the **idle** command. The meaning of **deadline** D is **false** if it is reached after time D. In Dijkstra's terminology [3] the command is called *miraculous*. The command **magic**, which is defined by $[\mathbf{false}]$, is miraculous in any environment and for all possible values of the variables. **magic** refines each command with respect to ρ, and cannot be implemented.

2.3 Compound Real-Time Commands

The language contains three compound commands: a variable block to introduce a new local variable, sequential composition, and parallel composition. Variable blocks and sequential composition are also part of the real-time language for sequential programs in [8]. Parallel composition is specific for concurrent programs and the most complex command of the language.

Command C	$in(C)$	$out(C)$
$\|[\text{ var } x \bullet C_1]\|$	$in(C_1) \setminus \{x\}$	$out(C_1) \setminus \{x\}$
$C_1; C_2$	$in(C_1) \cup in(C_2)$	$out(C_1) \cup out(C_2)$
$C_1 \parallel C_2$	$in(C_1) \setminus out(C_2)$ $\cup in(C_2) \setminus out(C_1)$	$out(C_1) \cup out(C_2)$

Fig. 3. Derived real-time commands

The table in Fig. 3 gives the minimal meaningful environments for the three commands. Note that in a parallel composition of two processes, an output variable of the parallel command may be an input variable for one process and an output for the other.

A variable block introduces a new local variable. The scope of the variable is the command inside the block. For this command the new variable is seen as an output variable. The allocation and deallocation of a new variable may take time. The new variable is given as a function from time to the universal value set $\mathcal{V}$.

Definition 4 (block). *Given a command C, a variable x, a meaningful environment ρ for $\|[\text{ var } x \bullet C]\|$ (see Fig. 3) such that x' is a fresh variable name that does not occur in ρ or C, and $\rho' = (in(\rho), out(\rho) \cup \{x'\})$, we define*
$$\mathcal{M}_\rho (\|[\text{ var } x \bullet C]\|) \triangleq \forall x' \in \text{Time} \to \mathcal{V} \bullet \mathcal{M}_{\rho'} (\textbf{idle};\ C\,[x'/x];\ \textbf{idle}).$$

Definition 5 (sequential composition). *Given commands C_1 and C_2, an environment ρ that is meaningful for C_1 and C_2, and a fresh variable τ' (that does not occur in ρ, C_1 or C_2), we define*
$$\mathcal{M}_\rho (C_1;\ C_2) \triangleq \exists \tau' \bullet \tau_0 \leq \tau' \leq \tau \wedge \mathcal{M}_\rho (C_1)\,[\tau'/\tau] \wedge \mathcal{M}_\rho (C_2)\,[\tau'/\tau_0].$$

The variable τ' stands for the finish time of C_1 and the start time of C_2. If C_1 does not terminate τ' is infinity and C_2 has no effect (see Definition 2).

Definition 6 (parallel composition). *Given commands C_1 and C_2, an environment ρ that is meaningful for $C_1 \parallel C_2$ (see Fig. 3), and fresh variables τ_1, τ_2 (that do not occur in ρ, C_1 or C_2), let $\rho_1 = (in(C_1), out(C_1))$ and $\rho_2 = (in(C_2), out(C_2))$, we define*
$$\mathcal{M}_\rho (C_1 \parallel C_2) \triangleq \exists \tau_1, \tau_2 \bullet \mathcal{M}_{\rho_1} (\textbf{idle};\ C_1;\ [\tau_1 = \tau_0];\ \infty\textbf{idle})$$
$$\wedge\ \mathcal{M}_{\rho_2} (\textbf{idle};\ C_2;\ [\tau_2 = \tau_0];\ \infty\textbf{idle})$$
$$\wedge\ max(\tau_1, \tau_2) < \infty \Rightarrow \tau < \infty$$
$$\wedge\ stable(out(\rho) \setminus out(C_1 \parallel C_2), [\tau_0 \ldots \tau]).$$

The variables τ_1 and τ_2 capture the finish times of C_1 and C_2, respectively. If both terminate then their parallel composition must terminate. The initial **idle** commands allow for the time to set up the parallel composition and the final ∞**idle** commands allow for the synchronisation of the two processes on termination. Note that one process may finish and the other never terminate in which case the ∞**idle** command following the first command does not terminate.

Parallel composition is defined for arbitrary commands. If both commands have output variables in common, it is possible that one process changes an output variable while the other process requires that the same output variable is stable in the same interval. Hence, the composed program is miraculous. To avoid the parallel composition of two non-miraculous commands leading to a miraculous composition, it makes sense to require that the sets of output variables of the two processes are disjoint: we call the commands C_1, C_2 *composable* if $out(C_1) \cap out(C_2) = \emptyset$.

Parallel composition is commutative and associative: $C_1 \parallel C_2 \sqsupseteq C_2 \parallel C_1$ and $(C_1 \parallel C_2) \parallel C_3 \sqsupseteq C_1 \parallel (C_2 \parallel C_3)$.

Definition 7 (pre- and post-idle invariant). *A command C is* pre-idle invariant *if $C \sqsupseteq$* (**idle**; C), *and it is* post-idle invariant *if $C \sqsupseteq (C;$ **idle**).

It is sufficient to show that C is refined by **idle**; C and C; **idle**, respectively. The other direction is trivial because $C \sqsupseteq$ (**skip**; C) $\sqsupseteq$ (C; **skip**) and **idle** $\sqsubseteq$ **skip**. For all commands C_1 and C_2, the parallel composition $C_1 \parallel C_2$ is pre- and post-idle invariant. If P does not constrain τ and Q does not constrain τ_0 then the specification command $\infty \vec{x}: [P, Q]$ is pre-idle invariant. If Q does not constrain τ and Q does not depend on the current value of input variables then the specification command $\infty \vec{x}: [P, Q]$ is post-idle invariant. For each pre- and post-idle invariant command C, we have $C \sqsupseteq$ (**idle**; C; **idle**) $\sqsubseteq$ ($C \parallel$ **skip**) $\sqsupseteq$ ($C \parallel$ **idle**).

3 Communication via Message Passing

For modelling asynchronous message passing systems, we use the same syntax and semantics as before but we introduce three new commands: a command that introduces a new channel, and the commands **send** and **receive** for sending and receiving a message.

We represent a channel c by two variables $c.sent$ and $c.rec$. As with other variables, $c.sent$ and $c.rec$ are traces over time. $c.sent(t)$ is the sequence of messages sent over channel c until time t, and $c.rec(t)$ is the sequence of messages received over this channel until time t.

The variable $c.sent$ is an output for the sending process and an input variable for the receiving process, whereas $c.rec$ is an input variable for the sending process and an output variable for the receiving process.

Command C	$in(C)$	$out(C)$
$[\![$ **chan** $c \bullet C_1]\!]$	$in(C_1) \setminus \{c.sent, c.rec\}$	$out(C_1) \setminus \{c.sent, c.rec\}$
$c :$ **send**$(\vec{x})$	$\{c.rec\}$	$\{c.sent, \vec{x}\}$
$c, \vec{x} :$ **receive**	$\{c.sent\}$	$\{c.rec, \vec{x}\}$

Fig. 4. The new commands and their input and output variables

The syntax and the minimal meaningful environments of the new commands are given in Fig. 4. In the remainder of this section, we define the semantics of these commands. We introduce a few notations about sequences to reason about the variables $c.sent$ and $c.receive$. We denote the set of all finite sequences of values of a set T by $seq(T)$. For two sequences σ_1 and σ_2, we denote by $\sigma_1 \leq \sigma_2$ that σ_1 is a prefix of σ_2. We append a value m to a sequence σ by $\sigma^\frown [m]$.

3.1 Introduction of a New Channel

With the introduction of a channel, we do not determine which model of channel we use, e.g. if we use a FIFO channel, or an unordered channel. This is done by the definition of the **send** and **receive** commands.

We do, however, assume some general properties about each channel: We assume that a newly introduced channel is initially empty. We assume that no sent message can be made "unsent", and no received message can be made "unreceived", i.e., $c.sent$ and $c.rec$ are monotonic with regard to the prefix relation. We formalise this by the channel invariant I that is stated below. Assume that $c'.sent$, $c'.rec$ do not occur in the environment ρ or in C. We define:

$$\mathcal{M}_\rho(\![\![\,\textbf{chan}\ c \bullet C\,]\!]\!) \ \widehat{=}\ \forall c'.sent, c'.rec \in \text{Time} \to \text{seq}(\mathcal{V}) \bullet$$
$$I \Rightarrow \mathcal{M}_{\rho'}(\textbf{idle};\ C\,[c'.sent, c'.rec/c.sent, c.rec]\,;\ \textbf{idle})$$

where $\rho' = \bigl(in(\rho) \cup \{c.sent, c.rec\}, out(\rho) \cup \{c.sent, c.rec\}\bigr)$ and $\mathcal{V}$ is as usual the universal value set and

$$I \ \widehat{=}\ \bigl(c'.sent_0 = c'.rec_0 = [\,] \land \forall \tau_1, \tau_2 \in \text{Time} \bullet \tau_1 \leq \tau_2 \Rightarrow$$
$$c'.sent(\tau_1) \leq c'.sent(\tau_2) \land c'.rec(\tau_1) \leq c'.rec(\tau_2)\bigr).$$

3.2 Sending and Receiving Messages

The variables $c.sent$ and $c.rec$ cannot be changed by an ordinary assignment command. A process (a command) is a sender for channel c if $c.sent$ is an output variable and $c.rec$ is an input variable. The value of $c.sent$ can only be changed by a **send** command and by a specification command. Analogously, a process is a receiver for channel c if $c.rec$ is an output variable and $c.sent$ is an input variable. The value of $c.rec$ can only be changed by a **receive** command and by a specification command. For each channel there is at most one sender and one receiver. This is ensured by the requirement that composable processes have disjoint sets of output variables.

To define these two commands uniformly for several models of channels, we define some predicates for each model of a channel: the predicate $clear(c)$ specifies when a message can be sent over channel c, the predicate $new(c)$ specifies when a message can be received, and if a message can be received, $next(c, m)$ specifies that the message m can be received next. (If the channel is unordered, the message m may not be unique.)

We now give the definitions of these predicates for unbounded FIFO channels and for n-buffered blocking channels. In both cases we assume, that the channels are reliable. Such predicates can be defined for other models of channel in a similar fashion, e.g. for lossy channels, unordered channels, overwriting channels etc.

Sending of a message is never blocked in an unbounded FIFO channel. Hence, the predicate $clear(c)$ is always true. A message can be received if $c.sent$ is strictly longer than $c.rec$. If this is the case, the next message to be received is the unreceived message that was sent first. Therefore, we define for an infinite FIFO channel c: $clear(c) \ \widehat{=}\ \textbf{true}$ and $new(c) \ \widehat{=}\ c.rec < c.sent$ and $next(c, m) \ \widehat{=}\ c.rec\,\widehat{}\,[m] \leq c.sent$.

Sending of a message is blocked in an n-buffered blocking channel if there are n messages buffered in the channel that are not yet received. Receiving a message is similar to a FIFO channel. For an n-buffered blocking channel c with $n \geq 1$, we define: $clear(c) \ \widehat{=}\ \#c.sent < \#c.rec + n$ and $new(c) \ \widehat{=}\ c.rec < c.sent$ and $next(c, m) \ \widehat{=}\ c.rec\,\widehat{}\,[m] \leq c.sent$, where $\#\sigma$ denotes the length of sequence σ.

Given these predicates, we are able to define the **send** command and the **receive** command uniformly for all models of channels. The command **await**(P) waits until the predicate P becomes true and is possibly non-terminating. If P does become true it is required to terminate immediately.

$$\textbf{await}(P) \;\widehat{=}\; \infty \begin{bmatrix} (\forall \tau' \bullet \tau_0 \leq \tau' < \tau \Rightarrow \neg P\,[\tau'/\tau]) \\ \wedge\, (\tau \neq \infty \Rightarrow P) \end{bmatrix}$$

According to our convention given after Definition 1, $P\,[\tau'/\tau]$ denotes the evaluation of P at time τ', and P denotes the evaluation of P at time τ.

$$c : \textbf{send}(m) \;\widehat{=}\; \textbf{await}(clear(c));\; c.sent\colon \begin{bmatrix} c.sent = c.sent_0\widehat{\;}[m] \end{bmatrix}$$

$$c, \vec{x} : \textbf{receive} \;\widehat{=}\; \textbf{await}(new(c));\; c.rec, \vec{x}\colon \begin{bmatrix} next(c_0, \vec{x}) \\ \wedge\, c.rec = c.rec_0\widehat{\;}[\vec{x}] \end{bmatrix}$$

The command **send** does not terminate if the channel is not cleared, and **receive** does not terminate if no message is sent.

From the above definitions and the monotonicity of $c.sent$ and $c.rec$, we can deduce that $c.sent$ and $c.rec$ change instantaneously, i.e., there is a time during the execution of the command such that the old value is valid until this time and the new value is valid from this time on. For the assignment command, we did not assume instantaneous change because it is impossible to implement for arbitrary variables. In the implementation of **send** and **receive**, mutual exclusion ensures the same overall effect as the instantaneous change.

There are several possibilities to cope with the different definitions of **send** and **receive**. If we only deal with systems with only one channel type, we can fix the appropriate definitions of **send** and **receive** in advance. If our model incorporates different channel models, we can use a new parameter in the introduction of a new channel. This parameter determines which model of channel is used and the definition of **send** and **receive** for this channel are adjusted appropriately.

4 Refinement

In the definition of parallel composition, an environment is split into two environments for the two processes. We now define how to join the environments of two processes to obtain a meaningful environment for the parallel composition of both. All variables that are input for one process and output for the other process become output variables of the composed process. For two environments ρ_1 and ρ_2, we define $\rho_1 \oplus \rho_2$ by

$$in(\rho_1 \oplus \rho_2) \;\widehat{=}\; (in(\rho_1) \setminus out(\rho_2)) \cup (in(\rho_2) \setminus out(\rho_1))$$
$$out(\rho_1 \oplus \rho_2) \;\widehat{=}\; out(\rho_1) \cup out(\rho_2)$$

The first law is specific for concurrent programs. It allows us to refine two processes in a parallel composition independently from each other, as long as the refined processes are composable (i.e. have disjoint sets of output variables). The parallel composition of the refined processes is then a refinement of the unrefined parallel composition.

Law 1 Let C_1, C_2, D_1, D_2 be commands such that $out(D_1 \parallel D_2) \subseteq out(C_1 \parallel C_2)$ and let ρ_1 be a meaningful environment for C_1 and D_1, and ρ_2 be a meaningful environment for C_2 and D_2 such that $out(\rho_1) \cap out(\rho_2) = \emptyset$ (this implies that C_1 and C_2 are composable and D_1 and D_2 are composable). Then we have that

$$C_1 \sqsubseteq_{\rho_1} D_1 \quad \text{and} \quad C_2 \sqsubseteq_{\rho_2} D_2 \quad \text{implies} \quad C_1 \parallel C_2 \sqsubseteq_{\rho_1 \oplus \rho_2} D_1 \parallel D_2$$

The next law allows us to split a specification command into two parallel specification commands.

Law 2 Given specification commands $\vec{x}\colon [P, \ Q]$, $\vec{x_1}\colon [P_1, \ Q_1]$ and $\vec{x_2}\colon [P_2, \ Q_2]$ with predicates P, P_1, P_2, Q, Q_1, Q_2 and variables $\vec{x}, \vec{x_1}, \vec{x_2}$ such that P, P_1, P_2 do not include initial (zero-subscripted) variables, and $\vec{x_1}\colon [P_1, \ Q_1]$ and $\vec{x_2}\colon [P_2, \ Q_2]$ are pre- and post-idle invariant. Assume that $P \Rightarrow P_1 \wedge P_2$, and $Q_1 \wedge Q_2 \Rightarrow Q$, and $\vec{x_1} \cup \vec{x_2} = \vec{x}$, and $\vec{x_1} \cap \vec{x_2} = \emptyset$. Then we have for each environment ρ that contains $\vec{x}$ as output variables:

$$\vec{x}\colon [P, \ Q] \sqsubseteq_\rho \vec{x_1}\colon [P_1, \ Q_1] \parallel \vec{x_2}\colon [P_2, \ Q_2]$$

Note that for some channel c, the vector $\vec{x}$ may contain both $c.sent$ and $c.rec$. By the law, we may split the specification command into a sending process C_1 (such that $\vec{x_1}$ contains $c.sent$) and a receiving process C_2 (such that $\vec{x_2}$ contains $c.rec$). The proofs of both laws are rather straightforward. Refinement laws for the sequential programs are given in [8].

5 An Example

We demonstrate the language and the refinement laws by means of an example. We use the example of a simple comparator, similar to the example in [12]. We have two input variables in_1, in_2 which are assumed to be stable in the time interval $[5\ldots 10]$. Provided that the program starts before time 5, it reads the values of the input variables in this interval and produces an output out that is **true** if the input values are equal and **false** if not.

We specify the program by $x_1, x_2, out\colon [P, \ Q]$ where

$P_1 \triangleq stable(\{in_1, in_2\}, [5\ldots 10])$ and $P_2 \triangleq \tau < 5$ and $P \triangleq P_1 \wedge P_2$
$Q \triangleq x_1 \in in_1(\!([5\ldots 10])\!) \wedge x_2 \in in_2(\!([5\ldots 10])\!) \wedge out = (x_1 = x_2)$

We consider the program in an environment ρ with input variables in_1, in_2 and output variables x_1, x_2, out.

We now refine this specification by splitting it into four sequentially composed specification commands. This step is known from the sequential real-time refinement calculus [8] and therefore not proved formally here.

$$x_1, x_2, out\colon [P, \ Q] \sqsubseteq_\rho$$
$$\{P\}; \ x_1, x_2\colon \begin{bmatrix} x_1 \in in_1(\!([5\ldots 10])\!) \wedge \\ x_2 \in in_2(\!([5\ldots 10])\!) \end{bmatrix}; \ out\colon [out = (x_1 = x_2)]$$

We now further refine the second and third commands in the sequential composition. This step can be proved formally by applying the definitions of sequential composition, the **delay until**, and the **deadline** command. We omit this proof as well because there is still no concurrency involved in this step. We define

$$Q_1 \mathrel{\hat{=}} x_1 \in in_1(\!| \,(\tau_0 \ldots \tau] \,|\!) \qquad \text{and} \qquad Q_2 \mathrel{\hat{=}} x_2 \in in_2(\!| \,(\tau_0 \ldots \tau] \,|\!)$$

Then the above sequence of four commands is refined by:

$\sqsubseteq_\rho \ \{P\};$
    delay until $5;\ x_1, x_2:\ [Q_1 \wedge Q_2]\ ;\ $**deadline** $10;$
    $out := (x_1 = x_2)$

We now apply the laws from the previous section to refine the specification command.

$x_1, x_2:\ [Q_1 \wedge Q_2] \sqsubseteq_\rho x_1:\ [Q_1] \parallel x_2:\ [Q_2]$ (by Law 2)
    $\sqsubseteq_\rho x_1:\ \mathbf{read}(in_1) \parallel x_2:\ \mathbf{read}(in_2)$ (by Law 1)

Hence, we have the final program: $\{stable(\{in_1, in_2\}, [5 \ldots 10]) \wedge \tau < 5\};$
                                           delay until $5;$
                                           $(x_1:\ \mathbf{read}(in_1) \parallel x_2:\ \mathbf{read}(in_2));$
                                           deadline $10;$
                                           $out := (x_1 = x_2)$

This program can be implemented using the **deadline** command as a directive for the timing constraint analysis. For the implemented program to satisfy the specification, it has to be ensured that the **deadline** is met. This is machine-dependent. As mentioned earlier, we can perform a machine-independent timing constraint analysis by extracting timing paths from the control flow graph of the program and determine a constraint for each path.

In this especially easy program, there is no interaction between the two concurrent tasks, and we can extract and analyse the timing paths as in the sequential case [5]. We can extract the following timing paths for this program.

$\{P_1 \wedge \tau < 5\};$ $\{P_1 \wedge \tau < 5\};$
delay until $5;$ **delay until** $5;$
$x_1:\ \mathbf{read}(in_1);$ $x_2:\ \mathbf{read}(in_2);$
deadline 10 **deadline** 10

Analysis of these paths reveals that the program satisfies all timing constraints if it is implemented on a machine that executes the above paths in less than 5 time units. This depends in particular on the concrete implementation of the **delay until** command on this machine.

6 Conclusion and Further Work

We have proposed a new language for modelling concurrent real-time programs. Together with the given predicative semantics, the language serves as a basis for a real-time refinement calculus. Due to the definition of the language, the laws from the sequential real-time refinement calculus [8] remain valid. In this paper, we gave examples for refinement laws that are specific for concurrent programs.

The **deadline** command provided by the language is not implementable but it can be seen as a directive in the final implementable program. The programs developed by the proposed method meet their specification under the assumption that all deadlines are met. This obviously depends on the machine on which the program is implemented. It is, however, possible to extract all timing paths from a program that end with a **deadline** command and analyse them. The result is a constraint on each path that can be checked by the programmer. This work was done for sequential programs in [5, 7] and is under way for the new language for concurrent programs.

Acknowledgements

We would like to thank Colin Fidge and Karl Lermer for their contribution to this paper and the anonymous referees for their detailed comments. The research was funded by the Australian Research Council Discovery Project DP0209722 "Derivation and timing analysis of concurrent real-time software".

References

1. R.-J. Back and J. von Wright. *Refinement Calculus: A Systematic Introduction.* Springer, 1998.
2. R. J. R. Back. A calculus of refinement for program derivations. *Acta Informatica*, 25:593–624, 1988.
3. E. W. Dijkstra. *A Discipline of Programming.* Prentice-Hall Series in Automatic Computation. Prentice Hall, 1976.
4. C. Fidge, I. Hayes, and G. Watson. The deadline command. *IEE Proceedings–Software*, 146(2):104–111, 1999.
5. S. Grundon, I. Hayes, and C. Fidge. Timing constraint analysis. In C. McDonald, editor, *Computer Science '98: Proc. 21st Australasian Computer Science Conference*, pages 575–586. Springer-Verlag, Singapore, 1998.
6. I. Hayes. Real-time program refinement using auxiliary variables. In M. Joseph, editor, *Proc. 6th International Symposium on Formal Techniques in Real-Time and Fault-Tolerant Systems*, volume 1926 of *LNCS*, pages 170–184. Springer, 2000.
7. I. J. Hayes, C. J. Fidge, and K. Lermer. Semantic characterisation of dead control-flow paths. *IEE Proceedings - Software*, 148(6):175-186, December 2001.
8. I. J. Hayes and M. Utting. A sequential real-time refinement calculus. *Acta Informatica*, 37:385–448, 2001.
9. E. C. R. Hehner. *A Practical Theory of Programming.* Springer, 1993.
10. J. Hooman and O. van Roosmalen. An approach to platform independent real-time programming: (1) formal description. *Real-Time Systems*, 19:61–85, 2000.
11. C. Morgan. *Programming from Specifications, 2nd edition.* International Series in Computer Science. Prentice Hall, 1994.
12. D. Scholefield, H. Zedan, and H. Jifeng. A specification-oriented semantics for the refinement of real-time systems. *Theoretical Computer Science*, 131(1):219–241, 1994.
13. N. Wirth. Program development by stepwise refinement. *Communications of the ACM*, 14(4):221–227, 1971.

Refinement Algebra
for Formal Bytecode Generation

Adolfo Duran, Ana Cavalcanti, and Augusto Sampaio

Centro de Informática,
Universidade Federal de Pernambuco,
Po Box 7851 50740-540 Recife PE Brazil
Fax:+55 81 32718438,
{aad,alcc,acas}@cin.ufpe.br

Abstract. In this paper we propose an strategy for the design of compilers correct by construction for object-oriented languages. The process is formalized within a single and uniform semantic framework of an object-oriented language based on a subset of sequential Java and its algebraic laws. The strategy is to reduce an arbitrary source program to a particular normal form which describes the behavior of the target machine. This behavior is defined by an interpreter written in the same language. From the interpreter we can capture the sequence of generated bytecodes of the target machine. The normal form reduction is formalized as algebraic transformations where the central notion is refinement of programs.

1 Introduction

The design of correct compilers for procedural languages is already understood; our main challenge is the development of an approach to deal with object-oriented features.

We propose an algebraic approach to construct a provably correct compiler for an object-oriented language called ROOL (for Refinement Object-oriented Language)[1, 2], which is similar to sequential Java and C++ [7].

We carry out compilation by a series of refinement steps identified with the reduction of an arbitrary source program to a program in a particular normal form: an interpreter executing target code. From the normal form program, we can capture the sequence of bytecodes for a ROOL Virtual Machine (RVM), which is a subset of the Java Virtual Machine (JVM).

This approach was originally described in [3] and has been further developed in [5]. It characterizes the compilation process within a uniform framework, where comparisons and translations between semantics are avoided. This constitutes the main advantage of our approach since it results in simplicity.

This paper is organized as follows. We first give an overview of ROOL, including some of its basic laws. Afterwards we explain the ROOL interpreter structure. Subsequently, we explain how we compile with compilation rules; we present an example to illustrate how the lemmas and basic laws are used to prove the compilation rules. Finally, we summarize the results achieved so far, and consider related work and topics for further research.

2 The ROOL Language and Its Laws

A program in ROOL consists of a sequence of class declarations, followed by a main command ($CDS \bullet c$). A class declaration has the form

    class N_1 **extends** N_2
        {**pri** $x_1 : T_1;$ }*   //*private attributes*
        {**prot** $x_2 : T_2;$ }*   //*protected attributes*
        {**pub** $x_3 : T_3;$ }*   //*public attributes*
        {**meth** $m \triangleq (pds \bullet s)$ **end**}* //*public methods*
        {**new** $\triangleq x := e$ **end**}*   //*Initializers*
    end

The clause **extends** determines the immediate superclass of N_1. If omitted, the built-in class **object** is regarded as the superclass. The visibility mechanism is similar to that of Java: the qualifiers **pri**, **prot**, and **pub** are used for private, protected, and public attributes. The clause **meth** declares a method. For simplicity, all methods are considered to be public. The list of parameters (pds) of a method is separated from its body by the symbol '$\bullet$'. The **new** clause declares initializers: methods called after creating an object of the class. Further details of ROOL and its semantics based on weakest precondition are given in [2].

The laws of ROOL are an algebraic semantics for this language and establish a sound basis for the design of correct compilers. In [1] many laws have been proved correct with respect to the weakest precondition of ROOL. Here we introduce a subset of the basic laws we use later on. We say that $CDS, x : T, N \triangleright c_1 = c_2$, when the commands c_1 and c_2 are equal, in the context of a sequence of class declarations CDS, visible attributes, parameters, local variables $x : T$, and class N. In what follows, we remove the context when it is not relevant for the law.

We use the abbreviation **skip** for the command that does nothing; its execution always terminates and leaves the state unchanged. To precede or follow a command by **skip** does not change its effect.

Law 1 (**skip**; c) = c = (c; **skip**)

The assignment of a variable to itself does not change anything.

Law 2 (v := v) = **skip**

If exactly one of the guards of a conditional is true, the corresponding command is selected for execution.

Law 3 If i and j range over $1..n$ and $\neg (b_i \wedge b_j)$ *with* $(i \neq j)$, then
    $[b_j];$ **if** $[]_{\langle 1 \leq i \leq n \rangle} b_i \rightarrow c_i$ **fi** $= [b_j];\ c_j$

The expression $[b_i]$ above is an assertion. Whenever the flow of control reaches an assertion, it is checked: if false, the program behaves like *miracle*; if true, execution continues normally. The command *miracle* is infeasible and cannot be implemented, but constitutes a useful theoretical concept for reasoning.

A **while** can be eliminated if an assertion before it implies that its condition does not hold initially.

Law 4 If $(b_1 \Rightarrow \neg b_2)$, then $[b_1]$; **while** $b_2 \bullet c$ **end** $= [b_1]$

If, on the contrary, the assertion before the **while** implies that its condition holds, it behaves like c followed by the whole iteration.

Law 5 If $(b_1 \Rightarrow b_2)$, then $[b_1]$; **while** $b_2 \bullet c$ **end** $= [b_1]$; c; **while** $b_2 \bullet c$ **end**

The symbol $\sqsubseteq$ denotes the refinement ordering on programs: $q \sqsubseteq r$ means that r is at least as good as q in the sense that the substitution of r for q in any context is an improvement or will leave things unchanged.

An assertion $[b]$ refines **skip**, as it behaves like miracle if b does not hold.

Law 6 **skip** $\sqsubseteq [b]$

If a declared variable is never used, its declaration has no effect.

Law 7 If x is not free in c, then **var** $x : T \bullet c$ **end** $= c$

Assigning to a variable just before the end of its scope is irrelevant.

Law 8 (**var** $x : T \bullet c$; $x := e$ **end**) $=$ (**var** $x : T \bullet c$ **end**)

Invoking a method is insignificant if the affected variables are just before the end of their scope.

Law 9 **var** $y : T_1, z : T_2 \bullet p; y.m(z);$ **end** $=$ **var** $y : T_1, z : T_2 \bullet p$ **end**

This is only a small fragment of the algebraic laws of ROOL. See [1] for a comprehensive set of laws.

3 Interpreter Structure

The RVM is characterized by a normal form, which is an interpreter-like program. The normal form (Figure 1) consists of a sequence of class declarations (CDS_{RVM}) followed by a main command named $I_{C,M}$. It describes the behavior of our virtual machine executing a stored program, in an iterated execution of a sequence of bytecodes stored in the global variable C, which represents the compiled program. Another global variable named M stores the initial value of the program variables. At the end of execution, the final values are copied back to M. Therefore, from the point of view of the interpreter execution, the observable data space is M.

More specifically, $I_{C,M}$ is a **var** block declaration that introduces three local variables. The main variable is rvm; the other two, op and k, are auxiliary: they are used to obtain the control information stored in rvm. The op variable is an integer whose value indicates the next bytecode instruction to be executed. The k variable is an instance of the *Control* class declared in CDS_{RVM}; its attributes are the pc register, *initial* and *final*. The last two attributes denote the interval comprising the bytecode stream of the current executing method.

CDS_{RVM} • **var** op, k, rvm : Int, Control, RoolVM •
$\quad rvm := $ **new** $RoolVM$; $rvm.SetClasses(C)$;
$\quad rvm.SetVar(M)$; $rvm.GetControl(k)$;
$\quad$ **while** $k.pc \geq k.initial \wedge k.pc < k.final$ •
$\quad\quad rvm.GetBcode(op)$;
$\quad\quad$ **if** $[]_{\langle 0 \leq i \leq n \rangle}\ op = i \rightarrow rvm.inst_i$ **fi**; $rvm.GetControl(k)$;
$\quad$ **end**;
$\quad rvm.GetVar(M)$;
end

Fig. 1. The ROOL Interpreter (CDS_{RVM} • $I_{C,M}$)

The **while** statement is executed until the program counter reaches a value beyond the current executing bytecode stream interval. In the body of the while statement, first the operation code (op) is obtained and then a conditional statement selects the corresponding method that implements that instruction.

The internal data structure of the interpreter is represented by the local variable rvm, an instance of $RoolVM$. This structure is basically a sequence of instances of $FrameInfo$ implementing the stack of frames named F. An instance of $FrameInfo$ holds the state of one ROOL method invocation. It includes its own pc register; its operand stack s; its current class cl, which is an instance of $ClassInfo$; its currently executing method mtd; and its list of local variables v.

An instance of $ClassInfo$ contains the following attributes: $name$, the class name; $super$, its superclass; $mtds$, a reference to the list of methods declared in the class; fds, a reference to the list of attributes declared in the class; cp, a reference to the constant pool which provides much of the essential information needed by a class; it contains entries for the names of referenced classes, methods and attributes, and for the integer constants.

Most of the data structures used to implement our interpreter employs sequences of objects. We assume the following operators to deal with sequences: $Y \frown Z$, the concatenation of sequence Y with sequence Z; $head\ y$, the leftmost element of sequence Y; $last\ Y$, the rightmost element of sequence Y; $front\ Y$, the sequence without the last element of Y; $tail\ Y$, the sequence without the head element of Y; $\#Y$, the number of elements of Y.

In order to refer to some components of our interpreter, we adopt the following abbreviations.

Definition 1 (Target Machine Components)
$\quad S \quad\stackrel{def}{=} (last\ rvm.F).s$
$\quad V[n] \stackrel{def}{=} (last\ rvm.F).v[n]$
$\quad PC \quad\stackrel{def}{=} (last\ rvm.F).pc$
$\quad CP[n] \stackrel{def}{=} (last\ rvm.F).cp[n]$

We denote by S the operand stack in the current frame; $V[n]$ designates the local variable whose location is n in the current frame; PC represents the current program counter; finally $CP[n]$ stands for the object stored in the constant pool of the current class, whose entry is given by the index n.

We now introduce abbreviations for update expressions over the operand stack.

Definition 2 (Abbreviations over the operand stack)

$$S \uparrow [e] \stackrel{def}{=} (rvm;\ F : (front\ F) \frown \langle (last\ F;\ S : S \frown \langle e \rangle) \rangle)$$
$$S \downarrow \stackrel{def}{=} (rvm;\ F : (front\ F) \frown \langle (last\ F;\ S : front\ S) \rangle)$$
$$S \| \stackrel{def}{=} (last\ rvm.F).(last\ S)$$
$$S_{uop} \stackrel{def}{=} (rvm;\ F : (front\ F) \frown \langle (last\ F;\ S : (front\ S) \frown \langle (\mathbf{new}\ DataInt;\ Info : \mathbf{uop}\,(last\ S).Info) \rangle) \rangle)$$
$$S_{bop} \stackrel{def}{=} (rvm;\ F : (front\ F) \frown \langle (last\ F;\ S : front(front\ S) \frown \langle (\mathbf{new}\ DataInt;\ Info : (last\ (front\ S)).Info\,\mathbf{bop}(last\ S).Info) \rangle) \rangle)$$

The abbreviation $S \uparrow [e]$ stands for an update expression in which e is pushed onto S. Similarly, $S \downarrow$ represents the update expression in which a value from the top of S is popped; $S\|$ depicts a copy of the value on the top of the stack; S_{uop} represents the update expression in which one integer value is popped from the top of the stack, the unary operator **uop** is applied to it, and the result is pushed back onto S. Finally, S_{bop} handles binary operators bop.

4 Compiling with Theorems

The compilation process consists in reducing by algebraic transformation an arbitrary program to the above normal form. The reduction theorems (stated here as rules) can be proved correct from the basic algebraic laws of ROOL. The correctness of the compiler follows from the correctness of each compilation rule. The compilation process involves three phases: simplification of expressions, data refinement, and control elimination, in this order.

In this section we give an overview of our approach to compilation. Moreover, we list the compilation rules to give an idea of how we can compile methods, classes, and imperative control structures.

4.1 Simplification of Expressions

The first task of the compilation process is the elimination of nested expressions. The expected outcome of this phase is a program formed of a sequence of assignments where each assignment operates through the operand stack. To do so, we need to refer to the variable rvm, which contains the data structure of our interpreter. Basically, the outcome is a program involving assignments of the form described by the following patterns. They are closely related to those used to define bytecode instructions of our stack-based machine.

Definition 3 (Patterns for the operand stack)
$$load_{se}(i) \stackrel{def}{=} rvm := S \uparrow [(\mathbf{new}\, DataInt;\; Info : i)]$$
$$store_{se}(i) \stackrel{def}{=} i := S\|.Info;\; rvm := S \downarrow$$
$$uop_{se} \stackrel{def}{=} rvm := S_{uop}$$
$$bop_{se} \stackrel{def}{=} rvm := S_{bop}$$

The pattern $load_{se}$ pushes an integer value onto the operand stack, whereas $store_{se}$ pops an integer value from the operand stack and assigns it to an integer variable. Since the operand stack consists of a sequence of objects, it is necessary to encapsulate integer values using instances of $DataInt$. The pattens uop_{se} and bop_{se} represent a group of patterns that implement the effect of the unary and binary operators, respectively.

The following rules rely on the context in which they will be applied. We use the notation $CDS_{RVM}, rvm : RoolVM, N \triangleright c \sqsubseteq c'$ to mean that the refinement step $c \sqsubseteq c'$ holds in the context of class declarations CDS_{RVM} and local variable $rvm : RoolVM$. Furthermore, the command c is assumed to be inside the class N which denotes the main command or a class in the sequence of class declaration (CDS) of the source program.

The next rule deals with the simplification of an assignment to an integer variable.

Rule 1 (Assignment of an integer variable)
$$CDS_{RVM}, rvm : RoolVM, N \triangleright (x := e) \quad \sqsubseteq \quad load_{se}(e);\; store_{se}(x);$$

The expression e above may be arbitrarily nested; we need to further simplify it until the resulting expressions consist only of a single variable or constant. For simplicity, we omit the context in the following rules.

The next rule handles a pattern whose argument is an application of binary operators.

Rule 2 (Binary operator) If S does not occur in e or f
$$load_{se}(e\; \mathbf{bop}\; f) \quad \sqsubseteq \quad load_{se}(e);\; load_{se}(f);\; bop_{se}$$
where **bop** represents an arbitrary binary operator.

The nested expression in $load_{se}(e\; \mathbf{bop}\; f)$ is replaced with a sequence of patterns which first load e, then load f, and finally perform the **bop** operation.

Object creation is just another instance of assignment.

Rule 3 (Object Creation - Simplification)
$$x := \mathbf{new}\; N \quad \sqsubseteq \quad load_o(\mathbf{new}\; N);\; store_o(x);$$

We use pattern $load_o(\mathbf{new}\; N)$ to push the new object onto the operand stack.

4.2 Data Refinement

Data refinement is the replacement of the abstract space of the source program by the concrete state of the target machine. The function Ψ is the symbol table which maps each variable of the source program to addresses in the local variables sequence, in such a way that $V[\Psi_x]$ holds the value of x. Similarly, we assume that Φ is the class table, which holds all instances of *ClassInfo* corresponding to the compiled class declarations. From these tables, we can build the function $\overline{\Psi\Phi}$ which carries out the data refinement on commands.

The treatment of class declarations is handled by the function $\overline{\omega}$, which associates a class declaration with an instance of *ClassInfo* recording the declarations of attributes and methods occurring in the class. The representation resulting from the compilation by $\overline{\omega}$ is incorporated in the class table Φ by the function $\overline{\Psi\Phi}$. The rather lengthy definition of $\overline{\omega}$ is by the induction on sequences of class declarations, and on the structure of classes.

We present below our main rule which states the correctness of the compilation process for a program $CDS \bullet c$.

Rule 4 (Compilation Process)
$$CDS_{RVM}\ CDS \bullet \overline{\Psi\Phi}(c) \sqsubseteq CDS_{RVM} \bullet \overline{\Psi\Phi \cup \overline{\omega}(CDS)}(c)$$

The source program $CDS \bullet c$ operates on a data space different from the data space of our normal form. Therefore, it does not make sense to compare them directly: $\overline{\Psi\Phi}$ performs the necessary change of data representation. Observe that $\Phi \cup \overline{\omega}(CDS)$ incorporates the compiled class declarations CDS in Φ.

In order to carry out the change of class references and data representation in a systematic way, we need to use the distributivity properties of $\overline{\Psi\Phi}$.

In the following, we introduce simple patterns over the operand stack introduced by the data refinement phase.

Definition 4 (Patterns introduced by the data refinement phase)
$$load_{dr}(\Psi_x) \stackrel{def}{=} rvm := S \uparrow [V[\Psi_x]]$$
$$new_o(\Phi_N) \stackrel{def}{=} \textbf{var}\ o:\ ObjectInfo \bullet$$
$$o := \textbf{new}\ ObjectInfo;\ o.create(CP[\Phi_N]);\ rvm := S \uparrow [o];$$
$$\textbf{end}$$

These patterns have no reference to variables or constants of the source program. The pattern $load_{dr}(\Psi_x)$ pushes onto the stack S the local variable whose location is given by Ψ_x. The pattern $new_o(\Phi_N)$ creates an object which is a representation of an instance of the class N; the new object is pushed onto S; Φ_N indicates the location of an instance of *ClassInfo* which represents the class N.

The next rules deal with patterns possibly introduced in the previous phase. The following rule deals with the loading of an integer variable.

Rule 5 (Load Integer - Data Refinement)
$$\overline{\Psi\Phi}(load_{se}(x)) \sqsubseteq load_{dr}(\Psi_x)$$

The pattern $load_{dr}(\Psi_x)$ uses Ψ_x to refer to location holding the value of x in V.

The rule below shows how we deal with object creation.

Rule 6 (Object Creation - Data Refinement)
$$\overline{\Psi\Phi}(load_o(\textbf{new}\ N)) \sqsubseteq new_o(\Phi_N)$$

The function $\overline{\Psi\Phi}$ eliminates the reference to N, a class of the source program.

4.3 Control Elimination

Control elimination consists of reducing the nested control structure of the source program to a single flat iteration. The outcome is a program in our normal form.

The following abbreviation defines the global variable C.

Definition 5 (Compiled Program)
$$C(\varrho, \beta) = (\textbf{new } \textit{ClassInfo}; \; CP : \varrho_\beta; \; \textit{mtds} : \langle(\textbf{new } \textit{MtdInfo}; \; \textit{bytecode} : \beta)\rangle)$$

This is an instance of *ClassInfo*, which contains only one *MtdInfo* that holds the bytecode stream β. The symbol table ϱ is the constant pool possibly referenced by the bytecode instructions in β. We also use $I_{C(\varrho,\beta),M}$ to refer to the ROOL interpreter executing the compiled program stored in $C(\varrho, \beta)$.

The reduction of **skip** states that its only effect is the PC increment.

Rule 7 (Skip)
   skip $\sqsubseteq$ $I_{C(\varrho,\beta),M}$
   where $\beta = [nop]$, and $\varrho = \emptyset$

The above β holds the bytecode stream containing the singleton operation *nop*.

The next rules deal with patterns introduced in the previous phases. The following rule considers the pattern that stores an integer variable.

Rule 8 (Store Integer)
   $store_{dr}(\Psi_x)$ $\sqsubseteq$ $I_{C(\varrho,\beta),M}$
   where $\beta = [store, \Psi_x]$, and $\varrho = \emptyset$

The first bytecode in β is the instruction *store*, followed by the index Ψ_x, representing the location of x in V.

The following rule deals with object creation.

Rule 9 (Object Creation)
   $new_{dr}(\Phi_N)$ $\sqsubseteq$ $I_{C(\varrho,\beta),M}$
   where $\beta = [new, \Phi_N]$, and $\varrho = \{\Phi_N \mapsto \Phi.cl\}$

The first bytecode is the instruction *new*, followed by the argument, the index in the constant pool of the class.

The reduction of sequential composition assumes that both arguments are already in the normal form.

Rule 10 (Sequential composition — $p; q$)
   $I_{C(\varrho_p,\beta_p),M}; \; I_{C(\varrho_q,\beta_q),M}$ $\sqsubseteq$ $I_{C(\varrho,\beta),M}$
   where $\beta = \beta_p \frown \beta_q$, and $\varrho = \varrho_p \cup \varrho_q$

We concatenate the bytecode streams of p and q given by β_p and β_q, respectively. We also join the symbol tables ($\varrho_p \cup \varrho_q$).

4.4 Lemmas

The basic rules of ROOL and the following lemmas are necessary to prove the compilation rules above. The introduction of assertions reveals the effect of the execution of a command, making explicit the contents of the internal data structure of our ROOL interpreter.

For convenience, we use $\ll PC : n;\ cl : p;\ mtd : m;\ V : l \gg$ as an abbreviation for the following update expression:

$$(\mathbf{new}\ RoolVM;\ (last\ F) : (\mathbf{new}\ FrameInfo;\ PC : n;\ cl : p;\ mtd : m;\ V : l))$$

The above update expression denotes an object of class $RoolVM$ whose top frame is an instance of $FrameInfo$; its program count PC has the value n; p represents the current class cl; m depicts the current executing method mtd; l is the list of local variables V.

The following lemma is related to the initialization of the rvm variable.

Lemma 1 (Initializing the local variable rvm)
$rvm := \mathbf{new}\ RoolVM;\ rvm.SetClasses(C)$
$=$
$rvm := \mathbf{new}\ RoolVM;\ rvm.SetClasses(C);$
$[rvm =\ll PC : 1;\ cl : C;\ mtd : (head\ C.mtds);\ V : null \gg]$

The assertion introduced here makes explicit the value of the attributes in the rvm's initial frame.

The next lemma shows the effect of the method call $rvm.SetVar(M)$.

Lemma 2 (Loading Initial Memory)
$[rvm =\ll PC : i;\ cl : C;\ mtd : (head\ C.mtds);\ V : null \gg];\ rvm.SetVar(M)$
$=$
$[rvm =\ll PC : i;\ cl : C;\ mtd : (head\ C.mtds);\ V : null \gg];\ rvm.SetVar(M);$
$[rvm =\ll PC : i;\ cl : C;\ mtd : (head\ C.mtds);\ V : M \gg]$

The last assertion shows the value of the list of local variables (V) as a copy of the global variable M.

The effect of the method call $rvm.GetControl(k)$ over the auxiliary variable k is made explicit by the following lemma.

Lemma 3 (Loading Control)
$[rvm =\ll PC : i;\ cl : C;\ mtd : (head\ C.mtds);\ V : M \gg];\ rvm.GetControl(k)$
$=$
$[rvm =\ll PC : i;\ cl : C;\ mtd : (head\ C.mtds);\ V : M \gg];\ rvm.GetControl(k);$
$[rvm =\ll PC : i;\ cl : C;\ mtd : (head\ C.mtds);\ V : M \gg];$
$[k.pc = i;\ k.Initial = v_1;\ k.Final = v_2;\ ]$
Where $v_1 = 1$ and $v_2 = (v_1 + (head\ C.mtds).Size)$.

The assertion introduced here shows that the value of the variable k is updated with the current program counter, and the interval denoted by v_1 and v_2.

The next lemma makes clear the value of the operation code of the next instruction to be executed.

Lemma 4 (Getting Operation Code)
$[rvm =\ll PC : i;\ cl : C;\ mtd : (head\ C.mtds);\ V : M \gg];\ rvm.GetBcode(op)$
$=$
$[rvm =\ll PC : i;\ cl : C;\ mtd : (head\ C.mtds);\ V : M \gg];\ rvm.GetBcode(op);$
$[rvm =\ll PC : i;\ cl : C;\ mtd : (head\ C.mtds);\ V : M \gg];\ [op = n]$
Where n denotes the operation code of the next instruction to be executed.

The last assertion makes explicit the value of the opcode.

The following lemma shows the effect of the *nop* instruction.

Lemma 5 (*Nop* Effect)
$[rvm =\ll PC : i;\ cl : C;\ mtd : (head\ C.mtds);\ V : M \gg];\ rvm.nop$
$=$
$[rvm =\ll PC : i;\ cl : C;\ mtd : (head\ C.mtds);\ V : M \gg];\ rvm.nop;$
$[rvm =\ll PC : i + 1;\ cl : C;\ mtd : (head\ C.mtds);\ V : M \gg]$

When $rvm.nop$ is executed, the program counter is incremented by 1.

The next lemma replaces the method call $rvm.GetVar(M)$ by an assignment corresponding to its effect.

Lemma 6 (*GetVar* Effect)
$[rvm =\ll PC : i;\ cl : C;\ mtd : (head\ C.mtds);\ V : l \gg];\ rvm.GetVar(M)$
$=$
$M := l$

M receives the list of local variables stored in the attribute V.

4.5 Proof Example

As an example of a proof of a compilation rule, we show how the lemmas and the basic laws are used to prove the Rule 7. We start from the right hand side (RHS) of the rule inequation. First, the Lemma 1 is applied to show the effect of initializing the variable rvm with the compiled program stored in C. Then, the Lemma 2 is applied to evidence the result of copying the global variable M into the rvm's current frame. After that, the Lemma 3 shows the values of the variables used in the **while** condition. Since the assertion before the **while** implies the satisfaction of the **while** condition, it can be unfold. Then, the Lemma 4 can be used to make explicit the value of the operation code of the current executing instruction.

RHS = {Lemma 1} {Lemma 2} {Lemma 3} {Law 2.5} {Lemma 4.1.4}

```
var op, k, rvm : Int, Control, RoolVM •
  rvm := new RoolVM; rvm.SetClasses(C);
  [rvm =≪ PC : 1; cl : C; mtd : (head C.mtds); V : null ≫];
  rvm.SetVar(M); [rvm =≪ PC : 1; cl : C; mtd : (head C.mtds); V : M ≫];
  rvm.GetControl(k); [k.pc = 1; k.Initial = 1; k.Final = 2];
  [rvm =≪ PC : 1; cl : C; mtd : (head C.mtds); V : M ≫]; rvm.GetBcode(op);
  [rvm =≪ PC : 1; cl : C; mtd : (head C.mtds); V : M ≫]; [op = 0];
  if []⟨0≤ i ≤ n⟩ op = i → rvm.inst$_i$ fi; rvm.GetControl(k);
  while k.pc ≥ k.Initial ∧ k.pc < k.Final •
    rvm.GetBcode(op); if []⟨0≤ i ≤ n⟩ op = i → rvm.inst$_i$ fi; rvm.GetControl(k);
  end;
  rvm.GetVar(M);
end
```

The assertion introduced just before the first **if** statement allows the selection of one command (Law 3); in this case, $rvm.nop$. Then, in order to show the effect of the $rvm.nop$, the Lemma 5 is used. Then, the Lemma 3 makes explicit the effect of the $rvm.GetControl(k)$, by showing the updated value of the variable k. At this point, the assertion before the **while** does not satisfy the **while** condition. Using the Law 4, we can eliminate the **while**. The Lemma 6 shows that the effect of the method call $rvm.GetVar(M)$ is just the useless assignment of the global variable M to itself, which can be eliminated (Law 2).

= {Law 3} {Lemma 5} {Lemma 3} {Law 4} {Lemma 6} {Law 2}

```
var op, k, rvm : Int, Control, RoolVM •
  rvm := newRoolVM; rvm.SetClasses(C);
  [rvm =≪ PC : 1; cl : C; mtd : (head C.mtds); V : null ≫]; rvm.SetVar(M);
  [rvm =≪ PC : 1; cl : C; mtd : (head C.mtds); V : M ≫];
  rvm.GetControl(k); [k.pc = 1; k.Initial = 1; k.Final = 2];
  [rvm =≪ PC : 1; cl : C; mtd : (head C.mtds); V : M ≫]; rvm.GetBcode(op);
  [rvm =≪ PC : 1; cl : C; mtd : (head C.mtds); V : M ≫]; rvm.nop;
  [rvm =≪ PC : 2; cl : C; mtd : (head C.mtds); V : M ≫]; rvm.GetControl(k);
end
```

Repeatedly applying the following laws we can eliminate every command that appears just before the end of the **var** block.

⊒ {Law 6} {Law 8} {Law 9} **var** op, k, rvm : $Int, Control, RoolVM$ • **end**
Using the Law 7 we can eliminate an empty **var** block.

= {Law 7} **skip**

This concludes our proof.

5 Conclusions

We have presented a framework that can be used to build a correct compiler for a Java-like language extending the approach described in [5]. We illustrate how compilation is carried out using compilation rules. Each transformation performed by the compilation rules brings the source program closer to our particular normal form, from which we can capture the sequence of generated bytecodes of the target machine.

Our strategy of proof based on assertions allows us to keep the object-oriented design of the interpreter. We carry out the proof of the rules at a more abstract level, without needing to expand the definition of the interpreter and its associated methods. This is necessary only when proving the lemmas.

In the literature, one can find several approaches related to the design of correct compilers. The majority deals with procedural languages, as the algebraic approach described in [4]. Recently, in [6] descriptions of the ASM models of Java and JVM are given and properties of JVM verification and execution of compiled Java programs are proved. The approach is based on verification instead of on calculation, as here.

A further topic for investigation is the mechanization of our approach. Due to its algebraic nature, a term rewrite system can be used to verify the compilation rules (reduction theorems). Furthermore, the compilation rules can be taken as rewrite rules to carry out compilation automatically. In this way, a prototype compiler can be obtained as a by-product of its own proof of correctness.

Acknowledgments

The research reported in this paper benefitted from discussions with our collaborators David Naumann and Paulo Borba. The authors are partly supported by CAPES and CNPq, grants 520763/98-0 (Ana Cavalcanti), 521039/95-9 (Augusto Sampaio), 680032/99-1 (CO-OP project, jointly funded by PROTEM-CC and the National Science Foundation), and PICDT/UFBA (Adolfo Duran).

References

1. Paulo Borba and Augusto Sampaio. Basic laws of rool: an object-oriented language. *Revista de Informática Teórica e Aplicada*, 7(I):49–68, 2000.
2. Ana Cavalcanti and David Naumann. A weakest precondition semantics for refinement of object-oriented programs. *IEEE Transactions on Software Enginnering*, 26(08):713–728, 2000.
3. C. A. R. Hoare, J. He, and A. Sampaio. Normal form approach to compiler design. *Acta Informatica*, 30:701–739, 1993.
4. M. Müller-Olm. *Modular Compiler Verification: A Refinement-Algebraic Approach Advocating Stepwise Abstraction*, volume 1283 of *LNCS*. Springer-Verlag, Heidelberg, Germany, 1997.
5. Augusto Sampaio. *An Algebraic Approach to Compiler Design*, volume 4 of *AMAST Series in Computing*. World Scientific, 1997.
6. R. Stärk, J. Schmid, and E. Börger. *Java and the Java Virtual Machine - Definition, Verification, Validation*. Springer-Verlag, 2001.
7. B. Stroustrup. *The C++ Programming Language*. Addison-Wesley, 1991.

Formal Modelling of Java GUI Event Handling

Jessica Chen

School of Computer Science, University of Windsor,
Windsor, Ont. Canada N9B 3P4
xjchen@cs.uwindsor.ca

Abstract. Programming in Java Swing and AWT can be quite error-prone due to the implicit nondeterminism caused by the complex event handling realized via multithreading. In this work, we provide a framework on formal modelling of Java GUI event handling in terms of labelled transition systems. The significance of the work is twofold: on one hand, it provides a formal basis for a better understanding and correct use of Java GUI event handling mechanism; on the other hand, it lays the ground work for formally reasoning about the correctness of a GUI-based Java application against certain properties that, due to the nondeterminism involved, may be hard to detect.

Keywords: Java Swing and AWT, Concurrency, Nondeterminism, Model Checking, Labelled Transition Systems.

1 Motivation

With the advances of software development and the increasing use of web programming technologies, more and more applications now make use of Graphical User Interface (GUI) to enhance user friendliness. In particular, as Java is gaining its increasing popularity, many web applications now involve graphical user interface developed with Java Swing and AWT.

However, programming in Java Swing and AWT can be quite error-prone due to the implicit nondeterminism caused by the complex event handling realized through the use of multiple threads. To write correct programs thus requires a good understanding of Java multithreading and the GUI event control. Such a good understanding is hard to achieve without a precise definition of the working context. In this paper, we define the operational semantics in terms of labelled transition systems for the behavior of a GUI-based Java application/applet at a lower level where event handling mechanism is explicitly specified. This is essential for the software programmers to get a better understanding of the internal event control and thus avoid potential errors in their coding.

No programmer can be perfect: both faults and errors are quite common in software industry practice. In order to detect system faults and errors, various static analysis techniques, formal verification techniques, and dynamic testing/debugging techniques have been explored. Although testing has always been our primary device to guarantee the quality of the systems, some concurrency control related errors are hard to find because the tests are not repeatable due to the nondeterminism involved. The Java GUI event systems are typically of this kind because of the implicitly employed multithreading in the GUI event handling. For these systems, software *verification* under certain formalisms and methodologies usually gives us higher confidence about the system. The formal model we defined for the Java event handling is the basis for formally reasoning about the correctness of the a GUI-based Java application/applet against certain properties that, due to the nondeterminism involved, may be hard to detect by ordinary testing techniques.

In the following, we first give in Section 2 a brief review of Java GUI event handling mechanism. Then we present our operational semantics followed by an example in Section 3 and 4. In Section 5 we discuss how to detect errors via labelled transition system. The related work is provided in Section 6 and we have Section 7 for conclusion and final remarks.

2   Java GUI Event Handling Mechanism

Common graphical user interactions include moving the mouse, clicking a button, typing in a text field, selecting an item from a menu, closing a window, etc. Java GUIs are event driven: when the user interacts with the GUI, some *events* are automatically generated and a proper piece of code may be executed as to handle each event.

A triggered event contains information about the *event type* and the *event context*.

- GUI events are classified into different types. For instance, single click on a button can trigger an action event, while moving the mouse around triggers lots of mouse events.
- The same user interaction on different GUI components may cause totally different reactions. The event context is the GUI component object on which the event is triggered.

An event listener is an object who listens for specific types of events generated on specific GUI objects. Each event listener has pre-defined methods (called *event handlers*) to be executed for the events that it listens to.

In order to have the Java run-time system process GUI events, the programmer needs to perform two tasks:

- register an event listener for each specific type of event on each specific GUI object;
- provide implementation of the event handlers to handle such events for each event listener.

Figure 1 shows a very simple Java application with Swing. It constructs a JFrame p which contains a JTextField t. l is an event listener object that is registered to listen to the action events on t. l handles such events by calling its method *actionPerformed* which sets t to be *non-editable*.

```java
import java.awt.*;
import java.awt.event.*;
import javax.swing.*;

public class NotSafeProg extends JFrame {
    private JTextField t;
    public NotSafeProg()      /* constructor */
    {
        /* call constructor of superclass JFrame with title "A Wrong Program" */
        super("A Wrong Program");
        t = new JTextField();    /* create a JTextField object t */
        /* add t to current JFrame object */
        getContentPane().add(t, BorderLayout.NORTH);
        TextFieldListener l = new TextFieldListener();   /* create a listener object */
        t.addActionListener(l);   /* register listener l for action events in t */
        setSize(200,100);
        setVisible(true);
        /* ......do something here...... */
        t.setEnabled(true);
    }
    private class TextFieldListener implements ActionListener {
        /* this method is automatically called when action events on t triggered */
        public void actionPerformed(ActionEvent e)
        {
            t.setEnabled(false);
        }
    }
    public static void main(String args[])
    {
        NotSafeProg p = new NotSafeProg();
        p.setDefaultCloseOperation(JFrame.EXIT_ON_CLOSE);
    }
}
```

Fig. 1. A Swing application with potential error

When the user interacts with the GUI, all triggered events are put into an event queue. An internal *dispatching thread* is dedicated to dispatch the events from the event queue: it keeps picking the events from the head of the event queue and dispatching it to the proper event listeners according to the event type and the associated event context. If there is no listener registered for this event type and context, the event will be simply ignored. If there are some listeners registered, then their corresponding predefined event handlers will be executed.

There is a special kind of events that requires the dispatching thread to perform by itself the *run()* method defined on the event context. We use *runnable* to denote this type.

The event context is not guaranteed to be thread-safe in general: When an event is dispatched to a listener, the event handler may be executed in a thread other than the one that performed the listener registration. The choice of which thread to use is made by the service provider. Furthermore, when an event is dispatched to multiple listeners, the service provider will normally choose to execute the event handlers concurrently in separate threads.

In the above example, the JFrame constructor is called by an implicitly created thread (we call it *main* below) to execute the *main()* method. Within this constructor, we have registered l for action events on t. However, the dispatching thread may assign a thread other than *main* to execute the event handler of l. This makes the concurrent executions of event handler and of the JFrame construction possible. As a consequence, while a separate thread is setting t to be *non-editable* according to the event handler, it is possible that the *main* thread will be trying to set t to be *editable*. This causes the simultaneous access to the same GUI object via different threads and hence implies potential errors.

Although here we have only shown a very simple example, the real applications may take quite complicated forms and thus make the potential errors hard to see by code walk through. Like in many concurrent systems, to detect such concurrency-related errors via ordinary testing techniques is also hard mainly because the tests are not repeatable.

3 Operational Semantics for the Event Handling

We define the operational semantics of the behavior of the Java GUI event handling mechanism in terms of labelled transition systems. Basically, a labelled transition system is a triple *(States,Labels,→)* where

- *States* is the set of possible states of the program computation;
- *Labels* is a set of labels showing the information about the state changes;
- →⊆ *State* × *Labels* × *State* is a transition relation that describes the system evolution. $(s, l, s') \in \rightarrow$ (also written as $s \xrightarrow{l} s'$) expresses that the system may evolve from state s to state s' with the information of the state change described in l.

A state in our setting consists of the state of objects, the state of event queue, the state of the registration, and the state of the execution state of the threads.

An object is represented by a couple (od, st) where od is an object identifier and st is an object state. An object state consists of a set of field name and field value pairs. Let P be a given GUI-based Java program under consideration.

- We use Fd to denote the set of field names used in P.
- We use V to denote the set of field values in P. For simplicity, we only consider integer and boolean values.
- We use Od to denote the set of object identifiers in P. Note that it includes the identifiers of all thread objects created in the program.
- $O \in Od \to (Fd \to V)$ is a state of objects in P.

An event is represented by a couple (gd, tp) where gd is a GUI object identifier to denote the event context, and tp is an event type name. An event queue is represented by a sequence of events.

- We use Gd to denote the set of GUI object identifiers in P. $Gd \subseteq Od$.
- We use TP to denote the set of type names of GUI events in P. This set includes the special name *runnable* for those events that request the dispatching thread to execute the *run()* method of the given runnable objects.
- $E \subseteq Gd \times TP$ is a set of events.
- $Q \in E^*$ is a sequence of events. Let $e \in E$ be an event. We use $head(Q)$ to denote the first event of Q; $enqueue(Q,e)$ to denote the event queue obtained from Q by adding e to the tail of the queue; $dequeue(Q)$ to denote the event queue obtained from Q by removing the head event.

An event listener registration is a triple (gd, tp, ld) where gd is the identifier of the GUI object, i.e. the context of the event; tp is the name of the event type; and ld is the identifier of the listener object. Such an event listener registration expresses that the object with identifier ld is registered to listen to the events of type tp on GUI object with identifier gd.

- We use Ld to denote the set of listener object identifiers. $Ld \subseteq Od$.
- $R \subseteq Gd \times TP \times Ld$ is a set of event listener registrations. Let $gd \in Gd$, $ty \in TP$. We use $reg(R, gd, tp)$ to denote the set of listener objects registered with gd and tp in R.

In this work, we consider only the following restricted set of atomic actions:

$$A = \{read(od, fd), write(od, fd, v), reg(gd, tp, ld), dereg(gd, tp, ld)$$
$$\mid od \in Od, fd \in Fd, v \in V, gd \in Gd, tp \in TP, ld \in Ld\}$$

A sequential program execution can be constructed as a process term [19] based on a set of atomic actions and a set of operators. For simplicity, we only consider the sequential execution operator denoted by a semicolon. Extension of this framework to include other operators such as choice, recursion, etc. is straightforward. For convenience, we assume that such a sequence is a sequence of actions ended by a special symbol *stop*.

- $SE \subseteq A^* \times \{stop\}$ is a set of sequential executions. Let $sm_i \in A$ for $1 \leq i \leq n$ and $n \geq 1$. We use $sm_1; \ldots; sm_n; stop$ to denote the program execution of a sequence $sm_1, \ldots, sm_n$ of actions.

A thread state records the current status of the execution of a thread. It is a pair *(td,se)* where *td* is the thread identifier and *se* is the program that *td* needs to execute.

- We use Td to denote the set of thread identifiers. It includes the special identifier dt for the *dispatching thread*. $Td \subseteq Od$.
- $T \in Td \to SE$ is a set of thread states.

A method registration is a triple *(ld,tp,se)* where *ld* is the identifier of the listener object, *tp* is an event type name, and *se* is the piece of program to be executed when listener *ld* handles an event of type *tp*.

- $M \in (Ld \times TP) \to SE$ is a set of method registrations. Let $ld \in Ld$, $tp \in TP$. We use *met(M,ld,tp)* to denote the piece of program for listener *ld* to handle events of type *tp*.

Given a program, the labelled transition system is a quadraple $\langle S, L, \to, s_0 \rangle$. where

$$S \subseteq O \times Q \times R \times T,$$

$s_0 \in S$ is the initial state,

$$L \subseteq Td \times (A \cup \{dispatch, runnable\}) \cup \{trigger(e) \mid e \in E\},$$

and O, Q, R, T, E, M, Td, A are as defined above.

The transition relation $\_ \to \_$ is defined as the least relation satisfying the following eight *structural rules*. All the structural rules have schema:

$$\frac{\text{ANTECEDENT}}{\text{CONSEQUENT}}$$

which is interpreted logically as: $\forall(\text{ANTECEDENT} \longrightarrow \text{CONSEQUENT})$, where $\forall(\ldots)$ stands for the universal closure of all free variables occurring in $(\ldots)$. Observe that, typically, ANTECEDENT, CONSEQUENT share free variables. In case the ANTECEDENT is missing, it is interpreted as *true*.

In the following, $od \in Od, fd \in Fd, v \in V, gd \in Gd, tp \in TP, k \geq 1, ld, l_1, \ldots, l_k \in Ld, sm, sm_1, \ldots, sm_k \in SE$.

Rule A1 (Dispatch with Listeners)

$$\frac{head(Q) = (od, tp) \wedge tp \neq runnable \wedge reg(R, od, tp) = \{l_1, \ldots, l_k\} \wedge \bigwedge_{1 \leq i \leq k} met(M, l_i, tp) = sm_i}{\langle O, Q, R, T \cup \{(dt, stop)\}\rangle \xrightarrow{(dt, dispatch)} \langle O, dequeue(Q), R, T \cup \{(dt, stop), (t_1, sm_1), \ldots, (t_k, sm_k)\}\rangle}$$

where t_i are new threads ($1 \leq i \leq k$), and T does not include the behavior of the dispatching thread.

The first rule is used to define the possible evolution of the system caused by the event dispatching of the dispatching thread when the first event of the event queue is a GUI event and there are listeners registered in the current R to handle it. In this case, the whole system makes the related transition corresponding to the one by the dispatching thread while all other threads remain in the same state. In the ending state of the system, the GUI event is removed from the event queue Q, and there are new threads generated to perform each of the handling tasks of the listeners registered for this event. Note that the dispatching thread should have no code to execute (i.e. in state $stop$) in order to dispatch events from the event queue, otherwise it has to execute its own code first.

Rule A2 (No Listener Dispatch)

$$\frac{head(Q) = (od, tp) \wedge tp \neq runnable \wedge reg(R, od, tp) = \emptyset}{\langle O, Q, R, T \cup \{(dt, stop)\}\rangle \xrightarrow{(dt, dispatch)} \langle O, dequeue(Q), R, T \cup \{(dt, stop)\}\rangle}$$

where T does not include the behavior of the dispatching thread.

Rule (A2) is used to define the possible evolution of the system caused by the event dispatching of the dispatching thread when the first event of the event queue is a GUI event and there is no listener registered in the current R to handle it. In this case, the GUI event is simply removed from the event queue Q and ignored.

Rule A3 (Runnable)

$$\frac{head(Q) = (od, tp) \wedge tp = runnable \wedge met(M, od, runnable) = sm}{\langle O, Q, R, T \cup \{(dt, stop)\}\rangle \xrightarrow{(dt, runnable)} \langle O, dequeue(Q), R, T \cup \{(dt, sm)\}\rangle}$$

where T does not include the behavior of the dispatching thread.

When the first element in the event queue is of type $runnable$, the dispatching thread will execute the related code, that is, the $run()$ method of the context object of the event. This is expressed by Rule (A3). Note that at the ending state, the dispatching thread is assigned the related code to perform, and thus no more available to dispatch events until the assigned code is completed.

Rule A4 (Trigger)

$$\frac{O(gd, visible) = true}{\langle O, Q, R, T\rangle \xrightarrow{trigger(gd, tp)} \langle O, enqueue(Q, (gd, tp)), R, T\rangle}$$

Rule (A4) expresses our simulation of the GUI input from the end users. An end user can trigger GUI events at any time as long as the context GUI object is currently visible by the end user. Here we use $O(od,f)$ to denote the value of field f of object od in the current state.

Rules (A5) and (A6) define the possible evolution of the system caused by an action to read from the main memory or write into the main memory. The thread that executes such an action can be either of a program thread or the dispatching thread that is executing a $run()$ method. Rules (A7) and (A8) show the possible system moves caused by the registration and deregistration of the event listeners to the specified event types on the specified GUI objects. For the lack of space, we do not present these structural rules formally.

Given an initial state, the above eight structural rules allow us to associate to it a labelled transition system whose states are those reachable from the initial state, via the transitions inferred by using the structural rules. The labelled transition system generated from the initial state describes all the possible evolutions, and hence constitutes our model of the system.

4 An Example

In the above given program, there are four objects that we are interested in (without confusion, we use the object reference names as their identifiers):

- the listener object l.
  we are interested only in the object identifier.
- the JFrame object p.
  we are interested only in its field $visible$, which is initially $false$.
- the JTextField object t.
  we are interested only in its field $visible$ which is initially $false$ and its field $enabled$ which is initially $true$.
- the implicit thread $main$ which is used to call the $main$ method.
  we are interested only in its object identifier.

Thus, we have

- $Ld = \{l\}$;
- $Gd = \{p, t\}$;
- $Td = \{main, dt\}$;
- TP contains all the names of the event types that can be triggered on GUI object p and t, such as $action\ event$ (denoted by ae below), $focus\ event$, $text\ event$.
- $M = \{(l, ae, write(t, enabled, false); stop)\}$

At the beginning, $s_0 = \langle O_0, [\ ], \emptyset, \{T_0\}\rangle$ where

- $O_0 = \{(l,\emptyset), (p,\{(visible, false)\}), (t,\{(visible, false), (enabled, true)\}), (main, \emptyset)\}$;
- $T_0 = (main,\ reg(t,\ ae,\ l); write(p, visible, true); write(t, visible, true),$
  $write(t, enabled, true); stop)$

From state s_0, we can apply Rule (A7) to obtain

$$s_0 \xrightarrow{(main, reg(t, ae, l))} s_1$$

where
$s_1 = \langle O_0, [\ ], \{(t, ae, l)\}, \{T_1\}\rangle$,
$T_1 = (main, write(p, visible, true); write(t, visible, true); write(t, enabled, true); stop)$.

This corresponds to the action performed by thread *main* to register l as the listener of the action event on t.

From state s_1, we can apply Rule (A6) twice to obtain

$$s_1 \xrightarrow{(main, write(p, visible, true))} s_2 \xrightarrow{(main, write(t, visible, true))} s_3$$

where
$s_3 = \langle O_1, [\ ], \{(t, ae, l)\}, \{T_2\}\rangle$
$T_2 = (main, write(t, enabled, true); stop)$
$O_1 = \{(l, \emptyset), (p, \{(visible, true)\}), (t, \{(visible, true), (enabled, true)\}), (main, \emptyset)\}$;

This corresponds to the *setVisible(true)* action performed by thread *main*.

Once GUI object t is set visible, user interactions may occur at any time. So, for example, from s_3 we can apply Rule (A4) to obtain

$$s_3 \xrightarrow{trigger(t, ae)} s_4$$

where

$$s_4 = \langle O_1, [(t, ae)], \{(t, ae, l)\}, \{T_2\}\rangle$$

5 Detecting Errors

The most prominent significance in defining operational semantics on the GUI event handling mechanism lies in formally reasoning about the correctness of the GUI-based programs.

As we know, process algebras e.g. CCS [19], CSP [13], ACP [1], have been well studied for describing concurrent and multi-process systems. For finite state processes (processes that can be interpreted on finite transition systems), various practical model checking tools have been developed to verify whether a process satisfies certain properties (see e.g. [3, 7, 10, 15, 18, 26]), where the properties actually characterize the requirements of the system and can be described in a formula of a modal/temporal logic such as CTL [9], μ-calculus [16, 25]. Since most of these tools are based on transition systems, we can make use of their techniques, or even reuse existing tools to verify certain properties over the transition systems we obtained for the GUI event handling.

For example, we know that *GUI update is not thread-safe*. We need to guarantee that at each moment, there is at most one thread accessing the GUI objects. This can be expressed as an *invariance* that *in the given transition system, there is no two consecutive actions (labels in our setting) (t_1, op_1) and (t_2, op_2) such that op_1 and op_2 both access some GUI objects, i.e. for some $t_1, t_2 \in Td$, $od_1, od_2 \in Gd$, $f_1, f_2 \in Fd$, $v_1, v_2 \in V$,*

$t_1 \neq t_2$,

$op_1 = write(od_1, f_1, v_1)$ or $op_1 = read(od_1, f_1)$,

$op_2 = write(od_2, f_2, v_2)$ or $op_2 = read(od_2, f_2)$.

This statement can be easily formulated in, for example, modal μ-calculus or action-based CTL [20]. Similarly, we can formulate an invariance to express that at each moment, there is at most one thread accessing an (not necessarily GUI) object field.

The violation of these invariance are mainly due to the nondeterministic assignment of the threads to execute the event handlers, and the possibility of hitting the related errors is relatively low. As a consequence, it becomes very hard, if not impossible, to detect them using ordinary testing techniques. Without the help of verification tools, such errors would easily slip into product in customers hands.

6 Related Work

Formal verification strongly relies on the formal specifications or formal models of the target systems. Such a formal specification or formal model can be derived either from the design documents or from the final code.

Formalism of design documents has been an important and active research direction [11, 17, 22]. Typically, since Unified Modeling Language (UML) [2] is well accepted by the software industries as graphical design notations, people have been studying the translations of UML descriptions into various formalisms. For example, in [11] it has been discussed the formalism of class diagrams in UML using Z [24]. In [17], operational semantics is provided to UML State Machine so that formal verification techniques can further apply.

Considering final code or programming languages, we have mainly two approaches.

- One is to provide automated translation of a program into a certain formal specification language so that the related verification technique can apply. For example, in [23], Shatz et al. described a tool to verify the correctness of Ada tasking programs using Petri Net. A translator from a concurrent extension of C++ into Promela [14] is presented in [4], and a translator from a subset of Java into Promela can be found in [12]. In both of these two works, the translated programs are then given to SPIN model checker (see e.g. [15]) as input to verify systems properties given in LTL [21]. In [6], we discussed a translation of a concurrency-sensitive subset of Java into CCS in order to verify systems properties given in model μ-calculus.
- Another approach is to provide formal semantics to some popular programming languages. For example, in [5, 8], the semantics of subsets of Java are defined directly with a set of structural rules. Our work actually followed this line of research. We have discussed the operational semantics of Java event handling mechanism which has not been addressed in the literature.

7 Conclusion and Final Remarks

Based on the Java language specification, we proposed a framework on the modeling of Java GUI event handling mechanism in labelled transition systems. The proposed operational semantics gives a precise definition of the behavior of the system with respect to the GUI events, and thus helps us to gain a better understanding of the system behavior and avoid incorrect programming. It can also be further developed for formal verification against certain required properties, such as deadlock/livelock freeness, fairness, eventualities, etc. Usually these kind of properties are very hard to test with general testing techniques.

As we mentioned, we have considered only the part of the graphical user interface of Java. To further combine this part of semantics on GUI with other parts on multithreading, stream socket etc. is possible as long as they all define the system models in labelled transition systems through structural rules.

We have adopted interleaving semantics in our interpretation. Of course, a truly concurrent semantics may also be considered. This can be accomplished by providing some additional structural rules. Our choice on interleaving semantics is based on the following three observations: (i) it is simple and the generated model is relatively small; (ii) we can easily check the satisfiability of some system properties that we are interested in against the given model; (iii) most of the existing formal verification tools are based on interleaving models.

Acknowledgements

This work is supported in part by the Natural Sciences and Engineering Research Council of Canada under grant number RGPIN 209774.

References

1. J. Bergstra and J. Klop. Process algebra for synchronous communication. *Information and Control*, 60:109–137, 1984.
2. G. Booch, I. Jacobson, and J. Rumbaugh. *The Unified Modeling Language User Guide*. Addison-Wesley, 1998.
3. G. Boudol, R. de Simone, V. Roy, and D. Vergamini. Process calculi, from theory to practice: Verification tools. In *Proc. of Workshop on Automatic Verification Methods for Finite State Systems, LNCS 407*. Springer-Verlag, 1990.
4. T. Cattel. Modeling and verification of sC++ applications. In *Proc. of the Tools and Algorithms for the Construction and Analysis of Systems, LNCS 1384*, pages 232–248. Springer-Verlag, 1998.
5. P. Cenciarelli, A. Knapp, B. Reus, and M. Wirsing. An event-based structural operational semantics of multi-threaded java. In *Formal Syntax and Semantics of Java, LNCS 1523*, pages 157–200. Springer-Verlag, 1999.
6. J. Chen. On verifying distributed multithreaded Java programs. *Software Quality Journal*, 8:321–341, 1999.
7. R. Cleaveland and S. Sims. The NCSU concurrency workbench. In *Computer-Aided Verification (CAV'96), LNCS 1102*, pages 394–397. Springer-Verlag, 1996.

8. E. Coscia and G. Reggio. A proposal for a semantics of a subset of multi-threaded "good" Java programs. In *Proc. of the OOPSLA'98 Workshop on Formal Underpinnings of the Java Paradigm*. Vancouver, Canada, October 1998.
9. E. A. Emerson. Temporal and modal logic. In *Handbook of Theoretical Computer Science*, volume B, chapter 16. Elsevier Science Publishers B.V., 1990.
10. E. A. Emerson. Automated temporal reasoning about reactive systems. In *Logics for Concurrency: Structure versus Automata, LNCS 1043*, pages 41–101. Springer-Verlag, 1996.
11. R. B. France, J. M. Bruel, M. M. Larrondo-Petrie, and M. Shroff. Exploring the semantics of UML type structures with Z. In *IFIP Proc. of Formal Methods in Open Object-based Distributed Systems*, pages 247–257. Chapman & Hall, 1997.
12. K. Havelund. Java PathFinder. In *The 6th International SPIN Workshop, LNCS 1680*. Springer-Verlag, 1999.
13. C. A. R. Hoare. *Communicating Sequential Processes*. Prentice Hall Int., London, 1985.
14. G. Holzmann. *The Design and Validation of Computer Protocols*. Prentice Hall, 1991.
15. G. Holzmann. The model checker SPIN. *IEEE Transactions on Software Engineering*, 23(5), May 1997.
16. D. Kozen. Results on the propositional μ-calculus. *Theoretical Computer Science*, 27(2):333–354, 1983.
17. J. Lilius and I. Paltor. Formalizing UML state machines for model checking. In *UML'99: Lecture Notes in Computer Science 1723*. Springer-Verlag, 1999.
18. K. L. McMillan. *Symbolic Model Checking*. Kluwer Academic Publishers, 1993.
19. R. Milner. *Communication and Concurrency*. Prentice Hall, London, 1989.
20. R. D. Nicola, A. Fantechi, S. Gnesi, and G. Ristori. An action based framework for verifying logical and behavioural properties of concurrent systems. *Computer Networks and ISDN Systems*, 25(7):761–778, Feb. 1993.
21. A. Pnueli. The temporal logic of programs. In *Proc. of 18th IEEE Symp. on Foundations of Computer Science*, pages 46–57. 1977.
22. G. Reggio, M. Cerioli, and E. Astesiano. Towards a rigorous semantics of UML supporting its multiview approach. In *Proceedings of FASE 2001, LNCS 2029*. Springer-Verlag, 2001.
23. S. Shatz, K. Mai, C. Black, and S. Tu. Design and implementation of a Petri Net based toolkit for Ada tasking analysis. *IEEE Transactions on Parallel and Distributed Systems*, 1(4), October 1990.
24. J. M. Spivey. *The Z Notation: A Reference Manual*. Prentice Hall, 1992.
25. C. Stirling. Modal and temporal logics. In *Handbook of Logic in Computer Science, Volume 2*, pages 477–563. Oxford University Press, 1992.
26. C. Stirling. Modal and temporal logics for processes. In *Logics for Concurrency: Structure versus Automata, LNCS, 1043*, pages 149–237. Springer-Verlag, 1996.

A New Algorithm for Service Interaction Detection

Ana Cavalli and Stéphane Maag

Institut National des Télécommunications,
9 rue Charles Fourier,
F-91011 Evry Cedex, France
phone : +33 1 60764474, fax : +33 1 60764711,
{Ana.Cavalli,Stephane.Maag}@int-evry.fr

Abstract. This paper presents a new formal method for telephony services engineering allowing feature interactions detection. System and service specifications are provided using the specification language SDL. These specifications are simulated in order to obtain finite state machines. An algorithm allowing to compare service scenarios according to marked transitions is proposed. The algorithm has been implemented and applied to a case study, a telecommunication system on Intelligent Network architecture including the Basic Call Service (BCS) and two supplementary: Originating Call Service (OCS) and Call Forward Unconditional (CFU). The results of this application are presented.

Keywords: Telecommunication service, Feature interaction, Finite State Machine, Intelligent Network

1 Introduction

The service interaction is one of the most critical problems in the telecommunications domain. In order to give an example of such problems, let two users A and B be subscribers of the service *Call Forward Unconditional*. A forwards his calls to B and the latter B forwards to A. Let us imagine a third user C who calls A or B. What happens to user C ? What happens for the telecommunication network ? The detection and resolution of these interactions become more and more complex and crucial. Indeed, the number of services (or features, we do not differentiate the two terms here) may be witnessed. In order to manage this complexity, different methods and techniques have been proposed: analysis of interactions at the early user-needs stage, or at the service specification stage, when designing and conceiving the environment supporting the services or at the service implementation stage [3].
Many types of feature interactions may be observed [5], this is the reason why it is very difficult to find a universal method to detect all possible interactions. It is therefore necessary to integrate different methods to be applied at the early stages of development [9], as well as, during later stages, when implementing specific environments [1].

We may notice that the number of service interactions is growing up through all these stages. Therefore, in order to be efficient, we present in this paper an analysis and a formal method for feature interactions detection based at the upper level of the life cycle, that is the specification phase. There exists several suitable formalisms to model protocols. For example, extended finite state machines [15], transition systems [16], labelled transition systems [4], process algebras [2] and Petri nets [17]. Many works tackle this problem and thus several analysis lead to the creation of detection methods based on different kind of specifications. The study presented in [6] leads to the use of Message Sequence Charts scenarios. However, a partial behavior of the system is described while we would like to perform a global behavior analysis. There are others methods allowing to detect some interactions (e.g. [7, 8, 13]) such as the ones using the feature requirements. In turn, requirements are expressed by properties. Nevertheless, one of the main drawbacks of the properties oriented approaches is that it is often very difficult to describe all the system properties by logic expressions. Furthermore, when we add new features to a system, it is sometimes necessary to rewrite some properties. That is why the choice of our study turns on a formal approach based on finite state machines.

We use a specification of services based on Extended Finite State Machines (EFSMs) to analyze and detect feature interactions. Work involving the same formal concepts is presented in [14]. The authors use a restriction function on automata that deprives the analysis of a specification part. However, no satisfying method is given allowing to show that the pruned part is negligible to the feature interaction detection. Our work consist in the detection of interactions based on comparison of scenarios with marked transitions. The main contribution of our work consists in the design of a new algorithm for the detection of interactions from the behavior of a telecommunication system. This algorithm has been implemented and applied to the feature interaction detection on an intelligent network architecture. It describes five services on the Basic Call Service (BCS) implemented in SDL [10], however we present here only the results dealing with the Originating Call Service (OCS) and the Call Forward Unconditional (CFU).

The article is organized as the following. Section 2 introduces the basic notions and the definitions illustrating the problematic. Section 3 describes the feature interaction detection algorithm. Section 4 presents the application of the case studied on a real telecommunication system. And finally, Section 5 concludes the article.

2 Basics

The Extended Finite State Machines (abbreviated by EFSM) are the basis of the specification processes in SDL (Specification and Description Language). The goal of SDL is to specify system behaviors from the representation of their functional properties and to describe their effective behavior. Therefore, this language is particularly suited to study systems that can be described by using the extended finite state machines. Our technique can also be applied on other mathematic models such as transition systems, labelled transition systems, process algebras and Petri nets. In our work, EFSMs (modeled by using SDL) are deployed into Finite State Machines.

Definition 1: A *Finite State Machine* (in short FSM) or *automaton*, is a quintuple $Aut = (s^0, D, \Sigma, Act_{Aut}, T)$ with:

- $s^0 \in \Sigma$ is the initial state of Aut,
- D is the set of Aut final states,
- Σ is the set of Aut states,
- Act_{Aut} is the set of Aut actions,
- $T \subset \Sigma \times Act_{Aut} \times \Sigma$ defines the set of transitions. □

An action of a FSM is composed by a primitive and data, as for instance *offhook(A)* which means that user A has offhooked. This notion of Finite State Machine allows to obtain the description of telecommunication system behaviors from SDL specifications. We use here the usual notion of telecommunication system in the sense that it provides a set $\mathcal{F}$ of features to some customers such that $\mathcal{F} \in \mathcal{P}(\{F_0, F_1, \ldots, F_n\})$. F_0 is the BCS on which the other value-added features F_i ($i \in I = \{1, \ldots, n\}$) are connected. A telecommunication system T_k is a finite state machine such that $T_k = BCS \bigoplus_{i \in I_k \subset I} F_i$. In our work, we assume that the connections are specified and that the finite state machines are given.

When we analyze the system features, we often mention the notion of *behavior*. However this behavior is not always formalized. There are several aspects that may define it. For instance, the *functional* aspects, which concern the sequences of possible states/events, and the *non-functional* aspects, with regard to any real time and performance aspects of the behavior. In this paper, we restrict our analysis to the functional aspects. *Execution sequences* (or *scenarios*) are a good and formal way in order to capture this kind of behavior. Next, we introduce this concept in our framework.

Definition 2: Let Aut be a finite state machine. A *scenario* s in Aut is a concatenation of elements in T, where data have been removed. Only primitives named *feature primitives* are kept. In our paper, we study feature interactions from the control part of the system behaviors. Therefore, we avoid the generation of multiple behaviors that are the same (e.g. user A or B offhooks and onhooks). We represent every Aut's scenario by $S(Aut)$. □

The feature interactions may have different causes and thus many definitions. In our work, feature interaction refers to situations where different features or instances of the same features influence each other. Generally, they can be observed when two telecommunication systems affect each other [12]. This mechanism is developed in the following section.

3 Feature Interaction Detection Algorithm

In order to analyze feature interactions, we need to obtain the whole studied system behavior. We generate all the behaviors in deploying and executing every cycle in the finite state machines.

3.1 Acyclic Paths and Simple Loops Generation in a Finite State Machine

The behaviors are usually cyclic in telecommunication systems, that is, when all the users onhook, the current state becomes the initial state, and we obtain the system like a huge strongly connected component. Therefore, for the automata analysis, we stop the scenarios execution when we reach the initial state back, defining then final states. In order to obtain every scenario of a FSM Aut, we first transform it in a Direct Acyclic Graph (DAG) Aut' in which the nodes are either Aut nodes or Strongly Connected Components (SCC) in Aut. To compute the partitions of finite state machines into SCCs, we apply the method developed by Tarjan [18] implemented in our laboratory. By a depth-first search, we obtain the acyclic paths in the finite state machine Aut'. Into the scenarios, some nodes represent some SCCs and then we need to deploy them in order to analyze the whole behavior. We generate for this reason every simple loop. We call simple loops the cycles which do not contain other cycles. We apply the following algorithm to the strongly connected components.

Scenario-Generation Algorithm
Input: N a strongly connected component in Aut, v a state in N.
Output: A set of scenarios in N starting from v.
1- Let v_i, be a node belonging to N, $(v_i, t_j, v_j) \in T_{Aut}$, where v_j is a node in N,
2- $\gamma(v_i) = \bigcup_{(v_i,t_j,v_j) \in T_{Aut}} (v_i, t_j, v_j)\gamma(v_j)$ where $\gamma(v_j) = \{\Lambda\}$ if v_j has already been visited by $\gamma(v_i)$. \ * $\{\Lambda\}$ illustrates the empty scenario *.
3- return $\gamma(v)$

We apply this last algorithm to the SCC represented in Figure 1 and to the state $v = 1$. We obtain the set $\gamma(1) = \{(1, a, 2, b, 3, c, 1), (1, a, 2, b, 3, d, 4, e, 1), (1, a, 2, b, 3, d, 4, f, 5, g, 3)\}$. Every simple loop in N is obtained from this last set by projecting the segments of scenarios. That is, in each element of $\gamma(v)$, we extract all the scenarios beginning from a state p and terminating to the same state p. In the previous case, we obtain the simple loops set $\{(1, a, 2, b, 3, c, 1), (1, a, 2, b, 3, d, 4, e, 1), (3, d, 4, f, 5, g, 3)\}$.

Proposition 1. This last algorithm allows to obtain all the simple loops in a strongly connected component.

Proof: By the SCC definition, all states are reachable from any states. From one state, we execute all the possible transitions. We thus may reach from this state all the other states in a recursive way and we eventually reach this same state. Therefore, all the simple loops are generated by any state. ∎

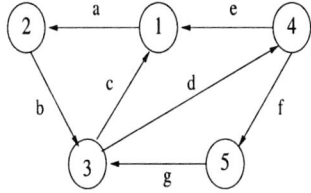

Fig. 1. A strongly connected component.

We obtain simple loops that allow to analyze interactions from the FSM scenarios. Nevertheless, in the general case, the set of all these scenarios has a infinite size, indeed, the SCC cycles may be executed infinitely. The method used here consists in, first of all, obtaining the acyclic paths in a DAG and in the second hand, analyzing the automaton SCC. This is detailed in the following.

3.2 Scenarios Analysis

Let our system be composed by two services F_1 and F_2 (different from the BCS) with some different primitives. The specification of this system is written in SDL and with ObjectGEODE [19] we generate three finite state machines A_1, A_2 and G. They respectively represent the feature F_1 and the BCS, the feature F_2 and the BCS, and the global system containing F_1, F_2 and the BCS.
Our work follows the idea that there exists a feature interaction between F_1 and F_2 if and only if the behavior of G does not respect the expected and defined behaviors of A_1 and A_2, according to Section 2.
In an informal manner, here is the procedure allowing the feature interaction detection we propose:

- First, we want to verify that the scenarios included in A_1 and A_2 are present in the scenarios set of G (having renamed the states if necessary). If this is not the case, it means that the service behavior, whose the scenario is the cause, has been modified. A feature interaction occurs.
- In the second hand, if the inclusion in the last step is verified, we also have to check that the scenarios of G non-executed previously can be produced by A_1 and A_2. The mixed execution of actions of A_1 and A_2 have to generate them. These scenarios correspond to the configurations where both services are active. Indeed, the other scenarios are checked by the previous step. The mixed execution of A_1 and A_2 may generate scenarios where only one service is activated, which are undesired. Therefore, we remove transitions that prevent to services from beeing triggered or do not cause the services to be triggered. In A_1 and A_2, we mark such transitions.

The first step of the procedure corresponds of preserving the A_1 and A_2 behaviors in the global system. The second step allows to guarantee that both features are activated in the scenarios of G not taken into account previously, and that these latters may be generated by the mixed execution of A_1 and A_2 actions. This combination is obtained by the *independent product* $A_1 * A_2$ of A_1 and A_2. The independent product allows to obtain all the interleaved behaviors of the automata A_1 and A_2.

Definition 3: Let $Aut_i = (s_i^0, D_i, \Sigma_i, Act_i, T_i)$, $i = 1,2$, be two finite state machines, we note $*$ the *independent product* between the two Aut_i, defined by:
$A_1 * A_2 = Aut = ((s_1^0, s_2^0), D_1 \times D_2, \Sigma_1 \times \Sigma_2, Act_1 \cup Act_2, T)$
with T obtained such that:
$(s_1, x_1, s'_1) \in T_1 \Longrightarrow \forall s_2 \in \Sigma_2, \ ((s_1, s_2), x_1, (s'_1, s_2)) \in T$
$(s_2, x_2, s'_2) \in T_2 \Longrightarrow \forall s_1 \in \Sigma_1, \ ((s_1, s_2), x_2, (s_1, s'_2)) \in T$

$\square$

We illustrate this product in Figure 2.

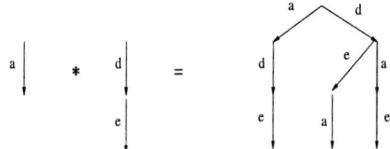

Fig. 2. Example of independent product $*$.

We need to check the inclusion of one set of scenarios in another set of scenarios. However, strongly connected components may exist. As follows, we give a method based on two SCCs obtained with scenario-generation algorithm in order to improve this analysis.

For every strongly connected component scc_i in Aut_1, let P_i^j be the j execution sequences from the initial state to scc_i. These P_i^j have to reach a scc_i' in Aut_2 such that the set of simple loops of scc_i is included in scc_i'. Furthermore, each state of the simple loops of these both strongly connected components must have the same outcoming and incoming transitions. Otherwise, $S(Aut_1) \nsubseteq S(Aut_2)$. Figure 3 shows an example where $S(Aut_1) \nsubseteq S(Aut_2)$.

By this technique, we check whether a set of scenarios is included in another one by analyzing the strongly connected components.

3.3 Feature Interactions Detection Strategy

We expound here our feature interaction detection method. First, we check whether the behaviors defined by each isolated automaton A_1 and A_2 are present in the finite state machine G. After that, we verify that the other scenarios in G, that is $S(G) \setminus \{S(A_1) \cup S(A_2)\}$ are included in $S(A_1 * A_2)$. As mentioned before, marked transitions in A_1 and A_2 do not have to be executed. The marked automaton A_i is noted $\overline{A_i}$. Formally, we can describe our feature interaction algorithm as follows.

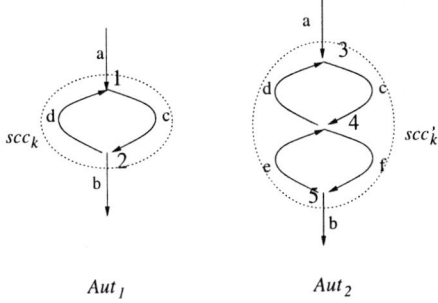

The simple loops of scc_k in Aut_1 are included in the one of scc'_k. However, in the state 2, the transition c is incoming, and b outcoming which is not the case for state 4. We infer $S(Aut_1) \nsubseteq S(Aut_2)$.

Fig. 3. Automata with different sets of scenarios.

Interactions-Detection Algorithm

Input: A_1, A_2 and G, three FSMs respectively representing F_1 and the BCS; F_2 and the BCS, F_1, F_2 and the BCS.
Output: "Interaction detected" or "No interaction detected".
1- **if** $S(A_1) \subset S(G)$ **and** $S(A_2) \subset S(G)$ **and** $S(G) \setminus \{S(A_1) \cup S(A_2)\} \bar{\subset} S(\overline{A_1} * \overline{A_2})$
2- **then** "no interaction detected"
3- **else** "interaction detected".

We note here $S(G) \setminus \{S(A_1) \cup S(A_2)\} \bar{\subset} S(\overline{A_1} * \overline{A_2})$ the inclusion which is true if and only if $\forall s \in S(G) \setminus \{S(A_1) \cup S(A_2)\}$ such that s does not execute marked transitions and reaches a final state of A_1 or A_2, we have $s \in S(A_1 * A_2)$. Indeed, if s does not reach neither a final state in A_1 nor in A_2, it means that s in G have not executed a excepted behavior in A_1 or A_2. That is a feature interaction occurs. In order to avoid the combinatory explosion problem when $\overline{A_1} * \overline{A_2}$ is generated, the inclusion $\bar{\subset}$ will be verified on-the-fly in $\overline{A_1}$ and $\overline{A_2}$.

This feature interaction detection algorithm is applied to a pair of services. It means that we analyze two-way interactions. However we also may be confronted with three-way (and even more) interactions although pairs of these features do not show any interaction. Let us imagine a party A, subscriber of the *Unlisted Number* service (the subscriber may hide his call number to a called party), that calls a party B, subscriber of an *Automatic Recall* of the last caller (the subscriber may automatically recall the last caller). User B is also a subscriber of *Itemized Billing* service. If every feature is activated and B uses the *Automatic Recall*, A's number appears on B's phone bill. This is clearly a violation of the intention of A's *Unlisted Number*. These cases are less common than two-way interactions but we may extend our algorithm in order to tackle this kind of interactions. Let A_1, A_2, A_3 and G be four finite state machines respectively containing the services F_1, F_2, F_3 and $\{F_1, F_2, F_3\}$. The last automaton G represents the global system. The reasoning is then the same than for the interactions-detection algorithm except that we focus on the G scenarios composed by behaviors belonging to A_1, A_2 and A_3 interleaved together. For this reason, we use the independent product between A_1, A_2 and A_3.

Property 2: Let A_1, A_2 and A_3 be three finite state machines, we have:
commutativity: $A_1 * A_2 = A_2 * A_1$,
associativity: $(A_1 * A_2) * A_3 = A_1 * (A_2 * A_3)$.

In order to extend our algorithm to three-way interactions detection we then use the independent product $A_1 * A_2 * A_3$ (also written $\bigotimes_{i \in \{1,2,3\}} A_i$) represented by $(A_1 * A_2) * A_3$. As before, we mark the transitions allowing the deactivation or non-activation of a service. The following algorithm allows to detect such interactions.

Three-Way-Interactions-Detection Algorithm
Input: A_1, A_2, A_3 and G, four FSMs that respectively represent F_1 and the BCS; F_2 and the BCS, F_3 and the BCS, F_1, F_2, F_3 and the BCS.
Output: "Interaction detected" or "No interaction detected".
1- if $S(A_1) \subset S(G)$ and $S(A_2) \subset S(G)$ and $S(A_3) \subset S(G)$ and $S(G) \setminus \{S(A_1 * A_2) \cup S(A_1 * A_3) \cup S(A_2 * A_3)\} \bar{\subset} S(\overline{A_1} * \overline{A_2} * \overline{A_3})$
2- then "no interaction detected"
3- else "interaction detected".

This algorithm allows to check whether the isolated behaviors of F_1, F_2 and F_3 are present in the global system G. Furthermore, the fourth inclusion verifies if the execution of F_1, F_2 and F_3 in a same G scenario has a sense with regard to the A_1, A_2 and A_3 specifications. Let us remark that Three-Way-Interactions-Detection Algorithm does not guarantee the Two-Way interactions detection covered with the Interactions-Detection Algorithm. Indeed, the scenarios only containing pairs of services behaviors are not covered there. By this way, we also may study four-way (and more) interactions in extending our method. We give in the following a method allowing to detect interactions between n features. This is an extension of Three-Way-Interactions-Detection Algorithm in which we detect interactions when n services are active.

N-Way-Interactions-Detection Algorithm
Input: $A_1, A_2, \ldots, A_n$ and G, $n+1$ FSMs that respectively represent F_1 and the BCS; F_2 and the BCS,... F_3 and the BCS, and the BCS with $F_1, \ldots, F_n$.
Output: "Interaction detected" or "No interaction detected".
1- if $\bigcup_{i \in \{1,\ldots,n\}} S(A_i) \subset S(G)$
and $S(G) \setminus \{ \bigcup_{i \in \{1,\ldots,n\}} S(\bigotimes_{j \in \{1,\ldots,n\}, j \neq i} A_j) \} \bar{\subset} S(\bigotimes_{i \in \{1,\ldots,n\}} \overline{A_i})$
2- then "no interaction detected"
3- else "interaction detected".

As before, this last algorithm does not guarantee k-Way-Interactions-Detection for $k \in \{2, \ldots, n-1\}$. However, when n increases, the number of N-Way interactions decreases. This method is used with a number n of features that allows to limit the number of k-Way interactions detection and thus improving the computation. Indeed, in order to detect every feature interaction between each service, it is necessary to tackle each k-Way interaction. Our approach enables to resolve this last point.

In order to apply our Interactions-Detection Algorithm, we illustrate a case of study in the following.

4 Application to a Case Study

In this section, we describe the experimental results obtained by an implementation of our algorithm. We present an application of the tool developed in our laboratory to a real telecommunication system upon an intelligent networks architecture [11]. The services integrated in this system are the Originating Call Service (OCS), Terminating Call Service (TCS), Call Forward Unconditional (CFU), Call Forward on Busyline (CFB) and the Automatic Call Back (ACB). The system is described using the SDL language [10] for the call treatment, the services invocation and for the customers management. The framework of this specification is described in Figure 4.

The global system whose we give few significantly numerals in Figure 5, has been simulated in using the exhaustive simulation mode and a startup file in order to obtain a complete reachability graph. The startup file allows to restrict the simulation and thus to avoid the combinatory explosion problem. Indeed, it is impossible to obtain the complete reachability graph, huge memory size is necessary for such a graph. Therefore, the startup file of the specification allows to activate only the Originating Call Service (OCS) and the Call Forward Unconditional (CFU), and to put the three others inactive. We also may reduce the number of the customers as three, U_1, U_2 and U_3.

Our tool needs three input files. The first one represents an automaton where OCS is lonely active, the second one illustrates the system with only CFU active, and the last one represents the global system containing the two services above. In order to mark the transitions of the two first finite state machines, a static insertion of a signal *fake* is provided in the SDL specification. This signal is sent when the service is unused as it is shown on Figure 6.

With the ObjectGEODE tool, we have simulated the three configurations and have obtained the three finite state machines A_1, A_2 and G whose the details are given in Figure 7.

We may underline that these three finite state machines A_1, A_2 and G do not contain neither deadlocks, nor livelocks. If this is the case, it would meant that the behavior is not correct, and then, an analysis of these scenarios reaching these deadlocks or livelocks would be necessary. From the formal method described in Section 3.2, we check $S(A_1) \subset S(G)$ and $S(A_2) \subset S(G)$. Our tool does not detect any anomalies when we verify both inclusions, it means that the F_1 and F_2 isolated behaviors are correctly respected in the global system. The A_1 and A_2 transitions have previously been marked and the implementation of our algorithm respectively provides us 228,157 and 507 scenarios in A_1, A_2 and G. The third inclusion takes into account 285 scenarios which we need to reproduce from the A_1 and A_2 behaviors in $A_1 * A_2$. We note that 124 errors

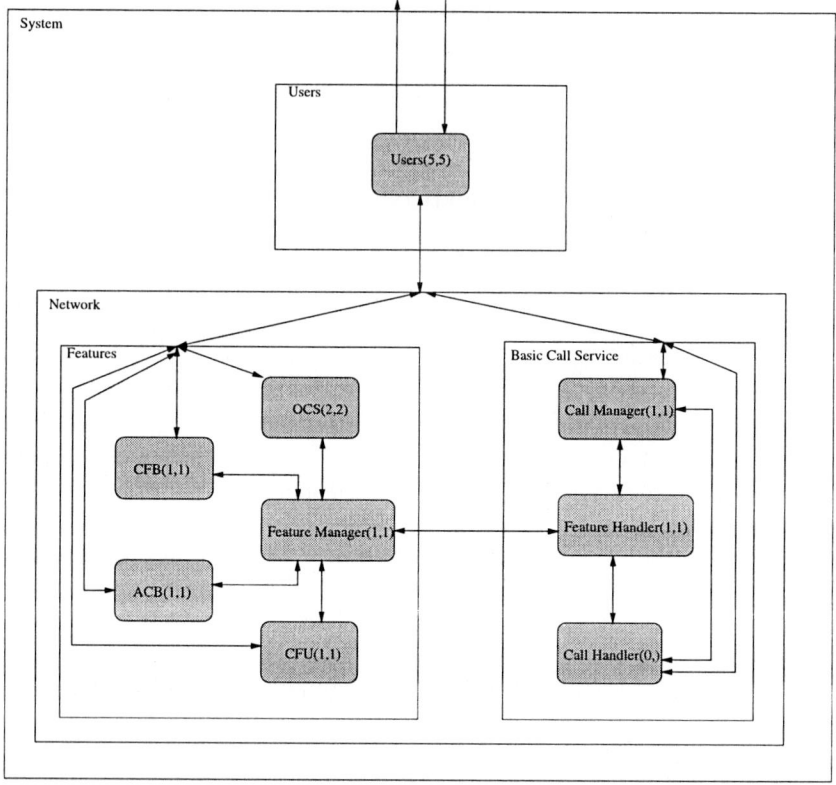

Fig. 4. Global Framework.

Lines	3,098
Blocks	4
Processes	9
Procedures	12
States	88
Signals	50
Macro definition	12
Timers	0

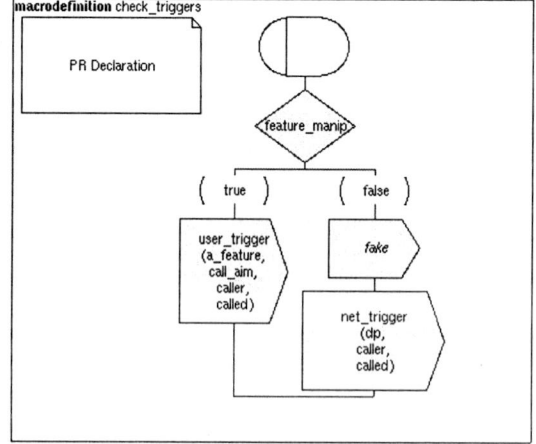

Fig. 5. Metrics of the service specification.

Fig. 6. Marks of the transitions in the SDL specification.

	A_1	A_2	G
Configurations	U_2 can activate and deactivate CFU to U_3.	U_1 can activate and deactivate OCS with U_3 in his blacklist.	U_1 and U_2 may respectively activate and deactivate OCS and CFU.
Number of States	17081	17629	18379
Number of Transitions	17571	18123	18907

Fig. 7. The three input automata allowing the interaction detection.

invalidate the inclusion. Therefore, we have analyzed the obtained results in order to observe the interactions we detected. Every scenario implied in the detection represents the same interaction, indeed, we reach the wished final states, but the *fake* transition is executed. We have studied the schema of the detected communication and we observe that the interaction is produced when the user U_1 is in line with U_3 whereas this latter is in the U_1's blacklist.

5 Conclusion

The contribution of our work is the definition of a formal method allowing to analyze the global behavior of a system containing several services in order to detect the feature interactions. We extend our algorithm in order to detect three-way interactions. This work has led to the implementation of a tool taking three finite state machines in input and allowing to detect the interactions. We applied our algorithm to a real case study in a system with an Intelligent Network architecture. The experimentation has been realized on the system containing the Call Forward Unconditional service and the Originating Call Service. We detect 124 scenarios that lead to the same interactions. One of the perspectives is to restrict the scenarios analysis in order to avoid the execution of all the scenarios which create a redundant interaction.

Furthermore, it is possible to study the desirable interactions with our method. Indeed, this could be obtained as a generalization of our algorithm by marking the transitions with different criteria. This would allow to reach objectives such as desirable interactions.

References

1. M. Amer, T. Gray, A. Karmouch, and S. Mankovskii. Feature-Interaction Resolution Using Fuzzy policies. *Feature Interactions in Telecommunications and Software systems VI*, 2000.
2. J. A. Bergstra, A. Ponse, and S. A. Smolka, editors. *Handbook of Process Algebra*. Elsevier, 2001.
3. T.F. Bowen, F.S. Dworak, C.H. Chow, N.D. Griffeth, G.E. Herman, and Y.-J. Lin. The Feature Interaction Problem in Telecommunication Systems. *Proceedings of the Seventh IEE International Conference on Software Engineering for Telecommunications Systems*, March 1989.
4. E. Brinksma. A Theory for Derivation of Tests. In *IFIP WG6.1 8th Int. Symp. On Protocol Specification, Testing and Verification*, 1998. North Holland.
5. E. J. Cameron, N. D. Griffeth, Y.-J. Lin, M. E. Nilson, W. K. Schnure, and H. Velthuijsen. A Feature Interaction Benchmark for IN and Beyond. Technical report, Bellcore and PTT Research, 1993.
6. R. Dssouli, S. Some, J.W. Guillery, and N. Rico. Detection of Feature Interactions with REST. In L.M.S. Logrippo P. Dini, R. Boutaba, editor, *4th Int. Workshop on Feature Interactions in Telecommunications Networks and Software Systems*, pages 271–283. IOS Press, June 1997. Netherland.
7. M. Frappier, A. Mili, and J. Desharnais. Defining and Detecting Feature Interactions. In R.S. Bird and L.G.L.T. Meertens, editors, *IFIP TC 2 Working Conference on Algorithmic Languages and Calculi*. Chapman and Hall, 1997.
8. P. Gibson, G. Hamilton, and D. Méry. A taxonomy for Triggered Interactions using Fair Object Semantics. In M.Calder and E.Magill, editors, *Feature Interaction in Telecommunications and Software Systems VI*. IOS Press, 2000.
9. J. Hassine, T. Kikuno, L. Logrippo, and M. Nakamura. Feature Interaction Filtering with Use Case Maps at Requirements Stage. *Feature Interactions in Telecommunications and Software systems VI*, 2000.
10. ITUT-T. Recommandation Z.100: CCITT Specification and Description Language (SDL). Technical report, IUT-T, 1999.
11. ITU-T. General Recommendations on Telephone Switching and Signalling, Intelligent Network, Q-Series Intelligent Network Q.1200-Q.1290. Technical report, ITU-T, 1993.
12. D. O. Keck and P. J. Kuehn. The Feature and Service Interaction Problem in Telecommunications Systems: A Survey. In *IEEE Transactions on Software Engineering*, volume 24, pages 779–795. TSE, October 1998.
13. F. Khendek and A. Sefidcon. A Pragmatic Approach for Feature Interaction Detection in Intelligent Networks. In *Proceedings of the IEEE International Conference on Computer Communications and Networks*, October 1999. Boston, Massachusetts.
14. T. F. LaPorta, D. Lee, Y.-J. Lin, and M. Yannakakis. Protocol Feature Interactions. *Proc. FORTE-PSTV, France*, 1998.
15. D. Lee and M. Yannakakis. Principles and Methods of Testing Finite State Machines - A Survey. *The Proceedings of IEEE*, 84(8):1090–1123, August 1996.
16. R. Milner. *Communication and Concurrency*. Prentice Hall, Englewood Cliffs, New Jersey, 1989.
17. A. Petri. *Kommunikation mit Automaten*. PhD thesis, Universitat Bonn, 1962.
18. R. Tarjan. *Depth-First Search And Linear Graph Algorithms*, volume 1. SIAM J. Computer, June 1972.
19. Verilog. *ObjectGEODE Simulator, Reference Manual*, 1997.

Specification of an Asynchronous On-chip Bus

Juha Plosila and Tiberiu Seceleanu

University of Turku, Dept. of Information Technology,
Lab. of Electronics and Communication Systems,
FIN-20014 Turku, Finland
tel: +358-2-3336953, fax: +358-2-3336950,
{Juha.Plosila, Tiberiu.Seceleanu}@utu.fi

Abstract. The latest improvements in the technology of digital devices allow designers to build whole systems on a single silicon chip. New problems arise in this context, one of them being the complexity of interconnections. Optimizing interfaces has become a tedious design step. Other problematic issues are global clock signal distribution and design composability, for which asynchronous design methodology proves to be a good solution. Formal methods can be used to verify the logical correctness of digital hardware. These methods are well-featured for asynchronous designs. This study introduces asynchronous bus modeling aspects in the formal framework of Action Systems.

1 Introduction

Modern deep sub-micron silicon technologies have given a real boost to system-on-chip (SOC) design research and development. A key issue in integrating a whole system into a single chip is to realize efficient and reliable interconnections between system modules on the chip, because the overall performance of the system is constrained by the properties of the interconnect. Furthermore, the time required to complete a design task depends strongly on the complexity of the different interconnections in the system. Optimizing interfaces has become a cumbersome process [9].

A common way to implement a digital system is to build it around a *bus* shared by the system modules. As the modules connected to the bus have uniform interfaces, the bus-based design approach offers a relatively rapid method to construct large systems-on-chip. In future high-performance systems, maintaining global synchrony will be increasingly difficult, if not impossible. A solution to this problem comes from the employment of asynchronous, or self-timed, design methodologies [3]. Enhanced modularity and composability is another advantage of self-timed approaches over synchronous ones. Therefore, the present study describes a self-timed bus structure. This means that all the components of a system employing the bus interact via handshakes on asynchronous communication channels, while locally they can operate synchronously, controlled by some local clock signal(s).

The integration of a complex digital system requires comprehensive know-how of verification and development of SOC solutions, both at the functional (behavioral) as well as at the physical levels. Because a system can be viewed as a composition of concurrent processes, formal methods of concurrent programming can be used to verify mathematically the logical correctness of digital hardware. The *Action Systems* framework is one of such formalisms. It has recently been applied to the area of self-timed and synchronous VLSI design [8, 10].

In this paper, we present an Action Systems-based specification of an on-chip bus targeted for SOC designs. While bus-related protocols have been studied before from a formal point of view [6, 7], our study goes one step further and describes the components of a bus-based system, including the central bus controller (arbiter) and the abstract models of the master and slave modules attached to the bus. The presented formal component specifications are templates which can fit a large range of actual devices. The integration of an asynchronous bus model into the Action Systems framework is a part of our current work on developing a formal design flow for complex systems-on-chip. In this flow, a design process from an abstract specification to a concrete implementable model is viewed as a sequence of correctness preserving refinement steps.

Instead of trying to develop a completely new bus specification, we prefer to adapt an existing standard bus to our needs. The *AMBA bus* specification [1] is an established, open bus standard that serves as a framework for SOC designs. We use many characteristics of this specification in our descriptions. However, mostly because AMBA is a *synchronous* bus, our *asynchronous* bus does not require some of the control issues described in [1]. On the other hand, we introduce several new control signals which are needed in asynchronous communication between system modules. Thus, our representation of the bus controller and the associated masters and slaves would show some differences concerning the interfaces with respect to the AMBA specification. For the matched signals, however, we will use the same notations as in [1].

2 Action Systems

The Action Systems formalism is based on an extended version of Dijkstra's language of *guarded commands* [5]. An *action* A is defined (for example) by

$$
\begin{aligned}
A ::=\ & x := x'.R && \text{(nondeterministic assignment)} \\
& A_1 \parallel A_2 && \text{(nondeterministic choice)} \\
& A_1;\ A_2 && \text{(sequential composition)} \\
& P \to A_1 && \text{(guarded action)} \\
& A_1\ //\ A_2 && \text{(prioritized composition)}
\end{aligned}
$$

where P and R are predicates, x is a variable or a list of variables, and A_1 and A_2 are actions. Semantically, an action A is defined by the *weakest precondition* for A to establish some post-condition Q, denoted wp(A, Q). The *guard* of an action, gA is defined by $gA \;\widehat{=}\; \neg\text{wp}(A, false)$. An action is said to be *enabled*, if its guard is *true*, *disabled* otherwise. Actions are considered *atomic*, meaning that whenever one is selected for execution, it will be completed without interference.

```
sys A(interface list) ::
|[
   var          local variable declaration
   const        local constant declaration
   expressions  expressions used to ease the readability
   actions      action list
   init         initialization of variables
   do           action composition od
]|
```

Fig. 1. A partial action system representation.

An *action system* $\mathcal{A}$ is an iterative composition of actions. It has the form shown in Fig. 1 [11]. Here, the *interface list* defines the global variables through which $\mathcal{A}$ communicates with other systems. The **var** and **const** clauses define the local variables and constants, visible only within $\mathcal{A}$. The **expressions** clause defines shorthand notations for some expressions used within $\mathcal{A}$. The items declared here are evaluated every time they are met during the execution of the system. The **actions** clause describes the atomic actions present in the system. A unique name is given for each action. An action can also be, partly or completely, composed of other actions defined in the **actions** clause. For instance: $A_4 : (A_1; A_2) [\!] A_3$. Here, the actions A_1, A_2, A_3 are called *included actions* with respect to the action A_4.

In the **init** clause, all the local and interface variables are initialized. For the latter, special care has to be devoted, as these variables have to be initialized with the same values in all the systems that share them.

The system's **do-od** loop contains a composition of the actions defined in the **actions** clause. The composition can be realized using the atomic operators ' $[\!]$ ' and ' $//$ ' and the *macro operators* such as the non-atomic sequential composition operator ' ; ' which is actually defined in terms of the non-deterministic choice (' $[\!]$ ') and an auxiliary local variable. In the loop, one enabled action is executed at the time. Parallel behavior is modeled by two or more actions that are enabled simultaneously and can be executed in any order without affecting the result of the computation.

Notation. A substitution operation within an action A is denoted by $A[e_{new}/e_{old}]$, where e_{old} refers to an element (variable, predicate, component action etc.) of the original action A, and e_{new} denotes the new element which replaces e_{old} in A. The same notation may also be used for action systems.

Composing action systems. The *parallel composition* of two action systems $\mathcal{A}_1$ and $\mathcal{A}_2$, denoted $\mathcal{A}_1 \parallel \mathcal{A}_2$, is defined as an action system whose loop has the form **do** $A_1 \parallel A_2$ **od**, where A_1 and A_2 represent the action compositions within the loops of the constituent systems $\mathcal{A}_1$ and $\mathcal{A}_2$, respectively. The composed system merges the global variables of the components keeping the local variables and action identifiers distinct.

Quantified composition. Any composition operator can be *quantified*. This applies to the different types of action compositions and the parallel composition of action systems. The notation is defined as follows:

$$[* \; i = 1..n : \mathcal{A}(i) \;] \;\widehat{=}\; \mathcal{A}[1/i] * \ldots * \mathcal{A}[n/i]$$
$$[\;\|\; i = 1..n : \mathcal{A}(i) \;] \;\widehat{=}\; \mathcal{A}[1/i] \;\|\; \ldots \;\|\; \mathcal{A}[n/i]$$

Here the asterisk '*' denotes any action constructor mentioned above. Note that in general the index variable does not have to run through a range of values. In this case, the set of values is defined explicitly, for example: $i \in \{5, 2, 6, 9\}$. The leftmost value is considered first, the rightmost value last. The actions $A(i)$ are called *parameterized* actions, and, naturally, i is the *parameter*. The same rules are valid for the action systems in the second definition above.

3 Bus Components

A bus is a cost-effective data communication connection between two or more communicating devices. It is composed of *data, address* and *control* signals. The components of a concrete bus-based system include *masters, slaves* and an *arbiter* [1, 4, 12]. A master is a module that actively requests services from passive modules connected to the bus, the slaves. The master devices request the bus from the central control unit, the arbiter, which grants the bus to only one master at a time. This requires dedicated request and grant wires between each master and the arbiter.

In this section, we describe the variables and communication protocols that we use to model an asynchronous bus inspired by the AMBA AHB [1], supporting up to 16 bus masters. The interface between the bus components in our approach is shown in Fig. 2. The actual Action System specifications of the components are presented later in section 4.

The asynchronous realization of the bus introduces more complex communication protocols than the synchronous one, mainly due to the fact that the participants to a given transfer have to know *when* data is actually ready to be either read or written. Hence, in asynchronous communication the active party

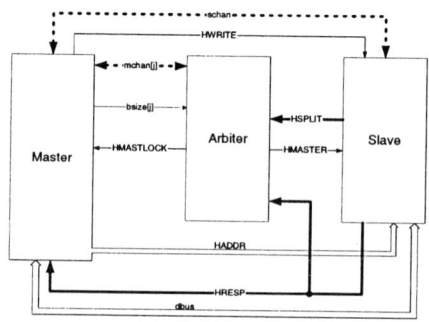

Fig. 2. System interconnections

sends a request signal to the passive party, which then responds by sending back an acknowledgement signal after completing the requested task.

Master-Arbiter communication. The asynchronous communication channel between the bus controller, i.e., the arbiter, and a master j, where $j = 0..15$ is a number identifying a particular master, is modeled by the 5-value variable $mchan[j]$ of the type $mchanType \,\widehat{=}\, \{\ hr,\ hrl,\ gr,\ done,\ idle\ \}$.

The initial value of $mchan[j]$ is $idle$. The master requests the bus from the arbiter by setting $mchan[j]$ to either hr (bus request) or hrl (request for a locked transfer). The arbiter responds eventually by setting the channel to gr (bus grant) and the control signal $HMASTLOCK$ according to the request. When the master has completed a transaction with a slave, it updates the signal $bsize[j]$ (burst size, $bsize[j] = 0..16$), which carries the number of data words still to be transferred between the master and the slave, and sets $mchan[j]$ to $done$. If $bsize[j] \neq 0$, the arbiter responds by setting the channel eventually back to gr. If $bsize[j] = 0$, i.e., the whole burst has been transferred, the arbiter initializes $mchan[j]$ to $idle$.

The values hr, hrl, and gr of $mchan[j]$ correspond to the AMBA AHB signals $HBUSREQx$, $HLOCKx$, and $HGRANTx$, respectively [1].

Master-Slave communication. The master-slave communication channel is modeled by the variable $schan$ of the type $schanType \,\widehat{=}\, \{req,\ ack\ \}$. This is accompanied by the natural-type variables $dbus$ and $HADDR$ that model the data and address signals of the bus, the boolean variable $HWRITE$ which specifies whether the master is reading ($HWRITE = false$) or writing ($HWRITE = true$) data, and the variable $HRESP$ of the type $SlaveResponseType \,\widehat{=}\, \{OKAY,\ ERROR,\ RETRY,\ SPLIT\ \}$ through which the selected slave signals the status of the latest transaction. All the mentioned variables are globally shared by all the masters and slaves in the system.

The address $HADDR$ of the AMBA AHB is composed of two parts: the N most significant bits represent the identification of the slave, while the remaining $32 - N$ bits, assuming a 32-bit address, represent a valid location in the memory space of the selected slave. Hence, in our abstract model $HADDR$ is a natural number with the range $0..2^{32} - 1$, from which the identification number $SlaveId$ of the selected slave is computed by: $SlaveId = HADDR/2^{32-N}$. The maximum number of slaves in the system is then 2^N. Observe that the model does not contain an explicit decoder which would generate the slave select signals $HSELx$ from the address $HADDR$ as in the original AMBA specification. Instead, a slave itself performs this selection based on the value of the address variable $HADDR$ which is shared by all the slaves.

Once the access to the bus is granted by the arbiter, the granted master first sets the $HWRITE$ signal, the slave address $HADDR$, and also data $dbus$ if $HWRITE = true$ indicating a write operation, and places the channel $schan$ to req. The selected slave tries to execute the requested operation and assigns then an appropriate value to $HRESP$. If $HRESP = OKAY$ and $HWRITE = false$ indicating a successful read operation, the slave also assigns a valid value to $dbus$. Then it acknowledges the master's request by setting $schan$ to ack. In the case of a successful read, the master stores the value of *dbus* set by the slave. The value of *bsize*[*j*] (burst size) is decremented by the master every time the slave gives an *OKAY* response. If an *ERROR* response is detected, the master either decrements *bsize*[*j*] or initializes it to 0. If the response is either *RETRY* or *SPLIT*, the value of *bsize*[*j*] is not changed.

When *HRESP* = *OKAY* and *HMASTLOCK* = *true*, i.e., a successful locked transfer event (write or read) took place, the master initiates immediately a new communication cycle with the slave, as long as the burst has not yet been completed (*bsize*[*j*] ≠ 0). If the slave sets *HRESP* to *ERROR* as the response to a locked transfer event, it is up to the master to decide whether to continue the locked burst with the slave or to interrupt it by assigning *bsize*[*j*] := 0 and communicating with the arbiter. In the case of any other response, or if the transfer process is not locked (*HMASTLOCK* = *false*), the master always communicates first with the arbiter which then decides whether the master still has the access to the bus or not.

Arbiter-Slave communication. The interface between the arbiter and the slaves consists of the shared variables *HMASTER* = 0 . .15, *HRESP* (defined above), and *HSPLIT*[0. .15] (array of booleans).

The arbiter assigns the identification number of the master that is currently accessing the bus to the variable *HMASTER* read by the slaves. The arbiter reads the value of the variable *HRESP* which is set by a slave as a response to a transaction requested by the granted master. If *HRESP* = *SPLIT*, the slave has decided to split the current transfer, i.e., to postpone a part of the transfer burst. In this case, the arbiter temporarily masks or disables the request signal of the current master. When the slave is later ready to continue the burst with a masked master *j*, it sets the boolean variable *HSPLIT*[*j*] to *true*. The arbiter then responds by removing the mask allowing the master *j* to access the bus again. If *HRESP* = *RETRY*, the slave wishes to retry the latest transaction with the master *HMASTER*. The arbiter gives the bus to this master immediately, provided there are no higher priority requests present.

4 Specification

In this section we illustrate characteristics of the three components of a bus system, the arbiter, the slaves and the masters. The last two are abstract templates that we show in Fig. 3 and Fig. 4, respectively.

We consider a fixed number of masters, 16, and a generic number of slaves, 2^N, with *SlaveId* running from 0 to $2^N - 1$. The whole bus-based system is then represented by the parallel composition:

$$\mathcal{A}rbiter$$
$$\| \; [\| \; j = 0. \; .15 : \; \mathcal{M}aster(j)[mchan[j], bsize[j]/mchan, bsize]$$
$$\| \; [\| \; i := 0. \; .2^N - 1 : \; \mathcal{S}lave(i)[i/SlaveId]]$$

In the composition, the $\mathcal{A}rbiter$ runs in parallel with the other system components, the masters and the slaves. We identify the master systems in the above

```
sys Slave (HADDR : natural 0. .2^32 − 1; HMASTER : natural 0. .15;
           dbus : natural; schan : SchanType;
           HSPLIT[16], HWRITE : bool; HRESP : SlaveResponseType) ::
|[
var  mem : natural; MastQ[16], busy : bool
const SlaveId := natural
actions S_1 : schan = req ∧ SlaveId = HADDR/2^{32−N} →
                    (¬busy → (HWRITE → mem := dbus
                              ‖ ¬HWRITE → dbus := d.d ∈ natural)
                     ‖ busy → skip);
                    busy := b.b ∈ {true, false}
           S_2 : busy → (HRESP, MastQ[HMASTER] := SPLIT, true
                         ‖ HRESP := RETRY)
                 ‖ ¬busy → HRESP := h.h ∈ {OKAY, ERROR}
           S_3 : S_1; S_2; HSPLIT[HMASTER], schan := false, ack
           S_4 : (∃j.MastQ[j]) → HSPLIT[j], MastQ[j] := true, false
     init MastQ, HWRITE, HSPLIT, busy := false; schan := ack;
          mem, HADDR, HMASTER, dbus := 0; HRESP := OKAY
     do  S_3//S_4 od
]|
```

Fig. 3. Asynchronous Slave Specification.

```
sys Master (mchan : MchanType; schan : SchanType; bsize : natural 0. .16;
            HMASTLOCK, HWRITE : bool; HADDR : natural 0. .2^32 − 1;
            dbus : natural; HRESP : SlaveResponseType) ::
|[
var  mem, ssel, addr : natural; write : bool;
actions  M_1 : mchan = idle →
                    write, bsize, ssel :=
                      w, b, s.(w ∈ bool) ∧ (1 ≤ b ≤ 16) ∧ (0 ≤ s ≤ 2^N − 1);
                    mchan := m.m ∈ {hr, hrl}
         M_2 : mchan = gr → HWRITE, addr := write, a.0 ≤ a ≤ 2^{32−N} − 1;
                    HADDR := 2^{32−N} · ssel + addr;
                    (HWRITE → dbus := db.db ∈ natural ‖ ¬HWRITE → skip);
                    schan := req
         M_3 : schan = ack →
                  ( HRESP = OKAY →
                        (¬HWRITE → mem := dbus ‖ HWRITE → skip); bsize := bsize − 1
                    ‖ HRESP = ERROR → bsize := b.(b = bsize − 1) ∨ (b = 0)
                    ‖ HRESP ∈ {SPLIT, RETRY} → skip);
         M_4 : (¬HMASTLOCK ∨ (bsize = 0) ∨ (HRESP ∈ {SPLIT, RETRY}) →
                    mchan[j] := done
                ‖ HMASTLOCK ∧ (bsize ≠ 0) ∧ (HRESP ∉ {SPLIT, RETRY}) →
                    skip)
         M_5 : M_3; M_4
    init bsize, mem, ssel, addr, HADDR, dbus := 0; mchan := idle; schan := ack;
         write, HMASTLOCK, HWRITE := false; HRESP := OKAY
    do  M_1 ‖ (M_2 ; M_5) od
]|
```

Fig. 4. Asynchronous Master Specification.

description by the corresponding channel they share with the arbiter ($mchan[j]$ and $bsize[j]$). The *SlaveId* number identifies the slaves.

Even though the arbiter that we analyze here is also a general template, we discuss it in more detail, as the generality only refers to the number of masters and slaves present in the system and not to the actual functionality of the arbiter, which is completely defined.

```
sys  Arbiter (mchan[16] : MchanType; HMASTER : natural 0. . 15;
     HMASTLOCK, HSPLIT[16] : bool; bsize[16] : natural 0. . 16;
     HRESP : SlaveResponseType) ::
|[
var   mask[16], disable[16], reserved : bool
const G₀ := {0, 1, 2, 3, 4}; G₁ := {5, 6, 7, 8, 9, 10, 11}; G₂ := {12, 13, 14, 15}
expressions Enabled(j, k) ≙ (∀i ∈ G_k \ {j} . ¬disable[i])
actions   Grant(j, k) :   (mchan[j] ∈ {hr, hrl}) ∧ (mask[j] ∨ HSPLIT[j])
                          ∧ Enabled(j, k) ∧ ¬reserved →
                               HMASTLOCK, HMASTER := (mchan[j] = hrl), j;
                               mask[j], reserved := true; disable[j] := false;
                               mchan[j] := gr
          ChkResp(j) :    mchan[j] = done →
                               (Split(j) [] Retry(j) [] Ok_or_Err(j));
                               reserved := false
          Split(j) :      HRESP = SPLIT → mask[j] := false; Req(j)
          Retry(j) :      HRESP = RETRY → disable[j] := true; Req(j)
          Ok_or_Err(j) :  HRESP ∈ {OKAY, ERROR} →
                               bsize[j] ≠ 0 → disable[j] := true; Req(j)
                               [] bsize[j] = 0 → mchan[j] := idle
          Req(j) :        ¬HMASTLOCK → mchan[j] := hr
                          [] HMASTLOCK → mchan[j] := hrl
init  mask := true; HSPLIT, disable, reserved, HMASTLOCK := false;
      mchan := idle; HRESP := OKAY; bsize, HMASTER := 0
do    [//k = 0. . 2 : [ [] j ∈ G_k : (Grant(j, k) [] ChkResp(j))]] od
]|
```

Fig. 5. Asynchronous Arbiter Specification.

4.1 Arbiter System

The representation of the bus controller, modeled by the system $\mathcal{A}rbiter$, is illustrated in Fig. 5. In this abstract model, we consider that the masters are organized in priority groups – we leave the details of the priority scheme to be decided at later design steps. If a master belongs to a higher priority group, it is allowed to interrupt the bus access of another master placed in a lower priority group. In the exemplification we give here, the masters are divided into three priority groups which are identified as the sets G_k, $k = 0..2$ declared in the **const** clause of the system $\mathcal{A}rbiter$. These sets contain the indices by which the arbiter identifies the masters in the system. The group G_0 contains the masters having the highest priority, the group G_2 the masters having the lowest priority.

In the **actions** clause of the system $\mathcal{A}rbiter$ we have specified six actions. The notation also provides a generic aspect, illustrated by the action parameters k and j. We describe the behavior of the controller with respect to a single master, and the parameters help generalizing, so that we cover all the other masters. In the following, we analyze the behavior of the arbiter by describing briefly the behavior of its actions. We refer to the actions without mentioning their parameters.

Action *Grant*. This action is responsible for granting the bus ownership to a requesting master ($mchan[j] \in \{$ hr, hrl $\}$). It is enabled if the request is not masked or the *HSPLIT* signal is active ($mask[j] \lor HSPLIT[j]$), the request is not blocked by another master in the same priority group ($Enabled(j, k)$), and the bus is not reserved ($\neg reserved$).

Action *ChkResp.* The second main action of the arbiter models the answer of the controller following the different possible results communicated by the operating slaves. The behavior is defined by the included actions, *Split, Retry, Ok_or_Error* and *Req*. The communication variable $mchan[j]$ is updated correspondingly in each situation characterized by a given *HRESP* value.

Action *Split.* The slave may decide not to answer immediately to the request coming from the current owner of the bus. We modeled this by assigning an arbitrary value to the slave's local variable *busy* (Fig. 3). If the slave issues a *SPLIT* response to the request of the master, the arbiter then inhibits the master from taking part in the arbitration process by setting the corresponding mask element to *false*. The value of every mask element is checked in the action *Grant*. Whenever the slave decides to allow the master to resume the split connection, it informs the arbiter by setting the corresponding element of the *HSPLIT* vector to *true*. This is also checked by the action *Grant* which then initializes the mask back to *true* next time the master in question obtains the access to the bus.

Action *Retry.* This action is enabled when the slave gives a *RETRY* response. It inhibits, by assigning $disable[j] := true$, any other master in the same priority group with the current owner of the bus to gain access. If there is no higher priority master requesting, the ownership of the bus will remain with the current master. The variable $disable[j]$ is set back to *false* by the corresponding *Grant* action when selected for execution next time.

Action *Ok_or_Error.* From the point of view of the arbiter, an *OKAY* or an *ERROR* answer from the operating slave bears the same significance. The decision in an error situation is taken by the master (action M_3, Fig. 4). The arbiter only checks the value of the corresponding *bsize* element and either initializes the specific channel to *idle*, or sets it back to the previous request state *hr* or *hrl* assigning also $disable[j] := true$ as in the case of the *RETRY* response.

Global behavior. The behavior of the arbiter is described further by the composition $[//k = 0..2 : [\parallel j \in G_k : (Grant(j,k) \parallel ChkResp(j))]]$ in the system's **do-od** loop. The actions within the innermost quantified composition deal with arbitration between masters coming from the same priority group. The outermost quantified composition describes the priority scheme.

5 Discussion

In the original AMBA bus specification [1] the bus is governed by a global clock. All the transfers relate to this signal which synchronizes the data transfers and the control lines. In the previous sections we described an asynchronous approach to bus control. Instead of the clock signal we introduced communication channels that identify the moments when data or control signals are valid on certain lines.

The transfers allowed on the synchronous bus are not only limited in size, but also, based on the clock frequency, in time. Thus, a sixteen-word transfer can be carried out in sixteen successive clock cycles if the master that controls it receives no interrupts. Knowing the clock frequency, one can establish a period of time in which a normal executed transfer takes place. In the asynchronous representation, even though the transfer size is also limited, one cannot be certain of the time period in which a sixteen-word transfer is completed, in an uninterrupted execution.

Even though, at this level of the description, the period of *time* in which a certain master controls the bus was ignored, we can also think of means by which one can control this aspect of the arbitration. For instance, a local synchronous counter can be attached to the arbiter so that it monitors, in steps that can be related to the actual time of the processing, the actual time a master has been accessing the bus. Another solution could be the employment of a specific master, which would implement the same counter. This master would have the highest priority in the system, and thus, could interrupt the access to the bus of any other master. By not addressing any slave, the interrupt requests sent by this master cannot be masked by a possible split or retry operation.

Refinement issues. The abstract bus specification, given above as an action system description, is intended to be developed into a hardware-realizable model in a stepwise manner using Refinement Calculus-based [2] *transformation rules*. Such a disciplined design flow yields a concrete system model which is a logically correct implementation of the initial abstract specification, satisfying possibly a set of auxiliary logical constraints which are necessary for successful circuit implementation [8, 10]. This lays a solid ground for the technology mapping process, where the final formal description is transformed into a layout of actual circuit components.

After the initial specification, the abstract bus arbiter and the involved masters and slaves are further decomposed or partitioned into compositions of action systems each of which describes some essential functional aspect of an original system component. Each decomposition step is a refinement, where a new communication channel is created between the separated parties. The majority of the introduced channels are local to the system components, which means that they do not change the bus itself. However, some transformations may involve the bus as well. For example, if the address decoding operation is extracted from the slaves, a new global control block is created for the bus. Splitting the variable *dbus*, which models the data bus between the masters and slaves, into two separate variables modeling write and read busses is an example of another kind of global refinement.

The decomposition procedure is followed by the *handshake expansion*, a nontrivial *data refinement* [2], where the description is brought closer to the circuit level by implementing each abstract communication channel with a set of boolean variables.

As an example, let us consider a master-arbiter channel $mchan$ (we have omitted the index j to make the notation simpler) which has 5 possible values $\{hr, hrl, gr, done, idle\}$. We can implement it using 5 boolean handshake variables or signals, say hr, hrl, gr, $done$, and $next$. They are related to the original variable by the following relations:

$R_1 \stackrel{\widehat{}}{=} (mchan = hr) \Leftrightarrow (hr \wedge \neg hrl \wedge \neg gr \wedge (\neg done \vee next))$
$R_2 \stackrel{\widehat{}}{=} (mchan = hrl) \Leftrightarrow (\neg hr \wedge hrl \wedge \neg gr \wedge (\neg done \vee next))$
$R_3 \stackrel{\widehat{}}{=} (mchan = gr) \Leftrightarrow ((hr \vee hrl) \wedge gr \wedge (\neg done \vee next))$
$R_4 \stackrel{\widehat{}}{=} (mchan = done) \Leftrightarrow$
$\qquad ((((hr \vee hrl) \wedge done) \vee (\neg hr \wedge \neg hrl \wedge \neg done)) \wedge gr \wedge \neg next)$
$R_5 \stackrel{\widehat{}}{=} (mchan = idle) \Leftrightarrow (\neg hr \wedge \neg hrl \wedge \neg gr \wedge \neg done \wedge \neg next)$

Hence, the resulting communication channel is considered idle when all of its handshake variables are *false* (R_5). The channel is put to a request state, when the master sets either *hr* or *hrl* to *true*, or when the arbiter decides to remove grant by setting the grant signal *gr* to *false* and asserting the *next* signal (R_1, R_2). The arbiter puts the channel to the grant state by setting *gr* to *true* as the response to the asserted request *hr* or *hrl*, or by setting the variable *next* to *true* as the response to the asserted *done* signal while keeping *gr* true (R_3). The *done* state indicates that the master has set either the variable *done* to *true*, or the request *hr* or *hrl* to *false* (R_4). In the former case, the master has just transmitted or received a data word, but the burst has not yet been completed. In the latter case, the last data of the burst has just been transmitted or received, which means that the arbiter can put the channel to the initial *idle* state.

The design flow continues, after the transformation of the communication channels, with the *circuit extraction*, where the formal description of each system component is stepwise refined into a concrete description from which an actual circuit implementation can be easily derived. The final phase in the Action Systems-based design flow is the *implementation* or *technology mapping* step, where the system units are refined into compositions of action systems each of which corresponds to either an actual circuit component in a component library available to the designer or a synthesizable hardware description language (HDL) model.

Observe that the design flow becomes more fluent, if our component library contains abstract action system models for large circuit components that have been verified formally beforehand. For example, we could have an entire bus master or slave, or a significant part of it, as a single library component. Furthermore, once the shared bus controller (arbiter) has been designed from an abstract specification to the circuit implementation, it is placed in a library and re-used from there. Then the design flow of a system built around the bus discussed in this paper would mainly consist of the decomposition phase, where the abstract models of the pre-defined library components are stepwise extracted from the initial system specification.

6 Conclusions

We presented in this study a formal abstract specification of an asynchronous bus structure within the Action Systems framework. The work originally started with the intention to describe a self-timed AMBA AHB bus, which, in comparison with similar approaches to bus modeling [4, 12], seemed to be a less complex structure. Due to the specifics of the self-timed architecture and high level of abstraction, the presented model does not contain all the characteristics of the original synchronous AMBA specification. Common aspects include for example the centralized arbitration scheme, the locked data transfer mode, and the handling of the slave's response signals including the split transfer feature.

One of the purposes of this study was to integrate the analyzed bus structure into our formal framework for digital hardware design as a platform to construct complex systems in a modular way. By representing the bus in the same framework with the other systems in a design process, we have the possibility to apply the same formal techniques to both the systems modeling the digital hardware devices and the systems describing the underlying connectivity. The successive transformations one needs to perform in order to bring the descriptions of these systems to concrete implementable levels are carried out in the formal framework of Action Systems, thus ensuring a correct derivation process.

Several aspects of bus design are left for future study. For instance, we did not specify in the presented model how the arbiter may terminate the ownership of the bus in the case of a prolonged access, although some possible scenarios were discussed. Modeling a system with two or more different busses interacting via bridge modules could be another interesting topic. Furthermore, developing a detailed formal design flow for actual bus-based digital systems with realistic master and slave systems is a challenging task. Substantial real-life case studies are needed to establish such a flow properly.

References

1. ARM Limited. AMBA Specification (Rev 2.0), 1999.
2. R. J. R. Back and J. von Wright. *Refinement calculus: A Systematic Introduction.* Springer. April 1998.
3. W. J. Bainbridge. *Asynchronous System-on-Chip Interconnect.* PhD. Thesis, University of Manchester, UK, 2000.
4. W. J. Bainbridge and S. B. Furber. Asynchronous Macrocell Interconnect Using MARBLE. In Proceedings of the 4th International Symposium on Advanced Research in Asynchronous Circuits and Systems (ASYNC '98) San Diego, CA, March 30 - April 2, 1998.
5. E. W. Dijkstra. *A Discipline of Programming.* Prentice-Hall International, 1976.
6. J. Hooman. *Verifying Part of the ACCESS.bus Protocol using PVS.* Proceedings 15th Conference on the Foundations of Software Technology and Theoretical Computer Science, LNCS 1026, Springer-Verlag, pages 96-110, 1995.
7. A. Mokkedem, R. Hosabettu, M. D. Jones, G. Gopalakrishnan, *Formalization and proof of a solution to the PCI 2.1 bus transaction ordering problem.* Formal Methods in Systems Design, vol. 16, no. 1, pp. 93-119, January 2000.
8. J. Plosila. *Self-Timed Circuit Design - The Action Systems Approach.* Ph.D. Thesis, University of Turku, Dept of Applied Physics, Turku, Finland, 1999.
9. C. Purtell-Tappen. *Platform Express to Accelerate Platform-Based System-on-Chip Design and Verification.* ECN Magazine, September 2001.
10. T. Seceleanu. *Systematic Design of Synchronous Digital Circuits.* Ph.D. Thesis, Abo Akademi, Turku, Finland, 2001.

11. T. Seceleanu, J. Plosila. *Hierarchical Action Systems*. Manuscript. To appear as Technical Report.
12. A. Zitouni et al. *Design of an Asynchronous VME bus Controller for Heterogeneous systems*. Dedicated Systems Magazine - 2000 Q3 (http://www.dedicatedsystems.com).

Analysis of a Security Protocol in μCRL

Jun Pang

Centrum voor Wiskunde en Informatica,
P.O. Box 94079, 1090 GB Amsterdam, The Netherlands
Jun.Pang@cwi.nl

Abstract. In this paper, we present how the process-algebraic language μCRL can be used to specify security protocols and discuss the analysis process using the μCRL toolset and CADP. To illustrate the feasibility of our approach, we analyzed the Needham-Schroeder public-key protocol and reproduced the error found by Gavin Lowe [7]. Two more definitions of authentication are also studied. We give some remarks on our approach and discuss some possible directions for future work.

1 Introduction

The security of communication between computers has become a hot research issue. A variety of security protocols based on cryptographic primitives are used to establish secure communication over insecure open networks. Unfortunately, security protocols often contain serious errors. Formal methods are mathematically based techniques for specifying and verifying software and hardware systems. Their mathematical underpinning allows formal methods to analyze systems in a more precise and non-ambiguous fashion. This makes it possible to use formal description and verification to obtain assurance that a protocol cannot be attacked by an intruder.

μCRL provide a notation for the specification and analysis of distributed systems in an algebraic fashion. This language extends the process algebra ACP [5] with equational *abstract data types*. The μCRL toolset [1], together with the CÆSAR ALDÉBARAN DEVELOPMENT PACKAGE (CADP) [4], which acts as a back-end for the μCRL toolset, features visualization, simulation, state space generation, model checking, theorem proving and state bit hashing capabilities. It has been successfully applied in the analysis of a wide range of protocols and distributed systems (see ¡http://www.cwi.nl/ mcrl/¿).

In this paper, we present how the process-algebraic language μCRL can be used to specify security protocols and discuss the analysis process. The behavior of agents of a security protocol can be modeled by processes. The abstract data types in μCRL can be used to abstract from the complex cryptographic primitives and to model the knowledge databases of agents. We define some *security actions* to indicate the critical points in the protocol and these *security actions* can contain the information relevant to the properties we want to verify. To illustrate the feasibility of our approach, we analyzed the Needham-Schroeder public-key protocol, and reproduced a known error. Our approach resembles the method used by Leduc and Germeau [6]. The μCRL toolset was used to generate the state spaces from specifications, and CADP was used to model check the requirements.

Related work. FDR, a model checker for CSP, is used to analyze the Needham-Schroeder public-key protocol in [7]. The agents of the protocol and an intruder are modeled as processes. FDR takes an implementation and a specification of the protocol as input, and checks whether the implementation refines the specification. A security error was discovered. They adapted the protocol to remove this error and detected no further attacks.

In [10], a finite state exploration tool, Murφ, is used to analyze several security protocols. A process is modeled by a set of related rules. The parallel composition of two processes is modeled by a simple union of the rules of the two processes. The correctness properties can be specified as invariants in Murφ. The Needham-Schroeder public-key protocol was analyzed. Murφ was able to reproduce the error described in [7].

How LOTOS can be used to specify security protocols is presented in [6]. Security properties can be modeled as safety properties and checked automatically by a model-based verification tool. This technique is illustrated on a concrete registration protocol. An error is found and corrected.

2 The Needham-Schroeder Public-Key Protocol

The Needham-Schroeder public-key protocol [11] aims to provide mutual authentication between an initiator A and a responder B, after which some session involving the exchange of messages can take place. Both the initiator and the responder want to be assured of the identity of the other. The formal presentation of this protocol can be decomposed into several parts. We present a simplified form of the protocol, which can be described in three steps: In step 1, the initiator A seeks to establish a connection with the responder B by selecting a nonce N_a, and sending it along with its identity to B, both encrypted with B's public key K_b. When B receives this message, it decrypts the message to obtain the knowledge of N_a. It then returns the nonce N_a with a new nonce N_b to A. Both nonces are encrypted with A's public key. When A receives this message, it decrypts it and concludes that it is talking to B, since only B should be able to decrypt A's initial message containing nonce N_a; B is authenticated. A returns the nonce N_b to B, encrypted with B's public key. In the same fashion, A is authenticated after step 3.

3 Analysis Process

Several approaches have been developed for analyzing security protocols. We take the *explicit intruder method* [3] as the basis of our analysis approach and adopt it with μCRL and its toolset. The whole process may have this sequence of steps: specify the protocol; model the intruder; state the correctness properties and verify the protocol.

3.1 Algebraic Specification

Each µCRL specification has two parts, one defines the data types and the other gives the specification of behavior. The data part expresses which kinds of data are used and the operations on them. By this, we can abstract away the complex cryptographic primitives, such as encryption and decryption. In µCRL, we model the knowledge database for agents as a set.

To verify the correctness of this protocol, normally we need to put the agents into a hostile environment by adding an intruder into the protocol. In µCRL, we can model an intruder as a process which can mimic attacks of a real-world intruder. We refer to a general set of modeling assumptions with wider applicability as the *Dolev-Yao model* [2]. The responder and initiator are linked together by communication channels. These channels are insecure, meaning that they can be eavesdropped by an intruder. Both of the responder and initiator are defined as a µCRL process. Due to space limitation, the specification in µCRL can be found in the full version of this paper [12].

3.2 Stating the Correctness Properties

Model checking is an automatic technique to determine whether a state transition system satisfies certain requirements. A requirement should be expressed as a temporal logic formula first. A model checker searches the reachable states of a labeled transition system to determine whether this formula holds. The temporal logic used by Evaluator[1] is called *regular alternation-free µ-calculus*. The syntax of this logic is given in [9].

Similar to what Leduc and Germeau did [6], we need to define some *security actions* (e.g. actions *I_running*, *I_commit*) for agents to determine the critical points in the specification. These actions can be parameterized with any data relevant to the properties we want to check. The parameters of these actions play an important role when model checking the properties. By this, we can abstract away from the details of communication and only focus on these actions. The correctness requirements of a security protocol are always related to authentication and rely on the fact that the intruder does not know some secret. In this paper, we study three kinds of authentication, and show that the Needham-Schroeder public-key protocol and its repaired version can or cannot guarantee secure communication at different level. The fact that the intruder does not know some secret can be characterized as safety properties.

3.3 Requirements of the Protocol

We catch three kinds of definition for authentication from [8] and formulate them in the *regular alternation-free µ-calculus*.

---
[1] A model checker among the CÆSAR ALDÉBARAN DEVELOPMENT PACKAGE.

The mostly investigated definition of authentication is: whenever A completes a run apparently with B, then B has recently been running the protocol apparently with A.

A3: $[(\neg\ \text{R\_running}(A,B))^* \cdot \text{I\_commit}(A,B)]$ False

A3 claims that the responder is correctly authenticated. It says that if an execution sequence does not contain an action $R\_running(A,B)$, then in the resulting state an initiator A cannot believe that it is talking with a responder B.

A4: $[(\neg\ \text{I\_running}(A,B))^* \cdot \text{R\_commit}(A,B)]$ False

In the same way, A4 claims that the initiator is correctly authenticated.

A stronger definition insists not only that the two agents agree on each other's state, but also a one-one relationship, meaning that the two agents agree upon all data values used in the run.

A1: $[(\neg\ \text{I\_commit}(A,B,N_a,N_b))^* \cdot \text{I\_commit}(A,B,N_a,N_b)]$
$\mu\ X \cdot (<T>T \wedge [\neg\ \text{R\_commit}(A,B,N_a,N_b)]\ X)$

It states that after an action $I\_commit(A,B,N_a,N_b)$, the reachability of an action $R\_commit(A,B,N_a,N_b)$ is inevitable.

A2: $[(\neg\ \text{I\_commit}(A,B,N_a,N_b))^* \cdot \text{R\_commit}(A,B,N_a,N_b)]$ False

A2 claims that the initiator is correctly authenticated.

A weaker definition is: whenever an agent A completes a run apparently with B, then agent B has recently been running the protocol. Note that agent B may run the protocol with some other agent and never have heard of A.

A5: $[(\neg\ \text{R\_running}(B))^* \cdot \text{I\_commit}(A,B)]$ False
A6: $[(\neg\ \text{I\_running}(A))^* \cdot \text{R\_commit}(A,B)]$ False

3.4 Verification Results

In our verification, we were able to discover the protocol error described in [7]. Property A3 was proved as *false* by the model checker. After fixing the protocol as Gavin Lowe did in [7], the repaired protocol was shown to satisfy the properties A3 and A4. Table 1 summarizes the verification result on all the properties listed in Section 3.3. It shows that both the protocol and its repaired version can satisfy weaker authentication (A5 and A6). The protocol satisfies neither A1 nor A2, while the repaired version satisfies A2 but not A1.

4 Conclusion and Future Work

This paper presents a formal approach to analyze security protocols in μCRL. We took the Needham-Schroeder public-key protocol as a case study. The known error can be reproduced by model checking. Furthermore, we also can study another two definitions of authentication.

Compared with works using general purpose verification methods to analyze security protocols, our approach has achieved some success. Encouraged by the work presented in this paper, we can list some further directions of research.

Table 1. Verification result on the properties

	A1	A2	A3	A4	A5	A6
NS-PKP	False	False	False	True	True	True
Repaired NS-PKP	False	True	True	True	True	True

1. Try to analyze other security protocols, and hope to discover new errors;
2. Apply our approach to more complicated e-commerce protocols, where security plays an important role, e.g. the electronic payment protocols;
3. Combine the approach with the design of new security protocols;
4. Applying techniques from process algebra and theorem proving for the formal analysis of security protocols.

References

1. S.C.C. Blom, W.J. Fokkink, J.F. Groote, I.Z. van Langevelde, B. Lisser and J.C. van de Pol. μCRL: A toolset for analysing algebraic specification. In *Proc. CAV'2001, LNCS* 2102, Springer-Verlag, pp. 250–254.
2. D. Dolev and A. Yao. On the security of public-key protocols. *IEEE Transactions on Information Theory 29(2)* (1983).
3. N. Durgin and J. Mitchell. Analysis of security protocols. In *Calculational System Design* (1999), ISO Press, pp. 369–395.
4. J.-C. Fernandez, H. Garavel, A. Kerbrat, L. Mounier, R. Mateescu and M. Sighireanu. CADP – a protocol validation and verification toolbox. In *Proc. CAV'1997, LNCS* 1102, Springer-Verlag, pp. 437–440.
5. W.J. Fokkink. *Introduction to Process Algebra*. Texts in Theoretical Computer Science. Springer-Verlag, 2000.
6. G. Leduc and F. Germeau. Verification of security protocols using Lotos-method and application. *Computer Communications 23* (2000), 1089–1103.
7. G. Lowe. Breaking and fixing the Needham-Schroeder public-key protocol using CSP and FDR. In *2nd International Workshop on Tools and Algorithms for the Construction and Analysis of Systems* (1996), Springer-Verlag, pp. 147–166.
8. G. Lowe. Some new attacks upon security protocols. In *9th IEEE Computer Security Foundations Workshop* (1996), IEEE Press, pp. 162–169.
9. R. Mateescu and M. Sighireanu. Efficient on-the-fly model-cheching for regular alternation-free mu-calculus. In *Proc. FMICS'2000*, pp. 65–86.
10. J. Mitchell, M. Mitchell and U. Stern. Automated analysis of cryptographic protocols using Murϕ. In *Proc. of IEEE Symposium on Security and Privacy* (1997), pp. 141–151.
11. R. Needham and M. Schroeder. Using encryption for authentication in large networks of computers. *Communications of the ACM 21* (1978), 120–126.
12. J. Pang. Analysis of a security protocol in μCRL. Tech. Rep. SEN-R0201, CWI, Amsterdam, 2002.

Developing a Spell-Checker for Tajik Using RAISE

Gafurov Davrondjon* and Tomasz Janowski

UNU/IIST, P.O. Box 3058, Macau
{gad,tj}@iist.unu.edu

Abstract. Tajik is spoken in the Republic of Tajikistan where it has been the official language since 1989, and the neighbouring areas of Uzbekistan and Kyrgyzstan.Tajik does not currently have a spell checker. This paper describes the process of developing such a spell checker using formal methods, in particular RAISE. The spell checker is supposed to: check the spelling of a given word according to the rules of the language and existing dictionaries; decompose correct words into prefixes, roots and suffixes; and suggest how to correct the words that are misspelled.

1 Introduction

Tajik is spoken in the Republic of Tajikistan where it has been the official language since 1989, and the neighbouring areas of Uzbekistan and Kyrgyzstan. It is closely related to the Persian used in Iran and Afghanistan (Farsi and Dari languages). Its script has evolved from Arabic (till 1930), Latin (from 1930 till 1940), to Cyrillic (since 1940). Tajik does not currently have a spell checker.

This paper describes the process of developing a spell checker for Tajik using formal methods, in particular RAISE [5,6]. The spell checker is supposed to: (1) check the spelling of a given text according to the rules of the language and existing dictionaries; (2) decompose correctly spelled words into prefixes, roots and suffixes; and (3) suggest how to correct the words that are misspelled. The development starts with formalising the rules for constructing Tajik words, on the level suitable to specify any language processor. Then we proceed via increasingly detailed descriptions, from abstract and non-executable, to concrete enough to be translated to software. The main source about the language is [4].

There are several arguments in favour of using formal methods to develop non-safety-critical systems. First, to gain some confidence that the system is fit for its purpose and performs its function reliably. Second, to ensure that the development has the largest possible potential for reuse. On the one hand, we would like to reuse the language model to build other processors for Tajik. On the other, by replacing the model we would like to re-apply the development to build spell checkers for other related languages.

The rest of this paper is as follows: Section 2 describes the language, Section 3 describes the model, Section 4 shows how to develop and the spell checker from this model, and Section 5 contains some conclusions.

---
* Technological University of Tajikistan, Dushanbe, Tajikistan.

2 Tajik Language

A word in Tajik is built with several roots, prefixes and suffixes. A prefix or a suffix alone do not express any meaning, and their presence is optional within a word. In contrast, a root is necessary and it can alone express meaning. The relationship between prefixes, roots and suffixes in a word is expressed through parts of speech. Tajik provides ten parts of speech, divided into stable and unstable, and assigns one or more of them to every word. A word whose root has an unstable part of speech cannot have any prefixes or suffixes. Composing the words from prefixes, suffixes and roots is subject to several constraints. First, the number of prefixes must not exceed three, and the number of suffixes must not exceed seven. Second, a prefix can only precede a root with particular parts of speech. Third, when a prefix precedes a root, the resulting word's part of speech may change. Fourth, prefixes can only precede each other in a particular order. Fifth, the allowed composition of suffixes depends on the part of speech of the root. If the root is preceded by a prefix, it depends on the part of speech resulting from the composition of the prefix and the root.

Consider the word бекорчиҳоро. The root of the word, кор, has two parts of speech: `ism` and `fel` (a noun and a verb). However, the prefix бе can only precede `ism`, and the resulting part of speech of the combined prefix and root is `sifat`. Then the word has three suffixes: чи, ҳо and ро, all of which expect `sifat` as the part of speech of the preceding part, and return `sifat` as a result.

3 Language Modelling

Tajik contains ten parts of speech (type `Speech`), including `verb`, and divides them into two classes: stable and unstable (function `is_stable`).

type	value

Speech ==
   ism | fel | sifat | shumora |
   jonishin | zarf | payvandak | ...
	verb: Speech = fel,
	 is_stable: Speech $\to$ **Bool**
	 is_stable(s) $\equiv$ s $\in$ {ism, fel, sifat, ... }

There are 17 different prefixes in Tajik (type `Prefix`) and six rules to decide when one prefix can precede another (function `can_prec`). A prefix-list (type `Prefixes`) is defined to obey such rules. Prefixes can only precede the roots that belong to certain parts of speech (function `before`), and may cause this part of speech to change (function `after`).

type	value

Prefix = {| t:**Text** • ispre(t) |},
 Prefixes = {| ps: Prefix* • ...|}
 value
   ispre: **Text** $\to$ **Bool**
   ispre(t) $\equiv$ t $\in$ {"bar", "me", ... }
	can_prec: Prefix $\times$ Prefix $\to$ **Bool**
	 can_prec(p1, p2) $\equiv$ (p1, p2) $\in$
	   {("bar", "me"), ("bar", "na"), ... },
	 before: Prefixes $\to$ Speech-**set**,
	 after: Prefixes$\times$Speech$\overset{\sim}{\to}$ Speech-**set**

A word can contain one or more roots (type `Root`) put one after another or separated by optional infixes (type `Infix`). Every (composed) root belongs to one or more parts of speech (function **speech**); stable and unstable parts of speech are never assigned simultaneously. A root which is a verb can occur in two different forms depending on the tense: **present** or **past** (function **tense**).

type
   Root, Infix,
   Part == none |
     root(Root) | infix(Infix),
   Roots = {| rs: Part* • ... |}

type
   Tense == past | present
value
   speech: Roots → Speech-set,
   tense: Roots → Tense

A verb also depends on the presence of the prefix "me". A table of speech (type **Table**) extends stable parts of speech to include four different forms of verbs: one for each combination of the values in **Tense** and **Me** (**yes** and **no**).

Tajik contains 150 suffixes (type **Suffix**), and many rules to decide which suffixes are allowed to succeed one another, one set of rules for each table of speech (function **can_suc**): **can_suc(t)(s)** contains the suffixes allowed to succeed **s** in a word that belongs to the table **t**. Every time a suffix is appended, it may change the table of speech of the word (function **change_table**). We declare a list of suffixes (type **Suffixes**) to obey such rules with respect to a given table of speech (function **iswf**), taking into account how this table will change.

type
   Suffix = {|t:**Text** • issuf(t) |},
   Suffixes = Suffix*
value
   issuf: **Text** → **Bool**
   issuf(t) ≡
     t ∈ {"ho", "on", "yon" ...},
   iswf: Table × Suffixes $\overset{\sim}{\to}$ **Bool**

type
   Me == yes | no,
   Table' == speech(Speech) |
     verb(tense: Tense, me: Me),
   Table = {| tb: Table' • ... |}
value
   can_suc: Table→(Suffix $\overrightarrow{m}$ Suffix-set),
   change_table: Table × Suffix → Table

The type **Word** is a record type with three fields for prefixes, roots and suffixes. The subtype makes sure that the prefix, if present, is allowed to precede the root (function **can_prec**) and the suffix, if present, is allowed to succeed the root and the prefix (function **can_suc**). In order for a prefix to precede a root, they must share at least one part of speech in the sets returned by **speech** and **before**. In order for a suffix to succeed a root, there must be at least one table in the set of tables for the prefix and root, for which this suffix is well-formed.

type
   Word'::
     ps: Prefixes
     rs: Roots ss: Suffixes,
   Word={|w:Word'•iswf(w)|}
value

iswf: Word' → **Bool**
iswf(w) ≡
   (ps(w) = ⟨⟩ ∨ can_prec(ps(w),rs(w))) ∧
   (ss(w) = ⟨⟩ ∨ can_suc(ps(w),rs(w),ss(w))),
can_prec: Prefixes × Roots → **Bool**,
can_suc: Prefixes × Roots × Suffixes → **Bool**

4 Developing the Spell Checker

The spell-checker receives a text t as input and decides if t represents a correct word in Tajik: respects the rules of the language described by the model in Sections 3. The function check tries to establish this by dividing t with indexes i and j such that: t(1) until t(i-1) is a correct prefix, t(i) until t(j) is a correct root, and t(j+1) until t(len t) is a correct suffix. The latter means there exists a table tb for the prefix and root such that the suffix is correct with respect to tb. Suppose speech, before and after are redefined for **Text**, then:

value
  check: **Text** → **Bool**
  check(t) ≡ t = "" ∨
    (∃ i, j: **Nat** • 1 ≤ i ∧ i < j ∧ j ≤ **len** t ∧
      let ps=substr(1,i−1,t), rs=substr(i,j,t), ss=substr(j+1,**len** t,t) **in**
        is_root(rs) ∧ (ps = "" ∨ is_prefix(ps)) ∧ (ss = "" ∨
        (∃ s: Speech • s ∈ after(ps,speech(rs)) ∩ before(ps)) ∧
          is_suffix(table(tense(rs), **if** ps = "me" **then** yes **else** no **end**, s), ss)
      ))
    end
)

In particular, with only 25 legal combinations of prefixes we decide to list them all and define is_prefix explicitly. In contrast, in order to check a root (is_root), we decide to use a dictionary implemented as a character tree: a tree consisting of the nodes with varying number of children, where each child is labelled by a character. By collecting all the characters along the path in the tree, the resulting text represents one possible root in the language. One particular tree is tajik: the tree to represent the dictionary of roots in Tajik.

type
  Node == empty |
    put(tense:Tense,
    speech:Speech-**set**),
  Trees = **Char** $\overrightarrow{m}$ Tree,
  Tree:: sub: Trees node: Node
value
  intree: **Text** × Tree → **Bool**

value
  tajik: Tree • ∀ t:**Text** •
    intree(t,tajik) ⇒
      tense(t)=tense(text2root(t)) ∧
      speech(t)=speech(text2root(t))
value
  is_root: **Text** → **Bool**
  is_root(t) ≡ intree(t,tajik)

If the input text t is correct, the spell-checker should produce the set of possible words, divided into prefixes, roots and suffixes, that t can represent. We calculate this set by first constructing the set of all valid roots inside t and then removing those roots that do not contain valid prefixes or suffixes.

If t is incorrect, the spell-checker should suggest possible corrections. We calculate such corrections by transforming t in various ways (assuming the errors of deleting a character, exchanging two adjacent characters, replacing a character by another one, or inserting one), then checking if the result is correct.

5 Conclusions

The paper describes our experience with developing a spell-checker for Tajik using formal methods, in particular RAISE. The spell-checker has been implemented with Visual Basic using the Windows (98/NT/2000) environment, relying on the modest dictionary of roots [3]. The prototype version can be obtained, including binaries, sources and dictionaries, from ftp.iist.unu.edu/pub/tajik.

This work has been undertaken to respond to the clear demand: until now, there was no spell-checking software for Tajik. It was also undertaken as a research project: we wanted to learn how formal methods can be used to develop language-processing applications, what are the benefits, limitations, and compromises one has to make in practice. But it was also undertaken as an engineering project: to obtain quality models that capture precisely the structure of words in Tajik – so that such models could be reused to develop other language processors for Tajik, and the models to develop spell-checking software – so that such models could be reused to develop spell-checkers for other languages with similar word structures. The full version of this paper is published as the UNU/IIST Technical Report [2]. The work is part of the project to develop Tajik language software, established jointly by the Tajik Academy of Science and Computer Centre of the Technological University of Tajikistan.

Possible future work includes improving the implementation by adding some new functionality (e.g. producing the break-down of a given correct text into prefixes, roots, and suffixes), improving precision of spell-checking (by adding more roots into the dictionary) and removing some limitations. One particular limitation is having to run the implementation in the Windows environments, instead of relying on public domain software. It would be useful to generate the C++ code directly from the RSL specification [1], and make this implementation available across different execution platforms, with all the functionality offered by the Visual Basic version but without the GUI interface.

References

1. Univan Ahn and Chris George. C++ Translator for RAISE Specification Language. Technical Report 220, UNU/IIST, P.O. Box 3058, Macau, November 2000.
2. Gafurov Davrondjon and Tomasz Janowski. Developing a Spell-Checker for Tajik using RAISE. Technical Report 252, UNU/IIST, P.O. Box 3058, Macau, May 2002.
3. И. Калонтаров. Лугати Орфографи. Ministry of Education of Republic of Tajikistan, 1959.
4. М. А. Исмаилов. Основы Автоматизированного Морфологического Анализа Слов Таджикского Языка. Institute of Mathematics of the Academy of Sciences of Tajikistan, 1994.
5. The RAISE Method Group. *The RAISE Specification Language*. Prentice Hall, 1992.
6. The RAISE Method Group. *The RAISE Development Method*. Prentice Hall, 1995.

M2Z: A Tool for Translating a Natural Language Software Specification into Z

Zarina Shukur, Abdullah Md. Zin, and Ainita Ban

Computer Science Dept, Fakulti Teknologi dan Sains Maklumat, Universiti Kebangsaan, Malaysia, 43600 Bangi, Selangor.

Abstract. This paper discusses the design of a tool for translating a natural language software specification into a formal specification. The input to the tool are basic information about the system to be specified and a statement describing the specification of the system written in the Malay language. The basic information is used as the basic knowledge about the system. By using this basic knowledge, the specification statement will be translated and semantically interpreted in order to produce an equivalent statement in Z.

Keywords: Formal methods, machine translation, linguistic, Z

1 Introduction

Software specification is normally written in a natural language. As with other documents that are written in a natural language, a software specification normally has a lot of ambiguouty, especially when it is read and interpreted by different people. The misunderstanding of a software specification due to these ambiguouties has been identified as one of the most important source of error in software development. For example, Boehm has stated that more than 60% of errors in software development is due to the error in understanding the software specification [1].

Formal notations that are based on mathematics, such as Z and VDM, have been considered to be more effective in representing software specifications. Although the benefit of using formal notations is generally accepted by most of software practitioners, formal notations are not widely used in software development [2]. Most of software developers are not familiar with mathematical notation and they find that writing matematical statements is too complicated [4].

A possible solution to this problem is by providing software developers with a tool that can aid in translating natural language statements into mathematical statements. A few such systems have been developed. Most of these systems were designed to translate natural language statements in English into statements in formal notation. This paper discusses the design of a tool that can help software engineers to translate natural language statements written in the Malay language into formal specification statements in Z.

2 Translating Natural Language Text into Formal Notations

In general, the approaches that have been used in developing tools to translate text from a natural language into a formal notation can be divided into two types [10]: knowledge-based approach and natural language processing approach. Knowledge based approach uses domain knowledge as the basis in analysing requirements for producing formal specifications. Examples of tools that were developed by using this approach are SPECIFIER [5] and Requirement Analysis [6].

Natural language processing approach combines the knowledge of linguistics and computer sciences. Examples of tools that produce formal specifications from natural language software specification by using this approach are NL2ACTL [3] and FORSEN [10].

3 Overview of M2Z

M2Z has been designed and developed to translate a software specification that is written in Malay into a formal specification in Z. It uses natural language processing technique in order to extract the information from Malay language. Nouns represent sets or types, verbs represent relation between the sets whilst adjectives represent modifiers.

If Saeki et al [7] used an object approach in manipulating and formalising informal requirements for software specification, this study adopts the concepts of entity relationship module for developing the prototype of M2Z as has been done by Vadera and Meziane in FORSEN [10]. Figure 1 shows the architecture of M2Z. It is similar to a machine language translation method. M2Z architecture uses indirect approach that is by implementing the knowledge of source language and target language.

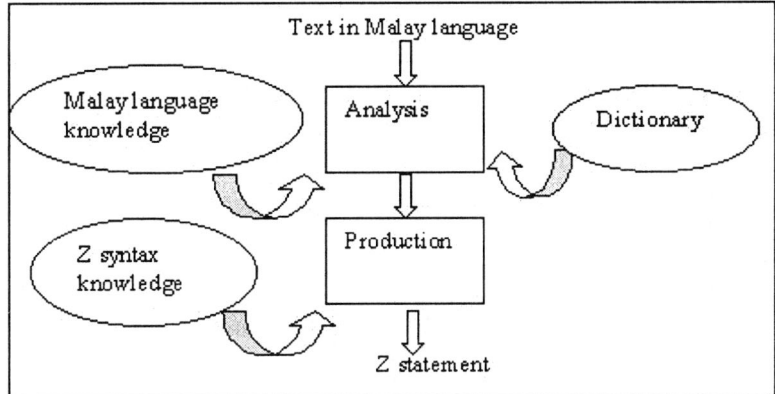

Fig. 1. Architecture of M2Z

The source text for M2Z used in this study is a structured Malay language. What this means is that the vocabulary and grammar are restricted. In order to carry out the study, some assumptions have been made:

- Source text is grammatically correct and meaningful.
- User is familiar with the writing of software specification for discrete problem.

Before the input text is entered, M2Z needs to be provided with basic information about the system. Basic information is information about the system being modeled whilst input text is sentences which describe requirement of the system, which is written in Malay language. Basic information of a model contains two types: data types and function types. They will be used as a basis to determine the respective set in the model.

4 Architecture of M2Z

Overall, the processes that are involved in M2Z can be divided into two phases as follows:
1. Analysis Phase
   This phase contains two steps. First is to lexically analyse the input, which is done by a lexical analyser and the result from this step is called *intermediate product*. Second, is to semantically interpret the intermediate product that will then produce a *conceptual model*.
2. Production Phase
   In this phase, Z statement is generated based on the information in *conceptual model*. This phase uses Z syntax rule as in Spivey [9].

Lexical Analysis
The role of lexical analyser is to read every word and then categorizes them into one of this classes; verbs, nouns, adjectives, symbols and stop words. The output from lexical analysis is called an intermediate product. For example, the sentence
   'setiap pelajar yang belajar di UKM mesti mengambil SKP2201'
(which means: all students that are studying at UKM must register for SKP2201), will be represented by an intermediate product as shown in Figure 2.

<Word Location>	<Item>	<Category>
0	∀	Symbol
1	pelajar	Noun
2	|	Symbol
3	belajar	Verb
4	UKM	Noun
5	•	Symbol
6	mengambil	Verb
7	SKP2201	Noun

Fig. 2. Example of intermediate product

Semantic Interpretation

In this study, semantic interpretation is carried out to identify the relation among entities in a Malay sentence. Therefore, modification approach is used. In this approach, the meaning of a sentence is expressed in its sub-component. Table 1 shows grammar rule and the use of modification approach in interpreting its semantic. The symbol * shows the semantic translation for the rule.

Table 1. Grammar Rule

Rule	Semantic Interpretation
A → FN FK	FN* (FK*)
FK → KK FN	KK* (FN*)
FK → KK	KK*
FN → KN	KN*
FA → KA	KA*

Conceptual model for intermediate product example in Figure 2 is as in Figure 3. Integer 1001 indicates that the respective id-item only have one argument.

\<Id Item\>	\<Argument 1\>	\<Argument 2\>
0	1	1001
2	3	1001
5	6	1001
3	1	4
6	1	7

Fig. 3. Conceptual model based on Intermediate product in Figure 2

Production Phase

Production phase is a process to produce source text from conceptual model. This phase consists of three tasks. The first task is to determine the possible form of type expression of a model. The second task is to generate the declaration. And the third task is to extract predicates from conceptual model by manipulating logical symbols in the model.

The result from the whole proces is an output text which is in the form of predicates. The occurrences of bar symbol ('|') in a conceptual model is important as it will be used to determine the predicate format of the output. Based on the conceptual model in Figure 3, the target text that will be produced in this phase is:

$$\forall\ p\text{:pelajar}\ |\ (p,\ UKM) \in \text{belajar} \bullet (p,\ SKP2201) \in \text{AmbilKursus}$$

5 Conclusion

In this paper we have described the design of M2Z, a tool to translate software specification that is written in the Malay language to formal specification in Z. M2Z is a research prototype. It is designed to be integrated into ZEdit [8], a WYSIWYG-based Z Editor. In order to make it compatible with most Z tools, the text that is generated by M2Z is presented in Latex form. In the present form, the tool suffers from a number of limitations. The natural language statement that is accepted by the tool is restricted to a certain grammar rule. Similarly, the formal specificatoion statement is limited to a certain data type. Hence, it is not yet ready to translate one complete software specification. We are in the process of improving the design of the tool by extending the grammar rule and the range of type of data that can be supported.

References

1. Boehm, B. W.: Software Engineering: R&D Trends and Defence needs. in Research directions in Software Technology. MIT Press. 44-86 (1979)
2. Dill, D. dan Rushby, J.: Acceptance of Formal Methods: Lesson from Hardware Design. IEEE Computer **29**(4) (1996) 23-24
3. Fantechi, A., Gnesi, S., Ristori, G., Carenini, M., Vanocchi, M. & Moreschni, P.: Assisting requirement formalization by means of natural language translation. in Formal Methods in System Design, Vol. 4, 243-263. Kluwer Academic Publishers (1994)
4. Holloway, C.M.:Why Engineers should consider formal methods? Proc. IAA/IEEE Digital Avionics Systems Conference. **1:** (1997) 1.3-16 - 1.3-22
5. Miriyala, K. & Harandi, M.T.:Automatic Derivation of Formal Software Specifications From Informal Descriptions. IEEE Transaction on Software Engineering **17**(10) (1991) 1126 -1142
6. Reubenstein, H.B. & Waters, R.C.: The Requirement Apprentice: Automated Assistance for Requirements Acquisition. IEEE Transaction on Software Engineering **17**(3) (1991) 226 -240
7. Saeki, M, Horai, H. & Enomoto, H.: Software development process from natural language specification. Proceedings of the 11th international conference on Software engineering, (1989) 64-73
8. Shukur, Z., Nantha, K.S, & Ban, A.: Developing WYSIWYG-based Z Editor with Natural Language Capabilities. Proceedings of the International Conference on Parallel and Distribution Processing Technique and Applications, (2001) 135-140.
9. Spivey, J.M.: The Z Notation: a reference manual. 2nd edn. Prentice Hall International Series in Computer Science. Prentice Hall (1992)
10. Vadera, S. & Meziane, F.: From English to Formal Specifications. The Computer Journal **37**(9) (1994) 753-761

Abstract Interpretation with a Theorem Prover

Hugh Anderson

Department of Computer Science, National University of Singapore
hugh@comp.nus.edu.sg

Abstract. This paper presents an approach to the implementation of the *abstract interpretation* style of program analysis by first constructing a logic for representing the process of abstract analysis, and then embedding this logic in the theorem prover **HOL**. Programs to be analysed undergo a two-phase process, first being mechanically transformed to an analysis *model*, and then this being used to test or verify program properties. A specific advantage of this approach is that it allows abstract interpretation to be used in a consistent framework with other analysis methods, such as Hoare Logic or exhaustive state space analysis.

1 Introduction

Software developments are often so complex that program developers are unsure of the behaviour of code they have constructed. Testing, though useful, cannot guarantee the behaviour of developed code unless the testing is exhaustive, and this is generally not possible for large software developments.

An alternative strategy is to attempt to confirm behaviours of code by analysis using representations of the semantics of the code components. In one approach, the operation of the program is represented in an abstract manner, and mathematical techniques are used to derive properties of the code. These properties may be considered to be partial specifications of the code. Examples of this approach include Hoare reasoning [8], and abstract interpretation, elaborated by Cousot and Halbwachs in [3]. Graf and Saidi have presented a method in [10] which automatically constructs abstract state graphs suitable for checking with a model checker.

This paper explores a transformational approach to analysis within a unified program development environment, by constructing a logic for analysis, coding this logic as a shallow embedding in the theorem prover **HOL** [6], and then using this to derive an efficient analysis model from a program. This model has a functional form and may be used to test and verify properties of a program.

This paper has the following structure: Sections 2 and 3 briefly introduce abstract interpretation and the mechanical theorem prover **HOL**. Section 4 presents elements of a logic for abstract interpretation analysis, showing a sample analysis of a program within the logic. Section 5 shows sample codings of logic elements in **HOL**, and section 6 is the conclusion.

2 Abstract Interpretation

The technique of abstract interpretation approximates the *exact* analysis of programs, by reasoning on some abstract semantics of the program. An example of abstract interpretation is found in the analysis of the semantics of a program restricted over a representation of program state given as a set of linear inequalities or equalities between the variables of the program. For example, consider two unsigned integer variables $x \geq 2$ and y and the assignments:

$$y := (x * x) + 1;$$
$$x := x + x;$$

An *exact* static analysis of the state of the program variables after these assignments may involve keeping track of a series of (x, y) pairs: $\{(4, 5), (8, 17), ...\}$ (depending on other program elements). However, it may also be given as a set of linear inequalities, written as:

$$\{y \geq x + 1\}$$

Note that this assertion is always true, but it tells us less about the behaviour of the assignment statements. The reason for doing this sort of software approximation is that further analysis on the machine state may be less computationally expensive.

Linear programming functions such as *convex-hull* and *projection* are also useful in this context. Consider the analysis of program state $\{Q\}$ at the beginning of this do-loop[1]:

$$\{y \geq 1 \wedge x = 2\}$$
$$\textbf{do } \{Q\} B \rightarrow$$
$$\qquad y := (x * x) + 1;$$
$$\qquad x := x + x;$$
$$\textbf{od}$$

If we were to consider the case of an *exact* representation of this state, $\{Q\}$ would either be (initially) $\{y \geq 1 \wedge x = 2\}$ or (on successive iterations) the values $(4, 5), (8, 17), ...$, which may be represented by the inequality $y \geq x + 1$.

In the case of the approximate abstract interpretation of this state, the convex hull of the equations $y \geq 1 \wedge x = 2$ and $y \geq x + 1$ may be used instead. We interpret this graphically in Figure 1, where the spaces represented by the two sets of equations are shown, and an enclosing (convex hull) half-space.

The convex hull for a larger set of inequalities involving large numbers of variables may be efficiently calculated using a linear programming software library such as the **cddlib** package found in Fukuda [4].

There is also a graphical interpretation of *projection*, where equations in an "n"-dimensional space are projected onto an "$n-1$"-dimensional space. For

---

[1] Note that here we switch between predicate and set representations of the linear inequalities when the meaning is clear, writing $\{y \geq 1 \wedge x = 2\}$ for the two linear equations $\{y \geq 1, x = 2\}$.

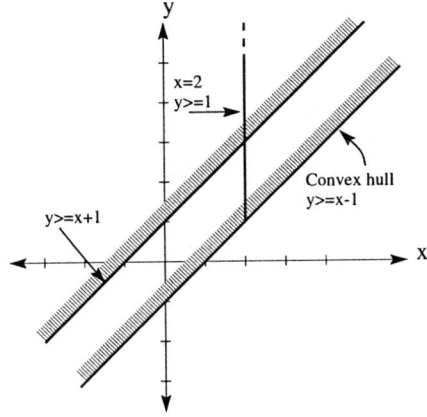

Fig. 1. The convex hull of $y \geq 1 \wedge x = 2$ and $y \geq x + 1$ is the half-space $y \geq x - 1$

example, the projection of $y \geq 1 \wedge x = 2$ onto y ($y = x^{\perp}$, the orthogonal complement of x) is $y \geq 1$.

In this paper, the particular abstract interpretation style described and implemented in **HOL** is the one just outlined, with the program state represented as sets of linear inequalities, and transformations using convex hull and projection.

3 The HOL Theorem Prover

HOL is a theorem prover assistant written by Mike Gordon in the mid 1980s, and derived from Milner's LCF [5]. **HOL** is implemented in the language **ML**, and it is common to develop **HOL** systems in a blend of **HOL** and **ML**, here called **HOL/ML**. **HOL** provides tools which only allow the construction of theorems which follow from original axioms and definitions. The core of **HOL** consists of 8 inference rules and 5 axioms, and all later proofs and theories are derived from these.

HOL supports both a forward proof style, in which we construct new theorems from existing ones by constructing functions in **HOL/ML** with existing theorems and axioms as parameters, and a backward proof style, in which we set up a goal, and then break it into (separately proved) subgoals. In **HOL**, the steps made during this backward reasoning process are called tactics.

3.1 Extending Theories in HOL

HOL operates in two modes, *draft* and *proof* mode. In draft mode it is possible to introduce (possibly) inconsistent axioms. In proof mode, this is not possible. Theories are extended through the addition of types, constants and inference rules, and this may lead to inconsistent theories. Back and Wright [2] discuss the use of conservative extensions to a theory to ensure consistency:

"The advantage of a conservative extension is that it has a standard model whenever the original theory has one. This means that a conservative extension can never introduce inconsistency."

The approach taken here is a mix; we include underived elements into the theory to access external efficient libraries, but after each use, a check is done of the derived result, to see if it is still consistent with the original.

4 A Logic for Analysis

In the logic presented here, programs may be represented in both a conventional *specification* style using pre and postcondition state representations, and in an *executable* style with a simple imperative language, along the lines given in [9]. For example the Morgan notation

$v\colon [\,\text{true}\,,\ v > 10\,]$

specifies that in the frame[2] v, for any precondition, the postcondition should be $v > 10$. This style of specification is commonly used in the context of the Refinement Calculus to construct code from specifications. For example, we may *refine* this specification using an *assignment introduction* refinement rule:

$\sqsubseteq$ Assignment introduction

$v := 11$

The $\sqsubseteq$ symbol in $S \sqsubseteq C$ indicates that C is a *refinement* of S. The refinement relation ordering is defined in weakest precondition terms by the requirement for $\text{post}(C) \Rightarrow \text{post}(S)$ for initial states satisfying $\text{pre}(S)$.

We introduce a similar logic for analysis, adopting similar notation, although our rules operate in a reverse manner, tending to derive (more abstract) specifications from code. The $\sqsupseteq$ symbol in $C \sqsupseteq S$ indicates that S is an *abstraction* of C. The abstraction relation ordering is the converse of refinement. If $C \sqsupseteq S$ and $C \sqsubseteq S$, then $C \equiv S$.

As an example, the previous code segment might be transformed for the purpose of program analysis, using one of many possible rules, as follows:

$\equiv$ Equivalent assignment postcondition introduction

$v\colon [\,P\,,\ \exists v' : P[v'/v] \wedge v = 11[v'/v]\,]$

The meaning attached to the notation $P[v'/v]$ is that of substitution, replacing each free occurrence of the variable v in an arbitrary formula P with the expression v'. Our example may be simplified to:

$\equiv$ Simplification

$v\colon [\,P\,,\ \exists v' : P[v'/v] \wedge v = 11\,]$

This may not seem all that interesting, however, it may be used in the context of program analysis by unifying P with true to get

---

[2] A *frame* indicates those variables or state elements that may change.

⊒   Unification - strengthen precondition/weaken postcondition
$$v\colon [\,\text{true}\,,\,v = 11\,]$$

That is - an assertion that the code segment $v := 11$ has a property matched by the specification $v\colon [\,\text{true}\,,\,v = 11\,]$. This analysis is one of many that might be performed on assignment code, and reflects a strongest postcondition style of program analysis. In this paper, two sample types of analysis rules are described:

1. **Equivalence analysis rules** - ≡ - In this sort of transformation rule, the program state is represented by predicates over the program variables, and program statements are transformed in relation to the way in which they transform these predicates.
2. **Abstraction analysis rules** - ⊒ - In this sort of transformation rule, an abstraction of the program state is represented by a set of linear inequalities reflecting the relationships between the variables in the program. Program statements are transformed in relation to the way they transform these linear inequalities.

The ⊒ abstraction transformations are used to transform either a code segment, or a specification, to some form more amenable to analysis. For example, we may only be interested in the relative values of variables in a program, and not their absolute values, or we may be only interested in a subset of the variables.

The ≡ equivalence transformation rules are used to transform the resultant abstract specifications to a final specification form. This final specification is an *analysis* of the original program - what it specifies is a (weaker) true assertion about the original specification.

Intermediate transformations of an original source program are considered to be models of the program at different levels of abstraction, and the goal of the transformation phase of the analysis process is to produce a functional abstract specification of the program. This specification is then executed to test properties of the program.

In the following section of the paper, sample rules for equivalence and abstraction are given, and then an example analysis uses these two sorts of rules to transform a small program. The resultant functional specification reveals an unexpected property of the code.

4.1 Equivalence Rules

In the equivalence rules, an attempt is made to capture all relevant behaviour of the program. The refinement calculus textbooks give detailed descriptions of rules suitable for program development which are not repeated here, however, here are two sample rules with specific application in the area of analysis of assignment statements.

1. An equivalence rule for the assignment $v := e$ using strongest postconditions:

    ≡   Equivalent assignment postcondition introduction
$$v\colon [\,P\,,\,\exists v' : P[v'/v] \wedge v = e[v'/v]\,]$$

2. An equivalence rule for the assignment $v := e$ using weakest preconditions:

$\equiv$ Equivalent assignment precondition introduction
$v\colon [\, P[e/v]\, ,\, P\,]$

There are other rules for loops, if statements and so on.

4.2 Abstraction Rules

As discussed in Section 2, the program state is represented here as a set of linear inequalities, and the transforming operations on these are standard linear programming ones such as *convex hull* or *projection* operations. The resultant expressions are computationally easy to evaluate, but may tell us *less* about our programs.

1. A rule for abstract interpretation style analysis of assignments of the form $v := e$ that are not invertible, such as $v := 0$:

   $\sqsupseteq$ Abstract ni-assignment postcondition introduction
   $v\colon [\, P\, ,\, \mathrm{proj}_{v^{\perp}}(P) \wedge v = e\,]$

   In this expression, the notation $\mathrm{proj}_{v^{\perp}}(P)$ represents the projection of the expression P onto the orthogonal complement of v.

2. A rule for assignments which are invertible, such as $v := v + 1$. We may generalize such assignments as $v := f(v)$, where f is an invertible function:

   $\equiv$ Abstract i-assignment postcondition introduction
   $v\colon [\, P\, ,\, P[f^{-1}(v)/v]\,]$

   In this expression, the notation f^{-1} represents the inverse of f. This rule may only be applied if $\exists f^{-1} \forall x : f(f^{-1}(x)) = x$.

3. A rule for projecting a specification $f\colon [\, \mathrm{true}\, ,\, Q\,]$ onto the orthogonal complement of (say) x. This sort of abstraction is used to perform analysis on a subset of the variables in a frame, while retaining as much information as possible about the frame:

   $\sqsupseteq$ Abstract projection onto $x^{\perp}$
   $g\colon [\, \mathrm{true}\, ,\, \mathrm{proj}_{x^{\perp}}(Q)\,]$

   In this expression g is defined by $g \cup x = f \wedge g \cap x = \{\}$ (i.e. the frame f without the variable x).

4. A rule for the *do-loop* **do** $B \rightarrow f: [P\,,\, Q]$ **od** introduces the conv(R) operator which returns the *convex hull* of R:

⊒ Abstract iteration postcondition introduction
$f: [R\,,\, R]$;
do $f: [\,\text{conv}(R \cup Q) \wedge B\,,\, Q\,]$ **od**;
$f: [\,\text{conv}(R \cup Q) \wedge \neg B\,,\, \text{conv}(R \cup Q) \wedge \neg B\,]$

The $f: [R\,,\, R]$ component of the refinement is an artifact to introduce a state variable name. The last component of the refinement retains information about the *do-loop*.

Note that we cannot mix refinement and abstraction rules and expect the resultant expression to still be a refinement of the original expression.

4.3 Example Analysis

In this section, a small example is analysed, demonstrating the two phases of analysis used in this approach. In the first *transformation* phase, a code implementation is given, and then transformed according to abstract analysis rules. In the second *execution* phase, the resultant specification is used to derive something possibly *bad* about the particular implementation - specifically that the result might be wrong in some circumstances.

In public key encryption schemes, large integer computations often have to be performed. For example, the evaluation of modulo(P^Q, N) where P, Q and N are all large numbers. A simple implementation might involve calculating first P^Q, and then performing a **mod()** (*modulo*) machine operation[3]. However, the calculation of P^Q may involve very large numbers, difficult to manipulate on a computer. The following code is another implementation of this specification, and calculates modulo(P^Q, N), leaving the result in variable c. A quality of this particular implementation is that the code never has to calculate P^Q - the largest calculation is always less than $N * P$:

$\|\,$ **var** $x, d : \mathbb{N}\bullet$
  $c, x, d := 1, 0, 0$;
  do $x \neq Q \rightarrow x, d := x + 1, c * P$;
    $c := \text{mod}(d, N)$
  od
$\,\|$

---

[3] Note that the mathematical expression modulo(x, y) = x if $y = 0$. This is different from the standard programmer's experience with the **mod()** operation which is that **mod(x,y)** is always less than y.

Applying abstraction rules to the assignments inside the do-loop results in this:

⊒ Abstract assignment postcondition introduction
var $x, d : \mathbb{N}$ •
$\quad c, x, d := 1, 0, 0;$
$\quad$ **do** $x \neq Q \to x, d, c\colon [\, M\ ,\ \mathcal{L}\,];$
$\quad\quad\quad x, d, c\colon [\, \mathcal{L}\ ,\ \text{proj}_{c^\perp}(\mathcal{L}) \land c < N\,]$
$\quad$ **od**

where $\mathcal{L}$ is $\text{proj}_{d^\perp}(M[x-1/x]) \land d = c * P$. Note also that the specification state variable M can stand for anything, awaiting later unification with some concrete state. The first assignment in the *do-loop* requires a mix of both invertible and non-invertible assignment rules. The second assignment uses the **mod()** operator, and information is lost here, as we only represent state using linear inequalities. As a result, the only retained effect of $c := \text{mod}(d, N)$ is that $c < N$. Application of the do-loop abstraction rule leads to:

⊒ Abstract iteration postcondition introduction
var $x, d : \mathbb{N}$ •
$\quad c, x, d := 1, 0, 0;$
$\quad x, d, c\colon [\, R\ ,\ R\,];$
$\quad$ **do** $x, d, c\colon [\, \mathcal{H} \land x \neq Q\ ,\ \mathcal{K}\,];$
$\quad\quad\quad x, d, c\colon [\, \mathcal{K}\ ,\ \text{proj}_{c^\perp}(\mathcal{K}) \land c < N\,]$
$\quad$ **od**;
$\quad x, d, c\colon [\, \mathcal{H} \land x = Q\ ,\ \mathcal{H} \land x = Q\,]$

Where $\mathcal{H}$ is shorthand for $\text{conv}(R \cup \text{proj}_{c^\perp}(d = c * P) \land c < N)$, and $\mathcal{K}$ is shorthand for $\mathcal{H} \land x - 1 \neq Q \land d = c * P$. After further simplification and abstractions including the projection onto $x^\perp d^\perp$, many of the terms disappear, resulting in this derivation of the original code:

≡ Simplification
var $x, d : \mathbb{N}$ •
$\quad x, d, c\colon [\, R\ ,\ \mathcal{S} \land c = 1\,];$
$\quad$ **do** $x, d, c\colon [\, \mathcal{T}\ ,\ \mathcal{T}\,];$
$\quad\quad\quad x, d, c\colon [\, \mathcal{T}\ ,\ \mathcal{T} \land c < N\,]$
$\quad$ **od**;
$\quad x, d, c\colon [\, \mathcal{T}\ ,\ \mathcal{T}\,]$

Where $\mathcal{T}$ is shorthand for $\text{conv}((\mathcal{S} \land c = 1) \cup c < N)$ and $\mathcal{S}$ is shorthand for $\text{proj}_{c^\perp}(R)$. In the prototype software, the order of application of rules can be modified by the user of the system, but the transformations are done automatically. If we now only consider the first and last conditions, a derived specification of the whole code segment is:

$\equiv$ Simplification
$x, d, c:$ $[\, R \,,\, \mathcal{T} \,]$

The view here is that an analysis *model* has been produced by the transformation rules. This model specifies true properties of the original program. In the practical application of the logic, input programs are encoded according to the transformation rules into linked **HOL/ML** functions representing the relationship between pre and postconditions of the derived specification. The functions then comprise an engine for abstract modeling of the behaviour of the program. This completes the transformation phase of this example.

In the execution phase, the model is executed to test the behaviour of the program in the specified abstract domain. For example, if R is unified with $N \leq 1$, the analysis reduces to:

$\sqsupset$ Unification
$x, d, c:$ $[\, N \leq 1 \,,\, c \leq N + 1 \,]$

This reveals a property of the implementation that was not apparent before, specifically that if $N \leq 1$, then c has a possibly incorrect value - it should always be less than N. The analysis process has pinpointed a problem with our code[4]. If R is unified with $N > 1$, then we verify that c will *always* be less than N:

$\sqsupset$ Unification
$x, d, c:$ $[\, N > 1 \,,\, c < N \,]$

At this stage a choice may be made to either accept the behaviour of the code or change/correct it.

Note that the end result of the transformation phase of analysis is a model of the functional behaviour of the original program with respect to the particular abstraction used. In this case, the relationship between c and N was of particular interest, and the penultimate analysis *model* was able to confirm that our desired property $(c < N)$ was guaranteed for $N > 1$.

5 On Using HOL

HOL is used in this development in two ways. Firstly as an expressive language in which to encode and simplify the transformations, and secondly to prove assertions made about pre or postconditions. The coding of the logic in **HOL/ML** is straightforward, often reducing to a simple translation from the mathematical representation of the element to a **HOL/ML** function. Some representative **HOL/ML** transforms are given in the next section to demonstrate the approach.

---
[4] If $N = 0$ and $Q = 0$, then the code returns $c = 1$, which is correct according to the mathematical definition of modulo$(P^0, 0)$, but is counter to an (unstated) assumption about the program that the resultant values will always be less than N.

5.1 Transforms in HOL

In the **HOL/ML** transform functions for an analysis tool, assertions about program state are manipulated as **HOL** *terms*. As an example of the techniques for constructing transform functions in **HOL/ML**, here are implementations of some of the transforms:

1. The first equivalence rule given for the assignment $v := e$ was:

    $\equiv$ Equivalent assignment postcondition introduction
    $$v: [\, P \,,\, \exists v' : P[v'/v] \wedge v = e[v'/v] \,]$$

    This may be interpreted as a transforming function which translates a precondition P to some postcondition. **HOL** has an embedded parser which can express this for us succinctly, and the following **HOL/ML** code is used for processing assignments of this form. The code defines a function with three parameters (P, e and v), and returns the required postcondition:

    ```
    fun FpAssign (P:Term.term) (e:Term.term) (v:Term.term) =
        --'?v0. ((\(^v). ^P)v0) /\ (^v=(\(^v). ^e)v0)'--;
    ```

2. The second equivalence rule for the assignment $v := e$ was:

    $\equiv$ Equivalence assignment precondition introduction
    $$v: [\, P[e/v] \,,\, P \,]$$

    This may be interpreted as a transforming function which translates a postcondition P to some precondition. The **HOL/ML** implementation is:

    ```
    fun RpAssign (P:Term.term) (e:Term.term) (v:Term.term) =
        --'(\(^v). ^P)^e'--;
    ```

In the chosen abstraction scheme, assertion state is represented by a linear set of inequalities. **HOL** has no native linear programming theory, but external libraries may be used, while still retaining high assurance that only true theorems may be proved. In this work, functions translate **HOL** terms to and from a structure representing a set of linear inequalities. Following this, various **LP**-based functions may be used to calculate the convex-hull or projection operations.

When using abstract interpretation analysis, the transform for assignment is optimized for various different types of expression. For example, an assignment like $x := x + 1$ is invertible, and involves no loss of state information, whereas an assignment like $x := a + b$ results in the loss of any relationships dependent on x', the previous value of x. Since our assertion state is represented by a linear set of inequalities we may remove the variable x' using projection. The code for projection is implemented separately from the **HOL** theory definitions, and may be subject to (programmer) error or inconsistency. For this reason, these external functions are called from **HOL**, and then tested afterwards for correctness within the **HOL** theory.

3. The first abstraction rule for non-invertible assignments was:

⊐ Abstract ni-assignment postcondition introduction
$v: \big[P,\ \text{proj}_{v\perp}(P) \wedge v = e \big]$

The following **HOL/ML** code is used for processing assignments of this form:

```
fun FpAbsNI (P:Term.term) (e:Term.term) (v:Term.term) =
    --'proj(^v,^P) /\ (^v=^e)'--;
```

5.2 Proof in HOL

The emphasis in the previous section was in the use of **HOL/ML** as an expressive and efficient language for encoding the analysis model. However this is only part of the usefulness of **HOL** in this application. During the process of analysis, it may be useful to prove programmer-supplied assertions about the program.

For example, in program code for sorting an array, an assertion about a partition of an array may be used to confirm that the sort program is working correctly. For example - we might know that the array is divided into a sorted *left-part* from $A[0]$ to $A[P-1]$ and a semi-sorted *right-part* in which the leftmost element $A[P]$ is the least element of the *right-part*, and that all elements in the *left-part* are less than or equal to all elements in the *right-part*. Given this, **HOL** may be used to prove that the array is now sorted from $A[0]$ to $A[P]$. The assertion to be proved is quite complex:

$$\vdash psorted\, A[0..P-1]$$
$$\wedge\, pminindex\, A[P..N-1]\, P$$
$$\wedge\, (\forall x\, y.\, x \in \{0..P-1\} \wedge y \in \{P..N-1\} \Rightarrow A[x] \leq A[y])$$
$$\Rightarrow psorted\, A[0..P]$$

A **HOL** proof script for this is as follows:

```
val assertionB = prove
   ((--'(psorted A (0..P-1)
       /\ pminindex A (P..N-1) P
       /\ (!x y. (0..P-1)x /\ (P..N-1)y ==> A[x]<=A[y]))
       ==>psorted A (0..P)'--),
   ARW_TAC[index_min_partition_DEF,inrange_def,sorted_DEF]
   THEN ('A[P-1]<=A[P]' by ZAP_TAC(arith_ss)[])
   THEN Cases_on 'j<P'
   THEN REPEAT (ZAP_TAC(arith_ss)[]));
```

A more complete explanation of this process of proof of assertions, and a **HOL** theory-of-arrays is found in [1].

6 Conclusion

This work is a part of a larger body of research into program analysis derived from Heintze, Jaffar and Voicu's [7] Conditional Hoare Logic reasoning framework. Various approaches to the management of a process of program analysis are being explored, and this paper reports on the notation and techniques used for representing abstract interpretation within the framework.

The end result of the analysis process is a model of the functional behaviour of the original program with respect to the particular abstraction used. This analysis *model* is used to confirm specific properties of the code under investigation through a testing process. In addition, the models may be directly manipulated in a program *proof* context, providing confirmation of user-supplied assertions.

The process takes place within a formal logic for analysis modeled on the refinement calculus, and the particular notation and methodology is of particular use when combined with other program analysis systems.

Acknowledgments

Thanks to Gill Dobbie, Dong Jin Song and the anonymous referees for their helpful and insightful comments on this paper.

References

1. H. Anderson. Partition theory for CHL. Internal report found at http://www.comp.nus.edu.sg/~hugh/chlproject/TheoryOfArrays.pdf, 2001.
2. R-J. Back and J. von Wright. *Refinement Calculus A Systematic Introduction.* Springer, 1998.
3. P. Cousot and N. Halbwachs. Automatic discovery of linear restraints among variables of a program. In *Association for Computer Machinery, SIGACT/SIGPLAN Symp on Principles of Programming Languages (POPL)*, pages 84–97, Jan 1978.
4. K. Fukuda and A. Prodon. Double description method revisited. In M. Deza, R. Euler, and I. Manoussakis, editors, *Combinatorics and Computer Science*, volume 1120, pages 91–111. Springer-Verlag, 1996.
5. Michael J. C. Gordon, R. Milner, and Christopher P. Wadsworth. *Edinburgh LCF: a mechanised logic of computation*, volume 78 of *Lecture Notes in Computer Science*. Springer-Verlag Inc., New York, NY, USA, 1979.
6. M. J. C. Gordon and T. F. Melham. *Introduction to HOL: A Theorem Proving Environment for Higher Order Logic.* Cambridge University Press, 1993.
7. N. Heintze, J. Jaffar, and R. Voicu. A framework for analysis and verification. In *Association for Computer Machinery, SIGACT/SIGPLAN Symp on Principles of Programming Languages (POPL)*, pages 26–39, Jan 2000.
8. C. A. R. Hoare. An axiomatic basis for computer programming. *Communications of the ACM*, 12:576–580, 1969.
9. C. C. Morgan. *Programming from Specifications.* Prentice Hall International Series in Computer Science, 1994.
10. S. Graf and H. Saidi. Construction of abstract state graphs with PVS. In O. Grumberg, editor, *Proc. 9th International Conference on Computer Aided Verification (CAV'97)*, volume 1254, pages 72–83. Springer Verlag, 1997.

Formal Reasoning about Hardware and Software Memory Models*

Abhik Roychoudhury

Department of of Computer Science, School of Computing,
S16 Level 5, 3 Science Drive 2,
National University of Singapore, Singapore 117543.
abhik@comp.nus.edu.sg

Abstract. The Java programming language allows multithreaded programming, where threads can be run on multiprocessor or uniprocessor platforms. The allowed behaviors of any multithreaded Java program on any implementation platform (multi- or uni-processor), are described in terms of a memory consistency model called the Java Memory Model (JMM). However, shared memory multiprocessors have a memory model of their own. To reason about the behavior of multithreaded Java programs on multiprocessors, we need a formal basis for understanding both the hardware memory model (of the multiprocessor platform) and the software memory model (the JMM). For this purpose, we have implemented formal executable specifications of the JMM and certain hardware memory models (such as TSO/PSO from SPARC). These executable specifications can be used for exhaustive search *i.e.* computing *all allowed behaviors* of test programs under the JMM and the hardware memory models. Consequently, we can compare the JMM with the hardware memory models (in terms of allowed behaviors). We show that such a comparison can help efficient and reliable multithreaded programming on multiprocessors. Results from comparing the current JMM with SPARC architecture memory models are presented.

1 Introduction

Memory consistency models have been used in shared-memory multiprocessors for many years. Given a number of processes accessing a shared store, a memory consistency model places restrictions on the order in which the processes can access (read/write) the shared store. This effectively restricts the values that can be returned on the read of a shared variable, and thereby provides a model of execution to the programmer. The simplest model of memory consistency was proposed by Lamport, and is called Sequential Consistency [11]. This model allows operations across threads to be interleaved in any order. Operations within each thread are however constrained to proceed in *program order*. For example, in the following multithreaded program initially we have u = v = 0.

---
* This work was partially supported by National University of Singapore Research Project R-252-000-095-112.

$$u:=1 \quad x:=v$$
$$v:=1 \quad y:=u$$

Then, a Sequentially Consistent execution of this program cannot return x = 1, y=0. This is possible if the writes to u, v are re-ordered.

Sequential consistency serves as a very simple and intuitive model of execution to the programmer. However, it disallows most compiler and hardware optimizations. For this reason, shared memory multiprocessors have employed *relaxed memory models* [2]. Examples of relaxed memory models include Total Store Order (TSO), Partial Store Order (PSO) and Relaxed Memory Order (RMO) in Sun SPARC architectures [6]. These memory models allow certain re-ordering of operations within a process/thread and allow more behaviors than Sequential Consistency *e.g.* x=1,y=0 in the above example is allowed under SPARC PSO and RMO models. This complicates the programming model at the cost of increased execution efficiency. Thus, people writing multithreaded programs for a shared-memory multiprocessor platform view the hardware memory model as an abstract description of the behaviors supported by the system.

Two recent developments have significantly increased the importance of multithreaded program usage on shared memory multiprocessors. First of all, the widespread use of commercial Symmetric Multiprocessors (SMP) clusters [3] has given shared memory parallelism new life. Secondly, multithreading has been integrated as a key feature of the popular Java programming language. Java supports multithreaded programming, where multiple threads can communicate via read/write of shared objects. These threads can then run on a single processor via a thread library, or on hardware multiprocessors.

Problem addressed. Execution of multithreaded Java programs on shared memory multiprocessors introduces a *new problem*. The semantics of multithreaded Java is given by a language level memory model, called the Java Memory model (henceforth called JMM) [9]. As in hardware memory models, the JMM is a set of abstract rules dictating the allowed ordering of read/write of shared variables. Any uniprocessor/multiprocessor implementation of Java multithreading must respect the JMM. The JMM is the first serious attempt to introduce a memory model at the language/software level. In this paper, we compare the behaviors allowed by the JMM with the behaviors allowed by hardware memory consistency models.

Typically, memory models are given as a set of abstract rules. A comparison of models M_1 and M_2 would proceed via human reasoning about which re-orderings are allowed by M_1 but disallowed by M_2 (and vice-versa). This approach is completely informal and extremely error-prone. In this paper, we advocate the use of formal specification and checking techniques for this purpose. In [16], we have developed a formal executable specification of the current JMM, while specification for hardware memory models have been developed in [8,14]. In this paper, we use these formal specifications for comparing hardware and software memory models. In particular, we craft test programs (using our informal understanding of the memory models), and then use the formal specifications to automatically generate all possible observed behaviors of the test programs under the two memory models. Thus, our method extends informal reasoning with formal specification and verification techniques.

Motivation. There are several reasons for studying such a comparison between software and hardware memory models. If the hardware memory model is weaker than the JMM (*i.e* allows more re-orderings than the JMM) then the Java Virtual Machine needs to insert memory barriers in the hardware instruction sequence. A memory barrier [5] prevents re-ordering of operations across the barrier and can make the multiprocessor execution comply to the JMM. Inserting these time-expensive memory barriers without understanding the JMM and hardware memory models can introduce unacceptable performance overheads. If all re-orderings allowed by the hardware memory model are also allowed by the JMM, then the JVM need not insert any memory barriers.

Comparing the JMM with hardware memory models is also useful for reasoning about low-level unsynchronized Java programs. Often, low-level libraries do not require a synchronization (i.e. lock acquisition) for every shared variable access. Examples of such programs include popular multithreaded Java software construction idioms *e.g.* the "Double-Checked Locking" idiom [17]. These programs allow different sets of behaviors on different multiprocessor platforms (with different memory models). We can formally reason about such low-level code by studying the memory models.

Organization. The rest of this paper is organized as follows. Section 2 recapitulates salient features of the Java Memory Model (JMM). Section 3 introduces the SPARC memory models, and our checker for these models. Section 4 outlines our methodology for studying the relationship between hardware and software memory models. Finally, section 5 describes the related work and conclusions.

2 A Checker for Java Memory Model

The Java programming language allows the user to write multithreaded programs. Java threads interact among themselves via shared variables. For any shared variable v, each thread (a) possesses a local copy of v and (b) is allowed to access the global master copy of v in main memory. The Java Memory Model (JMM) essentially imposes constraints on the interaction of the threads with the master copy of the variables and thus with each other. The model defines the following *actions* for reading/writing the local/master copy of v in thread t.

- $\text{use}_t(v)$: Read from the local copy of v in t
- $\text{assign}_t(v)$: Write into the local copy of v in t
- $\text{read}_t(v)$: Initiate reading from master copy of v to local copy of v in t.
- $\text{load}_t(v)$: Complete reading from master copy of v to local copy of v in t.
- $\text{store}_t(v)$: Initiate writing the local copy of v in t into master copy of v
- $\text{write}_t(v)$: Complete writing the local copy of v in t into master copy of v

Apart from the above actions, each thread t may perform lock/unlock on shared variables, denoted lock$_t$ and unlock$_t$ respectively.

Among the eight actions mentioned above, a thread in a Java program invokes only four of them: use, assign, lock, and unlock. Each thread invokes these actions in its program order. The other four (load, store, read, and write) are invoked arbitrarily by the multithreading implementation, subject to *temporal ordering constraints* specified in the JMM. For example, let the program running in a thread be assign u, 1; assign v, 2 (a sequence of two writes). Then, the two assign statements are executed in program order. However, this does not affect the master copy of the shared variables u, v. The master copy is updated based on store/write actions. These are issued in any order which preserves the temporal ordering constraints specified in the JMM. For example, the JMM allows the following execution assign u,1; assign v,2; store v,2; write v,2; store u,1; write u,1 where writes to u, v are completed out of order.

A major difficulty in reasoning about the JMM (as reported in [15]) lies in these ordering constraints. They are given in an informal, rule-based, declarative style. It is difficult to reason how multiple rules determine the applicability/non-applicability of an action. Our formal operational specification (presented in [16]) avoids this difficulty by modeling each action as a guarded command. We present a brief overview of this work below.

We model each action as a guarded command of the form $\mathcal{G} \to \mathcal{B}$, where the guard $\mathcal{G}$ is first evaluated; if $\mathcal{G}$ is true, then the body $\mathcal{B}$ is executed atomically. Our model is an asynchronous concurrent composition of n Java threads $Th_1, \ldots, Th_n$ and a single main memory process MM. Communication among processes takes place via shared data. Each process can perform a set of *actions*, each of which is modeled by a guarded command. The asynchronous concurrent composition of these processes is the union of the guarded commands of the constituent processes. At any time step, the processes Th_i and MM can execute either a *program action* or a *platform action*. In particular, an action invoked by the program running as thread Th_i is called a program action. The actions use$_i$, assign$_i$, lock$_i$, and unlock$_i$ are program actions. On the other hand, an action which is performed by the underlying multithreading implementation is called a platform action. The actions load$_i$, store$_i$, read$_i$, and write$_i$ are platform actions. Typically, the purpose of executing platform actions is to enable those program actions which are currently disabled.

Since our model is expressed in guarded-command notation, the Murφ model checker [7] is a candidate implementation vehicle[1]. However, we want to program the traversal strategy of the search space of multithreaded executions (for efficient checking and validation). This programming capability is very naturally supported in a general purpose logic programming system where computation proceeds by search. A prototype checker based on our executable memory model has been built using XSB, a memo-table based logic programming system [18]. The checker could be used in two modes. Either we could search the entire search space consisting of all allowed execution traces of program actions and platform

---

[1] Murφ supports a guarded-command based specification language

actions in the threads of a program; or we could input rules to prune the search space based on some scheduling algorithm.

3 A Checker for SPARC Memory Models

In this section, we give a brief overview of memory models appearing in hardware multiprocessors, in particular SPARC memory models. Based on formal executable specification of these memory models [8, 14], we have developed an invariant checker. This checker can be used to verify invariants or to generate all possible behaviors of low-level SPARC code.

The SPARC multiprocessor architecture defines three different memory models: Total Store Order (TSO), Partial Store Order (PSO) and Relaxed Memory Order (RMO) [6]. In terms of allowed behaviors $TSO \subseteq PSO \subseteq RMO$. That is, for any program P, the set of possible behaviors of P under TSO (PSO) is included in the set of possible behaviors of P under PSO (RMO). In describing each of the memory models, we assume that the instructions in each processor are issued in program order. However, these instructions may be completed out of order. Thus, each of these memory models are *weaker* than Sequential Consistency [11] where instructions must always be completed in the order in which they are issued. In the subsequent discussions we denote ld to denote a memory read instruction and st to denote a memory write instruction. Furthermore, note that all the memory models allow only those re-orderings which do not violate the data-flow dependencies in a processor *e.g.* the sequence st u; ld u can never be completed out-of-order since this would change the value of u read by ld.

In the TSO memory model, the restrictions are as follows: (a) a ld operation is ordered with respect to subsequent ld and st operations (b) a st operation is ordered with respect to subsequent st operations. Thus this execution model allows a sequence of instructions st u; ld v (a write to variable u, followed by a read of variable v) to be completed out-of-order. The PSO memory model relaxes the TSO model by removing the second restriction of TSO. Thus, two write operations to different variables st u; st v may be executed out-of-order. The RMO model relaxes PSO by removing both the restrictions of TSO.

An executable model of a shared memory multiprocessor system considers each of the processors as well as the shared memory as a separate process. The combined model is the asynchronous concurrent composition of these processes. Given a parallel program $P_1 \parallel \ldots \parallel P_k$ which is run on processors $Proc_1, \ldots, Proc_k$, processor $Proc_i$ executes the instructions in P_i in program order. The effect of the memory model (delaying/re-ordering of certain instructions) is captured in the following manner. Any processor $Proc_i$ maintains a buffer of incomplete instructions called the *Store buffer*, denoted SB_i. These are non-blocking instructions, *i.e.* instructions which were issued but which have not been completed. The shared memory process can then complete any instruction in any store buffer SB_i in a manner consistent with the memory model.

As a concrete example, let us consider the TSO memory model. It allows writes (st instructions) to be delayed, but not re-ordered. Given a multiprocessor program $P_1 \parallel \ldots \parallel P_k$, any processor $Proc_i$ issues instructions of P_i in program order as follows:

- a st instruction (write operation) is appended into the store buffer SB_i,
- a ld u instruction (reading some variable u) executes as follows. If SB_i contains incomplete writes to u then the value of the last incomplete write to u in SB_i is returned. Otherwise, the value of u is read from the memory.
- all other instructions (corresponding to computation) proceed as usual.

Concurrently, the shared memory process is allowed to complete the first instruction of any of the k store buffers $SB_1 \ldots SB_k$. This corresponds to the delaying of writes as allowed in TSO. To model the re-ordering of writes as allowed in PSO, the shared memory process can be allowed to complete a write instruction in SB_i which is not the first instruction in SB_i.

Based on these executable specifications, we have implemented a checker for the TSO and PSO memory models from SPARC. Given a multiprocessor program, it can generate all observed behaviors under TSO/PSO by computing the set of reachable states. Therefore, it can be used for model checking [4] of invariant properties *i.e.* checking whether an invariant holds in all reachable states. We have used the checker to automatically verify invariants in low-level SPARC code such as verifying mutual exclusion in implementation of spin locks (a lock where the check for whether lock is acquired is done by busy waiting), Dekker's algorithm etc. Many of these code fragments are available in the SPARC architecture manual [6]. However, at this point we move away from the description of the JMM/SPARC checkers and concentrate on how to use these checkers for comparing software/hardware memory models.

4 Relationship between Memory Models

In this section, we present our methodology for comparing the current JMM with hardware memory models. As a concrete example, we consider the SPARC memory models which were discussed in the last section. We show that such a comparison is useful for (a) obtaining efficient multithreading implementation on multiprocessors, and (b) reasoning about low-level unsynchronized multithreaded Java programs.

4.1 Avoiding Redundant Memory Barriers

We want to find out which hardware memory models are stronger than the JMM. A JVM can then execute without introducing *memory barriers* [5] on all such multiprocessor platforms. Recall that a memory barrier is a time-expensive hardware instruction such that in any code if a memory barrier I appears between instructions I_1 and I_2, instruction I_1 must complete before I_2 begins. To clarify the different components of a multiprocessor implementation of Java multithreading, refer to Figure 1. The JVM implementer needs to ensure that re-orderings caused by the multiprocessor platform do not violate the Java Memory Model.

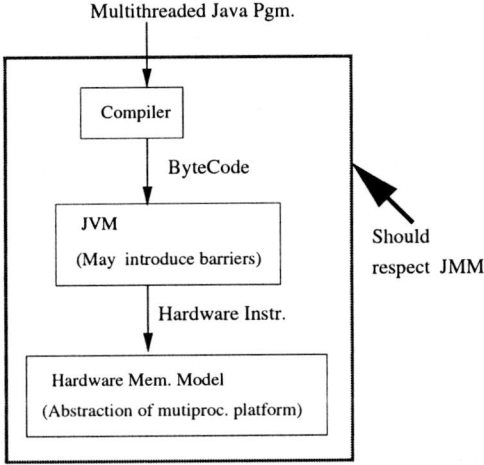

Fig. 1. Multiprocessor implementation of Java multithreading

Our methodology for comparing hardware and software memory models consists of the following steps:

1. Develop formal executable specifications of both the software and the hardware memory models M_s and M_h.
2. Select one/several terminating test program(s) P to expose the re-orderings allowed by the hardware memory model M_h. These test programs are obtained by our *informal* understanding of which re-orderings allowed by M_h.
3. Use the executable specifications of (1) to perform exhaustive state space exploration (as in model checking of invariants) of (a) P executed on M_s and (b) P executed on M_h. This step performs automated *formal* reasoning.
4. Check the set of possible values of the data variables of P on termination in the two cases. This allows us to compare the allowed behaviors of M_h and M_s.

Comparing JMM with TSO. As an illustrative example, let us compare the current JMM with the SPARC TSO memory model. In the TSO model, re-orderings of the following are not allowed: ld → ld/st, st → st. Only the re-ordering of st → ld is allowed. Thus, if st u appears before ld v in program order, they may be completed out of order.

To capture the delayed completion of stores allowed by TSO, consider the test program in Figure 2. It forms the heart of Dekker's algorithm. Assuming sequential consistency, we verify that the values of reg1 and reg2 at the end of execution must satisfy reg1 = 1 ∨ reg2 = 1. This is because in any sequentially consistent execution at least one of the loads will be executed last; this load will return 1 (instead of 0). We then use our implementation of the executable model of TSO to find all possible behaviors allowed by TSO. We find that under

Initially: u = v = 0

    Thread 1   Thread 2
    st u, 1   st v, 1
    ld v, reg1   ld u, reg2

Seq. Consistency: reg1 = 1 ∨ reg2 = 1
TSO : reg1 = 0 or 1, reg2 = 0 or 1

Fig. 2. Test program showing delayed completion of writes

TSO there is one *additional* behavior: reg1 = reg2 = 0. This is possible only because both the ld instructions may complete ahead of the st instructions.[2]

We now want to check whether the Java Memory Model (JMM) allows delayed completion of writes as in TSO. In particular, we want to perform exhaustive state space exploration of the test program in Figure 2 to find out all possible values of reg1, reg2 allowed by JMM. To do so, we must express each of the threads as a sequence of JMM actions (*i.e.* use, assign, lock, unlock). Note that in the JMM, assign denotes the beginning of a write operation, whereas use denotes the end of a read operation. On the other hand, in weak memory models, ld/st denote the beginning of read/write operations; these operations may complete out-of-order. Thus, we can map a st instruction to an assign action (both denote beginning of a write). Also, we can map a ld instruction to a use action provided the ld is blocking (which is the case in TSO and PSO models). Consequently, the test program of Figure 2 is reduced to

    assign u,1   assign v,1
    use v   use u

We use our JMM checker to find *all* possible values of u and v in the local copies of the two threads. Our checker shows that the local copy of v in thread 1 as well as the local copy of u in thread 2 can be 0 or 1 at the end of execution. This shows that the JMM allows delayed completion of writes as in TSO.

In a similar fashion we have compared the JMM with other memory models such as SPARC PSO. We find that JMM also allows the re-ordering of writes which are allowed in PSO (and not in TSO). Since both delaying and re-ordering of writes are allowed by JMM, therefore a JVM can execute on TSO/PSO memory models without inserting memory barriers. Such a conclusion cannot be reached for the RMO memory model, for which memory barriers will be needed.

A crucial step in the above methodology is the selection of the terminating test programs, which is done informally. However, we can formally check whether a set of selected test programs is complete with respect to the re-orderings allowed by a given hardware memory model M_h. In particular, for each of the re-orderings allowed by M_h we construct a separate terminating test program.

---

[2] In fact, to ensure that Dekker's algorithm works correctly on TSO, a memory barrier instruction needs to be inserted. This is however orthogonal to the memory model comparison we discuss here.

Thus, for the PSO model which allows the re-orderings st → ld and st → st, we will construct two separate test programs. To check whether a given test program P exercises a given re-ordering r, we can simply use exhaustive state space exploration. Each test program P comes with a set of observable variables $\overline{V}$ whose values we will observe on termination. We then exhaustively check all possible values of $\overline{V}$ when P is executed under (a) sequential consistency (b) relaxation of sequential consistency with re-ordering r enabled.[3] If the two sets of possible values of $\overline{V}$ are different, then we can conclude that test program P can be used to check the presence/absence of re-ordering r.

4.2 Reasoning about Unsynchronized Programs

We have discussed how the formal executable specification of hardware/software memory models can help avoid time-consuming barrier instructions in multi-threaded program execution. We now discuss how it can be used to analyze the behavior of low-level unsynchronized Java code. Typically, most Java programs are *"properly synchronized"*, that is, locks are acquired before any shared variable access. Since synchronization (acquiring/releasing of locks) is an time-consuming operation, low-level libraries sometimes avoid synchronization. In these programs, the programmers avoid synchronization with the assumption of sequential consistency *i.e.* they assume that the program will behave expectedly if the underlying platform is sequentially consistent. Unfortunately, the current JMM (as well as any future improvements) is (will be) weaker than Sequential Consistency.[4] Hence, it is necessary to incorporate an executable specification of JMM into verification of unsynchronized Java programs [16].

```
         Initially A = B = 0

         Thread 1    Thread 2
         ─────────────────────
         A = 1;      if (B == 1)
         B = 1;        C = A
```

Fig. 3. An example of Unsynchronized Code

Verifying unsynchronized code with respect to the JMM is not enough. Consider the simple example in Figure 3 where A and B are shared variables. This program is unsynchronized since shared variables A, B are read/written without acquiring locks. The programmer will however expect the value of C to be 1 on termination. This arises from the programmer's expectation of Sequential Consistency: each thread is expected to proceed in program order. By considering

---

[3] The underlying model allows a re-ordering $r = a \to b$ if it generates *more* behaviors by allowing an operation of type b to bypass an operation of type a.

[4] This is because the JMM represents all possible program behaviors on all possible platforms: uni- and multi-processor; see [1] for potential revisions to the current JMM.

the formal executable specification of the JMM we can conclude that C can be 0 or 1. This is because JMM allows the writes to A and B to be re-ordered. However, this merely means that the returned value of C may be 0 or 1 on certain (not all) implementations. Uni-processor implementations guarantee Sequential Consistency. To find out which multi-processor platforms allow C to be both 0 or 1 we need to consider the hardware memory model of the platform in question.

Methodology. To reason about behaviors of an unsynchronized program P we first use our JMM checker. This returns *all possible behaviors* of P in any implementation of Java multithreading. If some of these behaviors are marked by the programmer as *"undesirable"*, then we can find whether these undesirable behaviors appear in the specific multiprocessor platform(s) we are interested in. This is because all the behaviors allowed by the JMM may not be manifested on all platforms. To find whether a specific "undesirable behavior" appears in a given multiprocessor platform, we then use the checker for the corresponding hardware memory model.

For example, for the program in figure 3, we first use our JMM checker to find that the returned value of C can be 0 or 1. However, if we convert the program to SPARC instructions and check whether C can be 0 in the TSO model, our TSO checker returns "no". This is because TSO allows writes to be delayed, not re-ordered. By executing writes to A, B in program order we must return C = 1. We then use our PSO checker to find whether C can be 0 in PSO implementations. The PSO checker returns "yes" since PSO allows write re-ordering.

An Example. We have used our JMM and TSO/PSO checkers to find allowed behaviors of a widely-known multithreaded program fragment: the "Double Checked Locking" idiom.[5] This program fragment (shown in Figure 4) is used for efficient lazy instantiation of a singleton class (a class with only one instance) by multiple threads. Any thread which invokes getInstance executes the code in Figure 4. If instance is null (*i.e.*, an instance of Singleton class has not yet been created), then the code forces synchronization and checks whether instance is null again within the critical section. In between the first instance == null check and the synchronization, another thread may invoke getInstance, find that instance is null, and then create an instance of the Singleton class. Hence we need the second instance == null check.

Our JMM checker finds *all possible behaviors* of two threads running the Double Checked Locking program in less than a second. This set of allowed behaviors (which are generated by our JMM checker) includes an execution trace in which a singleton object with garbage datafields is returned by a thread. This amounts to an instantiation routine returning a partially instantiated object. The question now is whether this undesirable behavior is manifested in all multiprocessor platforms. We verify the absence of this undesirable behavior in the TSO model using our TSO checker in 0.01 seconds. On the other hand, our PSO checker detects in 0.02 seconds that this undesirable behavior is allowed in the

---

[5] See [10, 17] for a discussion of its use, and [15, 16] for a detailed explanation

```
            private static Singleton instance = null;
            ....    // the other fields
            public static Singleton getInstance()
            {
               if (instance == null){
                   synchronized (Singleton.class) {
                       if (instance == null)
                           instance = new Singleton();
                   }
               }
               return instance;
            }
```

Fig. 4. Double-checked locking

PSO memory model. All experiments were conducted on a Pentium-4 1.3 GHz workstation with 1 GB of memory.

5 Discussions

In this paper, we employed formal specification and verification techniques to study the relationship between hardware and software memory models. Hardware memory models describe the behaviors allowed by multiprocessor implementations, while software/language level memory models (such as the JMM) describe behaviors allowed by multithreading implementations. Efficient and reliable execution of multithreaded programs on multiprocessors is the main motivation of our study on memory models. We showed how a formal understanding of the memory models can (a) avoid unnecessary memory barrier instruction executions (leading to higher efficiency) and (b) allow reasoning about low-level multithreaded code (leading to higher reliability). To the best of our knowledge, such an comparison between hardware and software memory models has not been studied formally. Performance/reliability issues in running Java on multiprocessor architectures have been informally discussed in [15]. We have used formal executable specification of the hardware/software memory models to compare their allowed behaviors. Our comparison employs state space exploration (as in model checking) to compute all possible behaviors of programs on two different memory models.

Note that in this paper we chose the current Java Memory Model (JMM) as the software memory model and the SPARC TSO/PSO as hardware memory models. However our methodology for comparing the behaviors of software/hardware memory models is *not* restricted to this choice. The JMM is currently undergoing revision by an expert group [1] and formal/informal specifications are being developed for the various candidates for the revised JMM [12, 13, 19]. Once the JMM revision is finalized, we plan to perform a full-fledged comparison of the revised JMM with various existing multiprocessor memory models

(SPARC TSO, SPARC PSO, DEC Alpha, IBM 370 etc) using the methodology presented in this paper.

References

1. Java Specification Request (JSR) 133. Java Memory Model and Thread Specification revision. In http://jcp.org/jsr/detail/133.jsp, 2001.
2. S.V. Adve and K. Gharachorloo. Shared memory consistency models: A tutorial. *IEEE Computer*, December 1996.
3. A. Charlesworth. Starfire: Extending the SMP envelope. *IEEE Micro*, 1998.
4. E.M. Clarke, E.A. Emerson, and A.P. Sistla. Automatic verification of finite-state concurrent systems using temporal logic specifications. *ACM Transactions on Programming Languages and Systems*, 8(2), 1986.
5. D.E. Culler and J. Pal Singh. *Parallel Computer Architecture: A Hardware/Software Approach*. Morgan Kaufmann Publishers, 1998.
6. D.L. Weaver and T. Germond, Prentice Hall Publishers. *The SPARC Architecture Manual : Version 9*, 1994.
7. D. L. Dill. The Murφ verification system. In *Computer Aided Verification (CAV), LNCS 1102*, 1996.
8. D.L. Dill, S. Park, and A. Nowatzyk. Formal specification of abstract memory models. In *Symposium on Research on Integrated Systems*. MIT Press, 1993.
9. J. Gosling, B. Joy, and G. Steele. *The Java Language Specification*. Chapter 17, Addison Wesley, 1996.
10. A. Holub. *Taming Java Threads*. Berkeley CA, APress, 2000.
11. L. Lamport. How to make a multiprocessor computer that correctly executes multiprocess programs. *IEEE Transactions on Computers*, 28(9), 1979.
12. J. Maessen, Arvind, and X. Shen. Improving the Java Memory Model using CRF. In *ACM OOPSLA*, 2000.
13. J. Manson and W. Pugh. Core semantics of multithreaded Java. In *ACM Java Grande Conference*, 2001.
14. S. Park and D.L. Dill. An executable specification and verifier for relaxed memory order. *IEEE Transactions on Computers*, 48(2), 1999.
15. W. Pugh. Fixing the Java Memory Model. In *ACM Java Grande Conference*, 1999.
16. A. Roychoudhury and T. Mitra. Specifying multithreaded Java semantics for program verification. In *ACM SIGSOFT International Conference on Software Engineering (ICSE)*, 2002.
17. D. Schmidt and T. Harrison. Double-checked locking: An optimization pattern for efficiently initializing and accessing thread-safe objects. In *3rd Annual Pattern Languages of Program Design conference*, 1996.
18. XSB. The XSB logic programming system v2.2, 2000. Available for downloading from http://xsb.sourceforge.net/.
19. Y. Yang, G. Gopalakrishnan, and G. Lindstrom. Formalizing the Java Memory Model for multithreaded program correctness and optimization. Technical Report UUCS-02-011, University of Utah, Department of Computer Science, 2002.

Slicing Hierarchical Automata
for Model Checking UML Statecharts *

Wang Ji, Dong Wei, and Qi Zhi-Chang

National Laboratory for Parallel and Distributed Processing, P.R. China
{ji.wang, dong.wei}@263.net

Abstract. Hierarchical Automata has been widely used in modeling dynamic aspects of reactive software, such as in UML Statecharts. At the same time, model checking is an automatic technique to ensure the correctness of software models, where state space explosion is the main obstacle to applying this technique in large scale applications. The paper presents a method for slicing hierarchical automata with respect to properties to be verified. The considered formalism is Extended Hierarchical Automata (EHA), in which a set of dependence relations is specified after analyzing characteristics such as hierarchy, concurrency and synchronization. We present the algorithm of slicing EHA based on the slicing criterion in terms of states and transitions. The algorithm can remove the hierarchies and concurrent states which are irrelevant to the property, and reduce the state space efficiently in model checking UML Statecharts.

1 Introduction

Hierarchical Automata has been one of the most important formalisms for modeling dynamic aspects of software systems. The most famous example is Statecharts, presented by Harel [1]. As an extension of finite automata by adding hierarchy, concurrency and communication to traditional finite automata, it is a powerful and flexible kind of state transition diagrams. UML Statecharts is a variant of Statemate Statecharts. It depicts the behaviors of an object in its life cycle, and acts as an important role in software analysis and modeling [2]. Nowadays, it is a challenge to verify whether the design specifications, which include UML Statecharts, satisfy the requirements.

Model checking is an automatic technique for verifying correctness properties of reactive systems. It verifies the modal/proposition properties of reactive systems through explicit state exploration or implicit fixpoint computation. Recently, there have been some studies in model checking Statecharts [3–6]. However, because of the characteristics such as concurrency and hierarchy, verification of Statecharts faces the state explosion problem seriously in model checking.

---
* Supported by National Natural Science Foundation of China Grants No. 69973051 and No. 90104007, 863 Hi-Tech Programme of China Grant No. 2001AA113202 and Huo Ying Dong Education Foundation Grant No. 71064.

The problem should be especially emphasized when the design specification of a large software system has been refined to the detailed stage (such as flight control system [7]). To deal with this problem, a few of the researches attempt to reduce the state space of model checking with the method of program slicing.

Program slicing is a technique extracting statements relevant to particular computation from program according to slicing criteria. Dwyer and Hatcliff present a method using control and data dependence to slice sequential programs for model checking[8]. Millett and Teitelbaum give an approach to slicing Promela codes for model checking, simulation, and protocol understanding [9]. Hatcliff and Corbett et al show how to slice multi-threaded JAVA programs for model checking [10]. It mainly focuses on the dependence relations that rise in the thread synchronization statements with locks. In [7], the Statecharts of RSML modeling language is reduced with the notion of slicing. Its purpose is to analyze and understand the design specification better. It assumes that there exists no variable in the model, and the actions can only generate events. It describes the control dependence and data dependence informally, and does not give the slicing algorithm.

Under the background of model checking UML Statecharts and slicing model checking, this paper presents a method to reduce the state space in model checking by slicing Extended Hierarchical Automata (EHA) [4, 6] with respect to the properties to be verified (see Fig. 1). The novelty in the paper is to define the dependence relations and present the slicing algorithm along with the structure of EHA. First, a set of dependence relations is defined through analyzing characteristics such as hierarchy, concurrency and synchronization in EHA. Based on these dependence relations, the algorithm of slicing EHA with the slicing criterion in terms of states and transitions is presented. One can extract slicing criterion from the property to be verified, and it is proved that the sliced EHA and the original one are equivalent for the property in model checking UML Statecharts. Furthermore the sliced one removes the hierarchies and concurrent states which are irrelevant to the property.

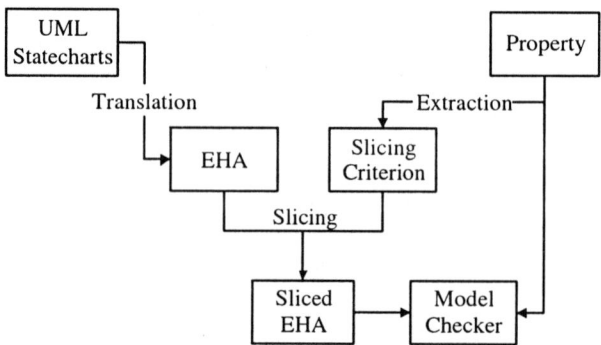

Fig. 1. Slicing EHA for Model Checking

The method presented in this paper can reduce the state space and the cost of constructing state space of dynamic formalisms such as UML Statecharts. After UML Statecharts has been translated into EHA according to [6], the result EHA can be sliced with respect to the property to be verified. Then the model checking algorithms can be used for the sliced EHA. The method is independent of the model checking algorithms, so it can be combined with other state reduction methods in model checking. More importantly, the proposed approach can be applied to verify the software dynamic models in automata with hierarchy and concurrency in a broad range.

The rest of the paper is organized as follows. Section 2 briefly introduces the syntax and semantics of Extended Hierarchical Automata. Section 3 defines a set of dependence relations in EHA. The algorithm of slicing EHA and the rules of extracting slicing criterion from Linear Temporal Logic (LTL) property are presented in section 4. Conclusion is given in section 5.

2 The Extended Hierarchical Automata

An Extended Hierarchical Automaton (EHA) is composed of a set of sequential automata, whose states can be mapped to a set of automata which refine it through a refine function. EHA can be regarded as a kind of abstract syntax of UML Statecharts, whose syntax is abstracted and the essential parts are reserved and presented structurally. This paper follows the definition of EHA in [6], which is an extension of the original one in [4].

Definition 1 (Sequential Automaton). *A sequential automaton A is a 4-tuple $(\sigma_A, s_A^0, \lambda_A, \delta_A)$, σ_A is a finite set of states, s_A^0 is the initial state, λ_A is a finite set of labels, and $\delta_A \subseteq \sigma_A \times \lambda_A \times \sigma_A$ is the transition relation.*

Definition 2 (Extended Hierarchical Automaton, EHA). *An EHA H is a 5-tuple (F, E, ρ, A_0, V), where F is a finite set of sequential automata, $\forall A_1, A_2 \in F, \sigma_{A_1} \cap \sigma_{A_2} = \emptyset$. E is a finite set of events. V is the set of variables. $\rho: \cup_{A \in F} \sigma_A \to 2^F$ is a refine function, which imposes a tree that satisfies: 1) there exists a unique root automaton $A_0 \in F$, and exists no state $s \in \cup_{A \in F} \sigma_A$ that $A_0 \in \rho(s)$; 2) every non-root automaton has exactly one ancestor state: $\forall A \in F \setminus \{A_0\}, \exists_1 s \in \cup_{A' \in F \setminus \{A\}} \sigma_{A'}, A \in \rho(s)$; 3) there are no cycles: $\forall s \in \cup_{A \in F} \sigma_A, s \notin \rho^*(s)$.*

A configuration denotes a global state of a hierarchical automaton, composed of the local states of the component sequential automata.

Definition 3 (Configuration). *A configuration of H is the set $Conf \subseteq \cup_{A \in F} \sigma_A$ such that: 1) $\exists_1 s \in \sigma_{A_0}, s \in Conf$; 2) $\forall s, A$, if $s \in Conf$ and $A \in \rho(s)$, then $\exists_1 s' \in A, s' \in Conf$.*

The operational semantics of an EHA is defined by a LTS (labelled transition system), which is a set of states connected with transitions. The state in the operational semantics of UML statecharts is called status, which consists of the configuration and its associated environment snapshot.

Definition 4 (Operational Semantics). *The operational semantics of an EHA H is a LTS* $T_H = (S, s_0, L, \rightarrow)$, *where S is the set of status of* T_H, s_0 *is the initial status,* $L : S \rightarrow 2^{AP}$ *labels a set of atomic propositions for each status,* $\rightarrow \subseteq S \times S$ *is the transition relation.*

A transition denotes an RTC-step completed by a maximal set of non-conflicting transitions of the sequential automata which respect priorities in UML Statecharts. The $\rightarrow$ relation is defined by a set of rules: progress rule, composition rule and stuttering rule. The semantics is defined based on the open model (which also includes closed model). For detail, please refer to [6]. We restrict the semantics within closed models when slicing EHA in this paper.

3 Dependence Relations in EHA

When slicing sequential programs, one mainly considers the control dependence and data dependence [11]. A method of slicing concurrent programs is presented in [12]. Because of the multiple control flows and data flows, it introduces three new types of primary program dependence, named the selection dependence, synchronization dependence, and communication dependence. However, the case becomes more complicated when slicing an EHA, because it has hierarchy besides concurrency and communication. There are states and transitions in syntax which are more complicated comparing with statements, and it is needed to select maximal non-conflict transition set in operational semantics. These features make it very difficult to slice an EHA when regarding states and transitions as basic units, and the slicing procedure may cost much time and space. Therefore, we investigate the dependence relations among states and transitions, but only remove the sequential automata from the original EHA to build the slice. The removed sequential automata should be irrelevant to the property to be verified.

Firstly, we define some functions and symbols which will be used in the following. Let $H = (F, E, \rho, A_0, V)$ be an EHA. $Src, Tar : \cup_{A \in F} \delta_A \rightarrow \cup_{A \in F} \sigma_A$, for $t = (s, l, s') \in \delta_A (A \in F)$, $Src(t) = s, Tar(t) = s'$. The variables of each state can be classified into three classes: referenced variables, updated variables and internal variables. The set of the referenced variables of a state s is denoted as $s.UV$. It includes all the variables which are referenced in the actions below s (including the actions of states and transitions of the sub-EHA of s, i.e. the EHA below s), and can be defined and referenced outside the sub-EHA of s. The set of the updated variables of s is denoted as $s.DV$. It includes all the variables which are assigned values in the actions below s, and can be defined and referenced outside the sub-EHA of s. $s.UV$ and $s.DV$ can be regarded as the input variables and output variables of a module s respectively. All of them are the global variables for s. The internal variables are local and can be used only below s. They can not be observed outside s. The internal variables of s may be the referenced or updated variables of some states below s. Similarly, $t.UV$ denotes the referenced variables in the action of transition t, and $t.DV$ denotes the variables which can be modified in the action of t. Furthermore, $t.CV$ denotes the variables referenced in the guard of t.

The events of each state can also be classified into three classes. $s.TE$ includes all the events which are generated outside s, and will be used as the trigger events of the transitions below s. $s.GE$ includes all the events which are generated in the actions below s, and can be used as the trigger events of the transitions outside s. There could be some internal events of s, which are generated in the actions below s and can only be used to enable the transitions below s. These events are invisible for the exterior. Similarly, $t.TE$ denotes the set of a single event which is the trigger event of t, and $t.GE$ denotes the set of events generated in the action of t.

A transition between non-basic states can be regarded as the transition from an exit state of a sequential automaton to an entering state of another sequential automaton. It is assumed that the trigger event of a transition can only be generated in the automata that are concurrent with this transition. This is consistent with the fact that events are mainly used for synchronization.

Definition 5 (Path). *A path in a sequential automaton $A \in F$ is a sequence of states and transitions $(s_1, t_1, s_2), (s_2, t_2, s_3), \ldots, (s_{k-1}, t_{k-1}, s_k)$, where $s_i \in \sigma_A, t_i \in \delta_A$, and $Src(t_i) = s_i, Tar(t_i) = s_{i+1}$, for $1 \leq i < k$.*

Definition 6 (Sequential Data-Dependence, $\rightarrow_{sdd}$). *If $A \in F$ and $u, v \in \sigma_A, r, t \in \delta_A$,*

1. $u \rightarrow_{sdd} v$ *iff there is a path* $P : (s_1 = v, t_1, s_2), (s_2, t_2, s_3), \ldots, (s_{k-1}, t_{k-1}, s_k = u)$ *in A such that* $(v.DV \cap u.UV) - ((\cup_{1 < i < k} s_i.DV) \cup (\cup_{1 \leq i < k} t_i.DV)) \neq \emptyset$.
2. $r \rightarrow_{sdd} v$ *iff there is a path* $P : (s_1 = v, t_1, s_2), (s_2, t_2, s_3), \ldots, (s_{k-1}, t_{k-1} = r, s_k))$ *in A such that* $(v.DV \cap r.UV) - ((\cup_{1 < i < k} s_i.DV) \cup (\cup_{1 \leq i < k-1} t_i.DV)) \neq \emptyset$.
3. $u \rightarrow_{sdd} t$ *iff there is a path* $P : (s_1, t_1 = t, s_2), (s_2, t_2, s_3), \ldots, (s_{k-1}, t_{k-1}, s_k = u)$ *in A such that* $(t.DV \cap u.UV) - ((\cup_{1 < i < k} s_i.DV) \cup (\cup_{1 < i < k} t_i.DV)) \neq \emptyset$.
4. $r \rightarrow_{sdd} t$ *iff there is a path* $P : (s_1, t_1 = t, s_2), (s_2, t_2, s_3), \ldots, (s_{k-1}, t_{k-1} = r, s_k)$ *in A such that* $(t.DV \cap r.UV) - ((\cup_{1 < i < k} s_i.DV) \cup (\cup_{1 < i < k-1} t_i.DV)) \neq \emptyset$.

Informally, if some variable computed in an element x (Here, the element could be a state or a transition. It is the same in the following.) has a direct influence on the value of some variable computed in the element y, and x and y are in the same sequential automaton, then y is sequential data-dependent on x. For the example EHA in Fig. 2, $s3 \rightarrow_{sdd} s1$. The transition from $s2$ to $s1$ is sequential data-dependent on $s3$.

Definition 7 (Parallel Data-Dependence, $\rightarrow_{pdd}$). *If $A, B \in F$ and $u \in \sigma_A, r \in \delta_A, v \in \sigma_B, t \in \delta_B$, and there are $C \in F$ and $s \in \sigma_C$ such that $A, B \in \rho(s)$, then $u \rightarrow_{pdd} v$ (or $u \rightarrow_{pdd} t$, or $r \rightarrow_{pdd} v$, or $r \rightarrow_{pdd} t$) iff $u.UV \cap v.DV \neq \emptyset$ (or $u.UV \cap t.DV \neq \emptyset$, or $r.UV \cap v.DV \neq \emptyset$, or $r.UV \cap t.DV \neq \emptyset$ respectively).*

Informally, if some variable computed in an element x has a direct influence on the value of some variable computed in the element y, and the automaton of

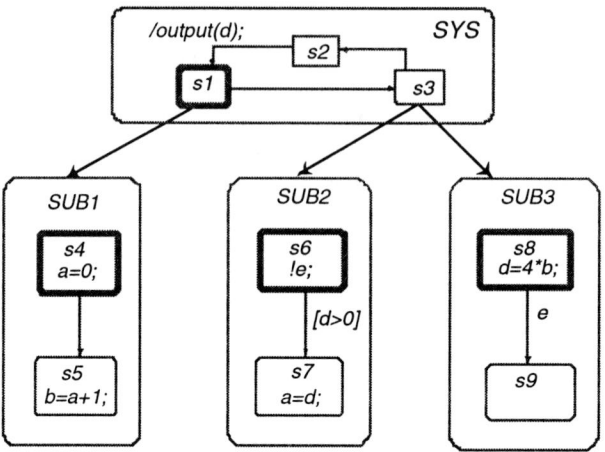

Fig. 2. An EHA example

x is concurrent with the automaton of y, then y is parallel data-dependent on x. In Fig. 2, $s7 \rightarrow_{pdd} s8$.

Definition 8 (Synchronization-Dependence, $\rightarrow_{sd}$). If $A, B \in F$ and $u \in \sigma_A, r \in \delta_A, v \in \sigma_B, t \in \delta_B$, and there are $C \in F$ and $s \in \sigma_C$ such that $A, B \in \rho(s)$, then $u \rightarrow_{sd} v$ (or $u \rightarrow_{sd} t$, or $r \rightarrow_{sd} v$, or $r \rightarrow_{sd} t$) iff $u.TE \cap v.GE \neq \emptyset$ (or $u.TE \cap t.GE \neq \emptyset$, or $r.TE \cap v.GE \neq \emptyset$, or $r.TE \cap t.GE \neq \emptyset$ respectively).

Informally, if the trigger event of some transition in an element x is generated by the action of the element y, and the automaton of x is concurrent with the automaton of y, then x is synchronization-dependent on y. In Fig. 2, the transition from $s8$ to $s9$ is synchronization-dependent on $s6$.

Definition 9 (Transition Control-Dependence, $\rightarrow_{tcd}$). Let $A \in F$ and $r \in \delta_A$.

1. For $v \in \sigma_A$, $r \rightarrow_{tcd} v$ iff there is a path $P: (s_1 = v, t_1, s_2), (s_2, t_2, s_3), \ldots, (s_{k-1}, t_{k-1} = r, s_k)$ in A such that $(v.DV \cap r.CV) - ((\cup_{1 \leq i < k} s_i.DV) \cup (\cup_{1 \leq i < k-1} t_i.DV)) \neq \emptyset$.
2. For $t \in \delta_A$, $r \rightarrow_{tcd} t$ iff there is a path $P: (s_1, t_1 = t, s_2), (s_2, t_2, s_3), \ldots, (s_{k-1}, t_{k-1} = r, s_k)$ in A such that $(t.DV \cap r.CV) - ((\cup_{1 \leq i < k} s_i.DV) \cup (\cup_{1 \leq i < k-1} t_i.DV)) \neq \emptyset$.
3. If $B, C \in F$ and $s \in \sigma_C$ satisfy $A, B \in \rho(s), v \in \sigma_B, t \in \delta_B$, then $r \rightarrow_{tcd} v$ (or $r \rightarrow_{tcd} t$) iff $r.CV \cap v.DV \neq \emptyset$ (or $r.CV \cap t.DV \neq \emptyset$).

Informally, if some variable computed in an element x has a direct influence on the truth of guard of transition r, then r is transition control-dependent on x. In Fig. 2, the transition from $s6$ to $s7$ is transition control-dependent on $s8$.

Definition 10 (Refinement Data-Dependence, $\rightarrow_{rdd}$). If $A \in F$ and $u \in \sigma_A, B \in \rho(u), v \in \sigma_B, t \in \delta_B$,

1. $u \to_{rdd} v$ iff $(v.DV \cap u.DV) \neq \emptyset$, or $u.GE \cap v.GE \neq \emptyset$.
2. $u \to_{rdd} t$ iff $(t.DV \cap u.DV) \neq \emptyset$, or $u.GE \cap t.GE \neq \emptyset$.

Informally, if an element x belongs to some direct sub-sequential automaton of state u, and the value of some variable computed in x is the value that u will return, or some event generated in x is used to synchronize with some concurrent state of u, then u is refinement data-dependent on x. In Fig. 2, $s3 \to_{rdd} s8$.

Definition 11 (Refinement Control-Dependence, $\to_{rcd}$). If $A, B \in F$, $u \in \sigma_A$, $v \in \sigma_B$, and v is the initial state of B, then $v \to_{rcd} u$ iff $B \in \rho(u)$.

Informally, if state v is the initial state of a direct sub-sequential automaton of state u, then v is refinement control-dependent on state u. In Fig. 2, $s4 \to_{rcd} s1$.

The dependence relation $\to_d$ is defined for EHA, which is the united set of these dependence relations (i.e., the united set of $\to_{sdd}$, $\to_{pdd}$, $\to_{sd}$, $\to_{tcd}$, $\to_{rdd}$ and $\to_{rcd}$). From the definitions of the dependence relations we can get if the sequential automaton of a state or transition is in the nth layer of an EHA, then the elements that the state or transition depends on will belong to the sequential automata that are local in $(n-1)^{th}$ to $(n+1)^{th}$ layer of the EHA, which will make the slicing efficient.

4 Slicing EHA for Model Checking UML Statecharts

The basic idea of slicing EHA is to search the states and transitions through the dependence relations according to the slicing criterion. The found states and transitions will have influence on the states and transitions in the slicing criterion. The units of the result slice are still the sequential automata. If some state or transition of a sequential automaton is included in the slice, then all the states and transitions of this automaton should be included in the slice. If some state is not depended on by any elements after the algorithm terminates, then the sub-EHA and actions of this state will not be included in the slice. If a transition is not depended on by any elements after the algorithm terminates, its action will be deleted.

4.1 Compute EHA Slice

Because there may be more than one state labels of interest appearing in the property to be verified, we adapt the slicing criterion concentrating on multiple states and transitions. Let $H = (F, E, \rho, A_0, V)$ be an EHA. For $A \in F$, the sets of sequential automata, states and transitions below A are defined respectively as following. $SE(A) = A \cup (\cup_{A' \in (\cup_{s \in \sigma_A} \rho(s))} SE(A'))$, $S(A) = \cup_{A' \in SE(A)} \sigma_{A'}$, $T(A) = \cup_{A' \in SE(A)} \delta_{A'}$.

Definition 12 (Slicing Criterion). A slicing criterion C of H is a tuple $< \{s_1, \ldots, s_k\}, \{t_1, \ldots, t_n\} >$, where $s_i \in S(A_0)$, $t_i \in T(A_0)$, and $s_i \neq s_j (1 \leq i, j \leq k, i \neq j)$, $t_i \neq t_j (1 \leq i, j \leq n, i \neq j)$.

The algorithm presented below computes the slice of an EHA with respect to the slicing criterion C according to the dependence relations in the EHA. In the algorithm, the set RS and RT keep the states and the transitions to be reserved in the final result slice respectively. IS and IT contain the states and the transitions respectively used to find the elements on which they depend. NS and NT contain the states and the transitions respectively found in each iteration, on which IS and IT depend. ES and ET contain the states and the transitions which are not included in NS and NT but belong to the sequential automata which include the new found elements in NS and NT. $Refine_R$ is a Boolean function used to determine whether the refinement information of the reserved elements should be kept in the slice.

At step 1, only the states and transitions in slicing criterion are included in RS and RT respectively. Assigning $True$ to their $Refine_R$ means their refined elements should be reserved. The elements in ES and ET are those elements which are in the same sequential automata with the elements in RS and RT, but are not included in the slicing criterion. Step 2 will find the states and transitions which are depended on by the elements in IS and IT. Step 3 searches the states and transitions which are not included in $(RS \cup NS)$ and $(RT \cup NT)$, but are in the same sequential automata with new elements of NS and NT. At step 4, IS and IT are reconstructed. Then they will include the elements which are found but do not belong to RS and RT, the elements which belong to RS and RT and need to be refined at the moment, and the initial states which need not be refined. $Refine_R$ is refreshed at step 5, and RS and RT are updated at step 6. If both of IS and IT are empty, the algorithm will terminate, otherwise return to step 2.

RS, IS, ES, NS: set of states; RT, IT, ET, NT: set of transitions.

1. Given the criterion $< \{s_1, \ldots, s_k\}, \{t_1, \ldots, t_n\} >$. Let

$$RS = \{s_1, \ldots, s_k\} \quad Refine_R(s) = True \ (for\ each\ s \in RS)$$
$$RT = \{t_1, \ldots, t_n\} \quad Refine_R(t) = True \ (for\ each\ t \in RT)$$

$$ES = \{s | \exists A \in F,\ ((\exists u \in RS, u \in \sigma_A) \vee (\exists t \in RT, t \in \delta_A))$$
$$\wedge (s \in \sigma_A \wedge s \notin RS)\}$$
$$ET = \{r | \exists A \in F,\ ((\exists u \in RS, u \in \sigma_A) \vee (\exists t \in RT, t \in \delta_A))$$
$$\wedge (r \in \delta_A \wedge r \notin RT)\}$$

Let $Refine_R(s) = False(s \in ES)$, $Refine_R(t) = False(t \in ET)$;
$RS = RS \cup ES$; $RT = RT \cup ET$; $IS = RS$; $IT = RT$.

2. *Compute the states and transitions which the existing states and transitions in IS and IT are dependent on by the following equations.*

$$NS = \{s | u \to_d s, u \in IS \land Refine_R(u)\} \cup$$
$$\{s | u \to_{rcd} s, u \in IS \land \neg Refine_R(u)\} \cup$$
$$\{s | t \to_d s, t \in IT \land Refine_R(t)\} \cup$$
$$\{s | t \to_{tcd} s \lor t \to_{sd} s, t \in IT \land \neg Refine_R(t)\}$$
$$NT = \{r | u \to_d r, u \in IS \land Refine_R(u)\} \cup$$
$$\{r | t \to_d r, t \in IT \land Refine_R(t)\} \cup$$
$$\{r | t \to_{tcd} r \lor t \to_{sd} r, t \in IT \land \neg Refine_R(t)\}$$

3. *Reconstruct ES and ET.*

$$ES = \{s | \exists A \in F, ((\exists u \in NS, u \in \sigma_A) \lor (\exists t \in NT, t \in \delta_A))$$
$$\land (s \in \sigma_A \land s \notin (RS \cup NS))\}$$
$$ET = \{r | \exists A \in F, ((\exists u \in NS, u \in \sigma_A) \lor (\exists t \in NT, t \in \delta_A))$$
$$\land (r \in \delta_A \land r \notin (RT \cup NT))\}$$

4. *Reconstruct IS and IT.*

$$IS = (NS - RS) \cup$$
$$\{s | s \in NS \land s \in RS \land \neg Refine_R(s)\} \cup$$
$$\{s | \exists A \in F, s \in ES \land s = s_A^0\}$$
$$IT = (NT - RT) \cup$$
$$\{t | t \in NT \land t \in RT \land \neg Refine_R(t)\} \cup ET$$

5. *For each* $s \in (NS \cup ES)$ *and* $t \in (NT \cup ET)$,

$$Refine_R(s) = \begin{cases} True & if\ s \in NS \\ False & if\ s \in ES \end{cases} \quad Refine_R(t) = \begin{cases} True & if\ t \in NT \\ False & if\ t \in ET \end{cases}$$

6. *Reconstruct RS and RT.*

$$RS = RS \cup NS \cup ES;\ RT = RT \cup NT \cup ET.$$

7. *If* $IS = \emptyset$ *and* $IT = \emptyset$, *then terminates; otherwise returns to step 2.*

Algorithm. The algorithm of slicing EHA

After the algorithm terminates, all the sequential automata whose states and transitions are included in RS and RT compose the slice of H according to criterion C. For any $s \in RS$, if $Refine_R(s) = False$, then we need not consider the sub-EHA of s and remove the entering and exit actions of s. For $t \in RT$, if $Refine_R(t) = False$, then remove the action of t.

If a state or a transition of some sequential automaton belongs to the slice, then all the states and transitions of this automaton belong to the slice. The sequential automaton which has no state or transition in the slice will be removed.

The slice is computed with the granularity of sequential automata. Obviously, for slicing criterion C, the slice of H is composed of the sequential automata that may affect the execution of the states or transitions in C. The slice obtained by this algorithm may not be the least slice.

Besides, one may use the following heuristics to improve the algorithm. When searching the dependence relations at step 2, if a new state s is found only through refinement control-dependence relation, and there are not any elements depending on s through other relations, then the algorithm will not search the elements which s is refinement data-dependent on in the next iteration when s is reserved in IS.

4.2 Extract Slicing Criteria from LTL Formulas

The properties to be verified are intended to be specified in LTL. The propositions appearing in the LTL formulas are of three forms: $x\ rop\ c$, in which rop is the relation operator (such as $>, <, \neq$, etc), is true if the relation between the value of variable x and constant c satisfies rop; $@s_i$, where s_i is the name of a state, is true when the current configuration includes s_i; $!e$ is true when event e has been generated and belongs to the event queue of current status. For the rules of constructing LTL formulas and their semantics, please refer to [6, 13].

Let LTL_{-X} be the subset of LTL formulas without the next time operator appearance. Given an EHA H and a LTL_{-X} property φ, it is desired to get the slicing criterion C_φ from φ. Slicing the EHA H with respect to C_φ should yield a smaller residual EHA that preserves the satisfaction of φ.

The following lemma [14] states that the satisfaction of LTL_{-X} formula φ for two φ-stuttering equivalent structures is the same.

Lemma 1. *Given a LTL_{-X} formula φ, if two structures M and M' are φ-stuttering equivalent, i.e. $M \sim_\varphi M'$, then $M, s_0 \models \varphi$ iff $M', s_0 \models \varphi$.*

One can extract the slicing criterion C_φ from a formula φ and guarantee that the LTS of the sliced EHA is φ-stuttering equivalent to the LTS of the original EHA. For a proposition $x\ rop\ c$, only the values of variable x may cause the change of its truth. This suggests that for each proposition $x\ rop\ c$ in a given property φ, each state or transition that assigns value to x should be included in the residual slice. For a proposition $@s_i$, it is obviously that s_i should be included in the slice. For the proposition $!e$, the states and transitions whose actions generate event e should be added to the slicing criterion.

Definition 13 (φ-Criterion). *Given a LTL_{-X} formula φ over EHA H, V and E are the set of all variables and events occurring in φ respectively. Define φ-criterion $C_\varphi = <\{s_1, \ldots, s_k\}, \{t_1, \ldots, t_n\}>$, $s_i \neq s_j (1 \leq i, j \leq k, i \neq j), t_i \neq t_j (1 \leq i, j \leq n, i \neq j)$, where $\{s_1, \ldots, s_k\}$ is the set of all states which assign values to variables in V or generate the events in E plus the set of all states appearing in state propositions of φ, and $\{t_1, \ldots, t_n\}$ is composed of the transitions whose actions contain assignments to variables in V or generations of events in E.*

The following theorem guarantees that the LTS of the sliced EHA is φ-stuttering equivalent to the LTS of the original EHA.

Theorem 1. *Given an EHA H and a LTL_{-X} formula φ. Let C_φ be the φ-criterion corresponding to φ, H_s be the result of slicing H with respect to C_φ, and M and M_s be the LTSs of H and H_s respectively. $M \sim_\varphi M_s$ holds.*

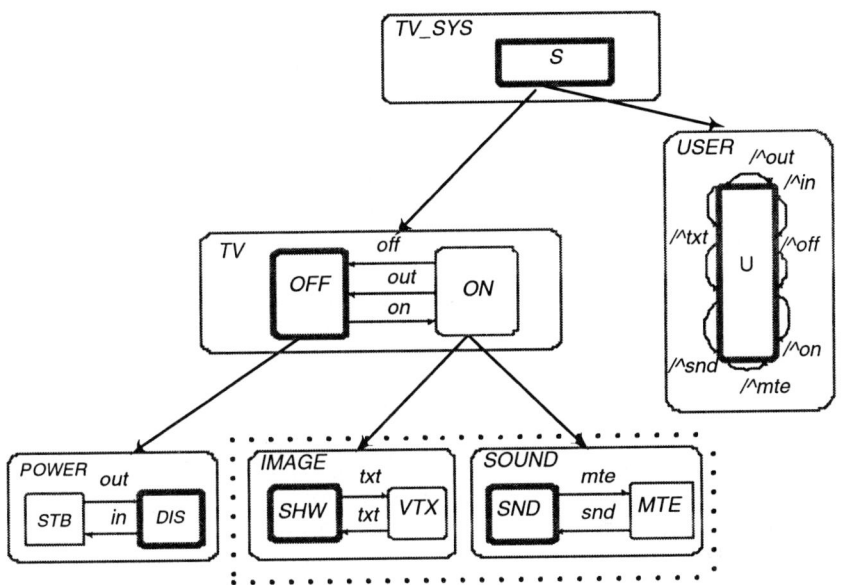

Fig. 3. The EHA of TV system

Fig. 3 depicts the EHA of a TV system as an example from [6]. If one wants to verify the property of $G(!out \rightarrow F(@DIS))$, the slicing criterion extracted from this property is $< \{DIS\}, \{t\} >$ where t is the transition generating event out in $USER$. After slicing, the sequential automata $IMAGE$ and $SOUND$ will be removed. The number of status of the LTS generated from the sliced EHA is 24, while that of the LTS generated from the original one is 48. With the improvement heuristics, the number of status of the final result slice will be 15.

5 Conclusion

This paper presents a method to reduce the state space in model checking by slicing Extended Hierarchical Automata (EHA) with respect to the properties to be verified. The novelty in the paper is to define the dependence relations and present the slicing algorithm along with the structure of EHA. Through finding the dependence relations in EHA and applying the slicing algorithm, one can compute the slice of the EHA according to the slicing criterion extracted from the LTL_{-X} property to be verified. The sliced EHA and the original one are equivalent with respect to the property in model checking UML Statecharts. Furthermore, the presented method can also be combined with the other state reduction methods in model checking.

References

1. D. Harel. Statecharts: A Visual Formalism for Complex Systems. Science of Computer Programming. Elsevier, 8(3): 231-274, 1987.
2. OMG Document ad/97-08-04. Rational Software et.al., 1997.
3. J. Lilius and I.P. Paltor. vUML: A Tool for Verifying UML Models. TUCS Technical Report No 272, 1999.
4. E. Mikk, Y. Lakhnech, M. Siegel, and G.J. Holzmann. Implementing Statecharts in PROMELA/SPIN. In Proceedings of Workshop on Industrial-Strength Formal Specification Techniques (WIFT' 98), 1998.
5. S. Gnesi and D. Latella. Model Checking UML Statecharts Diagrams Using JACK. In Proceedings of the 4th IEEE International Symposium on High-Assurance Systems Engineering, 1999.
6. W. Dong, J. Wang, X. Qi and Z.C. Qi. Model Checking UML Statecharts. In Proceedings of the Eighth Asia-Pacific Software Engineering Conference (APSEC 2001). IEEE Computer Society Press, December 2001.
7. M.P.E. Heimdahl and M. Whalen. Reduction and Slicing of Hierarchical State Machines. In Proceedings of the Fifth ACM SIGSOFT Symposium on the Foundations of Software Engineering, September 1997.
8. M.B. Dwyer and J. Hatcliff. Slicing Software for Model Construction. In ACM SIGPLAN Workshop on Partial Evaluation and Program Manipulation, 1999.
9. Lynette I. Millett and Tim Teitelbaum. Slicing Promela and its Applications to Model Checking, simulation, and protocol understanding. In Proceedings of the SPIN 98 Workshop in Paris, France, November 1998.
10. John Hatcliff, James Corbett, Matthew Dwyer, Stefan Sokolowski, and Hongjun Zheng. A Formal Study of Slicing for Multi-Threaded Programs with JVM Concurrency Primitives. In Proceedings of the International Symposium on Static Analysis (SAS'99), September 1999.
11. M. Weiser. Program Slicing. IEEE Trans. Softw. Eng, SE(10), 4, 1984.
12. J. Cheng. Slicing Concurrent Programs - A Graph-Theoretical Approach. In Proceedings of the First International Workshop on Automated Algorithmic Debugging, LNCS, Vol.749. Springer-Verlag, May 1993.
13. A. Puneli. The Temporal Semantics of Concurrent Programs. Theoretical Computer Science 13: 45-60, 1981.
14. Edmund M. Clarke, Orna Grumberg and Doron Peled. Model Checking, MIT Press, 1999.

Formal Verification
of a SONET Telecom System Block

M. Hasan Zobair and Sofiène Tahar

Concordia University, Montreal, Quebec, H3G 1M8 Canada
{mh_zobai,tahar}@ece.concordia.ca

Abstract. In this paper, we describe the formal verification of an industrial hardware design from PMC-Sierra, Inc. The design under investigation is a Telecom System Block which processes a portion of the SONET (Synchronous Optical Network) line overhead of a received data stream. We adopted a hierarchical modeling and verification approach which follows the natural design hierarchy. The formal specification and verification have been carried out based on MDGs (Multiway Decision Graphs), a new decision diagram subsuming the traditional binary decision diagrams and allowing abstract data and functions. The verification has been performed using both model checking and equivalence checking. To measure the performance of the MDG based model checker, we also conducted a comparative verification of the same design using Cadence FormalCheck tool.

1 Introduction

Simulation-based methods are currently used by the industrial community for system-level verification, since it can handle the entire design at a time. Simulation, however, cannot provide a high coverage ratio due to the exponential number of test cases to be developed and verified. This handicap is the reason, new methods are needed for the economical and reliable verification of digital systems. Formal verification [7] have recently paved a path, showing the utility of finding bugs early in the design cycle. Formal verification techniques are usually classified in two categories [7]: interactive theorem proving and automatic decision diagram based model checking and equivalence checking. In model checking, one checks if the design satisfies some properties (formal specification). With equivalence checking, we check if two designs exhibit the same behavior. The latter techniques have been successfully applied to real industrial design. However, since most tools are based on Binary Decisio n Diagrams (BDDs), they require the design to be described at the Boolean level. In practice, they often fail to verify a large-scale design because of the so-called state space explosion [7].

In this paper, we present a methodology for the formal verification of a real industrial design using the Multiway Decision Graphs (MDG) tools. MDGs subsume the traditional binary decision diagrams while extending them with abstract data sorts and uninterrupted function symbols [6]. The design we considered is a Telecom System Block (TSB) from PMC-Sierra, Inc., called RASE—Receive, Automatic Protection Switch Control, Synchronization Status Extraction and Bit Error Rate Monitor [8]. The main aspect of this paper is to illustrate the ability to carry out the verification of an industrial size design using MDGs. Furthermore, we conducted a comparison between the experimental results obtained with the MDG model checker and the model checking of the same design using Cadence FormalCheck [5].

There exists a few related works on the application of MDG tools in hardware verification of real systems. For instance, Tahar *et al.* [9] verified the Fairisle ATM (Asynchronous Transfer Mode) Switch Fabric using MDGs which has about 4200 equivalent gates implemented in Xilinx FPGAs. In comparison to this design, our investigated design represents with its 11400 equivalent gates [8] a significant larger case study. Other major differences between our work and the one presented in [9] are as follows:

1) Unlike the design presented in [9] in which the authors used an academic ATM switch fabric designed at Cambridge University, our work presents a design which is a commercial product.

2) We applied both safety and liveness properties model checking on the investigated design, but for the work in [9], the authors applied only invariant (safety) property checking on the system. In difference to [9], we were hence able to make a direct comparison with model checking tools such as FormalCheck [5].

Another notable related work is the one done by Balakrishnan *et al.* [2]. The authors used the MDG tools to model and verify an Embedded System of a mouse control application based on the PIC 16C71 Microcontroller from Microchip Technology, Inc. Although this represents the sole commercial design verified by MDGs before our work, its application is concerned with software assembly aspects rather than hardware design and implementation.

The rest of this paper is organized as follows: Section 2 gives an overview of Multiway Decision Graphs (MDGs). Section 3 describes the functionality of the RASE TSB. Section 4 describes our hierarchical verification methodology. Section 5 presents a comparison of the verification process between MDG and Cadence FormalCheck. Section 6 finally concludes the paper.

2 Multiway Decision Graphs

Multiway Decision Graphs (MDGs) [6] have been proposed to solve the state space explosion problem of ROBDD (Reduced Ordered Binary Decision Diagram) [4] based verification tools. While accommodating a higher level of abstraction as with theorem proving, the MDG tools offer automation in the verification process like ROBDD based tools. An MDG is a finite, directed acyclic graph [6]. An internal node of an MDG can be a variable of concrete sort with its edge labels being the individual constants in the enumeration of the sort; or it can be a variable of abstract sort and its edges are labeled abstract terms of the same sort; or it can be a cross-term (whose function symbol is a cross-operator).

Variables of concrete and abstract sort can be used to model control and data signals, respectively, while uninterpreted function symbols and cross-operators denote data operations and feedback from the datapath to the control circuitry, respectively. Hence, a data signal can be represented by a single variable of abstract sort, rather than a vector of Boolean variables, and data operations can be viewed as black boxes and represented by uninterpreted function symbols. An MDG may have only one leaf node denoted as **T**, which means all paths in an MDG are true formulae. Thus, MDGs essentially represent relations rather than functions in a canonical form. MDGs can also represent sets of states. Like ROBDDs, MDGs must be reduced and ordered. The underlying logic of the MDGs is a subset of many-sorted first-order logic [6].

In MDG-based verification, abstract descriptions of state machines, called Abstract State Machines (ASM) [6] are used to model the system. An ASM is obtained by letting some data inputs, states or output variables be of abstract sort, and the datapath operations be uninterpreted function symbols. They admit non-finite state machines as models in addition to their intended finite interpretations. This makes it possible to verify a circuit at the RTL functional model. The MDG tools [12] provide algorithms for equivalence checking, invariant checking and model checking, which are based on the reachability analysis of all states. The equivalence verification procedures are combinational and sequential verification. The model checking supports a first-order temporal logic, called $\mathcal{L}_{MDG}$ (*next_let_formula*) [10], which is an extension of universally quantified branching time first-order temporal logic. The MDG tools run on a Prolog platform and accepts a Prolog-style HDL as its input language, called MDG-HDL [12], which allows the use of abstract variables for representing data signals. MDG-HDL supports structural descriptions, behavioral descriptions, or a mixture of structural and behavioral description. It also comes with a library of basic hardware components, such as logic gates, multiplexers, bus drivers, etc.

The MDG tools have some significant practical limitations: For instance, due to the non-interpretation of data operators, the reachability analysis of abstract states may not terminate. If this situation occurs, a dedicated heuristic has to be used from a set of algorithms developed in [1] and [11]. Another practical drawback of the MDG tools with respect to an industrial setting is that they do not accept VHDL or Verilog HDL as input language. However a project is currently underway to translate Verilog to MDG-HDL which will be available in the near future. This paper is to advocate MDG, we will hence use small examples from the RASE TSB model to illustrate the MDG modeling of behavior and structure.

3 The RASE Telecom System Block

The design under investigation is the RASE Telecom System Block (TSB). It processes a portion of the SONET (Synchronous Optical Network) [3] line overhead of a received SONET data stream. The RASE TSB consists of three types of components: Transport overhead extraction and manipulation, Bit Error Rate

Monitoring (BERM) and Interrupt Server (see Figure 1) [8]. In addition to these blocks, it has an interface to a Common Bus Interface (CBI) block which is used mainly for the configuration and testing of the TSB interface and two inputs/outputs multiplexers. The transport overhead extraction and manipulation functions are implemented by three sub-modules (Transport Overhead bytes extractor, Automatic Protection Switch (APS) control and Synchronization Status filtering).

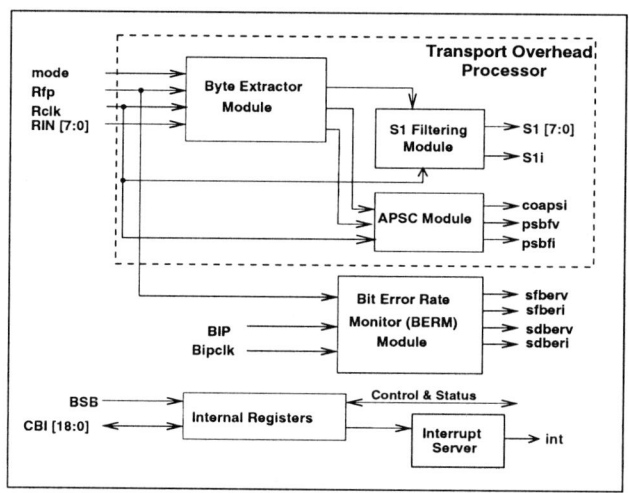

Fig. 1. The RASE Telecom System Block

The RASE TSB extracts the Automatic Protection Switch (APS) bytes, i.e., K1 and K2 bytes, and the Synchronization Status byte, i.e, S1 byte, from a SONET frame (see Figure 2). After extracting the above bytes, it processes them according to some requirements set by the SONET standard. The RASE TSB also performs Bit Error Rate Monitoring using the Bit Interleaved Parity (BIP)-24/8 line of a frame, i.e., B2 bytes (Figure 2). The received line BIP error detection code is based on the line overhead and synchronous payload envelope of the received data stream.

We propose a hierarchical approach to model the TSB behavior at different levels of the design hierarchy which in turn enables the verification process to be done at different levels. Inspired by [8], we derived a behavioral model of the RASE TSB which consists of five main functional blocks – Transport Overhead Extractor (TOH), Automatic Protection Switch (APS), Synchronization Status Filtering, Bit Error Rate Monitoring (BERM) and Interrupt Server.

3.1 MDG Modeling of the RASE Implementation

In this section, we describe the implementation of the TSB at the Register Transfer Level (RTL). For MDG-based verification we translated the original

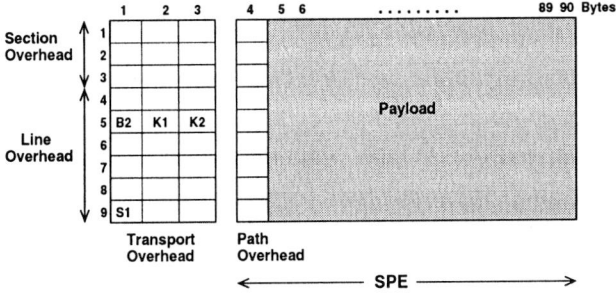

Fig. 2. The STS-1 SONET frame structure

VHDL models into very similar models using MDG-HDL. One of the major advantages in using MDGs is the ability to handle abstract descriptions. This avoids all the ponderous procedure of defining each bit of a vector of Boolean variables. Rather, a vector of Boolean variable can be viewed as a single abstract variable. Another advantage in using MDGs is the ability to represent data operations by *uninterpreted* function symbols. This enables the arithmetic and logical blocks to be viewed as black boxes. To handle the complexity of the design, we hence adopted a module abstraction technique for the RTL model. We can illustrate the idea of module abstraction in MDGs using an example (see Figure 3) from our case study.

The circuit in the example is performing data operations over two operands of different size. It is concatenating 5-bits for matching the size of the operands to be used for addition and extracting twelve bits from the least significant bit positions of the output by truncating the upper bits. Using MDG-HDL, we can

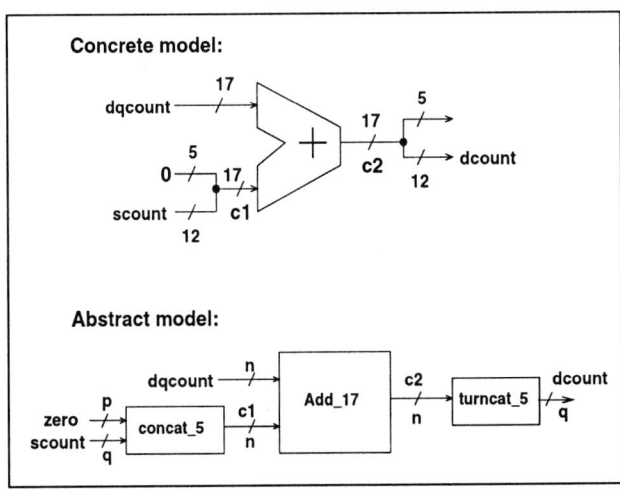

Fig. 3. An example of module abstraction

abstract the width of the datapath as well as the functionality of the original model. The data operations (e.g., addition, concatenation) can be modeled using *uninterpreted* function symbols applied to the operands (e.g. *Add_17, Concat_5*).

3.2 MDG Modeling of the RASE Behavior

Based on the product documentation [8] provided to us, we derived a high-level MDG behavioral model of the RASE TSB using Abstract State Machines (ASMs). To illustrate the behavioral modeling approach adopted for the RASE TSB, we are presenting here only the BIP counting abstract state machine and its pseudo-MDG-HDL model (see Figure 4). The BIP line counter has three possible states—S0, S1 and S2. The state variable *Bcount*, of abstract sort *worda12*, stores the count value of the BIP line. The symbols *st* and *bip* are the inputs to the state machine. They represent the saturation threshold value of the counter and the received BIP line, respectively. In state S0, the counter has been initialized to *zero* which is a generic constant of abstract sort *worda12*. After initialization, if the input $bip =$ "1" then the next state will be S1. The uninterpreted function inc_12 of type[1] [$worda12 \rightarrow worda12$] denotes the increment-by-one operation of abstract words. When the count value is equal to the saturation threshold value *st*, there will be a transition to state S2. In state S2, the value of the counter will remain unchanged until *Bcount* is not equal to *st*.

An abstract state machine can have an infinite number of states due to the abstract nature of some variables and function symbols. The reachability analysis algorithm of the MDG tools is based on the abstract implicit state enumeration [6]. Due to the *non-termination* of abstract state enumeration all states may not be reached [1]. To illustrate this limitation of MDG-based verification, we can look at the example of Figure 4, where a generic constant *zero* of the abstract sort denotes the initial value of *Bcount*. The MDG representing the set of reachable states of the BIP counting ASM (see Figure 4) would contain states of the form (*Bcount, inc_2(... inc_2(zero)...)*) for the number of infinite iterations. As a consequence, there is no finite MDG representation of the set of reachable states and the reachability algorithm will not terminate, since the structure of the MDG will become arbitrarily large. This typical form of non-termination can be avoided by using some heuristic techniques described, e.g., in [1]. One such methods is based on the *generalization* of initial state that causes divergence, like the variable *Bcount* in Figure 4. Rather than starting the reachability analysis with an abstract constant *zero* as the initial value of *Bcount*, a *fresh*[2] abstract variable (e.g., C) is assigned to *Bcount* at the beginning of the analysis.

4   Verification of the RASE TSB

To carry out the verification of the system, we need to define a proper environment of the system. The functional simulation for the TSB was performed

---
[1] The notation $f: [\alpha \rightarrow \beta]$ implies that the function f has argument of sort α and range of sort β.
[2] A *fresh* variable is disjoint from all other variables.

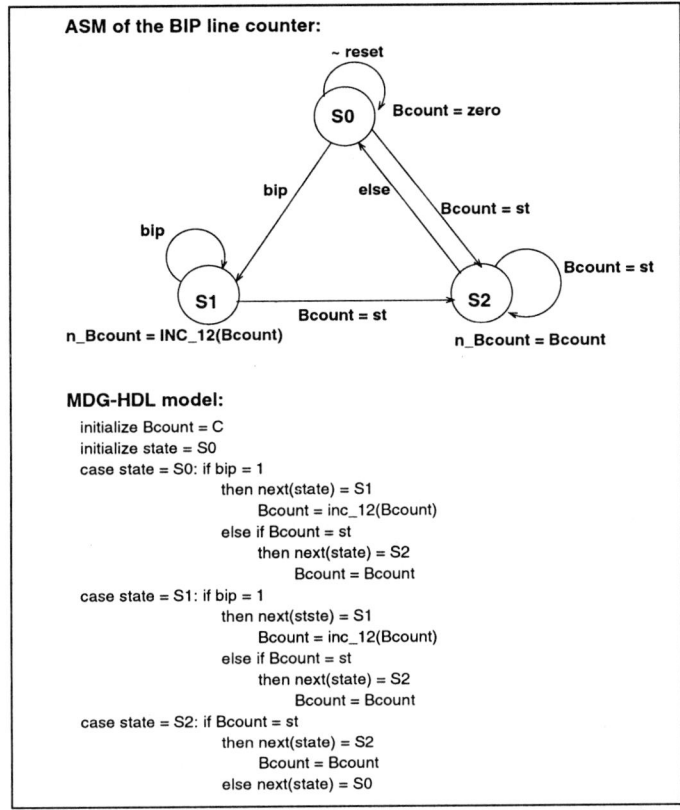

Fig. 4. Example of an ASM with its MDG-HDL model

using a VHDL test bench. In the simulation, two different types of data structure had been used. These data structures are implemented for two different functions: the SONET frame data information and the BIP line data. For the formal verification, we are interested in five control blocks only to eliminate the possibility of state space explosion. During our modeling of the verification environment, we eliminated those blocks which have no effect on the functionality of the TSB. In contrast to simulation, formal verification has a built-in technique that allows a non-deterministic choice of values for the primary inputs. This non-deterministic choice of data structure will eliminate the use of deterministic data structure as used for simulation. After establishing a proper environment, we performed model checking and equivalence checking of the TSB. This will be described in the following subsections.

4.1 Model Checking of the RASE TSB

We first applied property checking to ascertain that both the specification and the implementation of the Telecom System Block satisfy some specific characteristics of the system. The verification of the properties has been carried out using the model checking facility of MDG tools [10].

The properties are described using a property specification language called $\mathcal{L}_{MDG}$ [10], which is a universally quantified first-order temporal logic. Due to space limitations, in the following, we present one sample safety property (Property 7) of the RASE TSB. A complete description of a longer list of properties can be found in [13].

Property 7: When the calculated Bit Error Rate (BER) counters ($dcount$ and $ccount$) exceed their programmable alarm declaration threshold value ($declare\_th$) and alarm clearing threshold value ($clear\_th$), respectively, an alarm ($berv$) will be triggered to indicate that the calculated BER on the SONET input data stream exceeds its programmable threshold value, i.e.,

$if\ ((Bipclk = 1)\ and\ (dcount > declare\_th)\ and\ (ccount > clear\_th))$
$then\ Always\ (berv = 1)$

where, $Bipclk$ is the BIP line referenced clock and, $dcount$ and $ccount$ counters count up to 4k depending on the configuration of the threshold values.

We applied model checking on both the block and top levels of the TSB. As there are five blocks in our TSB design, we grouped the properties into five block level properties and finally merged them into a set of twelve properties featuring the top level verification of the TSB.

The experimental results from the verification of some specific properties for the implementation are given in Table 2, including the CPU time in seconds, memory usage in MB and the number of state variables. Experimental results of the full set of properties checked on both the behavioral specification and implementation models can be found in [13]. All experimental results have been carried out on a Sun Ultra Sparc 2 machine with 768 MB of memory.

4.2 Equivalence Checking of the RASE TSB

Once a certain confidence in the correctness of the models has been established, we proceed with the verification of the RASE TSB models using equivalence checking following a hierarchical approach. For instance, we verified that the RTL implementation of each module complied with the specification of its behavioral model. Thanks to the many abstractions we adopted to the overall RASE TSB, we also succeeded to verify the top level specification of the RASE TSB against its total implementation. Experimental results, including CPU time, memory usage and number of MDG nodes generated, for the equivalence checking between the behavioral models against their RTL implementations are given in Table 1, including the CPU time in seconds, memory usage in MB and the number of MDG nodes generated.

The verifications of the first four modules consumed less CPU time and memory, because they are less complex and have less abstract state variables and cross-operators than those of the last three modules (see Table 1). The BERM module consumed more CPU time and memory during the verification as it performs complex arithmetic operations on abstract data. On the other hand, the verification of the TOH Process module consumed less CPU time and memory, even though it needs more MDG components to model than the BERM module. This is because of the fact that the TOH Process module is a state machine based design and in contrast to BERM does not perform any complex data operation. To model the complex arithmetic operations of the BERM, we need more abstract state variables and uninterpreted functions, especially cross-operators, which have significant effects on the verification of this module. As the top level of the design comprises all the bottom level sub-modules, it obviously takes more CPU time and memory during the verification process than the other modules.

Table 1. Equivalence checking results

Property	CPU time (sec.)	Memory (MB)	MDG Nodes
TOH Extraction	3.88	2.33	2806
APSC module	17.37	7.91	9974
SSF module	22.22	6.81	14831
Interrupt server	0.48	0.09	180
BERM module	80.53	21.31	35799
TOH Pro. module	89.03	27.79	60068
RASE TSB	437.15	47.36	135658

5 Comparison with FormalCheck

One of the motivations of this work was to compare the model checking of the RASE TSB using the MDG model checker with existing commercial model checking tools, here Cadence FormalCheck [5]. The performance criteria of the comparison were CPU-time, memory usages and state variables. During our verification in FormalCheck, we setup the verification environment of the system in such a way that it reduces the state space and speeds up the verification process. To do so, we eliminated some blocks which do not affect the behavior of the system. Based on the design hierarchy, we organized the verification in FormalCheck such that model checking of the lower level modules will be done in first place. Finally, we integrated all sub-modules into a top level structural model of the RASE TSB and performed the model checking on it. In our performance comparison between FormalCheck and MDG model checking, we consider only the top level verification. The summary of the comparison between these two verification systems are given in Table 2, where '*' means that the verification did not terminate after a substantial run-time (several days). While performing the property checking on the top level model of the RASE TSB using FormalCheck, some of the properties verifications (Properties 5, 7, 8, 9, 10 and 12) did not terminate. These properties were taking too much CPU time and memory, even though we used different tool guided reduction and abstraction techniques in FormalCheck. The number of state variables used in FormalCheck are less than

MDG, because FormalCheck has a built-in state reduction technique which was not available within the MDG system when we worked on this project.

Properties 7, 8 and 12 belong to the BERM module, which is the largest and most complex module of the RASE TSB. The BERM module has several control state variables which perform complex arithmetic operations between large sized data. The verification of Properties 7, 8 and 12 did not terminate within a substantial CPU time as these three properties are dealing with control signals having width of 24 bits to 12 bits. Moreover, some complex data operations between large sized state variables were involved. In general, if the control information needs n bits, then it is impossible to reduce the datapath width to less than n. Hence, in this case ROBDD based datapath reduction technique is no more feasible. On the other hand, using the MDG-based approach, we naturally allow the abstract representation of data while the control information is extracted from the datapath using cross-operators. ROBDD [4] have proved to be a powerful tool for automated hardware verification. However, they require a Boolean representation of the circuit and the size of an ROBDD grows exponentially with the width of the Boolean variables. Therefore, ROBDD-based verification cannot be directly applied to a mixed control-datapath design which has large data words. The verification of the BERM module falls into the above mentioned category which comprises lots of wide state variables, e.g., 12-bits, 24-bits. There are ways to deal with this problem: the first one is to reduce the complexity of the design by means of data abstraction and the second one is to represent hardware designs at different levels of abstraction, and verify the designs hierarchically. In contrast to MDG FormalCheck, which is an ROBDD based tool, does not support datapath abstraction. Because of this limitation in FormalCheck the verification of Properties 7, 8 and 12 encountered the state space explosion considering 12-bits and 24-bits state variables. In both cases we used a hierarchical verification approach depending on the design hierarchy.

Our experimental results show that FormalCheck whose underlying structure is automata oriented [7] is more efficient in verifying FSM-based modules, i.e., concrete variables, than the MDG tools. For instance, Table 2 shows that Properties 1, 2, 3, 4, 6 and 11 take less verification time in FormalCheck than in the MDG tools. These properties are related to the APSC, Synchronization status and TOH Extraction modules which are completely FSM-based designs. Properties 5, 9 and 10 did not terminate on the top level using FormalCheck, as these properties are verifying the integrated functionality of several modules.

Human effort to formal verification of any design is an important issue to the industrial community. In FormalCheck, we do not need manual intervention for variable ordering while for MDG tools, we used manual variable ordering since no heuristic ordering algorithm is available in the current version. The translation of the original VHDL design description to MDG-HDL structural model took about one man-month. In contrast to this, no time was spent on the RTL modeling for FormalCheck which accepts the original VHDL structural model without any translation.

Table 2. Model checking results using MDG and FormalCheck

Property	MDG			FormalCheck		
	Time (sec.)	Memory (MB)	State variables	Time (sec.)	Memory (MB)	State variables
Property 1	82.47	15.60	57	60	16.08	54
Property 2	82.62	14.98	57	32	12.81	71
Property 6	81.65	15.80	55	10	11.75	28
Property 7	82.54	15.86	57	*	*	*
Property 8	64.30	15.72	57	*	*	*
Property 9	78.06	16.65	55	*	*	*

6 Conclusions

In this paper, we demonstrated that the MDG tools have the capability to verify a moderate size industrial Telecom hardware, the RASE TSB. Based on the product document provided by the PMC-Sierra Inc., we derived a behavioral model of the Telecom System Block. The specification was given as English text which was modeled in terms of Abstract State Machines using MDG-HDL. To handle the complexity of the RTL model, the module was abstracted by using MDG based abstract sorts and uninterpreted functions. We adopted a hierarchical verification approach to verify the whole TSB through MDG-based equivalence and model checking. Our verification did not find any errors in the existing design.

Although some of the ideas presented in this paper may be well known, this is the first time a prototype tool MDG has been applied to a commercial Telecom system. Unlike other conventional EDA tools, applying MDG to a design verification is not straight forward or well defined. To apply this tool, specially for a design like the RASE TSB, one needs to come up with a methodology "how to apply MDG" to this kind of large Telecom hardware. On the other hand, one of the motivations of this work was to compare the verification of the TSB using MDGs with the verification done by an existing commercialized formal verification tool, Cadence FormalCheck. The verification in FormalCheck has one major practical advantage over MDG, namely the VHDL/Verilog front-end which enables the integration with the design flow. The MDG-based approach can handle arbitrary data widths using abstract sort and uninterpreted functions which is a solution to the state space explosion problem. On the other hand, our experimental results show that in some cases FormalCheck fails short due to state space explosion for wider datapath.

Acknowledgments

We would like to thank PMC-Sierra, Inc. for providing us with the documentation and HDL models of the RASE TSB. We are in particular grateful to Jean

Lamarche from PMC-Sierra, whose cooperation contributed to the maturity of this work.

References

1. O. Ait-Mohamed, X. Song, E. Cerny. On the nontermination of MDG-based abstract state enumeration. In Proc. IFIP Conference on Correct Hardware and Verification Methods, Montreal, Canada, October 1997, pp. 218-235.
2. S. Balakrishnan and S. Tahar. A Hierarchical Approach to the Formal Verification of Embedded Systems Using MDGs, In Proc. IEEE 9th Great Lakes Symposium on VLSI, Ann Arbor, Michigan, USA, March 1999, IEEE Computer Society Press, pp. 284-287.
3. Bell Communication Research (BellCORE). SONET Transport Systems: Common Generic Criteria. GR-253-CORE, issue 2, December 1995.
4. R.E. Bryant. Graph-Based Algorithms for Boolean Function Manipulation. In IEEE Transactions on Computers, Vol. C-35, No. 8, August 1986, pp. 677-691.
5. Cadence Design Systems, Inc. Formal Verification Using Affirma FormalCheck Manual. Version 2.3, August 1999.
6. F. Corella, Z. Zhou, X. Song, M. Langevin and E. Cerny. Multiway Decision Graphs for Automated Hardware Verification. Formal Methods in System Design, Vol. 10, February 1997, pp. 7-46.
7. C. Kern and M. Greenstreet. Formal Verification in Hardware Design: A Survey. ACM Transactions on Design Automation of Electronic Systems, Vol. 4, April 1999, pp. 123-193.
8. PMC-Sierra Inc. Receive, APS, Synchronization Status and BERM Telecom System Block. Engineering Document. Issue 4, January 29, 1998.
9. S. Tahar, X. Song, E. Cerny, Z. Zhou, M. Langevin and O. Ait- Mohamed. Modeling and Verification of the Fairisle ATM Switch Fabric using MDGs. IEEE Transactions on CAD of Integrated Circuits and Systems, Vol. 18, No. 7, July 1999, pp. 956-972.
10. Y. Xu, E. Cerny, X. Song, F. Corella, O. Mohamed. Model Checking for First-Order Temporal Logic using Multiway Decision Graphs. In Computer Aided Verification, LNCS 1427, Springer Verlag, 1998, pp. 219-231.
11. Z. Zhou, X. Song, S. Tahar, E. Cerny, F. Corella, M. Langevin. Formal Verification of the Island Tunnel Controller using Multiway Decision Graphs. In Formal Methods in Computer-Aided Design, LNCS 1166, Springer Verlag, 1996, pp. 233-246.
12. Z. Zhou and N. Boulerice. MDG Tools (v1.0) User's Manual. Dept. of Information and Operation Research, University of Montreal, Canada, 1996.
13. M.H. Zobair. Modeling and Formal Verification of a Telecom System Block using MDGs. M.A.Sc. Thesis, Concordia University, Department of Electrical and Computer Engineering, Montreal, Canada, April 2001.

Enabling Hardware Verification through Design Changes

Amr T. Abdel-Hamid[1], Sofiène Tahar[1], and John Harrison[2]

[1] Concordia University, Montreal, Quebec, H3G 1M8 Canada
{at_abdel,tahar}@ece.concordia.ca
[2] Intel Corporation, Hillsboro, OR 97124, USA
johnh@ichips.intel.com

Abstract. The IEEE-754 floating-point standard, used in nearly all floating-point applications, is considered as one of the most important standards. Deep datapath and algorithm complexity have made the verification of such floating-point units a very hard task. Theorem proving, offers a good solution to handle such verification tasks. In this paper, we stress on the design changes performed for the sake of formalizing and verifying the IEEE-754 table-driven exponential function in all abstraction levels of the design flow. While verifying the VHDL code implementation against a high-level abstract specification, we were faced by two main problems: (1) the large abstraction gap between the two models; and (2) the flatness of the VHDL code, making it intractable to model and formally verify. We have therefore proposed a hierarchical methodology to solve such modeling problem, and experimented it on our verification task using the HOL theorem proving environment.

1 Introduction

Designs are getting larger and larger, more complex every day. Simulation, although widely used, could never give the verification coverage needed. There are two full coverage approaches, brute-force and special-purpose simulation, which fail to give even a fair coverage ratio for a moderate design and also less accurate, as sometimes faults occur where they are least expected. It is becoming clear that the "quality" of the validation achieved by traditional simulation is rapidly deteriorating as the VLSI technology progresses.

Formal verification methods [10] have sometimes been accused of a lack of ability to get into a whole industrial product design cycle. Working on the same design path of most electronic products, we discuss in this paper the design changes performed for the sake of formalizing and verifying the IEEE-754 table-driven exponential function at all abstraction levels of the design flow. The Floating-point functions are a main building block in nearly any modern microprocessor. As an example of such circuits, we used the IEEE-754 exponential function with symmetric 32 bits for both input and output. The IEEE-754 exponential function was specified first formally in [7]. This behavioral specification was written in a high level *while language*, and was intended mainly to be verified against a more abstract mathematical description of the exponential function

[12]. Starting from this behavioral specification Bui et al. [2] developed an RTL (Register Transfer Level) implementation of the design using VHDL. We were also interested in the development of a formal proof that a synthesized logic gate implementation also implies this RTL design.

In this exercise, we were faced by two problems: (1) the main intend of the specification, written in the *while language*, was to prove it against a more abstract arithmetic specification. This caused a large gap between this specification and the implementation it should be verified against. As the mathematical nature of the behavioral model was clearly unrelated to the lower level VHDL implementation. Unlike the implementation, we had to formalize the specification without making any kind of changes in it to insure system integrity. So, to solve such a problem we introduced a new level between the specification and the implementation, called *modular* behavioral specification, which will be discussed afterwards throughly in the paper; (2) the VHDL code provided was too flat to be modeled efficiently. Even if we succeed such a modeling, it would be too large to be verified. This problem was solved by reconstructing the RTL implementation in a more modular manner trying to minimize the interconnections between such modules.

In this work, we use the HOL theorem proving system [6] for specifying and verifying the floating-point design at hand. The HOL theorem prover is an interactive proof assistant for higher-order logic developed at Cambridge University by Gordon et al. [6]. It was explicitly designed for the formal verification of hardware, though it has also been applied to other areas including software verification and formalization of pure mathematics.

There exists very few related work in the open literature on the impact of design changes on the formal verification process. For instance, Curzon et al. [5] introduced this idea in the context of interactive proof. By using the HOL theorem prover, they suggested that the cost of verification of an ATM (Asynchronous Transfer Mode) switch in terms of time can be reduced by making appropriate design changes. For example, they redesigned the arbiter module to reset correctly if the cells and frame start occur close together. The authors noted the factors that were increasing the verification cost, where particular aspects of the behavioral specification were lengthening the verification task by a significant amounts. Zobair et al. [13] used a similar approach to investigate whether the same design changes would also reduce the verification cost while using the MDG tools [4]. Both of the above works have shown that design modifications and redesign for verifiability would have a significant effect on the speed and effort of the verification task. They also defined some design change rules similar to those discussed in this paper.

Other related work to ours is dealing with the verification of the floating-point algorithms and designs in general. For instance, Miner [11] formalized the IEEE-854 floating-point standard in PVS. He used this formalization to verify abstract mathematical descriptions of the main real operations and their relation to the corresponding floating-point implementations. Carreno [3] defined and then formalized the same IEEE-854 standard in HOL. The most related work among these efforts, however, is the one of Harrison [8] who defined and formalized real numbers using HOL. Then he developed a generic floating-point library to define and verify the most fundamental terms and lemmas of IEEE-754 standard [7]. This former library was used by him to formalize and verify floating-point algorithms against behavioral specification of the square root [9] and the exponential function [7].

The organization of the paper is as follows. We will start in Section 2 by describing the Table-Driven exponential function algorithm, whose formal specification and implementation are discussed throughout this paper. Section 3 introduces our methodology and shows how hierarchical and modular techniques were used to ease the verification task. Section 4 shows the specification formalization, and discusses the new modular specification level added as well as the design changes done on the implementation for easing the verification. Section 5 describes the formal verification process and summarizes the experimental results. Finally, conclusions are drawn in Section 6.

2   The IEEE-754 Exponential Function

In this section, we give an introduction to the IEEE-754 exponential function whose formal specification and design are discussed in the rest of the paper.

Using an approximate polynomial expansion, Tang [12] has developed an algorithm for computing the floating-point exponential function using what he calls a *Table-Driven* approach. In this approach, the input is first reduced to a certain working range, $[-log\ 2/2^{L+1}, log\ 2/2^{L+1}]$, where L is an integer larger than or equal to 1, chosen beforehand, (for instance, L = 4 for single precision [12]). Then this input x is considered to be composed of:

$$x = \frac{(32 * m + j) * (log2)}{32} + (r1 + r2)$$

where m and j are integers, and $r1$ and $r2$ are real numbers, $|\ r1 + r2\ | < ((\log 2)/64)$.

Starting from this equation, the exponential function can be constructed as follows:

$$x = (m * log2) + \frac{(j * log2)}{32} + r$$

where $r = r1 + r2$. The exponential of x will hence be equal to

$$exp(x) = exp((m * log2) + \frac{(j * log2)}{32} + r)$$

$$= 2^m + 2^{\frac{j}{32}} + exp(r)$$

The main objective of the algorithm is to isolate m and j, and to evaluate the approximating polynomial. According to Tang, four steps are needed to compute this exponential function:

Step 1. Filter any out-of-bounds inputs that occur. As mentioned before, x should be a number between $[-(log2/32),(log2/32)]$.

Step 2. Start the computation by first calculating N,

$$N = INTEGER(X * INVL)$$

where $INVL$ is a floating-point constant approximately equal to $32/log2$ in our case, and INTEGER is the default IEEE-754 round-to-nearest mode. This N is composed of two parts,

$$N = N1 + N2$$

where $N1 = 32 * m$, and $N2 = j$

So, the variables m and j can be derived from the previous result as follows:

$$j = N2$$

$$m = \frac{N1}{32}$$

Given the value of N, $r1$ and $r2$ can be calculated as discussed in [12].

Step 3. Compute the polynomial $p(r)$, similar to the Taylor expansion showed above.

Step 4. The values of $2^{j/32}$, $j = 0, 1, ...32$, are calculated beforehand and are represented by two working-precision numbers (single precision in our case), *Slead* and *Strail*. The sum approximates $2^{j/32}$ to roughly double the working precision. Finally $exp(x)$ is calculated as follows:

$$S = Slead(j) + Strail(j)$$

$$exp(x) = 2^m + (Slead(j) + (Strail(j) + S * p(r)))$$

3   Modeling and Verification Methodology

The verification process for the Table-Driven exponential function will be performed on many levels. Harrison [7] formalized and verified that a behavioral specification, an abstract algorithmic description he developed for the design, implies an abstract mathematical description of the IEEE-754 Table-Driven floating-point exponential function [12]. Starting from this behavioral specification, written in a *while-language*, Bui et al. [2] developed an RTL (Register Transfer Level) implementation of the design. The goal of this work is the modeling and verification of the latter implementation with respect to the behavioral specification designed by [7] using HOL. We were also interested in the development of a formal proof that the logic gate implementation, machine synthesized using the Synopsys tool, implies the RTL implementation.

As soon as we started the verification project, we noticed that there was a large abstraction gap between the high level behavioral specification and the RTL implementation. Trying to build the formal proof between the two levels, we found that such a gap cannot be bridged in one move. Another problem was that the flat behavioral specification itself cannot be modified or changed to facilitate the verification task.

On the other hand, it was noticed that the VHDL RTL implementation was very flat to be verified. The very high number of small modules and connections would make the modeling of such design in HOL a very long process, and it will nearly make the verification against the specification intractable. For these reasons, we rebuilt the RTL implementation of the design to a modular version. The code was redesigned into a smaller number of sub-modules to achieve the partitions needed for the modeling process. These modules were chosen to meet the following criteria:

1) *Self containing*: meaning the verification of one module does not affect the others in the same environment except by the input and output signals.

2) *Minimal communicating signals*: where the interfaces between such modules were minimized and kept as simple as possible. This would lead to extending the self containing property above, as well as less signals as possible in the heavy populated system level design.

Encountering the above problems, we introduced a new specification level, *the modular behavioral specification*. This level was placed between the modular RTL implementation and the abstract (flat) behavioral specification as shown in Figure 1 below. This new specification level was modeled using a closer modular composition as of the lower RTL design, yet its modules were described internally at a higher abstraction level as used in the original (flat) behavioral specification. It hence acted as the bridge that shorten the distance between the two design levels. Given the proposed design changes, the overall modeling and verification process is described in Figure 1, where the shaded boxes are the material provided by [7], and [2], while the white ones represent those developed in this work.

In Figure 1, we modeled the behavioral specification provided in [7] in HOL. We then proved that the modular behavioral specification implies the higher level abstract specification adopted from the one built by Harrison. We then built the modular VHDL code of the RTL level, after applying the design changes mentioned above. We then modeled this RTL implementation in HOL. Furthermore, we proved hierarchically that the synthesized gate level implementation implies the modular RTL description. Finally, all proof stages were linked in a single global proof covering the whole design cycle of the floating-point exponential function. In the next sections, we will describe the formal specification and verification of the IEEE exponential function design based on the proposed approach, respectively..

4 Formal Specification of IEEE-754 Exponential Function

In this section, we focus on the formal specification of the IEEE-754 exponential function through out the different abstraction levels. Due to space limitations, we will give a sketch of the main design change issues, while further specification details can be found in [1].

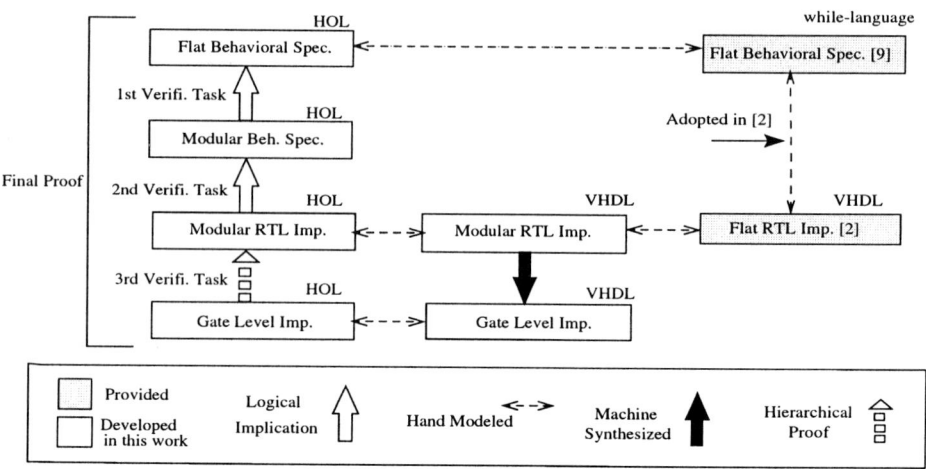

Fig. 1. The exponential function verification project

As mentioned earlier, the specification introduced in [7] was intended mainly to verify a higher level mathematical implementation of the design. This provided a large gap between this specification and the implementation it should be verified against. Unlike the implementation, we had to formalize the specification, written originally in *while language* (Figure 2), without making any changes in it to insure system integrity.

To introduce a modular behavioral specification, we have divided this specification into six intermediate blocks (modules), similar to those used for the RTL implementation, where the conjunction of these blocks (Figure 3) represents the full specification of the code described in Figure 2. It should be noted, that the mathematical operators (such as '*', '+', and '/') in Figure 2 are bit vector operations and not mathematical real numbers operators. Trying to achieve maximum modularity for the design, we have tried to minimize the interfaces between different modules. This helped us to divide the verification tasks into well-defined smaller ones. Each of these blocks was also divided into smaller specifications giving us smaller sub-specifications clearly related to the goals needed to be proved.

The six modules composing the new level are completely responsible for checking the input X value and computing the result of the exponential function (see Figure 3). These blocks are:

1) m and j computing block (M_J_SPEC): responsible for half of Step 2 (cf. Section 2) by computing the values of m and j. Its input is the number X and its outputs are J, M, N, and $N1$.

2) $r1$ and $r2$ block ($R1\_R2\_SPEC$): responsible for the second half of Step 2, it computes the values of $r1$ and $r2$. Its inputs are X, $N1$, $N2$ (equal to J) and its outputs are the two floating-point numbers $R1$ and $R2$.

```
Int_32 = Int(32)
Int_2e9 = Int (2 EXP 9)
Int_2e9 = Int (2 EXP 9)
Plus_one = float (0, 127, 0)
THRESHOLD_1 = float (0, 134, 6066890)
THRESHOLD_2 = float (0, 102, 0)
Inv_L = float (0, 121, 3240448)
L1 = float (0, 121, 3240448)
L2 = float (0, 102, 4177550)
A1 = float (0, 126, 68)
A2 = float (0, 124, 2796268)
var x:float, E:float, R1:float, R2:float, R:float, P:float,
Q:float,S:float, E1:float, N:Int, N1:Int, N2:Int, M:Int, J:Int;
```

/* Checking block */

```
if Isnan (X) then E:= X
else if X == Plus_infinity  then E:= Plus_infinity
else if X == Minus_infinity then E:= Plus_Zero
else if (abs(x) > THRESHOLD_1 then
if X > Plus_Zero then E:= Plus_infinity
else E:= Plus_Zero  else if abs(X) < THRESHOLD_2 then E:= Plus_one + X
else ( N:= INTRND (X * Inv_L);
```

/* m and j computing block */

```
N2:= N \% Int_32;
N1:= N - N2;   M:= N1 / Int_32;   J:= N2;
```

/* r1 and r2 block */

```
if abs (N) Int_2e9 then
R1:= (X-Tofloat(N1) * L1) - Tofloat (N2) * L1
else    R1:= X - Tofloat(N) * L1;
R2:= Tofloat(N) * L2;
R:= R1 + R2;
Q:= R * R (A1 + R * A2);
p(r) block P:= R1 + (R2 + Q);
```

/* Slead and Strail block */

```
S:= S_Lead(J) + S_Trail(J);
```

/* Exponent calculation block */

```
E1:= S_Lead(J) + (S_Trail(J) + S * P);
```

Fig. 2. Behavioral specification of the exponential function in *while language* [7]

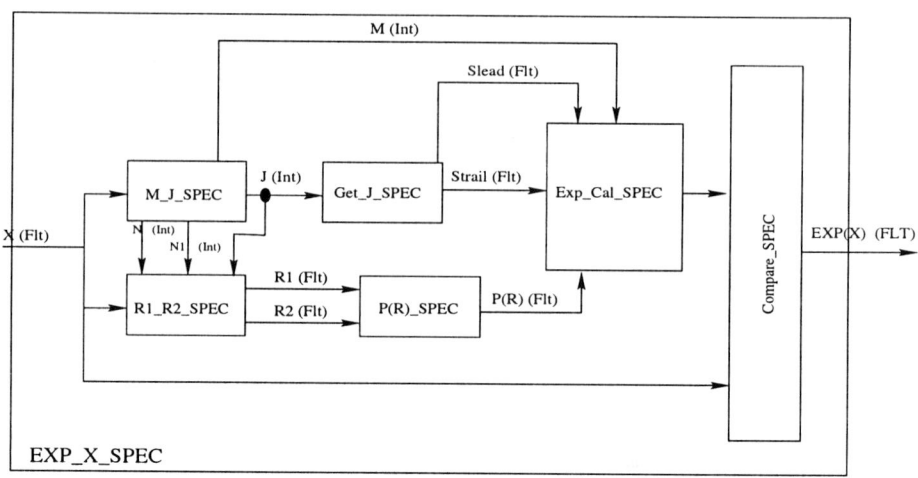

Fig. 3. Modular organization of the exponential function specification

3) *p(r) block (P_R_SPEC)*: computes the value of *p(r)*. It takes *R*1 and *R*2 and outputs *P_R*.

4) *Slead and Strail block (Ge_J_SPEC)*: a floating-point multiplexer module, where the value of *J* decides which values for Strail and Slead should be chosen. Its input is just the number *J* and its outputs are Slead and Strail.

5) *Exponent calculation block (Exp_Cal_SPEC)*: this is the main computational block where the exponential function is computed. It takes *Slead, Strail, M* and *P(R)* as its inputs and outputs *EXP(X)*.

6) *Checking block (Compare_SPEC)*: the compare and decision module. According to the value of input *X*, this module decides whether to choose the computed value of the exponent or another output as NAN (Not-A-Number). It takes *X* and the computed exponent as its inputs and outputs *EXP(X)*.

The top level of this system specification in HOL looks as follows:

```
⊢def  IEEE_EXP_SPEC Xs Xe Xm EXP_s EXP_e EXP_m =
∃ Ns Ne Nm Ms Me Mm Js Je Jm N1s N1e N1m R1s R1e R1m...
(M_J_SPEC Xs Xe Xm Ns Ne Nm Ms Me Mm Js Je Jm..)∧
(R1_R2_MOD_SPEC Xs Xe Xm Ns Ne Nm ..)∧
(Get_J_SPEC Js Je Jm Strail_s Strail_e Strail_m ..)∧
(P_R_SPEC R1_s R1_e R1_m R2_sR2_eR2_mPR_sPR_ePR_m)∧
(EXP_CAL_MOD_SPEC Strail_s Strail_e Strail_m ..)∧
(Compare_SPEC EXP_1_s EXP_1_e EXP_1_m Xs Xe Xm EXP_s EXP_e EXP_m)
```

In line with the behavioral specification, we also adopted a modular modeling of the IEEE-754 exponential function implementation. In fact, since the original VHDL implementation code developed by Bui *et al.* [2] was too flat as well, we performed a number of design changes, which keep the same code properties but make the design easier to model and verify. We have aimed mainly in our changes to reduce the logic complexity by introducing a hierarchical (modular) design architecture which reduced the complexity of the circuit. Also, in some modules the code has been changed to perform the same function, while being less complex.

Thanks to the above design changes, it became easier to move the new VHDL code into HOL notation. The HOL, top level model of our implementation is given as follows, which is now nearly a one-to-one mapping from the new VHDL model:

$\vdash_{def}$ IEEE_EXP_IMP Xs Xe Xm EXP_s EXP_e EXP_m =
∃ Ns Ne Nm Ms Me Mm Js Je Jm N1s N1e N1m...
(M_J_IMP Xs Xe Xm Ns Ne Nm Ms Me Mm Js Je Jm N1s N1e N1m) ∧
(R1_R2_MOD_IMP Xs Xe Xm Ns Ne Nm N1s N1e N1m ..) ∧
(Get_J_IMP Js Je Jm Strail_s Strail_e Strail_m ..) ∧
(P_R_IMP R1_s R1_e R1_m R2_s R2_eR2_m PR_s PR_e PR_m) ∧
(EXP_CAL_MOD_IMP Slead_s Slead_e Slead_m ..) ∧
(Compare_IMP EXP_1_s EXP_1_e EXP_1_m Xs Xe Xm EXP_s EXP_e EXP_m)

The above RTL modules show obviously one-to-one correspondence with the proposed modular behavioral specification. Moreover, there is a high level of regularity in these six modules where floating-point operations, like addition, multiplication, are the main sub-modules in all of them. This will help us in the reuse of the developed models and theories in building the lower levels of such specification. Each of the six modules was modeled further as a conjunction of lower level components.

After fully modeling the specification and implementation of the system, the next task was the verification process, which will be discussed in the next section along with the experimental results. The high similarity between the implementation at high levels and the specification considerably eased the verification task.

5 Formal Verification of the Exponential Function

So far, we modeled in HOL the IEEE-754 Table-Driven exponential function at different levels of abstraction, including the introduction of modular layers. The next step is to verify these different levels using a hierarchical proof approach in HOL.

Let X be the input and EXP the exponential output, our final goal is:

∀ X EXP.
assuming $\frac{-log2}{32} \leq X \leq \frac{log2}{32}$.
(EXP_GATE_IMP X EXP $\Longrightarrow$ EXP_BEH_SPEC X EXP)

This goal implies that if X meets the boundry conditions specified, $\frac{-log2}{32} \leq X \leq \frac{log2}{32}$, then the gate implementation, EXP_GATE_IMP, should imply the high level behavioral specification, EXP_BEH_SPEC.

Obviously, this goal cannot be reached directly, due to the very high abstraction gap between the gate and behavioral levels as described above. Using the design changes done, the proof scheme was changed to hierarchically prove that the gate level implies the more abstract RTL. Then the new introduced modular specification was proved to imply the higher level abstract specification modeled in HOL. The RTL afterwards, was related, by a formal proof, to the modular behavioral specification. This latter proof gave us the ability to prove the whole design path of the circuit, starting from the gate level implementation of the design up to the behavioral specification proposed in [7]. The assumption that X in its boundaries is made by the boundry module within both the specification and the implementation. So the goal would be the following:

$$\vdash_{thm} \forall X\ EXP.\ IEEE\_EXP\_GATE\_IMP\ X\ EXP \quad (1)$$
$$\implies IEEE\_EXP\_RTL\_IMP\ X\ EXP$$

$$\vdash_{thm} \forall X\ EXP.\ IEEE\_EXP\_RTL\_IMP\ X\ EXP \quad (2)$$
$$\implies IEEE\_EXP\_MOD\_BHV\_SPEC\ X\ EXP$$

$$\vdash_{thm} \forall X\ EXP.\ IEEE\_EXP\_MOD\_BHV\_SPEC\ X\ EXP \quad (3)$$
$$\implies IEEE\_EXP\_BHV\_SPEC\ X\ EXP$$

Finally using equations (1), (2) and (3), we can reach the final goal stated again in equation (4):

$$\vdash_{thm} \forall\ X\ EXP.\ IEEE\_EXP\_GATE\_IMP\ X\ EXP \quad (4)$$
$$\implies IEEE\_EXP\_BHV\_SPEC\ X\ EXP$$

A summary of the verification times for the whole system is given in Table 1. All experiments have been carried out on a Sun Ultra SPARC 2 workstation with a 296 MHz processor and 768 MB of memory. In the table, we have showed the verification time of two main building blocks, the floating-point adder and multiplier. These modules took a very high verification time, but due to the high reusability of pre-proven theorems and lemmas, other building blocks and even the main module required much less verification time. Also, it can be seen that the verification time for four of the six m ain modules are much smaller, as all these modules' building blocks were pre-proved, making the final task shorter. The sum of the times of the systems showed here will be less than the total verification time as there were some lemmas verified to achieve the final proof goal. The whole code was composed of nearly 4600 lines.

6 Conclusions

Most verification and testing tools will fail short to verify a circuit with a deep datapath. The IEEE-754 Table-Driven exponential function with its 32 bit input and 32 bit output implementation would be considered an impossible task for exhaustive simulation. Model Checking techniques will not go a lot further as

Table 1. Verification times of different system modules

Module Name	Verification Time (sec.)
Floating-Point Addition	60.50
Floating-Point Multiplication	30.54
M_J Module	2.12
R1_R2 Module	5.62
P_R Module	3.42
EXP_Cal Module	1.97
IEEE_EXP Module	5.29
Total Verification Time	**214.20**

the deep datapath means a huge state space causing a *state space explosion* problem. Also, the main module and most of its sub-modules' properties cannot be covered easily with, e.g., CTL properties.

In this paper, we have demonstrated the use of HOL to model the behavioral and RTL specifications for the IEEE-754 Table-Driven exponential function in a modular form. We have showed that adding new levels in the design path, as in the case of the intermediate behavioral specification, or changing the design to modular blocks, would ease both the modeling and verification processes. Finally, using *hierarchical verification*, we have been able to develop a formal proof indicating the correctness of the implementation using the HOL tool.

The main lessons for the design changes enabling formal verification are:

1) Modules performing the same function or highly interacting should be placed in the same module to minimize system blocks interfaces.

2) Create a boundry at the system, where the number of sub-modules in the main modules should not exceed it. As this would complicate the verification of the blocks afterwards.

3) Create easily localized modules, so that the module could be redesigned with minimal changes in the system verification task, as well as minimizing the main connections to other modules.

One of the very important advantages of the hierarchical verification lies in the fact that the change of a module or more will not mean the re-proof of the whole system. It only means the re-proof that the new module meets the same specification that the older version did. This may mean a lot for a tight time-to-market in a fast moving technology like microelectronics. As an example, our proof can always be used with the changing technology as long as we prove that the lower modules, gates for instance, are still satisfying the same properties.

References

1. A.T. Abdel-Hamid. A Hierarchical Verification of the IEEE-754 Table-Driven Floating-Point Exponential Function using HOL. M.A.Sc. Thesis, Concordia University, Department of Electrical and Computer Engineering, Montreal, Canada, April 2001.

2. H.T. Bui, B. Khalaf, and S. Tahar. Table-Driven Floating-Point Exponential Function. Proc. IEEE Canadian Conference on Electrical & Computer Engineering, May 1999, pp. 450-455.
3. V.A. Carreno. Interpretation of IEEE-854 Floating-Point Standard and Definition in the HOL system. NASA Technical Memorandum 110189, September 1995.
4. F. Corella, Z. Zhou, X. Song, M. Langevin and E. Cerny. Multiway Decision Graphs for Automated Hardware Verification. Formal Methods in System Design, vol. 10, February 1997, pp. 7-46.
5. P. Curzon and I. Leslie. Improving Hardware Designs whilst Simplifying their Proof. In Designing Correct Circuits, Workshops in Computing, British Computer Society, 1996.
6. M.J.C. Gordon and T.F.Melham. Introduction to HOL: a Theorem Proving Environment for Higher-order Logic. Cambridge University Press, 1993.
7. J.R. Harrison. Floating Point Verification in HOL Light: The Exponential Function. Technical Report number 428, University of Cambridge Computer Laboratory. UK, June 1997.
8. J.R. Harrison. Theorem Proving with the Real Numbers. Technical Report number 408, University of Cambridge Computer Laboratory, December 1996.
9. J.R. Harrison. Verifying the Accuracy of Polynomial Approximations in HOL. In Theorem Proving in Higher Order Logics, LNCS 1275, Springer Verlag, 1997, pp. 137-152.
10. C. Kern, and M. R. Greenstreat. Formal verification in Hardware Design: A Survey. ACM transactions on Design Automation of Electronic Systems, vol. 4, no. 2, April 1999, pp. 123-193.
11. P.S. Miner. Defining the IEEE-854 Floating-Point Standard in PVS. NASA Technical Memorandum 110167, June 1995.
12. P.T.P. Tang. Table-Driven Implementation of the Exponential Function in IEEE Floating-Point Arithmetic. ACM Transactions on Mathematical Software, vol. 15, no. 2, 1989, pp. 144-157.
13. M. Hasan, S. Tahar, and P. Curzon. Impact of Design Changes on Verification Using MDGs. Proc. IEEE Canadian Conference on Electrical & Computer Engineering, Halifax, Nova Scotia, Canada, May 2000, pp. 173-178.

Specification-Based Test Generation for Security-Critical Systems Using Mutations*

Guido Wimmel and Jan Jürjens

Department of Computer Science, Munich University of Technology,
Boltzmannstr. 3, D-85748 Garching, Germany
phone: +49-89-28917340, fax: +49-89-28917307
wimmel|juerjens@in.tum.de

Abstract. In specification-based testing, test sequences are generated from an abstract system specification to provide confidence in the correctness of an implementation. For security-critical systems, finding tests likely to detect possible vulnerabilities is particularly difficult, as they usually involve subtle and complex execution scenarios and consideration of domain-specific concepts such as cryptography and random numbers. We present research aiming to generate test sequences for transaction systems from a formal security model supported by the CASE tool AUTO-FOCUS. The test sequences are determined with respect to the system's required security properties, using mutations of the system specification and attack scenarios. To be able to apply them to an existing implementation, the abstract test sequences are concretized.

Keywords. Test Case Generation, E-Commerce Systems, Security-Critical Systems, Formal Methods, Test Specification, Validation and Analysis, Computer-aided Software Engineering (CASE), AutoFocus.

1 Introduction

Security aspects are playing an increasingly important role in the development of distributed systems. However, developing security-critical systems is very difficult. Although undetected vulnerabilities can cause enormous damage, often security-related requirements are only formulated imprecisely and considered in the development in an ad-hoc manner. Controlling the quality of such Applications is a hard problem, and in many cases vulnerabilities are found after the system has been put into operation.

Formal models can contribute to achieving high confidence in a system's security. A large number of modelling and verification approaches has been proposed (see [GSG99] for an overview), ranging from specifications in general languages such as CSP or TLA to protocol-specific formalisms such as CASPER (a protocol definition language that can be translated to CSP) or BAN (a logic modelling the actions and beliefs of the parties during execution of the protocol).

---
* This work was partially supported by the German Ministry of Economics within the FairPay project.

Our work presented in [WW01,JW01a] aims to integrate security aspects into systems development, based on formal models reflecting the security requirements and threat scenarios. Important concepts are tool support and use of description techniques understandable for non-expert software engineers.

However, in general the actual implementation is very complex. To allow proofs of security properties, abstraction techniques are used: in models of cryptographic transactions, messages, keys and random numbers are usually represented by abstract data entities which can be arguments to abstract operations such as encryption or hashing, and part of the actual messages exchanged may have been left out. Besides, as the security model is usually developed independently of the implementation (mostly after the implementation, though this is not desirable), it cannot be concluded from the correctness of a security model that the implementation is secure.

Confidence in the correctness of an implementation can be gained by extensive testing. Testing for security holes is usually restricted to penetration testing (a so-called "tiger-team" of experts manually tries to break the system or tools such as SATAN are used to search for known vulnerabilities). This approach is not satisfactory as it depends largely on the skill of the employed tiger team or the knowledge encoded into the tool, which does not consider application-specific security requirements.

In this paper, we show how to complement this approach by generating test sequences from a security specification. The aim is to find those test sequences that are most likely to detect possible vulnerabilities. For this purpose, we adapt methods from classical specification-based testing to the application domain of security-critical systems. Specifically, we include domain-specific concepts such as cryptography, knowledge of or access to secrets, and threat scenarios. Test sequences likely to detect vulnerabilities are computed using mutations of the specification that lead to violation of the security requirements. Besides, we show how to translate the abstract test sequences derived from the security model to concrete test sequences that can be applied to an existing implementation. For modelling and test case generation, we use the tool AUTOFOCUS.

This paper is organised as follows. In Section 2 we introduce AUTOFOCUS and show how to specify security-critical systems using an extension of AUTOFOCUS models. In Section 3 we describe our approach of generating security-related test sequences from such specifications and their concretization to implementation test sequences. We end with references to related work (Section 4) and conclude in Section 5. We use examples from a case study about CEPS [CEP01], a proposed global standard for purse cards. The case study is explained in more detail in the long version of this paper [WJ02].

2 Security Models in AUTOFOCUS

AUTOFOCUS is a CASE tool for graphically specifying distributed systems with a simple, formally defined semantics based on the formal method Focus [BS01]. It offers standard, easy-to-use description techniques for an end-user, who need not necessarily be a formal methods expert. It features simulation, code generation, test sequence generation and formal verification of the modelled systems.

Systems are specified in AUTOFOCUS using static and dynamic views conceptually similar to those offered in UML-RT. To model security-critical systems, we included security aspects into its description techniques. We briefly explain the extensions together with an abstract syntax for the relevant subset of AUTOFOCUS (excluding hierarchy). [WW01,JW01a] give more motivation and examples on security modelling.

System Structure Diagrams and Attack Scenarios. System Structure Diagrams (SSDs) are similar to UML component diagrams and describe the structure and interfaces of a system. In the SSD view, a system consists of a number of communicating components, which have input and output ports for receiving and sending messages. The ports are connected via directed channels.

In the abstract syntax, an SSD is a triple (Comp, Ports, Channels), where ports p are associated to components by $\mathsf{comp}(p) \in \mathsf{Comp}$, and channels ch are associated to source and destination ports by $\mathsf{sourceP}(ch) \in \mathsf{Ports}$ and $\mathsf{destP}(ch) \in \mathsf{Ports}$. A component c can have local variables $v \in \mathbf{lVar}$ (where **lVar** is a set of variable names) such that $\mathsf{comp}(v) = c$.

For security-critical systems, we have to assume the presence of an attacker trying to exploit security holes. The capabilities of the attacker are defined using threat scenarios incorporated into the specification, which should result from a risk analysis. For this purpose, we define a set $\mathsf{SecAttr} = \{\mathsf{critical}, \mathsf{public}, \mathsf{replace}, \mathsf{node}\}$ of security attributes covering the possible threats from the abstract viewpoint of SSDs, and a mapping $\mathsf{secattrSSD} : (\mathsf{Comp} \cup \mathsf{Channels}) \to \mathcal{P}(\mathsf{SecAttr})$ associating a set of security attributes to any component or channel (here $\mathcal{P}(X)$ is the power-set of X). Based on the security attributes, the relevant threat scenarios for the system can be generated automatically by AUTOFOCUS. The meaning of the security attributes is as follows:

- If critical $\in \mathsf{secattrSSD}(c)$ for a component or a channel c, security-critical information is processed in the component or transmitted via the channel. This is used as an indication that security verification and testing must focus on these parts of the model.
- If public $\in \mathsf{secattrSSD}(ch)$, then ch is a channel whose messages can be accessed and manipulated by the attacker. The corresponding threat scenario is obtained by replacing ch by a set of additional channels such that the communication on ch passes through a component "Intruder".
- If public $\in \mathsf{secattrSSD}(c)$ for a component c, c can be replaced by an internal attacker having access to all secrets contained in c (e.g., the attacker can access and manipulate the program)
- If replace $\in \mathsf{secattrSSD}(c)$ for a component c, c can be replaced by an attacker not knowing the secrets of c (e.g., the attacker tries to simulate the behaviour of c without having access to it).
- If node $\in \mathsf{secattrSSD}(c)$ for a component c, then c is an encapsulated component, to whose internals an attacker has no access.

Fig. 1 shows the SSD from the CEPS electronic purse study. We modelled the load transaction, so the relevant components are the purse card Card, the load security application module LSAM and the issuer's back-end system Issuer. The corresponding threat scenario contains an additional component Intruder, with all public connections redirected through it.

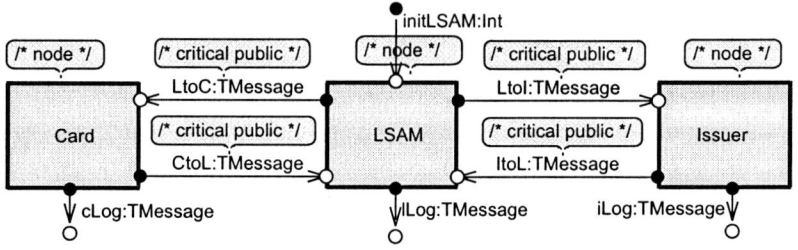

Fig. 1. System Structure Diagram with Security Attributes

Data Types and Cryptography. AUTOFOCUS offers hierarchical data types that are defined using a functional language. For models of security-critical transactions, data types for keys, messages and cryptographic operations are provided, as follows:

```
data TKey = EmptyKey | K1 | K2 | ... | Kn;
data TMessage = Empty | Msg1(...) | ... | Msgn(...)
  | Encr(getEncKey:TKey, getEncMsg:TMessage)
  | Mac(getMacKey:TKey, getMacMsg: TMessage)
  | Hash(getHashMsg:TMessage) | Key(TKey);
fun verifyMac(k,Mac(k1,msg),msg1) = ((k == k1) && (msg == msg1))
  | verifyMac(x,y,z) = False;
```

{K1,...,Kn} in the definition of type TKey is the set of key names, and the Msg1, ..., Msgn stand for possible message types used in the protocol (for example, Init(getInitM:Int) for an initialisation message m taking one integer parameter (the amount) that can be accessed via the expression getInitM(m). Encr, Mac and Hash represent encryption, computation of a message authentication code (MAC) and cryptographic hashing, and verifyMac is a function definition representing MAC verification.

Additionally, for each component c it is specified by knows(c) which set of keys c currently "knows" (initially, this is determined by the threat scenario) and by access(c) which set of keys it is allowed to know.

Behavioural Specification - State Transition Diagrams. To specify the behaviour of the components, we use AUTOFOCUS State Transition Diagrams

(STDs). STDs are state machines similar to a simplified fragment of Harel's statecharts. Formally, an STD is a pair (States, Transitions). Additionally, we fix a set **iVar** of transition-local input variables and denote with **Exp** the set of expressions in the Quest functional language, which can in particular contain the input and local variables.

Each transition $t \in$ Transitions is associated with source and target state source(t),target$(t) \in$ States, a precondition (guard) pre$(t) \in$ **Exp**, a sequence inp(t) of input expressions (p, x), where $p \in$ Ports and $x \in$ **iVar** (reading values from ports), a sequence outp(t) of output expressions (p, d), where $d \in$ **Exp** is an expression output to $p \in$ Ports when t is fired, and a sequence post(t) of postconditions (v, d), where $d \in$ **Exp** is an expression to be assigned to the variable $v \in$ **lVar** when t is fired.

We assume that for each component C in an SSD, there is an STD D that defines its behaviour. In the concrete syntax of STDs, the transitions are annotated with "pre(t):inp(t):outp(t):post(t)", where inp(t) is denoted as "$p_1?x_1; p_2?x_2; \ldots$", outp(t) as "$p_1!d_1; p_2!d_2; \ldots$" and post(t) as "$v_1 = d_1; v_2 = d_2; \ldots$".

As for the SSDs, we associate security attributes to the states and transitions of an STD by defining a mapping secattrSTD : States $\cup$ Transitions $\to \mathcal{P}$(SecAttr):

- If critical $\in$ secattrSTD(t), where $t \in$ Transitions, t is considered security-critical. A faulty implementation of t can lead to violations of security properties, making such transitions the focus of test sequence generation.
- If critical $\in$ secattrSTD(s), where $s \in$ States, then computations where state s is reached are considered security-critical.

The other security attributes have no meaning for states and transitions. In particular, we do not mark states or transitions with public, assuming that an intruder can either manipulate the complete behaviour of a component or not manipulate it at all. Note that the Intruder's behaviour must be specified as well. For the CEPS study we modelled a general intruder being able to inhibit, forward, store and fake cryptographic messages.

Security Requirements. In addition to the threat scenario, the security requirements have to be stated. Security requirements are formulated as first order predicates over execution sequences. Alternatively, formulas in temporal logic can be used, as they can be converted to such predicates. Formally, an execution sequence σ is a valuation of the ports, local variables and components for each execution step: σ : (Ports $\cup$ lVar $\cup$ Comp) $\times \mathbb{N} \to$ **Exp**. For a component c, $\sigma(c, t)$ evaluates to its current control state. Along the lines of [WLPS00], the semantics of an AUTOFOCUS system model can be given as a predicate Ψ, such that $\Psi(\sigma) = true$ if and only if σ is a valid execution sequence of the system.

To facilitate the formulation of security requirements, we defined functions operating on cryptographic messages which can also make use of the knowledge knows(c) available to the components. Besides, AUTOFOCUS supports specification patterns that can be used to build a library of generic security requirements. More detail can be found in [WJ02].

3 Generating Test Sequences for Vulnerabilities

In specification-based testing (see e.g. [DBG01] as a more recent example of the many approaches documented in the literature), test sequences are generated from a specification and used to verify the implementation. To test an implementation for vulnerabilities, we compute test sequences from the security model covering possible violations of the security requirements.

In terms of the above specification framework, a test sequence is a projection of an execution sequence σ to the ports, describing the input/output behaviour. Test scenarios are given by test case specifications, formulated as predicates $\Phi_i(\sigma)$. Test sequences for Φ_i are valid executions fulfilling the Φ_i and can be computed as solutions to $\Psi \wedge \Phi_i$. In AUTOFOCUS, a constraint solver is used for this purpose [LP00]. To ensure termination of the search (provided the expressions on the transitions terminate), σ must be limited by a maximum length.

3.1 Vulnerability Coverage Using Mutations

As it is not feasible to exhaustively test every behaviour of a security-critical system, first appropriate test case specifications have to be selected. For security testing, the aim is to cover a large number of possible vulnerabilities.

One can use structural coverage criteria such as state or transition coverage on the models [OXL99] and restrict them to those marked "critical", but this has the drawback that it does not take into account the security requirements.

The difficulty with defining coverage criteria related to the security requirements is that they are mostly universal properties. Such security requirements Φ_i can only be used to verify the model, not the implementation. If a trace fulfilling $\neg\Phi_i$ is found, the model violates the requirement and must be corrected. Otherwise, Φ_i cannot be used to select relevant traces, as *all* traces satisfy Φ_i.

In this case, mutation testing resp. fault injection techniques [Off95, VM98] prove to be promising approaches. In mutation testing, errors are introduced into a program (leading to a set of mutants), and the quality of a test suite is measured by its ability to distinguish the mutants from the original program (to "kill" the mutants). Fault injection works in a similar way, but is often also used for reliability evaluation (determining if a program tolerates a perturbation of the code or data states).

We introduce errors into the specification of the security-related behaviour, generate the threat scenarios and determine if and how the introduced errors can lead to security violations. The introduced errors can correspond to errors in the implementation or to attacks leading to such errors, e.g. subjecting a smart-card to environmental stress.

In our formal framework, mutations are generated by selecting a transition t of the STD of a component to be tested and applying a mutation function $\epsilon : \mathbf{Exp} \to \mathcal{P}(\mathbf{Exp})$ either to the precondition $pre(t)$, or to one of the output expressions or postconditions. This leads to a set of mutated transitions t'_j.

The mutation function ϵ can be based on general mutations for expressions and operands (e.g. operator or operand replacement) proposed for Ada by Offutt

$e \in \mathbf{Exp}$	$\epsilon(e)$	
a of type Bool	$\epsilon(a) \cup \neg a \cup \mathbf{true}$	missing or wrongly implemented condition
$a == b$	$\{(a{==}y)\|y{\in}\epsilon(b)\} \cup \{(x{==}b)\|x{\in}\epsilon(a)\} \cup$ **true**	faulty check, e.g. for an identity of a party
$a \wedge b$	(analogous to $a == b$, possibly also $(a \vee y), (x \vee b)$ ($\wedge$ replaced by $\vee$),...)	boolean operator replacement
	(similarly for other boolean operators)	
$\mathsf{Encr}(k, a)$	$\{\mathsf{Encr}(k', a)\|k' \in \mathsf{knows}(c)\} \cup$ $\{\mathsf{Encr}(k, x)\|x \in \epsilon(a)\}$	key confusion
$\mathsf{Mac}(k,a), \mathsf{Hash}(a)$	(analogous to $\mathsf{Encr}(k, a)$)	
$\mathsf{Key}(k)$	$\{\mathsf{Key}(k')\|k' \in \mathsf{knows}(c)\}$	
$\mathsf{verifyMac}(a)$	$\{\mathsf{verifyMac}(x)\|x \in \epsilon(a)\} \cup \mathbf{true}$	faulty MAC verification
$\mathsf{Msg1}(a_1,\ldots,a_n)$	$\{\mathsf{Msg1}(x_1, a_2, \ldots, a_n)\|x_1 \in \epsilon(a_1)\} \cup \ldots$ $\cup \{\mathsf{Msg1}(a_1, a_2, \ldots, x_n)\|x_n \in \epsilon(a_n)\}$ $\cup \mathsf{Empty}$	corrupted message
$\mathsf{is\_Msg1}(a)$	$\{is\_Msg1(x)\|x \in \epsilon(a)\} \cup \mathbf{true}$	missing type check

Fig. 2. Possible mutations

[OVJ96]. For security testing, ϵ should be based on common programming errors likely to lead to vulnerabilities, such as missing plausibility checks or wrong use of identities [AKS96]. In addition, in our model cryptography must be considered, leading to mutations corresponding to confusion of keys or secrets or missing or wrongly implemented verification of authentication codes.

Figure 2 shows such mutations, based on the AUTOFOCUS model described in Section 2. The actual mutation function ϵ to be applied depends on the available time and computing power. Only part of the proposed mutations can be selected (e.g. only replacement of boolean (sub-)expressions by **true** corresponding to missing checks), or other mutations (e.g. from [OVJ96]) can be added.

Now, we proceed as follows. For the component c to be tested, we determine the set of mutated STDs (derived by replacing a transition t with t'_j). The transitions t are chosen from the transitions marked critical. We now generate the threat scenarios, but take the mutated version of c instead of the original one. This way, we obtain a mutated system model Ψ'. For each security requirement Φ_i, we then try to compute a system run satisfying $\Psi' \wedge \neg \Phi_i$ using the test sequence generator. If this is successful, the mutation of t to t'_j introduces a vulnerability with respect to Φ_i and the trace σ shows how it can be exploited.

The input data to c from all traces σ determined this way gives us a test suite for c, covering possible vulnerabilities with respect to the security properties and the attack scenario. To determine the expected outputs, we use the original specification of c as an oracle.

Example. To demonstrate test sequence generation for the CEPS Card component, we chose a small subset of the mutations explained: subterms in the preconditions of critical transitions can be replaced by **true** (first line of Fig. 2).

This results in 9 mutations, 4 of which lead to test sequences violating security requirements (e.g. the omission of a MAC verification makes it possible that different amounts are credited according to the card's and issuer's log entries). The corresponding test sequences are computed by AUTOFOCUS in approx. 300s and depicted as AUTOFOCUS EETs (Extended Event Traces, showing the communication between the components in a similar way as message sequence charts). More detail can be found in [WJ02].

3.2 Concretization of Abstract Tests

The abstract test sequences computed from the formal security specification still have to be translated to concrete test data (i.e., byte sequences) that can be used to test the actual implementation. In many cases, concretization can be achieved using straightforward mappings between abstract and concrete test data [DBG01], and executing the test using a test driver that passes the inputs to the component to be tested and verifies if the outputs are as expected. However, testing security-critical systems involves additional complications:

- In formal specifications, cryptographic primitives are usually modelled symbolically, rather than as sequences of bytes, to make verification feasible (see [AJ01] for a justification of this general approach). The test driver must map these symbols to sequences of bytes in a consistent way. Conversely, sequences of bytes created and output by the tested component (e.g. random values such as nonces or session keys) must be stored by the test driver and used in place of the symbols in the test data of the remainder of the execution.
- Sometimes, values (such as transaction numbers or time stamps) are abstracted away in formal specifications to simplify verification (and because they are seen to be independent from a security property at hand). These have to be included in the concrete test data in a consistent way.
- If encryption is used, the test driver must know the corresponding keys and encryption algorithms to be able to compute the encrypted input data and verify encrypted output data.
- Hash values or message authentication codes contained in the output data can only be verified when the complete data that was hashed is available to the test driver.

We fix a set of transaction variables TransV and define a concretization of abstract messages by mapping each message type M in the data type definitions (see Section 2, e.g. Init) to a sequence concrete$(M) : d_1^M, d_2^M, \ldots, d_{n_M}^M$ of concrete data elements $d_i^M \in \mathbb{Z} \cup$ TransV $\cup$ **Exp**. d_i^M can be

- an integer value (corresponding to a constant sequence of bytes)
- a transaction variable (used to represent transaction data such as timestamps to be stored by the test driver)
- an AUTOFOCUS expression, in which message M can be referenced by "this"

In the last case, the expression is evaluated and the result is again concretized. The transaction variables $v \in \mathsf{TransV}$ are associated with a set $\mathsf{values}(v) \subseteq \mathbb{Z}$ of possible values. In addition, each data element has to be assigned a field length, which we omit here for simplification. Keys k are mapped directly to a transaction variable $\mathsf{concrete}(k) : d_1^k \in \mathsf{TransV}$. The actual concretization, i.e. the values for the d_i^M and $\mathsf{values}(v)$ must be provided by the developer.

An algorithm for the test driver is given in Fig. 3. It uses the algorithms **gen_sequence** and **verify_sequence** to generate concrete test data from abstract input messages to a component, resp. to compare abstract output messages to the test data received. In **verify_sequence**, $first(s)$ denotes the prefix of s corresponding to d_i^M, $removefirst(s)$ denotes the remaining part of s.

The idea of the algorithm is as follows. Constants in $\mathsf{concrete}(M)$ are passed directly to the implementation or compared to the received data. If a transaction variable v appears in $\mathsf{concrete}(M)$ for an input message, either a new concrete value is chosen for v and sent, or an already chosen value from the store *store* is sent. When data is received corresponding to v, it is either compared to the value already chosen, or the received value is added to the store. Encrypted messages, hashes and message authentication codes can be computed on sending using the data available. On reception, it is possible that the concrete byte sequence for a key or part of the data to be hashed is not yet available to the test driver, so for verification, in **gen_sequence** arbitrary concrete values that may not correspond to the actual values would be chosen and added to the store. In this case, instead a condition is added to *conditions*. The conditions are verified by the test driver as soon as they become evaluatable. The processing of messages by the test driver is repeated for each step of the test sequence (sending or receiving a message M_{abstr} to/from port p of the component under test). Note that if more than one transaction is to be tested using a single test sequence, the store must be reset between the transactions. Besides, in some cases a fixed prolog to the test sequences may have to be generated by the test driver.

Example. The first message sent from the LSAM to the Card in the CEPS model is of the form Init(getInitM : Int). The concretization mapping for Init is $\mathsf{concrete}(\mathsf{Init}) = 90, 50, 00, 00, 18, 17, DTHR_{LDA}, CURR_{LDA}, \ldots, \mathsf{getInitM}(\mathsf{this}), 00$, where $DTHR_{LDA}$ (transaction date/time) and $CURR_{LDA}$ (currency code) are transaction variables for which the possible values are defined. For example, $\mathsf{values}(DTHR_{LDA}) = \{x \in \mathbb{Z} : x \text{ is BCD coded date/time}\}$. Thus, the test driver translates a message Init(10) to the card e.g. to the byte sequence 90,50,00,00,18,17,02,04,04,09,01,0C,CC,0E,...,<u>00,00,00,0A</u>,00 (the underlined part corresponds to the transaction amount 10).

Similarly, if a reply is expected, the concretization is compared to the actual byte sequence received. In the example test sequence from [WJ02], the concretization of the expected reply contains a transaction identifier NT_{CEP}, which is stored so it can be sent out in later messages, a MAC $S1$ that can be verified, and a hash value h that is added to the constraints to be checked at a later execution step. For more detail, see [WJ02].

VAR $store : \mathcal{P}(\text{TransV} \times \mathbb{Z})$, $conditions : \mathcal{P}(\textbf{Exp}) = \emptyset$;

algorithm do_test
for each step (p, M_{abstr}) in test sequence
    if input message: send $gen\_sequence(M_{abstr})$ to p
    else wait for output s on p (fail on timeout)
        if $verify_sequence(M_{abstr}, s) = $ **false**: fail
    if $\exists\, c \in conditions$: c evaluatable and $\textsf{evaluate}(c) = $ **false**: fail

algorithm gen_sequence(M_{abstr})
{compute concrete data from abstract message M_{abstr}}
$s \leftarrow \epsilon$
if $M_{abstr} = \textsf{Encr}(k, x)$ or $M_{abstr} = \textsf{Mac}(k, x)$ or $M_{abstr} = \textsf{Hash}(x)$:
    $concr\_msg \leftarrow \textsf{gen\_sequence}(x)$
    if $M_{abstr} = \textsf{Encr}(k, x)$ or $M_{abstr} = \textsf{Mac}(k, x)$: $concr\_key \leftarrow \textsf{gen\_sequence}(k)$
    apply encryption, mac generation or hashing to $concr\_msg$; append to s
else determine message type M of M_{abstr}; $(d_1^M, \ldots, d_{n_M}^M) \leftarrow \textsf{concrete}(M)$
    for $i \in \{1 \ldots n_M\}$:
        if $d_i^M \in \mathbb{Z}$: append d_i^M to s
        elseif $d_i^M \in \textsf{TransV}$:
            if $\exists y : (d_i^M, y) \in store$: append y to s
            else choose $y \in \textsf{values}(d_i^M)$; append y to s, $store \leftarrow store \cup (d_i^M, y)$
        elseif $d_i^M \in \textbf{Exp}$: append $\textsf{gen\_sequence}(\textsf{evaluate}(d_i^M[\textbf{this} \leftarrow M_{abstr}]))$ to s
return s

algorithm verify_sequence(M_{abstr}, s)
{verify concrete data s w.r.t. abstract message M_{abstr}}
if $M_{abstr} = \textsf{Encr}(k, x)$:
    if $\exists concr\_key : (k, concr\_key) \in store$:
        $concr\_msg \leftarrow \textsf{decrypt}(concr\_key, s)$; $\textsf{verify\_sequence}(x, concr\_msg)$
    else $conditions \leftarrow conditions \cup \{\textsf{verify\_sequence}(M_{abstr}, s)\}$
elseif $M_{abstr} = \textsf{Mac}(k, x)$ or $M_{abstr} = \textsf{Hash}(x)$:
    if $\textsf{gen\_sequence}(x)$ computable without changing store
        and $\exists concr\_key : (k, concr\_key) \in store$ (for $M_{abstr} = \textsf{Mac}(k, x)$):
        $concr\_msg \leftarrow \textsf{gen\_sequence}(x)$; compare hash/mac of $concr\_msg$ to s
    else $conditions \leftarrow conditions \cup \{\textsf{verify\_sequence}(M_{abstr}, s)\}$
else determine message type M of M_{abstr}; $(d_1^M, \ldots, d_{n_M}^M) \leftarrow \textsf{concrete}(M)$
    for $i \in \{1 \ldots n_M\}$:
        if $d_i^M \in \mathbb{Z}$: compare($first(s), d_i^M$); $s \leftarrow removefirst(s)$
        elseif $d_i^M \in \textsf{TransV}$:
            if $\exists y : (d_i^M, y) \in store$: compare($first(s), y$); $s \leftarrow removefirst(s)$
            else $store \leftarrow store \cup (d_i^M, first(s))$; $s \leftarrow removefirst(s)$
        elseif $d_i^M \in \textbf{Exp}$:
            $\textsf{verify\_sequence}(\textsf{evaluate}(d_i^M[\textbf{this} \leftarrow M_{abstr}]), first(s))$
            $s \leftarrow removefirst(s)$
return false if any comparison failed

Fig. 3. Test Driver Algorithm

4 Related Work

There has been extensive research into specification-based testing, including [DF93,PS97,HNS97]; a complete overview has to be omitted. Here we used [LP00] as it has been built into the tool AUTOFOCUS; one could also have used a different approach.

Some of that work has been applied to safety-critical systems; our focus, however, is to adapt these concepts to the domain of security-critical systems with its specific characteristics as explained in Section 1 (most prominently, the use of cryptography). To the best of our knowledge, this is the first published work using formally generated test-sequences for security-critical systems, apart from [JW01b] which concerns testing of firewalls.

Dushina et al. explain concretization in their Genevieve framework [DBG01], but do not address the specific issues we explained in Section 3.2. The AVA approach [VM98] is conceptually similar to the fault insertion explained in Section 3.1, but the focus is on identifying critical statements rather than finding test sequences (for which random distributions are used), and it does not consider cryptographic mechanisms.

5 Conclusion

We presented work on generating test sequences for transaction systems from a formal security model supported by the CASE tool AUTOFOCUS. Going beyond classical specification-based conformance testing, the test sequences are determined with respect to stated security requirements. Using mutations of the system specification and attack scenarios, test sequences are generated that give increased confidence that a system meets the relevant security requirements. We gave results on concretizing abstract test sequences, to be able to apply them to existing implementations. The problem of test case explosion is handled in so far as only system parts considered as security-critical are tested.

The proposed method seems suitable to be applied to the application domain of security-critical systems, since it allows to find tests likely to detect possible vulnerabilities even in complex execution scenarios. Consideration of domain-specific concepts such as cryptography and random numbers is supported. Given that security aspects are playing an increasingly important role in the development of distributed systems, having a way to do methodological testing of security-critical systems should be a worthwhile goal.

In general, it is infeasible to establish completely that an implementation faithfully implements its specification. So even given a specification that is proved secure, our approach of ensuring on the implementation level that a system satisfies certain critical security requirements seems to be indispensable.

We explained our approach at the example of the CEPS purchase transaction protocol; it is applicable to security-critical systems in general. Note that our approach only aims to find vulnerabilities that can be detected at the level of abstraction of a given specification (which may however be lowered by refining the specification). Although we had to choose a method of generating test-sequences from formal specifications, the general approach is independent from the specific method, and also from the formal semantics of the used method AUTOFOCUS.

References

[AJ01] M. Abadi and J. Jürjens. Formal eavesdropping and its computational interpretation. In *TACS '01*, volume 2215 of *LNCS*. Springer, 2001.

[AKS96] T. Aslam, I. Krsul, and E. Spafford. Use of A Taxonomy of Security Faults. In *19th National Information Systems Security Conference*, Baltimore, 1996.

[BS01] M. Broy and K. Stolen, editors. *Specification and Development of Interactive Systems*. Springer, 2001.

[CEP01] CEPSCO. Common Electronic Purse Specifications, 2001. Available at http://www.cepsco.com.

[DBG01] J. Dushina, M. Benjamin, and D. Geist. Semi-Formal Test Generation with Genevieve. In *DAC*, 2001.

[DF93] J. Dick and A. Faivre. Automating the generation and sequencing of test cases from model-based specifications. In *FME '93*, pages 268–284, 1993.

[GSG99] S. Gritzalis, D. Spinellis, and P. Georgiadis. Security protocols over open networks and distributed systems. *Comp. Communic.*, 22(8):695–707, 1999.

[HNS97] S. Helke, T. Neustupny, and T. Santen. Automating Test Case Generation from Z Specifications with Isabelle. In *ZUM '97*, volume 1212 of *LNCS*, pages 52–71. Springer, 1997.

[JW01a] Jan Jürjens and Guido Wimmel. Security modelling for electronic commerce: The Common Electronic Purse Specifications. In *First IFIP conference on e-commerce, e-business, and e-government (I3E)*. Kluwer, 2001.

[JW01b] Jan Jürjens and Guido Wimmel. Specification-based testing of firewalls. In *Andrei Ershov 4th International Conference "Perspectives of System Informatics" (PSI'01)*, LNCS. Springer, 2001.

[LP00] H. Lötzbeyer and A. Pretschner. Testing concurrent reactive systems with constraint logic programming. In *2nd Workshop on Rule-Based Constraint Reasoning and Programming*, Singapore, 2000.

[Off95] J. Offutt. Practical Mutation Testing. In *12th International Conference on Testing Computer Software*, 1995.

[OVJ96] J. Offutt, J. Voas, and J.Payne. Mutation Operators for Ada. Technical Report ISSE-TR-96-09, George Mason University, 1996.

[OXL99] J. Offutt, Y. Xiong, and S. Liu. Criteria for Generating Specification-based Tests. In *IEEE Conf. on Engineering of Complex Computer Systems*, 1999.

[PS97] J. Peleska and M. Siegel. Test automation of safety-critical reactive systems. *South African Computer Jounal*, 19:53–77, 1997.

[VM98] J. Voas and G. McGraw. *Software Fault Injection: Inoculating Programs Against Errors*. Wiley, 1998.

[WJ02] G. Wimmel and J. Jürjens. Specification-Based Test Generation for Security-Critical Systems Using Mutations, 2002. Long version, available at http://www4.in.tum.de/~wimmel/.

[WLPS00] G. Wimmel, H. Lötzbeyer, A. Pretschner, and O. Slotosch. Specification Based Test Sequence Generation with Propositional Logic. *Journal on Software Testing Verification and Reliability*, 10, 2000.

[WW01] G. Wimmel and A. Wißpeintner. Extended description techniques for security engineering. In *IFIP SEC*, 2001.

A Formal Definition of Function Points for Automated Measurement of B Specifications

Hassan Diab, Marc Frappier, and Richard St-Denis

Département de mathématiques et d'informatique, Université de Sherbrooke,
Sherbrooke, Québec, Canada, J1K 2R1
Phone: (819) 821 8000 ext. 2096, Fax: (819) 821 8200
{Hassan.Diab, Marc.Frappier, Richard.St-Denis}@dmi.usherb.ca

Abstract. This paper proposes a formalization of the IFPUG Function Point (FP) definition for automated measurement of B specifications. This formal definition allows to: i) reduce the variance in FP counts due to rater interpretation of the IFPUG FP informal definition; ii) provide a better understanding of how the IFPUG FP definition should be applied; iii) automate the FP counts for B specifications, which can reduce measurement costs; and iv) identify specific holes in the IFPUG FP definition. We propose modifications to ensure completeness.

1 Introduction

Functional software size is an essential component for managing and controlling a software development project. FP analysis is one of the prominent industrial methods to measure functional size. It does not depend on a particular functional specification notation or on a system implementation. Albrecht proposed the first definition of this measure [2]. Its users are now structured as a user group, the International Function Point Users Group (IFPUG), which provides a Counting Practice Manual (CPM) [10]. Their definition of FP is the following: *"A function point is a synthetic metric that is comprised of the weighted totals of the inputs, outputs, inquiries, logical files or user data groups, and interfaces belonging to an application."*

The FP measure may be used to: estimate development effort, by relating it with FP; evaluate software quality, by computing defect density; evaluate software productivity; manage outsourcing contracts, by determining annual maintenance cost per FP; and to compare systems, specified in different languages, in terms of productivity, quality, and maintenance costs.

IFPUG FP have several weaknesses. First, the counting rules are given in plain natural language and are subject to interpretation by measurers. This problem introduces some variances on FP count depending on the rater. Studies noted a difference varying from 11% to 30 % between several counts of the same specification [8, 12, 13]. Furthermore, variations from 400% to 2 000% are observed between the FP count of an initial specification and FP count of the resulting system [9]. Moreover, FP calculation is mostly a manual process which is quite expensive. Typically, an expert can count 57 unadjusted function points per hour. For some companies with a large software portfolio (e.g., 325 000 FP), it would take around three person-years to precisely measure their portfolio.

Since the root of these weaknesses is the lack of a precise definition for the IFPUG FP method, our goal in this paper is to provide a clear and unambiguous definition for computing the *unadjusted function points* of IFPUG FP. The IFPUG CPM provides rules for counting the unadjusted function points [10]. It is these rules that must be formalized. In [7], the adequacy of several formal specification languages for the formalization of IFPUG FP has been evaluated. It was found that the B notation [1] provides some details which are essential to automatically compute the number of FP. The B method is a formal, industrial software development method for specification, design, and implementation of software products.

Since software requirement specifications depend on the language in use, the drawback of the general applicability of IFPUG FP is the lack of a direct representation of some IFPUG concepts within any specification language, the B notation in particular. It is unlikely that different measurers will consistently use the same mapping between B and IFPUG FP. For instance, Data Element Types (DET) and Record Element Types (RET) in IFPUG FP do not directly map to B concepts. The weights of function and data components in IFPUG FP are computed based on the number of DETs, RETs, and files. So any misuse of the counting rules for identifying these elements may negatively affect the measurement results. Therefore, mapping rules between B and IFPUG FP are required.

When using B in large scale projects, it is important to connect B to software metrics for an effective software engineering management. Our formal definition allows users of the B method to exploit the advantages due to the use of FP. For instance, an interesting research would be to take a number of B case studies, count the number of FP of each, and check what the implementation turns out to cost. The variation induced by implementation decisions could be an interesting factor and may mean that we should look at classes of problems.

In addition, our formal definition allows the automation of unadjusted FP counting for B specifications. It removes measurement variance and ensures perfect repeatability, because the formal definition is objective and independent of the measurer interpretation. Furthermore, the formal definition of IFPUG FP has allowed us to verify the completeness of the IFPUG FP counting rules. Interestingly, we have found that some components of a specification do not fall into any category in the IFPUG CPM. Hence, the IFPUG CPM definitions are incomplete. We have proposed modifications to ensure completeness.

This paper is structured as follows. Sections 2 and 3 provide overviews of IFPUG FP and the B method. Sections 4 and 5 provide the formal definition of IFPUG FP concepts within the B notation. Section 6 briefly describes how components are weighed. Section 7 introduces the algorithm of the unadjusted FP counting for B specifications. Section 8 introduces a case study. Finally, Section 9 concludes with an appraisal of this work.

2 Overview of Functions Points

In this section, we introduce the basic concepts of IFPUG FP as defined in the IFPUG CPM version 4.1. The following equation describes how function points, denoted by FP, are counted: $FP = UFP*VAF$.

The variable UFP denotes the number of unadjusted FP and the variable VAF denotes the value adjustment factor. The variable UFP is determined using two main categories of components: data components (e.g., files, database relations) and function components or elementary processes (updates, inquiries, reports). Data components are further divided in two categories of file: *external interface files* (EIF) and *internal logical files* (ILF). Note that in the rest of this paper we refer to a file as a data group. Elementary processes are divided into three categories: *external inputs* (EI), *external outputs* (EO), and *external inquiries* (EQ). To compute UFP, each component c is assigned a weight w_c according to its category (EIF, ILF, EI, EO, or EQ) and other parameters: for data components, these parameters are the number of data element types (DET) and the number of record element types (RET); for function components, they are the number of DET and the number of EIF and ILF referenced. The UFP is simply the sum of the component weights: $UFP = \sum_c w_c$.

The following equation describes the calculation of VAF which is determined by evaluating 14 factors, f_i, on a scale of 0 to 5 : $VAF = 0.65 + 0.01*\sum_{i=1}^{14} f_i$. There are also rules to evaluate each factor, but they are not easily formalizable. Indeed, they directly depend on human judgment of the technical elements that may have an impact on the system complexity, data communications, application type, and performance objectives for instance. It should be noted that the effort required to evaluate VAF only represents a small percentage of the total effort for FP count. Furthermore, these factors have been removed from the FP techniques that have been recently proposed, COSMIC Full Function Points [3] in particular. Hence, there is little interest for their formalization.

3 Overview of the B Method

The B method is founded on first order logic, set theory, and the theory of refinement. It is representative of the family of methods known as model oriented which represent a software by data, characterized by their invariant properties, and by services which handle these data [1]. The B method uses three notations as a specification language for software development: the mathematical notation, the generalized substitution notation, and the abstract machine notation. Set theory is the primarily mathematical notation used in B. It allows to specify the data and the software properties. Unlike classical set theory, the set theory of B is typed: a set consists of elements having all the same fundamental structure. The generalized substitution notation allows to describe the services of a software. In other words, it allows to describe the actions that a software can carry out to fulfill its functions.

The abstract machine notation allows to define sets, constants, variables, and operations which abstractly represent the data and services of a software. By doing this, it defines the operational interface of a software because it provides the mode and use conditions of its components. The sets and constants of an abstract machine represent immutable data. There are two kinds of set: abstract set and enumerated set. The definition of abstract set elements is deferred to the implementation. An enumerated set is a set defined by a complete list of its elements. The constants are characterized by a predicate of the mathematical notation. The variables of an abstract machine represent the modifiable data. As for the constants, variables are defined by a predicate called an invariant, which defines the properties that their actual values must always satisfy.

Finally, the B method includes various kinds of access relations between machines. The main relations are: **includes, uses, sees, imports,** and **extends**. Each relation imposes constraints on the access mode from the referencing machine to the referenced machine components.

3.1 Example of a B Specification

In this section, we use the B specification language to model the transactions of a simplified version of a library system (see Fig. 1). Only three transactions are modeled: `Acquire, ListBookAuthor,` and `FlagBadMember`. The last transaction is given in Section 5. Note that we will use this example in the rest of this paper to illustrate the application of our definition.

The machine in Fig. 1 describes the state variables, their invariant, and operations. The name of the machine, `Library`, is given in the first clause. `Library` has one input parameter `MaxLoanDuration`. The **SETS** clause defines the abstract sets of `Library`. The state of `Library` is defined by ten variables given in the **VARIABLES** clause. Each variable has a type given in the **INVARIANT** clause. The **INITIALIZATION** clause defines the initial state of the machine. A value is assigned to each variable by using an *elementary substitution*. Machine `Library` has several operations defined in the **OPERATIONS** clause. The main substitution of those operations is a *precondition substitution* of the form **PRE** p **THEN** S **END**, where p is a condition and S a set of elementary substitutions. This construct means that the elementary substitution (corresponding to S) is only well-defined when p holds.

4 Formal Definition Summary

The definitions provided in this paper are based on a *syntactic* analysis of B specifications. Moreover, we assume that the machines have been flattened. In other words, we consider that the access relations have been replaced by virtual machines. A virtual machine is the machine resulting from the use of an access relation between two machines. For instance, assume that a machine M_1 *includes* a machine M_2. We consider the resulting machine M_1' contains M_1 and M_2. The flattening of a specification changes its structure but it does not change its behavior from the user viewpoint. Therefore, no bias is introduced in the counting when using the flattened specification, since the functional measure is produced from the user viewpoint [10].

MACHINE *Library (MaxLoanDuration)*

CONSTRAINTS
  $MaxLoanDuration \in \mathbb{N}$
SETS
  $BOOK;\ TITLE;\ AUTHOR;\ DATE;\ MEMBER;$
  $LOAN\_STATUS = \{\ InLibrary,\ Loaned\ \};$
  $MEM\_STATUS = \{\ Bad,\ Good\ \}$
VARIABLES
  member, book, title, author; acquisitionDate, borrower,
  lastLoanDate, loanStatus, loanCount, memStatus,
INVARIANT
  $member \subseteq MEMBER \land book \subseteq BOOK \land title \in book \rightarrow TITLE \land$
  $author \in book \rightarrow AUTHOR \land acquisitionDate \in book \rightarrow DATE \land$
  $borrower \in book \nrightarrow member \land lastLoanDate \in book \nrightarrow DATE \land$
  $loanStatus \in book \rightarrow LOAN\_STATUS \land loanCount \in book \rightarrow \mathbb{N} \land$
  $memStatus \in member \rightarrow MEM\_STATUS$
INITIALIZATION
  $member := \emptyset\ ||\ book := \emptyset\ ||\ title := \emptyset\ ||\ author := \emptyset\ ||$
  $acquisitionDate := \emptyset\ ||\ borrower := \emptyset\ ||\ lastLoanDate := \emptyset\ ||$
  $loanStatus := \emptyset\ ||\ memStatus := \emptyset\ ||\ loanCount := \emptyset$
OPERATIONS
$Acquire(bbookid, btitle, bauthor, bdate) \triangleq$
  PRE
    $bbookid \in BOOK - book \land book \neq BOOK \land btitle \in TITLE \land$
    $bauthor \in AUTHOR \land bdate \in DATE$
  THEN
    $book := book \cup \{bbookid\}\ ||\ title(bbookid) := btitle\ ||$
    $author(bbookid) := bauthor\ ||\ acquisitionDate(bbookid) := bdate\ ||$
    $loanStatus(bbookid) := InLibrary\ ||\ loanCount(bbookid) := 0$
  END;
END;
$authorlist \leftarrow ListBookAuthor(bauthor) \triangleq$
  PRE
    $bauthor \in AUTHOR$
  THEN
    ANY *bookseq* **WHERE**
      $bookseq \in \text{seq}(TITLE \times \mathbb{N}) \land$
      $\textbf{ran}(bookseq) = \{\ tt, nn\ |\ tt \in TITLE \land nn \in \mathbb{N} \land$
              $\exists\ bbookid\ .\ (bbookid \in author^{-1}[\{bauthor\}] \land$
              $tt = title(bbookid) \land nn = loanCount(bbookid))\} \land$
      $sorted(bookseq, \textbf{prj1}(TITLE, \mathbb{N}))$
    THEN
      $authorlist := \{(bookseq \mapsto \textbf{card}(\textbf{dom}(bookseq)))\}$
    END
  END
END

Fig. 1. Sample B specification of a library system

Table 1 presents IFPUG FP concepts as defined in the IFPUG CPM version 4.1. The first column introduces each concept with a name and a brief description. The second column presents our interpretation of each concept within the B notation.

Table 1. The interpretation of FP concepts within the B notation

IFPUG CPM concepts	B notation
boundary	set of operations
elementary process	operation
data group (file)	subset of an abstract set
Data Element Type (DET)	variable S or a function variable f from S to T
Record Element Type (RET)	DETs are partitioned in two RETs: total and partial function variables

For instance, the *application boundary* in the IFPUG CPM corresponds to a set of operations in B specifications, because, given a set of operations, it possible to derive the set of data components which are modified or referenced by these operations. Therefore, the input of the FP counting process consists of the text of B specifications and the set of operation names to count. We denote the application boundary by F.

5 Classifying Components

In this section, we provide formal rules of the IFPUG FP definition allowing to identify the IFPUG FP component types for B specifications. Our rules are provided using conventional mathematical notations

Data Group and Data Element Types (DET). Typical examples of a data group in IFPUG FP are a group of logically related data or a relation in a relational database. It corresponds to a variable S which is a subset of an abstract set AS (i.e., $S \subseteq AS$) and the domain of a variable f which is a partial function to some other set T.

Let $\mathcal{AS}$ be the set of all abstract sets defined in a specification A. Let $\mathcal{V}$ be the set of all variables defined in A. Let $\mathcal{FV}$ be the set of all variables defined as functions in A. We denote by DG the set of data groups in specification A. It is defined as follows.

$$DG \triangleq \{S \mid S \in \mathcal{V} \land \exists\, AS, f, T : AS \in \mathcal{AS} \land S \subseteq AS \land f \in S \nrightarrow T\} \tag{1}$$

A DET in IFPUG FP is an attribute of a data group, defined as the smallest information that has a meaning. It corresponds to either a variable S, which is a subset of an abstract set AS (i.e., $S \subseteq AS$), or a variable f, which is a function from S to some other set T. We denote by $DET(S)$ the set of DETs of a data group $S \in DG$. It is defined as follows.

$$DET(S) \triangleq \{S\} \cup \{f \mid f \in \mathcal{FV} \land \exists T : f \in S \twoheadrightarrow T\} \qquad (2)$$

Record Element Types (RET). The DETs of a data group are partitioned into RETs based on the IFPUG FP definition. RETs are classified as either mandatory or optional. *"Optional subgroups are those that the user has the option of using one or none of the subgroups during an elementary process that adds or creates an instance of the data. Mandatory subgroups are subgroups where the user must use at least one."*

Obviously, it is possible to classify a DET as either optional or mandatory using the INVARIANT clause of a B specification. However, we do not know how to partition the DETs into RETs using only the specification text itself. It seems that this choice must be made by the user (which may be a subjective choice). A compromise is to define by default one RET which contains all the mandatory DETs of a data group and one RET which contains all the optional DETs of the data group.

Formally, let $\mathcal{PFV}$ be the set of all machine variables defined as partial functions and $\mathcal{TFV}$ be the set of all machine variables defined as total functions. Let $RET_m(S)$ be the mandatory RET of a data group S and $RET_o(S)$ be the optional RET of a data group S. Rules 3 and 4 provide the formal definitions of mandatory and optional RETs, respectively.

$$RET_m(S) \triangleq \{S\} \cup \{v \mid v \in DET(S) \land v \in \mathcal{TFV}\} \qquad (3)$$

$$RET_o(S) \triangleq \{v \mid v \in DET(S) \land v \in \mathcal{PFV}\} \qquad (4)$$

Internal Logical Files (ILF) and External Interface Files (EIF). A data group may be classified as an ILF or EIF. Rules 5 and 6 allow to classify the type of a data group. We denote by ILF and EIF the set of internal logical files and set of external interface files of a boundary F, respectively. We define ILF (resp. EIF) as the set of data groups which are maintained (resp. consulted without modification) by at least one operation of F.

$$ILF \triangleq \{S \mid S \in DG \land \exists o : o \in F \land maintains(o, S)\} \qquad (5)$$

$$EIF \triangleq \{S \mid S \in DG \land \exists o : o \in F \land consults(o, S) \land \\ \neg(\exists o : o \in F \land maintains(o, S))\} \qquad (6)$$

where $maintains(o, S)$ denotes that operation o maintains data group S and $consults(o, S)$ denotes that operation o consults data group S without changes.

An operation o is said to maintain a data group S if and only if there exists an elementary substitution b in o such that the left-hand side of b, $LHS(b)$, is a DET of S. Predicate $maintains(o, S)$ is defined as follows. Let B_o be the set of elementary substitutions appearing in the definition of operation o.

$$maintains(o, S) \Leftrightarrow \exists b, v : b \in B_o \land v \in DET(S) \land v = LHS(b) \qquad (7)$$

An operation o is said to consult a data group S if and only if o does not maintain S and there exists a DET v of S such that v occurs in the definition of o. Let $occurs(v, o)$ be that DET v appears in operation o. Predicate $consults(o, S)$ is defined as follows.

$$consults(o, S) \Leftrightarrow \exists\, v : v \in DET(S) \;\land\; occurs(v, o) \;\land\; \neg maintains(o, S) \tag{8}$$

By applying rules 1 to 8 to the library example, we conclude that: i) the subsets `book` and `member` are data groups classified as ILF; and ii) `book`, `title`, `author`, `acquisitionDate`, `borrower`, `lastLoanDate`, and `loanStatus`, (resp. `member` and `memStatus`) are DETs of `book` (resp. `member`). Finally, `book`, contains two RETs: $RET_o(\text{book})$ and $RET_m(\text{book})$ and `member` has one RET: $RET_m(\text{member})$.

External Inputs (EI). An EI is an elementary process that maintains data or control information. It corresponds to an operation in the B language that has inputs and maintains at least one ILF. Let EI be the set of external inputs of a specification. Let $inParam(o, p)$ denote that p is an input parameter of operation o and let $outParam(o, p)$ denote that p is an output parameter of operation o. Set EI is defined as follows.

$$EI \triangleq \{o \mid o \in F \;\land\; (\exists\, p, S : inParam(o, p) \;\land\; S \in DG \;\land\; maintains(o, S)) \;\land\; \neg(\exists\, p' : outParam(o, p'))\} \tag{9}$$

External Ouputs (EO). An EO is an elementary process that *derives* data or control information sent to outside the application boundary and possibly maintains data within the boundary. It corresponds to an operation o within the boundary that: i) has at least one output parameter considered as a derived data; ii) has at least one output parameter and there is no input parameter; or iii) has at least one output parameter and maintains an ILF; Let $derives(o, p)$ denote that operation o has a derived data p. Let EO be the set of external outputs of a specification. Set EO is defined as follows.

$$EO \triangleq \{o \mid o \in F \;\land\; \exists\, p : outParam(o, p) \;\land\; (\; derives(o, p) \;\lor\; \neg(\exists\, q : inParam(o, q)) \;\lor\; (\exists\, S : S \in ILF \;\land\; maintains(o, S))\;)\} \tag{10}$$

A detailed description of the formalization of the concept derived data is outside the scope of this paper. The reader may consult [4] for a more detailed description of this formalization.

By applying rules 9 and 10 to the library example, we conclude that `Acquire` is an EI and `ListBookAuthor` is an EO.

Completeness of IFPUG FP. In [4], a truth table, that summarizes how operations in B specification are classified in the IFPUG FP context, has been built. This table indicates the category in which an operation is classified according to our interpretation of the IFPUG CPM definitions and proposes extension to the IFPUG CPM definitions in order to have a more complete classification. Based on this table, we have been able to identify some cases that are not explicitly covered in the IFPUG CPM. Furthermore, an operation, that maintains the internal system state and has no input/output parameters, is not defined or discussed in IFPUG CPM. We believe that it should be counted as an EI. For instance, the operation `FlagBadMember` sets the status of all the members who are the current borrowers of overdue books to Bad. The operation has no input, but it modifies the system state in a way which can be recognized by the user.

$\text{FlagBadMember} \triangleq$
  $memStatus := memStatus \triangleleft$
  $\{\ bmemberid,\ newStatus\ |\ bmemberid \in member\ \wedge$
  $newStatus \in MEM\_STATUS \wedge \exists\ bbookid\ .\ (\ bbookid \in book\ \wedge$
  $bmemberid = borrower(bbookid) \wedge newStatus = Bad\ \wedge$
  $currentDate - lastLoanDate(bbookid) > MaxLoanDuration\ )\ \}$

To count operations of this kind, we propose to modify rule 9 as follows.

$$EI' \triangleq \{o\ |\ o \in F\ \wedge\ \exists\ S : S \in DG\ \wedge\ maintains(o, S)\ \wedge\ \neg(\exists\ p : outParam(o, p))\} \quad (11)$$

6 Weighing Components

The last step of the IFPUG FP count is to compute component weights. The weight (complexity level) of a data group (i.e., an ILF or an EIF) depends on the number of DETs and the number of RETs. We have already defined how to compute DETs and RETs of a data group in Section 5.1. The weight of a transaction (i.e., an EI, an EO, or an EQ) depends on the number of DETs and DGs referenced by function components. Additional details about the formal rules that identify the DETs and DGs referenced by a transaction are described in [4].

Once the referenced DETs, RETs, and DGs are known, we can compute a complexity level for each component type (ILF, EIF, EI, EO, or EQ) by using the complexity level tables of components as defined in IFPUG CPM.

In Section 5, we have defined the DETs, RETs, referenced DETs, and DGs as finite sets. In order to compute a complexity level for data or function components, we need to compute the number of elements in each finite set defined in the formal rules. To do so, we use the cardinality of a finite set E, denoted by **card**(E). For instance, we use **card**$(DET(S))$ to calculate the number of DETs of S.

7 The UFP Counting Algorithm

To compute the number of unadjusted function points (UFP) for a B specification that has been flattened, the only information needed as input (aside from the specification itself), is the list of operations included in the boundary F. This list can be provided in either of the following forms. i) A list of machine names : in that case, all operations of these machines are considered to be included in the boundary F. ii) A list of machine names and, for each machine name, a list of operation names : in that case, only the operations specifically identified are included in F.

The counting algorithm is composed of six steps, as described below. In each step, one or several formal rules, given so far, are used to compute the FP components. For instance, rule 1 is used in step 1 to compute the set of data groups DG. Recall that the formal rules are based on a syntactic analysis of a B specification.

1. Compute set DG for all the machines identified in the input
2. Compute sets RET and DET for each data group in DG
3. Compute sets EI, EO, and EQ
4. Compute sets ILF and EIF
5. Compute the weight of each element of ILF, EIF, EI, EO, and EQ
6. Compute the sum of the weights to obtain UFP

8 Case Study

In this section, we provide an illustration of the suitability and objectivity of our definitions by applying them to the full version of the library system, presented in [4] and comparing the results with three other counts. The first two counts were obtained with the IFPUG FP definitions, using two different user viewpoints. The third count is derived using a definition of IFPUG FP for use case diagrams from the UML notation. The details of this last approach are provided in [14]. The informal description of the library system is provided in [14].

For the library system, we see at least two viewpoints. In the first viewpoint, there are three data groups (book, reservation, and member). In the second viewpoint, reservation and book are considered to form a single data group, because reservations do not exist without books. Hence, they are sufficiently logically related to form a single data group. This choice has a significant impact on the UFP count, because the number of referenced data groups is used in the calculation of transaction weights.

The UFPs of the library system are: 91, 88, 75, and 112 using B formal rules, CPM1 (viewpoint 1), CPM2 (viewpoint 2), and Use cases of [14], respectively. Two people participated in the counts: the first three were made by the same person; the last count was made by another. The UFP count using our formal rules is 91, which is very close to the IFPUG CPM count based on the first viewpoint (88). The 3.4 % difference arises from the evaluation of function component complexity.

The CPM2 count is very different from both the B count (21 %) and the CPM1 count (17 %), due to the fact that books and reservations are combined into a single data group. It is an example of the subjectivity of the function point measure as defined in the IFPUG CPM.

Finally, the UCD (Use Case Diagram) count is significantly higher than the B count (23 %), because it identifies more function components (26 instead of 19). In the UCD approach of [14], function components are identified using events from sequence diagrams. The UCD model presented in [14] decomposes some B operations into several events, which results into a higher number of function components in the UCD count. If another UCD specification style was used in [14], the difference could be smaller.

9 Conclusion

The idea of this work was to show the subjectivity and incompleteness of the IFPUG FP definition, on the one hand. On the other hand, it was to provide a formal basis that can be used to develop a tool supporting the counting of FP for B specifications. The main contributions of this study are:

- removing the variance between measures in order to facilitate the validation and evaluation of the measure accuracy;
- providing a better understanding about the application of the IFPUG FP counting rules;
- identifying holes and ensure completeness of the IFPUG FP counting rules which is very helpful for IFPUG users and authors;
- connecting the B language to software metrics;
- increasing the objectivity of the IFPUG FP counting rules;
- providing a basis for the development of a tool that supports the FP measure in order to reduce measurement cost.

The formal rules provided in this paper are, however, specific to the B notation, hence automation is directly applicable to a B specification. Furthermore, these rules might be indirectly applicable to a specification written in OMT or UML, using translation rules from object-oriented notation to the B notation. We also hope that these rules, being formal, will help in reducing the subjectivity of FP counts in other specification languages, because they are more precise than IFPUG CPM counting rules. We also identified cases which were not covered by the IFPUG CPM rules. Therefore, it was necessary to propose modifications to take those cases into account and ensure the completeness of our formal rules.

The interpretation we made of the IFPUG CPM rules is perhaps not exactly the same as the ones used by some experts in the field. However, there is probably no universal agreement on a single interpretation of the IFPUG CPM rules. What is most important is that FP becomes an objective measure, repeatable and free of measurement variance due to human interpretation. That can only improve all activities based on FP measurement. The actual number of FP for a system is not in itself of interest for software managers. What is interesting is cost, quality and productivity. The interest in FP lies in its ability to predict cost, to compute quality ratio (defect / FP), productivity ratio (FP / effort), to benchmark and compare systems based on size (ex: system A is twice as big as system B). The less variance there is in FP measurement, the more reliable these management measures become.

From an analytical viewpoint, there are some open issues to resolve with the formalization of the IFPUG FP definition. More research is needed in order to address the following problems: i) our rules of a data group are based on a classical specification style in B. They may not properly identify a data group if the specification is written in another style; and ii) more investigations are needed to provide an objective definition of derived data and distinguish between optional RETs and mandatory RETs.

References

1. Abrial, J.-R.: *The B-Book*, Cambridge University Press, 1996.
2. Albrecht, A.J. and Gaffney, J.E. Jr.: Software function, source lines of code, and development effort prediction: a software science validation, *IEEE Transactions on Software Engineering*, **SE-9** (6) 639-648, 1983.
3. COSMIC FFP Measurement Manual, version 2.1, Laboratoire de Recherche en Gestion des Logiciels (LRGL), Université du Québec à Montréal, Québec, Canada, May 2001. http://www.cosmicon.com.
4. Diab, H.: Counting Function Points From B Specifications, Technical Report 246, Dépt. de mathématiques et d'informatique, Université de Sherbrooke, Québec, Canada, January 1999.
5. Dreger, J.B.: *Function points analysis*, Prentice-Hall, 1989.
6. Facon P., Laleau R., and Nguyen H. P.: Mapping Object Conceptual Diagrams into B Specifications. In: *Methods Integration Workshop*, Springer-Verlag, 1996.
7. Frappier, M.: An Overview of Formal Specification Languages and their Adequacy for Formalizing the Definition of Function Points, Technical Report, Département de mathématiques et d'informatique, Université de Sherbrooke, Sherbrooke, February, 1999.
8. Furey, S. and Kitchenham, B.: Point/counterpoint function points, *IEEE Software*, **14** (2) 28–33, 1997.
9. Habrias, H.: *La mesure du logiciel*, Teknea, 1994.
10. IFPUG: Function Points Counting Practices Manual, Release 4.1, International Function Points Users Group, 1999. http://www.ifpug.org
11. Jeffery, D.R. and Low, G.C.: Comparison of function point counting techniques, *IEEE Transactions on Software Engineering*, **SE-19** (5) 529–532, 1993.
12. Kemerer, C.F. and Porter, B.S.: Improving the reliability of function point measurement: An empirical study, *IEEE Transactions on Software Engineering*, **18** (11) 1011–1024, 1992.
13. Kemerer, C.F.: Reliability of function point measurement: A field experiment, *Communications of the ACM*, **36** (2) 85–97, 1993.
14. Labyad, S., Frappier, M., St-Denis, and R., Déry, D.: Calcul des points de fonction à partir du diagramme de cas d'utilisation de la notation UML, in 9th *International Workshop on Software Measurement*, September 1999.

Machine Code Type Safety

Fan Guo, YiYun Chen, and RongGui Hu

Department of Computer Science and Technology,
University of Science and Technology of China, Hefei 230026
(fguo@mail.ustc.edu.cn)

Abstract. Fundamental safety properties of machine code such as memory safety could be subsumed by type safety, so if the code is type safe, then it satisfies the fundamental safety policy. We present a new approach based on ELF logical framework to check type safety of machine code, and implement a prototype system to do experiments on sample programs.

1 Introduction

With the development of Internet, each node of the network faces two kinds of menace. Firstly, servers providing services have to be assured safe, otherwise, hackers could find the hole and exploit it, then control the machine; on the other hand, before running the third-party application and plug-ins, the host has to assure that these codes are safe and they would not destroy the local critical data. When could we say "machine code is safe", how can we assure it is safe? In fact, the same machine code maybe safe on some hosts, but unsafe on others, because safety is relative to the local safety policy. We said "machine code is unsafe", when the code violates the local safety policy.

At the very minimum, any safety policy for untrusty machine code running locally must guarantee three kind of fundamental safety properties [1],which are *memory safety, Stack safety and Control flow safety*. *Type safety* could subsume those fundamental safety properties by encoding them in the typing discipline, which is a way of assigning intention to raw data and code, and annotations have to be produced to do that. Compilers for high level programming language typically accumulate much information about a program during the compiler process, and traditionally, this additional information is discarded. We could obtain this information through parsing or program analysis and use them as the annotation of the object code. Then after encoding the annotation in the typing discipline, we could check whether the code obeys the typing discipline, that is, whether the code is type safety.

There are many researches concerning *Type Safety* such as TAL[2,3] and PCC[4,5] which have some common points: by analyzing the type of code blocks, use Type Theory to decide whether the block is type safe according to the semantics of the code. We bring forward another method, not to analysis the type of a whole code block, but to check whether each instruction to be executed violates the safety policy, by enforcing the type condition on each valid memory address and tracking memory state information changed by the semantics of each instruction. Our approach predigest the type checking process because the type information is only encoded to be the representation belonging to simple typed-λcalculus type which is easy to be checked.

2   Our Approach

In our approach, the whole valid memory address space is looked upon as address space with type. Each safe visit to a memory address must satisfy three conditions:
1) each memory address has definite type; 2) read-write bytes must be consistent with the size of the memory address type; 3) if the instruction is indirect addressing, then the computed address to be visited must satisfy the above two conditions.

We use symbolic expression to track the changes of the value and the type of machine registers and memory address, analysis the change of the whole memory state mirror before and after an instruction is executed according to the updated semantics of the instruction. And the type system of memory addresses and machine registers are subject to the type system of the high-level program language such as C and SML, which has simple representation, and the simple type system facilitates the whole type checking process. In our experiments, we use a sub type system of C language to assign the type to each valid memory address and machine registers.

Figure 1 gives the syntax of a logical system in the sub type system of C Language. The basic type is int and void, and void type is only used in the return type of function type. Type constructors include array, pointer and function type. Besides the basic terms, we must provide the basic axioms and inference rules used to check type correctness and type inference. Figure 2 gives the axioms and inference rules according to our simple type system. With the above logic syntax, axioms and inference rules, we informally describe our approach on the simple type system. To formally describe the whole logic system, we use a simplified ELF logic representation framework [7] to formalize the terms, axioms and inference rules, as Fig. 3 shows.

$$\begin{aligned}
\bullet &::= \text{int} \mid \text{void} \mid \text{arr} \bullet \text{num} \mid \text{ptr} \bullet \mid \bullet_1 \bullet_2 \\
e &::= \text{num} \mid \text{mem} \mid \text{add } e_1 \, e_2 \mid \text{sub } e_1 \, e_2 \mid \text{mul } e_1 \, e_2 \\
&\mid \text{div } e_1 \, e_2 \mid \text{sel4 } e \\
re &::= \text{lt } e_1 \, e_2 \mid \text{gt } e_1 \, e_2 \mid \text{eq } e_1 \, e_2 \mid \text{neq } e_1 \, e_2 \mid \\
&\mid \text{ge } e_1 \, e_2 \mid \text{le } e_1 \, e_2 \\
ass &::= \text{saferd4 } e \mid \text{type } e \bullet \mid \text{safewr4 } e \mid \text{size} \bullet \text{num}
\end{aligned}$$

Fig. 1. Logical syntax

Figure 4 describes the idea of the type check algorithm. The whole type checking procedure, which based on the idea of Necula[5], is looked upon as a set of subgoals. Subgoals are judgements produced through the analysis of the annotation of object code, which consist of sub-subgoals and at last reduce to axioms and basic inference rules. The subgoals is denoted by labels, so that the whole type checking procedure is a sequence of labels, each of which denotes either a subgoal or an axiom or an inference rule, resulting in the greatly decreased size of the representation of the procedure.

$$\frac{}{\triangleright \text{size int } 4}\text{szint} \qquad \frac{}{\triangleright \forall T.\text{size }(\text{ptr } T)\ 4}\text{szptr}$$

$$\frac{\triangleright \text{type } A\ (\text{arr } T\ N)\quad \triangleright \text{lt } O\ N\quad \triangleright \text{ge } O\ 0\quad \triangleright \text{size } T\ 4}{\triangleright \text{saferd4 }(\text{add } A\ (\text{mul } O\ 4))}\text{rdarr4}$$

$$\frac{\triangleright \text{type } A\ T \qquad \triangleright \text{size } T\ 4}{\triangleright \text{saferd4 } A}\text{rd4}$$

$$\frac{\triangleright \text{type } A\ (\text{ptr } T)\quad \triangleright \text{type }(\text{sel4 } A)\ T\quad \triangleright \text{size } T\ 4}{\triangleright \text{saferd4 }(\text{sel4 } A)}\text{rdptr4}$$

Fig. 2. Axioms and inference rules

Kind	K	::= Type | A→K
Families0	A	::= a | $A_1 \bullet A_2$
Families1	B	::= $aM_1..M_n$ | $B1 \bullet B2$ | $\bullet x{:}A.B$
Objects	M	::= $\lambda x{:}A.M$ | $cM_1..M_n$ | $xM_1...M_n$

Fig. 3. Simplified ELF

$solve(aM_1..M_n)\qquad\qquad = subgoals(B, aM_1..M_n)$

$subgoals(B_1 \bullet B_2)\qquad\qquad = subgoals(B_2, B) \bullet solve(B_1)$
$subgoals(\bullet x{:}A.B_p, B)\qquad = \exists x{:}A.subgoals(B_p, B)$
$subgoals(aM_1..M_n', aM_1..M_n) = M_1' \cong M2...M_n' \cong M_n$

Fig. 4. Type check algorithm

For example, supposed a goal "saferd4 A'" has to be proved. And a subgoal "typeass A' int" exists. The prove procedure is :

```
solve(saferd4 A')
= subgoals(•A:exp.(•T:ty.typeass A T•size T 4)•
   saferd4 A, saferd4 A)
= ∃A:exp.(saferd4 A'≅ saferd4 A)∧∃T:ty.solve(typeass A T)
   ∧ solve(size T 4)
```

Firstly *solve* is used, the inference rule *rd4*, *rdarr4*, *rdptr4* matches, since all of them has the last assertion like "saferd4 (...)". Then *subgoals* is called on rule *rd4*. After decomposing the rule, the sub goals are either axioms or equalities whose expression on the two sides are identical, so that the goal is proved successfully.

Based on our approach to assure the type safety of machine code, we implements a prototype system. Fig. 5 describes the architecture of the system. The prototype system is implemented on Redhat Linux 6.2, using ELF binary format, based on IA32 architecture [8]. Certifying compiler is implemented based on LCC [7].

3 Conclusion

Type safety subsumes the fundamental safety properties such as memory safety, control flow safety and stack safety. If the object code is type safe, we say the code satisfies the fundamental safety policy.

We provide a new approach to check type safety of object code, using the type checking technique based on ELF framework, and implement a prototype system. The approach does not consider the type of a code block, but analyzes the semantics of each machine instruction, by enforcing type conditions on the accessible memory address and tracking the whole memory state with symbolic expressions, to check whether the object code is type safe.

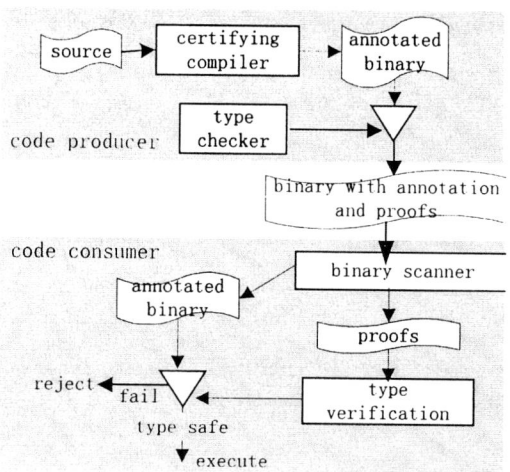

Fig. 5. Architecture of the prototype system

References

1. Dexter Kozen. Language-Based Security. In M. Kutylowski, L. Pacholski, and T. Wierzbicki, editors, *Proc. Conf. Mathematical Foundations of Computer Science (MFCS'99)*, volume 1672 of *Lecture Notes in Computer Science*, pages 284--298. Springer-Verlag, September 1999.

2. Greg Morrisett, David Walker, Karl Crary, and Neal Glew. From System F to Typed Assembly Language. In *ACM* Transactions on Programming Languages and Systems, 21(3):528-569, May 1999.
3. Greg Morrisett, Karl Crary, Neal Glew, Dan Grossman, Richard Samuels, Frederick Smith, David Walker, Stephanie Weirich, and Steve Zdancewic. TALx86: A Realistic Typed *Assembly Language. In the* 1999 ACM SIGPLAN Workshop on Compiler Support for System Software, pages 25-35, Atlanta, GA, USA, May 1999
4. George C. Necula. Ph.D. Thesis Compiling with Proofs. Carnegie Mellon University, September 1998.
5. George C. Necula, S. P. Rahul. Oracle-Based Checking of Untrusted Software. In Proceedings of the 28th ACM Symposium on Principles of Programming Languages (POPL01), London, January 2001.
6. Robert Harper, Furio Honsell, Gordon Plotkin. Logic Programming in the LF Logical Framework. Found at . http://citeseer.nj.nec.com/pfenning91logic.html
7. LCC, A Retargetable Compiler for ANSI C. Found at http://www.cs.princeton.edu/software/lcc/.
8. Intel 80386 Programmer's Reference Manual HTML translation–0.9 version. http://www.intel.com

On the Formalized Semantics of Static Modeling Elements in UML

Yan-Bing Jiang, Wei-Zhong Shao, Zhi-Yi Ma, and Yao-Dong Feng

The Department of Computer Science & Technology, Peking University,
Beijing, P.R. China 100871
jyb@cs.pku.edu.cn

Abstract. Along with the research and application of UML in depth, people in software development have cognized that the semantics of UML mainly described in nature language have some drawbacks such as ambiguity and scarcity of accuracy etc. In this paper, we first summarize the necessary of a kind of formalized semantics and previous studies, then provide some semantics of static modeling elements in UML on principle of conciseness, clarity, intelligibility and practicality from two aspects of extension and intension. Thus we provide an effective method of apprehending these modeling elements in depth quickly and exactly, and a basis for the study the semantics of static diagram, translation between elements and models, and the model extension.

1 Introduction

The object-oriented methodology has become the dominant modeling technique in current software development, but a universal accepted mathematics basis of object-oriented methodology has not been formed yet, in despite of vast and instructive research on this domain. Early research considered class is kind of extension to abstract data type. Subsequent research mainly discussed the mathematics meanings of the main mechanism in Object-Oriented theory. Because these studies were based on different methods and mathematics tools, a unified mathematics basis has not come into being.

For example, in 1993, Huang Tao and his fellows put forward a kind of formalized object semantics model, which describes an object as a set of operations, attributes and sequence of operations and provides a kind of formalized definition from two aspects of static constrain and time constrain. On this basis, they provided the formal semantics of object aggregation and inheritance etc. This method is still worth learning and referring. [10,11]

But during a long period of time, the researches on the formal semantics were always the patent of computer theory researchers, whose main purpose is to provide a kind of firm mathematics base for Object-Oriented methodology. For lack of the software engineering researcher's participation, these research products are hard to be accepted by software developers, and can not be applied into the practice of software development.

Some researchers in software engineering have found that the formalization have some merit such as proficiency, straightness and elimination of ambiguity, and introduce formal methods to the object-oriented modeling technology. For instance, in 1997, James Odell and Guus Ramackerss published a paper named *Toward a Formalization of OO Analysis*, which uses plain mathematics knowledge to describe the basic Object-Oriented concepts and makes the software analyst and designer understand the object-oriented theory easier and deeper. But this paper only formalizes the most basic concepts, such as object, class and association etc.[4]

In the middle of 1990's, the Unified Modeling Language (UML) [1,2,3] came into being and issued. Soon this modeling language drew the age of "method war" and became the dominant modeling language in software industry. But from beginning the criticism to UML never ceased and one of the focus problems is the formalization of semantics of UML. One of the purposes of constructing formal modeling language is to avoid the ambiguity and inconsistency that are inherent in nature language, and make the information in models being transferred effectively and accurately. Although UML has prescribed the formal syntax, most of its semantics is described in nature language, which causes different explanations of same modeling element. Some object-oriented authors and methodologists have criticized this problem and begun to research on the formal semantics. One of the representational research organizations is the pUML group (precise UML group) in Britain. In addition, many research institutions and individuals also put forward their opinions to the formalization of UML.[5]

According to the literatures about UML's formalization published recent years, we can see that although they use different mathematics methods to research the formal semantics of different diagrams, the principle they embody are same, that is, they adopt a kind of straightaway formal method, try their best to make most software developers understand easily, and want to affect the future revision of UML.

2 The Necessity of UML's Formal Semantics

The research on UML's formal semantics has deep and instructive meaning no matter from the point of view of studying and applying UML, theory researching, or developing CASE tools. The detailed aspects as follows:

1. Clarity: The formally stated semantics can act as a point of reference to resolve disagreements over intended interpretation and to clear up confusion over the precise meaning of a construct.

2. Equivalence and consistency: A precise semantics provides an unambiguous basis from which to compare and contrast the UML with other techniques and notations, and for ensuring consistency between its different components.

3. Extensibility: The soundness of extensions to the UML can be verified (as encourage by the UML authors).

4. Refinement and conversion: The correctness of design steps in the UML can be verified and precisely documented. Formalization can provide accurate rules and theory basis for conversion between models.

5. Proof: Formalization can be used in justified proofs and rigorous analysis of a model described in UML.

6. Tools: The tools that make use of semantics, for example a code generator or consistency checker, require that semantics to be precise, whether it be expressed as part of the standard or invented in the code by the tool developer.[5]

Usually the researches of the object-oriented formal semantics have two purposes: one is to provide firm theory basis for object-oriented methodology; the other is to solve real problems existing in object-oriented method and technology. The studies that aim to the latter purpose pay attention to the degree of comprehensible and the capabilities to resolve real problems. Recent years' research on the formal semantics almost fell into the latter purpose. These researches are different and follow different methods. If the researchers aim to the latter purpose, the mathematics tools that will be used in the researches should be prudently considered, because we should not ignore most people's capability of understanding these formal methods and only emphasize their theory value. Our work towards the formalization also follows the second purpose, that is, to solve real problems in object-oriented methods by simple mathematics tools (such as set, function, relationship and diagrams etc.).

The main purpose of this paper is to provide formal semantics of static modeling elements in UML and discuss the mapping between some concepts. By defining the formal semantics of these concepts, the ambiguity, obscurity and inconsistency that go with nature language would be eliminated or alleviated, and the modelers and users of UML would grasp these elements' meaning deeply and quickly and use them properly in the practice of object-orient modeling. In addition, formal definition of static modeling element is basis of discussing the semantics of static structure diagram in next step.

Interpretation of Syntax and Semantics in UML

UML is kind of modeling language, rather that a programming language, but the methods and ideas in classical formal semantics can be used for reference to study the formal semantics in UML. In UML1.4, One of common techniques for specification of languages is to first define the syntax of the language and then to describe its static and dynamic semantics. The syntax defines what constructs exist in the language and how the constructs are built up in terms of other constructs. Sometimes, especially if the language has a graphic syntax, it is important to define the syntax in a notation independent way, that is, to define the abstract syntax of the language. The concrete syntax is then defined by mapping the notation onto the abstract syntax. The static semantics of a language defines how an instance of a construct should be connected to other instances to be meaningful, and the dynamic semantics define the meaning of a well-formed construct. [1]

It can be inferred that UML uses denotational semantics to describe semantics of the language. But different from the classical denotational semantics, it uses OCL, a relatively formal language, and nature language to describe the static semantics, while the description of dynamic semantics completely resorts to nature language. The revisers of UML1.4 admit in the specification that although it is easier for us to understand dynamic semantics by describing them precisely, now they still use natural language to describe dynamic semantics. Currently, the dynamic semantics are not considered essential for the development of tools; however, this will probably change in the future.

3 Two Aspects of Phraseology Description

In 1950's, formal linguist C. K. Ogden put forward a semantics triangle as showed in Fig. 1.

There are two aspects in describing the meaning of a phrase, that is, extension and intension. A phrase's intension is its meaning or its complete concept, while a phrase's extension is the set of things fitting to its concept. A phrase's intension decides whether a thing belongs to the extension of the phrase. Extension is the external exhibition of a phrase, while the intension is the internal reason why these things aggregate together. In the remainder part of this paper, the external and internal semantics of some UML's modeling elements are provided.

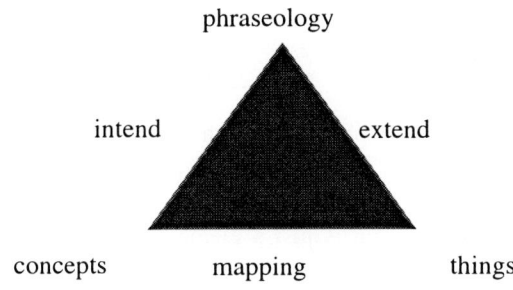

Fig. 1. Semantics triangle

4 Formal Semantics of Some Common Modeling Elements in UML

The semantics of some modeling elements can be completely described either from aspects of extension or intension. Some elements' semantics can only partly be reflected from aspects of extension or intension, which need to be integrated together to get the complete semantics of these elements. The aspects of extension or intension of other elements are hard to described, of which semantics is described only by the other aspects. These model elements' description in nature language is given before formal descriptions to make contrast, and the figures are provided in the place necessary.

4.1 Class and Object

The purpose of a class is to declare a collection of methods, operations, and attributes that fully describe the structure and behavior of objects. All objects instantiated from a class will have attribute values matching the attributes of the full class descriptor and support the operations found in the full class descriptor. [1]

According to the semantics of nature language provided in UML, the formal definition of class and object are given as follows:

Class (Intension): INTENSION(Class) = (A, X, {UNKNOW}), A represents the set of attributes of the class, and X represents the set of operations of the class. {UNKNOW} is components the user defined, such as responsibility etc, which can be omitted in most circumstances. To simplify problems, in the following discussion, Class = (A, X) or INTENSION(Class) = (A, X), more deeply, A = {a | a = <attriname, attritype>}, X = {x | x = <opname, sign>}, which represents a attribute is composed of attribute name and attribute type, and a operation is composed of operation name and its signature.

Object(Intension): INTENSION(Object)=(A, A' ,X), in which A represents the set of object's attributes, X is the set of object's operations, and $A' \subseteq A \times V$. Here V is the set of values that the object's all attributes might have, A' is a mapping from an attribute to its value.

According to these two definitions, the extension of a class and object is provided.

Class(Extension): EXTENTION(Class)={ob| INTENSION(Class)∈ Isa(ob) }.

In this definition, Isa:{ob1,ob2,....} $\longrightarrow 2^{\{Class1,Class2,Class3,....\}}$. Isa is a function that maps an object into a class it belongs to.

If and only if (iff) $A_{Class1} \subseteq A_{ob1}$ and $X_{Class1} \subseteq X_{ob1}$, class1∈ Isa(ob1).(Here A_{Class1} and A_{ob1} represent Class1 and Ob1's attributes respectively .)

The extension of a class may be denoted as EXTEND(Class).

The object extension definition is just a element of a set, and is omitted in this paper.

On this point, the static structure of class and object is formally defined from the aspects of intension and extension. From the aspect of intension, class is a set of description of attributions and operations, while object is an instance of a class and have attribute values of its own. From aspect of extension, a class is a set of objects that have same attributes and operations, while an object is an element of this set.

4.2 Generalization (for Class)

Generalization is the taxonomic relationship between a more general element (the parent) and a more specific element (the child) that is fully consistent with the first element and that adds additional information. It is used for classes, packages, use cases, and other elements. [1]

Class Generalization (Intension): Consider two classes: Class1 and Class2, if $A_{Class1} \subseteq A_{Class2}$ and $X_{Class1} \subseteq X_{Class2}$, then Class1 is the generalization of Class2, or Class2 is specification of Class1. This relationship can be formally denoted as INTEND(Class1) ℘ INTEND(Class2).

Class Generalization (Extension): Consider two classes: Class1 and Class2, if EXTEND(Class1) ⊇ EXTEND(Class2), then Class1 is the generalization of Class2, or Class2 is specification of Class1. This relationship can be formally denoted as EXTEND(Class1) ℘ EXTEND(Class2).

From the definitions above, it can be concluded that in common circumstances, the set of parent class include more elements than the one of child class, but the features of father class is less than the child class. Just because less feature (or constrain) exist in the father class than in the child class, it contains more instances.

In addition, four concepts associated with generalization are defined in UML:

Overlapping: An element may have two or more children from the set as ancestors. An instance may be a direct or indirect instance of two or more of the children.

Disjoint: No element may have two children in the set as ancestors. No instance may be a direct or indirect instance of tow of the children.

Complete: All children have been specified (whether or not shown). No additional children are expected.

Incomplete: Some children have been specified, but the list is known to be incomplete. There are additional children that are not yet in the model. This is a statement about the model itself. Note that this is not the same as the ellipsis, which states that additional children exist in the model but are not shown on the current diagram. [1]

Here gives the formal definitions of these concepts:

Overlapping and Disjoint (Intension): Consider class Class, SubClass1 and SubClass2. INTEND(Class) ≠ INTEND(SubClass1) and INTEND(Class) ≠ INTEND(SubClass2), if there is an object ob, which makes $A_{ob} \supseteq A_{Subclass1} \wedge X_{ob} \supseteq X_{subClass1} \wedge A_{ob} \supseteq A_{Subclass2} \wedge X_{ob} \supseteq X_{subClass1}$, then SubClass1 and SubClass2 are Overlapping, else are Disjoint.

Overlapping and Disjoint (Extension): Consider class Class, SubClass1 and SubClass2. EXTEND(Class) ≠ EXTEND(SubClass1) and EXTEND(Class) ≠ EXTEND(SubClass2), if there is an object ob, which makes $ob \in EXTEND(SubClass1) \wedge ob \in EXTEND(SubClass2)$, then SubClass1 and SubClass2 are Overlapping, else are Disjoint.

Complete and Incomplete (Extension): Consider class Class, SubClass1, SubClass2,...SubClassn, EXTEND(Class) ≠ EXTEND(SubClass1), EXTEND(Class) ≠ EXTEND(SubClass2)... and EXTEND(Class) ≠ EXTEND(SubClassn), if EXTEND(SubClass1) ∪ EXTEND(SubClass2) ∪ ... ∪ EXTEND(SubClassn)= EXTEND(Class), then the generalization between Class and its subclass is complete, else is incomplete.

The intention definition of complete and incomplete is omitted because it is hard to describe.

The following is the definition of multi-generalization from aspects of extension and intension:

Multi-Generalization (Intension): Consider class Class1, Class2 and SubClass, if $A_{Class1} \subseteq A_{SubClass} \wedge A_{Class2} \subseteq A_{SubClass} \wedge X_{Class1} \subseteq X_{SubClass} \wedge X_{Class2} \subseteq X_{SubClass}$, then the generalization between SubClass and its super class is multi-generalization.

Multi-Generalization (Extension): Consider class Class1, Class2 and SubClass, if $EXTEND(SubClass) \subseteq (EXTEND(Class1) \cap EXTEND(Class2))$, then the generalization between SubClass and its super class is multi-generalization.

4.3 Binary Association and Other Extend Association

An association defines a semantic relationship between classifiers. The instances of an association are a set of tuples relating instances of the classifiers. Each tuple value may appear at most once.[1]

The above concept of association is about classifiers, while following formal definition is limited to class.

Binary Association (Extension): Consider class Class1, Class2, if there is a binary relationship: $\{<a,b>|<a,b> \in EXTEND(Class1) \times EXTEND(Class2)\}$, then there is an association between Class1 and Class2, which is denoted as EXTEND(Class1)~EXTEND(Class2).

Binary Association (Intension): Consider class Class1, Class2, if there is a binary relationship:
$\{<attri,ob>|<attri,ob> \in A_{ob1} \times EXTEND(Class2), ob1 \in EXTEND(Class1)\}$, then there is an association between Class1 and Class2, which is denoted as INTEND(Class1)~ INTEND(Class2).

According to these definitions, from the aspect of extension, association is considered to be a subset of descartes product of the instance of two classes, while from aspect of intension, association is banding an attribute of a object of a class with an instance of the other class. The external aspect of association is usually used in the analysis phrases, while the intension aspect of it is often used in design or implementation phrases.

After given the formal definition of association, it is easy to conduct the definition of association's ends, for example, multiplicity and navigation etc. These contents are omitted in this paper.

Some Kinds of Extending Association
N-ary Association
An n-ary association is an association among three or more classifiers (a single classifier may appear more than once). Each instance of the association is an n-tuple of values from the respective classifier. A binary association is a special case with its own notation.[1]

Here gives a definition of 3-ary association:

3-ary Association (Extension): Consider class Class1, Class2 and Class3, if the there is trinary relationship:
$\{<a,b,c>|<a,b,c> \in EXTEND(Class1) \times EXTEND(Class2) \times EXTEND(Class3)\}$, then there are association among these three classes, which is denoted as EXTEND(Class1)~ EXTEND(Class2) ~EXTEND(Class3).

Transition from Trinary Association to Binary Association:
The following is a function mapping trinary association to binary association.

$\delta : EXTEND(Class1) \times EXTEND(Class2) \times EXTEND(Class3)$
$\rightarrow (EXTEND(Class1) \times EXTEND(MClass)) \times (EXTEND(Class2) \times EXTEND(MClass))$
$\times (EXTEND(Class3) \times EXTEND(MClass))$,

in which $\delta(<a,b,c>) = <<a,d>,<b,d>,<c,d>>$, $a \in EXTEND(Class1)$, $b \in EXTEND(Class2), c \in EXTEND(Class3), d \in EXTEND(MClass)$.

Association Class
An association class is an association that also has class properties (or a class that has association properties). Even though it is drawn as an association and a class, it is really just a single model element.[1]

Association Class(Extension): Consider class Class1,Class2 and Aclass, if there is a set of relation:

$\{<<a,b>,c>|<<a,b>,c> \in (EXTEND(Class1) \times EXTEND(Class2)) \times EXTEND(AClass)$, and for any $<a,b>$, there is only one c}, then there is association class AClass between Class1 and Class2, which is denoted as $EXTEND(Class1) \underset{\sim}{\overset{EXTEND\ (AClass\ )}{}} EXTEND(Class2)$.

Transition from an Association Class to Binary Association:
The following is a function mapping an association class to a binary association.

$\delta : (EXTEND(Class1) \times EXTEND(Class2)) \times EXTEND(AClass)$
$\rightarrow ((EXTEND(Class1) \times EXTEND(AClass)) \times (EXTEND(Class2) \times EXTEND(AClass))$

in which $\delta(<<a,b>,c>) = <<a,c>,<b,c>>$, $a \in EXTEND(Class1)$, $b \in EXTEND(Class2)$, $c \in EXTEND(AClass)$, and for any $<a,b>$, there is only one c.

Association with Qualifier
A qualifier is an attribute or list of attributes whose values serve to partition the set of instances associated with an instance across an association. The qualifiers are attributes of the association.[1]

Association with Qualifier (Extension): Consider class ClassA and ClassB, and EXTEND(ClassA)=A, EXTEND(ClassB)= B, if any instance of association between classA and ClassB, that is $<a,b>, a \in A, b \in B$, each belong to following set: $A_1 \times B_1 \cup A_2 \times B_2 \cup A_3 \times B_3 \ldots \cup A_n \times B_n$ ($A_1, A_2, A_3 \ldots A_n \subset A$, and disjoint with each other, $B_1, B_2, B_3 \ldots B_n \subset B$, and disjoint with each other too), then there is an association with qualifier between ClassA and ClassB.

Association with Qualifier (Intension): Consider ClassA and ClassB, there are a set $Q_B \subseteq ATTR(ClassB)$, which means Q_B is a subset of ClassB's attributes. EXTEND(ClassA)=A, EXTEND(ClassB)= B, if there are following relationship among A, B and $Q_B : <<a,q>,b> \in (A \times Q_B) \times B$ in which $a \in A$, $b \in B$, $q \in Q_B$ and $A'_{Q_B} \subseteq A_B$, which means pairs of the value of attributes of Q_B and it's value include in pairs of the value of attributes of B and it's value, then there is an association with qualifier between ClassA and ClassB, which is denoted as ClassA| Q_B ---ClassB.

Xor-Association: An xor-constraint indicates a situation in which only one of several potential associations may be instantiated at one time for any single instance.[1]

Xor-Association (Extension): Consider class ClassA, ClassB and ClassC, if there are following set of relation R, $R \subseteq EXTEND(ClassA_1) \times EXTEND(ClassB) \cup EXTEND(ClassA_2) \times EXTEND(ClassC)$, $EXTEND(ClassA_1) \subset EXTEND(ClassA)$, $EXTEND(ClassA_2) \subset EXTEND(ClassA)$, and $EXTEND(ClassA_1) \cap$

EXTEND(ClassA$_2$) = Φ , EXTEND(ClassA$_1$) $\cup$ EXTEND(ClassA$_2$) = EXTEND(ClassA), then there are a xor-association between ClassA ,ClassB and ClassC.

4.4 Aggregation

In UML, aggregation means a whole-part relationship. There two kind of aggregation in UML. Many object-oriented methodologists disagree with this mode, which have so many faintness and incompleteness that cannot capture all whole-part relationship in reality. Further more, it is hard to research aggregation with formal methods. So the formal semantics of aggregation is omitted in this paper.

4.5 Roles

A classifier role is a specific role played by a participant in a collaboration. It specifies a restricted view of a classifier, defined by what is required in the collaboration.[1]

Roles (Extension): there is a class ClassA , of which a role is R, then (EXTEND(R) $\subseteq$ EXTENDClassA).

Roles (Intension): there is a class ClassA , of which a role is R, INTEND(ClassA)=(A,X), INTEND(R)=(A$_R$,X$_R$), then A$_R$ $\subseteq$ A and X$_R$ $\subseteq$ X.

The concept of roles can not be formally defined from aspects of intension or extension. To get the completely concepts of roles, we need to integrate the two aspects. From aspect of extension, role is the subset of all instance of its class; while from aspect of intension, role is subset of attributes and operations of its class.

4.6 Powertype

A Powertype is a user-defined metaelement whose instances are classes in the model.

Powertype(intension): for class ClassA, of which powertype is the set: S $\subset 2^{\text{EXTEND(ClassA)}}$.

4.7 Template Class

A template is the descriptor for a class with one or more unbound formal parameters. It defines a family of classes, each class specified by binding the parameters to actual values. Typically, the parameters represent attribute types; however, they can also represent integers, other types, or even operations. Attributes and operations within the template are defined in terms of the formal parameters so they too become bound when the template itself is bound to actual values.[1]

Template Class (Intension): template class is: TC=(A,X,P,Q), in which A is TC's attributes; X is TC's operations; P is set of parameters, that is

$P=\{p|p\in \text{TYPE} \vee p\in \text{VALUE}\}$, p can either be a type or a value; and $Q\subset (A\bigcup X)\times P$, which shows relations between parameters and attributes or operations.

Template Class (Extension): consider template class $TC=(A,X,P,Q)$, and class $C=(A,X)$, there is a function $\beta: TC \longrightarrow \{C_i | i=1..n\}$, then $EXTEND(TC)=\bigcup_{i=1}^{n} EXTEND(C_i)$ which maps TC into a set of possible class.

4.8 Interface

Interface is a class that has no attribute and method. The formal definition is omitted in this paper.

4.9 Type

Type may be a class that has no operation and method but attributes. The formal definition is omitted in this paper.

4.10 Metaclass

A metaclass is a class whose instances are classes.

The intension definition of metaclass is same as class the one of class. The extension definition of metaclass is showed as follows.

Metaclass(Extension): $MetaClass=\{Class | INTENSION(MetaClass) \in Isa(Class)\}$, in which $Isa:\{ob1,ob2,....\} \longrightarrow 2^{\{Class1,Class2,Class3,....\}}$.

5 Conclusions and Expectation

UML run short of a simple, effective, rigid and formal semantics. To reduce the ambiguity in the description of nature language to the least, sentences in UML specification are made very lengthy and obscurity. This description of semantics has incurred much criticism from experts and scholars. Since UML has taken on the role of modeling standard all over the world, the problems above are more obvious in no-English-speaking countries.

In this paper we try to provide a series of simple, direct and clear definitions to some of static modeling elements of UML. To achieve this target, some formal techniques are imported. Our purpose is not to establish the formal theory basis of object-oriented methodology, but to use formalization as a bridge to make the semantics of these modeling elements clearer and more rigorous and less amphibolous, and hence to make sure to quickly and correctly master and use these modeling elements. The purpose of formalization is to make things simple, while not complex; is to make developer with moderate level of mathematics knowledge quickly and precisely grasp the mathematics basis behind these static modeling elements to transfer and communicate their modeling idea quickly, while not to define series of enigmatic formalization theory to close the door on the people who have not deep level of background of mathematics.

OMG has noticed the necessity of formal semantics in UML, but what time can formal semantics be written into the specification still depends on the appeal from experts and scholars and balance to other aspects. We wish the idea and content of this paper can be noticed by some experts of this field.

References

1. OMG Unified Modeling Language Specification 1.3,1.4
2. Grady Booch, James Rumbaugh, Ivar Jacobson: The Unified Modeling Language User Guide, Addisin Longman, Inc 1999
3. James Rumbaugh, Ivar Jacobson, Grady Booch: The Unified Modeling Language Reference Manual, Addisin Longman,Inc 1999
4. James Odell,Guus Ramackers, Toward a Formalization of OO Analysis, Journal of Object-Oriented Programming, July 1997
5. Andy Eavants,Stauart Kent, Core Meta-Modelling Semantics of UML: The pUML Approach, UML'99---The Unfied Modeling Language Beyond the Standard Springer October 1999
6. Shao WeiZhong, Yang FuQing, Analysis of Object-Oriented Systems, TsingHua University Press,1998
7. Cheng YunYi, The Basis of Formal Semantics, University of Science & Technology of China Press, 1994
8. Chai XiaoXi, Cheng Ping Object-Oriented Technology, XiDian University Press, 1995
9. LI Liu-ying ,WANG Ji, QI Zhi-chang, An Operational Semantics for UML StateChart Diagrams,Journal of Software, 2001, 12(12)
10. Feng YuLing, Li Jing, Huang Tao, Object Semantics Theory and Constraints Reasoning, Chinese J. Computers, 1993, Vol 16, No.11
11. Huang Tao, Feng YuLing, Li Jing, A Formal Semantics Model For object, Journal of Software,1995, Vol.6, Supplement

From a B Specification to UML StateChart Diagrams

Ahmed Hammad, Bruno Tatibouët,
Jean-Christophe Voisinet, and Wu Weiping

Laboratoire d'Informatique de l'université de Franche-Comté,
16, route de Gray 25030 Besançon cedex,
{hammad, tatibouet, voisinet, wu}@lifc.univ-fcomte.fr
http://lifc.univ-fcomte.fr

Abstract. B is a formal method (and a specification language) which enables the automatic generation of an executable code through a succession of refinements stemming from an abstract specification. The industrial tools provide support for all the development process (type-checking facilities, automatic and interactive proof support, ...). A B specification requires a certain knowledge of mathematical notations (Classical logic and sets) as well as specific terminology (generalized substitutions, B keywords) which may in all likelihood leave a non-specialist of the B notation in the dark. To address this problem, we will extract graphic elements from B specification in an effort to render it more understandable to the novice. These visual elements are illustrated in a UML statechart diagrams.

1 Introduction

Many works [4][8][12][9][10] have been carried out over the past few years regarding the generation of B specifications from OMT or UML diagrams. The advantages of such an approach are obvious: the modeling is conducted outside the framework of the B specification and thus allows to ignore this specification. The disadvantages are primarily due to the two following factors: the first being that, as notation B is not object oriented, the generated abstract specification from UML modeling is necessarily removed from what it would have been were B taken into account; the second, that the B specification remains incomplete, requiring the addition of missing elements that must be proved, after which remains the process of writing the refinements.

Given the difficulty in overcoming the disadvantages of this approach, one could infer that the developers might choose rather to directly write their specifications in B. We can see then the benefit of extracting from the B specification the information in order to understand and document it. This would enable the non-specialist to validate the accuracy of the formal specification. These elements would be presented in a graphic modeling notation, that is, UML (Unified Modeling Language) [11] along with certain constraints written in the OCL

(Object Constraint Language) [14]. UML-OCL is a standard of OMG[1] (Object Management Group). In this article we shall describe the extraction of diagrams of states transitions or State charts [6] who show a behavioral view of variables manipulated in the specification B.

One of the objectives of our works is to study the implemented of techniques which allow to assist the not specialist of the formal B method in the understanding of this one And to favour the communication among the various actors of the development by allowing to show the B specifications by means of UML diagrams .

Following a brief presentation of method B, which can be found in section 2 and a presentation of UML statecharts diagrams (section 3), we will present the extraction method of the visual elements of B specification, Then we apply the rules of extraction to a small example (Section 4). These visual elements are expressed under the shape of a diagram of states transitions. In our conclusion (Section 6), we will examine the limits of our work as well as the prospects of their development.

2 Overall View of B Method

The B method [1][7], developed by Jean-Raymond Abrial, is a formal method which allows an incremental development process (also known as a refining process) which stems from an abstract specification. This method is used in the following situations :

- For developing dependable software; in this case, automatic coding generation is included in the refining process
- To facilitate a system analysis (systems engineering)

The B method has tree development stages : the specification, the refinement, and the implementation. Development in the B method is centred around the concept of machines : an abstract machine - MACHINE, a refinemement machine - REFINEMENT, and an implementation machine - IMPLEMENTATION. Machines are similar to modules encapsuling their internal state. Machines provide a section for initialising their internal state and operations for accessing and manipulating it.

The developer starts off with translating an informal specification into an abstract MACHINE. The evolution of a state of a machine may only occur through its invocation by the operations of the machine. The abstract machines are divided into three parts: the machines that describe the level of the most abstract specification, the refinement machine ,similar to the abstract machine, but is usually more deterministic, which describe the intermediary stages between the specification and the code, and, finally, the implementation machine maps directly to a programming language such as C or Ada. In this paper, we only focus on the features of abstract machines and refinements which are relevant to our discussion.

---

[1] http://www.omg.org

```
MACHINE
    <Nom>
SETS
    <Sets>
VARIABLES
    <Variables>
INVARIANT
    <Invariant>
INITIALISATION
    <Initialisation of variables>
EVENTS
    <Events>
END
```

Fig. 1. General shape simplified of a B event system

The abstract machines are composed of three elements, the first being the declarative part, the second, the composition of the machines, the third, operational part. The declarative part enables the description of the state of an abstract machine through variables, constants, sets, and especially the properties whose specific purpose is the verification of the machine's state. The latter is based on the set theory and predicate logic. The compositional clauses (EXTENDS, INCLUDES, IMPORTS, PROMOTES, SEES, and USES) allow the description of different connections between abstract machines, with each clause introducing the rules of visibility on the variables and the operations of the abstract machines in question. As for the operational part, it contains the initialization and the operations of the abstract machine, and is based on the language of generalized substitutions.

The method B allows also to specify and to verify reactive systems by systems of events [2] (figure 1). The events are activated automatically when a condition, called guard, is satisfied.

3 Statecharts Diagrams

3.1 Introduction

The finished states machines through transition states diagrams have been used for a long time with various methods. This modelisation is especially adapted to the description of the dynamism of a determinist system. Conception/ design methods and particularly the UML language have integrated this style of diagram in order to modelise the behaviour of an object.

3.2 Presentation

These diagrams are used to represent finished states automates, as states graphs, linked each other thanks to oriented arcs which describe transitions. They make possible the description of an object or a component states changes, in relation to interactions with other objects/components or with other actors.

UML offers a graphic representation which reveals the significant elements in the life of an object : states, transitions, events and actions :

- A *state* represent a condition or a situation in the life of an object when it meets some conditions, carries out some actions or waits for some vents. Its characteristics are duration and stability. Its represents an instantaneous conjunction for the relevant characteristics values of an object.
- An *event* is the specification of occur which happens throughout time and which releases the state change of an object.
- A *transition* is a relation between two states which means that one object goes from a state to another when a well identified event occurs. A transition represents the instantaneous passage from a state to another and it occurs thanks to an event. In other word, it is the arrival of an event that affects the transition. Transitions can be automatic as well when one does not mention the event which releases them. In addition to specify a specific event, it is also possible to affect a condition with the help of "guards". Those are Boolean notations expressed in natural language (and in square brackets).
- An *action* is an operation whose the execution leads to the modification of a state from an object to given value in return.

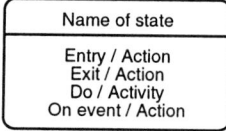

Fig. 2. Notation of a state

3.3 Notation

State. A state is represented by a rectangle with rounded corners (Fig. 2):

1. An action corresponds to an operation available in the object whose states are represented.
2. Actions peculiar to a state can be directly documented within the state.
3. UML defines a certain number of fields which permit to describe actions in a state :
   - *entry / action* : action executed at the entry of the state
   - *exit / action* : action executed at the exit of the state
   - *on event / action* : action executed each time the event happens.
   - *do / activity* : a recurrent or significant action which is executed in the state.

4. Many types of states are existing :
   - Initial state : is a pseudo-state which defines the starting point by default for the states machine or the under-state. It is represented with a black ring.
   - Final state : is a pseudo-state which indicates that the execution of states machine is finished. It is represented with a black ring surrounded by a circle.
   - Sequential state : In a states machine, states are sequential by default. Only one state is active at a given time.
   - Composite state and under-state : a composite states corresponds to a complex situation and is divided among under-states. It is an elemnet which structures transition states diagrams (It is a state which includes others states and transitions).
   - Concurrentiel states : concurrentiel states are active simultaneously.
   - Historical state : an historical state is a pseudo-state which memorizes the latest state of the states machine..

Transition. A transition is represented by an arrow the origin of which is connected with the state source and the destination of which is connected to the target state. She is decorated by the name of the event release mechanism and possibly a condition of release (guard) and a list of actions to be made. The condition of release is expressed between brackets after the name of the event and the list of actions is separated from both previous elements by the character "/".

4 Extraction of Statechart Diagrams

4.1 Introduction

In [3], the extraction of finite state machines is clarified, this with the aim of verifying properties of temporal logic by Model-Checking. Our aim is documentation, clarity and understanding of a B specification on the one hand, statecharts diagrams wich allow you to have a synthetical (overall) and graphical view of tne dynamic behavior of the system on the other hand.

4.2 Approach

In every B machine is associated a package of UML classes and in every variable of the machine is associated a class. In the oriented object modelling, a statechart diagram is connected with a class of the model.

The basic idea is schematised in fig 3. All the abstract or refined machines are represented by a statechart diagram including a great state, the name of which is that of the machine in question. Every variable is represented by a composite state included in that of the machine. These states are concurrent connected by the conjunction AND.

The statechart diagram of the refined machine includes the statechart diagram of variables used in the machine source.

For every machine, we use the VARIABLES and SETS clauses to select variables having a significant dynamic behavior susceptible to be represented by a statechart diagram. Variables represented are used those in the INVARIANT part. In this part, we deduct the various states of the concerned variable. The clause INITIALISATION informs us about the initial state for each of the selected variables. The clause EVENTS describes the events which allow the changes of states of the various variables.

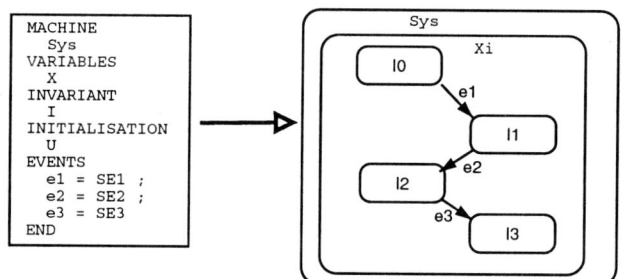

Fig. 3. The basic idea

We illustrate our approach by the example which follows:

4.3 The Example of the Robot

Presentation. The physical system to control is schematised in Fig. 4. It composed of three devices:

- A component arrival device called Da,
- A component evacuation device called De,
- A component transportation device, called Dt, which composed of an arm provided with pliers : the arm has three movements (vertical, horizontal and in-depth) and the pliers also have a movement of opening and closing
- None of three devices can contain more than a component at the same moment.

Principles of Functioning. Components arrive on the device Da, Dt makes the load of these components from Da and unload them on De. Component are evacuated then automatically. Dt can load a component only if it is free (vid) and that Da is busy (occ) (a component arrived). He can unload a component on the device of evacuation De only if this one is free (vid).

- Loading : A component can arrive at an arrival device only if it is free (vid)

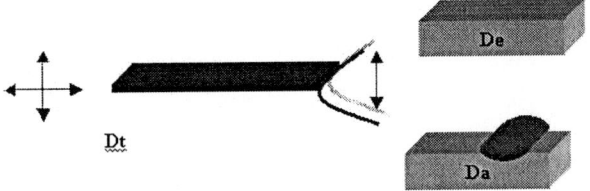

Fig. 4. The robot

- Movements :
    - *Dt* unload in high position,
    - *Dt* load in low position,
    - *Dt* must hold a component to go up,
    - *Dt* must be empty to go down.

In order not to make this presentation too complicate, we shall not present the modeling of the pliers movements.

4.4 Extraction of Statechart Diagram from the Abstract System

The abstract machine (Fig. 5) describes the device *Dt*. The ASCII notation of method B is used : "&" is the *and* between predicates and ":" is the *set membership* operator. In the clause EVENTS we find the events *chgt* and *dchgt* which correspond respectively to the load and dumping components by the device *Dt*. We notice that the *chgt* event made pass *Dt* of the state empty (vid) to the busy state (occ), on the other hand the *dchgt* event realizes the opposite.

```
MACHINE Robot0
VARIABLES dt0
INVARIANT
   dt0 : {vid, occ}
INITIALISATION
   dt0 := vid
EVENTS
   Chgt = SELECT dt0:= vid THEN dt0:=occ END
   Dchgt = SELECT dt0:= occ THEN dt0:=vid END
END
```

Fig. 5. Abstract machine

The diagram extracts (Fig. 6), as indicated in our approach, consists of the great state *Robot0* which describes the machine *Robot0* and the *Dt0* state which describes the variable *Dt0*. We notice that this variable has two states vid and occ, the event *chgt* made pass the variable *Dt0* of the state vid in occ and *dchgt* of occ in vid.

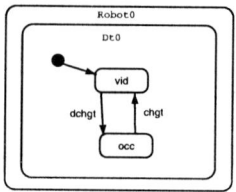

Fig. 6. Statechart of the Robot0

4.5 Extraction of Statechart Diagrams from a Refined Systems

First Refinement. In the first refinement (Fig. 7), we introduce the arrival device represented by the variable $Da1$. This variable possesses two states: space (vid) when there is no component on the arrival device and occupied (occ) as soon as a component arrived on this last one. This event is described in the EVENTS clause by arr_p. The *chgt* event expresses the following property : "The pliers can load only if there is a component on Da and that if Dt is empty". It describes the change of state in simultaneous of a variables $Da1$ (occ in vid) and $Dt1$ (vid in occ). The event *dchgt* is unchanged with regard to the abstract system.

```
MACHINE Robot1 REFINES Robot0
VARIABLE Dt1, Da1
INVARIANT
  Dt1 = Dt0 & Da : {vid, occ}
INITIALISATION
  Dt1, Da1 := vid, vid
EVENTS
  chgt = SELECT Da1=occ & Dt1=vid THEN Da1, Dt1 : = vid, occ END
  dchgt = SELECT Dt1=occ THEN Dt1 := vid END
  arr_p = SELECT Da1=vid THEN Da1 := occ END
END
```

Fig. 7. First refinement of the Robot

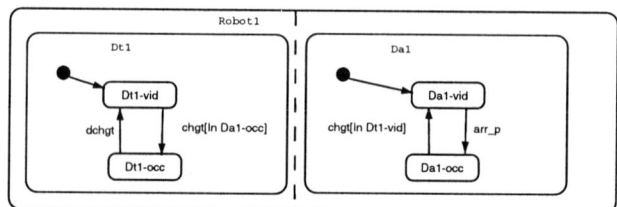

Fig. 8. Statechart for the first refinement of the Robot

The extracted diagram (Fig. 8) consists of a great state Robot1 (which corresponds to the machine Robot1). This state consists of two composite and concurrent states (Dt1 and Da1). For Dt1, the passage of the empty state (vid) in occupied (occ) is activated by the *chgt* event which is conditioned by a guard inter state [In Da1-occ] which means that Da1 is in the occupied state (Da1-occ). The event *arr_p* makes pass the variable Da1 of empty (Da1-vid) in occupied (Da1-occ). The expression Da1=occ (Dt1=vid is expressed by the guard [In Da1-occ] added to the *chgt* event of the state Dt1 and [In Dt1-vid] for the *chgt* event of the state Da1.

Second Refinement. In the second refinement (Fig. 9), we introduce the variable De2 which identifies the evacuation device De. The event *evac* made to pass the variable De2 of occupied (occ) to empty (vid). The events *chgt* and *arr_p* remain unchanged with regard to the first refinement. The dchgt event expresses the following property : "The pliers can unload only on a empty evacuation device".

```
MACHINE Robot2 REFINES Robot1
VARIABLE Dt2, Da2, De2
INVARIANT
   Dt2 = Dt1 & Da2 = Da1 & De2 : {vid, occ}
INITIALISATION
   Dt2, Da2, De2 := vid, vid, vid
EVENTS
   chgt = SELECT Da2=occ & Dt2=vid
          THEN Da2, Dt2 : = vid, occ END
   dchgt = SELECT Dt2=occ & De2=vid
          THEN Dt2, De2 : = vid, occ END
   arr_p = SELECT Da2=vid THEN Da2 := occ END
   evac = SELECT De2=occ THEN De2 := vid END
END
```

Fig. 9. Second refinement of the Robot

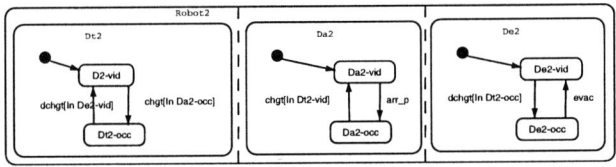

Fig. 10. Statechart for the second refinement of the Robot

The diagram extracted (Fig. 10) from the machine Robot2 is a great Robot0 state including three concurrent states which are: Dt2, Da2 and De2. Dt2 is Dt1's refinement, with there more the *dchgt* event [In De2-vid] who is extracted from the expression Dt2=occ & De2=vid. Da2 is unchanged with regard to the statechart diagram of the first refinement. De2 is a new state which models the behavior of the variable De2 (evacuation device). We finds two under states which are De2-vid who corresponds to De2=vid (evacuation device is empty) and De2-occ. The event *dchgt* of the machine Robot2, we extracts the transition which leaves the state De2-vid to De2-occ, by the event *dchgt*[In Dt2-occ].

```
MACHINE Robot3 REFINES Robot2
VARIABLE Dt3, Da3, De3, posdt3
INVARIANT
  Dt3 = Dt2 & Da3 = Da2 & De3 = De2 & posdt3 : {vid, occ}
INITIALISATION
  Dt3, Da3, De3, posdt3 := vid, vid, vid, bas
EVENTS
  chgt = SELECT Dt3 = vid & Da3 = occ & posdt3 = bas
         THEN Dt3, Da3 : = occ, vid END
  dchgt = SELECT Dt3=occ & De3 = vid & posdt3 = haut
          THEN Dt3, De3 := vid, occ END
  arr_p = SELECT Da3=vid THEN Da3 := occ END
  evac = SELECT De3 = occ THEN De3 :=vid END
  mont = SELECT De3 = occ & posdt3 = bas THEN posdt3 := haut END
  desc = SELECT De3 = vid & posdt3 = haut THEN posdt3 := bas END
END
```

Fig. 11. Third refinement of the Robot

Third Refinement. In this machine (Fig. 11), we introduces the variable posdt3 which models the position of the pliers (high and low). This to specify the following properties: " The pliers can not go down loaded" and " The pliers can not go up if it is empty ". They are specified by the events mont and desc.

In the diagram (Fig. 12), these two properties are described by the following events:

In Dt3 :	dchgt[In De3-vid And PosDt3-haur],
	chgt[In Da3-occ And posDt3-bas]
In Da3 :	chgt[In Dt3-vid And PosDT3-bas]
In De3 :	dchgt[In Dt3-occ And PosDt3-haut]
In PosDt3 :	desc[In Dt3-vid], mont[In Dt3-occ]

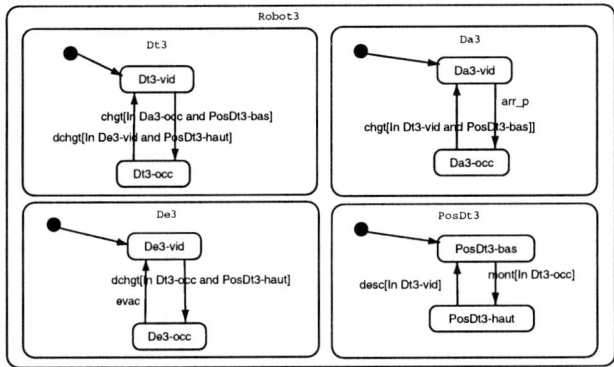

Fig. 12. Statechart for the third refinement of the Robot

5 Conclusion and Further Works

The proposition described in this document is based on the use of the object notations to facilitate the understanding and inform the formal specification. The proposed approach is the extraction of the UML diagrams from a specification B. One so obtains two additional views of the development:

- a UML view which describes in a synthetic and intuitive way the various aspects of the future system allowing a good understanding and documentation of the model builds allowing the validation of the B specification by an expert of the domain not mastering B.
- a B view which defines in a precise and rigorous way all the component of the system allowing a fine analysis and an understanding without ambiguity of the specified model.

In this article we have outlined a possible approach for the extraction of elements of information in a B specification. These elements of information are shown in the UML statechart diagrams. To test the validity of this approach (demonstrated on a creditable number of examples, to begin with), an experimental tool is developed parallel to this method. At present, this study is limited to the extraction of diagrams from a sub set of the B language. At this level, we treat that one under sufficient set of B. It would be interesting to extract the other UML diagrams (sequences, activities, usecase) to have a global and graphic view of the B specification.

In the present case, which is certain to evolve, and in the case where UML notations and B coexist with relative independence, the study of the idea of passing from one notation to another with the help of adequate tools would be extremely useful. This work corroborates the case studies which we have conducted in order to compare specifications between B and UML [5][13]. Future prospects for the generation of UML models from B specification might include:

- the generation of other kinds of diagrams

- the treatment of more complex properties,
- the treatment of a complete B project (composition of machines, refinement, and implementation)
- the study of the forming of a connection between reengineering and that which is obtained through derivation, indispensable in the context of an iterative process.

Our approach here is experimental, treating the extraction of statechart diagrams from the B specifications on an example. We think that this example is susceptible to serve as a guide in the development of a methodology.

References

1. J.R. Abrial - The B Book : Assigning Programs to Meanings - Cambridge University Press, 1996 - ISBN 0521-496195.
2. J.R Abrial, L. Mussat. Introducing dynamic constraints in B. In Second Conference on the B method, France, volume 1393 of LNCS, pages 83-128. Springer Verlag, April 1998.
3. D. Bert, F. Cave. Construction of finite labelled transition systems from B abstract systems. In proc. of IFM'2000, volume 1945 of LNCS, pages 235-254, Springer Verlag, November 2000.
4. P. Facon, R. Laleau, and H.P. Nguyen. - Mapping object diagrams into B specifications. - In A. Bryant and L. Semmens, editors, Methods Integration Workshop, Electronic Workshops in Computing (eWiC), Leeds (UK), March 1996. Springer-Verlag.
5. A. Hammad, B. Tatibouët, Formal and visual specification language, Information System Engineering (ISE 2001), USA, Las Vegas, p. 173-179, (25-28 juin 2001).
6. D. Harel. Statecharts. A visual formalism for complex systems. Science of computer programming, 8:231-274, 1987.
7. K. Lano - The B Language and Method : A Guide to Practical Formal Development - Springer-Verlag - 1996 - ISBN 3-540-19977-2.
8. K. Lano, H. Houghton, P. Wheeler - Formal Methods and Object Technology : Integrating Formal and Structured Methods in Object-Oriented System Development - Springer-Verlag - 1996 - ISBN 3-540-19977-2.
9. E. Meyer, J. Souquieres. A Systematic approach to Transform OMT Diagrams to a B specification. FM'99 Vol. 1 LNCS 1708, pp. 875-895, 1999.
10. E. Meyer - Développements formels par objets : utilisation conjointe de B et d'UML - Doctorat de l'université de Nancy 2 - Mars 2001.
11. J. Rumbaugh, I. Jacobson, G. Booch - The Unified Modeling Language Reference Manual - Addison Wesley - 1998 - ISBN 0-201-30998-X.
12. E. Sekerinsky - Graphical Design of Reactive Systems - B'98 : Recent Advances in the Development and Use of the B-Method - 2nd Conference on the B-Method. LNCS 1393. Montpellier. April 1998.
13. B. Tatibouët, A. Hammad, Une utilisation conjointe de B et UML sur l'étude de cas du robot type, Second Conférence d'Ingénierie des Systemes (AFIS 2001), France, Toulouse, p. 285-290, (25-28 juin 2001).
14. J. Warmer, A. Kleppe - The Object Constraint Language : Precise Modeling with UML - Addison Wesley - 1999 - ISBN 0-201-37940-6.

Formalizing UML Models with Object-Z*

Huaikou Miao, Ling Liu, and Li Li

School of Computer Engineering and Science, Shanghai University,
Shanghai, 200072, China
hkmiao@yc.shu.edu.cn, liuling@mail.shu.edu.cn

Abstract. The Unified Modeling Language (UML) has been developed as a standard language for object-oriented designs. Through its graphical and intuitive diagrams, software analysis and design process become easy. However, this graphical notation lacks precisely defined semantics. It is difficult to determine whether the design is consistent, unambiguous and complete. This paper provides a method of formalizing UML models. It gives the transforming rules from UML models to Object-Z constructs. With this method, the semantics of UML models are directly expressed in formal language Object-Z. The UML class, sequence and statechart diagrams are formalized using this method. A tool OZRose is developed to automate the transforming process.

1 Introduction

The Unified Modeling Language (UML) is rapidly becoming a standard object-oriented modeling notation. The latest UML Version 1.3 [1] gives its syntax and semantics in a combination of natural language (English), UML notation and Object Constraint Language (OCL) [1]. However, UML and OCL are semi-formal notations. This means that UML and OCL have a rather precise syntax but an informal semantics. The lack of formal precise semantics limits applications of UML and makes rigorous analysis of semantic properties captured by the models difficult.

In order to define a formal semantics for the UML, many researchers have devoted considerable effort. The PUML group has identified three general approaches for the formalization of the OO modeling concepts of UML [2]: supplemental, OO-extended formal notation, and methods integration approaches. In the supplemental approach the informal UML model is expressed directly using a formal specification language[3,4,5] (e.g. LSL). In the OO-extended formal language approach, an existing formal notation (e.g. Z) is extended with OO features (e.g. Object-Z), in an attempt to formalize the UML metamodel [6,7]. In the methods integration approach, informal OO modeling techniques are made more precise and amenable to rigorous analysis by integrating them with a suitable formal specification notation. Evans used this approach [8,9] to formalize UML. Kim and Carrington[10,11] extended the approach of Evans. They formalized the syntax of UML class diagram with Z schema and used Object-Z[12] to formalize the semantics of UML class diagram and statechart diagram.

This paper adopts the supplemental approach and uses Object-Z to formalize the UML models. It borrows some ideas of formalizing the semantics of UML class dia-

---
* This work is supported by National Natural Science Foundation of China (No. 60173030).

gram and statechart diagram from [10, 11]. But, this paper describes UML syntax construct with Object-Z constructs and presents the rules of formalizing static and dynamic models in UML. Here, the approach to formalizing class diagram presented is different from [10]. It unifies the representation of association class and takes the class diagram as a schema. For the statechart diagram, we give more detailed transforming rules than the work in [11]. Furthermore, This paper gives the detailed rules of formalizing UML sequence diagram. This method provides a comprehensive and clear way of transforming UML models into Object-Z constructs. It reduces the complexity of formalizing UML models.

The rest of this paper is arranged as follows. Section 2 describes the formalization of UML class diagram. Section 3 describes the formalization of UML sequence diagram. Section 4 specifies the formalization of UML statechart diagram. Section 5 introduces the OZRose tool developed by our research group. Section 6 gives the conclusion for this work.

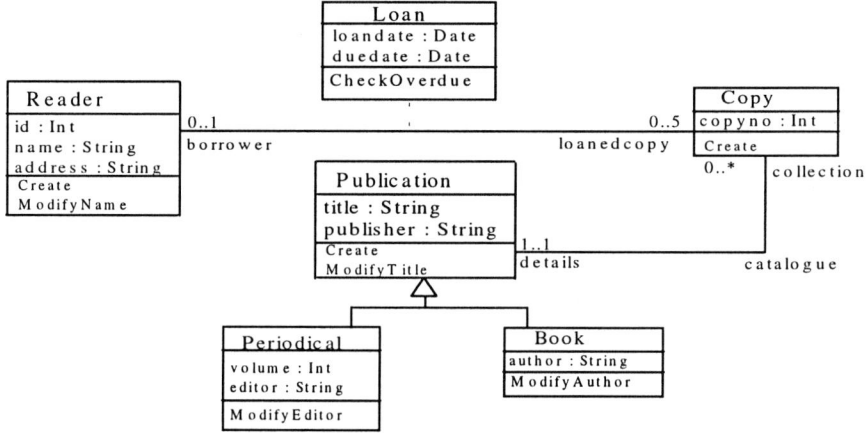

Fig. 1. A UML class diagram for the Library system

2 Formalizing the UML Class Diagram

A UML class diagram shows static aspect of a system. It is composed of class, association, association class and generalization. Figure 1 gives a UML class diagram for a Libragry system[10].

2.1 Class

Define the Syntax of UML Class. Semantically, a class in UML defines a set of objects with the same properties. In this sense, the UML class construct can be expressed with Object-Z class construct. So, the syntax definition of Object-Z class is used to define the UML class construct. The syntax of Object-Z class is shown as

```
┌─ClassName[FormalParameters]──────────┐
│ [VisibilityLists]                    │
│ [InheritedClasses]                   │
│ [LocalDefinitions]                   │
│ [StateSchemas]                       │
│ [InitialStateSchemas]                │
│ [OperationSchemas]                   │
└──────────────────────────────────────┘
```

Transforming Rules for UML Classes. The UML class name is used as the Object-Z class name. All attributes of the UML class are declared as state variables in the state schema of the corresponding Object-Z class. The data type of these attributes are declared as basic Object-Z data type or given type. Each operation in the UML class is transformed into an operation schema within this Object-Z class.

With these rules, the classes in the library system can be formalized as following forms.

[Int, String, Date]

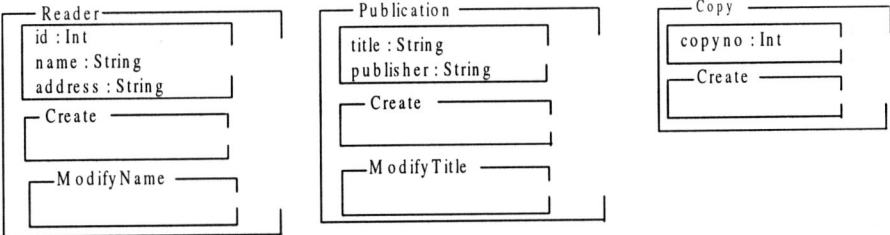

Generalization. In UML class diagram, generalization means the inheriting relation between a class and its subclasses. This relation can be expressed with the inherited class part of Object-Z class. In the library system example, class *Publication* is declared as the inherited part of these two classes definition.

2.2 Association

In UML, the relationships between classes are described as associations. These associations can be divided into three kinds: aggregation association, composition association and common association.

Semantically, an association is a set of object pairs. In this sense, we transform each association to an Object-Z schema, in which the association relationship is formalized as a relation between the associated classes.

The syntax of association is defined as follows.

```
┌─ SchemaName[FormalParameters] ─────────┐
[ │ Declaration                            │
  ├────────────────────────────────────┐   │
  │ PredicateList                    ] │   │
  └────────────────────────────────────┘   │
```

In order to distinguish the association type, a free type is defined as follows.
ASSOTYPE := common | aggregation | composition

The Transforming Rules for UML Association. An association name is used as schema name. In the declaration part of an Object-Z schema a relation is declared. Its name is the role names connected with a dash. Its type is a relation between associated classes. A variable is declared with type ASSOTYPE for indicating the association type. The multiplicity constraint is described in the predicate part of the Object-Z schema.

Using these rules, the association *catalogue* in library system can be formalized as the following schema.

```
┌─ catalogue ──────────────────────────────┐
│ collection-details : Copy ↔ Publication  │
│ assotype : ASSOTYPE                      │
├──────────────────────────────────────────┤
│ assotype = common                        │
│ ∀c : Copy • #({c} ◁ collection-details) = 1 │
└──────────────────────────────────────────┘
```

2.3 Association Class

The UML association class is a special structure that has class-like properties as well as association-like properties. It can be transformed into an Object-Z class. All attributes and the association relationship are represented as the attributes of state schema. The multiplicity constraints are stated in the predication part of the state schema. The methods are translated to operation schemas. Following Object-Z specification specifies the association class *Loan* in Figure 1.

```
┌─ Loan ──────────────────────────────────────┐
│ ┌─────────────────────────────────────────┐ │
│ │ Loandate : Date                         │ │
│ │ duedate : Date                          │ │
│ │ borrower-loanedcopy : Reader ↔ Copy     │ │
│ │ assotype : ASSOTYPE                     │ │
│ ├─────────────────────────────────────────┤ │
│ │ assotype = common                       │ │
│ │ ∀r : Reader • #({r} ◁ borrower-loanedcopy) ⩽ 5 │ │
│ │ ∀c : Copy • #(borrower-loanedcopy ▷ {c}) ⩽ 1 │ │
│ └─────────────────────────────────────────┘ │
│ ┌─ CheckOverdue ──────────────────────────┐ │
│ │                                         │ │
│ └─────────────────────────────────────────┘ │
└─────────────────────────────────────────────┘
```

2.4 Class Diagram

Semantically, a UML class diagram is a set of objects and relationships between these objects. So, The class diagram can be transformed into an Object-Z schema. The declaration part of the schema states all objects and relationships in the class diagrams. The predicate part of the schema gives the constraints on these objects and relationships. For Figure 1, the corresponding Object-Z schema is represented as follows.

```
┌── Library ──────────────────────────────────┐
│ readers : P Reader                          │
│ copies : P Copy                             │
│ publications : P Publication                │
│ periodicals : P Periodical                  │
│ books : P Book                              │
│ loans : P Loan                              │
│ cata : catalogue                            │
├─────────────────────────────────────────────┤
│ periodicals ∪ books ⊆ publications          │
│ cata.collection-details ⊆ copys × publications │
└─────────────────────────────────────────────┘
```

3 Formalizing UML Sequence Diagram

A sequence diagram shows an interaction arranged in time sequence. An interaction is defined in the context of collaboration. The interaction specifies the communication patterns between the roles. More precisely, it contains a set of partially ordered Message, each specifying one communication, e.g. what signal to be sent or what operation to be invoked, as well as the roles to be played by the sender and the receiver, respectively [1].

A sequence diagram has two dimensions: 1) the vertical dimension represents time and 2) the horizontal dimension represents different objects. Figure 2 gives an instance of UML sequence diagram.

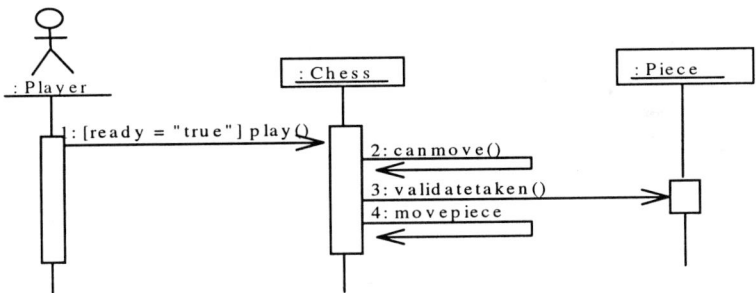

Fig. 2. A UML sequence diagram for Playchess system

3.1 Message

In a sequence diagram a message is shown as a horizontal solid arrow from the lifeline of one object to the lifeline of another object. The arrow is labeled with the name of the message and its argument values or argument expression. It may also be labeled with a guard condition and sequence number that is used to show the sequence of the message in the overall interaction. There are three kinds of messages: simple message, asynchronous message and synchronous message.

Semantically, a message is a communication between two objects that conveys information with the expectation that action will ensue. It specifies the roles that the sender and the receiver objects must conform to, as well as the action that will be stimulated.

From the semantics of a message, it can map to an Object-Z schema. The type of a message and the objects it connects can be stated in the declaration part of an Object-Z schema. The guard conditions and the actions it stimulates can be specified in the predicate part of this schema.

The Transforming Rules for a Message in Sequence Diagram. A message name is represented as schema name. If the message is labeled with a sequence number, this sequence number is put at the end of the schema name. The message parameters are transformed into formal parameters of the schema. In the schema declaration part, the sender and receiver objects connected by the message are declared as attributes *sender* and *receiver*. If the message is sent to and received from a same object, attribute *selfsr* is declared. The variables involved in guard condition are represented as input variables in the schema. An attribute *order* is also defined in the state schema to represent the sequence number for this message. Furthermore, the message type should be defined as a free type that contains three values - Simple, Asynchronous and Synchronous. In the predicate part of this Object-Z schema, the guard conditions of this message and the actions it stimulates are specified.

Using these rules, the messages in Figure 2 can be formalized as follows.
MESSAGETYPE ::= Simple | Asynchronous | Synchronous

```
┌─ play1 ──────────────────────┐   ┌─ validatetaken3 ─────────────┐
│ sender : Player              │   │ sender : Chess               │
│ receiver : Chess             │   │ receiver : Piece             │
│ ready? : Boolean             │   │ msgtype : MESSAGETYPE        │
│ msgtype : MESSAGETYPE        │   │ order : N                    │
│ order : N                    │   ├──────────────────────────────┤
├──────────────────────────────┤   │ msgtype = Simple             │
│ msgtype = Simple             │   │ receiver.validatetaken()     │
│ ready? => receiver.play()    │   │ order = 3                    │
│ order = 1                    │   │                              │
└──────────────────────────────┘   └──────────────────────────────┘

┌─ canmove2 ───────────────────┐   ┌─ movepiece4 ─────────────────┐
│ selfsr : Chess               │   │ selfsr : Chess               │
│ msytype : MESSAGETYPE        │   │ msgtype : MESSAGETYPE        │
│ order : N                    │   │ order : N                    │
├──────────────────────────────┤   ├──────────────────────────────┤
│ msgtype = Simple             │   │ msgtype = Simple             │
│ selfsr.canmove()             │   │ selfsr.move()                │
│ order = 2                    │   │ order = 4                    │
└──────────────────────────────┘   └──────────────────────────────┘
```

3.2 Sequence Diagram

Semantically, a sequence diagram presents an interaction, which is a set of messages between classifier roles within a collaboration to effect a desired operation or result. In this sense, the sequence diagram can be seen as a set of messages.

The Transforming Rules for Sequence Diagram. A key word "Seq" following the sequence diagram name is used as the name of Object-Z schema. The declaration part of the schema states all instance of the messages in this sequence diagram. The predicate part of the schema represents the sequence of sending messages. For Figure 2, the sequence diagram is formalized as follows.

```
┌─SeqPlaychess ─────────────────────────────┐
│ play : play1                              │
│ canmove : canmove2                        │
│ validatetaken : validatetaken3            │
│ movepiece : movepiece4                    │
├───────────────────────────────────────────┤
│ play.order < canmove.order                │
│ canmove.order < validatetaken.order       │
│ validatetaken.order < movepiece.order     │
└───────────────────────────────────────────┘
```

4   Formalizing UML Statechart Diagram

A statechart diagram can be used to describe the behavior of a model element such as an object or an interaction. Specially, it describes possible sequence of states and actions through which the element can proceed during its lifetime as a result of reacting to discrete events. Figure 3 gives an instance of an UML statechart diagram.

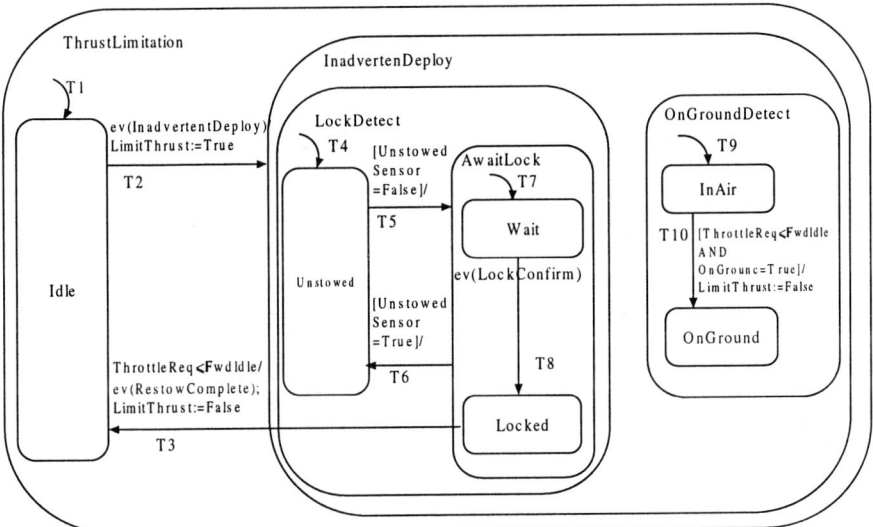

Fig. 3. The statechart diagram of Thrust Limitation

4.1   State

Semantically, a state is a condition during the life of an object or an interaction during which it satisfies some condition, performs some action, or waits for some event. A composite state is a state that, in contrast to a simple state, has a graphical decomposition [1]. A state models the static structure for an object ongoing some activities.

Transforming Rules for State:
- A composite state is translated to an attribute defined in the state schema of an Object-Z class. The name of this attribute is the state name. The type of this attribute is a free type that consists of all its substates.

- An initial state is transformed into the initial state within the Object-Z class corresponding to this statechart diagram.
- If a state declared entry, exit or do actions, these actions should be transformed into operation schemas within this Object-Z class. The detailed steps of transforming are: The action label followed by state name is used as operation names. The state conditions prior to performing this action are used as preconditions of this operation. The ongoing action and the changes after performing this action are used as postconditions of this operation.

For figure3, the states can be formalized as follows.

```
ThrustLimitation ::= Idle | InadvertentDeploy
InadvertentSub ::= LockDetect | OnGroundDetect
LockDetectSub ::= Unstowed | AwaitLock
AwaitLockSub ::= Wait | Locked
OnGroundDetectSub ::= InAir | OnGround
```

─── ThrustLimitationClass ───
| thrustlimitation : ThrustLimitation
| inadvertent : InadvertentSub
| lockdetect : LockDetectSub
| awaitlock : AwaitLockSub
| ongrounddetect : OnGroundDetectSub
| [other attributes of the class]

─── INIT ───
| thrustlimitation = Idle
| inadvertent = LockDetect
| lockdetect = Unstowed
| awaitlock = Wait
| ongrounddetect = InAir

4.2 Transition

Semantically, a transition is a relationship between two states indicating that an object in the first state will enter the second state and perform specific actions when a specified event occurs provided that certain specified conditions are satisfied. [1]. A transition may have a name. It follows the general format:

event-name '(' comma-seqarated-parameter-list ')' '[' guard-condition ']' '/' action-expression

The guard-condition specifies the condition to fire the event. The action-expression is executed if and when the transition fires.

Transforming Rules for Transition:
- Since events in a statechart diagram are not limit to an object. It may be used in the whole software system. A global variable is used to express the event. This global variable is defined as an Object-Z axiom with the name *eventvar*. The type of this global variable is specified with a free type that contains all events in the system. Through assigning concrete value to this variable, the event involved in a transition can be represented.
- A transition is transformed into an operation schema in the Object-Z class corresponding to this statechart diagram. The transition name is used as the operation name. The state variables affected by this transition and some input / output variables are declared in this operation schema. The source state, event and guard condi-

tion of this transition are described as precondition in the predicate of the operation schema. The target state, actions of this transition are represented as postcondition in the predicate of this schema.

- A guard conditions can be transformed into the predicate of the operation schema within the Object-Z class. If this condition is determined by outside environment, an input variable should be defined in this operation.
- An action in a transition can be transformed into postcondition of an operation schema within Object-Z class. If this action denotes an operation of the class the operation name can be directly used to represent this action. If this action changes the value of some parameter, an output variable should be defined.
- If a transition comes from or enters to a composite state, the precondition or postcondition in an operation schema within the Object-Z class should include a composite state. The default transition in each composite state means the initial value of each composite state, so, it does not need to be concerned.

Using above rules, the Figure 3 can be formalized as following form.

ThrustLimitation ::= Idle | InadvertentDeploy
InadvertentSub ::= LockDetect | OnGroundDetect
LockDetectSub ::= Unstowed | AwaitLock
AwaitLockSub ::= Wait | Locked
OnGroundDetectSub ::= InAir | OnGround
EVPARAMETER ::= InadvertendDeploy | RestowComplete | LockConfirm
EVENTTYPE ::= ev<<EVPARAMETER>>

| eventvar : EVENTTYPE

___ ThrustLimitationClass _____
| thrustlimitation : ThrustLimitation
| inadvertent : InadvertentSub
| lockdetect : LockDetectSub
| awaitlock : AwaitLockSub
| ongrounddetect : OnGroundDetectSub
| [other attributes of the class]
| ___ INIT ___
| | thrustlimitation = Idle
| | inadvertent = LockDetect
| | lockdetect = Unstowed
| | awaitlock = Wait
| | ongrounddetect = InAir

$T2 \cong [\Delta(\text{thrustlimitation}); \text{LimitThrust}! : \text{Boolean} | \text{thrustlimitation} = \text{Idle} \land$
$\quad \text{eventvar} = \text{ev}<<\text{InadvertentDeploy}>> \land \text{LimitThrust}! = \text{True} \land$
$\quad \text{thrustlimitation}' = \text{InadvertentDeploy}]$

$T3 \cong [\Delta(\text{thrustlimitation, awaitlock}); \text{ThrottleReq}?, \text{Fwdldle}?:\mathbb{N} ;$
$\quad \text{LimitThrust}!:\text{Boolean}|\text{thrustlimitation} = \text{InadvertentDeploy} \land \text{awaitlock} = \text{Locked} \land$
$\quad \text{ThrottleReq}? < \text{Fwdldle}? \land \text{eventvar} = \text{ev}<<\text{RestowComplete}>> \land$
$\quad \text{LimitThrust}! = \text{False} \land \text{thrustlimitation}' = \text{Idle}]$

$T5 \cong [\Delta(\text{lockdetect}); \text{UnstowedSensor}? : \text{Boolean} | \text{lockdetect} = \text{Unstowed} \land$
$\quad \text{UnstowedSensor}? = \text{False} \land \text{lockdetect}' = \text{AwaitLock}]$

$T6 \cong [\Delta(\text{lockdetect}); \text{UnstowedSensor}? : \text{Boolean} | \text{lockdetect} = \text{AwaitLock} \land$
$\quad \text{UnstowedSensor}? = \text{True} \land \text{lockdetect}' = \text{Unstowed}]$

$T8 \cong [\Delta(\text{awaitlock})|\text{awaitlock} = \text{Wait} \land \text{eventvar} = \text{ev}<<\text{LockConfirm}>> \land \text{awaitlock}' = \text{locked}]$

$T10 \cong [\Delta(\text{ongrounddetect}); \text{ThrottleReq}?, \text{Fwdldle}? : \mathbb{N}; \text{OnGround}? : \text{Boolean};$
$\quad \text{LimitThrust}! : \text{Boolean} | \text{ongrounddetect} = \text{InAir} \land \text{ThrottleReq}? < \text{Fwdldle}? \land$
$\quad \text{OnGround}? = \text{True} \land \text{LimitThrust}! = \text{False} \land \text{ongrounddetect}' = \text{OnGround}]$

5 OZRose – A Tool for Transforming UML Models into Object-Z

In the above sections, we describe the method of formalizing UML models to corresponding Object-Z constructs. In order to support this method of formalization, we have developed a tool, OZRose, to automate this transforming process. This tool utilizes the Rational Rose to edit UML models. When the UML models have been built, the tool extracts the information of these models and transforms them to the ASCII format of Object-Z.

5.1 The Framework of OZRose

The framework of OZRose is presented in Figure4.

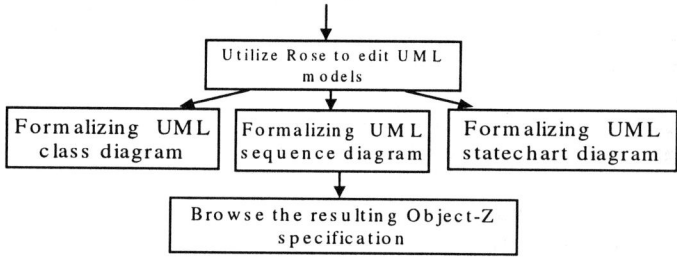

Fig. 4. The framework of OZRose

This tool makes an AddIn component in the Rational Rose environment. When customer has finished the edition of UML models, he or she can use this AddIn component to start the formalizing process for UML. After complete the formalizing process, the resulted Object-Z specification can be browsed.

5.2 The Executing Process of OZRose

The executing process of OZRose is displayed in following pictures.
  1) Start OZRose, and select the UML diagram that needs to be formalized.
  2) When a UML diagram is selected, you can open an existed file for this model or start Rational Rose to edit this model. For the limit of paper size, we omit the interface of Rational Rose edit
  3) When the edit process is completed, press "OZSL file" button in the first picture. This tool will begin the formalizing process. When this formalizing process is completed, press "preview file" button to preview the resulted Object-Z specification. Figure 6 gives the interface of preview.

Formalizing UML Models with Object-Z   533

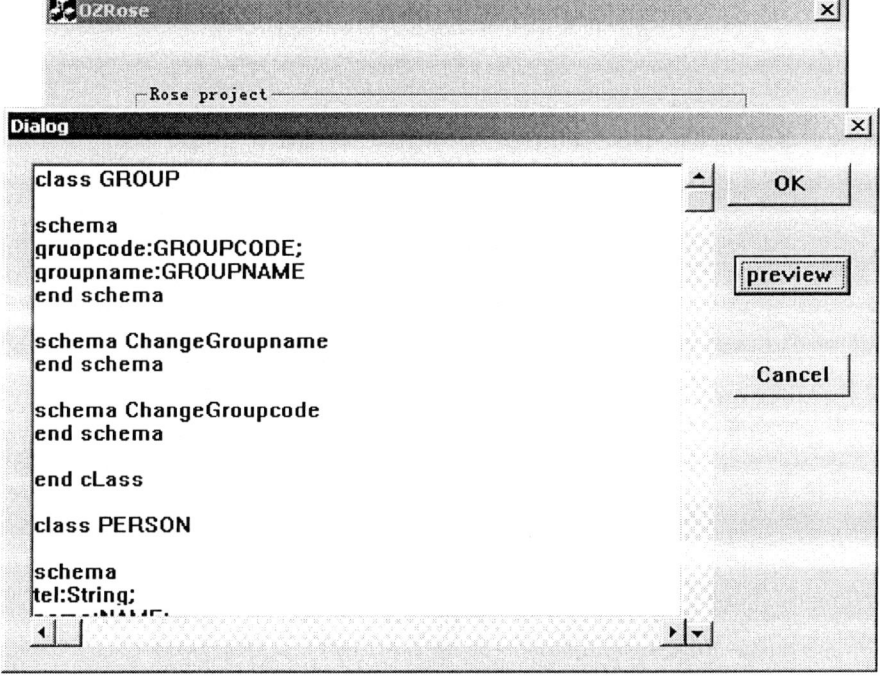

Fig. 5. The main interface of OZRose

Fig. 6. The preview interface of OZRose

6 Conclusion

This paper introduces the method of formalizing UML class, sequence and statechart diagram in detail. The method describes the approaches of formalizing UML static and dynamic models. It provides an unified way of formalizing UML models. In order to support our methods, we also have implemented a tool OZRose. This tool makes the formalization easy to take.

Besides the above works, we also need to do the researches on formalizing UML. These researches include formalizing other models and core modeling constructs in UML. A more mature supporting environment for the formalizing of UML needs to be developed

References

[1] Object Management Group, OMG Unified Modeling Language Specification, Version 1.3, June 1999, http://www.rational.com.
[2] R. B. France, A. Evans, K. Lano, and B. Rumpe, Developing the UML as a Formal Modeling Notation, Computer Standards and Interfaces, No 19, pp. 325-334, 1998.
[3] M. Bickford and D. Guaspari, Odyssey Research Associates Report No. 10, 1998.
[4] A. Hamie, "A Formal Semantics for Checking and Analysing UML Models", in Proceedings of the OOPSLA'98 Workshop on Formalizing UML. Why? How?, edited by L. Andrade, A. Moreira, A. Deshpande, and S. Kent, 1998.
[5] A. Hamie, J. Howse, and S. Kent, "Interpreting the Object Constraint Language", in Proceedings of Asia Pacific Conference in Software Engineering, IEEE Press, 1998.
[6] S. Mann and M. Klar, "A Metamodel for Object-Oriented Statecharts", in Proc. 2nd Workshop on Rigorous Object-Oriented Methods, ROOM 2, University of Bradford, 1998.
[7] M. Gogolla and M. Richters, "Equivalence Rules for UML Class Diagrams", in The Unified Modeling Language, UML'98 – Beyond the Notation. First International Workshop, Mulhouse, France, Jun 1998, edited by J. Bézivin and P. – A. Muller, LNCS Vol. 1618, pp. 87-96. Springer, 1998.
[8] A. Evans and T. Clark, "Foundations of the Unified Modeling Language", in Proc. of the 2nd BCS-FACS Northern Formal Methods Workshop, Ilkley, UK, 23-24 September 1997, 1997.
[9] A. Evans, "Reasoning with the Unified Modeling Language", in Proc. Workshop on Industrial-Strength Formal Specification Techniques (WIFT'98), 1998.
[10] S-K. Kim and D. Carrington, Formalizing the UML class diagram using Object-Z, Proc 2nd IEEE conference on UML: UML'99, LNCS, No 1723, pp. 83-98, 1999.
[11] S-K. Kim and D. Carrington,, An Integrated Framework with UML and Object-Z for Developing a Precise and Understandable Specification: The Light Control Case Study, In *Seventh Asia-Pacific Software Engineering Conference*, pages 240-248, December 2000. IEEE Computer Society. Los Alamitos, California.
[12] R. Duke, G. Rose and G. Smith, Object-Z: a Specification Language Advocated for the Description of Standards. Technique Report No. 94-45, December 1994.

Using Transition Systems to Unify UML Models

Zhiming Liu[1]*, Xiaoshan Li[2], and Jifeng He[1]

[1] International Institute for Software Technology, The United Nations University, Macau
{lzm,hjf}@iist.unu.edu
[2] Faculty of Science and Technology, The University of Macau, Macau
xsl@umac.mo

Abstract. The Unified Modeling Language (UML) is the de-facto standard modeling language for the development of software with broad ranges of applications. It supports for modeling a software at different stages during its development: requirement analysis, design and implementation. The models to produce for an object-oriented requirement analysis are a *conceptual class model* and a *use-case model*. This paper proposes a method to combine these two models by using a classic *transition system*. Then we can reason about and refine such systems with well established methods and tools.

Keywords: Object-orientation, UML, Conceptual model, Use-case model, Transition systems

1 Introduction

Object-orientation is now a popular approach in software industries. (UML) [3, 14] is the de-facto standard modeling language for the development of software with broad application ranges, covering the early development stages of requirement analysis and with strong support for design and implementation [3, 5].

The the requirement specification of a system consists of a *conceptual model* and a *use-case model*. The conceptual model represents the domain concepts as *classes* and their relationships as *associations*. It determines the possible *objects* and relationships between these objects. Requirement analysis is not usually concerned very much about what an object does or how it behaves [5]. Therefore, a conceptual model is mainly used as a *static model* of the *structure* of the application domain. A use-case model contains a number of *use cases*, each specifying a pattern of interactions between some users and the system.

A main problem with UML is that its does not yet have a well established semantics. It is impossible to check consistency or to reason about relationship among the different UML diagrams used in a development of a system. Problems concerning consistency between models for different views are classified as *horizontal consistency* and those about models at different levels of abstraction as *vertical consistency* [8].

Syntactic consistency conditions are expressed in UML in terms of the wellformedness rules of OCL (Object Constraint Language). There is currently a lot of active

---
* On leave from the University of Leicester, England.

research on formalization of UML to deal with semantic consistency. However, most of it focuses on translating a individual UML notation into an existing formal notation. For example, a class diagram is in Z or VDM, e.g. [19], and an interaction diagram or a statechart is translated into a CSP specification [8].

This paper proposes a method for specifying and reasoning about the UML conceptual model and the use cases of a system. It is based on the well known notation of *transition systems* [10] of the form $\mathcal{S} \stackrel{def}{=} (\Gamma, Inv, Init, P)$, where

- Γ is a set of declared state variables with known value domains. These variables and their data domains are constructed from the conceptual model.
- Inv is a state predicate called the *invariant* of the system. It has to be true during the operation of the system. This is determined by the conceptual model too.
- $Init$ is a state predicate determining the initial states of the system. It is established by the installation of the system.
- P is a set of state transitions that models the execution of the use use cases.

Both syntactic and semantic consistency between a conceptual model and a use-case model can be taken into account in this combined model.

After this introduction, a syntax and a semantics for a conceptual model are defined in Section 2. The syntax follows the traditional graph definitions. The semantics of a conceptual model is defined in terms of the variables, their value domains and the object diagrams as the state space of the model. Section 3 defines a syntax and semantics of the a use-case model. The semantics of a use case is defined based on the semantics of the conceptual model and how it carries out state transitions. This will lead to a combination of a conceptual model and a use case model into a transition system. Finally conclusion and discussion are given in Section 4. Small but illustrative examples are used through out the discussion.

2 Conceptual Model

One of the main artifacts to produce in an OO analysis is a conceptual class diagram. Such a diagram captures the physical *concepts* and their *relations* in the application domain. In UML, a concept is represented by a *class* with a given name. An instance of a concept is called an *object* of the corresponding class. A relation between two concepts are denoted by an *association*. In addition to associations between concepts, a concept may have some *properties* represented by *attributes*. For example, **Account** has a *balance* as an attribute.

A class represents a set of objects. A system requirement specification is concerned with what the system does as a whole rather than what an individual object does, how an object behaves, or how an attribute of an object is represented. The decision on the later issues should be deferred to the design stage when a use case is realized by decomposing its *responsibilities* and assigning them to appropriate objects. Use case decomposition and responsibility assignment are carried out according to the *knowledge* that the objects maintain[1]. *What an object can do depends on what it knows, though an object does not*

---

[1] This is the main idea of the design pattern called *Expert Pattern*.

have to do all what it can do. What an object knows is determined by its attributes and associations with other objects. Only when the responsibilities of the objects are decided in design, can the directions of the associations (i.e. *navigation* and *visibility*) and the methods of the classes be determined. This indicates that at this level an association has no direction or equivalently two directions and a class has no methods. This observation on conceptual models enables us to avoid from recursive definition of objects and method calls and to keep the theory simple [11].

2.1 Conceptual Class Diagram

To define a syntax for class diagrams, we assume three disjoint sets of names **CN**, **AN**, and **AttrN** to denote classes, associations and attributes. For each $A \in \mathbf{AN}$, we assume a unique name $A^{-1} \in \mathbf{AN}$ called the *inverse* of A, and $(A^{-1})^{-1} = A$.

Each attribute of an object takes a value in a *type of pure data* called a *data type*. Examples of data types include types of natural numbers **N**, Boolean values **Bool**, etc. Let $\mathcal{T}$ denote the set of the data types.

Definition 1. (Conceptual Class Diagram). A conceptual class diagram is a tuple: $\Delta = \langle \mathcal{C}, Ass, Att, \triangleleft\!\!\!- \rangle$, where

- $\mathcal{C}$ is a nonempty finite subset of **CN**, called the *classes* or *concepts* of Δ.
- Ass is a partial function $Ass : \mathcal{C} \multimap (\mathbf{AN} \multimap \mathbb{PN} \times \mathbb{PN} \times \mathcal{C})$ such that

$$Ass(C_2)(A^{-1}) = \langle M_2, M_1, C_1 \rangle \text{ iff } Ass(C_1)(A) = \langle M_1, M_2, C_2 \rangle$$

where $\mathbb{PN}$ is the powerset of **N**.
If $Ass(C_1)(A) = \langle M_1, M_2, C_2 \rangle$, then A is called an *association* between C_1 and C_2, M_1 and M_2 are called the cardinalities of C_1 and C_2 in A. An association A is in general denoted by $A : (C_1, M_1, M_2, C_2)$. We use $AssN(C_1, C_2)$ to denote the set of all the associations between C_1 and C_2.
- Att is a partial function $Att : \mathcal{C} \multimap (\mathbf{AttrN} \multimap \mathcal{T})$. We use $C.a : \mathbf{T}$ to denote $Att(C)(a) = \mathbf{T}$, and call a an *attribute* of C and $\mathbf{T}$ the *type* of a. We use $attV(C)$ to denote the set $\{a : \mathbf{T} \mid Att(C)(a) = \mathbf{T}\}$ of all the attributes of C.
- $\triangleleft\!\!\!-\; \subseteq \mathcal{C} \times \mathcal{C}$ is the *direct generalization relation* between classes. We use $C_1 \triangleleft\!\!\!- C_2$ to denote $(C_1, C_2) \in\; \triangleleft\!\!\!-$ and say that C_1 is a *direct superclass* of C_2, and C_2 is a *direct subclass* of C_1.

Definition 1 allows more than one association between two classes, a same name for associations between two different pairs of classes, and a same attribute name for attributes of different classes. In Figure 1, we give two class diagrams $Bank1$ and $Bank2$ for two possible banking systems. We only show either an association or its inverse, but not both in a diagram.

2.2 Semantics of Class Conceptual Diagrams

A class diagram specifies a family of types to represent the *data domain* of an application. Each class name C in a conceptual class diagram Δ is associated with a *class* of *objects*

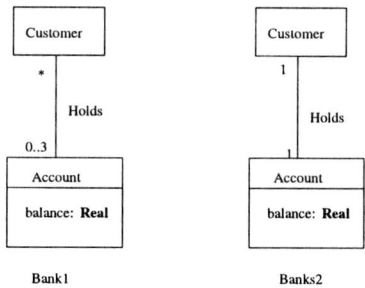

Fig. 1. An example of class diagram

in the application domain. Let us assume a set $\mathcal{O}$ of objects in the universe. Therefore, Δ assigns each $C \in \mathcal{C}$ a non-empty subset **C** of $\mathcal{O}$. We call **C** the *object type* of C [1]. The generalization relation ◁— in a class diagram defines a sub-superclass <: relation between the classes contained in Δ:

SUBT-1: $\mathbf{C} <: \mathcal{O}$ for each $C \in \mathcal{C}$.
SUBT-2: $\mathbf{C} <: \mathbf{C}$ for each $C \in \mathbf{CN}$.
SUBT-3: $\mathbf{C}_1 <: \mathbf{C}_2$ if C_2 ◁— C_1 is contained in Δ.
SUBT-4: $\mathbf{C}_1 <: \mathbf{C}_3$ if $\mathbf{C}_1 <: \mathbf{C}_2$ and $\mathbf{C}_2 <: \mathbf{C}_3$.

The meaning of $\mathbf{C}_1 <: \mathbf{C}_2$ is defined as the set inclusion $\mathbf{C}_1 \subseteq \mathbf{C}_2$. In general, for two list of types $\underline{\mathbf{T}}_1 = \mathbf{T}_{11}\ldots\mathbf{T}_{1n}$ and $\underline{\mathbf{T}}_2 = \mathbf{T}_{21}\ldots\mathbf{T}_{2m}$, let

$$\underline{\mathbf{T}}_1 <: \underline{\mathbf{T}}_2 \stackrel{def}{=} m = n \wedge \forall i : 1..n \bullet (\mathbf{T}_{1i} <: \mathbf{T}_{2i})$$

We require that a class diagram satisfies the following conditions.

1. The generalization is acyclic:

$$W_1(\Delta) \stackrel{def}{=} C_1 \triangleleft\!\!\!- C_2 \Rightarrow C_1 \neq C_2$$

2. The attribute names of a class are all distinct:

$$W_2(\Delta) \stackrel{def}{=} \forall C \in \mathbf{CN} \bullet dist(\pi_1(attV(C)))$$

where $\pi_1(attV(C))$ is the list of attribute names of C, and $dist$ is true if all these names are distinct.

3. An attribute name assigned to a class C_2 should not be assigned to its subclass C_1:

$$W_3(\Delta) \stackrel{def}{=} \begin{pmatrix} C_1 <: C_2 \\ \wedge\ C_1 \neq C_2 \end{pmatrix} \Rightarrow \pi_1(attV(C_1)) \cap \pi_1(attV(C_2)) = \emptyset$$

4. Similarly, any association name assigned to a class C_2 should not be assigned to its subclasses:

$$W_4(\Delta) \stackrel{def}{=} \begin{pmatrix} C_1 <: C_2 \\ \wedge\ C_1 \neq C_2 \end{pmatrix} \Rightarrow \begin{pmatrix} \forall C \in \mathbf{CN}\bullet \\ (AssN(C_1,C) \cap AssN(C_2,C) = \emptyset) \end{pmatrix}$$

5. Different associations between the same pair of classes should have different names: for any $C_1, C_2 \in \mathcal{C}$ and $A_1, A_2 \in \mathbf{AN}$:

$$W_5(\Delta) \stackrel{def}{=} \left(\begin{array}{c} (Ass(C_1)(A_1) = \langle M_{11}, M_{12}, C_2 \rangle) \\ \wedge (Ass(C_1)(A_2) = \langle M_{21}, M_{22}, C_2 \rangle) \end{array} \right) \Rightarrow A_1 \equiv A_2$$

A class diagram Δ is *well-formed* if it satisfies

$$W(\Delta) \stackrel{def}{=} W_1(\Delta) \wedge W_2(\Delta) \wedge W_3(\Delta) \wedge W_4(\Delta) \wedge W_5(\Delta)$$

A class diagram Δ also identifies the following sets of variables that use cases operate on.

1. $\mathbf{CV} \stackrel{def}{=} \{C : \mathbb{P}\mathbf{C} \mid C \in \mathcal{C}\}$ in which each C records the current set of objects of class **C** existing in the system.
2. $\mathbf{AV} \stackrel{def}{=} \{A : \mathbb{P}(\mathbf{C}_1 \times \mathbf{C}_2) \mid A : (C_1, M_1, M_2, C_2)\}$ in which each A records the links between objects existing in the system.

We call variables in $\mathbf{CV} \cup \mathbf{AV}$ variables in Δ too. In general, we use $type(e)$ to denote the type of an expression e, and $type(\underline{e})$ the list of types of $type(e)$.

2.3 Object Diagrams as System States

In UML, an object diagram of a class diagram Δ consists of some objects and links between these objects. The objects have to be instances of classes in the class diagram, and the links have to be instances of associations in the class diagrams. In our formalization, we define an object diagram as a *state* of the variables in Δ.

Definition 2. (Object Diagram). Let $\Delta = \langle \mathcal{C}, Ass, Att, \triangleleft\!\!-\!\!\rangle$ be a conceptual class diagram. An *object diagram* σ is a *state* over the variables $\mathbf{V} \stackrel{def}{=} \mathbf{CV} \cup \mathbf{AV}$, that is a mapping from variables in $\mathbf{CV} \cup \mathbf{AV}$ to values of their types:

- For each $C \in \mathbf{CV}$, the value $\sigma[C]$ of C in state σ is a subset of **C**.
- For each $A : (C_1, M_1, M_2, C_2) \in \mathbf{AV}$, the value $\sigma[A]$ of A in state σ is a subset of $\mathbf{C}_1 \times \mathbf{C}_2$.
- For each $C \in \mathbf{CV}$, each $a : \mathbf{T} \in att(C)$, and each $o \in \sigma[C]$, $o.a$ is a variable too and its value $\sigma[o.a]$ in state σ is taken from **T**.
  Let **Att** be a state variable that takes values of sets of the form $\{o.a_1 : \mathbf{T}_1, \ldots, o.a_n : \mathbf{T}_n\}$. Its value $\sigma[\mathbf{Att}]$ in a state σ is $\{o.a : \mathbf{T} \mid \exists C \in \mathcal{C}.(o \in \sigma[C] \wedge (a : \mathbf{T}) \in Att(C))\}$. Unlike **CV** and **AV** that are fixed for a class diagram, **Att** changes during the operation of the system that the class diagram models.

An example of an object diagram of $Bank1$ in Figure 1 is given in Figure 2.

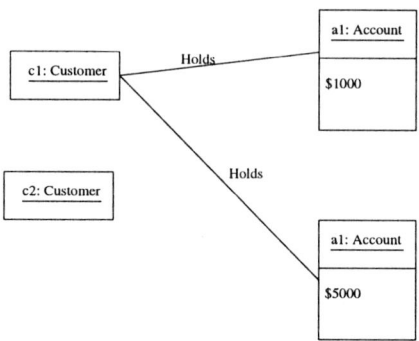

Fig. 2. An example of an object model

2.4 State Assertions

An application may require some property always holds during the execution of the system. For example, Figure 1 shows that a customer is allowed to have up to 3 accounts in a "big bank" modeled by diagram $Bank1$, while a customer has one and only one account in a "small" bank modeled by $Bank2$. In general, we can use predicate over $\mathbf{V} \cup \mathbf{Att}$ to specify a state constraint.

For an association $A : \mathbb{P}(\mathbf{C}_1 \times \mathbf{C}_2)$ and an objects $o_1 \in \mathbf{C}_1$, let

$$A(o_1) \stackrel{def}{=} \{o_2 \mid o_2 \in \mathbf{C}_2 \wedge (o_1, o_2) \in A\}$$

Apart from the syntactical constraint expressed in Definition 1 and the well-formed condition $W(\Delta)$, the following *state invariants* must be met by any valid state of Δ: for any classes C, C_1, C_2, and any association $A : (C_1, M_1, M_2, C_2)$ in Δ,

$$\theta_1 \stackrel{def}{=} \begin{pmatrix} \forall A : \mathbb{P}(\mathbf{C}_1 \times \mathbf{C}_2) \in \mathbf{AV}, \\ \forall o_1 : \mathbf{C}_1, o_2 : \mathbf{C}_2 \end{pmatrix} \bullet ((o_1, o_2) \in A \Rightarrow (o_1 \in C_1 \wedge o_2 \in C_2))$$

$$\theta_2 \stackrel{def}{=} \forall A \in \mathbf{AV}, o_1 \in C_1, o_2 \in C_2 \bullet (\mid A(o_1) \mid \in M_2 \wedge \mid A^{-1}(o_2) \mid \in M_1)$$

$$\theta_3 \stackrel{def}{=} \begin{pmatrix} \forall A : \mathbb{P}(\mathbf{C}_1 \times \mathbf{C}_2) \in \mathbf{AV}, \\ \forall o_1 : \mathbf{C}_1, o_2 \in \mathbf{C}_2 \end{pmatrix} \bullet ((c_1, c_2) \in A \Leftrightarrow (c_2, c_1) \in A^{-1})$$

$$\theta_4 \stackrel{def}{=} \mathbf{C}_1 <: \mathbf{C}_2 \Rightarrow \mathbf{C}_1 \subseteq \mathbf{C}_2$$

where M_1 and M_2 are the cardinalities of C_1 and C_2 in A.

Property θ_1 ensures that associations only link currently existing objects in a state, and all links of a object must be removed as well if this object is removed from the system; θ_2 characterizes the cardinalities of the roles in an association; θ_3 asserts that an association is of no direction; and θ_4 describes the inheritance. A *valid object diagram* of a conceptual class diagram Δ is state σ of Δ that satisfies $\theta \stackrel{def}{=} \theta_1 \wedge \theta_2 \wedge \theta_3 \wedge \theta_4$.

Definition 3. (Semantics of a Conceptual Diagram). The semantics of a conceptual class diagram Δ is the set of all its valid object diagrams, denoted by $[\![\Delta]\!]$.

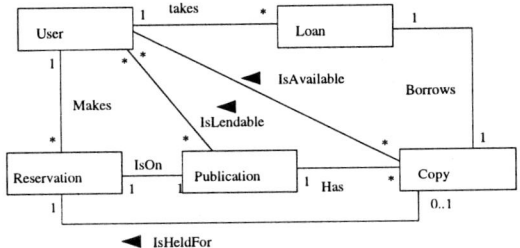

Fig. 3. A class diagram for a library system

The object diagram in Figure 2, is a state of $Bank1$ but not a state of $Bank2$ in Figure 1.

The constraint θ of Δ is enforced by the diagram itself. However, only classes, associations, and their cardinalities are not enough to express all constraints that the application requires. For example, the diagram in Figure 3 does not describe the property that a copy being held for a reservation must be a copy of the publication reserved by the reservation. This property cannot be represented by drawing elements. In UML, it can only be represented by a *comment* in text. In our model, this constraint can be described as the state assertion:

$$\begin{pmatrix} \forall c \in Copy, \\ \forall r \in Reservation, \\ \forall p \in Publication \end{pmatrix} \bullet (IsHeldFor(c,r) \wedge IsOn(r,p) \Rightarrow Has(p,c))$$

where we used the convention $R(a,b)$ for $<a,b> \in R$ for a relation R. This constraint can be written in terms of the algebra of relations $IsHeldFor \circ IsOn \subseteq Has^{-1}$, where $\circ$ is the *composition* operation of relations.

Properties of *associative classes*, *abstract classes* and *aggregation associations* can be captured and reasoned about in terms of state constraints [17].

2.5 Conceptual Models

Definition 4. (Conceptual Model). A conceptual model $CM = \langle \Delta, Inv \rangle$ where Δ is a conceptual class diagram and Inv is a state constraint over Δ.

A state property ψ of a conceptual model can be reasoned about by proving the implication $\theta \wedge Inv \Rightarrow \psi$ in the relational calculus. We denote by $CM \models \psi$ that CM satisfies ψ. This also allows us to define transformations between conceptual diagrams that preserve a state constraint.

3 Use-Case Model

Given a conceptual model CM, an object diagram represents a snapshot of the system at a moment of time. The execution of an *atomic use case* will change the system from one state into another. Such an atomic use case is called a *system operation*. It changes a system's object diagram by creating new objects, deleting old objects; forming or breaking links between objects; or modifying attributes of objects. However, the system only executes a system operation when it is called by an actor. Therefore, we should also model actions performed by the actors.

3.1 System Operations

To define an operation, we use the notion of *designs* in [13]. A design is a predicate that relates the initial values of state variables to their final values. It takes the form of $p(x) \vdash R(x, x')$

$$(p(x) \vdash R(x, x')) \stackrel{def}{=} ok \wedge p(x) \Rightarrow R(x, x') \wedge ok'$$

where x represents the value of x in the initial state and x' represents the value of x in the final state. Such a design asserts that the precondition p must be true before the operation starts, and the post-condition R holds when the operation terminates. However, a particular operation only changes part of the system variables. Thus, its design is always *framed* with the set of the variables it changes and it takes the form:

$$X : (p \vdash R) \stackrel{def}{=} p \Rightarrow R \wedge (\underline{w}' = \underline{w})$$

where $\underline{w}$ contains all the system's variables but those in X.

A system operation operates on the following variables.

1. It may change a class variable $C : \mathbb{P}\mathbf{C} \in \mathbf{CV}$ by creating a new object or deleting an existing object.
2. It may change an association variable $A : \mathbb{P}(\mathbf{C}_1 \times \mathbf{C}_2) \in \mathbf{AV}$ by forming a new link or breaking an existing link between two objects.
3. The value of **Att** will be changed when a new object is created or an old one is deleted.
4. An attribute $o.a$ in the current value of **Att** may be modified or read, e.g. changing or outputting the name of an existing person.
5. A system operation will be executed when some input value parameters are provided and will output some results to some variables. Therefore, an operation is specified as a procedure with a list $\underline{x} : \mathbf{T}_1$ of *formal value parameters* and a list $\underline{y} : \mathbf{T}_2$ of *formal result parameters*. Such a procedure can only be executed when it is called by an *actor object* that provides the *actual* value and result parameters. We use **val** to denotes the set of all actual value parameters and **res** the set of all actual result parameters for the calls to the system operations. These two sets of parameters are also variables that are accesses by the execution of the system operations. We require that these variables do not introduce new class types.
6. The actors decide the protocol in which they interact with the system. Local control variables are need for sequencing, choices and iterations. A control variable is of a simple data type.

We have **V** to be the set that contains the variables identified in items 1-4. Let **U** be the set of variables that contains the actual parameters and control variables identified in items 5 and 6, and **P** the set of formal parameters required for the specification of the system operations. We define $\varGamma \stackrel{def}{=} \mathbf{V} \cup \mathbf{U}$, and $\varOmega \stackrel{def}{=} \mathbf{V} \cup \mathbf{P}$. Now a system operation is defined in the form

$$op[\underline{x} : \mathbf{T}_1;\ \underline{y} : \mathbf{T}_2] :: \mathbf{Pre} : P;\ \mathbf{Post} : R$$

where op is the name of the operation, $\underline{x} : \mathbf{T}_1$ and $\underline{y} : \mathbf{T}_2$ the formal value and result parameters, P is a predicate over $\varOmega$ that defines the precondition, R is a predicate over variables in $\varOmega$ and their primed versions $\varOmega'$ that defines the post condition.

The semantics of operation op is defined as a design

$$op \stackrel{def}{=} X : (P \vdash R)$$

where, P and R only contain variables in $\varGamma$, and X is the set of variables that can be modified by op.

3.2 Actors Operations

An actor's operation may modify actual value parameters in **val** and read values from actual result parameters in **res**. It of course may modify and read a control variable. We call these operations that only access variables in $\mathbf{U}$ *control operations*. A control operation has no effect on the object diagrams of the conceptual model. Such an operation is in general a guarded design of the form

$$g \longrightarrow X : (Pre \vdash Post) \stackrel{def}{=} g \wedge (X : Pre \vdash Post)$$

This operation can only take place in a state that assigns g to $true$. Remember that such an operation only contains variables in $\mathbf{U}$.

Actors have to call system operations to carry out a use case. It is possible that one or more actors call an operation for a number of times as well as different system operations. To define system operation calls by actors, we introduce a set **Actor** of names to represent the set of individual actors (or users) involved in the system. A *call* to a system operation $op[\underline{x} : \mathbf{T}_1;\ \underline{y} : \mathbf{T}_2] :: \mathbf{Pre} : P;\ \mathbf{Post} : R$ by an actor u is an operation of the form $op_u(\underline{val};\ \underline{res})$:

$$op_u(\underline{val};\ \underline{res}) \stackrel{def}{=} W(op(\underline{val};\ \underline{res})) \Rightarrow op[\underline{val}/\underline{x};\ \underline{res}/\underline{y}],\ \text{where}$$
$$W(op_u(\underline{val};\ \underline{res})) \stackrel{def}{=} (type(\underline{val}) <: \underline{\mathbf{T}}_1) \wedge (\underline{\mathbf{T}}_2 <: type(\underline{res}))$$

where $op[\underline{val}/\underline{x};\ \underline{res}/\underline{y}]$ is obtained from the design of $op[\underline{x} : \underline{\mathbf{T}}_1;\ \underline{y} : \underline{\mathbf{T}}_2]$ by substituting $\underline{x}$ and $\underline{y}$ with $\underline{val}$ and $\underline{res}$ respectively.

This definition implies that it is the caller's responsibility to ensure the correctness of the types of the actual parameters. If a call is not well-formed, the system behaves chaotically. Of course, a system operation can be *refined* to handle unwell-formed calls as exceptions.

For concurrent applications, an actor u can make a number of calls simultaneously: $op_u^1(\underline{val}_1;\ \underline{res}_1) \wedge op_u^1(\underline{val}_2;\ \underline{res}_2)$. In general, we allow to conjoin two actors actions by conjunction $\wedge$. Such an operation is called an *joint operation*.

A call to a system operation by an actor can be conditional and in the form of $g \longrightarrow op_u(\underline{val};\ \underline{res})$, where g only contains variables in **U**. A non-conditional call is a special conditional call in which the guard is *true*.

In summary, an operation of an actor is either a control operation, a conditional call or an joint action to a system operations. The use cases of a system are then specified by giving a set **Actor** of actors, a set of system operations **OP** and a set of actors operations (also called *actions*) **UA**.

Some readers may wonder how sequential composition of two actors operations specified. This can be done by using a control variable ℓ:

$$P_1;\ P_2 \stackrel{def}{=} \{(\ell = c_1) \longrightarrow P_1 \wedge (\ell' = c_2), (\ell = c_2) \longrightarrow P_2 \wedge (\ell' = c_3)\}$$

where c_1, c_2 and c_3 represent the *labels* of commands, and it is required that $\ell = c_1$ initially.

For example, we can specify system operations $FindUser[Id : \mathbf{N};\ u : \mathbf{User}]$, $FindCopy[Id_1 : \mathbf{N};\ c : \mathbf{Copy}]$, $Loan[u : (\mathbf{User}, c : \mathbf{Copy}]$ for a library system [18]. Actor librarian L can carry out the use case $LendCopy_L(i_1, i_2)$ by the protocol

$FindUser_L(i_1;\ u);\ (u \neq null) \longrightarrow FindCopy_L(i_2;\ c);$
$(c \neq null) \longrightarrow Loan_L(u, c)$

This use case defines the behaviour of the process of lending a copy to a user. The librarian first inputs the identifications of the user and the copy. He/she then calls the system operation $FindUser$ which returns the user object if found otherwise $null$. If the user is found, the librarian then calls the system operation $FindCopy$ which returns the copy if found otherwise $null$. If the copy is found, the librarian calls the system operation $Loan$ that creates a loan and record the user and copy on the loan.

This specification is only correct if no other actor tries to lend the same copy to another user at the same time. In that case $FindCopy_L$ and $Loan_L$ should be carried out together atomically as $(u \neq null) \longrightarrow FindCopy_L(i_2;\ c) \wedge Loan_L(u, c)$.

3.3 Constructing a System Specification

Given a conceptual model $CM = (\Delta, Inv)$, a set of systems operations **OP**, a set **Actor** of actors, and a set **UA** of actors operations, we construct

- The set Γ of variables that the actors operations operate on.
- An initial condition $Init$ which define the set of states from which the system can start to work.

The system is then specified by the transition system $\mathcal{S} \stackrel{def}{=} (\Gamma, Inv, \mathbf{OP}, Init, \mathbf{UA})$. $\mathcal{S}$ is well formed if every operation call in **UA** is a call to an operation in **OP** from an actor in **Actor**:

$$W(\mathcal{S}) \stackrel{def}{=} \forall op_u(op_u \in \mathbf{UA} \Rightarrow op \in \mathbf{OP} \wedge u \in \mathbf{Actor})$$

The semantics of $\mathcal{S}$ is defined to be all the possible execution sequences of the operations in **UA**. Formally, an execution of $\mathcal{S}$ is an infinite sequence of states, $\sigma_0, \sigma_1 \ldots$, such that

- σ_0 satisfies $Init$.
- Each step (σ_i, σ_{i+1}) is a carried out by an operation in **UA**, i.e., there is an operation $op_u \in$ **UA** such that σ_i satisfies the precondition of op_u and its guard and (σ_i, σ_{i+1}) satisfies the post-condition of op_u.

Each execution of S in an interleaving of a set of *scenarios* of use cases. The invariant properties Inv can be prove by showing that for each $op_u \in$ **UA**,

$$Pre \wedge g \wedge Inv \wedge Post \Rightarrow Inv'$$

where Pre and $Post$ are the precondition and post condition of op_u, g is the guard of op_u, and Inv' is the predicate obtained from Inv by replacing its variables with their primed versions.

From the work [10] about the definition of Hoar's CSP specification by transition systems, we can also write the specification of use cases in the notation of CSP.

Let each operation call $op_u(\underline{val}; \underline{res})$ be an event triggered by actor u, and let $\mathcal{D}(op_u(\underline{val}; \underline{res}))$ denote the design of $op_u(\underline{val}; \underline{res})$ defined in this section. Define a CSP command

$$op_u(\underline{val}; \underline{res}) \longrightarrow (\mathcal{D}(op_u(\underline{val}; \underline{res})); out_u!(\underline{res}))$$

The meaning of this command is that once an interaction op_u between actor u and the system occurs, the system carries out the operation according to the design of the operation to change its state and outputs results to the actor.

Such a CSP command can be guarded by a Boolean expression too in the form

$$b \wedge op_u(\underline{val}; \underline{res}) \longrightarrow (\mathcal{D}(op_u(\underline{val}; \underline{res})); out_u!(\underline{res}))$$

Then sequential composition ";", external choices "[]", non-deterministic choice "⊓", and recursion can be defined to form a specification of a use case as a CSP process. The use-case model is then given as the interleaving composition of the specified use cases in the form $U_1 ||| \ldots ||| U_m$, where each $U_i, i = 1, \ldots, U_m$, is a CSP process specification of a use case. Examples of specifications of use cases are given in the full version of the paper [17].

4 Conclusion and Discussion

We have provided a method to formally combine a conceptual models and a use-cases model of UML to form a system specification. The combined model is the well-known notation of transition systems [10] for general reactive systems. This is well justified as an object-oriented system is in nature a concurrent and reactive system.

The advantage of using a well-established model is that we do not have to develop or study new semantics and tools for verification. Methods and tools for specification and verification of transition system are well-established, e.g. [10, 4, 7]. Furthermore, this model is already extended to deal with real-time and fault-tolerance [10, 15]. Furthermore, the model of transition systems is isomorphic to that of the statecharts which is a part of UML.

The main difference between our work and that in [19, 8, 6] is that we study formal semantic relationships between different models of UML, rather than only formalization of individual diagrams. The paper [9] also treats a class as a set of objects and an association as a relation between objects. However, it does not consider use cases. Our work also shares some common ideas with [2] in the treatment of use cases. However, we have a different understand about a conceptual model and have addressed the clear relationships between the UML models. We have also provided a working procedure for building a system specification from UML models.

In our related work [18], we used case studies to demonstrate that the formalization supports building up a model step by step. In [16], a specification language is developed with which we can write a specification as a Java-like program. Based on the model in this paper, that language can be extended to deal with concurrency

We have developed a model for requirement analysis in this paper, a specification language in [16] and a model for object-oriented programming in [11]. Further work is needed to close the gap between requirement analysis and programming by providing a method to transform a use-case model to a design model. Progress in this direction is made in [12].

References

1. M. Abadi and L. Cardelli. *A Theory of Objects*. Springer, 1996.
2. R.J.R. Back, L. Petre, and I.P. Paltor. Formalizing UML use cases in the refinement calculus. Technical Report 279, Turku Centre for Computer Science, Turku, Finland, May 1999.
3. G. Booch, J. Rumbaugh, and I. Jacobson. *The Unified Modelling Language User Guide*. Addison-Wesley, 1999.
4. E. Clarke, E.A. Emerson, and A.P. Sistla. Automatic verification of finite-state concurrent systems using temporal logic specifications. *ACM Transactions on Programming Languages and Systems*, 8(2):244–263, 1986.
5. D. D'Souza and A.C. Wills. *Objects, Components and Framework with UML: The Catalysis Approach*. Addison-Wesley, 1998.
6. A. Egyed. Scalable consistency checking between diagrams: The Viewintegra approach. In *Proc. of the 16th IEEE International Conference on Automated Software Engineering*, San Diego, USA, 2001.
7. U. Engberg, P. Grønning, and L. Lamport. Mechanical verification of concurrent systems with TLA. In G. Bochmann, editor, *Proceedings of the 4th International Conference on Computer Aided Verification, Lecture Notes in Computer Science 663*, pages 44–55. Springer-Verlag, Montreal, Canada, 1992.
8. G. Engels, J.M. Kuster, R. Heckel, and L. Groenewewegen. A methodology for specifying and analyzing consistency of object-oriented behavioral models. In *The Proc. of International Conference on Foundation of Software Engineering, FSE-10*, Austria, 2001.
9. D. Harel and B. Rumpe. Modeling languages: Syntax, semantics and all that stuff - part I: The basic stuff. Technical Report MCS00-16, Faculty of Mathematics and Computer Science, The Weizmann Institute of Science, Israel, September 2000.
10. T. Henzinger, Z. Manna, and A. Pnueli. Temporal proof methodologies for timed transition systems. *Information and Computation*, 112(2):273–337, 1994.
11. J. He, Z. Liu, and X. Li. A relational model for object-oriented programming. Technical Report UNU/IIST Report No 231, UNU/IIST, P.O. Box 3058, Macau, March 2001.

12. J. He, Z. Liu, and X. Li. Towards a refinement calculus for object-oriented systems. To appear at ICCI02 as a Keynote Talk, August 19-20, 2002, Alberta, Canada, 2002.
13. C.A.R. Hoare and J. He. *Unifying theories of programming.* Prentice-Hall International, 1998.
14. I. Jacobson, G. Booch, and J. Rumbaugh. *The Unified Software Development Process.* Addison-Wesley, 1999.
15. Z. Liu and M. Joseph. Specification and verification of fault-tolerance, timing and scheduling. *ACM Transactions on Languages and Systems*, 21(1):46–89, 1999.
16. Z. Liu, X. Li, J. He, and Y. Chen. A relational model for object-oriented analysis. Technical Report UNU/IIST Repor No 258, UNU/IIST, P.O. Box 3058, Macau, July 2002.
17. Z. Liu, X. Li, and J. He. Using transition systems to unify *uml* models. Technical report, Dept. of Maths and Computer Science, the University of leicester, England., May 2002.
18. X. Li, Z. Liu, and J. He. Formal and use-case driven requirement analysis in UML. In *COMPSAC01*, pages 215–224, Illinois, USA, October 2001. IEEE Computer Society.
19. The pUML Group. The precise UML web site: /http://www.cs.york.ac.uk/puml. 1999.

A Formal Metamodeling Approach to a Transformation between the UML State Machine and Object-Z

Soon-Kyeong Kim and David Carrington

School of Information Technology and Electrical Engineering
The University of Queensland, Brisbane, 4072, Australia
soon@itee.uq.edu.au, davec@itee.uq.edu.au

Abstract. A significant problem with currently suggested approaches for transforming between models in different languages is that the transformation is often described imprecisely, with the result that the overall transformation task may be imprecise, incomplete and inconsistent. This paper presents a formal metamodeling approach for transforming between UML and Object-Z. In the paper, the two languages are defined in terms of their formal metamodels, and a systematic transformation between the models is provided at the meta-level in terms of formal mapping functions. As a consequence, we can provide a precise, consistent and complete transformation between them.

1 Introduction

Two significant problems exist with current approaches [2, 3, 4, 11, 12, 15, 16] to transform a model in one modeling (or specification) language to another:
- the languages often lack a precise description for their syntax and semantics
- the transformation is often described imprecisely at the model level.

Moreover, it is often difficult to verify the transformation is correct in terms of the transformation rules given. This means that the overall transformation task may be imprecise, incomplete or inconsistent. An incomplete or inconsistent transformation can cause unexpected behavioral consequences [5]. Consequently, the confidence of the developer is reduced, making the transformation approach unreliable.

To overcome these problems, this paper introduces a formal metamodeling approach to integrate two languages: UML [13] and Object-Z [1, 14]. In this approach, the UML metamodel is first formalized using Object-Z. A formal metamodel of Object-Z is developed by adopting the metamodeling architecture used for the UML metamodel. Given these metamodels, a systematic transformation between these two languages is defined at the meta-level in terms of formal transformation rules.

Previously we presented our formal metamodel based approach for the static part of UML (the UML class constructs) [6]. We have applied the same approach to the dynamic part of UML (the UML state machine) [8]. This paper presents a more complete version of our work describing an extended Object-Z metamodel and formal transformation rules between the UML state machine and Object-Z. It should be noted that in this paper it is not our intention to show how the transformed Object-Z model of a UML model can be used for rigorous analysis of the UML model, rather we focus on describing our metamodel-based (formal) transformation approach precisely.

The advantages of the metamodel-based transformation can be summarized as follows: the transformation is defined in a systematic way at the meta-level, not the model-level; the semantic and syntactic structure is preserved during the transformation; inconsistency and incompleteness of the transformation can be verified in a systematic manner based on the metamodels of the languages; since the syntactic structure is preserved during the transformation, a systematic trace between the models in the two different languages is possible; and when the metamodel of a language is incomplete in terms of its semantics, mapping the language to another provides an extended semantic domain of that language.

The structure of the rest of this paper is as follows. Section 2 presents background materials. Section 3 introduces a formal mapping between the two languages. Section 4 draws some conclusions.

2 Background

This section presents background material to make this paper self-contained: a partial description in Object-Z of the core model elements of the UML state machine borrowed from [9] and a partial Object-Z metamodel defining core modeling concepts in Object-Z extending (the initial version of) the Object-Z metamodel presented in [8]. In this paper, we assume that all types are already defined as distinct Object-Z classes.

2.1 An Object-Z Model of the UML State Machine

State: State inherits from StateVertex and has associations with StateMachine, Action, Event and Transition: *stateMachine, entry, doActivity, exit, deferrableEvent,* and *internal* (Fig. 1).

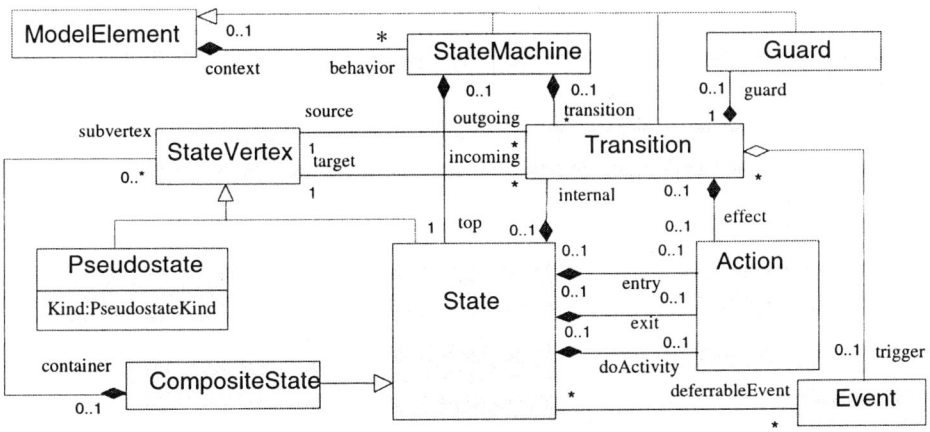

Fig. 1. Core modeling elements of the UML State Machine

```
┌─State─────────────────────────────────────────────────┐
│ StateVertex                                           │
│ ┌───────────────────────────────────────────────────┐ │
│ │ stateMachine : ℙ StateMachine                     │ │
│ │ entry : ℙ↓ Action ©                               │ │
│ │ doActivity : ℙ↓ Action ©                          │ │
│ │ exit : ℙ↓ Action ©                                │ │
│ │ deferrableEvent : ℙ↓ Event                        │ │
│ │ internal : ℙ Transition ©                         │ │
│ ├───────────────────────────────────────────────────┤ │
│ │ {# stateMachine, # entry, # exit, # doActivity} ⊆ {0, 1} │
│ │ ...                                               │ │
│ └───────────────────────────────────────────────────┘ │
└───────────────────────────────────────────────────────┘
```

Event and Action: Event and Action inherit from ModelElement. Event has parameters and associations to Transition and State.

```
┌─Event──────────────────────┐   ┌─Action────────────────────┐
│ ModelElement               │   │ ModelElement              │
│ ┌────────────────────────┐ │   │ ┌───────────────────────┐ │
│ │ transition : ℙ Transition │ │ │ isAsynchronous : Boolean │
│ │ state : ℙ↓ State        │ │   │ │ entryState : ℙ State  │ │
│ │ parameters : seq Parameter © │ │ exitState : ℙ State   │ │
│ │ ...                    │ │   │ │ activityState : ℙ State│ │
│ │                        │ │   │ │ ...                   │ │
│ └────────────────────────┘ │   │ └───────────────────────┘ │
└────────────────────────────┘   └───────────────────────────┘
```

CompositeState: CompositeState has two attributes *isConcurrent* and *isRegion* representing whether it is decomposed into two or more orthogonal regions and whether it is a substate of a concurrent state respectively [13]. It inherits from State and has a composition association to StateVertex. The static semantics (e.g. there must be at least two composite substates in a concurrent composite state) are formalized as invariants in the predicate of the following Object-Z class.

Transition: Transition has a source and a target state vertex. It also can have a guard, a trigger event, effect actions, and a state for internal transitions.

```
┌─CompositeState──────────────┐   ┌─Transition─────────────────┐
│ State                       │   │ ModelElement               │
│ ┌─────────────────────────┐ │   │ ┌────────────────────────┐ │
│ │ isConcurrent : Boolean  │ │   │ │ stateMachine : ℙ StateMachine │
│ │ isRegion : Boolean      │ │   │ │ source : ↓ StateVertex │ │
│ │ subvertex : ℙ ↓ StateVertex © │ │ target : ↓ StateVertex │ │
│ ├─────────────────────────┤ │   │ │ guard : ℙ Guard ©      │ │
│ │ isConcurrent ⇒          │ │   │ │ trigger : ℙ↓ Event     │ │
│ │  #{ s: subvertex |      │ │   │ │ effect : ℙ↓ Action ©   │ │
│ │    s ∈ CompositeState } ≥ 2 │ │ state : ℙ↓ State       │ │
│ │ ...                     │ │   │ │ ...                    │ │
│ └─────────────────────────┘ │   │ └────────────────────────┘ │
└─────────────────────────────┘   └────────────────────────────┘
```

StateMachine: StateMachine has composition relationships to State and Transition, and an aggregation relationship to ModelElement which is the context of the state machine.

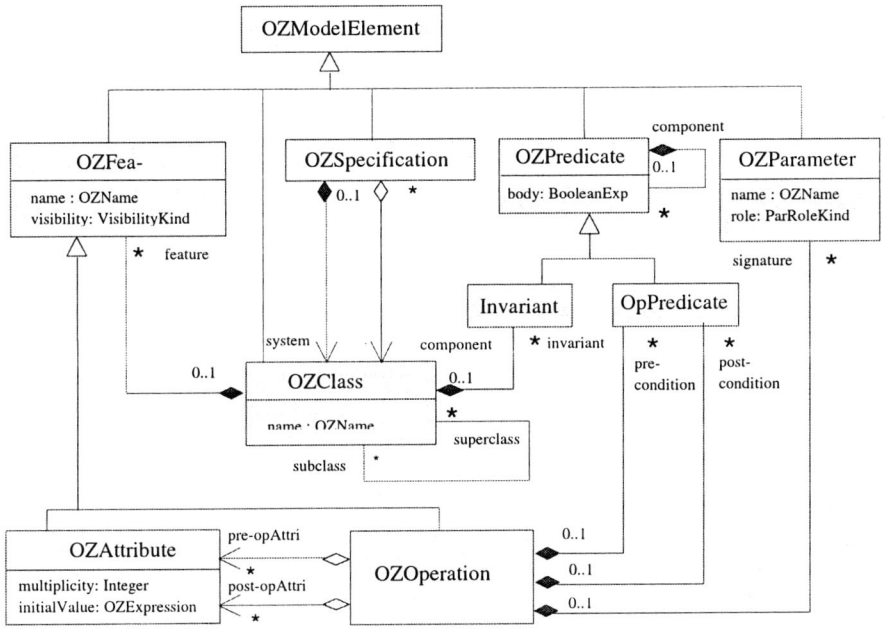

Fig. 2. A class diagram showing the structure of core model elements in Object-Z

2.2 The Object-Z Metamodel Defining core Modeling Concepts

Fig. 2 is a UML class diagram showing the abstract syntax of core modeling constructs in Object-Z.

The Object-Z class *OZClass* is a formal description for classes in Object-Z. The attribute *superclass* maintains inheritance information. Each class has its own features, i.e. attributes and operations defining static and dynamic behaviors of its instances.

─OZClass─────────────────────
OZModelElement
─────────────────────────────
superclass : $\mathbb{P}$ OZClass
features : $\mathbb{P}$ ↓OZFeature ©
invariant : $\mathbb{P}$ Invariant ©
─────────────────────────────

Attributes: Object-Z attributes can be further classified into pure and relationship attributes depending on their roles (Fig. 3). Pure attributes are those not modeling relationships between classes. On the other hand, relationship attributes model relationships between classes using the instantiation mechanism in Object-Z. Like UML, relationships between objects can be common reference relationships, shared or unshared whole-part relationships. For this, we define an enumeration type, *RelationshipKind*, which has *reference*, *sharedOwner* and *unsharedOwner* as its values.

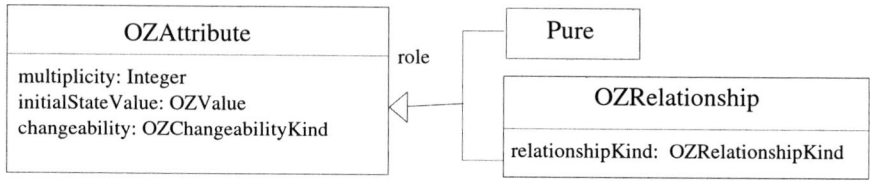

Fig. 3. A class diagram showing a classification of attributes in Object-Z

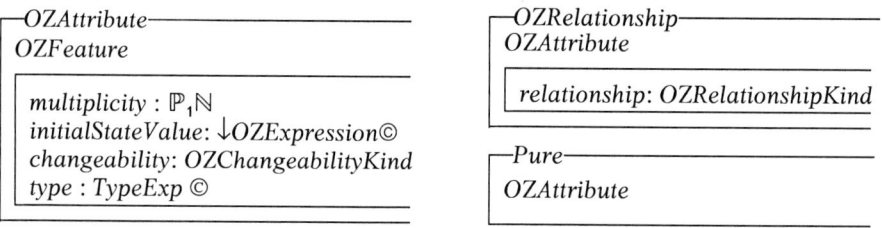

Operations: Operations in Object-Z can be classified as local or interaction (Fig. 4). Local operations model the local behavior of objects. Interaction operations model interactions with other objects. Obviously, interaction operations are related to relationship attributes.

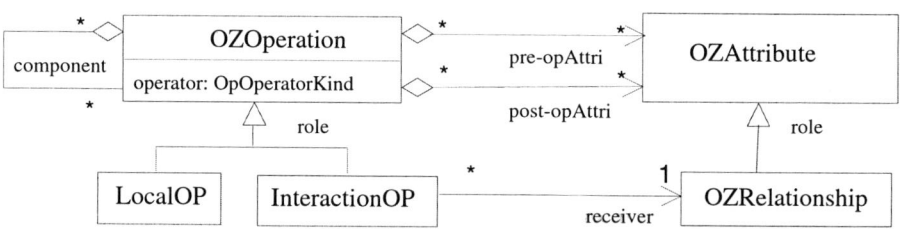

Fig. 4. A class diagram showing a classification of operations in Object-Z

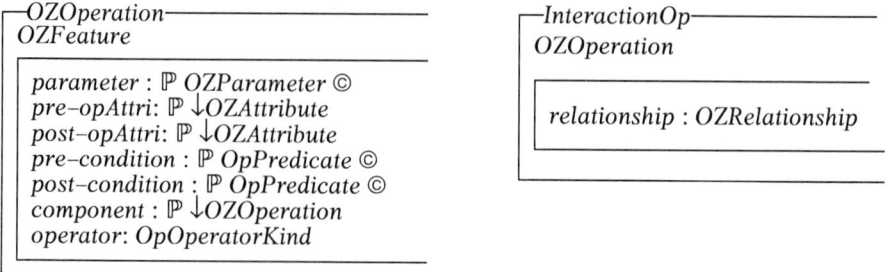

3   A Formal Mapping between the UML State Machine and Object-Z

When the context of a state machine is a class, the state machine as a whole describes the behavior of the class (Fig. 5). In Object-Z the behavior of a class (or, to be precise, an object of the class) can be modeled in terms of its attributes and operations. Consequently we transform the UML state machine in terms of attributes and operations in Object-Z (Fig. 5 shows this semantic mapping). To provide a direct syntactical mapping between the two languages, however, the syntactic structure of the Object-Z metamodel presented in Fig. 2 is extended according to that of the UML state machine. This enables us to preserve the syntactic structure of the two languages during the transformation and makes the translation process systematic and precise.

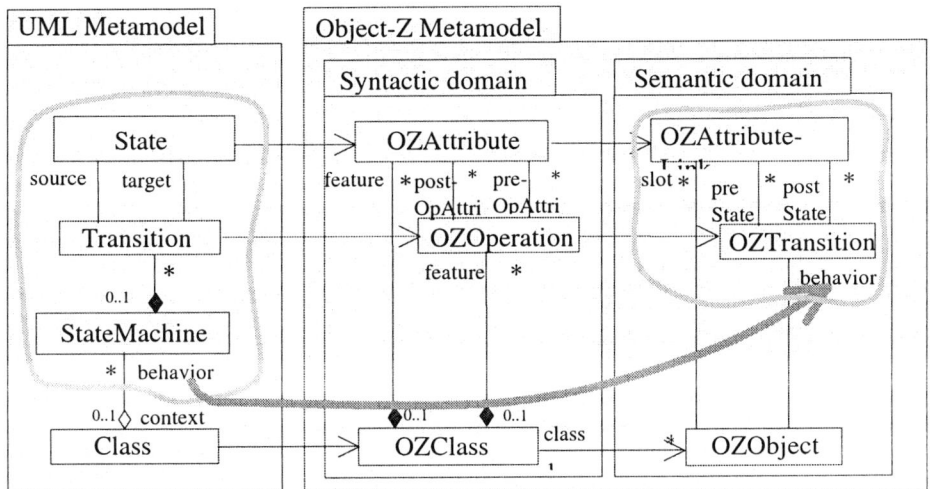

Fig. 5. Semantic comparability between UML State machines and Object-Z

Detailed transformation rules are as follows (we refer readers to [10] for a complete description of transformation rules and case studies developed using the rules).

States : A state in the state machine is a condition during the lifetime of an object. The condition can be either a passive situation, e.g. an object waiting for some event to occur, or an active situation, e.g. the object is performing some actions or activities. As claimed, in Object-Z such a behavioral state of an object can be modeled with an attribute. Although standard Object-Z does not explicitly distinguish whether an attribute models a static or a behavioral state of the object, to provide a direct syntactical mapping between the two languages, we extend the attribute structure of Object-Z by classifying pure attributes into static or behavioral state attributes. Behavioral state attributes model the notion of states in the state machine, e.g. capturing a situation in which the object is doing or waiting for some actions (see Fig. 6 for this extension).

A formal description of the metaclass BehavioralState is given below. Since behavioral attributes model observable states of objects, they are visible. The possible values of the attributes are Boolean values. When a behavioral state attribute is *true*, it means that the object is in that behavioral state, which is regarded as an *active* state in UML. Since states in the state machine can be contained by a composite state, the metaclass BehavioralState has an attribute *container* of type itself. We also define an attribute *isConcurrency* of type StateConcurrencyKind to formalize the concept of composite states in the state machine and their concurrency. These attributes are used to formalize the static semantics of the UML state.

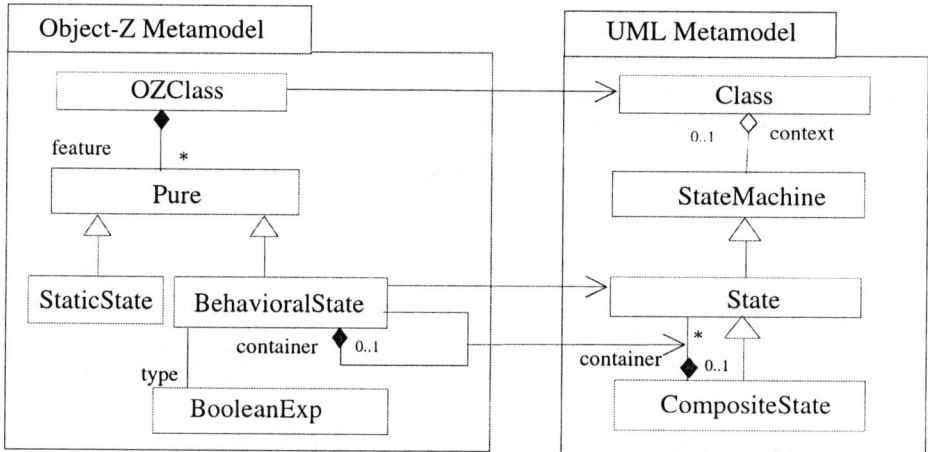

Fig. 6. A class diagram showing an extended structure of attributes in Object-Z

$StateConcurrencyKind ::== simple \mid concurrentComp \mid nonConcurrentComp$

─ BehavioralState ─────────────────────────
Pure
──────────────────────────────────────
container : $\mathbb{P}$ BehavioralState ⓒ
isConcurrency : StateConcurrencyKind
──────────────────────────────────────
# container ≤ 1 ∧ type ∈ BooleanType ∧ visibility = visible
type.evaluate = true ⇒
[1] (∀ c: container • c.evaluate = true)
[2] isConcurrent = concurrentComp ⇒
     (∀ s: BehavioralState | self ∈ s.container • s.type.evaluate = true)
[3] isConcurrent = nonConcurrentComp ⇒
     #{s: BehavioralState | self ∈ s.container ∧ s.type.evaluate = true} = 1
──────────────────────────────────────

The invariants defined in the predicate formalize the static semantics of states:

[1] When a state is *true* meaning active in the UML terminology, its container state should be also *true*.
[2] For a concurrent composite state, when it is *true*, all its contained states should be *true*.

[3] For a non-concurrent composite state, when it is *true*, only one of its contained states should be *true* at one time.

The state hierarchy is also formalized by these invariants.

The function *mapUMLStateToOZ* takes a UML state and returns a behavioral attribute of Object-Z. The corresponding behavioral state attribute of the UML container becomes the container of the Object-Z behavioral state attribute (see [10] for a complete description of the functions).

$\mid mapUMLStateToOZ : \downarrow State \rightarrow BehavioralState$

We map all states defined in a state machine to Object-Z. We restrict the context of the state machine to a UML class defined within a given UML class diagram. In this context, each state defined in the state machine maps to a distinct behavioral attribute of the Object-Z class corresponding to the UML class. The function *mapUMLStateMachineToOZ* is a formal description of this rule. It should be noted that the function *mapUMLStateMachineToOZ* is not completely defined yet and it needs to be extended with respect to other model elements of the state machine, e.g. transitions, events, and actions (see [10] for a complete description of the function).

$\mid mapUMLStateMachineToOZ : UMLStateMachine \rightarrow OZClass$

Events : An event represents the reception of a signal or a request to invoke an operation (a call event) [13]. From an object's point of view, responding to such a request should be modeled as an operation (we call this operation an *event acceptor operation*). Consequently, we transform each event into an event acceptor operation. Since the reception of an event is a local behavior of the receiving object, event acceptor operations inherit from local operations in the Object-Z metamodel (see the metaclass EventAccptOP in Fig. 7).

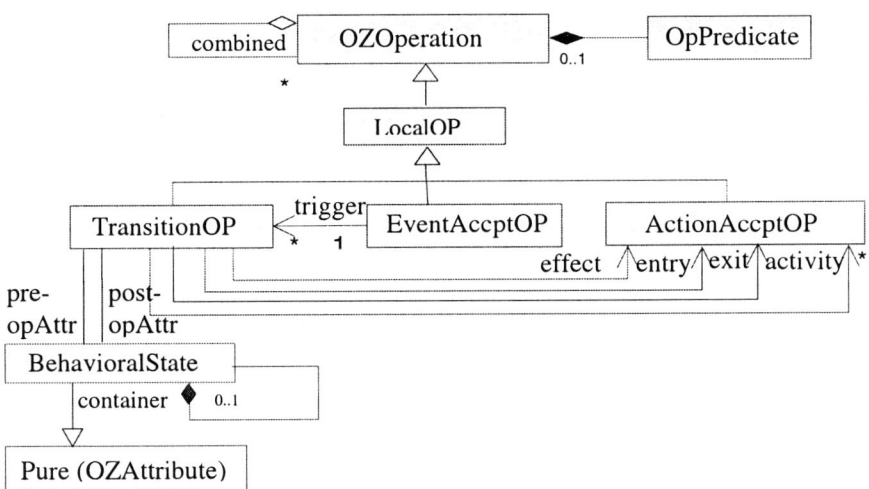

Fig. 7. A class diagram showing an extended structure of operations in Object-Z

Prior to formalizing event acceptor operations, we extend the Object-Z class *OZOperation* defined in Section 2 as below. The secondary attribute called *allComponent* holds all operation components recursively used to define the operation.

─ *OZOperation* ──────────────
...
Δ
allComponent : $\mathbb{P}$ *OZOperation*
─────────────────────────
allComponent = *component* ∪
  ∪ {*c*: *component* •
   c.allComponent}
─────────────────────────

─ *EventAcceptOP* ──────────────
LocalOP
─────────────────────────
triggeredTranOp :
    $\mathbb{P}$ *TransitionOP*
─────────────────────────
triggeredTranOp =
  {*c*: *allComponent* |
   c.component = ∅}
─────────────────────────

The Object-Z class *EventAcceptOP* is a formal description of the metaclass EventAcceptOP. Since the reception of an event results in firing transitions, an event acceptor operation contains a set of operations defined for the transitions.

─ *EventAcceptOP* ──────────────────────────────
LocalOP
───
triggeredTranOp : $\mathbb{P}$ *TransitionOP*
───
triggeredTranOp = {*c*: *allComponent* | *c.component* = ∅}
───

We map each event of a state machine to an event acceptor operation of Object-Z. The function *mapUMLEventToOZ* takes a UML event and returns an event acceptor operation of Object-Z. The parameters of the event map to those of the event acceptor operation. The Object-Z operations corresponding to the transitions that the event fires are defined as the triggered transition operations of the event acceptor operation (see the Object-Z class *TransitionOp* for the definition of transition operations and the mapping function *mapUMLTransitionToOZ* later in this section). The conditions of change events are formalized as the pre-condition of their event acceptor operations. When an event triggers more than one transition, their transition operations are combined by the following rules within the event acceptor operation.

When the source states of transitions are contained in the same composite state (note that in this case the composite state is always non-concurrent), only one of the transitions can be fired at any time. Consequently, we combine the transition operations using the choice operator ([]) in Object-Z. Therefore, there should exist a component operation in the set *allComponent* of the event acceptor operation that combines the transition operations using the choice operator ([]).

When the source states of transitions are contained in different composite states, the transition operations are combined depending on the concurrency of the least common ancestor of the source states. For example, when the least common ancestor of two transitions is concurrent, the transition operations are combined using the conjunction operator (∧). Otherwise, the operations are combined using the choice operator. Since Object-Z operations are combined recursively using other operations, the operations actually combined as a component in the set *allComponent* of the event acceptor operation are those containing not only the transition operations of the two transitions but also the transition operations of all other transitions defined in the state configuration of the least common ancestor and also fired by the event. In this way, we can formalize transitions triggered by the same event with respect to their state hierarchy and concurrency (see [10] for a complete description of the function).

$$| \; mapUMLEventToOZ : \downarrow Event \rightarrow EventAcceptOP$$

Actions: An action is a specification of an executable statement in UML [13], so we formalize actions in UML as operations in Object-Z (we call these operations *action acceptor operations*). We extend the Object-Z metamodel accordingly (see Fig. 7).

$$\begin{array}{l} \rule{0pt}{2ex}ActionAcceptOP \rule{5cm}{0.4pt} \\ LocalOP \\ \rule{10cm}{0.4pt} \end{array}$$

The function *mapUMLActionToOZ* takes a UML action and returns an action acceptor operation of Object-Z. When a call action invokes an operation defined in the same class, we directly map the Object-Z operation corresponding to the operation as the action acceptor operation. Note that it is assumed that the Object-Z class *Action* defined in Section 2 has an additional attribute *target* of type Instance (see [7]) which holds the target instances of the action. Also note that since the argument and script of actions are expressions which can be defined using any description language, no further rules are given for these constructs (see [10] for details of the function).

$$| \; mapUMLActionToOZ : \downarrow Action \rightarrow \downarrow OZOperation$$

Transitions: A transition has two aspects. First, it presents a change in the state of an object. Second, it also presents the execution of actions, e.g., exit, entry, or effect actions, or activities associated with the transition. We formalize the object behavior presented by transitions using class operations in Object-Z (we call these operations *transition operations*). Fig. 7 shows this extension to the Object-Z metamodel.

The Object-Z class *TransitionOP* is a formal description of transition operations and has two behavioral state attributes *source* and *target* representing the source and target states of the transition respectively. Since the source state is a condition to fire the transition, the attribute *source* is defined as a pre-operation attribute of the transition operation and its value is used as a pre-condition of the operation. Similarly, the attribute *target* is defined as a post-operation attribute and it value is used as a post-condition of the operation. The class has an action operation representing its effect and a set of action operations presenting the exit actions of the states in the full hierarchy of the source state (see the secondary attribute *explicitSourceState* in [9] for the concept of the state hierarchy). It also has two sets of action operations *stateEntry* and *stateActivity* presenting the entry actions and the activities of the states in the full hierarchy of the target state respectively. Finally, it includes an attribute called *actionSequence* formalizing the execution sequence of actions. The action operations are combined in the following sequence: the exit actions of the source states, the effect action stated in the transition, the entry actions stated in the target states, and the activities stated in the target states (see invariant [1]). The components of a transition operation are the action acceptor operations corresponding to the actions associated with the transition (see invariant [2]).

$$
\begin{array}{l}
\rule{4cm}{0.4pt}\ \textit{TransitionOP}\rule{6cm}{0.4pt}\\
\textit{LocalOP}\\[4pt]
\quad\begin{array}{l}
source : BehavioralState\\
target : \mathbb{P}\ BehavioralState\\
stateExit : seq \downarrow OZOperation\\
effect : seq \downarrow OZOperation\\
stateEntry : seq \downarrow OZOperation\\
stateActivity : seq \downarrow OZOperation\\
actionSequence : seq \downarrow OZOperation\\[4pt]
source \in pre\text{-}opAttr \wedge target \subseteq post\text{-}opAttr \wedge \#\ effect = 1\\
{[1]}\ stateExit\ \frown\ effect\ \frown\ stateEntry\ \frown\ stateActivity = actionSequence\\
{[2]}\ ran\ actionSequence = allComponent
\end{array}
\end{array}
$$

State changes: The source and target states of a transition are used to define those of the transition operation. That is, the Object-Z behavioral state attribute corresponding to the source state of the transition is defined as the source state of the transition operation. On the other hand, the target state is transformed by the following rules: When the target state of the transition is a simple state (not a composite state), its corresponding Object-Z behavioral state attribute is defined as the target state of the transition operation. When the target state of the transition is a composite state, the initial state in the composite state or each of the concurrent regions (if the composite state is concurrent) is the target state of the transition unless the initial state is a history state. When the initial state or each of the concurrent regions is also a composite state, this rule applies to the rest of the full hierarchy of the target state (see the secondary attribute *explicitTargetState* in [9] for the concept of this state hierarchy). In this case, the final target state is the inner-most state (or states) in the full hierarchy of the initial state (or each of the concurrent regions) so that their corresponding Object-Z behavioral state attribute (or attributes) are defined as the target states of the transition operation. The rest of the state hierarchy of the target state (or states) is formalized with the behavioral state attributes. When entering a shallow or a deep history state (see [9] for the concept of history states), the inner-most states in the full hierarchy of the shallow or the deep state are used to define the target state of the transition operation.

Guards: When a guard condition exists, it is translated as the pre-condition of the transition operation.

Entry and exit actions and activities: For the exit actions of the source states and the entry and activity actions of the target states, their corresponding Object-Z action acceptor operations are defined as the exit, entry, and activity operations of the transition operation respectively.

Effect Action: If a transition has an effect action, its corresponding Object-Z action acceptor operation is defined as the effect operation of the transition operation.

We extend the Object-Z class *CompositeState* defined in Section 2 by defining three additional secondary attributes *allDefaultStates*, *allShallowHistoryStates*, and *allDeepHistoryStates* which return states in the full hierarchy of the initial state, the shallow or the deep history state respectively. When a transition enters a composite state, these attributes are used to define the target scope of the transition.

$$
\begin{array}{|l}
\hline
\text{CompositeState} \\
\ldots \\
\begin{array}{|l}
\hline
[Attributes] \\
\Delta \\
allDefaultStates : \mathbb{P}\!\downarrow State \\
allShallowHistoryStates : \mathbb{P}\!\downarrow State \\
allDeepHistoryStates : \mathbb{P}\!\downarrow State \\
\hline
\end{array} \\
\hline
\end{array}
$$

We formalize the transformation rules defined for transitions in terms of a formal function *mapUMLTransitionToOZ* (see [10] for a complete description of the function).

$$mapUMLTransitionToOZ : Transition \rightarrow TransitionOP$$

4 Conclusions

In this paper, we describe a formal Object-Z model of the UML metamodel and an extended metamodel for Object-Z. Given these two metamodels, we present a formal transformation between the two languages at the meta-level. With previous work [6], we are able to integrate both static and dynamic models in UML into a single Object-Z specification that provides an integrated semantic basis for semantic consistency checks between the UML models. Examples of the semantic consistency checks include: checking that invariants are preserved, that no conflicts exist between invariants defined in the static model and guards defined in the dynamic models, and that no inconsistencies exist between object behaviors defined in terms of both operation specifications and state machines. On the other hand, transforming an Object-Z specification to UML enables us to visualize various aspects of the Object-Z specification. Although we do not discuss tools in this paper, existing tools for one language can be effectively used to help the analysis activity on models in the other language.

References

[1] R. Duke and G. Rose, *Formal Object-Oriented Specification Using Object-Z*, Macmillan, 2000.
[2] S. Dupuy, Y. Ledru, and M. Chabre-Peccoud. Translating the OMT Dynamic Model into Object-Z. in *ZUM'98- The Z Formal Specification Notation, 12th International Conference of Z users, LNCS. No. 1498,* Springer-Verlag. pp. 347-366, 1998.

[3] R. France, J. Wu, M. M. Larrondo-Petrie, and J.-M. Bruel, A Tale of Two Case Studies: Using Integrated Methods to Support Rigorous Requirements Specification, *Proc. of the BCS FACS Methods Integration Workshop*, 1996.

[4] H. Ledang and J. Souquieres, Contributions for Modeling UML State-Charts in B, *Proc. IFM2002*, LNCS, No. 2335, pp. 109-127, 2002

[5] W. McUmber and B. Cheng. A General Framework for Formalizing UML with Formal Languages. in *IEEE Conference on Software Engineering*, pp. 433-442, 2001.

[6] S-K. Kim and D. Carrington, A Formal Mapping between UML Models and Object-Z Specifications, *ZB2000*, LNCS, No. 1878, pp. 2-21, 2000.

[7] S-K. Kim and D. Carrington, A Formal Denotational Semantics of UML in Object-Z, *the special issue of the journal of l'Objet*, Vol. 7 (1), pp. 323-362, 2001

[8] S-K. Kim, D. Carrington, and R. Duke. A Metamodel-Based Transformation between UML and Object-Z. in *HCC'01 2001 IEEE Symposium on Visual Languages and Formal Methods*, IEEE Press. pp. 112-119, 2001.

[9] S-K. Kim and D. Carrington. A Formal Model of the UML Metamodel: the UML State Machine and its Integrity Constraints. *Proc. of ZB 2002*. LNCS. 2272, pp. 497-516, 2002

[10] S-K. Kim and D. Carrington. A Formal Metamodeling Approach Linking UML and Object-Z, SVRC, The University of Queensland, Technical Report 02-23, 2002

[11] J. Lilius and I. P. Paltor, Formalizing UML state machines for model checking, *Proc. UML'99*, LNCS, No. 1723, pp. 430-445, 1999.

[12] E. Meyer and J. Souquieres, A Systematic Approach to Transform OMT Diagrams to a B Specification, *FM'99*, Vol. 1, LNCS 1708, pp. 875-895, Springer-Verlag, 1999.

[13] OMG, *Unified Modeling Language Specification*, version 1.3, 1999, http://www.omg.org

[14] G. Smith. *The Object-Z Specification Language. Advances in Formal Methods*. Kluwer Academic Publishers, 2000.

[15] E. Wang, H. Richter and B. Chen, Formalizing and Integrating the Dynamic Model with OMT, *Proc. 19th International Conference on Software Engineering*, pp. 45 - 55, 1997.

[16] R. Wieringa, E. Dubois, and S. Huyts. Integrating Semi-formal and Formal Requirements. in *Advanced Information Systems Engineering*, LNCS. No. *1250*, Springer. pp. 19-32, 1997.

A UML Approach to the Design of Open Distributed Systems

Behzad Bordbar, John Derrick, and Gill Waters

Computing Laboratory, University of Kent, Canterbury, CT2 7NF, UK
{B.Bordbar,J.Derrick,G.Waters}@ukc.ac.uk

Abstract. The design of distributed systems is a highly complicated and non-trivial task. Introduction of multiple types of media into distributed systems causes a dramatic increase in the complexity of design. To deal with the inherent complexity of systems, two approaches have received considerable attention; ODP and UML. Open Distributed Processing (ODP) is a joint ITU/ISO standardisation framework for constructing distributed systems. Unified Modelling Language (UML) is a de facto standard for visualising, specifying, designing, and documenting object-oriented systems.
This paper presents a case study using a UML approach for the design and specification of distributed systems based on ODP. The purpose of the case study is to try this approach on a large system containing multiple types of media. The case study is carried out on an Interactive Multimedia Kiosk (IMK) example. IMKs integrate different types of media such as text, graphics, audio, video, animation and sound in the form of a large system; this provides an ideal subject for case study.

1 Introduction

There have been dramatic recent developments in the area of distributed systems fuelled by the birth of new applications in our daily life, such as different web-based products and the introduction of multimedia systems into day-to-day amenities such as shopping centres, transport facilities and leisure establishments. However, the design of distributed systems is a highly non-trivial task. In particular, introduction of different media types into systems increases the complexity of the design and results in the creation of a new set of problems such as performance related Quality of Service (QoS), portability and interoperability.

To ease the burden of dealing with the complexity of distributed systems, two approaches have received considerable attention; ODP and UML. The Reference Model for Open Distributed Processing (RM-ODP) [7] is a joint ITU/ISO standardisation framework for constructing distributed systems in a multi-vendor environment. Significant features of ODP include *object based* specification and programming, use of *transparencies* to hide aspects of distribution and its use of *viewpoints*. ODP viewpoints are used to help partition the complexity in distributed systems design. Each viewpoint considers the specification of a distributed system from a particular perspective, and of particular relevance to QoS specification is the *computational viewpoint*. This viewpoint is concerned with the algorithms and data flows which provide the distributed system function. It represents the system and its environment in terms of objects which interact by transfer of information via interfaces.

Since modern distributed systems are object-based, there has been considerable interest in the use of the Unified Modelling Language (UML) [14]. Indeed, UML has quickly emerged as the standard object-oriented analysis and design notation. However, because it attempts to provide notation for most aspects of object-oriented design, users can select from a rich variety of design diagrams in UML and there are few guidelines on how precisely the design is defined.

The RM-ODP presents a framework for constructing distributed systems and defines viewpoints with associated viewpoint languages. However, ODP does not prescribe a specification or design notation within those viewpoints. Thus, there is a need for a specification and modelling language to instantiate the viewpoints and UML is as an ideal candidate for such a language. Various approaches to integrate UML and ODP have been described in [13, 10, 12, 1, 2]. In [2], we presented a UML based method for modelling distributed systems in a framework complying with the RM-ODP. To address the performance issues, in [2] we elaborate on specification of the QoS aspects of the system as a part of the attributes of the entities of the system.

One major objective of introducing a design method for distributed systems is to cope with large examples involving different types of media in sufficient details to enable evaluation of the system in terms of performance, consistency, etc. In this paper we illustrate our approach via specification of static aspects of *Interactive Multimedia Kiosks* (IMKs). We also model the IMK via a UML based but non-ODP approach, COMET [6] and compare the result. We also compare UML and ODP and explain the contribution of our approach to bridging the gap between them.

The paper is organised as follows. The next section introduces IMKs and introduces our running example. Section 3 and 4 uses our running example to provide a brief introduction to ODP and reviews the design method of [2]. Section 5 applies the design method to the IMKs. We shall make a comparison between RM-ODP, UML and the method of [2] in section 6 by pointing out some of the concepts of RM-ODP that are missing from UML and the way that they are introduced into our UML model. Section 6 also presents a model of IMK via COMET [6] to compare it with our method. Finally, we conclude in section 7.

2 Interactive Multimedia Kiosk

An *Interactive Multimedia Kiosk* (IMK) [5] is a public stand that supplies text, graphics, video, animation and sound information to the user. Our example Museum Information Kiosk (MIK) is a real-time coordination of display of information related to a museum offering visitors interactive input, which is based upon one used by Blair and Stefani in [3]. Its function can be divided into three phases as follows.

The welcome phase: The visitor is presented with a welcoming video sequence with associated audio explanation. This phase is terminated when the user presses the start key.
The menu phase: A menu is displayed and a short video and audio message is played repeatedly, which invites the user to select a presentation. This phase is terminated when a user selects a choice from the keyboard.
The conference phase: A sequence of N images accompanied by an associated audio commentary is presented. The exact location of the presented work in the museum building is displayed in a separate window. The audio commentary is divided into N subunits and presented in synchronisation with the corresponding image. The next image is presented when the audio commentary of the previous image has finished. The new audio commentary starts two seconds after the display of the image. In addition, the access map is displayed simultaneously with the first picture of the conference. On termination of the presentation, the application returns to the menu phase.

The user can temporarily suspend and resume the conference phase with a toggle key with values *suspend* and *resume*. The duration of such a suspension is limited to 30 seconds. At the end of the 30 seconds if the user has not pressed *resume*, the presentation resumes automatically. It is possible to leave the menu or conference phases by pressing a *kill* button, which transfers the system to the welcome phase. There is a timeout of 5 minutes in the menu phase within which if the user has not made a choice, the system assumes that he/she has left and returns to the welcome phase.

3 Open Distributed Processing

The Reference Model for Open Distributed Processing (RM-ODP) [7] describes an architecture for building open distributed systems [9] in a multi-vendor environment. Central to the RM-ODP is the concept of *viewpoints*. Viewpoints partition a system specification into a number of partial descriptions, each targeted towards a particular audience to avoid the wide scope and inherent complexity of the domain. The reference model defines five viewpoints: *enterprise, information, computational, engineering* and *technology*. The following subsection explains the computational viewpoint, which is the focus of this paper. Further information regarding both the reference model and its approach to using viewpoints can be found in [7, 9, 11].

3.1 ODP Computational Viewpoint of the IMK

The computational viewpoint deals with the logical partitioning of the distributed system into a series of interacting entities, which are referred to as *objects*. To avoid confusion with the word "object", which is also a reserved word in UML, we use the term computational object, or *compobj* for short. For example, the computational viewpoint of the MIK system of Section 2 contains ten compobjs, see [3]. *Welcome Audio/Video producer* produces audio and video frames which must be presented via the *Welcome Audio/Video consumer* while the system is in the welcome phase. The audio producer of the phase Menu and Conference are modelled via compobjs *Menu audio producer* and *Conference audio producer*. *Audio Presenter* models the compobj that consumes the audio, for example, a speaker broadcasting sound. There is a *Keyboard* compobj for entering data and an external *Clock* compobj. Finally, there are three image sources modelled as compobjs *Conference images*, *Access map image* and *Menu image*, which refer to the corresponding repositories of images.

To perform a service in a distributed environment, the computational objects involved need to access one another, through (possibly multiple) *interfaces*. An interface is known to its environment by its *interface reference*. For example, consider Fig. 1, which depicts the subsystem of the MIK dealing with welcome phase. The compobj *Welcome Audio/ Video Producer* has two interfaces *WelcomeAvControl* and *WelcomeAvOut*. Each interface of a compobj is depicted via a "T" shape attached to it.

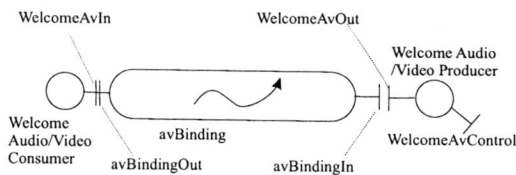

Fig. 1. Audio/Video subsystem for the welcome phase

In order for interactions between objects to occur, the interfaces of the relevant objects are associated by the formation of a *binding*, which can be implicit or explicit. In an implicit there is no term for expressing the binding action. In an *explicit binding* the binding itself is encapsulated as an object which provides the infrastructure resources supporting the communication [3, 7]. We shall refer to such objects as *bindobj* to distinguish them from compobjs. For example, the binding between the producer and consumer in the welcome phase of Fig. 1 is modelled by a bindobj called *avBindin*. Bindobjs, like compobjs, interact with the environment via interfaces. The bindobj *avBinding* has two stream interfaces: *avBindingIn* receives the audio/video frames from the environment; following the binding action, frames are delivered on the interface *avBindingOut*.

4 A UML Approach to Computational Viewpoint Modelling

The static architecture of the UML is based on a four layered structure of *user object, model, metamodel* and *metametamodel* [14]. The metametamodel defines the language for specifying metamodel structure. A metamodel, which is an instance of the metametamodel, defines the language for specifying the model. Models, which are instances of the metamodel, define the language used to describe an information domain from which user objects, describing a specific application domain, are specified. As a result, each layer defines a method of specification of the layer below. In this paper we shall only be dealing with the bottom three layers.

Similarly, a three layered structure for ODP can be considered. One can think of the "Computational viewpoint of RM-ODP" as a top layer which describes the computational aspects of the architecture for building open distributed systems. Such descriptions result in a second layer which is a template specifying the Specific Domain of Application (SDoA). The SDoA models the computational aspects of applications with some common features. For each application that belongs to the SDoA the "computational specification of an application " can be created with the help of the corresponding template.

Inspired by the above three layer structure, [2] models the computational viewpoint as a UML diagram, which we call the Computational Metamodel Diagram (CMD). Different computational entities and their relationship are modelled in the CMD. For each Specific Domain of Application (SDoA), for example IMKs, [2] presents a heuristic for modifying the CMD and creating a class diagram which models the static aspects of the system. We shall refer to such class diagrams as the Computational Class Diagrams (CCD). As a result, the CCD models the "Computational Specification of a SDoA". The CCD serves as a template for modelling static aspects of the computational viewpoint of applications which belong to the Specific Domain of Application (SDoA). As a result, by applying a heuristic to CCD, for each such application, an object diagram called the *Computational Object Diagram* (COD) is created which models the static aspects of the computational viewpoint of such application. In this section, we shall apply the modelling approach of [2] to the design of IMKs.

4.1 Computational Metamodel Diagram

Fig. 2 is a part of the Computational Metamodel Diagram (CMD) of [2], which models the computational viewpoint of RM-ODP via a UML class diagram. The CMD consists of a number of classes modelling different entities of the computational viewpoint. For example, the class *SystemComponent* embodies classes of computational objects and binding objects. The class *Infs* represents interfaces to computational or binding objects. Different types of interfaces are modelled via three sub-classes *OpInfs*, *StrInfs* and *SigInfs* corresponding to operational interfaces, stream interfaces and signal interfaces in the computational model, respectively. The association between *SystemComponent* and *Infs* models interfaces assigned to computational or binding objects.

As an example, we shall explain the class *SystemComponent* which has five attributes. *Name* identifies the *SystemComponent*. *Role* is used to differentiate between computational objects and binding objects, and has type *enumeration* (*enum*) which lists the set of possible values. The names of the interfaces of each computational or binding object are listed by the attribute *InfNames*.

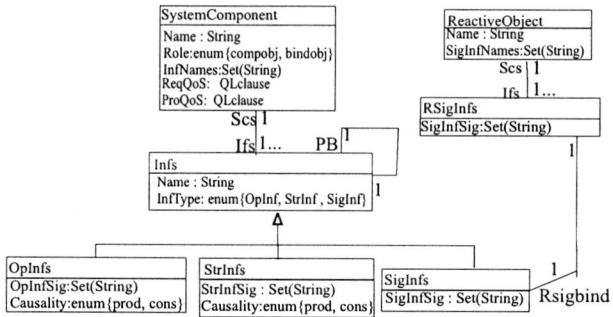

Fig. 2. A part of the Computational Metamodel Diagram

Attributes *ReqQos* and *ProQoS* of the class *SystemComponent* model *required* and *provided* QoS, respectively. The QoS *provided* to the environment by the computational object and the QoS *required* by the object from its environment [3]. We specify each of these attributes via QL [3]. As a result, the type of such attributes is specified as QL clauses (*QLclause*).

5   IMK as a Specific Domain of Application

This section focuses on the Interactive Multimedia Kiosk (IMK) as a Specific Domain of Application (SDoA) to produce its Computational Class Diagram. The CCD acts as a template for instantiation of object diagram of different applications such as the MIK belonging to the SDoA IMK.

5.1   Computational Class Diagram for IMK Systems

A heuristic for the creation of Computational Class Diagrams (CCD) from the CMD of Fig. 2 is explained in [2]. This section sketches the method of creation of part of the CCD of the IMK. To avoid confusion, for the rest of the section the word *metaclass* refers to the CMD. First, we start from metaclass *SystemComponent* and create classes *AudioProducer*, *VideoProducer*, *ImageProducer* and *AudioVideoProducer* which model the resources which are manipulated to produce sounds, graphics, pictures and video clips files. For example, the class *AudioProducer* which is created from the template metaclass *SystemComponent* of Fig. 2 has the usual attributes of the metaclass *SystemComponent*. Moreover, it has the additional attribute *ListOfAudioFiles* which gives the list of audio files. There is also a method *SizeOfAudioFiles()* assigning to each file its size. The files produced via objects from the above classes are transferred through interfaces to consumer objects *AudioConsumer*, *VideoConsumer* and *AudioVideoConsumer* which model windows and speakers that broadcast Audio, Video and AudioVideo files into the user environment. They are all created from template metaclasses *SystemComponent*.

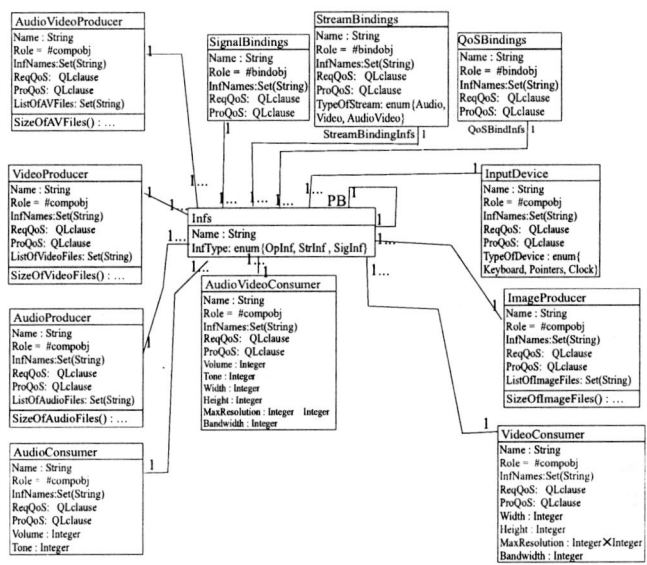

Fig. 3. A part of the CCD of the Interactive Multimedia Kiosk

The next stage is to create *bindobjs StreamBindings*, *SignalBindings* and *QoSBindings*. *StreamBindings* deal with transferring continuous media. To check the performance of the binding the class *QoSBindings* is created which interacts with a control mechanism. Signals are carried through *SignalBindings*.

The user can interact with an IMK through Keyboards and Pointers like mice, trackballs or trackpads. Such devices are modelled via the class *InputDevice* which is also created from the metaclass *SystemComponent* of Fig. 2.

5.2 Computational Object Diagram of the Museum Information Kiosk

To produce a model of the computational viewpoint of the Museum Information Kiosk, which is an example of an Information Multimedia Kiosk, [2] presents a heuristic similar to the heuristic explained above. For the purpose of explanation, Fig. 4 depicts the part of the COD which corresponds to the Audio/Video subsystem of Fig. 1. First, objects *welcomeAVConsumer* and *welcomeAVProducer* from the classes *AudioVideoConsumer* and *AudioVideoProducer* are created. Each of these objects includes the attributes of the corresponding class. For example, the object with name *welcomeAVConsumer* is a computational object with Role = #compobj. It has only one interface *welcomeAvIn* and no provided or required QoS.

Similarly, we need to create binding objects *avBindings* from *StreamBindings* and interface objects *welcomeAVIn*, *avBindIn*, etc. . The provides and required QoS of *avBinding* is as follows. The binding object *avBinding* will provide a throughput of 25 frames per sec and 5 packet per sec, with a delay of between

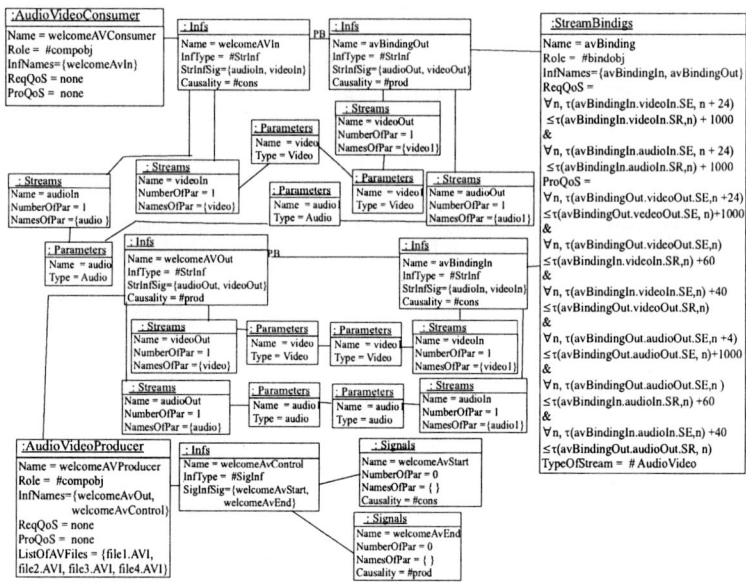

Fig. 4. Computational Object Diagram for the video stream

40 and 60 msec per frames/packets for video/audio, respectively. It must receive the audio frames at a rate of 25 frames per sec and audio packets at a rate of 5 packets per sec from the producer.

6 Discussion

There are certain concepts of RM-ODP that cannot be found in UML directly also there are a set of notions in UML that cannot be mapped directly to RM-ODP. A comparison between UML and RM-ODP is drawn in [11]. In the current section we shall discuss some of the differences between UML and RM-ODP as explained in [11] and the way that our approach addresses such issues. We also compare our approach to that of COMET.

Types and classes: The RM-ODP differentiates between types and classes. In the UML, the designer can specify a type as a stereotype of class, which seems a convenient way of modelling. We are currently working towards integrating stereotypes into our research. Stereotypes are particularly helpful for the creation of UML profiles [4], which facilitate use of existing tools. This put a great emphasis on the issue of types. As a result, in this paper, we have implemented the idea of type system of RM-ODP in our UML models. Each attribute and method of our classes or objects or metaclasses must have a type which is either a basic type such as *Integer*, *String*, ... or other types which are defined in RM-ODP such as *video*, *audio* which are types for streams. This results in models which are called *strongly typed* in the terminology of UML [14]. We use OCL to impose constraints on models [2]. Having a strongly typed model is required for writing OCL expressions as OCL is a typed language. Now, the issue of type checking can be resolved by applying the type checking algorithms of RM-ODP to all attributes and methods of the objects in the model.

Interfaces: An interface in the UML can not be directly instantiated. In our approach, we have modelled interfaces as separate classes *Infs*. As a result, using our heuristics we can create interfaces from such classes. There is an attribute *Name* in *Infs* that, in line with RM-ODP, is an identifier for an interface object. An attribute *InfType* is included that can be used to create different types of interface stream, signal and operational. In addition, all details of different types of interfaces are modelled via subclasses of *Infs* of CMD of Fig. 2 according to the instruction in RM-ODP.

Binding: In the UML there is no direct equivalent for the notion of a binding. The RM-ODP introduces two types of binding: *compound* and *primitive*. The compound binding action of the RM-ODP is performed by a binding object. Compound bindings are modelled as objects which are instantiated from *SystemComponent* in CMD with the role of *bindobj*. Our detailed specification of bindobjs allows us to specify complex real-time systems precisely. A primitive binding action allows binding of two interfaces of the same or different computational objects. The primitive binding between interfaces (*Infs*) is denoted by the self association called *PB* the metaclass *Infs*. In the CMD model of Fig. 2, the primitive binding actions instantiate the association from class *Infs* into itself. The RM-ODP requires the primitive binding to be between interfaces of the same type with complementary causality, which is implemented via an OCL invariant, see [2].

The attribute *Name*: One of the features of our approach, see CMD of Fig. 2, is that we have included an attribute *Name : String* in *SystemComponent, ReactiveObject, Signal,...* referring to the name of such entities. This might seems slightly strange in the eye of a UML modeller, since normally names of objects appear in the first upper box of an instantiated object. The motivation for this is the fact that in the RM-ODP *names are identifiers of corresponding entities*. To emphasise this we have included *Name* as an attributes. This also facilitates writing OCL expressions on the classes and metaclasses.

Layered structure: A central issue in our method is the use of a layered structure CMD, CCD, and COD which is inspired by UML and RM-ODP. We have tried to mimic the way that a modeller will use RM-ODP to produce ODP compliant design. Similarly, the CMD lays the pattern for creation of CODs. Now, it poses a question that, starting from scratch without application of our layered approach, what would the final model of the static aspects of the system look like? To answer this question, we have modelled the MIK via *C*oncurrent *O*bject *M*odelling and architectural design me*T*hod (COMET) [6].

Modelling MIK via COMET: COMET [6] is an object oriented software development process and the full COMET life cycle includes *requirements modelling, analysis, design, construction, integration* and *testing*. The COMET depicts a static model of the system via class diagrams. One of the challenges of the creation of the static model is to identify the concepts involved. To assist the designer in this respect, COMET presents a method called *Object Structuring Criteria* [6], which assists the designer in structuring the system into suitable categories of objects. Fig. 5 presents a static model of the Museum Information Kiosk (MIK) derived from COMET. The *keyboard* is modelled as an *input device interface*, which means that it is an interface software entity interacting with the hardware device keyboard. *Image Producer* and *Audio/Video Producer* are *output device interfaces* which interact with hardware devices such as monitors and speakers. COMET refers to *voice files*, *images*, *access maps* and *menu* as *entities*. *Local Control* is a *coordinator*, which facilitates lip synchronisation between *Image Producer* and *Audio Producer*. To ensure the correct functionality of the system, a *state dependent control* called *Central Control* is provided. Both

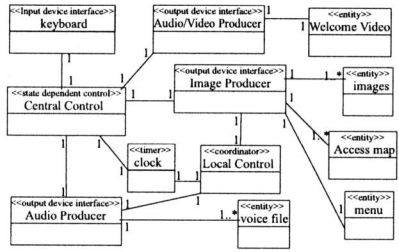

Fig. 5. A class diagram for MIK using classification method of COMET

Central Control and *Local Control* need to be aware of the time of the system, as a result a *timer* class *clock* is included.

Comparison: There are some similarities between our approach and the COMET. The COMET uses diagrams such as Object Structuring Criteria (OSC) of [6] as a template for identifying the concepts involved and structuring them into class diagrams such as Fig. 5. Similarly, we use the CMD of Fig. 2 to produce the CCD of Fig. 3. There are clearly some overlaps between CMD and OSC. However, it seems that the categorisation of concepts in OSC is inspired by engineering aspects of the system. For example, *control, application logic* of [6] page 161, resemble the components which are expected to appear in the final low level design of the system. We believe that this prevents a COMET user from modelling at a higher level of abstraction. As a result, our approach has the advantage of avoiding the complexity of design in early stages by abstraction into more general categories of objects. Later, relying on heuristics, each high level category can mapped into the CCD classes, which are fine grained objects related to a specific group of applications. The process of such mapping is carried over single classes, which enables the user to avoid dealing with large complex systems. Being ODP based, our approach rapidly results in a more precise design. For example, COMET does not address the issue of binding as a part of OSC. As a result, if the model requires to address issues related to binding, such as QoS for delivery of streams between two interfaces, suitable modelling course of action must be taken in further iteration development stages.

7 Related Work and Conclusion

A number of researchers are working on integrations of UML and RM-ODP. Many of them are interested in UML in the context of enterprise specification. Aagadel and Milosevic [1] study the way that enterprise viewpoints can be used as a part of software development cycle via UML. They also elaborate on different enterprise modelling concepts in terms of UML. Linington [10] uses UML to specify the enterprise viewpoint specifications of RM-ODP. Steen and Derrick [12] present a metamodel UML core for the enterprise viewpoint in the RM-ODP and also study the extent that UML can be applied for the specification of the enterprise viewpoint.

Other papers concentrate on specific applications. Oldewick and Berre [13] apply a methodology based on RM-ODP and UML to geographical information systems. Kande et al. [8] apply UML to specify service components of telecommunications management networking systems which are originally modelled in the framework of RM-ODP.

In this paper, we have applied the method of [2] to an Interactive Multimedia Kiosk example. We have presented a class diagram from which UML models of different IMK applications such as MIKs can be created. Our case study demonstrates that our approach is successfully applicable to systems containing multiple types of media. Our example in [2] illustrated simple audio and video channels; the case study of this paper encompases a larger range of media types such as text, graphics, animation and sound files. We have also addressed the issue of extensibility by demonstrating that the method is applicable to large examples. It is straightforward to follow the method explained in the paper to present a UML model of a central database system interacting with more than one IMK.

Doing the case study, we observed that the challenging part of the implementation of our process is the creation of the Computational Class Diagram (CCD). Since creation of the CCD requires a detailed knowledge of the Specific Domain of Application (SDoA). For example, to instantiate the CCD of the IMK, we have to know what *compobj, bindobj,* ... are involved and what their attributes are. In other words, like any other modelling task, it is essential to obtain a deep understanding of the SDoA. However, our method has the advantage of directing the modeller to search for the information and also recording such information in UML diagrams in a manner which complies the RM-ODP. The heuristic nature of our approach suggests that there is clear scope to develop tailored tools based on existing UML tools.

The paper has made a comparison between UML and ODP and shows that the approach [2] bridges the gap between specification via UML and ODP. The paper also applies a non-ODP (COMET) approach to the modelling of the application and draws a comparison with our method. We argue that our approach not only results in a more precise models, but also it avoids the complexity of design by starting at a higher level of conceptual modeling and follows the refinement of the model focusing on smaller and more manageable components of the system.

We are currently working on creation of a UML profile [4] which implements our method. In future we are planning to address the behavioural aspects of such distributed systems and also apply our approach to modelling of multicasting.

References

1. J. O. Aagedal and Z. Milosevic, *ODP Enterprise Language: UML Perspective*, 3rd International Enterprise Distributed Object Computing Conference (EDOC'99), Mannheim, Germany, pp. 27-30, 1999.
2. B. Bordbar, J. Derrick and A.G. Waters, *Using UML to specify QoS Constraints in ODP*, accepted for publication in Computer Networks and ISDN Systems.
3. G. Blair and J.- B. Stefani, *Open Distributed Processing and Multimedia*, Addison-Wesley, 1997
4. S. Cook, *The UML Family: Profiles, Prefaces and Packages* Proceeding of UML 2000-The Unified Modelling Language: Advancing the Standard (October 2000), pp. 255-265.
5. M. Cranston, D. J. Clayton and P. J. Farrands *Design and Implementation Consideration for an Interactive Multimedia Kiosk: Where to Start*, Proc. of the 13th Annual Conference of the Australian Society for Computer Learning in Tertiary (ASCILTE), Adelaide S. A., pp. 101-112.
6. H. Gomaa, *Designing Concurrent, Distributed and Real-Time Applications with UML*, Addison-Wesley Object Technology series, 2000.
7. *ITU Recommendation X.901-904 ISO/IEC 10746 1-4*. Open Distributed Processing Reference Model - Parts 1-4, July 1995.
8. M.M. Kande, S. Mazaher, O. Prnjat, L. Sacks and M. Wittig, *Applying UML to Design an Inter-Domain Service Management Application*, UML 98, LNCS 1618, pp. 200-214, Springer, 1999.
9. P. F. Linington, *RM-ODP: The Architecture*, In K. Raymond and E. Armstrong, editors, IFIP TC6 International conference on Open Distributed Processing, pp. 15-33, Brisbane, Australia, February1995. Chapman and Hall.
10. P. F. Linington, *Options for expressing ODP Enterprise Communities and their Policies by using UML*, Proceedings of the Third International Enterprise Distributed Object Computing Conference, pages 72-82. IEEE, September 1999.
11. J. R. Putman, *Architecting with RM-ODP*, Prentice Hall, 2001.
12. M.W.A. Steen and J. Derrick, *ODP Enterprise viewpoint specification*, Computer Standards and Interfaces, Vol. 22, 165-189, 2000.
13. J. Oldevik and A.-J. Berre, *UML based methodology for distributed systems*, 2nd International Enterprise Distributed Object Computing Conference (EDOC 98) San Diego
14. *UML 1.3 Documentation*, Rational Rose Resource Centre, 1999.

A Semantic Model of Real-Time UML*

Subash Shankar

City University of New York (CUNY), New York, NY 10021, USA
`subash.shankar@hunter.cuny.edu`

Abstract. This paper describes a formal framework for expressing the semantics of UML augmented with real-time constructs. The approach is based on a two-dimensional temporal logic to independently capture control-flow as well as time-flow. The goal is to provide a simple, intuitive, and validatable semantics that can be used for further formal analysis.

1 Introduction

The Unified Modeling Language (UML) is the defacto standard for expressing OO software. One common way of modeling OO software with UML is to use statecharts for object behavior and sequence diagrams for inter-object communication. The OMG has recently produced a draft specification that augments UML with *profiles* for various system issues including time [3]. The key feature of these profiles is that they are intended to be used independently in a 'mix-and-match' manner. The real-time profile includes support for clocks, timers, and several new timing marks for time-related message attributes.

There have been many attempts to provide formal semantics for UML, particularly for statecharts. However, numerous semantic ambiguities complicate the problem; in fact, [7] discusses 21 statechart variants. The obvious approach, providing a semantics for one selected combination of statechart variant and profiles, is thus of limited use. This paper provides an alternative approach of showing how to extend *any* semantics with real-time constructs, in keeping with the UML goal of allowing the modeler to arbitrarily combine profiles.

Propositional temporal logics (PTLs) are the predominant logical formalism for specification and verification of program properties. It is conceptually simple to model statecharts using PTL by mapping statechart state-transitions onto PTL time-transitions. For example, a transition from state s_0 to s_1 is modeled by a PTL formula whose English reading is: 'if the system is currently at s_0, it will be at s_1 next time'. However, it is then not possible to also represent state transitions that take time. The fundamental problem is that there are two distinct notions of flow: micro-time as objects make instantaneous state transitions, and macro-time as objects communicate with each other. The presence of these two distinct time modalities is further complicated by UML constructs that rely on both modalities (*e.g.*, when an otherwise instantaneous transition

---

* This research was supported in part by PSC-CUNY grant 63389-00-32

must wait for a trigger event). We approach this problem by introducing a two-dimensional temporal logic that can be used to capture the semantics of both transition types. The dimensions of the logic independently capture micro-time (referred to as state), as well as macro-time (referred to as time).

2 The UML Variant

As mentioned earlier, we use statecharts to model the states that an object transitions through, and sequence diagrams to model inter-object messages. The primary goal in this paper is to show how the formal semantics of such a model can be extended to cover some real-time constructs similar to those in the UML real-time profile. In particular, our goal is not to provide yet another statechart variant with a new semantics. Thus, we first stipulate one statechart variant.

We assume that the statechart has been flattened to eliminate hierarchy. Suppose there is a transition, t, from state s_1 to s_2, which is labeled by $ev[c]/a$. Then, if the object is in state s_1 and the trigger event ev is received while the guard condition c is satisfied, the object emits event a and transitions to state s_2. The guard condition is evaluated only once when the trigger occurs, and the transition is not taken if it is false on that evaluation - ev needs to be retriggered for the guard to be evaluated again. Harel's original definition of statecharts ([1]) and most variants assume the *perfect synchrony hypothesis*, which essentially states that the transition occurs instantaneously.

Sequence diagrams are used to represent inter-object events, which we do not distinguish from messages. UML and its real-time profile associate each event with various *timing mark* attributes. We use a discrete model of time.

The perfect synchrony hypothesis ensures that transitions occur instantaneously (unless otherwise stated), while constraints based on timing marks may be used for transitions that require time. Thus, there are three types of statechart transitions: instantaneous, timed where the time is a function of the transition, and timed where the time is derived from sequence diagram annotations for the triggering event. This paper denotes the micro-time instantaneous transitions as state transitions, and the macro-time timed transitions as time transitions.

3 The Two-Dimensional Temporal Logic $\mathcal{L}_2$

PTL syntax consists of a countable number of propositions, $\mathcal{A}$, traditional operators: ¬ (not), ∧ (and), ∨ (or), → (implication), and ↔ (iff), and temporal operators: ○ (next), □ (always), ◇ (eventually), and $\mathcal{U}$ (strong until). ○, □, and ◇ are unary operators, while $\mathcal{U}$ is dyadic. As usual, $\mathcal{U}$ is strong, thus asserting that the second operand holds now or at some future time. For notational simplicity, interval superscripts are used (*e.g.*, $\square^{[2,10]}$ is read as 'all times between 2 and 10 time units (inclusive) from now'). Similarly, $\circ^n$ indicates n ○ symbols.

In PTL, time is a sequence of non-negative integers, with propositions varying over time. In the two-dimensional logic $\mathcal{L}_2$, propositions vary over time X state. Fig. 1 shows this grid and 3 example propositions on this grid. Each timepoint in $\mathcal{L}_2$ contains its own full complement of states, and $\mathcal{L}_2$ contains a full set of temporal operators for states as well as timepoints: $\bar{\circ}$, $\bar{\Box}$, $\bar{\Diamond}$, $\bar{\mathcal{U}}$, $\hat{\circ}$, $\hat{\Box}$, $\hat{\Diamond}$, and $\hat{\mathcal{U}}$. State and time operators are distinguished by having bars or carets, respectively.

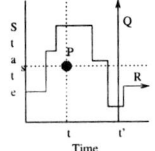

Fig. 1. Space for $\mathcal{L}_2$

Variables	Domain	English Reading
$at_{i,j}$	boolean	State machine i is in state j
$occur_i$	boolean	Event i has occurred
$send_i$	integer	The time that message i was sent
rec_i	integer	The time that message i was received
$start_i$	integer	The time that the operation for message i started
end_i	integer	The time that the operation for message i finishes

Fig. 2. Variables in TRL's Formal Semantics

Model-theoretic semantics for $\mathcal{L}_2$ are given in [5]. Satisfiability and validity are defined using an anchored rather than floating notion (that is, all formulas are expressed with respect to time and state 0): A $\mathcal{L}_2$ formula F is said to be *satisfiable* if there is some model $\mathcal{M}$ modeling F at time and state 0. Similarly, a $\mathcal{L}_2$ formula F is said to be *valid* if F is satisfiable by every model $\mathcal{M}$. For example, in Fig. 1, the following formulas hold: $\hat{\circ}^t \bar{\circ}^s P$, $\hat{\circ}^{t'} \bar{\Box} Q$, and $\hat{\Box} \bar{\Diamond} R$.

4 Translating the UML Model into $\mathcal{L}_2$

Fig. 2 lists variables used in the semantics. Denote by n_S, the number of statecharts in the model, and define a *step* macro indicating an [eventual] transition from s_j to s_k in statechart i: $step(i,j,k) \equiv at_{i,j} \bar{\mathcal{U}} at_{i,k}$. The translation of UML into $\mathcal{L}_2$ consists of global formulas corresponding to properties of all statecharts, and local formulas corresponding to individual transitions in a statechart.

Global Formulas. Global formulas deal with initial state, final state, and control flow. All statecharts start in their initial state s_0:

$$\bigwedge_{i=1}^{n_S} at_{i,0} \tag{1}$$

Similarly, the final state global formula ensures that once a statechart transitions to its final state (denoted s_f), it does not restart:

$$(\bigwedge_{i=1}^{n_S} \hat{\Box}\bar{\Box}(at_{i,f} \to \bar{\circ} at_{i,f})) \wedge (\bigwedge_{i=1}^{n_S} \hat{\Box}(\bar{\Diamond} at_{i,f} \to \hat{\circ} at_{i,f})) \tag{2}$$

Control flow formulas ensure that illegal control flows do not occur. If statechart i is in state s_j waiting for a trigger, it does not change states except when the trigger occurs. The actual state transition is modeled through local formulas, while the global formula prevents the transition from occurring on time changes:

$$\hat{\Box}(\bar{\Diamond}\bar{\Box} at_{i,j} \to \hat{\circ} at_{i,j}) \tag{3}$$

A statechart can not be in two states at once:

$$\hat{\Box}\bar{\Box}(at_{i,j} \to \neg at_{i,k}) for j \neq k \tag{4}$$

Local Formulas. For each transition in the model, there are two components in its formalization: the actual state transition, and the actions performed on the transition. There are three types of transitions: triggerless, time-triggered (*i.e.*, timeout), and regular transitions with triggers, guards, and actions, as shown in Fig. 3. For all three types of transitions, the statechart is assumed to be deterministic, either by having only one outgoing transition from each state or by having mutually exclusive guard conditions on outgoing transitions.

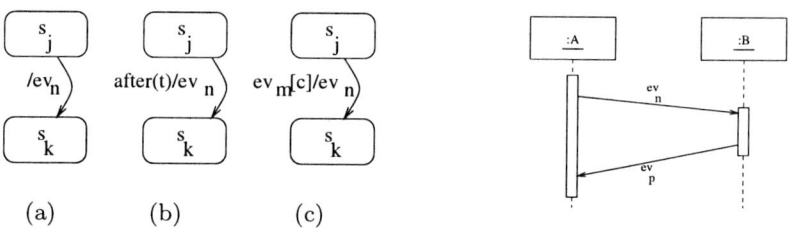

Fig. 3. Transitions: (a) Triggerless (b) Timed (c) Regular   **Fig. 4.** Sequence Diagram

We first formalize the actual state transitions for the three types. It is simple to capture the transitions for the triggerless transition (Fig. 3(a)):

$$\Box\bar\Box(at_{i,j} \to step(i,j,k)) \qquad (5)$$

Since statecharts run concurrently, (5) does not specify the exact state in which the transition occurs or impose any restrictions on statechart execution (*e.g.*, two statecharts may execute synchronously, or be arbitrarily interleaved).

For time-triggered transitions (Fig. 3(b)), statechart i stays in s_j for the remaining states in the current timepoint and all states in the next $t-1$ timepoints:

$$[\Box\bar\Box(at_{i,j} \to \bar\Box at_{i,j})] \land [\Box(enterState(i,j) \to ((\bigwedge_{p=1}^{t-1} \widehat{\circ}^p \bar\Box at_{i,j}) \land \widehat{\circ}^t at_{i,k}))] \qquad (6)$$

where $enterState(i,j)$ is defined to hold at the first point in which state s_j is reached (for positive-time and zero-time cases):

$$\Box(\widehat{\circ} enterState(i,j) \leftrightarrow (\widehat{\circ}(\neg at_{i,j} \land \bar\Diamond at_{i,j}) \lor (\bar\Diamond\bar\Box \neg at_{i,j} \land \widehat{\circ} at_{i,j})))$$

$$enterState(i,j) \leftrightarrow (\neg at_{i,j} \land \bar\Diamond at_{i,j})$$

The full transition (Fig. 3(c)) occurs only if the trigger ev_m occurs and c holds, at which point the the transition may be immediately taken:

$$\Box\bar\Box((at_{i,j} \land occur_m \land c) \to step(i,j,k)) \qquad (7)$$

In addition to taking the transition, the statechart must also perform an operation and emit event ev_n, possibly subject to real-time constraints. The actions are illustrated in Fig. 4, and they are formalized by:

$$\Box(\bar\Diamond(at_{i,j} \land occur_m \land c) \leftrightarrow (\widehat{\circ}^{start_n - send_n} occur_n \land \widehat{\circ}^{rec_p - send_n} occur_p)) \qquad (8)$$

5 Conclusions and Further Research

The primary goal of this paper (presented in more detail in [5]) is to illustrate a simple, intuitive formalism that captures the semantics of micro-time statechart transitions and macro-time constructs similar to those in the real-time profile. We believe that $\mathcal{L}_2$ is well suited towards these goals, as shown by the relative conciseness, simplicity, and independence of concerns in the axioms of Section 4. Simplicity and intuition are, of course, in the eye of the beholder; however, we have provided a similar formalization of VHDL in prior work ([6]), and been able to validate the correctness of the semantics against the LRM ([4]).

There are many statechart semantics in the literature, with many of them providing a detailed operational semantics that essentially translates statecharts into state transition machines (*i.e.*, a Kripke model). The key feature of our two-dimensional approach is that it allows us to augment *any* state-based statechart semantics with real-time constraints. If these state machines are then integrated with real-time constructs from sequence diagrams, it is simple to generate the semantics of the resulting model using the two-dimensional approach of this paper. Thus, we believe that our independence goal is also met.

To the best of our knowledge, the closest related work is [2], which models statecharts using first-order temporal logic. However, every transition must be timed, and instantaneous transitions are disallowed. Conversely, the use of a first order temporal logic allows for directly modeling continuous time, though the price for this greater expressive power is undecidability.

We are currently pursuing further research along several lines. First, we are implementing proof procedures for $\mathcal{L}_2$, and plan on using the resulting systems to prove properties of real-time UML diagrams. Second, we are extending our semantics to cover other real-time constructs in the real-time profile, such as the attributes of timing mechanisms (*e.g.*, skew, drift). Finally, we are applying our proof procedures to several real-time applications expressed using UML.

References

1. D. Harel. Statecharts: A visual formalism for complex systems. *Science of Computer Programming*, 8:231–274, 1987.
2. L. Lavazza, G. Quaroni, and M. Venturelli. Combining UML and formal notations for modelling real-time systems. In *Foundations of Software Engineering (FSE)*, pages 196–206, 2001.
3. Object Management Group. *UML Profile for Schedulability, Performance, and Time Specification, Draft Adopted Specification*, January 2002.
4. S. Shankar. *Formal Verification of VHDL Designs Using Temporal Logics*. PhD thesis, University of Minnesota, 1998.
5. S. Shankar. A formal semantics for UML with real-time constructs. Technical Report TR-200209, Dept. of Computer Science, City University of New York (CUNY), 2002.
6. S. Shankar and J. Slagle. A polymodal semantics for VHDL. In *Advances in Hardware Design and Verification (CHARME)*, pages 88–105. Chapman & Hall, 1997.
7. M. von der Beeck. A comparison of statecharts variants. In *Formal Techniques in Real Time and Fault Tolerant Systems (FTRTFT)*, pages 128–148, 1994.

Research on Ontology-Oriented Domain Analysis on MIS

Zhong Ming [1,2], Shi-xian Li[1], and Xiu-rong Fang[1]

[1] College of Information Science and Technology, SUN yat-sen University, P.R.C. 510275
[2] College of Information Engineering, SHENZHEN University, P.R.C. 518060
mingz@szu.edu.cn, nslsx@zsu.edu.cn

Abstract. A new approach of domain analysis——ontology-oriented MIS domain analysis is presented in this paper. It deals with how to apply the new knowledge representative method ——ontologies with objects to describe domain model, to store the existing domain knowledge and to facilitate the reuse of domain knowledge. The key technology is to define the domain model and the domain ontologies knowledge base(DOKB).

1 Introduction

Domain engineering analyzes the specific domain, forming a domain model by identifying the common features and changeable characters of application systems, making choices and abstraction among the objects and operations which represent those common features. The common software framework in the domain according to the domain model can be produced. Based on the domain model the reusable components can be identified, used and organized. The organization of this paper is as follow: section 2 introduces the related work. Section 3 describes the main idea of ontology-oriented domain analyzing on MIS. Section 4 is the summary .

2 Related Work

Domain analyzing has been shown effective by practice[2,3]and found many applications. The Feature-Oriented Domain Analysis——FODA is a typical domain analyzing method[3]. KAPTUR put forward by Computer Technology Associates is also famous. Genesis method was put forward by Don Batory[3]. Design Recovery method[3] collects design information from source codes, organizes this information and elicits a feasible design. The ontology oriented method is put forward in the Eagle Project[1]. The domain analyzing can be considered as the process of eliciting knowledge. This inspired us to introduce the way of knowledge elicitation, knowledge representation and knowledge maintaining in artificial intelligence to domain analyzing. We will use ONONET created in the Eagle project[1] to build up domain model on MIS(Management Information System).

3 Ontology-Oriented Domain Analyzing on MIS

3.1 Why do We Need Ontology?

There is a new way of knowledge representation—ontology. What is an ontology? An ontology is a specification of a conceptualization. The word "ontology" seems to generate a lot of controversy in discussions about AI. It has a long history in philosophy, in which it refers to the subject of existence. In the context of knowledge sharing, we use the term ontology to mean a specification of a conceptualization. That is, an ontology is a description (like a formal specification of a program) of the concepts and relationships that can exist for an agent or a community of agents. This definition is consistent with the usage of ontology as set-of-concept-definitions, but more general. And it certainly has second meaning which is quite different from its original meaning.

When we describe a domain, we find that the pure object oriented language is not efficient to represent the complex relationships among objects. Many object-oriented methods define an object using some language. These methods do not attach importance to the relationships among objects. They only use some key words such as "association, using" to express the logical relationships or reference relationships.

In the real world, it is sometimes more important to describe the relationship than to describe the entities. Similarly, the relationships may be very complicated in a domain. If we encapsulate the relationships within objects, then we go against the developers and domain experts to understand the domain knowledge. Therefore, we extract the relationships from objects.

Peter Chen put forward Entity-Relation diagram to describe the relationship among objects in 1970s. But E-R diagram emphases on static description, it is difficult to describe the many to many relationship and the dynamic description. On the other hand, ontology emphases on the essential concepts and the relationships among these concepts. It is not enough to just be concerned on the single object. Sometimes we should master the relations among objects. So we introduce ontology to represent the relationships. At the same time, we give the syntax and semantics to relationships. We build up the domain knowledge base to support the domain analyzing on MIS.

3.2 How to Introduce Ontology?

We consider relationship as an independent knowledge unit represented by ontology. We also use ontology to organize objects. Ontology can be used to represent all relationships except inheritance. The ontology we use here is different from other ontology. The objects are considered the basic elements of ontology. It is propitious to represent a large scale domain model if we consider the objects that have structure to be the elements of ontology. By using ontology and objects to describe the domain model, the structure of the domain model is like a network, the inheritance relationships are the vertical relationships and the ontology relationships are the horizontal relationships. An ontology can have their own inheritance relationships. As described above, the ontologies is a network composited by objects sites and the relationships between these objects. Because inheritance relationships exist among objects, the ontologies composited by objects also have inheritance relationships. Ontologies can be nested just like the molecules which can composite a polymer.

The scope of our research is confined to the MIS domain. The MIS domain model built up using ontology oriented method is called INFORM. As described above, in INFORM we use ontologies to organize objects.

Definition 1: Three basic objects:

1 Activity object: An activity object is a procedure of data processing, or a abstract action. Activity object defines the input data, output data and processing operations. The formula is:

$$\text{Activity object} \rightarrow \text{many input data} + \text{many output data} + \text{single operation}$$

2 Role object: A role is a organization ,a position or a program. A role object describes the activity that might execute and establish the priority of data accessing, its formula is:

$$\text{Role object} \rightarrow \text{many activities} + \text{many (data, priority)}$$

3 Data object: A data object is a structuring data, it defines a group of attributes and operations on these attributes.

$$\text{Data object} \rightarrow \text{data structure} + \text{many activities}$$

We can infer 7 kinds of relationships among the three basic objects:

Definition 2: Seven relationships:
1 Relationships among many roles
2 Relationships among many data
3 Relationships among many activities
4 Relationships between many roles and many activities
5 Relationships between many roles and many data
6 Relationships between many data and many activities
7 Relationships among many roles , activities and many data

In INFORM, We define the following relationships:

Definition 3: the main relationships in INFORM
1 Organize (role, community relationships, role)
2 Include (activity, include, activity)
3 DataTransfer (role A, data set, role B)
4 The data processing relationships are as follows:
   A. DataPro(data set, activity, data set)
   B. RolePro(data set, (role, activity) , data set)
   C. ToolPro(data set, (activity, tool), data set)
   D. MixPro(data set , (role, activity, tool), data set)

3.3 Definition of Ontology and Its Inheritance Relationship

Definition 4: An ontology can be represented as a septuple *(N, F, P, A, B, R, M)*, where N is the name of ontology, F is the name of the father of the ontology, P is a pointer that point to the relationships which the ontology becomes involved with other entities. A is the attributes set of the ontology. B represents the set of objects which consists of ontology. R is a grid of ontologies, M is a methods set that is attached to the ontology.

Definition 5: Let r be a ontology relationship, then $op(r)$ represents the relationship symbol of r. $Arity(r)$ represents the number of parameters of r. $Arity/n(r)$ represents the nth parameter.

Definition 6: Let b_1, b_2 be two objects. $b_1 < b_2$ ($b_2 > b_1$) represents that b_1 is an ancestor of b_2, $b_1 \le b_2$ ($b_1 \ge b_2$) represents $b_1 = b_2$ or $b_1 < b_2$.

Among the septuple, N, B, R are the most important. Therefore, we can use (N, B, R) to represent an ontology.

In INFORM, the element of ontology is the object. Since objects have a hierarchical structure, so we can define the inheritance of ontology based on objects inheritance.

Definition 7: Let $O_1 = (N_1, B_1, R_1)$ and $O_2 = (N_2, B_2, R_2)$, O_1 and O_2 are entities. We say there is a map between O_1 and O_2, if:

(1) Mapping M consists of three local mappings: $M(O_1) = M(N_1) \cup M(B_1) \cup M(R_1)$
(2) $M(N_1) = N_2$
(3) $M(B_1) = \cup \{ M(e_1) \mid e_1 \in B_1 \}$, where for each element of e_1, there is one and only one element of e_2 such that $M(e1) = e_2 \ge e_1$
(4) $M(R1) = \cup \{ M(r_1) \mid r_1 \in R_1 \}$, where for each relationship of R_1, there is a relationship $r_2 \in R_2$ such that
  (a) $op(r_1) = op(r_2)$,
  (b) $arity(r_1) = arity(r_2)$,
  (c) For $i = 1$ to $arity(r_1)$, if $arity/i$ is a set, then for each element $e_1 \in arity/i(r_1)$, there is one and only one element $e_2 \in arity/i(r_2)$, such that $M(e1) = e_2 \ge e_1$, otherwise, let $e_3 = arity/i(r_1)$, $e_4 = arity/i(r_2)$, then $M(e3) = e_4 \ge e_3$

Definition 8: Let $O_1 = (N_1, F_1, A_1, B_1, R_1, S_1)$ and $O_2 = (N_2, F_2, A_2, B_2, R_2, S_2)$, O_1 and O_2 are ontologies. We say O_1 is the father of O_2 if:
(1) $F_2 = N_1$,
(2) A_1 is a subset of A_2,
(3) S_1 is a subset of S_2 and
(4) There is a mapping from (N_1, B_1, R_1) to (N_2, B_2, R_2).

3.4 The Improvement of ONONET

It is difficult for a user who does not know very well of the concrete application system to use *DOKB* which is defined by *ONONET* program code. In order to make the *ONONET* easy to be understood, we add some description content to it.

The Ontolingua project provides formal description and informal description of ontology. The informal description is in natural language and easy to be read. So we improve the *ONONET* by two points:

1. We add an informal description part to *ONONET* program in order that the users can select the modules that already exist in the *DOKB*. The informal description part contains system introduction and general description. The system introduction contains the aim of the requirements definition, the scope of system and system types. The general description points out the system functions.

2. Adding keywords to each module of *ONONET* program so that users can use them in query.

The improved *ONONET* is called *ONONET'*, its definition is following:
```
<ONONET' program> : : = ONONET' (<program name>)
                      { <module>; }1n
                      {<introduction>}
                      {<general description>}
                      END_OF_ONONET'
<introduction> : : = Introduction
                    Purpose:;
                    Scope:;
                    System_category:;
                End_of_Introduction
<general description> : : = General_description
                    General_function:;
                    End_of_General_Introduction
```
Furthermore, a sentence of "<keyword> : : = Key;" is added to the definition of ontology and object.

4 Summary

A specific domain—MIS is discussed in this paper. We have researched how to apply the new knowledge representative method—ontologies with objects to describe the MIS domain model, to store the existing domain knowledge and to facilitate the reuse of domain knowledge. We have defined the general model to support the system modeling. The key technology that defines the domain model and the domain ontologies knowledge base *(DOKB)* is explored in this paper.

References

[1] 1. R.LU, Z.JIN. Domain Modeling-Based Software Engineering. Kluwer Academic Publishers. 2000
[2] Jag Sodhi, Prince Sodhi. Software Reuse: Domain Analysis and Design Processes. McGraw-Hill Companies, Inc. 1998
[3] Jacobson I, Griss M, Josson P. Software Reuse: Architecture Process and Organization for Business Success. 1998
[4] Scott A. DeLoach, Thomas C.Hartrum. A Theory-Based Representation for Object-Oriented Domain Models. IEEE TRANSACTIONS ON SOFTWARE ENGINEERING, VOL.26,NO.6,JUNE 2000
[5] Trygve Reenskaug, P.Wold and O.A.Lehne, The OOram Software Engineering Method,1996

A Requirements Description Model Based on Conditional Directed Graphs

Zaobin Gan, Chuanbo Chen, and Xiandeng Pei

College of Computer Sci. & Tech., Huazhong University of Sci. & Tech.,
Wuhan 430074,PR China
ganzk@public.wh.hb.cn

Abstract: On the basis of set theory and graph theory, this paper defines some conceptions of business flows, and proposes a requirements description model based on conditional directed graphs (CDGRD). The model focuses on business flows that are described by means of conditional directed graphs. A business flow can be described by some rectangles (activities) and some lines with arrowheads (conditions), the description approach distinctly illustrates the logical relationships among business elements, such as diversified static data, dynamic data and processing flows, which are used in the course of every business implementation. Finally, an application instance of the presented model is given in a large-sized enterprise information system project.

1 Introduction

As application software systems become more complicated and larger, software requirements analysis becomes more important and difficult. It is rather significant which requirements description method we adopt in order to reduce the loss and inconsistency of information, and improve the quality and automation of requirements analysis. At present, some methods, such as structured analysis, object-oriented analysis [1], etc, are in common use. The structured analysis approach is a data-oriented method, which is based on data flows, and its representative simulation tools are data flow diagrams, data dictionaries, and original process specification illustrations. The object-oriented analysis approach takes objects and their services as modeling standards. There are some main simulative elements, for instance, objects, classes, properties, relationships, methods, messages transfer, and so on. The two approaches pay attention to requirements description and do not support requirements specification automation. The object-oriented analysis cannot be effectively performed, and its immaturity is slowing down the adoption of object-oriented analysis [2,3,4]. In recent years, many scholars have introduced the conception of goal in different stages of requirements analysis. A goal-oriented requirements analysis method has been coming out. The goals have different effect and status in every kind of goal-based requirements analysis methods. Now, a united goal-oriented requirement analysis method has not been established, which still requires further study [5,6,7].

Rest of the paper is organized as follows. In section 2, we define some conceptions of business flows on the basis of set theory and graph theory. A requirements description model based on CDG is presented in section 3. A practical case study is given in section 4. Section 5 concludes the features of the presented description model and points to future work.

2 Mathematical Descriptions of Business Flows

In an enterprise, any kind of business has a corresponding business process, and the business process is made up of a few business activities (steps). We consider the whole business flows as a business requirements set, and it can be defined as:

$W = \{w_1, w_2, ..., w_n\}$, where w_i stands for a business flow. Any business flow can be expressed as a pair $<n_i, A_i>$, where n_i is the business process's name and A_i represents a set that consists of all activities abstracted from the business flow w_i.

If there are m activities in the business flow w_i, in other word, the business flow w_i is made up of m steps. Then the set A_i can be defined as:

$A_i = \{a_{i1}, a_{i2}, ..., a_{im}\}$, where, a_{ij} represents an activity in the business flow w_i, and a_{ij} can be defined by a quintuple $<n, C, R, D, S>$, here n is the activity's name; C is a set of the activity's beginning and end condition; R stands for a set that consists of the user roles having the operation authority to the activity; D is a set that is made up of the data objects processed in the activity, and can be expressed:

$D = \{d_1, d_2, ..., d_n\}$, where d_i is a vector:

$d_i = ($ the name of data object, data type, length, whether it is null or not, whether it is a keyword or not, value field, origin $)$. In this context, certain property of the data objects can be null, the properties in the vector d_i can also be added or modified.

The S in this quintuple is a set of conversion condition from activity a_{ij} to activity a_{ik} ($j = 1,2, ..., m, k = 1,2, ..., m, j \neq k$).

In the light of the implementation sequence of business flows, business flows can be classified as:

1. Serial business flows: In a business flow, all activities are serially implemented by sequence.

2. Parallel business flows: During the implementation of a business flow, different activities are allowed to perform concurrently.

3. Compound business flows: In a business flow, certain activity is a sub-process.

4. Feedback business flows: In the course of the implementation of a business flow, the business flow can feed back to re-handle the implemented activities.

3 Business-Oriented CDGRD Model

Several kinds of nodes in conditional directed graphs can be defined as:
Definition 1. *Real* node: In conditional directed graphs, an activity node that represents the activity of business flows is called a *real* node and it is expressed by a rectangle;

Definition 2. *Joint* nodes: In conditional directed graphs, a node that links several activities is called a *joint* node and can be expressed by a circle. A *joint* node has two kinds: a *split* node and *a join* node.

Definition 3. *Split* nodes: if an activity has several arrowheads directing several subsequent activities, then the *joint* node is called a *split* node, as shown in Fig.1 (a). By the end of the activity 'A', if subsequent activity 'B' and 'C' are in ready status simultaneously, then the *split* node is called an *and-split* node; if subsequent activity 'B' or 'C' is in ready status, then the *split* node is called an *or-split* node.

Definition 4. *Join* nodes: If several activities direct a subsequence activity simultaneously, then the *joint* node is called a *join* node, as shown in Fig.1 (b). If 'C' is in order status just when its all preceding activity 'A' and 'B' have entirely been completed, then the *join* node is called an *and-join* node; if 'C' is in order status just when its preceding activity 'A' or 'B' has been completed, then the *join* node is called an *or-join* node.

An *and-split (join)* node is expressed by " ⊕ ", and an *or-split (join)* node is expressed by " ⊖ ", as shown in Fig. 2.

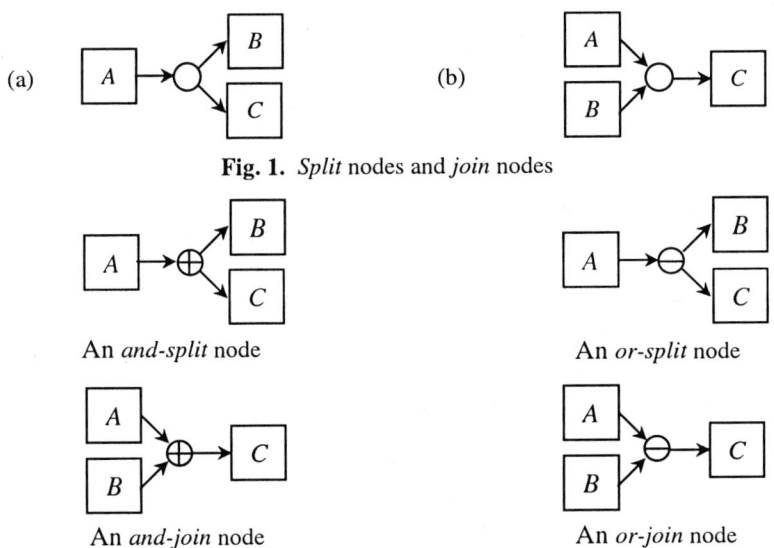

Fig. 1. *Split* nodes and *join* nodes

An *and-split* node   An *or-split* node

An *and-join* node   An *or-join* node

Fig.2. *And-split (join)* nodes and *or-split (join)* nodes

In the course of requirements analysis, the method of conditional directed graphs is adopted to describe business flows. The description approach distinctly illustrates the logical relationships among business elements, such as diversified static data, dynamic data and processing flows, which are used in the course of every business implementation. A rectangle in conditional directed graphs represents one activity (step) of a business flow, every line with arrowhead expresses the relationship between one activity and another, that is to say, it is the set of conversion condition from one activity to another. Therefore, a business flow model can be expressed by a series of rectangles (activities) and lines with arrowhead (conditions). So, according to the formal description of section 2, we can describe conditional directed graphs of all business flows.

4 An Application Instance

In a large-sized hydropower enterprise, its businesses management is very complicated, including production process management, material management, production real time information management, human resource and payment management, and office automation management, and so on. In this section, an application of the model is introduced in detail in the example of the second work sheet on management in the production process. The second work sheet management business mainly consists of seven activities: *'application'*, *'signature'*, *'permission'*, *'work'*, *'postponement'*, *'cancel'*, and *'logout'*. As mentioned above the model, the business logic activities and restriction conditions in the business flow are described respectively, as shown in Fig. 3.

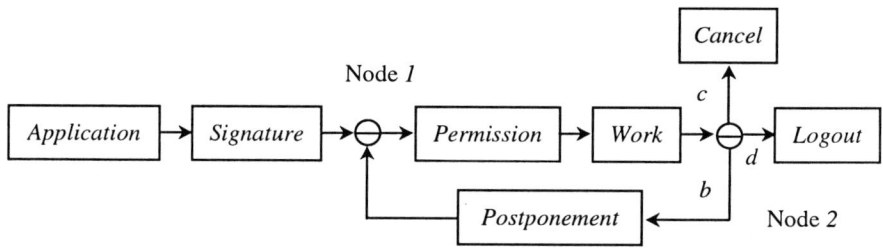

Fig.3. The conditional directed graph of the second work sheet business

The activities set of the second work sheet business is defined as:
A = {*'application'*, *'signature'*, *'permission'*, *'work'*, *'postponement'*, *'cancel'*, *'logout'*}.

Here, an activity can be expressed by a quintuple $< n, C, R, D, S >$. We take an example for the activity *1* (*'application'*), n = {*'application'*}; C = {having legal authorization of application; inputting the value of all data object in D in the activity; signature attestation}; R = {all user roles who have application authority of the second work sheet}; and D = {(work team, character type, 20, no, no, , manual input) ,(work task, character type,500, no, no, no, manual input) ,...}.

The line with arrowhead between *'application'* and *'signature'* represents the conversion condition set S, which can be expressed as:
S = {meeting the end condition of *'application'* activity; signatory validate}.

For the description of *joint* nodes, the keystone is the definition of constraint condition. Here is an example of *or-split* node 2, when the different conversion condition is met, the *'work'* can respectively switch to *'cancel'*, *'postponement'* or *'logout'*. So the conversion condition set that is represent by arrowhead b, c, d can be defined as:

S_b = {The work scheduled time is over, but the work is not be finished.}; S_c = {Within the work scheduled time, but the work condition cannot be met, the work should be stopped.}; S_d = {Within the work scheduled time, the work is finished.}.

The description shows as above: when the '*logout*' is over, it stands that the work sheet is normally completed; when the '*cancel*' is ended, it indicates that the work sheet is ended, but the work is not finished; when '*postponement*' is newly accepted, it can switch to '*permission*', and then continue to work.

5 Conclusions and Future Work

This paper presented an approach for formalizing problem analysis, the approach focuses on business processes analysis and description by means of conditional directed graphs. It can help to minimize discrepancy of requirements analysis, improve accuracy of requirement analysis, to offer some good testing cases to system testers, to optimize or reengineer some inconsequence business flows in enterprises, to provide software engineers with some experienced knowledge, to avoid the aimlessness of requirements analysis and effectively improve the requirements analysis quality and automation.

Up to now, we have developed a prototype system that can analyze syntax and accessibility of the formal description model, verify users requirements, and automatically generate requirements specifications according to documentation templates given by analysts. In the meantime, the documentation templates and the CDGRD model can be refined and modified. With regard to future work, we intend to improve the system to automate the CDGRD model construction, that is, it can automatically transform a scenario to CDGRD and guide analysts constructing a scenario of a problem.

References

1. Pressman R. S.: Software Engineering: A Practitioner's Approach. 4th Edn.. McGraw-Hill, 1997
2. Basili V.R., Briand L.C., Malo W.L.: How Reuse Influences Productivity in Object Oriented Systems. Communications of the ACM, 39 (10): 104–116, 1996
3. Wang S.: A Synthesis of Natural Language, Semantic Network and Objects for Business Process Modeling. Canadian Journal of Administrative Sciences, 14 (1): 79 – 92, 1997
4. Northrop M.: Object-Oriented Development. In: Software Engineering, IEEE Computer Society Press, Los Alamitos, pages: 148-159,1997
5. Anton A.I.: Goal-based Requirements Analysis. In Proceedings of the International Conference on Requirements Engineering, pages: 136-144, 1996
6. Darimont R., Van Lamsweerde A. and Leitier E.: Managing Conflicts in Goal-Driven Requirements Engineering. IEEE Transactions on Software Engineering, 24 (11): 908-926, 1998
7. Lee J., Xue N.L.: Analyzing User Requirements by Use Cases: a Goal-Driven Approach. IEEE Software, 16 (4): 92-101, 1999

Introducing Reference Semantics via Refinement

Graeme Smith

Software Verification Research Centre, University of Queensland, Australia
smith@svrc.uq.edu.au

Abstract. Two types of semantics have been given to object-oriented formal specification languages. *Value semantics* denote a class by a set of values representing its objects. *Reference semantics* denote a class by a set of references, or pointers, to values representing its objects. While adopting the former facilitates formal reasoning, adopting the latter facilitates transformation to object-oriented code. In this paper, we propose a combined approach using value semantics for abstract specification and reasoning, and then refining to a reference semantics before transforming specification to code.

1 Introduction

Research on object-oriented formal specification languages has gone through two main phases of development.

The first phase focussed on extending existing formal specification languages with object-oriented constructs in order to enhance modularity and reusability. These constructs included classes, objects, inheritance and polymorphism. A number of new formal languages were developed, notable among which are those which extend VDM or Z [21, 13]. The goal was to make formal methods more applicable to larger-scale systems and industrial problems [5, 15].

The languages developed in this phase of research, including MooZ [20], ZEST [23] and early versions of VDM++ [8] and Object-Z [2, 4], have a *value semantics*, i.e., a semantics in which a class is denoted by a set of values. Each value in such a set corresponds to an object of the class at some stage of its evolution. Such a semantics is conservatively based on that of the language being extended and hence introduces no additional complexity to the semantic basis.

The second phase of research saw the inclusion of object references in object-oriented formal specification languages. Object references work in the same manner as pointers in programming languages. They introduce the possibility of object sharing (through aliasing) and non-trivial, recursively defined structures (since objects may reference objects which also reference them). Existing object-oriented formal specification languages such as VDM++ and Object-Z were extended with object references [14, 6, 7, 18]. The goal was to make the transition from formal specification to code easier [9].

To incorporate object references, the new versions of the languages developed in this phase of research have a *reference semantics*, i.e., a semantics in which a class is denoted by a set of references to values (denoting objects). Such a semantics is a major departure from that of the language being extended and hence much effort has subsequently gone into developing suitable semantics [10].

The additional complexity of reference semantics has had a large impact on developing methods for reasoning about specifications [11], refining specifications [3] and encoding languages in tools such as theorem provers [16]. Although object references enable an easy transition from specification to object-oriented code, they hinder the abstract representation of systems and hence unnecessarily complicate refinement and reasoning.

In this paper, we propose a step *backward* to the languages with value semantics for abstractly specifying systems as part of a step *forward* to a new approach to formal object-oriented development. This approach involves refining value-semantics specifications to specifications with reference semantics. This allows reasoning to be carried out in the absence of object references, but allows the addition of references through refinement in order to ease the transition to code. To illustrate our approach, we use the Object-Z specification language for which both value and reference semantics exist. This distinguishes our work from similar work in the refinement calculus where explicit stores are introduced during refinement to model mappings from references to values [22,1]. In Section 2, we introduce the value-semantics version of Object-Z and in Section 3, the reference-semantics version. In Section 4, we illustrate through a simple case study how a value-semantics specification can be refined to a one with a reference semantics.

2 Value Semantics

The early work on Object-Z [2,4] adopts a value semantics [17]. The main extension to Z is syntactic: the introduction of a class schema. A class schema encapsulates a single state schema with its associated initial state schema and all the operations which can change its variables. For example, the following specifies a generic node which has two state variables, $empty$ denoting whether or not a value has been inserted into the node and val denoting the value.

$\underline{\quad Node[T] \quad}$
$empty : \mathbb{B}$
$val : T$

$\underline{\quad \textsc{Init} \quad}$
$empty$

$\underline{\quad Insert \quad}$
$\Delta(empty, val)$
$v? : T$
$empty \wedge val' = v? \wedge \neg\, empty'$

Initially, the node is empty and a value $v?$ can be inserted into it via the operation $Insert$. The Δ-list of this operation indicates that it is able to change the variables *empty* and *val*. The operation can occur when *empty* is true, and results in *empty* being false and *val* taking the value $v?$.

Like schemas in Z, a class schema can be used as a type: its instances are values denoting possible objects of the class. For example, a generic list could be defined as a non-empty sequence of node objects as follows ($\text{seq}_\infty X$ extends the Z definition $\text{seq } X$ of finite sequences of type X, i.e., finite functions whose domain is a contiguous set of natural numbers with least element 1 and whose range is X, to possibly infinite sequences, i.e., $\text{seq}_\infty X == \text{seq } X \cup \mathbb{N} \to X$).

┌─ *List*[T] ──
│ ┌──────────────────────────┐ ┌─ INIT ──────────────
│ │ $list : \text{seq}_\infty \text{ Node}[T]$ │ │ $\forall\, n : \text{ran } list \bullet n.\text{INIT}$
│ ├──────────────────────────┤ └─────────────────────
│ │ $list \neq \langle\,\rangle$ │
│ └──────────────────────────┘
│
│ ┌─ *Insert* ──────────────────────────
│ │ $\Delta(list)$
│ │ $v? : T$
│ ├─────────────────────────────────────
│ │ $\exists\, i : \text{dom } list \bullet$
│ │ $\quad (\forall\, j : 1\,..\,i-1 \bullet \neg\, list(j).empty) \land$
│ │ $\quad list(i).\text{Insert} \land$
│ │ $\quad \{i\} \mathbin{\lhd\!\!\!\!-} list' = \{i\} \mathbin{\lhd\!\!\!\!-} list$
│ └─────────────────────────────────────
└──

The class *List* denotes the functionality of a (possibly bounded) list abstractly by defining a possibly infinite sequence of nodes, the non-empty nodes of which denote the actual list. A finite sequence models a bounded list and an infinite sequence, an unbounded list.

Initially, each node n in the list satisfies the initial state of the class *Node*, i.e., it is empty. The operation *Insert* chooses a node such that all other nodes before it in the sequence are not empty, and inserts a value $v?$ into that node. The fact that a node must be empty for an insertion to take place (as defined in class *Node*) ensures that the selected node is the first empty one in the sequence. The final line of the operation ensures that all other nodes are unchanged ($\mathbin{\lhd\!\!\!\!-}$ is domain subtraction). It is needed since the inclusion of *list* in the Δ-list allows *list* to change arbitrarily unless otherwise constrained.

3 Reference Semantics

More recent work on Object-Z [6, 7, 18] adopts a reference semantics [10]. This enables a style of specification which more closely reflects implementation in an object-oriented programming language. In particular, it allows object sharing and non-trivial, recursive structures to be defined. For example, a list could be specified recursively by the variables associated with the node at the head of the list together with a pointer to the tail of the list (as in Fig. 1).

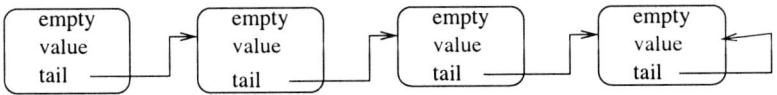

Fig. 1. Recursively defined list

A reference-semantics specification in Object-Z is

$$
\begin{array}{l}
\underline{\ List^*[T]\ } \\
\begin{array}{|l}
\begin{array}{|l}
empty : \mathbb{B} \\
val : T \\
tail : List^*[T]
\end{array} \\
\hline
tail = self \lor tail \in List^*[T]_{\copyright} \\
\hline
Insert \mathrel{\widehat{=}} \big[\,\Delta(empty, val)\ v?: T \mid empty \land val' = v? \land \neg\, empty'\,\big] \\
\quad [\!]\ \ [\neg\, empty\,] \land tail.Insert
\end{array}
\end{array}
\qquad
\begin{array}{l}
\underline{\ I\textsc{nit}\ } \\
empty \land tail.I\textsc{nit}
\end{array}
$$

Classes in the reference-semantics version of Object-Z have an implicitly declared constant *self* denoting a reference to the current object. This is used in class *List** to specify that *tail* may point to the current object (when there is no tail). In all other cases, the tail list and all objects referenced either directly or indirectly from it must be "contained" by the current list (denoted by the $\copyright$ symbol decorating the type). Containment is a means of controlling aliasing among references. An object may be directly contained by only one other object and may not contain itself. Hence, circularities in the structure of list are precluded.

The initial state schema and operation *Insert* are defined recursively.

Initially, the list's head is empty and the list's tail is in an initial state. Since the list's tail is a list, this means it's head element is also empty and it's tail is also in an initial state, and so on.

The operation *Insert* is specified by an operation expression (rather than a schema) using the operators for disjoining ($[\!]$) and conjoining ($\land$) operations. It inserts a value $v?$ into the head element of the list (when it is empty), or performs an insert operation on the tail of the list when it's head element is not empty.

The meaning of *INIT* and *Insert* can be given using fixed point theory as shown by Smith [19]. *INIT* can be shown to be equivalent to

$$
\begin{array}{l}
\underline{\ I\textsc{nit}\ } \\
\exists s : \mathrm{seq}_\infty\ List^*[T] \bullet \\
\quad s(1) = self \land (\forall\, i : \mathrm{dom}\, s \setminus \{1\} \bullet s(i) = s(i-1).tail) \land \\
\quad s \in \mathrm{seq}\ List^*[T] \Rightarrow s(\#s).tail = s(\#s) \land \\
\quad (\forall\, i : \mathrm{dom}\, s \bullet s(i).empty)
\end{array}
$$

and *Insert* can be shown to be equivalent to

$Insert \mathrel{\widehat{=}} [\!] \, s : \text{seq}_\infty \, List^*[T]; \, i : \text{dom} \, s \mid p \bullet s(i).NodeInsert$

where p is the predicate $s(1) = self \land (\forall j : \text{dom} \, s \setminus \{1\} \bullet s(j) = s(j-1).tail) \land s \in \text{seq} \, List^*[T] \Rightarrow s(\#s).tail = s(\#s) \land (\forall j : 1 \mathinner{\ldotp\ldotp} i-1 \bullet \neg \, s(j).empty)$ and $NodeInsert \mathrel{\widehat{=}} [\, \Delta(empty, val) \, v? : T \mid empty \land val' = v? \land \neg \, empty'\,]$.

4 Refinement

Refinement in reference-semantics Object-Z is defined in terms of simulation rules by Derrick and Boiten [3]. Downward simulation is defined as follows.

> An Object-Z class C is a downward simulation of a class A if there is a retrieve relation R such that every abstract operation AOp of A is recast into a concrete operation COP of C and the following hold.
>
> **DS.1** $\forall \, C.INIT \bullet \exists \, A.INIT \bullet R$
> **DS.2** $\forall \, A.STATE; \, C.STATE \bullet R \Longrightarrow (\text{pre} \, AOp \Longleftrightarrow \text{pre} \, COp)$
> **DS.3** $\forall \, A.STATE; \, C.STATE; \, C.STATE' \bullet$
> $\qquad\qquad R \land COp \Longrightarrow (\exists \, A.STATE' \bullet R' \land AOp)$

That is, the initial state predicate can be stronger in the concrete class (**DS.1**)), as can operation postconditions (**DS.3**). Operation preconditions (i.e., the predicate pre Op for an operation Op) can neither be weaker nor stronger (**DS.2**).

This definition is simply that for a *blocking* model of operations, i.e., where an operation Op cannot occur unless pre Op is true, and is therefore independent of the semantics adopted (see Josephs [12], for example, for a similar definition). Hence, we would like to use it show that *List* of Section 2 is refined by *List** of Section 3. The refinement is done in three phases (see Fig. 2) each comprising one or more refinement steps consistent with downward simulation. These phases represent a general strategy for refining from value semantics to reference semantics.

Phase 1 In the first phase, all object values are changed to references. Hence, the sequence of nodes in *List* becomes a sequence of references to nodes.

Phase 2 In the second phase, references are added between objects where appropriate. Hence, references are added linking each node to the next in the list. A self reference is added to the final node in a finite list.

Phase 3 In the third phase, the class describing the system is replaced by the class of an object which is connected via references to all other objects in the system. In the list example, the class refined from *List* is replaced by a class describing the list from the head node, i.e., *List**.

4.1   Phase 1: Replacing Object Values with References

To accomplish the first phase of refinement in Object-Z, any operation schemas in which operations are applied to objects must be replaced by equivalent operation expressions. This is necessary since the reference-semantics version of Object-Z does not support operation application in schemas [18].

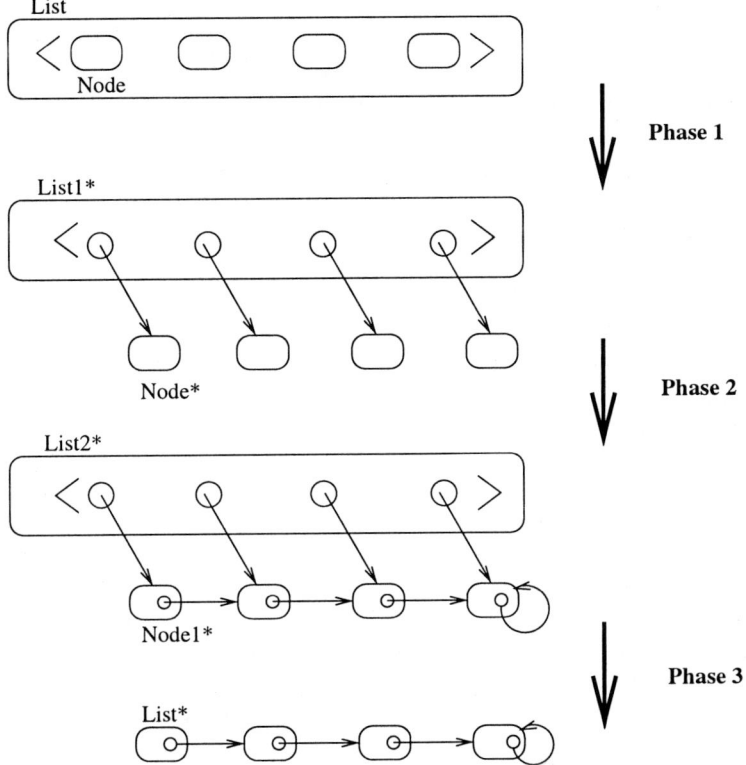

Fig. 2. Refinement of *List* to *List**

The operation *Insert* of *List*, can be replaced by

$$Insert \mathrel{\widehat{=}} \big[\,\Delta(list)\,\big] \wedge \big(\,[\!]\; i : \operatorname{dom} list \mid p \bullet list(i).Insert\big)$$

where p is $(\forall j : 1\mathinner{\ldotp\ldotp} i - 1 \bullet \neg\; list(j).empty) \wedge \{i\} \triangleleft list' = \{i\} \triangleleft list$.

The main step in this phase of refinement is then to replace all classes C in the specification by a new class with reference semantics. In the case where C has no declared objects, the definition of the new class is syntactically identical to C. The new class is therefore trivially a refinement of C under the identity retrieve relation. In the case where C declares objects, these declarations are changed to refer to the new classes. Furthermore,

- since, in a value semantics, different declarations always refer to different objects, all declared references must be contained by C and an invariant must be added that all declared references are distinct, and
- since, in a value semantics, values are changed by operation application but in a reference semantics, references are not, a schema $\big[\,a' = a\,\big]$ must be conjoined with any operation application $a.Op$.

The resulting classes are again trivially a refinement under the retrieve relation which equates the state variables of the corresponding declared objects. Such a retrieve relation is necessary since the semantic representations of the objects in the different semantics are not directly comparable.

Applying these steps to our example specification, results in a class $Node*$ defined syntactically identically to $Node$, and a class $List1*$ defined as follows. (Note that the conjunction of the schema $\left[\,list'(i) = list(i)\,\right]$ with $list(i).Insert$ has allowed us to remove $Insert$'s Δ-list and simplify its definition.)

$$
\begin{array}{|l}
\underline{List1*[T]}\\[4pt]
\quad\begin{array}{|l}
\underline{}\\
list : \text{seq}_\infty\ Node*[T]_{©}\\
\hline
list \neq \langle\,\rangle\\
\forall\, i,j : \text{dom}\ list \bullet i \neq j \Rightarrow list(i) \neq list(j)\\[4pt]
\quad\begin{array}{|l}\underline{I\text{NIT}}\\ \forall\, n : \text{ran}\ list \bullet n.I\text{NIT}\end{array}\\[6pt]
Insert \mathrel{\widehat{=}} [\!]\ i : \text{dom}\ list\ |\ \forall\, j : 1\,..\,i-1 \bullet \neg\ list(j).empty \bullet list(i).Insert
\end{array}
\end{array}
$$

The retrieve relations for these refinements are, respectively, $Node.empty = Node*.empty \land Node.val = Node*.val$ and $\text{dom}\,List.list = \text{dom}\,List1*.list \land (\forall i : \text{dom}\,List.list \bullet List.list(i).empty = List1*.list(i).empty \land List.list(i).val = List1*.list(i).val)$. The latter relates the value-semantics nodes to the reference-semantics nodes by equating the values of their state variables ($empty$ and val).

4.2 Phase 2: Adding References between Objects

For the second phase, we need to add references to classes and constraints on references reflecting the desired system structure. We begin by refining the class $Node*$ to a class $Node1*$ which has an added reference $next : Node1*[T]$ denoting the next node in the list, and strengthens the state invariant as follows.

$$
\begin{array}{|l}
\underline{Node1*[T]}\\[4pt]
\quad\begin{array}{|l}
empty : \mathbb{B}\\
val : T\\
next : Node1*[T]\\
\hline
next = self \lor next \in Node1*[T]_{©}
\end{array}
\qquad
\begin{array}{|l}
\underline{I\text{NIT}}\\
empty
\end{array}\\[10pt]
\quad\begin{array}{|l}
\underline{Insert}\\
\Delta(empty, val)\\
v? : T\\
\hline
empty \land \neg\ empty' \land val' = v?
\end{array}
\end{array}
$$

Node1* is a downward simulation of *Node** under the retrieve relation which identifies the variables *empty* and *val*, i.e., $Node^*.empty = Node1^*.empty \land Node^*.val = Node1^*.val$.

The state invariant of a class is implicitly conjoined to the initial state predicate and the precondition and postcondition of each operation. To show that the precondition of *Insert* is not strengthened under the retrieve relation, we need to show **DS.2** holds. That is,

$$\forall Node^*.\text{STATE}; Node1^*.\text{STATE} \bullet$$
$$Node^*.empty = Node1^*.empty \land Node^*.val = Node1^*.val \Rightarrow$$
$$(Node^*.empty \Leftrightarrow Node1^*.empty \land Node1^*.Inv)$$

where $Inv \mathrel{\widehat{=}} [\, next = self \lor next \in Node1^*[T]_\copyright\,]$. This trivially holds since the declaration of *Node1*.STATE* introduces the invariant *Inv* on the variables of *Node1**. In general, invariants can be added during refinement provided they do not constrain variables related (by the retrieve relation) to variables that are changed by the abstract operations [3].

To complete this phase, we refine the class *List1** by adding an invariant linking the nodes in the list in the appropriate way. That is, the next node of each node in the list, except the last in the case of a finite list, is that which occurs after it in the list. The next node of the last node of a finite list is itself. Once again, the invariant does not strengthen the precondition under the retrieve relation which in this case is the identity relation, i.e, $List1^*.list = List2^*.list$.

List2*[T]

$list : \text{seq}_\infty Node1^*[T]_\copyright$

$list \neq \langle\rangle$
$\forall i,j : \text{dom } list \bullet i \neq j \Rightarrow list(i) \neq list(j)$
$\forall i : \text{dom } list \bullet$
  $list(i).next = list(i+1) \lor$
  $(list \in \text{seq } Node1^*[T] \land i = \#list \land list(i).next = list(i))$

INIT
$\forall n : \text{ran } list \bullet n.\text{INIT}$

$Insert \mathrel{\widehat{=}} [\!]\, i : \text{dom } list \mid \forall j : 1 .. i-1 \bullet \neg\, list(j).empty \bullet list(i).Insert$

4.3 Phase 3: Replacing the System Class with an Object Class

The final phase involves removing the system class needed in a value semantics specification to relate the objects in the specified system. It is replaced by the class of one of the objects from which all others can be referenced. In cases where the value-semantics system class specifies an actual object of the specified system, this final phase may be unnecessary.

In our example, we want to replace the class $List2^*$ with the class $List^*$ of Section 3 (see Fig. 2). We begin by introducing a new variable $head$ as an alias to the head node of the list and redefine I_{NIT} and $Insert$ in terms of $head$. This is done by adding an existentially quantified variable s to both I_{NIT} and $Insert$ which denotes a sequence of nodes starting with $head$ and such that each other node in the sequence is the $next$ node of it predecessor in the sequence.

$List3^*[T]$

$list : \text{seq}_\infty\ Node1^*[T]_\copyright$
$head : Node1^*[T]_\copyright$

$list \neq \langle \rangle$
$\forall i, j : \text{dom}\ list \bullet i \neq j \Rightarrow list(i) \neq list(j)$
$\forall i : \text{dom}\ list \bullet$
  $\quad list(i).next = list(i+1) \lor$
  $\quad\quad (list \in \text{seq}\ Node1^*[T] \land i = \#list \land list(i).next = list(i))$
$head = list(1)$

I_{NIT}
$\exists s : \text{seq}_\infty\ Node1^*[T] \bullet$
  $\quad s(1) = head \land$
  $\quad (\forall i : \text{dom}\ s \setminus \{1\} \bullet s(i) = s(i-1).next) \land$
  $\quad s \in \text{seq}\ Node1^*[T] \Rightarrow s(\#s).next = s(\#s) \land$
  $\quad (\forall i : \text{dom}\ s \bullet s(i).I_{NIT})$

$Insert \mathrel{\widehat=} [\![\, s : \text{seq}_\infty\ Node1^*[T];\ i : \text{dom}\ s\ |$
  $\quad s(1) = head \land$
  $\quad (\forall j : \text{dom}\ s \setminus \{1\} \bullet s(j) = s(j-1).next) \land$
  $\quad s \in \text{seq}\ Node1^*[T] \Rightarrow s(\#s).next = s(\#s) \land$
  $\quad (\forall j : 1\mathinner{\ldotp\ldotp} i-1 \bullet \neg\ s(j).empty) \bullet$
  $\quad\quad s(i).Insert$

$List3^*$ is a downward simulation of $List2^*$ under the retrieve relation $List2^*.list = List3^*.list$.

Since $list$ is no longer used in the initial state schema or operation $Insert$, the class can be further refined by removing this variable. The invariants in terms of $list$ do not constrain $head$ and can be removed as well. In particular, the invariant that nodes in the list are distinct is captured by the invariant of $Node1^*$ which precludes circular list structures.

In the case where one or more of the invariants did constrain $head$, they would need to be redefined in terms of $head$.

The following class, $List4^*$, is a downward simulation of $List3^*$ under the retrieve relation $List3^*.head = List4^*.head$.

Introducing Reference Semantics via Refinement   597

―― $List4*[T]$ ――――――――――――――――――――――――――

  ―― $head : Node1*[T]_{©}$ ―――――――――――――――――――――

  ―― INIT ―――――――――――――――――――――――――――
  $\exists\, s : \text{seq}_{\infty}\, Node1*[T] \bullet$
    $s(1) = head \,\wedge$
    $(\forall\, i : \text{dom}\, s \setminus \{1\} \bullet s(i) = s(i-1).next) \,\wedge$
    $s \in \text{seq}\, Node1*[T] \Rightarrow s(\#s).next = s(\#s) \,\wedge$
    $(\forall\, i : \text{dom}\, s \bullet s(i).\text{INIT})$
  ―――――――――――――――――――――――――――――

  $Insert \,\widehat{=}\, [\!]\, s : \text{seq}_{\infty}\, Node1*[T];\ i : \text{dom}\, s \,|$
    $s(1) = head \,\wedge$
    $(\forall\, j : \text{dom}\, s \setminus \{1\} \bullet s(j) = s(j-1).next) \,\wedge$
    $s \in \text{seq}\, Node1*[T] \Rightarrow s(\#s).next = s(\#s) \,\wedge$
    $(\forall\, j : 1\,..\,i-1 \bullet \neg\, s(j).empty) \bullet$
        $s(i).Insert$
―――――――――――――――――――――――――――――――

Our system class $List4*$ now comprises a single contained object. Such a class can be refined to a class C with the single object declaration $a : A_{©}$ replaced by the state declarations of A, and with all occurrences of a, A, $a.\text{INIT}$ and $a.Op$ replaced by $self$, C, and the definitions of INIT and Op respectively. Hence, class $List4*$ is refined by

―― $List5*[T]$ ――――――――――――――――――――――――――

  $empty : \mathbb{B}$
  $val : T$
  $next : List5*[T]$
  ―――――――――――――――――――――――――――――
  $next = self \,\vee\, next \in List5*[T]_{©}$

  ―― INIT ―――――――――――――――――――――――――――
  $\exists\, s : \text{seq}_{\infty}\, List5*[T] \bullet$
    $s(1) = self \,\wedge$
    $(\forall\, i : \text{dom}\, s \setminus \{1\} \bullet s(i) = s(i-1).next) \,\wedge$
    $s \in \text{seq}\, List5*[T] \Rightarrow s(\#s).next = s(\#s) \,\wedge$
    $(\forall\, i : \text{dom}\, s \bullet s(i).empty)$
  ―――――――――――――――――――――――――――――

  $Insert \,\widehat{=}\, [\!]\, s : \text{seq}_{\infty}\, List5*[T];\ i : \text{dom}\, s \,|$
    $s(1) = self \,\wedge$
    $(\forall\, j : \text{dom}\, s \setminus \{1\} \bullet s(j) = s(j-1).next) \,\wedge$
    $s \in \text{seq}\, List5*[T] \Rightarrow s(\#s).next = s(\#s) \,\wedge$
    $(\forall\, j : 1\,..\,i-1 \bullet \neg\, s(j).empty) \bullet$
        $s(i).NodeInsert$
―――――――――――――――――――――――――――――――

where $NodeInsert \,\widehat{=}\, [\,\Delta(empty, val)\ v? : T \,|\, empty \,\wedge\, val' = v?\, \wedge\, \neg\, empty'\,]$.

Given that $self.x = x$ for each state variable x, $List5^*$ is a downward simulation of $List4^*$ under the retrieve relation $List4^*.head = List5^*.self$.

With $next$ renamed to $tail$, the initial state schema and operation $Insert$ of $List5^*$ are the equivalent schemas of those of $List^*$ derived using fixed point theory in Section 3. Hence, under the retrieve relation $List5^*.empty = List^*.empty \land List5^*.val = List^*.val \land List5^*.next = List^*.tail$, we can refine $List5^*$ to $List^*$.

5 Conclusion

In this paper, we have shown how to refine an object-oriented formal specification with a value semantics to one with a reference semantics. This process allows an abstract specification to be written in a value semantics in order to facilitate reasoning, and then be refined to a concrete specification with a reference semantics in order to facilitate transformation to code.

The general process was illustrated using a simple case study. This case study involved the introduction of recursion. Other refinements to reference semantics could involve the introduction of object sharing. The refinement steps were justified with respect to the definition of downward simulation in Object-Z. A set of rules proved sound with respect to this definition, or that of upward simulation, could be developed to aid the specifier by removing much of the proof burden.

Acknowledgements

Thanks to John Derrick for discussions which led to this work and Ian Hayes for his constructive comments on an earlier draft of this paper. This work was funded by a University of Queensland External Support Enabling Grant.

References

1. P. Bancroft and I.J.Hayes. Type extension and refinement. In L. Groves and S. Reeves, editors, *Formal Methods Pacific (FMP'97)*, pages 23–39. Springer-Verlag, 1997.
2. D. Carrington, D. Duke, R. Duke, P. King, G. Rose, and G. Smith. Object-Z: An object-oriented extension to Z. In S. Voung, editor, *Formal Description Techniques (FORTE'89)*, pages 281–296. North-Holland, 1989.
3. J. Derrick and E. Boiten. *Refinement in Z and Object-Z, Foundations and Advanced Applications*. Springer-Verlag, 2001.
4. R. Duke, P. King, G. Rose, and G. Smith. The Object-Z specification language. In T. Korson, V. Vaishnavi, and B. Meyer, editors, *Technology of Object-Oriented Languages and Systems (TOOLS 5)*, pages 465–483. Prentice Hall, 1991.
5. R. Duke, G. Rose, and G. Smith. Transferring formal techniques to industry: A case study. In J. Quemada, J. Mañas, and E. Vazquez, editors, *Formal Description Techniques (FORTE'90)*, pages 279–286. North-Holland, 1990.
6. R. Duke, G. Rose, and G. Smith. Object-Z: A specification language advocated for the description of standards. *Computer Standards and Interfaces*, 17:511–533, 1995.

7. R. Duke and G. Rose. *Formal Object-Oriented Specification using Object-Z.* MacMillan, 2000.
8. E.H. Dürr and J. van Katwijk. VDM++ – A formal specification language for object-oriented designs. In B. Meyer, G. Heeg, and B. Magnusson, editors, *Technology of Object-oriented Languages and Systems (TOOLS Europe 92)*, pages 63–78. Prentice-Hall, 1992.
9. A. Griffiths. From Object-Z to Eiffel: a rigorous development method. In C. Mingins, R. Duke, and B. Meyer, editors, *Technology of Object-Oriented Languages and Systems (TOOLS 18)*, pages 293–308. Prentice Hall, 1995.
10. A. Griffiths. An extended semantic foundation for Object-Z. In *1996 Asia-Pacific Software Engineering Conference (APSEC'96)*, pages 194–207. IEEE Computer Society Press, 1996.
11. A. Griffiths. Modular reasoning in Object-Z. In Wai Wong and K. Leung, editors, *Asia-Pacific Software Engineering Conference and International Computer Science Conference (APSEC '97/ICSC '97)*, pages 140–149. IEEE Computer Society Press, 1997.
12. M.B. Josephs. A state-based approach to communicating processes. *Distributed Computing*, 3:9–18, 1988.
13. K. Lano and H. Haughton, editors. *Object-Oriented Specification Case Studies.* Object-Oriented Series. Prentice Hall, 1993.
14. K. Lano. *Formal Object-Oriented Development.* Springer-Verlag, 1995.
15. K. Rosenberg. The adoption of formal methods within OTC. In K. Parker and G. Rose, editors, *Formal Description Techniques (FORTE'91)*, pages 85–92, 1991.
16. G. Smith, F. Kammüller, and T. Santen. Encoding Object-Z in Isabelle/HOL. In D. Bert, J.P. Bowen, M.C. Henson, and K. Robinson, editors, *International Conference of Z and B Users (ZB 2002)*, volume 2272 of *Lecture Notes in Computer Science*, pages 82–99. Springer-Verlag, 2002.
17. G. Smith. A fully abstract semantics of classes for Object-Z. *Formal Aspects of Computing*, 7(3):289–313, 1995.
18. G. Smith. *The Object-Z Specification Language.* Advances in Formal Methods. Kluwer Academic Publishers, 2000.
19. G. Smith. Recursive schema definitions in Object-Z. In A. Galloway J. Bowen, S. Dunne and S. King, editors, *International Conference of B and Z Users (ZB 2000)*, volume 1878 of *Lecture Notes in Computer Science*, pages 42–58. Springer-Verlag, 2000.
20. S.R.L.Meira and A.L.C. Cavalcanti. Modular object-oriented Z specifications. In *Z User Meeting 1990*, Workshops in Computing, pages 173–192. Springer-Verlag, 1990.
21. S. Stepney, R. Barden, and D. Cooper, editors. *Object-Orientation in Z.* Workshops in Computing. Springer-Verlag, 1992.
22. M. Utting. Reasoning about aliasing. In *Australian Refinement Workshop (ARW 95)*, pages 195–211, School of Computer Science and Engineering, The Univeristy of New South Wales, 1995.
23. H.B. Zadeh and S. Stepney. *ZEST – Z Extended with Structuring: A User's Guide, PROST-Objects, BT.7004.0.20.13, Issue 2*, 1996.

Soundness, Completeness and Non-redundancy of Operational Semantics for Verilog Based on Denotational Semantics

Zhu Huibiao[1], Jonathan P. Bowen[1], and He Jifeng[2]*

[1] Centre for Applied Formal Methods,
South Bank University, SCISM, 103 Borough Road, London SE1 0AA, UK
{huibiaz,bowenjp}@sbu.ac.uk
http://www.cafm.sbu.ac.uk/
[2] United Nations University, UNU/IIST, P.O. Box 3058, Macau, China
jifeng@iist.unu.edu
http://www.iist.unu.edu/

Abstract. This paper investigates three significant questions of Verilog's operational semantics: *soundness*, *completeness* and *non-redundancy*. Our understanding for these three questions is denotational-based. We provide an operational semantics for Verilog and prove that our operational semantics is sound, complete and non-redundant.

1 Introduction

Modern hardware design typically uses a hardware description language (HDL) to express designs at various levels of abstraction. An HDL is a high level programming language, with usual programming constructs such as assignments, conditionals and iterations, and appropriate extensions for real-time, concurrency and data structures suitable for modelling hardware. Verilog is an HDL that has been standardized and widely used in industry [6]. Verilog programs can exhibit a rich variety of behaviours, including event-driven computation, shared-variable concurrency and simulator-based interpretation.

The semantics for Verilog is very important because Verilog is widely used in industry. At UNU/IIST, the operational semantics has been explored in [1, 3, 4, 7]. Verilog's denotational semantics [9] has also been explored based on the operational semantics using Duration Calculus [8]. We have already investigated the derivation of denotational semantics from operational semantics for Verilog [10]. We also derived the operational semantics for Verilog from its denotational semantics [11].

Regarding operational semantics, there are three typical questions we should face:

(1) By which rule can we say our operational semantics is sound?
(2) How can we guarantee our operational semantics is complete?
(3) How can we say there will not be any redundant rules among all our transition rules?

---
* On leave from East China Normal University, Shanghai, China

This paper considers the soundness, completeness and non-redundancy of operational semantics for Verilog. Our approach is denotational-based. An operational semantics is called sound if it is consistent with the denotational model that has already been formulated. Regarding the transition rules of an operational semantics, there may be too few transitions. The completeness of an operational semantics is to check if the transitions are sufficient. There may also be too many transitions in a transition system. Redundant rules may add new extra features to our language, but these features actually do not exist in our language originally. Therefore we want to detect and avoid these redundant rules in our transition system.

This paper is organised as follows. Section 2 introduces the language and presents an operational semantics for Verilog. Assignment is regarded as an atomic action in this paper. Section 3 is devoted to the soundness of our operational semantics. We give a definition of the completeness and non-redundancy for operational semantics in section 4 and 5 respectively. The operational semantics for Verilog is proved to be sound, complete and non-redundant based on our denotational semantics. We give a brief introduction of our denotational semantics in the appendix.

Our discussion for soundness, completeness and non-redundancy focuses on a narrow area, which is denotational-based. Therefore, soundness, completeness and non-redundancy in this paper is called *D-soundness*, *D-completeness* and *D-non-redundancy* respectively. Here, "*D-*" indicates our understanding for these three questions is based on denotational semantics.

2 Operational Semantics for Verilog

There are some previous work [1, 3, 4, 7] about operational semantics for Verilog, where assignment is not regarded as an atomic action in these previous work. Our operational semantics provided below treats assignment as an atomic action.

2.1 Syntax for Verilog

The language discussed in this paper is a subset of Verilog [6]. It contains the following categories of syntactic elements introduced in [2].

$P ::= x := e \mid P \,;\, P \mid \textbf{if } b \textbf{ then } P \textbf{ else } P \mid \textbf{while } b \textbf{ do } P \mid c\, P \mid P \parallel P$

$c\, P$ denotes a timing controlled statement, and c is a time control used for scheduling.

$c ::= \#n \mid @(\eta), \quad \text{where} \quad \eta ::= v \mid \uparrow v \mid \downarrow v$

Time delay $\#n$ suspends the execution for exactly n time units. n is treated as an integer in this paper. An event guard $@(\uparrow v)$ is fired by the increase of the value of v, whereas $@(\downarrow v)$ is triggered by a decrease in v. Any change of v awakes the guard $@(v)$.

To accommodate the expansion laws of parallel construct, the language is equipped with a hybrid control event $@(g)$:

$g ::= \eta \mid g \textit{ or } g \mid g \textit{ and } g \mid g \textit{ and } \neg g$

and the guarded choice $(@(g_1)\, P_1)[\!] \ldots [\!](@(g_n)\, P_n)$ [9].

2.2 Transition Types

There are two types of configuration:
$$< P, \sigma, \sigma' > \quad \text{and} \quad < P, \sigma, \emptyset >$$
where:
(1) the first component P is a program text representing the program that remains to be executed.
(2) The second component σ indicates the initial state of an atomic action.
(3) When assignment is executed, σ and σ' identify the state changes within the assignment, where σ' represents the current state after the execution of assignment. If the third component is $\emptyset$, it means the previous atomic action ends and the new atomic action has not been scheduled.

The transition rules for Verilog can be grouped into the following categories:

T_1 Instantaneous transition
This type of transition models the execution of assignment. The new state contributed by assignment is stored in σ'.
$$< P, \sigma, \emptyset > \longrightarrow < P', \sigma, \sigma' >, \quad \text{where } \sigma' = f(\sigma)$$

T_2 Time event transition
(1) A transition can be fired by the sequential predecessor.
$$< P, \sigma, \sigma' > \xrightarrow{<\sigma,\sigma'>}_c < P', \sigma', \emptyset >$$
Here c is the triggered condition. It has the form $c(\sigma, \sigma')$, where σ and σ' are from $\xrightarrow{<\sigma,\sigma'>}_c$. If $\xrightarrow{<\sigma,\sigma'>}_c$ has no triggered condition, the triggered condition can be considered as **true**.
(2) A transition can be fired by its parallel partner.
$$< P, \sigma, \emptyset > \xrightarrow{<\sigma,\sigma'>}_c < P', \sigma', \emptyset >$$

T_3 Time advancing transition
If process P cannot do any other transitions at the moment, time will advance. We regard the unit of time advancing is 1.
$$< P, \sigma, \emptyset > \xrightarrow{1} < P', \sigma, \emptyset >$$

2.3 Operational Semantics for Verilog

Assignment $x := e$ can be scheduled at once. It can also allow the environment to do some atomic actions. Assignment cannot let time advance.

T_1 $\quad < x := e, \sigma, \emptyset > \longrightarrow < E, \sigma, \sigma[e/x] >$ $\hfill$ (*assign-1*)
$\quad$ where $\sigma[e/x]$ is the same as σ except the value of variable x is now associated with the value e.

T_2 $\quad < x := e, \sigma, \sigma' > \xrightarrow{<\sigma,\sigma'>} < x := e, \sigma', \emptyset >$ $\hfill$ (*assign-2*)
$\quad < x := e, \sigma, \emptyset > \xrightarrow{<\sigma,\sigma'>} < x := e, \sigma', \emptyset >$ $\hfill$ (*assign-3*)
Here "E" represents the empty process.

The event guard $@(g)$ can be immediately fired after it is scheduled to execute, it is actually triggered by the execution of its prior action. Another case is the guard waits to be fired by its environment. Time can also advance before the event becomes enabled.

$\mathbf{T_2}$ $<@(g), \sigma, \sigma'> \xrightarrow{<\sigma,\sigma'>}_{fire(g)} <\mathbf{E}, \sigma', \emptyset>$ (guard-1)

$<@(g), \sigma, \sigma'> \xrightarrow{<\sigma,\sigma'>}_{\neg fire(g)} <@(g), \sigma', \emptyset>$ (guard-2)

$<@(g), \sigma, \emptyset> \xrightarrow{<\sigma,\sigma'>}_{fire(g)} <\mathbf{E}, \sigma', \emptyset>$ (guard-3)

$<@(g), \sigma, \emptyset> \xrightarrow{<\sigma,\sigma'>}_{\neg fire(g)} <@(g), \sigma', \emptyset>$ (guard-4)

$\mathbf{T_3}$ $<@(g), \sigma, \emptyset> \xrightarrow{1} <@(g), \sigma, \emptyset>$ (guard-5)

Here, $fire(g)(\sigma, \sigma')$ is used to indicate the transition from state σ to state σ' can awake the guard $@(g)$, where σ, σ' are from $\xrightarrow{<\sigma,\sigma'>}$.

The transition rules for $\#n$, sequential composition, conditional, iteration and guarded choice can be found in [12]. In order to let our operational model for $P \parallel Q$ be consistent with the denotational model, we add the virtual process $flash$ to the end of each component, i.e., we regard the behaviour of $P \parallel Q$ as that of $(P; flash) \parallel (Q; flash)$. For $flash$, its denotational semantics is briefly described in the appendix. Its operational semantics is as follows:

$<flash, \sigma, \sigma'> \xrightarrow{<\sigma,\sigma'>} <\mathbf{E}, \sigma, \emptyset>$
$<flash, \sigma, \emptyset>$ can be regarded as $<\mathbf{E}, \sigma, \emptyset>$.

Below are the transition rules for parallel process $P \parallel Q$.

$\mathbf{T_1}$ If one of them can perform an instantaneous action, the whole process can also make this transition.
If $<P, \sigma, \emptyset> \longrightarrow <P', \sigma, \sigma'>$, then $<P \parallel Q, \sigma, \emptyset> \longrightarrow <P' \parallel Q, \sigma, \sigma'>$
If $<Q, \sigma, \emptyset> \longrightarrow <Q', \sigma, \sigma'>$, then $<P \parallel Q, \sigma, \emptyset> \longrightarrow <P \parallel Q', \sigma, \sigma'>$

$\mathbf{T_2}$ (1) $P \parallel Q$ can perform a triggered action caused by its predecessor.
If $<P, \sigma, \sigma'> \xrightarrow{<\sigma,\sigma'>}_{c1} <P', \sigma', \emptyset>$ and $<Q, \sigma, \sigma'> \xrightarrow{<\sigma,\sigma'>}_{c2} <Q', \sigma', \emptyset>$
then $<P \parallel Q, \sigma, \sigma'> \xrightarrow{<\sigma,\sigma'>}_{c1 \wedge c2} <P' \parallel Q', \sigma', \emptyset>$

(2) $P \parallel Q$ can perform a triggered action only caused by P.
If $<P, \sigma, \sigma'> \xrightarrow{<\sigma,\sigma'>}_{c1} <P', \sigma', \emptyset>$ and $<Q, \sigma, \emptyset> \xrightarrow{<\sigma,\sigma'>}_{c2} <Q', \sigma', \emptyset>$
then $<P \parallel Q, \sigma, \sigma'> \xrightarrow{<\sigma,\sigma'>}_{c1 \wedge c2} <P' \parallel Q', \sigma', \emptyset>$

(3) $P \parallel Q$ can perform a triggered action only caused by Q.
If $<P, \sigma, \emptyset> \xrightarrow{<\sigma,\sigma'>}_{c1} <P', \sigma', \emptyset>$ and $<Q, \sigma, \sigma'> \xrightarrow{<\sigma,\sigma'>}_{c2} <Q', \sigma', \emptyset>$
then $<P \parallel Q, \sigma, \sigma'> \xrightarrow{<\sigma,\sigma'>}_{c1 \wedge c2} <P' \parallel Q', \sigma', \emptyset>$

(4) $P \parallel Q$ allows the environment to perform an atomic action.
If $<P, \sigma, \emptyset> \xrightarrow{<\sigma,\sigma'>}_{c1} <P', \sigma', \emptyset>$ and $<Q, \sigma, \emptyset> \xrightarrow{<\sigma,\sigma'>}_{c2} <Q', \sigma', \emptyset>$
then $<P \parallel Q, \sigma, \emptyset> \xrightarrow{<\sigma,\sigma'>}_{c1 \wedge c2} <P' \parallel Q', \sigma', \emptyset>$

Remark: We regard $<P \parallel \mathbf{E}, \sigma, \emptyset>$ and $<\mathbf{E} \parallel P, \sigma, \emptyset>$ as $<P, \sigma, \emptyset>$.
Hence, $<\mathbf{E} \parallel \mathbf{E}, \sigma, \emptyset>$ is considered as $<\mathbf{E}, \sigma, \emptyset>$.

$\mathbf{T_3}$ $P \parallel Q$ allows time to advance **iff** both components do so.
If $<P, \sigma, \emptyset> \xrightarrow{1} <P', \sigma, \emptyset>$ and $<Q, \sigma, \emptyset> \xrightarrow{1} <Q', \sigma, \emptyset>$
then $<P \parallel Q, \sigma, \emptyset> \xrightarrow{1} <P' \parallel Q', \sigma, \emptyset>$ □

We have formulated an operational semantics for Verilog. Next we use $\Longrightarrow_c$ to specify an atomic action.

Definition 2.1. (Atomic action)

$<P,\sigma,\sigma'> \Longrightarrow_c <Q,\sigma',\emptyset> =_{df} <P,\sigma,\sigma'> \xrightarrow{<\sigma,\sigma'>}_c <Q,\sigma',\emptyset>$

$<P,\sigma,\emptyset> \Longrightarrow_c <Q,\sigma',\emptyset> =_{df} <P,\sigma,\emptyset> \longrightarrow <P',\sigma,\sigma'> \wedge$
$<P',\sigma,\sigma'> \xrightarrow{<\sigma,\sigma'>}_c <Q,\sigma',\emptyset>$ □

The phase semantics of the atomic action $<P,\sigma,\emptyset> \Longrightarrow_c <Q,\sigma',\emptyset>$ is the sequential composition of the corresponding two phase semantics.

In order to show the denotational-based soundness and completeness for Verilog operational semantics in the next two sections, our discussion for parallel process $P \parallel Q$ under state $<P \parallel Q, \sigma, \emptyset>$ will only focus on the atomic transition $<P \parallel Q, \sigma, \emptyset> \Longrightarrow_c <P' \parallel Q', \sigma', \emptyset>$.

The predicate $first\_par(<P,\sigma,\emptyset>)$ indicates if the first transition for program P under $<P,\sigma,\emptyset>$ is caused by a parallel process; it is defined as follows:

Definition 2.2. (*first_par*)

$first\_par(<P,\sigma,\emptyset>)$

$=_{df} \begin{cases} \text{false}, & \text{if } P = x := e, @(g), \#n \\ \text{false}, & \text{if } P = (@(g_1)\,P_1)\|\ldots\|(@(g_n)\,P_n) \\ \text{true}, & \text{if } P = P_1 \parallel Q_1 \\ first\_par(<P_1,\sigma,\emptyset>), & \text{if } P = P_1; Q_1 \\ first\_par(<P_1,\sigma,\emptyset>) \triangleleft b(\sigma) & \text{if } P = \text{if } b \text{ then } P_1 \text{ else } Q_1 \\ \triangleright first\_par(<Q_1,\sigma,\emptyset>), & \\ b(\sigma) \wedge first\_par(<P_1,\sigma,\emptyset>), & \text{if } P = \text{while } b \text{ do } P_1 \end{cases}$

We use the following two programs to illustrate the function of *first_par*.

$first\_par(<x := 1; @(\uparrow y), \sigma, \emptyset>) = \text{false}$,
$first\_par(<x := 1 \parallel y := 1 ; @(\uparrow y), \sigma, \emptyset>) = \text{true}$.

2.4 Transition Condition and Phase Semantics

The relationship between a transition and the variables in the denotational model can be described by the following diagram of an example transition, where the denotational model is briefly introduced in the appendix.

$\pi_2(last(\overleftarrow{tr}))$ $ttr2$ $\pi_2(last(\overrightarrow{tr}))$ $ttr2'$
$\uparrow$ $\uparrow$ $\uparrow$ $\uparrow$
$<P,\quad \sigma,\quad \sigma'>$ $\xrightarrow{<\sigma,\sigma'>}_c$ $<P',\quad \sigma',\quad \emptyset>$

We define a transition condition $\text{Cond}_{i,j}$ and its corresponding phase semantics for each type of transition. Here $\text{Cond}_{i,j}$ stands for the transition condition for the j-th transition of type $\mathbf{T}_i$.

$\mathbf{T}_1\ <P,\sigma,\emptyset> \longrightarrow <P',\sigma,\sigma'>$, where $\sigma' = f(\sigma)$

$$\mathbf{Cond}_{1,1} =_{df} \overrightarrow{tr} = \overleftarrow{tr} \wedge ttr = null \wedge$$
$$ttr1' = \pi_2(last(\overleftarrow{tr})) \wedge ttr2' = f(\pi_2(last(\overleftarrow{tr})))$$

$\mathbf{T_2}$ (1) $< P, \sigma, \sigma' > \xrightarrow{<\sigma, \sigma'>}_c < P', \sigma', \emptyset >$
$\mathbf{Cond}_{2,1} =_{df} c(ttr1, ttr2) \wedge ttr \neq null \wedge ttr' = null \wedge \mathbf{attach1}$, where:
$\mathbf{attach1} =_{df} \overrightarrow{tr} = \overleftarrow{tr} \triangleleft \pi_2(last(\overleftarrow{tr})) = ttr2 \triangleright \overrightarrow{tr} = \overleftarrow{tr}\widehat{} < (\overleftarrow{time}, ttr2, 1) >$

(2) $< P, \sigma, \emptyset > \xrightarrow{<\sigma, \sigma'>}_c < P', \sigma', \emptyset >$
$\mathbf{Cond}_{2,2} =_{df} ttr = null \wedge ttr' = null \wedge c(\pi_2(last(\overleftarrow{tr})), \pi_2(last(\overrightarrow{tr})))$
$$\wedge \left(\overrightarrow{tr} = \overleftarrow{tr} \vee \begin{pmatrix} \pi_1(\overrightarrow{tr} - \overleftarrow{tr}) = \overleftarrow{time} \wedge \\ \pi_3(\overrightarrow{tr} - \overleftarrow{tr}) = 0 \end{pmatrix} \right)$$

The above two types of transitions have the instantaneous feature. The corresponding phase semantics of each transition can be expressed as $Inst(\mathbf{Cond}_{i,j})$, where $Inst(\mathbf{X}) =_{df} \mathbf{H}(true \vdash \neg wait' \wedge \delta(time) = 0 \wedge \mathbf{X})$

$\mathbf{T_3}$ $< P, \sigma, \emptyset > \xrightarrow{1} < P', \sigma, \emptyset >$
$\mathbf{Cond}_{3,1} =_{df} \overrightarrow{tr} = \overleftarrow{tr} \wedge ttr = null \wedge ttr' = null$

Its phase semantics is:

$$\mathbf{phase3} =_{df} \mathbf{H}(true \vdash \mathbf{Cond}_{3,1} \wedge (\delta(time) < 1 \triangleleft wait' \triangleright \delta(time) = 1))$$

3 Soundness

A model is called sound if it is consistent with another model that has already been formulated. For Verilog, as we have already formulated the denotational model, the correctness of operational semantics should depend on its consistency with our denotational model. Therefore our understanding of soundness for operational semantics is based on denotational analysis.

First we introduce the notion of configuration condition. It links the configuration state with the denotational state.

Definition 3.1. (Configuration Condition)
$Condition(< P, \sigma, \sigma' >) =_{df} ttr \neq null$
$Condition(< P, \sigma, \emptyset >) =_{df} ttr = null$ □

Example 3.2: Consider the execution of $x := e$ under state $< x := e, \sigma, \emptyset >$. There are two execution branches from the state $< x := e, \sigma, \emptyset >$.

$< x := e, \sigma, \emptyset > \longrightarrow < \mathbf{E}, \sigma, \sigma[e/x] >$ (1)

$< x := e, \sigma, \emptyset > \xrightarrow{<\sigma, \sigma'>} < x := e, \sigma', \emptyset >$ (2)

On the other hand, from the denotational view, we can prove:

$Inst(\mathbf{Cond}_{1,1}) ; II \Rightarrow ttr = null \wedge x := e$ (3)
$Inst(\mathbf{Cond}_{2,2}) ; x := e \Rightarrow ttr = null \wedge x := e$ (4)

Here $Inst(\mathbf{Cond}_{1,1})$ and $Inst(\mathbf{Cond}_{2,2})$ are the phase semantics of the above two transitions. We regard the denotational semantics of the empty process $\mathbf{E}$ as II. Therefore logical formulae (3) and (4) are consistent with transitions (1) and (2) respectively. This leads to the definition of soundness for operational semantics. □

Definition 3.3. (Soundness)
An operational semantics is considered *sound*, based on denotational semantics iff

for any transition $<P,\alpha> \xrightarrow{\beta} <P',\alpha'>$
it satisfies $sem\ ;\ P' \Rightarrow Condition(<P,\alpha>) \wedge P$ (∗)

where:
(1) sem is the phase semantics of transition $<P,\alpha> \xrightarrow{\beta} <P',\alpha'>$.
(2) If $<P,\alpha>$ has the form $<P,\sigma,\sigma'>$ OR
$<P,\alpha>$ has the form $<P,\sigma,\emptyset>$ AND $\neg first\_par(<P,\sigma,\emptyset>)$,
then $\xrightarrow{\beta}$ can be of the transition form $\longrightarrow$, $\xrightarrow{<\sigma,\sigma'>}_c$ or $\xrightarrow{1}$.
(3) If $<P,\alpha>$ has the form $<P,\sigma,\emptyset>$ AND $first\_par(<P,\sigma,\emptyset>)$,
then $\xrightarrow{\beta}$ can only be of the atomic action transition $\Longrightarrow_c$.

Here, "⇒" represents logical implication. P and P' appearing in a configuration stand for the syntax, whereas P and P' in (∗) above stand for the denotational semantics. □

Theorem 3.4: The operational semantics for Verilog that appeared in section 2.3 is sound. □

4 Completeness

Although our transition system is proved to be sound, we still need to check if our transition rules are sufficient. If the transition rules for a language are insufficient, this may generate a new and unintended class of terminal state. Therefore, it is worthy to investigate if our transition rules for Verilog are sufficient. Our approach for completeness is also by denotational analysis.

Example 4.1 (Incompleteness)
There are five transition rules for event guard @(g) (see section 2.3). If we omit the time advancing rule for @(g) (*guard-5*), we may find that the rest of the rules for @(g) are not complete. Consider the case $<@(g), \sigma, \emptyset>$. Originally we have:

$(sem_{2,3}\ ;\ II) \vee (sem_{2,4}\ ;\ @(g)) \vee (sem_{3,1}\ ;\ @(g)) = (ttr = null) \wedge @(g)$
Now we have $(sem_{2,3}\ ;\ II) \vee (sem_{2,4}\ ;\ @(g)) \neq (ttr = null) \wedge @(g)$.

Here $sem_{2,3}$, $sem_{2,4}$ and $sem_{3,1}$ are the phase semantics of the three transitions (*guard-3*, *guard-4*, *guard-5*) under $<@(g), \sigma, \emptyset>$ respectively. This inequation indicates the rest of the transition rules for @(g) after omitting *guard-5* are not complete. □

Example 4.2 (Completeness)
There are three transition rules for assignment (see section 2.3, *assign-1*, *assign-2*, *assign-3*). From the denotational view, we can prove :

$(Inst(\mathbf{Cond}_{1,1})\ ;\ II) \vee (Inst(\mathbf{Cond}_{2,2})\ ;\ x := e) = (ttr = null) \wedge x := e$ (3)
$Inst(\mathbf{Cond}_{2,1})\ ;\ x := e = (ttr \neq null) \wedge x := e$ (4)

Here $Inst(\mathbf{Cond}_{1,1})$, $Inst(\mathbf{Cond}_{2,1})$ and $Inst(\mathbf{Cond}_{2,2})$ are the phase semantics of transition *assign-1*, *assign-2* and *assign-3* respectively. These two equations indicate the transition rules at state $< x := e, \sigma, \emptyset >$ and $< x := e, \sigma, \sigma' >$ are complete respectively. This comes to the definition of completeness based on denotational semantics.□

Definition 4.3. (Completeness of Transition Rules for Program)
The transition rules for program P are called *complete*, based on denotational semantics iff for every configuration $< P, \alpha >$, it should satisfy
$$\bigvee_i (sem_i \ ; \ P_i) \ = \ Condition(< P, \alpha >) \wedge P$$
where:
(1) sem_i is the phase semantics of the transition $< P, \alpha > \xrightarrow{\beta_i} < P_i, \alpha_i >$.
(2) If $< P, \alpha >$ has the form $< P, \sigma, \sigma' >$ **OR**
$< P, \alpha >$ has the form $< P, \sigma, \emptyset >$ **AND** $\neg first\_par(< P, \sigma, \emptyset >)$,
then $\xrightarrow{\beta_i}$ can be of the transition form $\longrightarrow$, $\xrightarrow{<\sigma,\sigma'>}_c$ or $\xrightarrow{1}$.
(3) If $< P, \alpha >$ has the form $< P, \sigma, \emptyset >$ **AND** $first\_par(< P, \sigma, \emptyset >)$,
then $\xrightarrow{\beta_i}$ can only be of the atomic action transition $\Longrightarrow_c$.
(4) i goes through all the transitions of process P under state $< P, \alpha >$. □

Remark: The empty process **E** cannot do any transitions under state $< \mathbf{E}, \sigma, \emptyset >$ (or $< \mathbf{E}, \sigma, \sigma' >$). We will not discuss the completeness for transition rules of empty process **E**.

The following diagram illustrates our intuitive understanding for completeness.

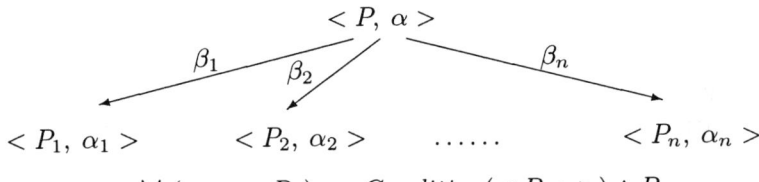

$$\bigvee_i (sem_i \ ; \ P_i) \ = \ Condition(< P, \alpha >) \wedge P$$

Definition 4.4. (Completeness of Operational Semantics)
An operational semantics is called complete if the transition rules for every program are complete. □

Theorem 4.5: The operational semantics for Verilog that appeared in section 2.3 is complete.

Proof. Here we give the proof of completeness for the transition rules of assignment. We only consider $x := e$ under state $< x := e, \sigma, \emptyset >$.

$(Inst(\mathbf{Cond}_{1,1}); II) \vee (Inst(\mathbf{Cond}_{2,2}); x := e)$ Def of $\mathbf{Cond}_{1,1}$, assign
$= (ttr = null \wedge assign(x,e)) \vee$ Def of $\mathbf{Cond}_{2,2}$, PL
$\quad (\ Inst(\mathbf{Cond}_{2,2}) \ ; \ hold(0) \ ; \ assign(x, e) \ )$
$= (ttr = null) \wedge (hold(0) \ ; \ assign(x,e))$ Def of $x := e$
$= (ttr = null) \wedge x := e$

For other statements, the proofs for the completeness of their transition rules are presented in [12]. □

5 Non-redundancy

Although our transition system for Verilog has been proved to be sound and complete, there may be too many transition rules. Therefore, we need to check if there are some redundant rules in our transition system. Redundant rules may add new features to our language, which we do not want. These new features actually do not exist in our language originally. Therefore, redundant rules may cause conflict for our understanding of a language. The following approach is a way to test if there are some redundant rules in our transition system. Our approach is by denotational analysis.

The transition rules for iteration are the same as the ones for conditional [12]. In the following discussion of non-redundancy we will omit iteration. We only focus on finite programs, but this does not mean our discussion loses generality.

In the first part of this section, we use the logical point of view to consider the transitions of a program. We want to represent the operational semantics of program P as a logical formula $O(P)$ [10]. In the second part, we use the notation $D(P)$ to represent the denotational semantics for program P. We plan to prove $D(P) = O(P)$, which can be considered as a way to test if there are no redundant rules for program P.

5.1 Logical Point of View for Operational Semantics

Definition 5.1: A configuration $< P, \sigma, \sigma' >$ (or $< P, \sigma, \emptyset >$) is called *a divergent state* if P can perform an infinite sequence of instantaneous transitions or self-triggered transitions, i.e., there exists an infinite set $\{D_i \mid i \in Nat\}$ of configurations such that $D_0 = < P, \sigma, \sigma' >$ (or $< P, \sigma, \emptyset >$), and for all i,
- either $D_i \longrightarrow D_{i+1}$
- or $D_i = < P_i, \sigma_i, \sigma'_i >$, $\sigma'_i \neq \emptyset$, $D_i \xrightarrow{<\sigma_i, \sigma'_i>}_{c_i} D_{i+1}$ □

Definition 5.2: A computational sequence of program P is an empty sequence or any finite sequence leading P to the other state; that is:
$$D_0 \xrightarrow{\delta_1} D_1 \ldots \ldots \xrightarrow{\delta_n} D_n$$
where $\xrightarrow{\delta_i}$ ($i = 1, \ldots, n$) can be an instantaneous transition ($\longrightarrow$), a triggered transition ($\xrightarrow{<\sigma, \sigma'>}_c$), or a time advancing transition ($\xrightarrow{1}$). □

If computational sequence seq is not empty, $seq[i]$ is the i-th transition ($D_{i-1} \xrightarrow{\delta_i} D_i$) of seq.

We write $cp[P]$ representing the set which contains all the computational sequences leading program P to terminating state or divergent state. $cp[P]_{ter}$ and $cp[P]_{div}$ stand for the sets which contain all the sequences leading program P to the terminating and divergent states correspondingly. Therefore, we have $cp[P] = cp[P]_{ter} \cup cp[P]_{div}$.

If a process terminates, its terminating state can be one of the following states:
$$< E, \sigma, \emptyset >, \qquad < E, \sigma, \sigma' >$$

Definition 5.3: Let seq stand for a computational sequence of program P. Suppose $len(seq) = n$, $sem(seq)$ is the semantics of the computational sequence seq, which can be defined as:
If $len(seq) = 0$, then $sem(seq) =_{df} II$.

If $len(seq) = 1$, then $sem(seq) =_{df} sem_1$.
Otherwise $sem(seq) =_{df} sem_1 ; \ldots ; sem_n$.
sem_i is the phase semantics of the i-th transition ($seq[i]$) of the computational sequence seq. $len(seq)$ indicates the length of the computation sequence, i.e., the number of transitions in the computation sequence. □

Definition 5.4. (Operational Semantics from Logical Point of View)
$$O(P) =_{df} \bigvee\nolimits_{seq \in cp[P]_{div}} (sem(seq) ; \bot) \lor \bigvee\nolimits_{seq \in cp[P]_{ter}} (sem(seq)).$$
where, $\bot =_{df} H(false \vdash true)$, which is the bottom element of the complete lattice HF under implication order. Here HF is the set containing all heathy formulae. □

5.2 Non-redundancy

Example 5.5: For assignment we originally have three transition rules (see section 2.3, *assign-1*, *assign-2*, *assign-3*). In the last two sections we have already proved that these transition rules are sound and complete. According to the logical point of view for operational semantics, we get the following result:
$$D(x := e) = O(x := e)$$
Now if we add another transition rule (*assign-4*) for $x := e$, we may find this rule is redundant.
$$< x := e, \sigma, \emptyset > \longrightarrow < x := e, \sigma, \sigma > \qquad (assign\text{-}4)$$
We can prove that this new rule is also sound. The current transition rules for $x := e$ (this newly added rule, together with its original three rules) are complete. But we find that this new rule will cause problems by the following analysis.

Let $\quad D_{2i+1} = <x := e, \sigma, \emptyset> \ (i = 0, 1, 2, \ldots)$ and
$\quad D_{2i} = <x := e, \sigma, \sigma> \ (i = 1, 2, 3, \ldots)$.

The sequence $D_1 \longrightarrow D_2 \xrightarrow{<\sigma, \sigma>} D_3 \longrightarrow \ldots$ indicates that $<x := e, \sigma, \emptyset>$ is a divergent state, which means $\bot \Rightarrow O(x := e)$. As $\bot$ is the bottom element of all healthy formulae (HF), which indicates that $O(x := e) = \bot$. But actually $x := e$ has no divergent behaviour, and $D(x := e) \neq \bot$. Assignment should satisfy $D(x := e) = O(x := e)$ actually. This newly added rule (*assign-4*) makes $O(x := e)$ different from $D(x := e)$. □

In our denotational model, the divergent part of the denotational semantics for program P stands for its divergent behaviour. As we only focus on finite programs in this subsection, which means we don't have iteration in our syntax. We find that $D(P)_{div} = false$ for any program P. This means that there are no sequences leading program P to the divergent state, i.e., $cp[P]_{div} = \emptyset$. But if there are some redundant rules which make P have some divergent behaviour, then $cp[P]_{div} \neq \emptyset$. This means $O(P)_{div} \neq false$, which also means $D(P) \neq O(P)$.

In order to link the transition rules with the denotational semantics and consider the denotational semantics as the starting point, we introduce $O(P)$, which is the logical point of view to characterise the operational semantics. If the transition system does not cause any extra new features, which do not exist in our language, $O(P)$ should be the same as $D(P)$ for any program P. Therefore, we use "$D(P) = O(P)$" as the definition of the non-redundancy of a transition system.

Definition 5.6. (Non-redundancy)
An operational semantics is called non-redundant, based on denotational semantics iff
$$D(P) = O(P), \quad \text{for any program } P. \qquad \Box$$
Theorem 5.7 If we exclude iteration in the syntax for Verilog, then
$$D(P) = O(P), \quad \text{for any program } P. \qquad \Box$$

This theorem indicates the operational semantics for Verilog that appeared in section 2.3 (omitting iteration) is non-redundant. Our understanding for non-redundancy is denotational-based.

The above approach is only a testing way to check if there are some redundant rules. That is, if $D(P) \neq O(P)$, this means that there may be too many transition rules because our original rules are assumed to be sound and complete. Then we need to look at the transition rules of P carefully and discover the redundant rules.

6 Conclusion

This paper discusses three significant aspects regard to an operational semantics for Verilog: (1) soundness, (2) completeness, (3) non-redundancy. Our understanding for these three aspects is new, based on denotational semantics. Therefore, soundness, completeness and non-redundancy is called *D-soundness*, *D-completeness* and *D-non-redundancy* respectively. Here "*D-*" indicates our approach is denotational-based. We give definitions for these three concepts and prove that the operational semantics for Verilog presented in this paper is sound and complete. Our operational semantics can also be proved to be non-redundant if we omit iteration in our syntax.

The denotational-based understanding of these three questions can be regarded as a general approach. Our approach could also be applied to the operational semantics of other languages. The work presented in this paper can be regarded as the extension of unifying theories [5] for Verilog.

References

1. J. P. Bowen, He Jifeng and Xu Qiwen. An Animatable Operational Semantics of the VERILOG Hardware Description Language. *Proc. ICFEM2000: 3rd IEEE International Conference on Formal Engineering Methods*, IEEE Computer Society Press, pp. 199–207, York, UK, September 2000.
2. M. J. C. Gordon. The Semantic Challenge of Verilog HDL. *Proc. Tenth Annual IEEE Symposium on Logic in Computer Science*, IEEE Computer Society Press, pp. 136–145, June 1995.
3. He Jifeng and Xu Qiwen. An Operational Semantics of a Simulator Algorithm. Technical Report 204, UNU/IIST, P.O. Box 3058, Macau, China, June 2000.
4. He Jifeng and Zhu Huibiao. Formalising Verilog. *Proc. IEEE International Conference on Electronics, Circuits and Systems*, IEEE Computer Society Press, pp. 412–415, Lebanon, December 2000.
5. C. A. R. Hoare and He Jifeng. *Unifying Theories of Programming*. Prentice Hall International Series in Computer Science, 1998.
6. IEEE *Standard Verilog Hardware Description Language*. IEEE Standard 1364-2001 (Revision of IEEE std 1364-1995), 2001.

7. Li Yongjian and He Jifeng. *Formalising VERILOG: Operational Semantics and Bisimulation.* Technical Report 217, UNU/IIST, P.O. Box 3058, Macau, China, November 2000.
8. Zhou Chaochen, C. A. R. Hoare and A. P. Ravn. A Calculus of Durations. *Information Processing Letters*, 40(5):269–276, 1991.
9. Zhu Huibiao and He Jifeng. A Semantics of Verilog using Duration Calculus. *Proc. International Conference on Software: Theory and Practice*, pp. 421–432, Beijing, China, August 2000.
10. Zhu Huibiao, J. P. Bowen and He Jifeng. From Operational Semantics to Denotational Semantics for Verilog. *Proc. CHARME 2001: 11th Advanced Research Working Conference on Correct Hardware Design and Verification Methods*, Springer-Verlag, LNCS 2144, pp. 449–464, Livingston, Scotland, UK, September 2001.
11. Zhu Huibiao, J. P. Bowen and He Jifeng. Deriving Operational Semantics from Denotational Semantics for Verilog. *Proc. APSEC 2001: 8th Asia-Pacific Software Engineering Conference*, IEEE Computer Society Press, pp. 177–184, Macau, China, December 2001.
12. Zhu Huibiao, J. P. Bowen and He Jifeng. *Soundness, Completeness and Non-redundancy of Operational Semantics for Verilog based on Denotational Semantics (Extended version).* Technical Report SBU-CISM-02-07, SCISM, South Bank University, London, UK, 2002.

Appendix

Our denotational semantic model contains a variable tr to describe the behaviour of a process, which is composed of a trace of *snapshots*. A snapshot is used to specify the behaviour of an atomic action, and expressed by a triple (t, σ, μ), where: (1) t indicates the time when the atomic action happens; (2) σ denotes the final values of program variables at the termination of an atomic action; (3) μ is the control flag indicating which process is in control: $\mu = 1$ states the atomic action is engaged by the process, whereas $\mu = 0$ implies it is performed by the environment.

The components of a snapshot can be selected using the projections:

$$\pi_1((t, \sigma, \mu)) =_{df} t \qquad \pi_2((t, \sigma, \mu)) =_{df} \sigma \qquad \pi_3((t, \sigma, \mu)) =_{df} \mu$$

A pair of variable $ttr =_{df} (ttr1, ttr2)$ is introduced to model the change made by an atomic action, where $ttr1$ stores the initial state of an atomic action, $ttr2$ stores the current state after the execution of the atomic action. Below is a formal description of the variables used by our denotational semantic model:

- $\overleftarrow{time}$ and $\overrightarrow{time}$ are the start point and the end point of a time interval over which the observation is recorded. We use $\delta(time)$ to represent the length of the time interval.
  $$\delta(time) =_{df} (\overrightarrow{time} - \overleftarrow{time})$$
- $\overleftarrow{tr}$ stands for the initial trace of a program over the interval which is passed by its predecessor. $\overrightarrow{tr}$ stands for the final trace of a program over the interval. $\overrightarrow{tr} - \overleftarrow{tr}$ stands for the sequence of snapshots contributed by the program itself and its environment during the interval.
- ttr and ttr' stand for the initial and final value of the variable ttr which are used to store the contribution of an atomic action over the interval.
- ok, ok' are boolean variables. $ok = true$ indicates that the process has started, and $ok' = true$ records the observation that the process has become stable.
- $wait, wait'$ are boolean variables. $wait = true$ indicates that the process starts in an intermediate state, and $wait' = true$ means the process is waiting. □

The following definitions are very important in our semantic model:
(1) Chop:
$$P \frown Q =_{df} \exists t, s, tt, \bullet \quad P[s/\overrightarrow{tr}, t/\overrightarrow{time}, tt/ttr'] \\ \land Q[s/\overleftarrow{tr}, t/\overleftarrow{time}, tt/ttr]$$

(2) Sequential composition:
Let P and Q be formulae. Define
$$P \,;\, Q =_{df} \exists w, o \bullet (\, P[w/wait', o/ok'] \frown Q[w/wait, o/ok]\,)$$

(3) Healthy formula:
A formula is called a *healthy formula* if it has the following form.
$$\mathbf{H}(Q \vdash W \triangleleft wait' \triangleright T)$$
where: (1) $\mathbf{H}(X) = II \triangleleft wait \triangleright (X \land R1)$; (2) $R1 =_{df} \overleftarrow{tr} \preceq \overrightarrow{tr}$; (3) II is the unit of sequential composition; (4) $P \triangleleft b \triangleright Q =_{df} P \land b \lor Q \land \neg b$; (5) $P \vdash R =_{df} (ok \land P) \Rightarrow (ok' \land R)$ □

Our denotational semantics of process P is described as:
$$\mathbf{H}(\neg P_{div} \vdash P_{wait} \triangleleft wait' \triangleright P_{ter})$$
where, P_{div}, P_{wait} and P_{ter} are the divergent, waiting and terminating behaviour of P respectively.

Assignment is considered as an atomic action in this paper. The execution of $x := e$ assigns the value e to x.
$$x := e =_{df} flash \,;\, hold(0) \,;\, assign(x, e)$$
where:

- $flash$ adds to the trace a new snapshot (made by its prior atomic action).
- $hold(n)$ indicates that the execution is held for exactly n time units.
- $assign(x, e)$ models the updating incurred by the assignment.

The definition for $flash$ can be found in [12]. The definitions for $hold(n)$, $assign(x, e)$ can be found in [10–12]. The detailed explanation of our denotational model can be found in [9–12].

Towards a Time Model for *Circus*

Adnan Sherif and He Jifeng [*]

The United Nations University,
International Institute for Software Technology,
Casa Silva Mendes, Est. do Engenheiro Trigo No. 4,
P.O Box 3058, Macau
Tel.:+853 - 712.930, Fax: +853 - 712.940
ams@iist.unu.edu, hjf@iist.unu.edu

Abstract. In this work we propose a time model for *Circus*. The model is an extension to the model proposed by the unifying theories of programming and used by *Circus*. We take a subset of *Circus* and study its semantics in the new model. We create an abstraction function that maps the timed model to the original model. The main objective of this mapping is to create a relation between the two models. This allows the exploration of some properties of the timed semantics in the untimed model. We study a toy example to illustrate the use of this mapping.

1 Introduction

Real time systems have always been a strong candidate for formal development methods. This fact rises due to the complexity and, usually, critical nature of these systems. The development of formal specification languages, and the adaptation of existing languages with time expressing capacity, was and still is a challenging task. Many languages such as DC [1], and RTL [4] are based on temporal logic and are powerful for expressing timed functionalities. Timed CSP [8] is an extension to the well known CSP [9]. Reed and Roscoe have developed several semantic models for the language [8].

Lately the combination of different languages and techniques have been adapted to obtain formalisms that can be used in a wider range of applications. *Circus* is a combination of CSP and Z [12]; it includes specification statements found in Morgan's refinement calculus [7] and Dijkstra's language of guarded commands [2]. *Circus* has a well-defined syntax and a formal semantics [15, 13] based on the unified theories of programming [3]. Case studies using the language are explored in [14] to show its power of expression. A development method for *Circus* using refinement is described in [10].

This paper aims to provide a model which is enriched with time in a conservative manner to the untimed *Circus* . We add some time operators to the language as well. A mapping between the two models is created with the objective of studying the properties of timed programs in the untimed model.

---

[*] On leave from East China Normal University, Shanghai. The work is partly supported by research grant 02104 of MoE P. R. of China

To define this model we adopt a simple language (CT^*). CT^* is a subset of *Circus*. For simplicity, we only consider actions, guarded commands and assignment from the original language. The fact that we are using a subset of the original language has no effect over the model, as the other constructs of the language are abstractions and declarations that have little effect over the model.

In the next section we give an informal introduction to the syntax and semantics of the language CT^*. In Section 3, we present the semantic model and give the formal semantics of CT^*. A relation between the timed model and the original model is explored in Section 4. We study a simple example and explore some properties in Section 5, and conclude in Section 6 with a discussion on future work.

2 CT^*:Informal Description

A CT^* program is formed by actions, commands and channel communication events. Figure 1 presents the BNF description of the syntax of CT^*.

$$
\begin{aligned}
\text{Action} \quad &::= Skip \mid Stop \mid Chaos \mid Wait\ t \\
&\mid \text{CommunicationAction} \mid b\ \&\ \text{Action} \\
&\mid \text{Action; Action} \mid \text{Action} \square \text{Action} \mid \text{Action} \sqcap \text{Action} \\
&\mid \text{Action} \|[\ CS\ ]\| \text{Action} \mid \text{Action} \setminus CS \mid \text{Command} \\
&\mid \text{Action} \stackrel{t}{\triangleright} \text{Action} \mid \mu N \bullet \text{Action}
\end{aligned}
$$

Communication ::= N CParameter*

CParameter ::= ?N | !e | .e

Command ::= N^+ := e | Action ◁ b ▷ Action

Fig. 1. CT^* syntax

In the syntax above, e stands for any expression, t stands for a positive integer time expression, N any valid name, N^+ a list of names and CS stands for a set of channel names.

A CT^* program is formed from one single action. An action can be a basic action, or a combination of one or more actions.

Skip, is a basic action that terminates immediately. *Stop* represents an abnormal termination which simply puts a program in an ever waiting state. *Chaos* is the worst action, nothing can be said about its behavior.

The action (*Wait* t) will be held for an amount of time determined by the positive integer expression t before terminating normally. Guarded actions (b & Action) are proceeded by a predicate which has to be *true* for the action to take place; otherwise the guarded action cannot be executed and the resulting behavior is similar to the action *Stop*.

An internal choice (Action ⊓ Action) selects one of the two actions in a non-deterministic manner, whereas the external choice (Action □ Action) waits for any of the two actions to interact with the environment. The first action that shows an interaction with the environment (either by synchronizing on an event or terminating) is the resulting action.

The sequential composition of two actions (Action; Action) will result in a new action that will behave as the first action followed immediately by the second action.

An action can be prefixed with a communication event (input or output) which will take place before the action starts. The action waits for the other actions that need to synchronize on the channel before the communication can take place. The parallel composition of two actions (Action⟦CS⟧Action) involves a set (CS) containing the events they need to synchronize on. A hiding operation also takes a set of events (CS). The set is to be excluded from the resulting observation; hidden events can no longer be seen by other actions.

The timeout construct (Action ▷^{t} Action) takes a positive integer value as the length of the timeout. The timeout operator acts as a time guarded choice. If the first action performs an observable event or terminates before the specified time elapses, it is chosen. Otherwise, the first action will be suspended and the only possible observations are those produced by the second action.

Assignment is a command; it simply assigns a value to a variable in the current state. If the variable already exists its value will be overwritten, otherwise it will be added to the current state and assigned the given value. The conditional command (Action ◁ b ▷ Action) associates two actions with a boolean expression b. If the expression evaluates to *true* then the first action is chosen, otherwise the second action is chosen.

3   The Semantic Model

The first question that had to be answered is: what model of time we would like to have, discrete time or continuous time? On one hand the second seems to be more appropriate for it is powerful to express time in both forms, and for the nature of time in the real world to be continuous. On the other hand, it cannot be implemented by a computer system. Unlike a continuous model, a discrete model is implementable, and therefore the untimed refinement rules can be extended in a more natural way. Following the main objective of making the model conservative we make a choice for the discrete model.

Similar approaches such as those in [6] and [5] use Extended Duration Calculus (EDC) to add continuous time to the language semantics. Both works, show clearly the elegance and powerful expression capacity of the EDC formulas. But both approaches make it clear that the new model cannot be easily related to the original untimed model. Proving properties in the new model is a laborious task.

A reactive system behavior can be studied with two observations. The initial observation shows the state of the environment before the program starts, and the second observations shows the state of the environment at the moment the program reaches a stable state. A stable state is either a termination state or a none termination state in which the program has no interaction with the environment [3]. The final observation registers the interaction of the program with the environment during and at the point of observation. This observation is registered in the form of a sequence of events that show the order in which the events occurred, and a set of refusals which indicate the events the program can refuse at the observation point.

In our approach we continue with the same pair of observations, at the initial and end of the program. But we enrich the observations on the interaction with environment, by adding time information. The interaction with the environment is recorded as a sequence of tuples, each element of the sequence denoting the observations over a single time unit. The first component of the tuple is a sequence of events which occurred during the time unit. The second component is the set of refused events at the end of the time unit.

The following is a formal description of the observation variables used by our model.

ok, ok' are boolean variables. When ok is true, it states that the program started and ok' indicates that the program is in a stable state.

$$ok, ok' : Boolean$$

$wait, wait'$ boolean variables. When $wait$ is true the program starts in an intermediate state. When $wait'$ is true the program has not terminated; when it is false, it indicates a final observation.

$$wait, wait' : Boolean$$

$state, state'$ A mapping from variable names to values. This mapping associates each user variable in the program to a value.

$$state, state' : N \rightarrow Value$$

The dashed variable represents the state of the program variables at the final observation.

tr, tr' A sequence of observations on the program interaction with its environment. tr records the observations that occurred before the program starts, and tr' records the final observation. Each element of the sequence represents an observation over one time unit. Each observation element is composed of a tuple, where the first element of the tuple is the sequence of events that occurred during the time unit, and the second one is the associated set of refusals at the end of the same time unit.

$$tr, tr' : \text{seq}(\text{seq } Event \times \mathbb{P} \, Event)$$

The type $Event$ represents all the possible events of a program. We also define a relation between two timed traces. We define a relation $Expands$ as follows

$$Expands(tr, tr') \cong (Front(tr) \preceq tr') \wedge (first(Last(tr)) \preceq first(tr'(\# \, tr)))$$

Given two timed traces, we state that the second expands the first if the initial part of the first timed trace is a subsequence of the second timed trace, and the untimed traces registered at the last time unit of the first timed trace is a subsequence of the traces registered at the same time in the second timed trace.

$trace'$ A sequence of events that occurred since the last observation. In this observation we are interested in recording only the events without time.

$$trace' : \text{seq } Event$$
$$trace' = Flat(tr') - Flat(tr)$$

where
$$Flat : \text{seq}(\text{seq } Event \times \mathbb{P}\, Event) \to \text{seq } Event$$
$$Flat(<>) = <>$$
$$Flat(< (el, ref) > \frown S) = el \frown Flat(S)$$

A single observation is given by the combination of the above variables. We will define our programs as predicates over the observation variables. We define a condition R that needs to be satisfied by all observations.

$$R(P) \cong P \wedge Expands(tr, tr')$$

The condition states that for all valid observations the final values of the timed trace (tr') are always an expansion of the initial timed traces (tr). We use the term $[\![P]\!]_{time}$ to stand for the timed semantic of a program P

3.1 Basic Actions

The semantics of the action *Skip* is given as a program that can only terminate normally, without consuming any time. It also has no interaction with the environment.

$$[\![Skip]\!]_{time} \cong (ok' \wedge \neg wait' \wedge tr' = tr \wedge state' = state) \qquad (1)$$

On the other hand the semantics of the action *Stop* is given as a predicate that waits for ever. Notice that *Stop* permits time to pass, but it does not interact with the environment ($trace' = <>$).

$$[\![Stop]\!]_{time} \cong (ok' \wedge wait' \wedge trace' = <>) \qquad (2)$$

The action *Chaos* is given as the predicate *true*. *Chaos* is the worst action and nothing can be said about it except that it also needs to satisfy the condition R.

$$[\![Chaos]\!]_{time} \cong R(true) \qquad (3)$$

The assignment assigns a value to a variable in the current state. If the variable does not exist it will be added, otherwise its value will be overwritten. The assignment operation is instantaneous and does not consume time.

$$[\![x := e]\!]_{time} \cong (ok' \wedge \neg wait' \wedge tr' = tr \wedge state' = state \oplus \{x \mapsto e\}) \qquad (4)$$

Wait: The only possible behavior for this action is to wait for the specified number of time units to pass before terminating immediately.

$$[\![Wait\ d]\!]_{time} \cong ((ok' \wedge wait' \wedge (\#tr' - \#tr) < d) \vee \\ (ok' \wedge \neg wait' \wedge (\#tr' - \#tr) = d)) \wedge \\ (trace' = <>) \qquad (5)$$

Communication: An action can engage in a communication if all the other actions involved in the same communication are ready to do so. We model this with the help of two predicates. $wait\_com(c)$ models the waiting state of an action to communicate on channel c. The only possible observation is that the communication channel cannot appear in the refusal set during the observation period. $term\_com(m)$ represents the act of the communication itself. It states clearly that the communication does not take any time ($\#tr' = \#tr$), but the event appears in the traces of the observation.

$$wait\_com(c) \cong ok' \wedge wait' \wedge possible(tr, tr', c) \wedge trace' = <>$$
$$term\_com(m) \cong ok' \wedge \neg wait' \wedge trace' = <m> \wedge \#tr' = \#tr$$

Where, $possible(tr, tr', c)$ returns true if the channel c is not contained in the refusal set of all the observations recorded from tr to tr'. The following is a definition of the function

$$possible(tr, tr', c) \cong \forall i : \#tr..\#tr' \bullet c \notin second(tr'(i))$$

The semantics of the output communication is given bellow. The definition describes two states for the communication semantics. The first is that the communication observation is in a waiting state. The second describes the case of a communication waiting for a time period before terminating with the event registered in the traces.

$$[\![c!e]\!]_{time} \cong wait\_com(c) \vee \\ (wait\_com(c) \circ (term\_com(c.e) \wedge state' = state)) \qquad (6)$$

We use ($\circ$) to stand for observation concatenation. It is defined as follows

$$A \circ B \cong \exists \bar{o} \bullet A(\bar{v}, \bar{o}) \wedge B(\bar{o}, \bar{v}')$$

Where $\bar{v}, \bar{v}'$ represent the vector of observation variables. We use the term $A(\bar{v}, \bar{v}')$ to denote the predicate that satisfies the vector of observation variables $\bar{v}$ as input and the vector $\bar{v}'$ as output. The concatenation states that there exists a vector of observation variables $\bar{o}$ such that this vector is the output of the first predicate and satisfies the input of the second predicate. The concatenation operator satisfies the following properties

$$(A \vee B) \circ C = (A \circ C) \vee (B \circ C)$$
$$(A \circ B) \circ C = A \circ (B \circ C)$$

We can define the input operation in a similar manner. The main difference is that when the communication takes place, the value transmitted on the channel is assigned to the variable used in the input command.

$$[\![c?x]\!]_{time} \cong wait\_com(c) \vee \\ (wait\_com(c) \circ (term\_com(c.e) \wedge state' = state \oplus [x \mapsto e])) \qquad (7)$$

The semantics of the communication prefix can be given with the help of the sequential composition. The action *comm* is either an input or output operation.

$$[\![commAction]\!]_{time} \mathrel{\widehat{=}} [\![comm;\ Action]\!]_{time} \tag{8}$$

Conditional Choice: We use the conditional choice operator exactly as defined in the unifying theories of programming [3].

3.2 Sequential Composition

The sequential composition has three possible states. The first shows that if the first action diverges then so does the sequential composition. The second state shows that the initial action is in a waiting state and therefore the following action can not start. The alternative behavior would be for the first action to terminate and the second to start immediately after.

$$\begin{aligned}[] [\![A;\ B]\!]_{time} \mathrel{\widehat{=}} & ([\![A]\!]_{time}[false/ok']) \vee \\ & ([\![A]\!]_{time} \wedge wait') \vee \\ & (([\![A]\!]_{time}[true, false/ok', wait']) \circ [\![B]\!]_{time}) \end{aligned} \tag{9}$$

3.3 Guarded Action

A guarded action has a predicate p which needs to be satisfied before the action can take place. If the predicate is *false* the only possible behavior of the resulting action is to wait for ever. But if the predicate evaluates to *true* then the result will be any possible behavior of the guarded action.

$$[\![p\ \&\ A]\!]_{time} \mathrel{\widehat{=}} ([\![A]\!]_{time} \triangleleft p \triangleright [\![Stop]\!]_{time}) \tag{10}$$

3.4 External Choice

The external choice between two actions is determined by the environment. The composed system will behave as either one of the two actions which ever reacts first to the environment. This can be expressed as two possible behaviors, either the system is in a waiting state and only internal behavior can take place or the system reacts to the environment after waiting for an external event which satisfies either one of the component actions or both, and in this case the choice is non-deterministic.

$$\begin{aligned}[] [\![A\ \Box\ B]\!]_{time} \mathrel{\widehat{=}} & ([\![A]\!]_{time} \wedge [\![B]\!]_{time} \wedge wait' \wedge trace' =<>) \vee \\ & (([\![A]\!]_{time} \wedge [\![B]\!]_{time} \wedge ok' \wedge wait' \wedge state' = state \wedge \\ & trace' =<>) \vee [\![Skip]\!]_{time}) \circ (([\![A]\!]_{time} \vee [\![B]\!]_{time}) \wedge \\ & (\neg wait' \vee (\neg(tr \preceq tr') \wedge trace' \neq <>))) \end{aligned} \tag{11}$$

The internal choice is specified just as in [3].

3.5 Recursion

To define recursion we need to define an ordering operator. An action A is as good as action B in the sense that it will meet all the operations and satisfy all the specifications satisfied by B. This relation is denoted by $A \sqsupseteq B$.

$$A \sqsupseteq B \triangleq [[\![A]\!]_{time} \Rightarrow [\![B]\!]_{time}] \qquad (12)$$

An action A is equal to an action B if

$$A = B \triangleq A \sqsupseteq B \wedge B \sqsupseteq A \qquad (13)$$

We notice that the set of observations in our model form a complete lattice with respect to the relation $\sqsupseteq$, having $[\![Chaos]\!]_{time}$ as its bottom element, $\sqcap$ as the greatest lower bound. So we can define the semantics of recursion as the *weakest fixed point* [3].

$$\mu X \bullet F(X) \triangleq \sqcap \{X \mid X \Rightarrow F(X)\} \qquad (14)$$

3.6 Timeout

The Timeout operator takes a time value and combines two actions such that, the first action should react to the environment within the given time period or the second action will take place. We can model this with the help of the external choice.

$$[\![A \stackrel{d}{\triangleright} B]\!]_{time} \triangleq [\![(A \;\square\; (Wait\; d;\; intB)) \setminus \{int\}]\!]_{time} \qquad (15)$$

The event int is taken to be an event that is not used by A and B or another event can be used. The main objective of adding this event is to trigger the external choice and force it to select the second option. It can only do the first option if the action A engages in a communication or terminates before the wait period d elapses. The event int is hidden from the rest of the environment.

For details of the semantic of the other operators of the language and the properties please refer to [11].

4 Linking *Circus* Models

Our proposed model is different from other approaches, we are interested in adding time information to the semantics of the language, but we will also like to preserve the untimed semantics of our programs in the time model. To show the relation between the two models we create a function L that given a set of timed observations related to a CT^* program P, the function returns the equivalent observation in the original model without time information. This function is defined as follows

$$L([\![P]\!]_{time}) \triangleq \exists\, obs \bullet [\![P]\!]_{time} \wedge trace' = Flat(tr') - Flat(tr) \wedge \\ ref' = second(Last(tr')) \qquad (16)$$

The function L maps the timed semantics of a program P to the untimed semantics of the *Circus* program. This is done by applying the *Flat* function to the timed traces to obtain the original model traces. A projection on the second element of the last entry in tr', results in the refusal set of the original model.

We also introduce a function R as an inverse function for L. This function takes as input a set of untimed observations and adds arbitrary time information.

$$R(\llbracket P \rrbracket) \cong \bigvee \{\llbracket Q \rrbracket_{time} \mid L(\llbracket Q \rrbracket_{time}) \sqsupseteq \llbracket P \rrbracket\} \tag{17}$$

We observe that the functions L and R form a *Galois connection* [3]. If we apply the mapping R to the result of applying the mapping L to a timed specification S, we will get a larger set of observation. The time information contained in S is lost and the result is a weaker specification.

$$S \sqsupseteq R(L(S))$$

This permits us to explore some properties of the timed language. Let us consider the following theorem.

Theorem 1. *A specification S is time insensitive if it satisfies the following equation*

$$R(L(S)) = S \tag{18}$$

The above theorem states that by applying the conjunction of the mapping functions to a specification S we obtain the same specification. Then the time information in the original specification is irrelevant to the behavior of the system. An example of such case is the action *Skip*. By applying the function L to the semantics of the constructs of CT^* we can obtain the equivalent *Circus* semantics.

$$L(\llbracket x := e \rrbracket_{time}) = \llbracket x := e \rrbracket \tag{19}$$
$$L(\llbracket Skip \rrbracket_{time}) = \llbracket Skip \rrbracket \tag{20}$$
$$L(\llbracket Stop \rrbracket_{time}) = \llbracket Stop \rrbracket \tag{21}$$
$$L(\llbracket Chaos \rrbracket_{time}) = \llbracket Chaos \rrbracket \tag{22}$$
$$L(\llbracket comm \rrbracket_{time}) = \llbracket comm \rrbracket \tag{23}$$
$$L(\llbracket Wait\ d \rrbracket_{time}) = \llbracket Stop \rrbracket \vee \llbracket Skip \rrbracket \tag{24}$$
$$L(\llbracket A \triangleleft b \triangleright B \rrbracket_{time}) \sqsupseteq L(\llbracket A \rrbracket_{time}) \triangleleft b \triangleright L(\llbracket B \rrbracket_{time}) \tag{25}$$
$$L(\llbracket p\&\ A \rrbracket_{time}) \sqsupseteq p\&\ L(\llbracket A \rrbracket_{time}) \tag{26}$$
$$L(\llbracket A \sqcap B \rrbracket_{time}) \sqsupseteq L(\llbracket A \rrbracket_{time}) \sqcap L(\llbracket B \rrbracket_{time}) \tag{27}$$
$$L(\llbracket A \square B \rrbracket_{time}) \sqsupseteq L(\llbracket A \rrbracket_{time}) \square L(\llbracket B \rrbracket_{time}) \tag{28}$$
$$L(\llbracket A;\ B \rrbracket_{time}) \sqsupseteq L(\llbracket A \rrbracket_{time}); L(\llbracket B \rrbracket_{time}) \tag{29}$$
$$L(\llbracket A \llbracket cs \rrbracket B \rrbracket_{time}) \sqsupseteq L(\llbracket A \rrbracket_{time}) \llbracket cs \rrbracket L(\llbracket B \rrbracket_{time}) \tag{30}$$
$$L(\llbracket A \backslash cs \rrbracket_{time}) \sqsupseteq L(\llbracket A \rrbracket_{time}) \backslash cs \tag{31}$$
$$L(\llbracket \mu X \bullet A(X) \rrbracket_{time}) \sqsupseteq \mu X' \bullet L(\llbracket A \rrbracket_{time})(X') \tag{32}$$
$$L(\llbracket A \stackrel{d}{\triangleright} B \rrbracket_{time}) = L(\llbracket (A \square (Wait\ d;\ intB)) \backslash \{int\} \rrbracket_{time}) \tag{33}$$

The relation between the models will permit us to explore properties of programs expressed in the untimed model. The parts of the program which are not time sensitive can be identified and explored in the untimed model. For programs with time information some properties can still be investigated in the untimed model. In the next section we explore this topic in more detail with the aid of an example.

5 Example

A one place buffer, takes as input a value from the input channel, stores this value in a local internal variable and then offers to communicate the same value on the output channel. The buffer has a main safety requirement. The buffer can not lose data, i.e. it should not allow the data to be over written by new input before an output is issued. The simple buffer is given in the following CT^* actions

$$Buffer \mathrel{\widehat{=}} in?xBuffer_{<x>}$$
$$Buffer_{<x>} \mathrel{\widehat{=}} out!xBuffer$$

To add some timing constraints we state that the input and output operations have a duration of 3 time units. We will add a waiting state at the end of each operation. The communication does not consume time. We can change the buffer example as follows

$$TBuffer \mathrel{\widehat{=}} in?x Wait\ 3;\ TBuffer_{<x>}$$
$$TBuffer_{<x>} \mathrel{\widehat{=}} out!x Wait\ 3;\ TBuffer$$

The safety property of the buffer can be specified by a function on traces. The function states that, the projection of the trace over the event *out* should be shorter or equal to the projection of the same trace over the event *in*. It also states that the projection of the *front* of the trace over the event *in* is shorter or equal to the projection of the same trace on the event *out*.

$$S(trace) \mathrel{\widehat{=}} Front(trace) \upharpoonright \{in\} \leq trace \upharpoonright \{out\} \land$$
$$trace \upharpoonright \{out\} \leq trace \upharpoonright \{in\}$$

We would like to check if our timed buffer still meets the safety requirement. Because the specification uses the untimed traces to state the property, we can use our mapping function L to obtain the time abstract version of the buffer, and then check if the abstract version of satisfies the specification. We define a relation sat_T to state that a timed program P satisfies an untimed specification S that only uses the traces.

$$P\ sat_T\ S \mathrel{\widehat{=}} L(P) \Rightarrow S$$

We need to prove that
$$L([\![TBuffer]\!]_{time}) \Rightarrow S$$

Where

$$L([\![TBuffer]\!]_{time})$$
$$\sqsupseteq$$
$$[\![in?x(Stop \sqcap Skip);\ out?x(Stop \sqcap Skip)]\!];\ L(TBuffer)$$

Because the program is a guarded recursive action. We can use the following
$$F(X) \sqsupseteq S \text{ iff } F(S) \sqsupseteq S$$
and
$$(\llbracket in?x(Stop \sqcap Skip); \ out?x(Stop \sqcap Skip) \rrbracket; \ S) \sqsupseteq S$$
$$implies$$
$$L(TBuffer) \sqsupseteq S$$

From the semantic definition of communication and the definition of sequential composition
$$\llbracket in?x(Stop \sqcap Skip); \ out?x(Stop \sqcap Skip) \rrbracket; \ S \Rightarrow (trace = <>) \lor$$
$$(trace = <in>) \lor$$
$$(trace < in \ out > \frown t'' \land$$
$$S(t'')$$

Therefore
$$L(\llbracket TBuffer \rrbracket_{time}) \ sat_T \ S$$

□

Notice that the abstraction function L when applied to $Wait \ d$, substitutes the wait command with non-deterministic choice between *skip* and *stop*. This actually introduces the deadlock state into the program. Therefore deadlock free property can not be explored with this abstraction function. A more suitable abstraction would be, to substitute $Wait \ d$ with a *Skip*. We are currently exploring this type of abstractions.

6 Conclusions

In this paper we presented a model for adding time to *Circus*. The new model is an extension to the original untimed model. We also show that the semantics of a program that has no time information is the same in both models. We have created a mapping from one model to the other, this mapping forms a Galois connection between the two models. Therefore we explored the possibility of reasoning on some properties of the system in one model, given a program semantics in the other model.

As future work, we are studying other mappings and the possible properties to be explored by these mappings. Therefore different mappings to the untimed model can be used according to the type of property to be explored. *Circus* has a semantic model implemented in Z, we are also interested in extending this semantics model in Z with time, we would like to use a tool such as ZEVES to study the model. We are also interested in rewriting the case studies of the steam boiler presented by Jim Woodcock and Ana Cavalcanti in [14]. The validation of the refinement laws introduced in [10] in the timed model is in our scope as well.

The model we presented uses discrete time. Requirements for control systems are usually expressed in continuous time. A mapping between the continuous time models and our implementation model is an interesting aspect to be explored. This mapping can be used to validate the timing requirements.

References

1. Z. Chaochen, C. A. R. Hoare, and A. P. Ravn. A Calculus of Duration. *Information Processing Letters.*, 40:269–276, 1991.
2. E. W. Dijkstra. Guarded Commands, Nondeterminacy and Formal Derivation of Programs. *Communications of the ACM*, 18(8), 1975.
3. C. A. R. Hoare and H. Jifeng. *Unifying Theories of Programming*. Prentice-Hall Series in Computer Science, 1998.
4. F. Jahanian, A. K. Mok, and D. A. Stuart. Formal specification of real-time systems. Technical Report TR-88-25, Department of Computer Science, University of Texas at Austin, June 1988.
5. He Jifeng and Victor Verbovskiy. Integrating CSP and DC. R 248, International Institute for Software Technology, The United Nation University, P.O. Box 3058, Macau, January 2002.
6. Li Li and He Jifeng. A Denotational Semantics of Timed RSL using Duration Calculus. R 168, International Institute for Software Technology, The United Nation University, P.O. Box 3058 Macau, July 1999.
7. C. Morgan. *Programming from Specifications*. Series in Computer Science. Prentice-Hall International, 2nd edition, 1994.
8. G. M. Reed and A. W. Roscoe. A timed model for communicating sequential processes. In *Proceedings of ICALP '86*, volume 226. Lecture Notes in Computer Science, 1986.
9. A. W. Roscoe. *The Theory and Practice of Concurrency*. Prentice-Hall International, 1998.
10. A. Sampaio, J. C. P. Woodcock, and A. L. C. Cavalcanti. Refinement in Circus. To appear in proceedings of FME2002, 2002.
11. Adnan Sherif and He Jifeng. Towards a Time Model for Circus. R 257, International Institute for Software Technology, The United Nation University, P.O. Box 3058, Macau, July 2002.
12. M. Spivey. *The Z Notation*. Prentice-Hall International, 2nd edition, 1992.
13. J. C. P. Woodcock and A. L. C. Cavalcanti. Circus: a concurrent refinement language. Technical report, Oxford University Computing Laboratory, Wolfson Building, Parks Road, Oxford OX1 3QD, UK, July 2001.
14. J. C. P. Woodcock and A. L. C. Cavalcanti. The steam boiler in a unified theory of Z and CSP. In *8th Asia-Pacific Software Engineering Conference (APSEC 2001)*, 2001.
15. J. C. P. Woodcock and A. L. C. Cavalcanti. The Semantics of Circus - a Concurrent Language for Refinement. In *ZB 2002: Formal Specification and Development in Z and B*, volume 2272 of *LNCS*. Springer, January 2002.

Author Index

Aalderink, Henri   226
Abdel-Hamid, Amr T.   459
Alagar, Vasu   92
Anderson, Hugh   411
Arenas, Alvaro E.   204
Attiogbé, J. Christian   120
Auguston, Mikhail   103

Back, Ralph-Johan   1
Ban, Ainita   406
Ben Ahmed, Samir   216
Bordbar, Behzad   561
Bowen, Jonathan P.   600
Bryant, Barrett R.   103
Burt, Carol C.   103
Butler, Michael   287

Campos, Sérgio   180
Cao, Fei   103
Carrington, David   548
Cavalcanti, Ana   347
Cavalli, Ana   371
Celiku, Orieta   299
Chang, Jiayue   98
Chen, Chuanbo   583
Chen, Feng   38
Chen, Jessica   359
Chen, Xuejun   80
Chen, YiYun   495
Chen, Zhenqiang   262

Davrondjon, Gafurov   401
Deng, Yi   275
Derrick, John   108, 561
Diab, Hassan   483
Dong, Jin Song   144, 156, 311
Dong, Wei   435
Du, Yuyue   221
Duran, Adolfo   347

Fang, Xiu-rong   578
Feng, Yao-Dong   38, 500
Frappier, Marc   483

Gan, Zaobin   583
Gao, Xiaolei   69

Goldson, Doug   323
Gorgulho, Gustavo   180
Guo, Fan   495

Hale, Mark A.   20
Hammad, Ahmed   511
Harrison, John   459
Hayes, Ian   335
He, Jifeng   168, 535, 600, 613
He, Xudong   275
Heisel, Maritta   57
Hu, RongGui   495
Huang, Jinfeng   226
Hughes, Arthur   24

Janowski, Tomasz   401
Jaray, Jacques   216
Jemni, Leila   216
Jiang, Changjun   221
Jiang, Yan-Bing   500
Jüllig, Richard   22
Jürjens, Jan   471

Kim, Soon-Kyeong   548

Lämmel, Ralf   92
Li, Guangyuan   231
Li, Li   523
Li, Shi-xian   48, 578
Li, Xiaoshan   535
Li, Yuan Fang   311
Liu, Jing   69
Liu, Ling   523
Liu, Shaoying   3
Liu, Ying   237
Liu, Yuan   262
Liu, Zhiming   535
Lukkien, Johan   226

Ma, Huadong   98
Ma, Zhi-Yi   500
Maag, Stéphane   371
Mei, Hong   38
Meira, Wagner, Jr.   180
Miao, Huaikou   69, 523
Miller, Tim   192

Ming, Zhong 578
Mo, Lian 275
Mosbahi, Olfa 216
Musser, David R. 132

Ng, Muan Yong 287

Olson, Andrew M. 103

Pang, Jun 396
Pei, Xiandeng 583
Pereira, Adriano 180
Peuker, Sibylle 335
Plosila, Juha 383

Qi, Zhi-Chang 435
Qin, Shengchao 168
Qiu, Zongyan 168

Raje, Rajeev R. 103
Reeve, Greg 323
Reeves, Steve 323
Roychoudhury, Abhik 423

Sampaio, Augusto 347
Santen, Thomas 57
Seceleanu, Tiberiu 383
Shankar, Subash 573
Shao, Wei-Zhong 500
Shao, Zhiqing 132
Sherif, Adnan 613
Shukur, Zarina 406
Smith, Graeme 108, 588
Song, Mark 180

Souquières, Jeanine 57
St-Denis, Richard 483
Strooper, Paul 192
Sun, Jing 156, 311
Sun, Jun 311

Taguchi, Kenji 144
Tahar, Sofiène 447, 459
Tang, Zhisong 231
Tatibouët, Bruno 511

Verschueren, Ad 226
Voisinet, Jean-Christophe 511

Wang, Hai 156, 311
Wang, Ji 435
Wang, Qianxiang 38
Waters, Gill 561
Wimmel, Guido 471
Woodcock, Jim 24
Wright, Joakim von 299
Wu, Weiping 511

Xu, Baowen 262

Yu, Huiqun 275

Zhang, Naixiao 168, 237
Zheng, Hong 48
Zhu, Hong 249
Zhu, Huibiao 600
Zin, Abdullah Md. 406
Zobair, M. Hasan 447

Lecture Notes in Computer Science

For information about Vols. 1–2425
please contact your bookseller or Springer-Verlag

Vol. 2343: I. Chong (Ed.), Information Networking. Proceedings, Part I, 2002. XIX, 729 pages. 2002.

Vol. 2344: I. Chong (Ed.), Information Networking. Proceedings, Part II, 2002. XX, 825 pages. 2002.

Vol. 2426: J.-M. Bruel, Z. Bellahsène (Eds.), Advances in Object-Oriented Information Systems.Procedings, 2002. IX, 314 pages. 2002.

Vol. 2427: M. Hannebauer, Autonomous Dynamic Reconfiguration in Multi-Agent Systems. XXI, 284 pages. 2002. (Subseries LNAI).

Vol. 2428: H. Hermanns, Interactive Markov Chains. XII, 217 pages. 2002.

Vol. 2429: P. Druschel, F. Kaashoek, A. Rowstron (Eds.), Peer-to-Peer Systems. Proceedings, 2002. IX, 339 pages. 2002.

Vol. 2430: T. Elomaa, H. Mannila, H. Toivonen (Eds.), Machine Learning: ECML 2002. Proceedings, 2002. XIII, 532 pages. 2002. (Subseries LNAI).

Vol. 2431: T. Elomaa, H. Mannila, H. Toivonen (Eds.), Principles of Data Mining and Knowledge Discovery. Proceedings, 2002. XIV, 514 pages. 2002. (Subseries LNAI).

Vol. 2432: R. Bergmann, Experience Management. XXI, 393 pages. 2002. (Subseries LNAI).

Vol. 2433: A.H. Chan, V. Gligor (Eds.), Information Security. Proceedings, 2002. XII, 502 pages. 2002.

Vol. 2434: S. Anderson, S. Bologna, M. Felici (Eds.), Computer Safety, Reliability and Security. Proceedings, 2002. XX, 347 pages. 2002.

Vol. 2435: Y. Manolopoulos, P. Návrat (Eds.), Advances in Databases and Information Systems. Proceedings, 2002. XIII, 415 pages. 2002.

Vol. 2436: J. Fong, C.T. Cheung, H.V. Leong, Q. Li (Eds.), Advances in Web-Based Learning. Proceedings, 2002. XIII, 434 pages. 2002.

Vol. 2437: G. Davida, Y. Frankel, O. Rees (Eds.), Infrastructure Security. Proceedings, 2002. XI, 339 pages. 2002.

Vol. 2438: M. Glesner, P. Zipf, M. Renovell (Eds.), Field-Programmable Logic and Applications. Proceedings, 2002. XXII, 1187 pages. 2002.

Vol. 2439: J.J. Merelo Guervós, P. Adamidis, H.-G. Beyer, J.-L. Fernández-Villacañas, H.-P. Schwefel (Eds.), Parallel Problem Solving from Nature – PPSN VII. Proceedings, 2002. XXII, 947 pages. 2002.

Vol. 2440: J.M. Haake, J.A. Pino (Eds.), Groupware: Design, Implementation and Use. Proceedings, 2002. XII, 285 pages. 2002.

Vol. 2441: Z. Hu, M. Rodríguez-Artalejo (Eds.), Functional and Logic Programming. Proceedings, 2002. X, 305 pages. 2002.

Vol. 2442: M. Yung (Ed.), Advances in Cryptology – CRYPTO 2002. Proceedings, 2002. XIV, 627 pages. 2002.

Vol. 2443: D. Scott (Ed.), Artificial Intelligence: Methodology, Systems, and Applications. Proceedings, 2002. X, 279 pages. 2002. (Subseries LNAI).

Vol. 2444: A. Buchmann, F. Casati, L. Fiege, M.-C. Hsu, M.-C. Shan (Eds.), Technologies for E-Services. Proceedings, 2002. X, 171 pages. 2002.

Vol. 2445: C. Anagnostopoulou, M. Ferrand, A. Smaill (Eds.), Music and Artificial Intelligence. Proceedings, 2002. VIII, 207 pages. 2002. (Subseries LNAI).

Vol. 2446: M. Klusch, S. Ossowski, O. Shehory (Eds.), Cooperative Information Agents VI. Proceedings, 2002. XI, 321 pages. 2002. (Subseries LNAI).

Vol. 2447: D.J. Hand, N.M. Adams, R.J. Bolton (Eds.), Pattern Detection and Discovery. Proceedings, 2002. XII, 227 pages. 2002. (Subseries LNAI).

Vol. 2448: P. Sojka, I. Kopeček, K. Pala (Eds.), Text, Speech and Dialogue. Proceedings, 2002. XII, 481 pages. 2002. (Subseries LNAI).

Vol. 2449: L. Van Gool (Ed.), Pattern Recognotion. Proceedings, 2002. XVI, 628 pages. 2002.

Vol. 2451: B. Hochet, A.J. Acosta, M.J. Bellido (Eds.), Integrated Circuit Design. Proceedings, 2002. XVI, 496 pages. 2002.

Vol. 2452: R. Guigó, D. Gusfield (Eds.), Algorithms in Bioinformatics. Proceedings, 2002. X, 554 pages. 2002.

Vol. 2453: A. Hameurlain, R. Cicchetti, R. Traunmüller (Eds.), Database and Expert Systems Applications. Proceedings, 2002. XVIII, 951 pages. 2002.

Vol. 2454: Y. Kambayashi, W. Winiwarter, M. Arikawa (Eds.), Data Warehousing and Knowledge Discovery. Proceedings, 2002. XIII, 339 pages. 2002.

Vol. 2455: K. Bauknecht, A M. Tjoa, G. Quirchmayr (Eds.), E-Commerce and Web Technologies. Proceedings, 2002. XIV, 414 pages. 2002.

Vol. 2456: R. Traunmüller, K. Lenk (Eds.), Electronic Government. Proceedings, 2002. XIII, 486 pages. 2002.

Vol. 2457: T. Yakhno (Ed.), Advances in Information Systems. Proceedings, 2002. XII, 436 pages. 2002.

Vol. 2458: M. Agosti, C. Thanos (Eds.), Research and Advanced Technology for Digital Libraries. Proceedings, 2002. XVI, 664 pages. 2002.

Vol. 2459: M.C. Calzarossa, S. Tucci (Eds.), Performance Evaluation of Complex Systems: Techniques and Tools. Proceedings, 2002. VIII, 501 pages. 2002.

Vol. 2460: J.-M. Jézéquel, H. Hussmann, S. Cook (Eds.), «UML» 2002 – The Unified Modeling Language. Proceedings, 2002. XII, 449 pages. 2002.

Vol. 2461: R. Möhring, R. Raman (Eds.), Algorithms – ESA 2002. Proceedings, 2002. XIV, 917 pages. 2002.

Vol. 2462: K. Jansen, S. Leonardi, V. Vazirani (Eds.), Approximation Algorithms for Combinatorial Optimization. Proceedings, 2002. VIII, 271 pages. 2002.

Vol. 2463: M. Dorigo, G. Di Caro, M. Sampels (Eds.), Ant Algorithms. Proceedings, 2002. XIII, 305 pages. 2002.

Vol. 2464: M. O'Neill, R.F.E. Sutcliffe, C. Ryan, M. Eaton, N. Griffith (Eds.), Artificial Intelligence and Cognitive Science. Proceedings, 2002. XI, 247 pages. 2002. (Subseries LNAI).

Vol. 2465: H. Arisawa, Y. Kambayashi, V. Kumar, H.C. Mayr, I. Hunt (Eds.), Conceptual Modeling for New Information Systems Technologies. Proceedings, 2001. XVII, 500 pages. 2002.

Vol. 2467: B. Christianson, B. Crispo, J.A. Malcolm, M. Roe (Eds.), Security Protocols. Proceedings, 2001. IX, 241 pages. 2002.

Vol. 2469: W. Damm, E.-R. Olderog (Eds.), Formal Techniques in Real-Time and Fault-Tolerant Systems. Proceedings, 2002. X, 455 pages. 2002.

Vol. 2470: P. Van Hentenryck (Ed.), Principles and Practice of Constraint Programming – CP 2002. Proceedings, 2002. XVI, 794 pages. 2002.

Vol. 2471: J. Bradfield (Ed.), Computer Science Logic. Proceedings, 2002. XII, 613 pages. 2002.

Vol. 2473: A. Gomez-Perez, V.R. Benjamins, Knowledge Engineering and Knowledge Management. Proceedings, 2002. XI, 402 pages. 2002. (Subseries LNAI).

Vol. 2474: D. Kranzlmüller, P. Kacsuk, J. Dongarra, J. Volkert (Eds.), Recent Advances in Parallel Virtual Machine and Message Passing Interface. Proceedings, 2002. XVI, 462 pages. 2002.

Vol. 2475: J.J. Alpigini, J.F. Peters, A. Skowron, N. Zhong (Eds.), Rough Sets and Current Trends in Computing. Proceedings, 2002. XV, 640 pages. 2002. (Subseries LNAI).

Vol. 2476: A.H.F. Laender, A.L. Oliveira (Eds.), String Processing and Information Retrieval. Proceedings, 2002. XI, 337 pages. 2002.

Vol. 2477: M.V. Hermenegildo, G. Puebla (Eds.), Static Analysis. Proceedings, 2002. XI, 527 pages. 2002.

Vol. 2478: M.J. Egenhofer, D.M. Mark (Eds.), Geographic Information Science. Proceedings, 2002. X, 363 pages. 2002.

Vol. 2479: M. Jarke, J. Koehler, G. Lakemeyer (Eds.), KI 2002: Advances in Artificial Intelligence. Proceedings, 2002. XIII, 327 pages. (Subseries LNAI).

Vol. 2480: Y. Han, S. Tai, D. Wikarski (Eds.), Engineering and Deployment of Cooperative Information Systems. Proceedings, 2002. XIII, 564 pages. 2002.

Vol. 2483: J.D.P. Rolim, S. Vadhan (Eds.), Randomization and Approximation Techniques in Computer Science. Proceedings, 2002. VIII, 275 pages. 2002.

Vol. 2484: P. Adriaans, H. Fernau, M. van Zaanen (Eds.), Grammatical Inference: Algorithms and Applications. Proceedings, 2002. IX, 315 pages. 2002. (Subseries LNAI).

Vol. 2486: M. Marinaro, R. Tagliaferri (Eds.), Neural Nets. Proceedings, 2002. IX, 253 pages. 2002.

Vol. 2487: D. Batory, C. Consel, W. Taha (Eds.), Generative Programming and Component Engineering. Proceedings, 2002. VIII, 335 pages. 2002.

Vol. 2488: T. Dohi, R. Kikinis (Eds), Medical Image Computing and Computer-Assisted Intervention – MICCAI 2002. Proceedings, Part I. XXIX, 807 pages. 2002.

Vol. 2489: T. Dohi, R. Kikinis (Eds), Medical Image Computing and Computer-Assisted Intervention – MICCAI 2002. Proceedings, Part II. XXIX, 693 pages. 2002.

Vol. 2491: A. Sangiovanni-Vincentelli, J. Sifakis (Eds.), Embedded Software. Proceedings, 2002. IX, 423 pages. 2002.

Vol. 2493: S. Bandini, B. Chopard, M. Tomassini (Eds.), Cellular Automata. Proceedings, 2002. XI, 369 pages. 2002.

Vol. 2495: C. George, H. Miao (Eds.), Formal Methods and Software Engineering. Proceedings, 2002. XI, 626 pages. 2002.

Vol. 2496: K.C. Almeroth, M. Hasan (Eds.), Management of Multimedia in the Internet. Proceedings, 2002. XI, 355 pages. 2002.

Vol. 2498: G. Borriello, L.E. Holmquist (Eds.), UbiComp 2002: Ubiquitous Computing. Proceedings, 2002. XV, 380 pages. 2002.

Vol. 2499: S.D. Richardson (Ed.), Machine Translation: From Research to Real Users. Proceedings, 2002. XXI, 254 pages. 2002. (Subseries LNAI).

Vol. 2502: D. Gollmann, G. Karjoth, M. Waidner (Eds.), Computer Security – ESORICS 2002. Proceedings, 2002. X, 281 pages. 2002.

Vol. 2503: S. Spaccapietra, S.T. March, Y. Kambayashi (Eds.), Conceptual Modeling – ER 2002. Proceedings, 2002. XX, 480 pages. 2002.

Vol. 2504: M.T. Escrig, F. Toledo, E. Golobardes (Eds.), Topics in Artificial Intelligence. Proceedings 2002. XI, 432 pages. 2002. (Subseries LNAI).

Vol. 2505: A. Corradini, H. Ehrig, H.-J. Kreowski, G. Rozenberg (Eds.), Graph Transformations. Proceedings, 2002. IX, 459 pages. 2002.

Vol. 2509: C.S. Calude, M.J. Dinneen, F. Peper (Eds.), Unconventional Models in Computation. Proceedings, 2002. VIII, 331 pages. 2002.

Vol. 2511: B. Stiller, M. Smirnow, M. Karsten, P. Reichl (Eds.), From QoS Provisioning to QoS Charging. Proceedings, 2002. XIV, 348 pages. 2002.

Vol. 2514: M. Baaz, A. Voronkov (Eds.), Logic for Programming, Artificial Intelligence, and Reasoning. Proceedings 2002. XIII, 465 pages. 2002. (Subseries LNAI).

Vol. 2516: A. Wespi, G. Vigna, L. Deri (Eds.), Recent Advances in Intrusion Detection. Proceedings, 2002. X, 327 pages. 2002.

Vol. 2521: A. Karmouch, T. Magedanz, J. Delgado (Eds.), Mobile Agents for Telecommunication Applications. Proceedings 2002. XII, 317 pages. 2002.

Vol. 2526: A. Colosimo, A. Giuliani, P. Sirabella (Eds.), Medical Data Analysis. Proceedings 2002. IX, 222 pages. 2002.